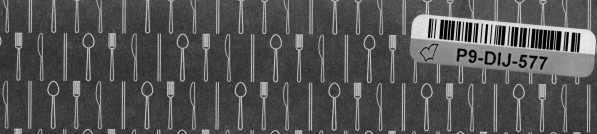

Lighthearted
at Home

Lighthearted
at Home

The Very Best of
Anne Lindsay

John Wiley & Sons Canada, Ltd.

Finding answers. For life.

Library and Archives Canada Cataloguing in Publication Data

Lindsay, Anne, 1943–
     Lighthearted at home : the very best of Anne Lindsay.

Includes index.
ISBN 978-0-470-16077-0

     1. Heart—Diseases—Diet therapy—Recipes. 2. Low-fat diet—Recipes.
I. Title.

RC684.D5L54 2009   641.5'6311   C2009-905190-7

Production Credits
Creative direction, cover & interior design: Ian Koo
Photographer: Lorella Zanelli
Food stylist: Adele Hagan
Composition: Adrian So, Mike Chan, Natalia Burobina, Pat Loi, Joanna Vieira
Printer: R.R. Donnelley

John Wiley & Sons Canada, Ltd.
6045 Freemont Blvd.
Mississauga, Ontario
L5R 4J3

Printed in the United States
1 2 3 4 5 RRD 14 13 12 11 10

To my grandchildren, who bring us pure joy—Pierce, Katie, Pippa and Elizabeth

Brief Table of Contents

Detailed Table of Contents

VEGETARIAN MAINS

PASTA AND NOODLES

POULTRY AND GAME

BEEF

BREADS AND MUFFINS

COOKIES, SQUARES AND BARS

DESSERTS

Preface

The Heart and Stroke Foundation of Canada is pleased to bring you *Lighthearted at Home: The Very Best of Anne Lindsay*.

If this is your first Anne Lindsay cookbook, you're in for a treat. Devoted readers have come to appreciate Anne's innovative heart-healthy recipes and smart ideas for flavourful, healthy eating options. An early champion of heart-healthy cuisine, Anne was on to something more than twenty years ago with her first *Lighthearted Cookbook*. Since then, over two million Canadians have turned to her for inspirational meal suggestions. This beautifully photographed book with updated nutrition information features more than five hundred of Anne's most delicious heart-healthy meals.

Anne Lindsay and the Heart and Stroke Foundation share a strong and successful history of providing Canadians with wholesome recipes, nutritional information and simple ways to eat heart healthy. In fact, Anne was one of the first food writers to convey the importance of good food in our overall health. It's a pleasure to collaborate again with this celebrated author. Nutrition and healthy eating has been a long-standing priority for the Heart and Stroke Foundation.

We are what we eat—and everyone benefits from eating well.

Nutritious balanced meals, which are lower in fat, sugar and sodium and include a wide variety of vegetables and fruit, are key to achieving and maintaining a healthy weight and reducing the risk of heart disease and stroke.

In its efforts to improve your overall heart health, the Foundation has developed a number of programs to help Canadians stay healthy:

- We are a proud partner with the Canadian Cancer Society in the *5 to 10 a Day* program, which encourages Canadians to consume at least 5 to 10 servings of vegetables and fruit a day as part of a healthy diet and lifestyle;

- *My Heart & Stroke Blood Pressure Action Plan*™ at heartandstroke.ca/bp is an online tool to help you manage and control your blood pressure, the number one risk factor for cardiovascular disease;

- *My Heart & Stroke Healthy Weight Action Plan*™ at heartandstroke.ca/hwplan, developed by nutrition experts, is a twelve-week online program that can help you achieve and maintain a healthy weight; and

- The Foundation's Health Check™ food information program makes it simple to identify healthy choices in the grocery store. Products that display the Health Check™ symbol have been reviewed by our dietitians and meet nutrition criteria based on recommendations in Canada's Food Guide.

An overall healthy lifestyle, together with regular physical activity, staying smoke-free, limiting alcohol consumption and managing stress, will also help you and your family enjoy life to the fullest. You can find more information on nutrition and health on our website at heartandstroke.ca.

Whether this is your first Anne Lindsay cookbook or an addition to your Anne Lindsay favourites, I know you'll enjoy finding new recipes—with so many to choose from, you'll have no shortage of variety.

Bob Brooks
Chair
Heart and Stroke Foundation of Canada

Acknowledgements

I would like to thank the great team who worked so hard to put together this cookbook. Thanks to all the folks at Wiley, led by my wonderful editor Leah Fairbank, including Lindsay Humphreys, Pamela Vokey, Alison MacLean and Katie Wolsley, as well as freelance editor Judy Phillips and indexer Mary Newberry. Also, I'd like to thank creative director Ian Koo, photographer Lorella Zanetti and food stylist Adele Hagan for the beautiful photographs.

Thanks to my agent and good friend Denise Schon for all her advice and support over many years. And to my good friend Shannon Graham, who has worked on all my books and tested yet again some of these recipes, and who is always there when needed. For all their work on the new nutritional analyses of the recipes, I'd like to thank Barbara Selley and Cathie Martin from Food Intelligence and give particular thanks to Carol Dombrow for her diligence and hard work not only on the nutritional analyses but also on the Introduction and Glossary.

I am honoured and pleased to have the Heart and Stroke Foundation of Canada involved with this book. Thanks to Sally Brown, CEO; Robert Brooks, Chair; Stephanie Lawrence, Manager of Communications, Health Check Program; and Tony Graham, long-time volunteer with the Foundation, for their enthusiasm for this book.

And many thanks to all of you, the readers and cooks who have bought and used my cookbooks over the years. I appreciate your e-mails and letters, and I hope to continue hearing from you.

As always, thanks to my husband, Bob, for his patience and support while I worked on this cookbook, and to my children and their spouses: Jeff and Karen, John and Jesse, Susie and Brendan. Love to you all, and happy cooking!

Anne Lindsay

Introduction

Since I was a little girl, pulling a chair up to the kitchen counter to "help" my mother, I've loved to cook. I remember the fun of making fudge on a rainy day or picking berries with the whole family then coming home to make pies or jam. And I've always loved to eat good-tasting, real food. In high school, I became fascinated by the science of nutrition. It was an easy decision for me to study home economics at university because it combined both nutrition and cooking. Later, when I had the opportunity to write cookbooks teamed with Canada's leading health organizations, it really was a dream come true. Even better was the reaction from readers—thank you for being so receptive to my cookbooks, for actually cooking from them and for writing to tell me what you think.

For me, enjoying and sharing good food with family and friends is one of life's greatest pleasures. I love to experience new tastes whether at home or out—it's exciting. I also get a huge amount of satisfaction from cooking something that tastes delicious and then sharing it with others.

However, you may be surprised to learn that I don't spend a lot of time cooking. I like flavourful but simple foods. If you have used my cookbooks, you know how often I use fresh herbs, spices, garlic, ginger, mustard, vinegars and lemon. I use good-quality ingredients, local whenever possible. This is in part because I value my health and the health of my family above everything else. Right from the beginning I have been passionate about creating delicious food that is good for you and easy to prepare.

As I've learned more about healthy eating over the years, my eating habits have changed. For example, I eat far less meat now than I used to. In fact, I've discovered that some of my favourite meals are vegetarian; I love vegetable curries, vegetarian chili and hearty bean soups. I eat almost no fried foods, few rich desserts, and I drink skim milk. Of course, these changes didn't happen overnight. They occurred gradually, and I felt better and better along the way. I still enjoy a huge variety of foods—I eat just about anything. But how I prepare food, and how much and how often I eat certain foods, have changed. I still love really good french fries; I just don't order them very often, and when I do, I share them with a friend.

It doesn't have to take any longer to cook a healthy meal than a less healthy one, but it does require a little planning, shopping and organizing. It means using a minimum of prepared and processed foods, and choosing these wisely. At a bare minimum, my kitchen is stocked with milk, cheese, eggs, bread, rice, pasta, frozen peas and corn, potatoes, carrots, onions and garlic, canned tomatoes, beans (black, kidney, chickpeas) and salmon. I grow fresh herbs and have spices, vinegars, mustards and olive oil on hand. With these basics alone I can make a quick pasta, stir-fry, hearty soup, salad or egg dish.

Truly, it's never been easier to eat well. The aisles of the grocery store look far different from what they did just a few years ago— and some of those changes have made healthy eating easier. Pre-washed baby spinach and lettuce, bagged coleslaw, skinless boneless chicken, peeled-and-cut squash and pineapple, sliced mushrooms, grated cheese, couscous and fresh pasta are just a few of the choices now available that let us cook a meal in a jiffy.

Having the family eat together has also been at the heart of my joy of cooking. I like to have music on, and I recruit help whenever I can. It helped a lot to frame cooking as a joy rather than a chore, and I discovered early on that when the kids helped to cook a meal, they were far more likely to enjoy eating it. Cooking together was a fantastic way to catch up on each other's day, especially with a non-communicative teenager!

My kids are all married now, and they have become great cooks. They cook healthy and interesting foods. Best of all, they invite me and my husband over for meals. I'm impressed by how they cope with life's busy schedules yet manage to make such great-tasting food. I'm a grandmother now, so once again I'm having fun with little ones in the kitchen. I love to see their faces light up with joy and wonder as they taste a food for the first time. I hope to repeat the cycle and help instil in my grandkids a love of good food; maybe they will get as hooked on cooking as I am.

Everyone has different tastes, and so I invite you to experiment and make the recipes in this book your own—taste the dishes during cooking and add more herbs, spices and seasonings to your liking. I hope these recipes will help you enjoy your time in the kitchen, and I especially hope you'll take part in the pleasure of sharing delicious, healthy meals with your friends and family.

Anne Lindsay
December 2009

Eating Well to Live Well
by the Heart and Stroke Foundation of Canada

Eating well is one of the best investments you can make for your overall health. A lifetime of healthy eating will help with your general well-being, vitality and energy, and help prevent many chronic diseases, especially if you are also physically active and don't smoke.

Good nutrition is important at every stage of our lives. What your children do today not only affects them now, as they are growing and developing, but also helps set healthy eating patterns that will continue into adulthood. Eating well is a long-term strategy that starts to pay off as soon as it is put into action—it is never too late to start, and it is always too early to quit.

However, eating well every day can be a challenge. We are bombarded with different nutrition information, some of it conflicting. Grocery stores, markets and restaurants present us with an overwhelming array of choices, and our busy schedules can make it tempting to forgo homemade meals from scratch and instead opt for easier, faster but less nutritious alternatives.

With some planning, including choosing your favourite recipes in advance and making the most of nutrition tools such as Canada's Food Guide and the Nutrition Facts tables while you grocery shop, you can enjoy healthy meals and snacks every day.

EATING WELL WITH CANADA'S FOOD GUIDE

Eating Well with Canada's Food Guide translates the science of nutrition and health into a healthy eating pattern. The Food Guide describes the *amount of food* you need each day and the *type of food*. It is important to remember that the Food Guide is just that—a guide; it provides the general direction to help you eat an overall healthy diet, while offering lots of options within each of the four food groups so you can make nutritious, delicious and interesting choices.

The recommended number of Food Guide servings is an average amount that you should aim to eat each day. The recommended number of daily servings is different for women and men, and also changes to suit the various stages of life. However, there are general healthy eating guidelines everyone can keep in mind to help make the most of dietary choices:

- Eat more vegetables and fruit, especially dark green and orange produce.
- Eat more whole-grain products.
- Drink 2 cups (500 mL) of skim, 1% or 2% milk every day.
- Try meat alternatives such as beans, lentils and tofu more often.
- Enjoy at least two servings of fish every week.
- Drink water to satisfy your thirst.

The Food Guide recommends a small amount (2 to 3 tbsp/25 to 45 mL) of unsaturated fat, such as vegetable oils (for example, canola oil, olive oil or soft non-hydrogenated margarine), each day. If you check the ingredient list for these types of fats when buying foods and you use these type of fats when preparing foods, you will likely meet your daily requirements.

NUTRITION LABELLING

Another valuable resource to help you make wise food choices is the Nutrition Facts table that appears on much of the food packaging found in grocery stores. This useful tool is packed with information, including the amount of calories and nutrients based on a product's serving size (keeping in mind that this may be more or less than what you yourself might consume in a serving). Look for a higher percent Daily Value for nutrients such as fibre, calcium, iron and vitamins and a lower percent Daily Value for fat and sodium. Make sure the serving sizes are the same when you are comparing products.

Most of us know it is important to limit the amount of saturated fat in our diet and to avoid trans fats. We also need to watch the amount of salt (sodium) we consume each day. Sodium is an essential nutrient, but most of us are getting too much of it—largely from processed foods and meals we eat out. However, even some of the basic ingredients we use to cook with can be loaded with sodium, including broths, canned tomatoes and other vegetables, and meat and poultry. This is where good label-reading skills come in handy—you can refer to the Nutrition Facts table to compare products and make wise choices.

Look for the Health Check™ symbol on food products. The symbol is your assurance that the products meet nutrient criteria developed by the Heart and Stroke Foundation's registered dietitians and are part of a healthy diet based on recommendations in the Food Guide.

GET ACTIVE

Being physically active is also part of a healthy lifestyle. People at a healthy weight who are very active will need extra servings from the four food groups to meet their energy needs. Building physical activity into your daily life will improve your health, make you feel better overall and help you fight disease.

MENU PLANNING

Planning your meals is one of the best ways to ensure you and your family meet your nutrition needs. This may seem easier said than done, but planning will save you time and money in the long run, as well as help you prepare balanced and tasty meals. Start by deciding which recipes you want to prepare for the week and then make a list of all of the ingredients you will need. By planning a week's worth of snacks and meals you will also be able to choose a good variety of foods from each food group to make sure you are getting the recommended daily number of servings for each one. Of course, you'll want to incorporate some of Anne's lighthearted recipes into your weekly meal planning.

To keep the planning to a minimum, arrange two or three weeks' worth of meals and snacks and then rotate them over a few months or even the year. You can make adjustments to take advantage of foods that are in season and specials at the grocery store. Holiday meal planning can be particularly challenging, but there are still many nutritious and delicious choices you can make, and remember to apply the rule of moderation—not deprivation—when it comes to treats for special occasions.

HELP KIDS DEVELOP A TASTE FOR HEALTHY EATING

Involving children in shopping, planning and preparing healthy meals is a great way to teach them how to make wise choices and interest them in the entire food experience. Making food fun and inclusive will encourage kids to be more interested in and aware of what they eat—lessons that will serve them well as they get older.

The best way to teach children how to eat well is to eat well yourself. Children need to eat the same foods as adults but in smaller amounts. By offering kids a wide variety of foods in small portions, you will encourage them to develop an appreciation for different flavours and textures. Prepare meals that include foods from each food group and make snacks count by providing healthy and appealing options.

KEEPING TEENAGERS ON TRACK

The older your children get, the more they will make decisions on their own, including what they eat and where they choose to eat it. Hopefully, many of those good eating habits you helped them develop when they were younger will have made an impression, but the lesson is by no means over. Good nutrition is likely not always top of mind to hungry, busy teenagers who are constantly faced with less than wholesome choices and advertising. Take advantage of any opportunity you can to influence what your teenager eats. Encourage teens to participate in regular family meals and stress the importance of starting the day with a good breakfast. Continue to involve them in family meal planning by giving them a say in the weekly menu and teaching them to make simple meals and snacks. Keep your fridge and cupboards stocked with a selection of healthy and interesting options so they get used to making healthy choices.

MAINTAINING HEALTHY EATING AS ADULTS

Healthy eating does not stop once you are an adult. In fact, it is just as important as ever to eat a well-balanced diet and to fit physical activity into your daily routine. We need fewer calories as we get older, but we still need the same nutrients. This means making sure you get your recommended number of daily servings from all four food groups while also keeping an eye on your portion sizes. Pay close attention to your intake of vegetables and fruit, whole grains and meat alternatives, and don't forget those two cups of milk. If you are pregnant or breastfeeding you will need extra calories.

Nearly everyone needs to reduce the amount of sodium in their diet. Always read the Nutrition Facts table before you purchase pre-packaged foods and try to select products with a lower amount of sodium. When eating at restaurants, ask if nutrition information is available so you can opt for a lower sodium and lower fat alternative. Food plays a very important role in helping to protect you from diseases, including heart disease and cancer. Reducing fat, increasing fibre and including antioxidant vitamins in your diet are key to lowering your risk for heart disease and nutrition-related cancers. All of this can be accomplished by eating simple, healthful meals and following the Food Guide.

ENJOY IT TOGETHER

Eating well is important for our health, and there are many nutritious choices that are sure to please all palates and suit any meal occasion. Eating is one of our greatest pleasures. A wholesome and delicious meal prepared with fresh ingredients and enjoyed with friends or family is about more than just providing fuel for our bodies. Cooking and sharing meals is an important part of our social lives. Meals are a time to slow down, providing us with an excuse to take a break from our daily busy lives and bringing us together for special occasions.

Savour everything you can about your eating experiences. Try a new recipe or put a new twist on an old favourite. Add texture and flavour to your food. When you have the time, delight in the preparation of your meals, including the presentation on the plate and the setting on the table. Be thankful for the nourishing food in front of you and the people around you to share it with.

Carol Dombrow, Registered Dietitian
Heart and Stroke Foundation
December 2009

SALSAS, DIPS AND SPREADS

Tomato and Cucumber Salsa

Serve this salsa with tacos or burritos or as a dip. A finely chopped sweet red, yellow or green pepper can also be added for extra colour and flavour.

1	large tomato, finely diced	1
1 cup	finely diced cucumber	250 mL
1	small green chili pepper (canned or fresh), chopped, or ¼ tsp (1 mL) crushed red pepper flakes	1
2 tbsp	minced onion	25 mL
1 tbsp	red or white wine vinegar	15 mL
1 tbsp	chopped fresh coriander (cilantro), plus more to taste	15 mL
Half	clove garlic, minced	Half
¼ tsp or less	salt and freshly ground pepper	1 mL or less

In bowl, combine tomato, cucumber, chili pepper, onion, vinegar, coriander and garlic; mix well. Transfer 1 cup (250 mL) of the tomato mixture to blender or food processor and purée; return to remaining mixture in bowl and combine. Season with salt, pepper and coriander.

MAKES 2 CUPS (500 mL)

MAKE AHEAD: Serve at room temperature within 3 hours or cover and refrigerate for up to 3 days.

PER 2 TBSP (25 mL): 4 calories, 0 g protein, 0 g total fat, 0 g saturated fat, 0 mg cholesterol, 1 g carbohydrate, 0 g fibre, 45 mg sodium, 34 mg potassium

---

Black Bean and Corn Salsa

Black bean and corn is a popular salsa combination. My daughter Susie serves it as a dip with baked chips and also uses it as a filling for quesadillas and wraps, or as a topping or filling for fajitas and tacos.

1	can (19 oz/540 mL) black beans, drained and rinsed	1
1 cup	corn kernels	250 mL
1	avocado, diced	1
1	large tomato, finely chopped	1
⅓ cup	finely chopped red onion	75 mL
⅓ cup	chopped fresh coriander (cilantro)	75 mL
¼ cup	fresh lime or lemon juice	50 mL
1 tbsp	olive oil	15 mL
1 tbsp	seeded, minced jalapeño pepper	15 mL
½ tsp	salt	2 mL

In bowl, combine beans, corn, avocado, tomato, onion and coriander. Sprinkle with lime juice, oil, jalapeño pepper and salt; toss lightly. Cover and refrigerate for up to 4 hours.

MAKES 4 CUPS (1 L)

PER ¼ CUP (50 mL): 65 calories, 2 g protein, 3 g total fat, 0 g saturated fat, 0 mg cholesterol, 8 g carbohydrate, 3 g fibre, 145 mg sodium, 210 mg potassium

Winter Salsa

Make this version of salsa in winter, when canned tomatoes are a better choice than fresh ones. Use the salsa as a dip with nachos or as a sauce for burritos. Adjust the amount of coriander according to taste. If fresh coriander isn't available, add fresh basil or parsley to taste.

1	can (19 oz/540 mL) tomatoes, drained and chopped	1
2 tsp	apple cider vinegar	10 mL
1½ tsp	each ground cumin and chili powder	7 mL
½ cup	chopped green onions	125 mL
1	clove garlic, minced	1
Half	sweet green pepper, chopped	Half
2 tbsp	chopped fresh coriander (cilantro), plus more to taste	25 mL
¼ tsp or less	salt and freshly ground pepper	1 mL or less

Combine tomatoes, vinegar, cumin, chili powder, onions, garlic, green pepper and coriander. Season with salt, pepper and coriander.

MAKES 2 CUPS (500 mL)

MAKE AHEAD: Cover and refrigerate for up to 4 days.

PER 2 TBSP (25 mL): 8 calories, 0 g protein, 0 g total fat, 0 g saturated fat, 0 mg cholesterol, 2 g carbohydrate, 0 g fibre, 32 mg sodium, 68 mg potassium

Tomato Salsa

Serve this Mexican staple as a topping for tacos or tostadas, over low-fat cottage cheese, as a low-fat dip with Belgian endive wedges or low-fat chips, as a filling for pita bread, or as an accompaniment to meats.

4	large tomatoes, diced	4
1	large sweet green pepper, diced	1
1	fresh hot chili pepper or 1 pickled jalapeño pepper or 2 canned green chili peppers, seeded and diced	1
¼ cup	chopped fresh coriander (cilantro), plus more to taste	50 mL
2 tbsp	grated onion	25 mL
1	clove garlic, minced	1
1 tsp	crushed dried oregano	5 mL
¼ tsp or less	salt and freshly ground pepper	1 mL or less

In bowl, combine tomatoes, green pepper, chili pepper, coriander, onion, garlic and oregano, mixing well. Season with salt, pepper and coriander.

MAKES 4 CUPS (1 L)

MAKE AHEAD: Cover and refrigerate for up to 3 days.

NOTE: One ½ cup (125 mL) serving is a very high source of vitamin C.

PER ½ CUP (125 mL): 26 calories, 1 g protein, 0 g total fat, 0 g saturated fat, 0 mg cholesterol, 6 g carbohydrate, 2 g fibre, 79 mg sodium, 279 mg potassium

Light and Easy Guacamole

Because avocado is high in fat, I use a mixture of green peas and avocado in my guacamole, without sacrificing the authentic flavour of a traditional Mexican dip. Serve with crudités, Belgian endive wedges or baked tortilla chips.

1⅔ cups	frozen peas (8 oz/250 g), thawed	400 mL
1	avocado	1
2	tomatoes, peeled, seeded and chopped	2
2	small cloves garlic, minced	2
¼ cup	minced red onion	50 mL
2 tbsp	fresh lemon juice	25 mL
1 tsp	chili powder	5 mL
½ tsp	each salt and ground cumin	2 mL
Pinch	cayenne pepper	Pinch

In food processor, purée peas until smooth. In bowl, mash avocado with fork; add peas, tomatoes, garlic, onion, lemon juice, chili powder, salt, cumin and cayenne pepper; mix until blended.

MAKES 2½ CUPS (625 mL)

VARIATION:

Avocado and Asparagus Guacamole
In asparagus season, use 8 oz (250 g) cooked asparagus instead of peas.

PER 2 TBSP (25 mL): 29 calories, 1 g protein, 2 g total fat, 0 g saturated fat, 0 mg cholesterol, 3 g carbohydrate, 1 g fibre, 75 mg sodium, 112 mg potassium

Hummus

This is the dip I make most often. I always keep a can of chickpeas in the cupboard so that I can make this at a moment's notice. Garnish with chopped fresh parsley or coriander, and serve with pita bread or sliced raw vegetables for dipping.

2	small cloves garlic	2
1	can (19 oz/540 mL) chickpeas, drained and rinsed	1
¼ cup	tahini (sesame seed paste) or peanut butter, or 1 tbsp (15 mL) sesame oil	50 mL
	Juice of 1 lemon	
2 tbsp	water	25 mL
1½ tsp	cumin	7 mL
¼ tsp or less	salt	1 mL or less
	Freshly ground pepper, hot pepper sauce	

In food processor, chop garlic; add chickpeas, tahini, lemon juice, water, cumin and salt. Process until smooth. Season with pepper and hot pepper sauce to taste.

MAKES 2 CUPS (500 mL)

MAKE AHEAD: Cover and refrigerate for up to 1 week.

PER 2 TBSP (25 mL): 53 calories, 2 g protein, 2 g total fat, 0 g saturated fat, 0 mg cholesterol, 6 g carbohydrate, 1 g fibre, 94 mg sodium, 73 mg potassium

Fresh Beet and Onion Dip

Susan Pacaud, who helped with some of the recipe testing for my book *Smart Cooking*, gave me the recipe for this wonderful and intriguingly bright pink dip.

2	green onions, finely chopped	2
¼ cup	grated peeled raw beet	50 mL
½ cup	low-fat plain yogurt or light sour cream	125 mL
½ cup	light cream cheese, softened, or quark	125 mL
2 tsp	fresh lemon juice	10 mL
¼ tsp	each salt and freshly ground pepper	1 mL

In small bowl, combine onions, beet, yogurt, cream cheese, lemon juice, salt and pepper; mix well.

MAKES 1¼ CUPS (300 mL)

MAKE AHEAD: Cover and refrigerate for up to 8 hours.

NOTE: When buying cream cheese, check the butterfat ("BF") content on the label. Sometimes packaged light cream cheese has nearly the same butterfat content as delicious local regular-fat cream cheese.

PER 1 TBSP (15 mL): 18 calories, 1 g protein, 1 g total fat, 1 g saturated fat, 4 mg cholesterol, 1 g carbohydrate, 0 g fibre, 76 mg sodium, 33 mg potassium

Green Onion Dip

My grandkids love this dip with raw vegetables. I like to add fresh basil or any other fresh herbs I have on hand. If you don't have a blender or food processor, use light sour cream or part light sour cream and part light cream cheese instead of the cottage cheese, and mix by hand. Add any other fresh herbs that you like—dill, basil, coriander.

1 cup	low-fat cottage cheese	250 mL
¼ cup	chopped green onions	50 mL
¼ cup	chopped fresh parsley	50 mL
½ cup	low-fat plain yogurt	125 mL
2 tbsp	freshly grated Parmesan cheese (optional)	25 mL
¼ tsp or less	salt and freshly ground pepper	1 mL or less

In blender or food processor, process cottage cheese, onions and parsley. Add yogurt and Parmesan cheese (if using); process just to mix. Season with salt and pepper. Refrigerate for at least 1 hour to chill.

MAKES 1½ CUPS (375 mL)

MAKE AHEAD: Cover and refrigerate for up to 2 days.

VARIATION:

Fresh Basil Dip
Add ½ cup (125 mL) chopped fresh basil.

PER 2 TBSP (25 mL): 21 calories, 3 g protein, 0 g total fat, 0 g saturated fat, 1 mg cholesterol, 1 g carbohydrate, 0 g fibre, 136 mg sodium, 53 mg potassium

Roasted Eggplant Dip

For the best flavour, barbecue the eggplants. They can also be baked in the oven, but don't microwave them for this recipe. Garnish the dip with sprigs of parsley and serve with small pita rounds or raw vegetables for dippers.

½ cup	low-fat plain yogurt (without gelatin), or ¼ cup (50 mL) light sour cream	125 mL
2	medium eggplants (each 1 lb/500 g)	2
¼ cup	chopped fresh parsley	50 mL
3 tbsp	fresh lemon juice	50 mL
2	green onions, minced	2
1	clove garlic, minced	1
1 tsp	sesame or olive oil	5 mL
½ tsp	each ground cumin and salt	2 mL
	Freshly ground pepper	

In cheesecloth-lined sieve set over bowl, drain yogurt in refrigerator for 4 hours or until yogurt amounts to ¼ cup (50 mL). Discard liquid. (Do not drain light sour cream, if using.)

Prick eggplants with fork. Grill over high heat for 1 hour or until blackened and blistered. (Or bake on baking sheet in 400°F/200°C oven for 40 to 45 minutes or until softened, turning once during baking.)

Cut eggplants in half and drain; scoop out flesh. Purée in food processor or mash until smooth to make about 1½ cups (375 mL). Stir in yogurt, parsley, lemon juice, onions, garlic, sesame oil, cumin, salt, and pepper to taste. Transfer to serving dish.

MAKES 2 CUPS (500 mL)

MAKE AHEAD: Cover and refrigerate for up to 2 days.

PER 1 TBSP (15 mL): 10 calories, 0 g protein, 0 g total fat, 0 g saturated fat, 0 mg cholesterol, 2 g carbohydrate, 0 g fibre, 40 mg sodium, 35 mg potassium

Minted Coriander Dipping Sauce

For a richer version of this dipping sauce, add some light sour cream; for a spicier version, add hot pepper sauce to taste.

½ cup	low-fat plain yogurt	125 mL
2 tbsp	each chopped fresh coriander (cilantro) and mint	25 mL
¼ tsp or less	salt and freshly ground pepper	1 mL or less

Combine yogurt, coriander and mint; season with salt and pepper.

MAKES ½ CUP (125 mL)

MAKE AHEAD: Cover and refrigerate for up to 3 days.

PER 2 TBSP (25 mL): 21 calories, 2 g protein, 1 g total fat, 0 g saturated fat, 2 mg cholesterol, 2 g carbohydrate, 0 g fibre, 169 mg sodium, 87 mg potassium

Roasted Red Pepper and Fresh Basil Dip

Serve this dip in the fall, when red peppers are plentiful and fresh basil is readily available. To save time, instead of roasting the peppers yourself, buy them already roasted—you'll find them at deli counters or in jars on the supermarket shelf. Be sure to drain thoroughly before using.

2	sweet red peppers	2
⅓ cup	light ricotta or cream cheese	75 mL
⅓ cup	chèvre (soft goat cheese)	75 mL
⅓ cup	chopped fresh basil*	75 mL
Pinch	cayenne pepper	Pinch
¼ tsp or less	salt and freshly ground pepper	1 mL or less

On baking sheet, bake red peppers in 400°F (200°C) oven for 30 minutes, turning once or twice, or until peppers are blackened and blistered. (Or barbecue until blistered.) Let cool then scrape off skin; discard seeds. Purée in food processor until smooth to make almost ¾ cup (175 mL). Add ricotta cheese, chèvre, basil and cayenne pepper; process until well blended. Season with salt and pepper.

MAKES 1½ CUPS (375 mL)

*If fresh basil isn't available, substitute ⅓ cup (75 mL) chopped fresh parsley and ½ tsp (2 mL) dried basil, or more to taste.

MAKE AHEAD: Cover and refrigerate for up to 2 days.

VARIATIONS:
Roasted Red Pepper and Fresh Basil Dip, Spinach and Artichoke Dip (halve the amount of yogurt), Herbed Cheese Spread and Smoked Salmon Spread are great as hors d'oeuvre fillings.

Stuffed Mushrooms
Remove stems from mushrooms. Spoon about 1 tsp (5 mL) dip or spread of your choice into each cap. Cover and refrigerate for up to 4 hours. Garnish each with a strip of smoked salmon, a tiny shrimp, or a sprig of fresh herb. Each recipe will fill 50 to 60 mushroom caps.

Stuffed Cherry Tomatoes
Slice tops off cherry tomatoes and scoop out seeds; fill with your choice of dip or spread. Garnish each with a sprig of fresh herb. Each recipe will fill at least 60 cherry tomatoes.

Filled Belgian Endive Spears
Scoop a spoonful of dip or spread onto the wider ends of Belgian endive spears. Garnish each with a strip of sun-dried tomato. Each recipe will fill at least 50 spears.

PER 1 TBSP (15 mL): 12 calories, 1 g protein, 1 g total fat, 0 g saturated fat, 1 mg cholesterol, 1 g carbohydrate, 0 g fibre, 37 mg sodium, 23 mg potassium

Spinach and Artichoke Dip

Serve this tasty dip with raw vegetables.

1	pkg (10 oz/300 g) frozen chopped spinach	1
1	can (14 oz/398 mL) artichoke hearts, drained	1
½ cup	light mayonnaise	125 mL
¼ cup	minced fresh dill or basil (or 1½ tsp/7 mL dried)	50 mL
1	small clove garlic, minced	1
1¼ cups	low-fat plain yogurt	300 mL
1 tsp or less	salt and freshly ground pepper	5 mL or less

Thaw spinach and squeeze out excess water. In food processor, process spinach and artichokes until coarsely chopped. Add mayonnaise, dill and garlic; process until mixed. Stir in yogurt; season with salt and pepper. If mixture is too thick, add more yogurt.

MAKES 3 CUPS (750 mL)

MAKE AHEAD: Cover and refrigerate for up to 1 day.

NOTE: I add the yogurt after combining the rest of the ingredients in the food processor because, when processed, the yogurt breaks down and thins.

PER 1 TBSP (15 mL): 19 calories, 1 g protein, 1 g total fat, 0 g saturated fat, 1 mg cholesterol, 2 g carbohydrate, 1 g fibre, 88 mg sodium, 66 mg potassium

Mexican Bean Dip

Kids love this as a filling for celery, as a dip with raw vegetables or as a sandwich spread along with lettuce, sliced tomato and cucumber inside pita pockets. Fresh or canned chilies (hot or mild) add even more flavour to this dip. For a party, sprinkle light shredded Cheddar cheese, sliced pitted black olives and finely diced tomato or red pepper over top.

1	can (14 oz/398 mL) refried, pinto or white kidney beans	1
⅓ cup	low-fat plain yogurt	75 mL
2	green onions, chopped	2
1	clove garlic, minced	1
1 tsp	each ground cumin and chili powder, plus more to taste	5 mL
2 tbsp	chopped fresh coriander (cilantro) or parsley	25 mL

In bowl, combine beans (if using pinto or kidney beans, drain well, rinse under cold water then mash or combine everything in a food processor), yogurt, onions, garlic, cumin and chili powder; mix well. Taste and add more cumin and chili powder if necessary, and coriander to taste. Just before serving, sprinkle with chopped coriander.

MAKES 2 CUPS (500 mL)

MAKE AHEAD: Cover and refrigerate for up to 2 days.

PER 2 TBSP (25 mL): 30 calories, 2 g protein, 0 g total fat, 0 g saturated fat, 2 mg cholesterol, 5 g carbohydrate, 2 g fibre, 85 mg sodium, 95 mg potassium

Herbed Cheese Spread

Two cups (500 mL) of quark, a low-fat soft cow's milk cheese, can also be used for this herbed spread instead of the yogurt and cream cheese. Spread this on Crostini (p. 28) or melba toast rounds and garnish with a thin strip of red pepper and a sprig of fresh basil or dill.

1 cup	low-fat plain yogurt	250 mL
1 cup	plain light cream cheese	250 mL
¼ cup	chopped fresh parsley	50 mL
¼ cup	chopped fresh dill or basil	50 mL
2	small cloves garlic, minced	2
2 tbsp	chopped chives or green onions	25 mL
½ tsp	salt	2 mL
	Freshly ground pepper	

In bowl, combine yogurt, cream cheese, parsley, dill, garlic, chives, salt, and pepper to taste; mix well.

MAKES 2 CUPS (500 mL)

MAKE AHEAD: Cover and refrigerate for up to 2 days.

PER 1 TBSP (15 mL): 21 calories, 1 g protein, 2 g total fat, 1 g saturated fat, 5 mg cholesterol, 1 g carbohydrate, 0 g fibre, 93 mg sodium, 33 mg potassium

Smoked Salmon Spread with Capers

You can use lox, cold smoked salmon or hot smoked salmon in this spread. I usually use the hot smoked salmon when I'm in British Columbia, where it is so readily available. I use at least 4 oz (125 g) of the hot smoked salmon (sold in chunks), cut into pieces or 2 oz of lox. Sometimes I use hot pepper sauce instead of horseradish, and I add extra fresh dill to taste.

1 cup	light ricotta or light cream cheese	250 mL
2 oz	smoked salmon, chopped (about ⅓ cup/75 mL)	60 g
2 tbsp	chopped fresh dill	25 mL
2 tbsp	drained capers	25 mL
2 tsp	fresh lemon juice	10 mL
2 tsp	ketchup	10 mL
1 tsp	prepared horseradish	5 mL
¼ tsp or less	salt and freshly ground pepper	1 mL or less

In blender or food processor, purée ricotta cheese until smooth. Add smoked salmon, dill, capers, lemon juice, ketchup and horseradish; using on/off motion, process until lightly mixed. Season with salt and pepper.

MAKES 1⅓ CUPS (325 mL)

VARIATION:

Wild Sockeye Salmon Spread
Substitute 1 can (7½ oz/213 g) wild sockeye salmon, drained and skin removed, for the smoked salmon. Reduce light ricotta or light cream cheese to ½ cup (125 mL) or to taste.

PER 1 TBSP (15 mL): 17 calories, 2 g protein, 1 g total fat, 0 g saturated fat, 2 mg cholesterol, 1 g carbohydrate, 0 g fibre, 93 mg sodium, 23 mg potassium

APPETIZERS AND SNACKS

Crudités with Creamy Fresh Dill Dip

The more colourful the selection of raw vegetables for this dish, the better—good options include snow peas, baby corn, zucchini, green and yellow beans, celery, fennel and purple peppers. If I'm using low-fat cottage cheese, I make this dip in a blender rather than a food processor, for a creamier, smoother consistency. If you don't have a blender, use quark (7% BF) or low-fat sour cream, rather than cottage cheese.

2	Belgian endive	2
4 oz	mushrooms	125 g
4	carrots, cut in strips	4
2	sweet red, yellow or green peppers, cut in strips	2
Half	small cauliflower, cut in florets	Half

CREAMY FRESH DILL DIP

½ cup	coarsely chopped fresh dill (or 2 tsp/10 mL dried)*	125 mL
2 tbsp	chopped fresh parsley	25 mL
1 cup	2% cottage cheese or light sour cream	250 mL
3 tbsp	low-fat plain yogurt or light cream cheese	50 mL
¼ tsp or less	salt and freshly ground pepper	1 mL or less

Separate endive leaves. Halve mushrooms, if large. Arrange endive, mushrooms, carrots, peppers and cauliflower on platter.

In blender, chop dill and parsley. Add cottage cheese, yogurt, and salt and pepper to taste; process until smooth. (Or finely chop dill and parsley, stir in light cottage cheese, yogurt, and salt and pepper.) Place dip in small bowl in centre of platter.

MAKES 1¼ CUPS (300 mL)

*If using dried dillweed, add an extra ¼ cup (50 mL) chopped fresh parsley.

MAKE AHEAD: Cover and refrigerate for up to 2 days.

VARIATION:

Creamy Herb Sauce
Creamy Fresh Dill Dip is delicious as a sauce, and it's low in fat. Fresh herbs add wonderful flavour to sauces; instead of fresh dill, try 1 to 2 tbsp (15 to 25 mL) chopped fresh tarragon, basil, or a combination of whatever fresh herbs you have on hand.

PER 1 TBSP (15 mL) DIP:
38 calories, 3 g protein,
3 g total fat, 1 g saturated fat,
8 mg cholesterol, 1 g carbohydrate,
0 g fibre, 158 mg sodium,
36 mg potassium

Tomato Bruschetta with Fresh Basil

I make this bruschetta often for lunch or a snack, especially on the weekends in August and September, when fresh tomatoes are sweet and juicy. If fresh basil isn't available, use 1 tsp (5 mL) dried and sprinkle with 2 tbsp (25 mL) grated Parmesan, or dot with soft chèvre and broil for 1 minute.

2	large tomatoes, diced (about 2 cups/500 mL)	2
¼ cup	chopped fresh basil, lightly packed	50 mL
1	clove garlic, minced	1
¼ tsp or less	salt and freshly ground pepper	1 mL or less
Half	loaf French or Italian bread or 1 baguette	Half
1	large clove garlic, halved	1
1 tbsp	olive oil	15 mL
2 tbsp	freshly grated Parmesan cheese (optional)	25 mL

In bowl, combine tomatoes, basil and minced garlic; add salt and pepper. Let stand for 15 minutes or up to 2 hours. Slice bread in 1-inch (2.5 cm) thick slices. Place on baking sheet and broil until lightly browned on each side. Rub cut side of garlic clove over one side of bread; brush with olive oil. Spoon tomato mixture over top. If using Parmesan, sprinkle with the Parmesan and broil for 1 minute.

MAKES 16 SLICES

PER SLICE: 50 calories, 1 g protein, 1 g total fat, 0 g saturated fat, 0 mg cholesterol, 8 g carbohydrate, 1 g fibre, 124 mg sodium, 68 mg potassium

Crab-Cucumber Rounds

Crisp cucumber slices, instead of pastry or bread, make refreshing low-calorie, low-fat canapé bases.

1	seedless English cucumber	1
1	can (6 oz/170 g) crabmeat*	1
2 tbsp	light sour cream or light cream cheese	25 mL
2 tbsp	chopped fresh chives or green onion	25 mL
¼ tsp or less	salt, freshly ground pepper and hot pepper sauce	1 mL or less
	Paprika	

Run tines of fork lengthwise along cucumber to make decorative edge; cut in ¼ inch (5 mm) thick slices. Drain crabmeat thoroughly. In bowl, mix crabmeat, sour cream and chives; season with salt, pepper and hot pepper sauce. Add more sour cream if necessary to hold mixture together. Place small spoonful of crab mixture onto each cucumber slice. Sprinkle with paprika.

MAKES 36 PIECES

*Imitation crabmeat also works well in this recipe. Chop and mix with 2 tbsp (25 mL) each light sour cream and light cream cheese.

MAKE AHEAD: Cover and refrigerate for up to 2 hours.

PER PIECE: 5 calories, 1 g protein, 0 g total fat, 0 g saturated fat, 4 mg cholesterol, 0 g carbohydrate, 0 g fibre, 51 mg sodium, 18 mg potassium

Mussels with Herbs and Garlic on the Half Shell

You can use any combination of fresh herbs, basil, coriander, dill or parsley to equal about ⅓ cup (75 mL) chopped. Add hot pepper sauce if you like.

2 lb	mussels	1 kg
1	sweet red pepper, finely chopped	1
1 tbsp	each fresh lemon and orange juice	15 mL
1 tbsp	olive oil	15 mL
1 tbsp	sodium-reduced soy sauce	15 mL
2	cloves garlic, minced	2
⅓ cup	chopped fresh basil and/or coriander	75 mL

Rinse mussels and pull off any hairy beards. Discard any mussels that are cracked or don't close after a minute or two when tapped. In large Dutch oven or heavy saucepan cook mussels with ¼ cup (50 mL) water, covered, over medium-high heat for 5 minutes or until mussels are open. Discard any mussels that don't open after another minute or two of cooking. Remove from heat and let cool.

In bowl, mix red pepper, lemon juice, orange juice, olive oil, soy sauce, garlic and basil. Separate mussels from the shells, reserving half the shell of each. Add mussels to garlic-herb mixture; stir to mix, cover and let stand at least 30 minutes or refrigerate for up to 8 hours.

To serve, place a mussel in each half shell; spoon herb-garlic mixture over; arrange on a large serving platter.

MAKES 45 TO 50 PIECES

PER PIECE: 9 calories, 1 g protein, 0 g total fat, 0 g saturated fat, 2 mg cholesterol, 1 g carbohydrate, 0 g fibre, 21 mg sodium, 16 mg potassium

Teriyaki Shrimp Wrapped with Snow Peas

This colourful, delicious hors d'oeuvre is very easy to prepare. Stick the toothpicks holding these tasty bites into a cauliflower for a novel presentation. Serve with Minted Coriander Dipping Sauce (p. 6) or on their own. Serve any remaining snow peas with a dip or spread, or split them down the centre and fill with light sour cream mixed with fresh chopped basil or dill.

1 lb	large raw shrimp (about 18)	500 g
2 tbsp	sodium-reduced soy sauce	25 mL
2 tbsp	sherry	25 mL
1 tbsp	sesame oil	15 mL
1 tbsp	grated gingerroot	15 mL
2 tsp	granulated sugar	10 mL
4 oz	snow peas	125 g

Peel each shrimp and remove black intestinal vein; place shrimp in bowl.

Combine soy sauce, sherry, oil, gingerroot and sugar, mixing well. Pour over shrimp; cover and refrigerate for 1 hour. Transfer shrimp and marinade to nonstick skillet; cook over medium-high heat for 3 to 5 minutes or until shrimp are pink and opaque. Let cool.

Trim snow peas and blanch in boiling water for 2 minutes or just until pliable. Drain and plunge into bowl of ice water to set colour and prevent further cooking. Drain.

Wrap 1 snow pea around each shrimp; secure with toothpick. Arrange on serving platter; cover and refrigerate until serving time.

MAKES 18 PIECES

MAKE AHEAD: Cook shrimp in marinade (don't drain); cover and refrigerate for up to 1 day. Assembled appetizers can be covered and refrigerated for up to 3 hours.

PER PIECE: 27 calories, 4 g protein, 1 g total fat, 0 g saturated fat, 37 mg cholesterol, 1 g carbohydrate, 0 g fibre, 73 mg sodium, 53 mg potassium

Endive with Chèvre and Shrimp

This easy-to-prepare appetizer looks fancy and tastes terrific. It's a favourite of my daughter, Susie. Sometimes she uses smoked salmon or trout instead of shrimp. Serve on a large platter along with cherry tomatoes.

4	Belgian endive	4
5 oz	chèvre (soft goat cheese)	140 g
⅓ cup	light ricotta cheese (5% MF) or light sour cream	75 mL
	Freshly ground pepper	
4 oz	small cooked salad shrimp	125 g
	Small sprigs fresh dill or chopped chives	

Divide endive into individual leaves; wash under cold running water and drain well.

In small bowl, combine chèvre, ricotta cheese, and pepper to taste; mix well.

Fill wide end of each endive leaf with cheese mixture; top with shrimp. Garnish with sprig of dill.

MAKES 30 APPETIZERS

MAKE AHEAD: Cover and refrigerate for up to 6 hours.

PER PIECE: 21 calories, 2 g protein, 1 g total fat, 1 g saturated fat, 8 mg cholesterol, 0 g carbohydrate, 0 g fibre, 30 mg sodium, 31 mg potassium

Thai Shrimp Salad in Mini Pita Pockets

Perfect for a cocktail party menu or with drinks before dinner, these easy-to-make hors d'oeuvres are one of my new favourites, mainly because of the fabulous flavour combination of fresh mint and fresh coriander.

2 tbsp	light mayonnaise	25 mL
1 tbsp	fresh lemon juice	15 mL
1 tsp	minced gingerroot	5 mL
Dash	hot pepper sauce	Dash
1 cup	cooked salad shrimp	250 mL
1 cup	bean sprouts	250 mL
½ cup	grated carrot	125 mL
¼ cup	coarsely chopped fresh mint	50 mL
¼ cup	chopped fresh coriander (cilantro)	50 mL
14	whole-wheat mini pitas, halved	14

In bowl, whisk together mayonnaise, lemon juice, gingerroot and hot pepper sauce. Add shrimp, bean sprouts, carrot, mint and coriander; mix gently. Spoon shrimp mixture into pita halves.

MAKES 28 PIECES

MAKE AHEAD: Cover and refrigerate mixture early in the day. Spoon into pita pockets up to 2 hours before serving.

VARIATION:
Instead of mini pitas, use Crostini (p. 28), or cucumber cups made by hollowing out cucumber rounds (leaving a base).

NOTE: Shrimp is very low in fat but does contain cholesterol. By combining the shrimp with other ingredients, the total cholesterol of this recipe is low and fits into a healthy diet.

PER PIECE: 24 calories, 2 g protein, 1 g total fat, 0 g saturated fat, 9 mg cholesterol, 3 g carbohydrate, 1 g fibre, 45 mg sodium, 34 mg potassium

Salmon Mousse with Dill

This is one recipe that I continue to make year after year. I always use fresh dill and usually use a ring mould or loaf pan—the mousse looks pretty once it's unmoulded, surrounded with melba toast or slices of French bread. However, it's just as delicious served straight from a shallow bowl. Be sure to use wild sockeye salmon, for its bright red colour.

MAKE AHEAD: Cover and refrigerate for up to 3 days.

PER 1 TBSP (15 mL): 17 calories, 2 g protein, 1 g total fat, 0 g saturated fat, 2 mg cholesterol, 1 g carbohydrate, 0 g fibre, 56 mg sodium, 40 mg potassium

2	cans (each 7¾ oz/220 g) sockeye salmon	2
1	envelope unflavoured gelatin	1
¾ cup	low-fat plain yogurt	175 mL
½ cup	light sour cream	125 mL
½ cup	finely chopped celery	125 mL
½ cup	chopped fresh dill (or 1 tsp/5 mL dried)*	125 mL
2 tbsp	grated onion	25 mL
1 tbsp	fresh lemon juice	15 mL
½ tsp	salt	2 mL
Dash	hot pepper sauce	Dash

Drain salmon liquid into measuring cup; add enough water to make ½ cup (125 mL). Pour into small saucepan. Sprinkle gelatin over top; let stand until softened, about 5 minutes. Warm over medium heat until dissolved. Let cool to room temperature. Stir in yogurt, sour cream, celery, dill, onion, lemon juice, salt and hot pepper sauce.

Remove skin from salmon (but not bones, as they contain calcium); mash salmon with fork or process in food processor. Mix into gelatin mixture. Spoon into lightly oiled 4-cup (1 L) mould. Cover and refrigerate until firm, at least 3 hours. Unmould onto serving plate.

MAKES 3½ CUPS (875 mL)

*If using dried dillweed, add ¼ cup (50 mL) finely chopped fresh parsley.

Crab Cakes with Lime Ginger Mayonnaise

Whenever I'm dining out and see crab cakes on the menu, I order them. Along with a green salad they make a yummy lunch. Yet, too often they are dry and made with not enough crabmeat. When I make them at home I use imitation crabmeat (unless I'm in British Columbia and can get fresh crab) and absolutely love them. Serve on individual plates on a bed of arugula, with a drizzle of Monda Rosenberg's Lime Ginger Mayonnaise (p. 323) over top.

¼ cup	light mayonnaise	50 mL
¼ cup	finely chopped green onions	50 mL
2 tbsp	finely chopped sweet red pepper	25 mL
2 tbsp	each chopped fresh parsley and dill	25 mL
1 tsp	Dijon mustard	5 mL
1 tsp	finely grated lemon rind	5 mL
¼ tsp	each freshly ground pepper and hot pepper sauce	1 mL
1	large egg, lightly beaten	1
1	pkg (8 oz/227 g) crab-flavoured pollock or imitation crabmeat or fresh crabmeat	1
1 cup	fine dry bread crumbs (divided)	250 mL
1	bunch fresh arugula or watercress (optional)	1
¼ cup	Monda Rosenberg's Lime Ginger Mayonnaise (p. 323) (optional)	50 mL

In bowl, stir together mayonnaise, onions, red pepper, parsley, dill, mustard, lemon rind, salt, pepper, hot pepper sauce and egg. Stir in ⅓ cup (75 mL) of the bread crumbs and all of the crabmeat; mix lightly until combined. Shape and press into 4 patties, about ½ inch (2 cm) thick. They will be soft, but if they do not hold their shape, add more bread crumbs and mayonnaise.

Place remaining bread crumbs on plate; press cakes lightly into crumbs to coat all sides.

Place on lightly oiled baking sheet and bake in 400°F (200°C) oven for 15 minutes until crisp and golden, turning half way through.

Serve on individual plates lined with arugula or watercress and drizzle with Lime Ginger Mayonnaise.

MAKES 4 SERVINGS

MAKE AHEAD: Refrigerate uncooked crab cakes, covered, for up to 4 hours; bake just before serving.

PER SERVING (not including Lime Ginger Mayonnaise): 228 calories, 11 g protein, 11 g total fat, 2 g saturated fat, 63 mg cholesterol, 21 g carbohydrate, 1 g fibre, 759 mg sodium, 149 mg potassium

Grilled Salmon Ribbons with Sesame and Coriander

Easy to eat without cutlery, this appetizer is great for a buffet, and goes well with Creamy Dill Sauce (p. 325). It can also be served as a main course.

16	wooden skewers	16
1 lb	skinless salmon fillet (1 inch/2.5 cm thick)	500 g
3 tbsp	fresh lemon juice	50 mL
1 tbsp	sesame oil	15 mL
2 tbsp	chopped fresh coriander (cilantro)	25 mL
1 to 2 tbsp	sesame seeds	15 to 25 mL

Soak wooden skewers in water to cover for at least 10 minutes to prevent scorching. Cut salmon into ¼-inch (5 mm) thick slices to make sixteen 6- × 1-inch (15 × 2.5 cm) strips. Thread salmon onto skewers. Place in single layer in shallow dish.

Combine lemon juice and sesame oil; pour over salmon. Sprinkle with coriander. Let marinate for 15 minutes. Arrange salmon on lightly greased broiling pan or grill; sprinkle with sesame seeds. Broil or grill 6 inches (15 cm) from heat for 3 to 5 minutes or until opaque.

MAKES 16 APPETIZER PIECES OR 4 MAIN-COURSE SERVINGS

MAKE AHEAD: Marinate salmon, covered, in the refrigerator for up to 4 hours.

NOTE: For recipes calling for sesame oil, use dark sesame oil, a strong-flavoured oil made from roasted sesame seeds. You'll find it in Asian food stores and many supermarkets.

PER PIECE: 63 calories, 6 g protein, 4 g total fat, 1 g saturated fat, 16 mg cholesterol, 0 g carbohydrate, 0 g fibre, 16 mg sodium, 101 mg potassium

Asian Salad Rolls

Perfect for a first course, because they can be prepared in advance, these wonderfully flavoured rolls look and taste terrific. For a bit more heat, add more red pepper flakes.

SAUCE

½ cup	unseasoned rice vinegar	125 mL
2 tbsp	sodium-reduced soy sauce	25 mL
2 tbsp	hoisin sauce	25 mL
1 tbsp	peanut butter	15 mL
2 tsp	granulated sugar	10 mL
1 tsp	grated gingerroot	5 mL
⅛ tsp	crushed red pepper flakes	0.5 mL

ROLLS

2 oz	rice noodles (rice vermicelli)	60 g
8	shiitake mushrooms (fresh or dried)	8
¼ cup	sodium-reduced chicken or vegetable broth	50 mL
8	small green onions, trimmed	8
16	rice paper wrappers (8-inch/20 cm rounds)	16
8	leaves Boston or leaf lettuce, halved	8
1¼ cups	bean sprouts	300 mL
2	small carrots, coarsely grated	2
1 cup	cooked small salad shrimp (optional)	250 mL
¼ cup	each fresh mint and coriander (cilantro), coarsely chopped	50 mL

SAUCE: In small bowl, combine rice vinegar, soy sauce, hoisin sauce, peanut butter, sugar, gingerroot and red pepper flakes.

ROLLS: In pot of boiling water, soak noodles for 2 minutes (or follow package instructions); drain and cool under cold water. Drain and transfer to bowl. Pour ¼ cup (50 mL) of the sauce over noodles and mix well; set aside.

If using dried mushrooms, soak in hot water until soft. Cut mushrooms into thin strips. In small saucepan, cook mushrooms in stock for 3 minutes or until tender. Cut green onions lengthwise into thin strips; cut into 3-inch (8 cm) lengths.

In large bowl of hot water, soak 1 rice paper wrapper for 2 minutes or until softened. Remove from water, place on work surface and fold in half. Place lettuce leaf on wrapper with top of lettuce extending slightly over fold of wrapper. Place a few slices of green onion on top to extend over wrapper slightly. Top with spoonful of noodles, then 2 mushroom pieces, a few bean sprouts, some carrot, shrimp, mint and coriander. Fold up rounded edge of wrapper, then roll wrapper around filling. Repeat with remaining wrappers.

Serve 2 rolls per person on individual plates. Pass remaining sauce separately, for dipping.

MAKES 8 SERVINGS

MAKE AHEAD: Cover and refrigerate rolls for up to 6 hours.

NOTE: Rice paper wrappers (usually from Thailand or Vietnam) are available at many grocery stores, as well as at specialty food shops and Asian markets.

PER SERVING: 128 calories, 3 g protein, 2 g total fat, 0 g saturated fat, 0 mg cholesterol, 26 g carbohydrate, 2 g fibre, 276 mg sodium, 203 mg potassium

Thai Pork Skewers

These strips of spicy meat make wonderful finger food—terrific as cocktail snacks or in a buffet. For a dinner party appetizer, serve with Thai Peanut Sauce (p. 329). They are also great barbecued and served as a main course. Fresh coriander adds a distinctive, lively flavour.

1 lb	thinly sliced pork	500 g
3 tbsp	chopped fresh coriander (cilantro)*	50 mL
2 tbsp	dry sherry or fresh lime juice	25 mL
1 tbsp	white wine vinegar	15 mL
1 tbsp	fish sauce or hoisin sauce	15 mL
1 tbsp	dark sesame oil	15 mL
1 tbsp	honey	15 mL
1 tbsp	sodium-reduced soy sauce	15 mL
2 tbsp	minced gingerroot	25 mL
1	large clove garlic, minced	1
¼ tsp	crushed red pepper flakes	1 mL
30	wooden skewers (or 48 toothpicks)	30

Trim fat from pork; slice pork into thin strips. In bowl, combine coriander, sherry, vinegar, fish sauce, sesame oil, honey, soy sauce, gingerroot, garlic and red pepper flakes. Add pork, stirring to coat. Cover and marinate in refrigerator for at least 2 hours.

Soak wooden skewers or toothpicks in water for 15 minutes. Thread pork strips onto skewers. Broil on broiler pan in single layer for 3 to 5 minutes or until browned.

MAKES 30 PIECES ON SKEWERS, 48 ON TOOTHPICKS

*If fresh coriander is unavailable, substitute parsley, adding 1 tsp (5 mL) each dried coriander and ground coriander.

MAKE AHEAD: Marinate pork in the refrigerator for up to 1 day. Or, once threaded on skewers, pour remaining marinade over, cover, and refrigerate for up to 4 hours.

VARIATION:
Substitute 1 lb (500 g) beef, chicken or turkey for the pork.

NOTE: Buy the pork either very thinly sliced or buy a 1-inch (2.5 cm) thick piece and slice it thinly across the grain. Cut strips to fit length of skewer or toothpick. If using skewers, bite-size lengths are ideal for cocktail snacks, 6-inch (15 cm) long pieces for a buffet or a main course.

Fish sauce, with its distinctive, pungent flavour, is a staple ingredient in Southeast Asian cooking and is available in Asian markets and some supermarkets. It keeps on the shelf for at least a year.

PER 1 OF 48 PIECES: 16 calories, 2 g protein, 1 g total fat, 0 g saturated fat, 5 mg cholesterol, 0 g carbohydrate, 0 g fibre, 24 mg sodium, 29 mg potassium

Roasted Red Pepper and Arugula Spirals

You can roast your own peppers or use the ones from a jar, available at most supermarkets. Instead of chèvre, you can use light, tub or plain cream cheese mixed with ¼ cup (50 mL) chopped fresh basil or coriander. Or mix chèvre with half its volume of light sour cream (to make it spreadable) and basil or coriander.

4	10-inch (25 cm) flour tortillas	4
½ cup	chèvre (soft goat cheese)	125 mL
4	roasted red peppers, well drained	4
Half	bunch arugula or enough watercress or lettuce to cover	Half

Spread each tortilla with cheese. Cut red peppers into 1-inch (2.5 cm) wide strips: arrange, in single layer, in row over cheese. Cover with arugula, leaving 1-inch (2.5 cm) border around edge.

Roll up tightly jelly-roll fashion. Wrap tightly in plastic wrap. Refrigerate for at least 1 hour. Cut each on the diagonal in 12 slices; discard or eat ends.

MAKES 40 PIECES

MAKE AHEAD: Refrigerate rolls for up to 6 hours before slicing.

NOTE: For instruction on how to roast red peppers, see page 22.

VARIATION:

Smoked Salmon and Cream Cheese Spirals
Spread flour tortilla with chèvre or herbed light cream cheese (store-bought is fine). Cover with a single layer of thin slices of smoked salmon, leaving about 1-inch (2.5 cm) border. Continue as in recipe.

PER PIECE: 33 calories, 1 g protein, 1 g total fat, 0 g saturated fat, 1 mg cholesterol, 5 g carbohydrate, 0 g fibre, 71 mg sodium, 25 mg potassium

Teriyaki Beef Rumaki

Wrap tender strips of marinated beef around crunchy water chestnuts for a delectable hot appetizer.

¾ lb	sirloin, round or flank steak, ½ inch (1 cm) thick	375 g
¼ cup	sodium-reduced soy sauce	50 mL
1	clove garlic, minced	1
1 tbsp	minced onion	15 mL
1 tbsp	granulated sugar	15 mL
1 tbsp	chopped gingerroot (or ½ tsp/2 mL ground ginger)	15 mL
¼ tsp	hot pepper sauce	1 mL
1	can (10 oz/284 mL) whole water chestnuts	1

Place meat in freezer for about 30 minutes or until firm, for easier slicing. Cut off any fat; slice meat across the grain into very thin strips about ⅛ inch (3 mm) thick and 3 inches (8 cm) long.

In bowl, combine soy sauce, garlic, onion, sugar, gingerroot and hot pepper sauce. Add meat, stirring to coat strips evenly. Marinate for 30 minutes at room temperature, stirring occasionally. Drain meat. Wrap 1 strip around each water chestnut and secure with toothpick.

Arrange on baking sheet; broil for 3 to 4 minutes or until piping hot and meat is medium-rare. (Or microwave on High for 3 to 4 minutes, rotating dish a quarter-turn halfway through cooking time.)

MAKES 25 TO 30 PIECES

MAKE AHEAD: Marinate meat for up to 2 days in refrigerator. Wrap meat around water chestnuts; cover and refrigerate for up to 6 hours.

PER PIECE: 26 calories, 3 g protein, 1 g total fat, 0 g saturated fat, 7 mg cholesterol, 2 g carbohydrate, 0 g fibre, 50 mg sodium, 55 mg potassium

Goat Cheese and Pesto Tortilla Pizzas

I first had these fabulous, crisp thin-crust pizzas at a barbecue at my friend Marilyn Short's house in Toronto. In the summer, I put out the toppings in small bowls, then let guests make their own pizzas and cook them on the barbecue. Makes a great lunch, just add a green salad.

8	soft 6-inch (15 cm) flour tortillas	8
1 tsp	olive oil	5 mL
1 cup	sliced mushrooms (Portobello or regular)	250 mL
⅓ cup	dry-packed sun-dried tomatoes (about 8)	75 mL
8	medium asparagus spears	8
¼ cup	pesto	50 mL
1 cup	shredded part-skim mozzarella cheese (4 oz/125 g)	250 mL
2 oz	chèvre (soft goat cheese), diced	60 g
1	roasted sweet red pepper (homemade or bottled), cut in thin strips	1
1 tbsp	sesame seeds	15 mL

Place tortillas on ungreased baking sheet. Bake in 350°F (180°C) oven for 5 minutes. Set aside.

In non-stick skillet, heat oil over medium-high heat; cook mushrooms for 5 to 8 minutes or until tender, stirring often. In bowl, pour boiling water over sun-dried tomatoes; let stand for 5 minutes. Drain well; cut in strips. Steam or boil asparagus for 3 minutes or until tender-crisp; drain. Cool under cold water; drain. Cut in 2-inch (5 cm) lengths.

Spread a little pesto on each tortilla; sprinkle with mushrooms, tomatoes, asparagus, mozzarella cheese, chèvre, red pepper and sesame seeds.

Barbecue over medium-high heat, covered, for 5 minutes or until cheese melts. Or bake on baking sheet in 400°F (200°C) oven for 8 minutes. Cut tortillas in quarters.

MAKES 16 SERVINGS

MAKE AHEAD: Bake tortillas and prepare toppings up to 6 hours in advance; refrigerate mushrooms and asparagus.

NOTE: Use store-bought pesto or, for a lower fat version, homemade (see p. 324).

NOTE: Buy bottled roasted red peppers or roast your own: Place peppers on barbecue grill or in 400°F (200°C) oven for 20 to 30 minutes (turning when one side is blackened) or until skins are blistered and peppers are soft. Let cool. Scrape skin from peppers; discard seeds.

PER SERVING: 117 calories, 5 g protein, 6 g total fat, 2 g saturated fat, 7 mg cholesterol, 11 g carbohydrate, 1 g fibre, 225 mg sodium, 123 mg potassium

Tortilla Pizza Triangles

You can make these cocktail tidbits in a jiffy using your favourite pizza toppings.

2	soft 9-inch (23 cm) flour tortillas	2
½ cup	tomato sauce	125 mL
½ tsp	dried oregano	2 mL
½ tsp	dried basil	2 mL
½ cup	shredded part-skim mozzarella cheese or crumbled chèvre (soft goat cheese)	125 mL
2	mushrooms, sliced	2
4	black olives, cut in strips	4
Quarter	sweet green pepper, cut in thin strips	Quarter

Using scissors or knife, cut tortillas into 2-inch (5 cm) triangles; place on baking sheet. Combine tomato sauce, oregano and basil; spread about 1 tsp (5 mL) over each triangle. Sprinkle with cheese, mushrooms, olives and green pepper. Bake in 400°F (200°C) oven for 3 to 5 minutes or until cheese melts. Serve hot.

MAKES 32 PIECES

NOTE: Soft flour tortillas are available at most supermarkets, either refrigerated or in the bakery section. They make a delicious, crisp pizza base.

VARIATIONS:

Tortilla Chips
Brush soft flour tortillas with olive oil. Arrange in single layer on baking sheet. Sprinkle with oregano, rosemary, sesame seeds or freshly grated Parmesan cheese. Bake in 375°F (190°C) oven for 3 to 5 minutes or until crisp. When cool, break into chip-size pieces.

Pita Chips
Instead of tortillas, separate pita bread into two rounds and prepare as in recipe.

PER PIECE: 18 calories, 1 g protein, 1 g total fat, 0 g saturated fat, 1 mg cholesterol, 2 g carbohydrate, 0 g fibre, 56 mg sodium, 24 mg potassium

---

Smoked Turkey-Wrapped Melon Balls

These juicy snacks make a nice addition to an hors d'oeuvres platter. They are delicious on their own or with Minted Coriander Dipping Sauce (p. 6). Prosciutto or thinly sliced ham can be used instead of turkey.

1	large cantaloupe	1
8 oz	thinly sliced smoked turkey	250 g
1	bunch fresh basil	1

Cut melon in half; scoop out seeds. Using melon baller, scoop out melon rounds. Cut turkey into strips about 1 inch (2.5 cm) wide and 5 inches (12 cm) long. Separate leaves from stems of basil. Cut large leaves in half. Wrap melon ball with a piece of basil, then a strip of turkey; fasten with toothpick.

MAKES 48 PIECES

MAKE AHEAD: Cover and refrigerate for up to 6 hours.

PER PIECE: 14 calories, 2 g protein, 0 g total fat, 0 g saturated fat, 4 mg cholesterol, 1 g carbohydrate, 0 g fibre, 50 mg sodium, 63 mg potassium

Cheese and Tomato Quesadillas

I keep a jar of pickled jalapeño peppers in the refrigerator to use in these zesty quesadillas.

4	soft 9-inch (23 cm) flour tortillas	4
¾ cup	shredded Danbo Light or part-skim mozzarella cheese	175 mL
1 oz	mild chèvre (soft goat cheese), diced	28 g
1	medium tomato, diced	1
1	green onion, chopped	1
2 tbsp	chopped pickled jalapeño pepper	25 mL
¼ cup	chopped fresh coriander (cilantro)	50 mL

Sprinkle half of each tortilla with Danbo and chèvre, tomato, green onion, jalapeño pepper and coriander. Fold uncovered half over filling and press edges together. Heat ungreased skillet over medium heat; cook quesadillas for 3 to 4 minutes on each side or until golden and cheese melts. To serve, cut each into 3 wedges.

MAKES 12 PIECES

MAKE AHEAD: Refrigerate filled and folded quesadillas, covered, for up to 3 hours before cooking.

NOTE: Quesadillas are folded flour tortillas filled with a savoury filling, often including melted cheese and chili peppers. Any cooked meats or chopped vegetables, or even refried beans, can also be added.

VARIATIONS:

Grilled or Barbecued Quesadillas
Grill over medium heat or coals for 2 to 3 minutes on each side or until golden and cheese melts.

Oven-Baked Quesadillas
Bake on baking sheet in 400°F (200°C) oven for 10 minutes or until golden and cheese melts.

Shrimp Quesadillas
Prepare Cheese and Tomato Quesadillas, omitting jalapeño pepper and adding ½ cup (125 mL) salad shrimp. Fresh dill can be used instead of coriander, if you like.

PER PIECE: 84 calories, 4 g protein, 3 g total fat, 1 g saturated fat, 5 mg cholesterol, 10 g carbohydrate, 1 g fibre, 204 mg sodium, 68 mg potassium

Sun-Dried Tomato and Caramelized Onion Toasts

Tender-sweet onions, full-flavoured dried tomatoes and balsamic vinegar make a delightful flavour combo. To save time, slice the onions in a food processor.

5 cups	thinly sliced cooking onions (1 lb/500 g)	1.25 L
1 cup	water	250 mL
¼ cup	chopped dry-packed sun-dried tomatoes	50 mL
2 tsp	granulated sugar	10 mL
¼ cup	chopped fresh parsley	50 mL
⅓ cup	freshly grated Parmesan cheese	75 mL
4 tsp	balsamic vinegar	20 mL
¼ tsp or less	salt and freshly ground pepper	1 mL or less
1	baguette (French bread stick)	1
2	cloves garlic, halved	2

In skillet, bring onions, water, tomatoes and sugar to a boil; reduce heat to low and simmer, uncovered, for 45 minutes or until onions are tender and only 1 tbsp (15 mL) liquid remains. Stir in parsley, half of the Parmesan, vinegar, and salt and pepper.

Meanwhile, slice bread into ½-inch (1 cm) thick rounds. Toast in 350°F (180°C) oven for 5 minutes. Rub one side of each round with cut side of garlic.

Spread each round with about 1 tsp (5 mL) onion mixture. Sprinkle with remaining cheese. Arrange on baking sheet. Broil for 2 to 3 minutes or until hot.

MAKES 36 PIECES

MAKE AHEAD: Cover and refrigerate onion mixture (omitting parsley) and toasted rounds for up to 2 days. Top rounds with onion mixture (adding parsley) and cheese up to 3 hours before serving.

PER PIECE: 30 calories, 1 g protein, 1 g total fat, 0 g saturated fat, 1 mg cholesterol, 5 g carbohydrate, 0 g fibre, 82 mg sodium, 42 mg potassium

Stuffed Mushroom Croustades

These mushroom appetizers are so delicious they'll disappear from the plate. Other savoury fillings are also wonderful nestled in the croustades—toasted bread cases that are much lower in fat and calories than pastry.

36	thin slices whole-wheat bread	36
36	medium mushrooms	36
1 cup	fresh whole-wheat bread crumbs	250 mL
1 to 2	large cloves garlic, chopped	1 to 2
¼ cup	chopped fresh parsley	50 mL
¼ tsp or less	salt and freshly ground pepper	1 mL or less
4 tsp	olive oil	20 mL
½ cup	shredded part-skim mozzarella cheese	125 mL

Using 2½-inch (6 cm) cookie cutter or glass, cut out 36 rounds of bread. Press each into small muffin cups. Bake in 300°F (150°C) oven for 20 to 25 minutes or until light brown. Let cool.

Remove stems from mushrooms. In food processor or bowl, combine bread crumbs, garlic, parsley, and salt and pepper; process until combined. Add olive oil and process just until mixed.

Spoon some stuffing into each mushroom cap; top with cheese. Place mushrooms into bread cases and place on ungreased baking sheet; bake in 400°F (200°C) oven for 10 minutes or until hot. If desired, broil for last minute. Serve hot.

MAKES 36 PIECES

MAKE AHEAD: Store bread croustades in an airtight container for up to 1 week. Refrigerate stuffed mushrooms, covered, for up to 1 day.

NOTE: Add the unused mushroom stems to soup for extra flavour and nutrients.

PER PIECE: 52 calories, 2 g protein, 2 g total fat, 0 g saturated fat, 1 mg cholesterol, 8 g carbohydrate, 1 g fibre, 111 mg sodium, 84 mg potassium

Marinated Mushrooms

Pass these zippy mushrooms on toothpicks with drinks or serve as part of a relish tray or salad plate.

⅔ cup	tarragon or white wine vinegar	150 mL
⅓ cup	canola oil	75 mL
2 tbsp	granulated sugar	25 mL
1 tsp	each dried basil and thyme	5 mL
½ tsp	salt	2 mL
2 tbsp	water	25 mL
Dash	hot pepper sauce	dash
¼ tsp	crushed red pepper flakes (optional)	1 mL
1	clove garlic, minced	1
	Freshly ground pepper	
1	onion, thinly sliced	1
1½ lb	medium mushrooms	750 g

In large bowl, combine vinegar, oil, sugar, basil, thyme, salt, water, hot pepper sauce, dried hot pepper flakes (if using), garlic, and pepper to taste; stir until well mixed.

Separate onion into rings. Trim bases off mushrooms. Add onions and mushrooms to vinegar mixture; mix lightly to coat. Cover and refrigerate for at least 8 hours or up to 2 days, stirring occasionally. Drain before serving.

MAKES 10 APPETIZER SERVINGS

MAKE AHEAD: Cover and refrigerate for up to 2 days. Stir occasionally and drain before serving.

VARIATION:

Marinated Mushrooms and Artichokes
Drain 1 can (14 oz/398 mL) artichokes. Cut in half and add to mushroom mixture before marinating.

PER SERVING: 69 calories, 1 g protein, 5 g total fat, 0 g saturated fat, 0 mg cholesterol, 6 g carbohydrate, 1 g fibre, 77 mg sodium, 250 mg potassium

Spicy Popcorn

When it comes to healthy eating, my downfall isn't dessert but salty, chip-like snacks. Popcorn is often my solution.

3 cups	plain popped corn	750 mL
2 tsp	soft margarine, melted	10 mL
½ tsp	chili powder	2 mL
¼ tsp	each ground cumin and salt	1 mL

Place popcorn in food-safe plastic bag. In small dish, stir together margarine, chili powder, cumin and salt; pour over popped corn and shake to mix.

MAKES 3 CUPS (750 mL)

PER 1 CUP (250 mL): 55 calories, 1 g protein, 3 g total fat, 0 g saturated fat, 0 mg cholesterol, 7 g carbohydrate, 1 g fibre, 234 mg sodium, 37 mg potassium

Candied Corn

This tasty recipe uses only a minimum of sugar and fat. For variety, add ¼ tsp (1 mL) cinnamon to the sugar mixture.

2 tbsp	packed brown sugar	25 mL
1 tbsp	soft margarine	15 mL
1 tbsp	corn syrup	15 mL
4 cups	plain popped corn	1 L

In microwaveable custard cup or small dish, combine sugar, margarine and corn syrup. Microwave on Medium for 20 seconds; stir. Microwave on Medium for another 30 seconds; stir. Pour over popped corn and toss to mix. Spread on baking sheet. Bake in 275°F (140°C) oven for 20 minutes, stirring every 5 minutes.

MAKES 4 CUPS (1 L)

MAKE AHEAD: Store in an airtight container for up to 1 day.

PER 1 CUP (250 mL): 96 calories, 1 g protein, 3 g total fat, 0 g saturated fat, 0 mg cholesterol, 17 g carbohydrate, 1 g fibre, 47 mg sodium, 50 mg potassium

Crostini

Crostini, Italian-style toasted bread rounds, are a nice change from crackers to top with your favourite spread. To reduce the fat even more, omit the oil and simply rub the toasted bread rounds with a cut clove of garlic.

1 tbsp	olive oil	15 mL
1	small clove garlic, minced	1
1	baguette (French bread stick)	1

Combine oil and garlic; set aside. Cut bread into ½-inch (2.5 cm) thick slices (if large, cut slices in half); place on baking sheet. Brush with oil and toast in 350°F (180°C) oven for 5 to 8 minutes or until crisp.

MAKES 36 SLICES

MAKE AHEAD: Store at room temperature in an airtight container for up to 3 days.

VARIATION:

Low-Salt Bagel Thins
These are another alternative to crackers and even to high-fat potato chips. With a serrated knife, slice bagel into very thin round slices. Place on baking sheet and brush very lightly with extra-virgin olive oil. Sprinkle with dried oregano to taste. Bake in 350°F (180°C) oven for 10 to 12 minutes or until golden and crisp. Bagel thins can be stored in an airtight container for up to 1 week.

PER SLICE: 23 calories, 1 g protein, 1 g total fat, 0 g saturated fat, 0 mg cholesterol, 4 g carbohydrate, 0 g fibre, 43 mg sodium, 8 mg potassium

Spiced Meatballs with Coriander Dipping Sauce

Middle Eastern seasonings, such as cinnamon, allspice and garlic, plus crunchy water chestnuts and juicy raisins, make these meatballs the best I've tasted; salt will never be missed. Fresh coriander is a perfect flavour match in the sauce. Don't substitute dried coriander for fresh; instead, use fresh Thai basil and add a bit of curry powder to taste.

NOTE: Bake rather than fry meatballs; not only is there less fat as a result, it's also much easier.

PER 1 PIECE: 26 calories, 2 g protein, 1 g total fat, 0 g saturated fat, 6 mg cholesterol, 2 g carbohydrate, 0 g fibre, 35 mg sodium, 57 mg potassium

MEATBALLS

¼ cup	raisins	50 mL
½ lb	lean ground lamb	250 g
⅓ cup	minced water chestnuts	75 mL
2 tbsp	minced green onions	25 mL
1	clove garlic, minced	1
½ tsp	ground allspice	2 mL
½ tsp	cinnamon	2 mL
	Freshly ground pepper	

CORIANDER DIPPING SAUCE

¾ cup	low-fat plain yogurt	175 mL
¼ cup	minced fresh coriander (cilantro), lightly packed	50 mL
¼ tsp or less	salt and freshly ground pepper	1 mL or less

MEATBALLS: Soak raisins in hot water for 15 minutes; drain and chop. In bowl, combine raisins, lamb, water chestnuts, onions, garlic, allspice, cinnamon and pepper; mix well.

Shape into 24 balls of 1 tbsp (15 mL) each. Arrange in single layer in ungreased baking dish. Bake, uncovered, in 400°F (200°C) oven for 15 to 20 minutes or until no longer pink inside.

CORIANDER DIPPING SAUCE: Meanwhile, in small bowl, combine yogurt, coriander, and salt and pepper; cover and refrigerate for at least 30 minutes to allow flavours to develop. Serve hot meatballs with toothpicks for dipping into sauce.

MAKES 24 MEATBALLS AND 1 CUP (250 mL) DIPPING SAUCE

SOUPS

Gazpacho

This Spanish cold soup is perfect for a sultry summer evening. It's easy to make in a blender or food processor. I like to pass around a bowl of homemade garlic bread croutons so each person can add their own. For an extra punch of flavour, use locally grown tomatoes from your local farmers' market.

1	clove garlic	1
Half	small onion, quartered	Half
1	sweet red pepper, seeded and cut in chunks	1
3	ripe tomatoes, quartered	3
1	cucumber, cut in chunks*	1
3 tbsp	chopped fresh basil or coriander (cilantro)	50 mL
¼ cup	wine vinegar	50 mL
2 tbsp	olive oil	25 mL
½ cup	sodium-reduced vegetable or chicken broth, or water (optional)	125 mL
¼ tsp or less	salt, freshly ground pepper and hot pepper sauce	1 mL or less
	Chopped fresh basil or coriander (cilantro)	

In blender with machine running, drop garlic into feed tube, then onion; when chopped, turn machine off. Add red pepper, tomatoes, cucumber, basil, vinegar and oil; blend just until chopped. (Or, finely chop garlic, vegetables and basil; add vinegar and oil.) Add up to ½ cup (125 mL) broth if desired. Cover and refrigerate until serving.

Taste and season with salt, pepper, hot pepper sauce and more vinegar, if necessary. If the mixture is too thick, add water, sodium-reduced broth or tomato juice. Sprinkle each serving with chopped fresh basil.

MAKES 6 SERVINGS, ¾ CUP (175 mL) EACH

*Peel cucumber only if skin is tough or waxy.

MAKE AHEAD: Cover and refrigerate for up to 1 day.

NOTE: One serving is a high source of vitamin C.

VARIATION:
To reduce the fat even more, use only 1 tsp (5 mL) olive oil.

PER SERVING: 66 calories, 1 g protein, 5 g total fat, 1 g saturated fat, 0 mg cholesterol, 6 g carbohydrate, 1 g fibre, 102 mg sodium, 251 mg potassium

Purée of Tomato Soup with Fresh Basil

This is one of my husband's favourite soups; he likes it cold, preferring it to gazpacho. Make it in the summer when garden tomatoes and basil are at their best.

2 lb	ripe tomatoes (about 5)	1 kg
1 tbsp	olive oil	15 mL
Half	Spanish onion, thinly sliced	Half
2 tsp	chopped fresh garlic	10 mL
¼ cup	chopped fresh basil	50 mL
¼ tsp	salt	1 mL
	Freshly ground pepper	
2 tbsp	light sour cream (optional)	25 mL
2 tbsp	chopped fresh chives	25 mL

Peel tomatoes by blanching in boiling water for 1 minute; peel off skins. Cut in half, then squeeze or scoop out seeds. In skillet, heat oil over medium heat; cook onion and garlic until tender, about 5 minutes.

In blender or food processor, purée tomatoes and onion mixture until smooth; stir in basil, salt, and pepper to taste. To serve hot, reheat but don't boil. Or, cover and refrigerate for at least 30 minutes and serve cold.

Garnish each bowlful with light sour cream (if using) and chives.

MAKES 6 SERVINGS, ½ CUP (125 mL) EACH

MAKE AHEAD: Cover and refrigerate for up to 2 days.

NOTE: For the most flavour, don't refrigerate tomatoes. Instead, store at room temperature out of direct sunlight or in a cool place (but not as cold as the refrigerator).

PER SERVING: 47 calories, 1 g protein, 3 g total fat, 0 g saturated fat, 0 mg cholesterol, 6 g carbohydrate, 2 g fibre, 104 mg sodium, 301 mg potassium

Chilled Melon and Yogurt Soup

A hint of ginger and fresh mint adds sparkle to this light, refreshing summer soup. Serve it as first course for brunch, lunch or dinner. A ripe cantaloupe is very flavourful; an unripe one is not, so choose one that has a sweet fragrance and yields slightly to pressure at the blossom end.

1	very ripe cantaloupe	1
1 cup	low-fat plain yogurt	250 mL
3 tbsp	fresh lemon juice	50 mL
½ tsp	grated gingerroot (or ¼ tsp/1 mL ground ginger)	2 mL
2 tbsp	chopped fresh mint	25 mL

Cut cantaloupe in half and remove seeds. Scoop out pulp into blender or food processor; purée to make about 1½ cups (375 mL). Add yogurt, lemon juice and gingerroot; process to mix. Refrigerate until serving. Divide among small bowls; top with sprinkling of mint.

MAKES 4 SERVINGS, ⅔ CUP (150 mL) EACH

MAKE AHEAD: Cover and refrigerate for up to 1 day.

NOTE: One serving provides 105% of the daily value for vitamin C and is a high source of vitamin A.

PER SERVING: 74 calories, 4 g protein, 1 g total fat, 1 g saturated fat, 4 mg cholesterol, 13 g carbohydrate, 1 g fibre, 59 mg sodium, 416 mg potassium

Chilled Cucumber Mint Soup

Refreshing and easy to make, this soup is a nice way to start a summer meal.

1	English cucumber, seeded	1
¼ cup	chopped green onion	50 mL
¼ cup	chopped fresh mint	50 mL
2 tbsp	coarsely chopped fresh coriander (cilantro) or parsley	25 mL
1½ cups	low-fat milk	375 mL
½ cup	light sour cream	125 mL
½ cup	low-fat plain yogurt	125 mL
¼ tsp or less	salt and freshly ground pepper	1 mL or less

In blender or food processor, purée cucumber, onion, mint and coriander; add milk and sour cream and process to mix. Stir in yogurt. Season with salt and pepper. Refrigerate for at least 1 hour before serving.

MAKES 6 SERVINGS, ¾ CUP (175 mL) EACH

MAKE AHEAD: Cover and refrigerate for up to 2 days.

PER SERVING: 70 calories, 4 g protein, 2 g total fat, 1 g saturated fat, 9 mg cholesterol, 9 g carbohydrate, 1 g fibre, 162 mg sodium, 277 mg potassium

Balkan Beet Cream Soup

This is one of my favourite soups for a first course or for a light meal along with a pasta or spinach salad and crusty bread. Save any leftover cooked beets for this flavourful chilled soup.

¼ cup	light sour cream	50 mL
¼ cup	low-fat cottage cheese	50 mL
2 cups	buttermilk	500 mL
2	medium beets, cooked, peeled and cubed	2
1	hard-cooked egg, peeled and chopped	1
One-third	English cucumber, diced (unpeeled)	One-third
½ cup	chopped fresh parsley	125 mL
3 tbsp	sliced radishes	50 mL
2 tbsp	chopped fresh chives or green onions	25 mL
¼ tsp or less	salt and freshly ground pepper	1 mL or less

In blender or food processor, combine sour cream and cottage cheese until smooth. Combine with buttermilk; refrigerate. Just before serving, divide beets among serving bowls. Stir egg, cucumber, parsley, radishes, chives, and salt and pepper to taste into buttermilk mixture; pour over beets.

MAKES 6 SERVINGS, ¾ CUP (175 mL) EACH

MAKE AHEAD: Cover and refrigerate buttermilk mixture, including vegetables, for up to 1 day.

NOTE: To cook beets, cut green tops from beets, leaving at least 1 inch (2.5 cm) of greens attached; don't trim off tapering root. (If beets are trimmed too close, colour and vitamins are leached into the cooking water.) Cook beets in boiling water or steam for 40 to 60 minutes or until tender when pierced with a fork. Drain under cold running water; slide off skins. Serve hot or let cool and add to salads.

PER SERVING: 77 calories, 6 g protein, 2 g total fat, 1 g saturated fat, 37 mg cholesterol, 8 g carbohydrate, 1 g fibre, 259 mg sodium, 286 mg potassium

Leek and Potato Soup

Entertaining is a breeze when you have the base for this smooth soup on hand in the freezer. Just thaw, add milk and serve hot or cold as a first course at a dinner party. For a lunch main course, top soup with garlic croutons, baby shrimp and chopped chives or green onions.

3	medium leeks	3
2	medium potatoes, peeled and cubed	2
1	clove garlic, minced	1
3 cups	sodium-reduced chicken or vegetable broth	750 mL
1½ cups	2% milk	375 mL
¼ tsp or less	salt and freshly ground pepper	1 mL or less
2 tbsp	minced fresh parsley or chives	25 mL

Trim all dark green parts from leeks. Cut lengthwise and spread apart; wash under cold running water. Slice thinly by hand or in food processor.

In saucepan, combine leeks, potatoes, garlic and chicken broth; simmer, partially covered, for 30 minutes or until vegetables are tender. Pour into blender or food processor; purée until smooth. Return soup to pan. Add milk, and salt and pepper; heat until hot. Sprinkle each serving with parsley.

MAKES 6 SERVINGS, 1 CUP (250 mL) EACH

VARIATIONS:

Vichyssoise
Substitute whole milk for 2% milk. Just before serving, add 1 tbsp (15 mL) fresh lemon juice, and salt and pepper to taste. Serve cold, garnished with chopped chives.

Zucchini and Watercress Vichyssoise
Reduce leeks to 2 small, add 1 lb (500 g) zucchini (about 4 small) sliced, and ½ cup (125 mL) packed watercress leaves. Cook zucchini along with leek-potato mixture. Add watercress to blender or food processor along with hot vegetables. Serve hot or cold.

Chunky Leek and Potato Soup
Add another potato; follow recipe except don't purée. Add any other vegetables you like, such as carrots, green beans, cabbage, sweet potatoes or broccoli. Omit milk if desired. For a creamier soup and extra calcium, reduce chicken broth to 2 cups (500 mL) and increase milk to 2½ cups (625 mL).

MAKE AHEAD: Cover and refrigerate purée for up to 2 days or freeze for up to 1 month. Reheat gently, then add milk; serve hot or cold.

NOTE: To reduce sodium, use water or Basic Chicken Stock (p. 62).

COMPARE:
One serving of Leek and Potato Soup made with:

	g fat	calories
2% milk	1	107
Whole milk	2	113
Light cream (10% BF)	6	148
Whipping cream (33% BF)	21	272

PER SERVING: 107 calories, 5 g protein, 1 g total fat, 1 g saturated fat, 5 mg cholesterol, 19 g carbohydrate, 1 g fibre, 409 mg sodium, 439 mg potassium

Mushroom Bisque with Tarragon

Easy to make, this creamy soup tastes so much better than anything out of a can. I usually double this recipe, as I like large servings.

8 oz	mushrooms	250 g
1 tbsp	canola or olive oil	15 mL
¼ cup	minced onion	50 mL
2 tbsp	all-purpose flour	25 mL
1 cup	sodium-reduced hot vegetable or chicken stock	250 mL
1½ cups	2% milk	375 mL
1 tsp	dried tarragon	5 mL
⅓ cup	minced fresh parsley	75 mL
¼ tsp or less	salt and freshly ground pepper	1 mL or less
1 tbsp	dry sherry (optional)	15 mL

Thinly slice 4 mushroom caps and set aside; coarsely chop remaining mushrooms (if using food processor, use on-off motion).

In saucepan, heat oil over medium-high heat; add onion and cook for 2 minutes, stirring occasionally. Add chopped mushrooms and cook for 10 minutes or until golden and no liquid remains, stirring often. Sprinkle with flour and stir until mixed. Whisk in hot broth and bring to boil, whisking constantly. Reduce heat to low and add milk, tarragon, parsley and reserved sliced mushrooms; cover and simmer for 5 minutes.

Season with salt and pepper. Stir in sherry (if using).

MAKES 4 SERVINGS, ¾ CUP (175 mL) EACH

VARIATION:

Wild Mushroom Soup
Break 10 g (½ cup/125 mL) dried porcini mushrooms into ¾-inch (2 cm) pieces. Pour ½ cup (125 mL) boiling water over mushrooms and let stand for 15 minutes. Prepare Mushroom Bisque with Tarragon, adding porcini mushrooms and soaking liquid along with the stock.

PER SERVING: 117 calories, 5 g protein, 6 g total fat, 1 g saturated fat, 7 mg cholesterol, 12 g carbohydrate, 2 g fibre, 303 mg sodium, 363 mg potassium

Doug Andison's Cream of Parsnip Soup with Ginger

This splendid soup is the creation of Doug Andison, my friend and good cook. He microwaves parsnips and leeks separately in large amounts, then freezes them in smaller portions so that he can prepare this soup easily at the last minute. He also likes to press the gingerroot through a garlic press instead of grating or chopping it, and might use cream instead of 2% milk.

1	onion (or whites of 2 leeks), chopped	1
4	medium parsnips, peeled and cubed (about 10 oz/280 g)	4
1 cup	water	250 mL
1 tbsp	canola or olive oil	15 mL
2 tbsp	all-purpose flour	25 mL
1 cup	sodium-reduced chicken or vegetable broth	250 mL
1½ tsp	finely grated fresh gingerroot	7 mL
¾ cup	2% milk	175 mL
¼ tsp or less	salt and freshly ground pepper	1 mL or less
	Chopped fresh coriander (cilantro) or parsley	

In saucepan, combine onion, parsnips and water; simmer, covered, for 8 to 10 minutes or until parsnips are tender. Purée in blender or food processor and set aside.

In saucepan, heat oil over medium heat; stir in flour and cook for 1 minute. Stir in broth and cook, stirring, until mixture comes to boil and thickens.

Add puréed parsnip mixture, gingerroot, milk, and salt and pepper. Stir to mix well and heat through. If too thick, thin with more milk or chicken broth.

Serve hot or cold. Sprinkle with chopped coriander to garnish.

MAKES 5 SERVINGS, ⅔ CUP (150 mL) EACH

NOTE: To reduce sodium, use water or Basic Chicken Stock (p. 62).

When adding milk to a hot soup, it is best to warm the milk gradually by slowly adding some of the hot mixture to it, then pouring it into the hot soup. The soup can be reheated, but don't let it boil.

MAKE AHEAD: Cover and refrigerate for up to 3 days.

VARIATION:

Carrot Soup with Ginger
Use carrots instead of parsnips. Add 1 tsp (5 mL) curry paste or powder to saucepan with oil, if desired.

PER SERVING: 129 calories, 3 g protein, 4 g total fat, 1 g saturated fat, 3 mg cholesterol, 22 g carbohydrate, 3 g fibre, 253 mg sodium, 420 mg potassium

Sweet Potato and Ginger Soup

Ginger, lime juice and coconut milk complement the mellow flavour of sweet potatoes. This is great served as a first course at a dinner party. If the soup is too thick, stir in extra sodium-reduced broth or light coconut milk.

6 cups	cubed peeled sweet potatoes (about 3 large)	1.5 L
3½ cups	sodium-reduced vegetable or chicken broth	875 mL
1 tbsp	minced gingerroot	15 mL
½ cup	light coconut milk	125 mL
3 tbsp	fresh lime juice	50 mL
½ tsp	salt	2 mL
¼ tsp	freshly ground pepper	1 mL
¼ cup	sliced almonds, toasted*	50 mL
¼ cup	chopped fresh coriander (cilantro)	50 mL

In saucepan, combine potatoes, stock and gingerroot; bring to boil. Reduce heat, cover and simmer for about 10 minutes or until potatoes are tender.

Transfer to food processor; purée until smooth. Return to saucepan; whisk in coconut milk, lime juice, salt and pepper. Cook over low heat just until heated through.

Ladle into bowls; sprinkle with almonds and coriander.

MAKES 8 SERVINGS, ¾ CUP (175 mL) EACH

*Toast almonds in skillet over medium-low heat for 3 to 5 minutes or until golden.

MAKE AHEAD: Cover and refrigerate for up to 1 day.

NOTE: To reduce sodium, use water or Basic Chicken Stock (p. 62).

A medium sweet potato is high in fibre and beta carotene and is a good source of vitamin C.

PER SERVING: 126 calories, 3 g protein, 3 g total fat, 1 g saturated fat, 0 mg cholesterol, 23 g carbohydrate, 4 g fibre, 380 mg sodium, 320 mg potassium

Broccoli Soup

This is one of the easiest and most nutritious ways to make soup—throw everything into the pot and cook until tender. With this method, the nutrients are retained rather than drained away with the cooking water; no fat is used to sauté the onions, as in many other recipes; and the soup thickens with a potato rather than with a flour-and-butter mixture. Since there isn't any other fat in the soup, I like to use 2% milk.

1	bunch broccoli	1
1	onion, chopped	1
2 cups	diced peeled potatoes	500 mL
1	clove garlic, minced	1
1½ cups	sodium-reduced vegetable broth or water	375 mL
½ tsp	dried thyme	2 mL
¼ tsp	freshly ground pepper	1 mL
Pinch	nutmeg	Pinch
1½ cups	2% milk	375 mL
¼ tsp or less	salt and freshly ground pepper	1 mL or less

Peel broccoli stems; coarsely chop stems and broccoli florets. In saucepan, combine broccoli, onion, potatoes, garlic, broth, thyme, pepper and nutmeg; bring to boil. Reduce heat, cover and simmer for 10 minutes or until potatoes are very tender.

In blender or food processor, purée soup in batches until smooth; return to pan. Add milk; heat through but do not boil. Season with salt and pepper.

MAKES 5 SERVINGS, 1 CUP (250 mL) EACH

MAKE AHEAD: Cover and refrigerate for up to 2 days. Reheat gently.

NOTE: Broccoli is packed with nutrients; one cup (250 mL) is an excellent source of folacin, vitamin C and beta carotene. It is also a source of calcium and iron and is high in fibre.

PER SERVING: 137 calories, 6 g protein, 2 g total fat, 1 g saturated fat, 6 mg cholesterol, 25 g carbohydrate, 3 g fibre, 321 mg sodium, 582 mg potassium

Old-Fashioned Quebec Pea Soup

Most pea soup recipes call for salt pork or a ham bone. To reduce fat, I don't use salt pork, but I often make it when I have a ham bone, though it can also be made without one. In Quebec, this soup is usually made with dried whole yellow peas. If they are unavailable, use yellow split peas. If available, use leaf savory, rather than ground.

2 cups	dried yellow whole or split peas	500 mL
10 cups	water	2.5 L
1	ham bone or 4 oz (125 g) ham, chopped	1
5	medium onions, chopped	5
3	medium carrots, peeled and chopped	3
2	stalks celery (including leaves), chopped	2
1 tsp	summer savory	5 mL
1	bay leaf	1
¼ tsp or less	salt and freshly ground pepper	1 mL or less

Rinse peas. In large soup pot, combine peas, water, ham bone or ham, onions, carrots, celery, summer savory and bay leaf; bring to boil. Skim off any scum. Cover and simmer for 3 hours or until peas are softened and soup has thickened. If soup is too thin, uncover and simmer 30 minutes longer. Season with salt and pepper. Discard bay leaf and ham bone.

MAKES 8 SERVINGS, 1¼ CUPS (300 mL) EACH

NOTE: One-quarter cup (50 mL) of dried peas (or ¾ cup/175 mL cooked) is a high source of soluble fibre (the kind that research has shown helps lower blood cholesterol), a good source of iron, and also supplies potassium and protein.

PER SERVING: 220 calories, 15 g protein, 2 g total fat, 0 g saturated fat, 8 mg cholesterol, 38 g carbohydrate, 6 g fibre, 264 mg sodium, 726 mg potassium

Split Pea Soup

I use the leftover bone from a cooked ham in this family favourite. Many cooks add carrots and other vegetables, but I don't—my mother said they take away from the flavour of peas. Taste the soup for seasoning just before serving. You might not want to add salt because there is often enough in the ham.

1	ham bone	1
8 oz	lean cooked ham*, cubed	250 g
10 cups	water	2.5 L
1¼ cups	split green peas (12 oz/375 g)	300 mL
4	onions, sliced	4
¼ tsp or less	salt and freshly ground pepper	1 mL or less

Remove any fat from ham bone. In large saucepan, combine ham bone, ham, water, peas and onions; bring to boil, skimming off any foam. Reduce heat and simmer, partially covered and stirring occasionally, for 2 to 3 hours or until peas are soft. If too thick; add more water. Season with salt and pepper.

MAKES 10 SERVINGS, ¾ CUP (175 mL) EACH

*Use the meat from the ham bone or, if nothing is left on the bone, buy ham.

MAKE AHEAD: Cover and refrigerate for up to 3 days. Soup tastes best if allowed to sit for at least 1 day. It will thicken upon cooling and standing, so add water to reach desired consistency when reheating.

NOTE: One serving is a high source of folacin and a high source of fibre.

PER SERVING: 128 calories, 10 g protein, 2 g total fat, 0 g saturated fat, 12 mg cholesterol, 19 g carbohydrate, 3 g fibre, 317 mg sodium, 376 mg potassium

Harvest Squash Soup

This is a delightful fall soup. If you don't peel the zucchini, the soup will be green in colour; if peeled, it will be pumpkin-coloured. You can use nearly any kind of squash instead of pumpkin. I've even made it using spaghetti squash and it always tastes terrific.

3 cups	peeled, cubed pumpkin or squash	750 mL
3 cups	cubed zucchini	750 mL
2	medium potatoes, peeled and cubed	2
1	large onion, sliced	1
2 cups	sodium-reduced vegetable or chicken broth	500 mL
1 tbsp	olive oil	15 mL
2 tbsp	chopped fresh parsley	25 mL
2	cloves garlic, chopped	2
¾ cup	2% milk	175 mL
1 tsp	dried basil (or 2 tbsp/25 mL chopped fresh)	5 mL
1 tbsp	fresh lemon juice	15 mL
¼ tsp or less	salt and freshly ground pepper	1 mL or less
	Shredded fresh basil, mint, or chopped fresh parsley	

In large saucepan, combine pumpkin, zucchini, potatoes, onion, broth, oil, parsley and garlic. Cover and simmer, stirring occasionally, for 45 minutes or until vegetables are tender. If stock simmers down, add water to reach original level.

In blender or food processor, purée mixture in batches. Return to saucepan. Add milk and basil; heat until hot. Stir in lemon juice, and salt and pepper. Garnish each serving with shredded basil.

MAKES 8 SERVINGS, ¾ CUP (175 mL) EACH

MAKE AHEAD: Cover and refrigerate puréed vegetable mixture for up to 3 days. Add milk, basil and remaining ingredients when reheating.

NOTE: To reduce sodium, use water or Basic Chicken Stock (p. 62).

Milk with at least 2% MF is best for this recipe; milk with 1% or less MF will result in a thinner, less creamy soup.

PER SERVING: 97 calories, 3 g protein, 2 g total fat, 1 g saturated fat, 2 mg cholesterol, 17 g carbohydrate, 3 g fibre, 204 mg sodium, 381 mg potassium

Italian Vegetable Soup with Pesto

Pesto, a vibrant Italian uncooked sauce made with fresh basil and garlic, adds exquisite flavour to this soup. This version of pesto has less oil than most, without any loss of flavour. Bottled pesto is available in most grocery stores. Add pesto directly to soup before serving or top each serving with a little spoonful.

1 tbsp	canola or olive oil	15 mL
1	onion, coarsely chopped	1
1½ cups	sodium-reduced chicken broth	375 mL
2½ cups	water	625 mL
2	carrots, thinly sliced	2
2	leeks (white part only), coarsely chopped	2
1	potato, diced	1
1	large stalk celery (including leaves), coarsely chopped	1
1	can (19 oz/540 mL) tomatoes undrained, chopped	1
1 cup	sliced green beans	250 mL
½ cup	coarsely chopped zucchini	125 mL
⅓ cup	broken medium egg noodles or spaghetti	75 mL
1	can (19 oz/540 mL) white beans*, drained and rinsed	1
¼ tsp or less	salt and freshly ground pepper	1 mL or less

PESTO

2	large cloves garlic	2
1 cup	lightly packed fresh basil**	250 mL
½ cup	freshly grated Parmesan cheese	125 mL
2 tbsp	olive oil	25 mL
¼ cup	hot soup liquid	50 mL

In skillet, heat oil over medium heat; add onion and cook, stirring, for 6 to 8 minutes or until tender.

In large pot, bring stock and water to boil. Add onion mixture, carrots, leeks, potato and celery; cover and simmer for 15 minutes. Add tomatoes, green beans, zucchini, egg noodles and white beans; cover and simmer for 10 to 15 minutes or until vegetables are tender, adding more water if needed. Season with salt and pepper.

PESTO: In food processor, chop garlic and basil. Add Parmesan and oil; process until smooth. Add enough of the warm soup liquid to make consistency of mayonnaise.

Ladle soup into individual bowls. Top each with spoonful of pesto.

MAKES 10 SERVINGS, 1 CUP (250 mL) EACH

*Or use 2 cups (500 mL) cooked white beans (see p. 118).

**If fresh basil is unavailable, substitute ¾ cup (175 mL) fresh Italian (flat-leaf) parsley and 2 tsp (10 mL) dried basil. The flavour isn't the same, but it is quite acceptable.

MAKE AHEAD: Cover and refrigerate for up to 2 days. Add pesto just before serving.

NOTE: To reduce sodium, use water or Basic Chicken Stock (p. 62).

One serving is a very high source of vitamin A and folacin and a high source of fibre.

PER SERVING: 166 calories, 7 g protein, 6 g total fat, 1 g saturated fat, 8 mg cholesterol, 22 g carbohydrate, 5 g fibre, 426 mg sodium, 503 mg potassium

Hearty Scotch Broth

In the winter, I like to serve this hearty soup for supper along with fresh bread and a salad. It's handy to have in the refrigerator for those rushed weekday dinners. If you can, make the soup in advance—not only does the flavour improve but when it is cool, any fat that has solidified on top can then be easily removed.

2 cups	chopped cooked lamb or 1½ lb (750g) raw lamb shanks	500 mL
8 cups	water	2 L
1	bay leaf	1
2	medium onions, chopped	2
2	stalks celery, diced	2
2	medium potatoes, peeled and diced	2
¼ cup	pearl or pot barley	50 mL
1½ cups	diced peeled rutabaga	375 mL
2 cups	chopped cabbage	500 mL
2	medium carrots, grated	2
½ cup	chopped fresh parsley	125 mL
¼ tsp or less	each salt and freshly ground pepper	1 mL or less

In large pot, combine lamb, water, bay leaf and onions; bring to boil. Cover, reduce heat and simmer for 1 hour. (If using cooked meat, simmer until onion is tender.) Skim fat from top and discard. Add celery, potatoes, barley and rutabaga; simmer for 15 minutes. Add cabbage and carrots; simmer until vegetables are tender, about 10 minutes. Remove lamb shanks; cut meat from bones and return to soup. Discard bone and bay leaf. Add parsley, salt and pepper.

MAKES 8 SERVINGS, 1 CUP (250 mL) EACH

MAKE AHEAD: Cover and refrigerate for up to 2 days. Skim off any fat and add parsley, salt and pepper before reheating.

NOTE: Because lamb has a stronger flavour than beef or poultry, it is particularly good for soups—a little meat will add a lot of flavour. You can use any cut of lamb; however, you might as well use less expensive cuts such as shank or shoulder, since the meat will become tender when simmered. If using shoulder, use only about 1 lb (500 g), as there will be much less bone than in shank.

VARIATION: For fat-restricted diets, make the broth first: bring lamb shank, water, bay leaf and 1 chopped onion to boil; simmer for 1 hour. Remove lamb and cut meat from bone; reserve. Refrigerate broth for 4 hours or overnight; skim all fat from top. Reheat broth; add remaining onion and continue as in recipe.

PER SERVING: 162 calories, 13 g protein, 3 g total fat, 1 g saturated fat, 38 mg cholesterol, 20 g carbohydrate, 3 g fibre, 127 mg sodium, 435 mg potassium

Vegetable Borscht

Give a flavour boost to any meal with small portions of this soup for a first course. Or serve larger bowlfuls for a main course. A dollop of light sour cream on top contrasts nicely with the colourful vegetables.

2	large fresh beets, peeled and finely chopped	2
1	onion, finely chopped	1
1	medium carrot, diced	1
1	large potato, peeled and diced	1
4 cups	sodium-reduced beef or vegetable broth	1 L
1	tomato, finely chopped	1
Quarter	small head cabbage, shredded	Quarter
2 tbsp	chopped fresh parsley	25 mL
½ tsp	dried dillweed	2 mL
1 tbsp	fresh lemon juice	15 mL
¼ tsp or less	salt and freshly ground pepper	1 mL or less
3 tbsp	light sour cream	50 mL

Chop all vegetables either in a food processor or by hand. In large saucepan, combine beets, onion, carrot, potato and broth; bring to boil. Reduce heat, cover and simmer for 30 minutes, skimming off any foam. Add tomato, cabbage, parsley and dill; simmer for 15 minutes or until vegetables are tender.

Season with lemon juice, salt and pepper. Ladle into individual bowls and top each serving with spoonful of sour cream.

MAKES 8 SERVINGS, 1 CUP (250 mL) EACH

MAKE AHEAD: Cover and refrigerate for up to 3 days or freeze for up to 3 weeks.

NOTE: One serving is a high source of vitamin A.

VARIATION: To reduce sodium, use water or homemade stock (p. 62).

PER SERVING: 70 calories, 3 g protein, 1 g total fat, 0 g saturated fat, 1 mg cholesterol, 13 g carbohydrate, 2 g fibre, 396 mg sodium, 347 mg potassium

Old-Fashioned Mushroom Barley Soup

Barley makes an excellent base for soups: it's inexpensive, filling and nutritious. Many butchers are delighted to cut up soup bones and give them away. This is a basic recipe; add any other vegetables you like, such as leeks, green beans, cabbage, turnip, sweet potato or squash.

8 cups	water	2 L
½ cup	pearl or pot barley	125 mL
1	large soup bone (beef or lamb)	1
1	bay leaf	1
3	large carrots, chopped	3
1	celery stalk (including leaves), chopped	1
1	large onion, chopped	1
1	large potato, peeled and diced	1
1	clove garlic, minced	1
¼ tsp	dried thyme	1 mL
1½ cups	coarsely chopped mushrooms	375 mL
¼ tsp or less	salt and freshly ground pepper	1 mL or less

In large pot, combine water, barley, soup bone and bay leaf; bring to boil. Reduce heat, cover and simmer for 1 hour. Add carrots, celery, onion, potato, garlic and thyme; simmer, covered, for 25 minutes. Add mushrooms and simmer for 5 minutes or until tender. Season with salt and pepper. Remove bay leaf and soup bone.

MAKES 8 HEARTY SERVINGS, 1¼ CUPS (300 mL) EACH

MAKE AHEAD: If possible, make this soup a day in advance, cover and refrigerate. Any fat from the soup bone will solidify on top and can then be easily removed.

NOTE: One serving is an excellent source of vitamin A.

Barley, a grain with a slightly nutty flavor and soft texture, is high in soluble fibre, which research has shown lowers blood cholesterol.

PER SERVING: 97 calories, 2 g protein, 0 g total fat, 0 g saturated fat, 0 mg cholesterol, 22 g carbohydrate, 3 g fibre, 104 mg sodium, 306 mg potassium

Three-Grain Vegetable Soup

This easy soup is economical to make, low in calories and packed with nutrients. You can use this recipe as a base and add a ham bone or a chicken carcass or vegetables of your choice. I use whatever vegetables I have on hand but always like to include rutabaga or parsnip, for they add a great deal of flavour. I like to use a combination of grains and legumes, but you can use one or two types to make a total of ½ cup (125 mL). Sometimes I add a fresh herb, such as basil, rosemary or dill, or sprinkle each serving with freshly grated Parmesan cheese.

2 tsp	canola or olive oil	10 mL
1	large onion, chopped	1
1 tbsp	minced fresh garlic	15 mL
6 cups	water	1.5 L
2 tbsp	each pearl or pot barley, bulgur, whole-grain rice and green lentils	25 mL
2	carrots, diced	2
2 cups	diced peeled rutabaga or parsnips	500 mL
2 cups	thinly sliced cabbage	500 mL
2 tsp	dried basil	10 mL
¼ cup	chopped fresh parsley	50 mL
¼ tsp or less	salt and freshly ground pepper	1 mL or less

In large saucepan, heat oil over medium heat; cook onion until tender, about 5 minutes. Add garlic, water, barley, bulgur, rice, lentils, carrots and rutabaga; bring to boil. Reduce heat, cover and simmer for 30 minutes. Add cabbage and basil; simmer for 10 to 15 minutes or until vegetables and grains are tender. Add parsley, and salt and pepper.

MAKES 6 SERVINGS, 1 CUP (250 mL) EACH

MAKE AHEAD: Cover and refrigerate for up to 2 days; add parsley when reheating.

NOTE: One serving of this soup is an excellent source of vitamin A and good source of vitamin C and folacin.

PER SERVING: 106 calories, 3 g protein, 2 g total fat, 0 g saturated fat, 0 mg cholesterol, 20 g carbohydrate, 4 g fibre, 131 mg sodium, 333 mg potassium

Beef 'n' Bean Minestrone

Packed with nutrients, this easy main-course soup is great to have on hand for those nights when everyone is on the run. The soup keeps well in the refrigerator for up to 3 days, ready and waiting for anyone to warm up a bowlful in the microwave. This version is lighter than many minestrone recipes because the vegetables aren't sautéed in oil.

8 oz	lean ground beef	250 g
1	large onion, diced	1
1	carrot, diced	1
1	stalk celery, diced	1
1	small zucchini (6 inches/15 cm), diced	1
2	tomatoes, diced, or 1 can (14 oz/398 mL) diced tomatoes, undrained	2
1	potato, peeled and diced	1
3	cloves garlic, minced	3
8 cups	water	2 L
¾ cup	small pasta	175 mL
1 tbsp	each dried oregano and basil (or 3 tbsp/50 mL each fresh)*	15 mL
1	can (19 oz/540 mL) white kidney beans, drained and rinsed	1
¼ cup	freshly grated Parmesan cheese	50 mL
½ cup	chopped fresh parsley	125 mL
¼ tsp or less	salt and freshly ground pepper	1 mL or less

In large saucepan, cook beef over medium heat until brown, breaking up with fork; drain off fat. Add onion; cook, stirring, for 3 minutes. Add carrot, celery, zucchini, tomatoes, potato and garlic; cook, stirring, for 3 minutes. Add water; bring to boil. Add pasta, oregano and basil; cook, uncovered, until pasta is tender but firm and vegetables are cooked, 10 to 12 minutes. Add kidney beans, Parmesan and parsley; season with salt and pepper.

MAKES 8 SERVINGS, 1¼ CUPS (300 mL) EACH

*If using fresh herbs, add just before serving.

NOTE: Pasta comes in many shapes and sizes. For this soup, choose shells (conchiglie), bows (farfalle) or small corkscrews (rotelle).

PER SERVING: 187 calories, 12 g protein, 4 g total fat, 2 g saturated fat, 18 mg cholesterol, 26 g carbohydrate, 6 g fibre, 306 mg sodium, 523 mg potassium

Portuguese Collard Soup

My Canadian-Portuguese friend, Albino Santos, taught me how to make this savoury soup. Collard greens are similar in shape to large beet greens and kale. This soup is so popular in Portugal that grocery stores there sell plastic bags full of thinly sliced collard leaves just for making this soup. Kale or spinach can be used if collard leaves are not available.

6 cups	water	1.5 L
5	large potatoes, peeled and coarsely chopped	5
1	large carrot, thinly sliced	1
14	large collard leaves	14
2 oz	chorizo (sweet smoked pork sausage), about 3½ inches (9 cm) long	60 g
1 tbsp	olive oil	15 mL
1 tsp	salt	5 mL
Dash	hot pepper sauce	Dash

In large saucepan, combine water, potatoes and carrot; simmer over medium heat until vegetables are tender. With a hand-held blender, purée in pot until smooth. (Or use slotted spoon to transfer potatoes and carrot to blender or food processor; blend until smooth and return to cooking liquid and stir until combined.)

Remove tough stems from collard leaves. Thinly slice leaves into ⅛-inch (3 mm) or less strips to make about 8 cups (2 L) lightly packed. (Or roll up 4 or 5 leaves at a time and slice crosswise in food processor.) Peel casing from sausage; slice sausage as thinly as possible (1/16 inch/1 mm thick).

Stir sliced collard leaves and sausage into soup; simmer, uncovered, for 10 minutes. Add oil, salt and hot pepper sauce. If soup is too thick, add more water.

MAKES 10 SERVINGS, 1 CUP (250 mL) EACH

MAKE AHEAD: Cover and refrigerate for up to 2 days.

NOTE: For a very low-fat soup, you can omit the oil without sacrificing flavour.

One serving is a very high source of vitamin A.

VARIATION:

Spinach Soup
Substitute 1 package (10 oz/284 g) fresh spinach, thinly sliced, for the collard leaves.

PER SERVING: 164 calories, 5 g protein, 2 g total fat, 0 g saturated fat, 4 mg cholesterol, 32 g carbohydrate, 3 g fibre, 317 mg sodium, 570 mg potassium

Curried Apple and Zucchini Soup

The lovely delicate flavour of this light cream soup makes it a good choice for a first course at a dinner party that has a variety of tastes and texture to follow. A woman I sat beside on an airplane flying from Vancouver to Toronto in the early 1980s, when I was writing my first cookbook, *Smart Cooking*, gave me this recipe. I wish I knew her name. It was one of the first recipes I cooked on CityLine TV with Marilyn Denis, as it was a favourite recipe of hers from my cookbook.

2 tbsp	olive oil	25 mL
2	apples, peeled, cored and chopped	2
1	large onion, chopped	1
1 to 3 tsp	curry powder (or 2 tbsp/25 mL medium-hot Indian curry paste)	5 to 15 mL
2 cups	each water and sodium-reduced chicken or vegetable broth	500 mL
3 cups	diced (unpeeled) zucchini (12 oz/375 g)	750 mL
¼ cup	rice	50 mL
½ tsp	salt	2 mL
1 cup	2% milk	250 mL

In saucepan, heat olive oil over medium-high heat; sauté apples and onion for 5 minutes or until softened. Sprinkle with curry powder; cook, stirring, for a few seconds. Pour in water and broth; bring to boil. Add zucchini, rice and salt; cover and simmer over low heat until zucchini and rice are very soft and soup is slightly thickened.

In batches, pour into blender or food processor; blend until smooth. Return to pan and add milk; heat through.

MAKES 10 SERVINGS, ¾ CUP (175 mL) EACH

MAKE AHEAD: Cover and refrigerate for up to 1 day or freeze for up to 1 month. (If freezing, add curry powder just before reheating soup.) Before reheating gently, stir soup with a whisk to regain consistency.

NOTE: To reduce sodium, substitute Basic Chicken Stock (p. 62) for sodium-reduced chicken or vegetable broth.

Milk with at least 2% MF is best for this recipe; milk with 1% or less MF will result in a thinner, less creamy soup.

PER SERVING: 82 calories, 2 g protein, 3 g total fat, 1 g saturated fat, 2 mg cholesterol, 11 g carbohydrate, 1 g fibre, 241 mg sodium, 215 mg potassium

Lentil Spinach Soup with Curried Yogurt

This soup is easy to make using either canned or dried lentils that you have precooked. The soup is packed with nutrients and along with toast and a salad makes a quick yet satisfying meal.

2 cups	sodium-reduced chicken or vegetable broth	500 mL
2 cups	water	500 mL
1	can (19 oz/540 mL) brown lentils, rinsed and drained, or 2 cups (500 mL) cooked*	1
2	stalks celery, chopped	2
2	small onions, minced	2
2	small cloves garlic, minced	2
4 cups	chopped fresh spinach, packed (10 oz/284 g bag)	1 L
1 tbsp	fresh lemon juice	15 mL
	Freshly ground pepper	

CURRIED YOGURT

¼ cup	low-fat plain yogurt	50 mL
1 tsp	curry powder	5 mL

In saucepan, bring broth, water, lentils, celery, onions and garlic to boil; reduce heat, cover and simmer for 5 minutes or until onions are tender. Add spinach and simmer for 3 minutes. Add lemon juice; season with pepper to taste. (If thicker soup is desired, remove half and purée in blender or food processor; return to saucepan and heat through.)

CURRIED YOGURT: Mix yogurt with curry powder.

Ladle soup into individual bowls; swirl dollop of curried yogurt into each.

MAKES 5 SERVINGS, 1 CUP (250 mL) EACH

*For 2 cups (500 mL) cooked lentils, cook ⅔ cup (150 mL) dried brown lentils with 4 cups (1 L) water, covered, for 25 minutes or until lentils are tender; drain.

NOTE: To reduce sodium, use Basic Chicken Stock (p. 62).

Inexpensive lentils are a nutrient bargain, packed with all the good things we need, such as protein, iron, the B vitamin niacin, complex carbohydrates and soluble fibre. They contain no cholesterol and very little fat. Dried lentils don't need to be soaked before cooking; red lentils cook in about 10 minutes, green in about 30 minutes.

PER SERVING: 100 calories, 8 g protein, 1 g total fat, 0 g saturated fat, 1 mg cholesterol, 18 g carbohydrate, 4 g fibre, 277 mg sodium, 559 mg potassium

Curried Pumpkin Soup

The recipe for this fall soup comes from my friends and good cooks Peter and Penny White. The soup has only an accent of curry so as not to mask the pumpkin and is best made ahead so that the flavours have time to develop.

1 tbsp	olive oil	15 mL
½ cup	finely chopped onion	125 mL
1	clove garlic, minced	1
8 oz	fresh mushrooms, sliced	250 g
2 tbsp	all-purpose flour	25 mL
1 to 2 tsp	curry powder or paste	5 to 10 mL
2 cups	sodium-reduced vegetable or chicken broth	500 mL
1	can (14 oz/398 mL) pumpkin or 2 cups (500 mL) cooked fresh pumpkin	1
1 tbsp	liquid honey	15 mL
	Freshly grated nutmeg	
2 cups	2% milk	500 mL

In large saucepan, heat oil over medium heat; cook onion, garlic and mushrooms for 8 to 10 minutes or until softened. Stir in flour and curry powder; cook for 1 minute over low heat, stirring, until well blended.

Gradually add broth, whisking until smooth. Stir in pumpkin and honey; season with nutmeg to taste. Cook over low heat for 15 minutes, stirring occasionally. Add milk and heat until hot.

MAKES 8 SERVINGS, ¾ CUP (175 mL) EACH

MAKE AHEAD: Cover and refrigerate for up to 2 days (omitting milk). When ready to serve, add milk and reheat gently.

NOTE: To reduce sodium, substitute Basic Chicken Stock (p. 62) for sodium-reduced chicken or vegetable broth.

PER SERVING: 97 calories, 4 g protein, 3 g total fat, 1 g saturated fat, 5 mg cholesterol, 14 g carbohydrate, 3 g fibre, 144 mg sodium, 304 mg potassium

Curried Cauliflower Soup

Cool and creamy, this is a wonderful soup for a warm day. For a fresher taste use curry paste instead of powder. For a special occasion, garnish with tiny salad shrimp and fresh chives.

1 tsp	canola or olive oil	5 mL
1 to 2 tsp	curry powder or paste	5 to 10 mL
1 to 2 tsp	ground cumin	5 to 10 mL
Half	cauliflower, cut in chunks (about 6 cups/1.5 L)	Half
1 cup	sliced peeled potato	250 mL
3½ cups	2% milk	875 mL
½ tsp	salt	2 mL
2 tbsp	chopped fresh chives or green onion	25 mL

In saucepan, heat oil over medium heat; stir in curry powder and cumin and cook 1 minute. Add cauliflower, potato and milk; bring to boil. Reduce heat; cover and simmer for 20 minutes or until tender. Purée in blender or food processor. Stir in salt.

Cover and refrigerate for 2 hours or until cold. If desired, thin with additional milk. Garnish with chives.

MAKES 6 SERVINGS, ¾ CUP (175 mL) EACH

NOTE: Use a Yukon Gold or baking potato, which is starchier than a new potato—it's the starch that thickens the soup.

PER SERVING: 122 calories, 7 g protein, 4 g total fat, 2 g saturated fat, 11 mg cholesterol, 15 g carbohydrate, 2 g fibre, 270 mg sodium, 438 mg potassium

Red Lentil Soup

Make this soup the centrepiece of a meal, perhaps along with grilled cheese sandwiches or a salad, depending on appetites. Use 2 tbsp (25 mL) each of chopped fresh thyme and oregano if available.

½ cup	dried red lentils	125 mL
2	small onions, coarsely chopped	2
4 cups	sodium-reduced vegetable or chicken broth	1 L
1	bay leaf	1
1	large clove garlic, minced	1
1 cup	sliced carrots	250 mL
2 tbsp	long-grain rice	25 mL
1	can (14 oz/398 mL) diced tomatoes, undrained	1
1 tsp	each crushed dried thyme and oregano	5 mL
1 tsp	ground cumin	5 mL
¼ cup	chopped fresh parsley and/or coriander (cilantro)	50 mL
¼ tsp or less	salt and freshly ground pepper	1 mL or less

Wash and drain lentils. In large saucepan, combine lentils, onions, broth, bay leaf and garlic; cover and simmer for 30 minutes. Add carrots, rice, tomatoes, thyme, oregano and cumin; simmer, covered, for 20 minutes or until carrots are tender and lentils are soft. Remove bay leaf. Add parsley and/or coriander; season with salt and pepper.

MAKES 8 SERVINGS, ¾ CUP (175 mL) EACH

MAKE AHEAD: Cover and refrigerate for up to 3 days or freeze for up to 1 month.

NOTE: To reduce sodium, substitute Basic Chicken Stock (p. 62) for sodium-reduced chicken or vegetable broth.

One serving is a very high source of vitamin A and folacin and a high source of iron.

PER SERVING: 89 calories, 5 g protein, 1 g total fat, 0 g saturated fat, 0 mg cholesterol, 17 g carbohydrate, 3 g fibre, 380 mg sodium, 307 mg potassium

Hot and Sour Soup

As its name implies, this soup tastes both hot and sour, thanks to chili paste and vinegar. The sharpness of ginger and saltiness of soy sauce also contribute to the soup's intriguing flavour. If you like a fiery hot soup, you will want to add more chili paste. Along with a salad, this makes a tasty lunch.

6	dried Chinese mushrooms	6
3 cups	sodium-reduced chicken broth	750 mL
3 cups	water	750 mL
¼ lb	lean boneless pork, cut in thin 1-inch (2.5 cm) strips	125 g
1 tbsp	grated gingerroot	15 mL
½ cup	julienned bamboo shoots	125 mL
1⅓ cups	diced firm tofu (8 oz/250 g)	325 mL
3 tbsp	unseasoned rice vinegar	50 mL
2 tbsp	sodium-reduced soy sauce	25 mL
1 tbsp	dark sesame oil	15 mL
1 tsp	chili paste	5 mL
2 tbsp	cornstarch	25 mL
½ tsp	granulated sugar	2 mL
2	green onions, thinly sliced	2

Soak dried mushrooms in enough warm water to cover for 15 minutes or until softened. Drain. Remove and discard stems; cut mushrooms into thin strips.

In large saucepan, bring broth to boil. Add mushrooms, pork and gingerroot; simmer, covered, for 10 minutes. Add bamboo shoots and tofu.

In small bowl, combine vinegar, soy sauce, sesame oil and chili paste; blend in cornstarch and sugar until smooth. Stir into soup; bring to boil. Reduce heat and simmer, stirring, for 2 minutes.

Sprinkle each serving with green onions.

MAKES 8 SERVINGS, ¾ CUP (175 mL) EACH

MAKE AHEAD: Cover and refrigerate for up to 2 days.

NOTE: Chinese mushrooms are the Chinese version of Japanese shiitake mushrooms, but with a stronger flavour. Do not substitute fresh mushrooms or the taste will suffer. Use the soaking liquid to flavour other dishes.

To reduce sodium, substitute Basic Chicken Stock (p. 62) for sodium-reduced chicken or vegetable broth.

VARIATION:

Hot and Sour Soup with Egg
Usually an egg is swirled into this soup, which adds body but can make the soup cloudy. I omit the egg because I usually serve the soup as an appetizer and I prefer a clear one. If you want to add an egg, gradually stir in 1 beaten egg just before serving.

PER SERVING: 89 calories, 7 g protein, 4 g total fat, 1 g saturated fat, 9 mg cholesterol, 7 g carbohydrate, 1 g fibre, 362 mg sodium, 261 mg potassium

Miso Soup with Tofu

This light Japanese soup is from Heather Epp, a chef who helped to test recipes for my *Light Kitchen* cookbook. Miso, a fermented soybean paste, is delicious as a soup base and is available in a wide variety of flavours and colours, though there are three basic types: barley, rice and soybean. Heather prefers a barley or brown rice miso for this soup; I use a brown soybean miso, but any type would work for this recipe.

1 tsp	sesame oil	5 mL
Half	onion, chopped	Half
1	large carrot, thinly sliced	1
3 cups	water	750 mL
2 tbsp	miso*	25 mL
1 tbsp	sodium-reduced soy sauce	15 mL
3	green onions, diagonally sliced	3
½ cup	diced firm tofu (3 oz/85 g)	125 mL

In saucepan, heat oil over medium heat; cook onion and carrot, stirring occasionally, for 5 to 7 minutes or until tender. Add water and bring to boil; reduce heat and simmer for 3 minutes. Remove from heat; stir in miso until dissolved. Add soy sauce, green onions and tofu. Serve hot.

MAKES 4 SERVINGS, ¾ CUP (175 mL) EACH

*When shopping for miso, look for lower-sodium varieties (220 mg or less per tsp). Miso is readily available at Japanese markets and health food stores.

MAKE AHEAD: Cover and refrigerate for up to 2 days; reheat over medium heat, but don't boil.

NOTE: Make your own sodium-reduced soy sauce by mixing regular naturally brewed soy sauce with an equal amount of water. It has just as much flavour if not more than the bottled sodium-reduced soy sauce and it's half the price.

PER SERVING: 70 calories, 4 g protein, 3 g total fat, 0 g saturated fat, 0 mg cholesterol, 7 g carbohydrate, 1 g fibre, 473 mg sodium, 172 mg potassium

Carrot and Corn Chowder

Hannah's Kitchen in Toronto is a popular lunch spot. Here is one of its delicious soup recipes from co-owner Susan Hughes.

1 tsp	olive oil	5 mL
1	onion, chopped	1
1	leek (white part only), thinly sliced	1
1½ cups	water or sodium-reduced vegetable broth	375 mL
1	potato, peeled and diced	1
3	medium carrots, peeled and diced	3
1	sweet potato, peeled and diced	1
½ cup	coarsely chopped fresh parsley	125 mL
2 tbsp	all-purpose flour	25 mL
1½ cups	low-fat milk	375 mL
1½ cups	corn kernels	375 mL
¼ tsp or less	salt and freshly ground pepper	1 mL or less
1 tbsp	fresh thyme (or 1 tsp/5 mL dried)	15 mL

In large nonstick saucepan, heat oil over medium heat; cook onion and leek, stirring occasionally, for 5 to 10 minutes or until onions are tender. Add a little of the water if necessary to prevent sticking.

Add 1¼ cups (300 mL) of the water, potato, carrots, sweet potato and half of the parsley; cover and simmer until vegetables are tender, about 15 minutes.

Mix flour with remaining ¼ cup (50 mL) water; stir into soup. Add milk; bring to simmer, stirring. Add corn, and salt and pepper. Add thyme and remaining parsley; simmer for 1 minute.

MAKES 6 SERVINGS, ¾ CUP (175 mL) EACH

MAKE AHEAD: Cover and refrigerate for up to 2 days, adding thyme and parsley when reheating.

PER SERVING: 137 calories, 5 g protein, 2 g total fat, 1 g saturated fat, 3 mg cholesterol, 27 g carbohydrate, 3 g fibre, 157 mg sodium, 470 mg potassium

Creamy Corn Chowder with Dill

I like to serve this soup for a casual lunch. I love the flavour with fresh dill; however, fresh basil and coriander also taste great. In corn season, use any leftover cooked corn instead of frozen corn. If serving as a main course, top each serving with grated Cheddar cheese, fresh tiny salad shrimp or chopped crabmeat. Serve with Shannon Graham's Crisp Cracker Bread (p. 349).

2 tsp	olive oil	10 mL
1	onion, chopped	1
1	carrot, chopped	1
1	stalk celery, chopped	1
1	potato, peeled and chopped	1
¼ cup	diced sweet red pepper (optional)	50 mL
½ tsp	dill seed	2 mL
1 cup	sodium-reduced vegetable or chicken broth	250 mL
1½ cups	2% milk	375 mL
1	can (14 oz/398 mL) creamed corn	1
1 cup	frozen corn kernels	250 mL
¼ tsp or less	salt and freshly ground pepper	1 mL or less
⅓ cup	chopped fresh dill	75 mL

In nonstick saucepan, heat oil over medium heat; cook onion, stirring for 2 minutes or until onion is softened. Stir in carrot, celery, potato, red pepper (if using), dill seed and broth; bring to a boil. Cover and simmer until vegetables are tender, about 10 minutes. Add milk, creamed and frozen corn; heat until hot. Stir in salt, pepper and fresh dill. If too thick, add milk or broth to taste.

MAKES 6 SERVINGS, 1 CUP (250 mL) EACH

MAKE AHEAD: Refrigerate for up to 2 days. Garnish with fresh dill just before serving.

PER SERVING: 162 calories, 5 g protein, 3 g total fat, 1 g saturated fat, 5 mg cholesterol, 31 g carbohydrate, 3 g fibre, 424 mg sodium, 439 mg potassium

Nova Scotia Seafood Chowder

This Maritime dish is from the Crawford family of Five Islands, Nova Scotia. Serve as a main course along with crusty rolls and a tossed green salad. It's also a great item to include in a dinner buffet or on a party menu, especially in winter. Try to make it early in the day to give the flavours a chance to develop. A food processor makes quick work of chopping the onions, celery and carrots.

1 tbsp	canola or olive oil	15 mL
1 cup	chopped onions	250 mL
2 cups	sodium-reduced chicken or vegetable broth, or clam juice	500 mL
1 cup	chopped celery	250 mL
1 cup	chopped carrots	250 mL
1 lb	haddock or tilapia fillets, cut in chunks	500 g
2 cups	whole milk	500 mL
⅓ cup	all-purpose flour	75 mL
1	can (5 oz/142 g) clams, undrained	1
4 oz	cooked small shrimp and/or lobster meat	125 g
¼ tsp or less	salt and freshly ground pepper	1 mL or less
1 to 2 tsp	Pernod (optional)	5 to 10 mL

In large saucepan, heat oil over low heat; add onions and cook for a few minutes, until softened. Stir in broth, celery and carrots; bring to boil. Reduce heat, cover and simmer for 20 minutes or until carrots are tender. Add fish; cover and cook for 5 minutes.

Stir about half of the milk into flour until smooth. Gradually stir flour mixture into soup; stir in remaining milk and simmer until thickened slightly. Stir in clams and shrimp and/or lobster; heat through. Season with salt and pepper. Add Pernod (if using).

MAKES 6 SERVINGS, 1¼ CUPS (300 mL) EACH

MAKE AHEAD: After adding fish fillets, cover and refrigerate for up to 1 day or freeze for up to 2 weeks. Thaw, then reheat before adding milk and continuing with recipe.

NOTE: To reduce sodium, use water or Basic Chicken Stock (p. 62).

Just one serving of this soup is a very high source of iron (39% of an adult's daily requirement), niacin (46% of an adult's daily requirement), vitamin B12 (greater than 100% of an adult's daily requirement), vitamin A (49% of an adult's daily requirement) and a high source of calcium.

VARIATION: For a creamier soup, use 1 cup (250 mL) chicken stock or clam juice and 3 cups (750 mL) whole milk.

PER SERVING: 224 calories, 26 g protein, 6 g total fat, 2 g saturated fat, 97 mg cholesterol, 15 g carbohydrate, 2 g fibre, 478 mg sodium, 699 mg potassium

Quick and Easy Fish Chowder

If you keep a package of fish fillets in your freezer, last-minute meals are a cinch to make. Any fresh or frozen fillets can be used in this chowder. If I have bacon on hand, I'll use it for its smoky flavour. Sometimes I add chopped carrot or celery, and I always add fresh dill when I have it.

1 tbsp	canola oil	15 mL
1	onion, chopped	1
3	potatoes, diced	3
2 cups	water	500 mL
1 lb	fresh or frozen fish fillets, cut in chunks	500 g
2 cups	2% milk	500 mL
1 cup	corn kernels	250 mL
¼ cup	coarsely chopped fresh parsley or dill	50 mL
¼ tsp or less	salt and freshly ground pepper	1 mL or less

In heavy saucepan, heat oil over medium heat. Add onion and cook for 5 minutes or until tender. Add potatoes and water; cover and simmer until potatoes are nearly tender, about 15 minutes.

Add fish; cover and cook until opaque, about 2 minutes for fresh, 10 minutes for frozen. Stir in milk and corn; simmer until hot. Add parsley; season with salt and pepper.

MAKES 4 MAIN-COURSE SERVINGS, 1½ CUPS (375 mL) EACH

NOTE: I peel the potatoes only if the skin is tough. Unpeeled potatoes have more fibre.

PER SERVING: 384 calories, 32 g protein, 9 g total fat, 2 g saturated fat, 46 mg cholesterol, 45 g carbohydrate, 4 g fibre, 271 mg sodium, 1402 mg potassium

Hearty Salmon Chowder

I first had this delicious soup when it was served to a group of food writers on a boat off British Columbia's Vancouver Island. We all asked for the recipe, which was from the *Lopez Island Cookbook*. Here it is, adapted slightly. You could also use 2% milk instead of evaporated milk; however, I like the flavour the evaporated milk imparts. It is a good chowder to prepare for camping and boat trips.

1	can (7½ oz/213 g) salmon	1
2 tsp	olive oil	10 mL
½ cup	each chopped onion and celery	125 mL
¼ cup	chopped sweet green pepper	50 mL
1	clove garlic, minced	1
3 cups	diced potatoes	750 mL
1 cup	diced carrots	250 mL
1 cup	each sodium-reduced chicken broth and water	250 mL
½ tsp	each coarse pepper and dill seed	2 mL
1 cup	diced zucchini	250 mL
1	can (370 mL) 2% evaporated milk	1
1	can (10 oz/284 mL) cream-style corn	1
	Freshly ground pepper	
½ cup	chopped fresh parsley	125 mL

Drain and flake salmon, reserving liquid.

In large nonstick or heavy saucepan, heat oil over medium heat; cook onion, celery, green pepper and garlic, stirring often, for 5 minutes or until vegetables are tender.

Add potatoes, carrots, broth, water, coarse pepper and dill seed; bring to boil. Reduce heat, cover and simmer for 20 minutes or until vegetables are tender. Add zucchini; simmer, covered, for 5 minutes.

Add salmon, reserved liquid, evaporated milk, corn, and pepper to taste. Cook over low heat just until heated through. Just before serving, stir in parsley.

MAKES 4 MAIN-COURSE SERVINGS OF 1¾ CUPS (425 ML) EACH OR 8 APPETIZER SERVINGS OF ¾ CUP (175 ML) EACH

NOTE: When using canned salmon, be sure to crush the bones and include them in the soup. The bones are an excellent source of calcium.

PER MAIN-COURSE SERVING:
372 calories, 21 g protein, 10 g total fat, 3 g saturated fat, 21 mg cholesterol, 51 g carbohydrate, 5 g fibre, 733 mg sodium, 1290 mg potassium

Creamy Oyster Chowder

Make this chowder for an easy supper or serve it as an appetizer course. I often omit the carrots and potatoes and increase the amount of celery. If the oysters are huge, cut them in half before adding to the soup.

1 tbsp	olive oil	15 mL
1	small onion, diced	1
1	stalk celery, diced	1
1	carrot, diced	1
2 tbsp	all-purpose flour	25 mL
½ cup	sodium-reduced fish stock or white wine	125 mL
1	can (5 oz/142 g) oysters or container (8 oz/225 g) fresh shucked oysters	1
1 cup	diced peeled baking or Yukon Gold potatoes	250 mL
¼ tsp	dried thyme (or 2 tsp/10 mL chopped fresh) (optional)	1 mL
2¼ cups	2% milk	550 mL
2 tbsp	chopped fresh parsley	25 mL
¼ tsp or less	salt and freshly ground pepper	1 mL or less

In large saucepan, heat oil over medium heat; cook onion, celery and carrot, covered, for 5 minutes. Blend in flour. Stirring constantly, gradually pour in stock or wine. Drain liquid from oysters into saucepan; set oysters aside. Add potatoes, thyme and milk; stir and bring to simmer. Reduce heat and simmer, covered, until potatoes are tender, about 10 minutes.

Add oysters and parsley; cook until heated through. Season with salt and pepper.

MAKES 3 MAIN-COURSE SERVINGS OF 1⅓ CUPS (325 ML) EACH OR 6 APPETIZER SERVINGS OF ⅔ CUP (150 mL) EACH

NOTE: Milk with at least 2% MF is best for this recipe; milk with 1% or less MF will result in a less creamy, thinner soup.

PER MAIN-COURSE SERVING:
253 calories, 11 g protein,
9 g total fat, 3 g saturated fat,
41 mg cholesterol,
28 g carbohydrate, 2 g fibre,
353 mg sodium, 699 mg potassium

Easy Tomato-Bean Chowder

I like this soup all year round: it's light enough for a summer supper, yet comforting and hearty enough for a cold winter day. Chopped fresh coriander livens up its flavour.

I often add other vegetables, such as cubed potatoes, corn, broccoli, celery, cabbage or mushrooms. Sometimes I use black beans instead of kidney beans or only one can of beans. As well, I might omit the chili powder and use fresh herbs, such as basil, instead. Go ahead—don't be afraid to experiment.

1 tbsp	olive oil	15 mL
3	medium onions, finely chopped	3
2 to 4 tsp	chili powder	10 to 20 mL
1	sweet red or green pepper, seeded and chopped	1
1	can (28 oz/796 mL) diced tomatoes	1
4 cups	water or sodium-reduced beef or vegetable broth	1 L
1	can (19 oz/540 mL) red kidney beans, drained and rinsed	1
1	can (19 oz/540 mL) chickpeas, drained and rinsed	1
¼ tsp or less	salt and freshly ground pepper	1 mL or less
½ cup	finely chopped fresh parsley and/or coriander (cilantro)	125 mL

In large heavy saucepan, heat oil over medium heat; add onions and cook until tender. Stir in chili powder, then red pepper and tomatoes. Add water; bring to boil. Reduce heat and simmer for 5 minutes. Add beans and chickpeas; simmer for 10 minutes. Season with salt and pepper. Ladle into individual bowls, sprinkling each serving with parsley or coriander.

MAKES 10 SERVINGS, 1 CUP (250 mL) EACH

MAKE AHEAD: Cover and refrigerate for up to 2 days. Reheat, then top with parsley or coriander.

NOTE: One serving is a very high source of folacin, vitamin C and fibre. One-half cup (125 mL) of cooked legumes, such as kidney beans or chickpeas, is a high source of fibre and contributes iron and protein to our diet.

In this recipe the canned kidney beans, chickpeas and tomatoes contribute about 300 mg of sodium per serving. To reduce the sodium, you can replace them with your own dried beans and chickpeas cooked without salt (see p. 118), and use tomatoes canned without salt.

If you want to substitute sodium-reduced broth for water, remember that it will add about 210 mg of sodium per serving.

PER SERVING: 134 calories, 6 g protein, 2 g total fat, 0 g saturated fat, 0 mg cholesterol, 23 g carbohydrate, 6 g fibre, 382 mg sodium, 455 mg potassium

Turkey Noodle Soup

Whenever you roast a turkey or chicken, make this comforting soup from the leftovers. Don't be put off by the long list of ingredients; it's really quite easy to prepare. I usually start the stock simmering while I'm making dinner one night, let it simmer for a few hours that evening, then finish it the next night. If you prefer, use rice instead of noodles.

STOCK

1	carcass from roast turkey (approx 11 lbs/5 kg)	1
10 to 15 cups	water*	2.5 to 3.75 L
1	bay leaf	1
1	stalk celery (including leaves), chopped	1
1	onion, quartered	1

SOUP

⅓ cup	broken noodles (½-inch/1 cm pieces)	75 mL
2	stalks celery (including leaves), chopped	2
1	carrot, chopped	1
3	green onions, sliced	3
⅓ cup	grated zucchini or frozen peas	75 mL
1 tsp	dried basil	5 mL
1 tsp	dried thyme	5 mL
Dash	hot pepper sauce	Dash
½ tsp or less	salt and freshly ground pepper	2 mL or less

STOCK: In stockpot or large saucepan, combine carcass, water, bay leaf, celery and onion. Simmer, covered, for 4 hours. Strain, reserving stock. Let bones cool, then pick out any meat and add to stock. (You should have about 6 cups/1.5 L.)

SOUP: In stockpot or saucepan, bring stock to boil; add noodles, celery, carrot, green onions, zucchini, basil and thyme; simmer for 10 minutes. Stir in hot pepper sauce; season with salt and pepper.

MAKES 8 SERVINGS, ¾ CUP (175 mL) EACH

*Water should cover the carcass. Use more for a larger bird.

VARIATIONS:
If you don't have a leftover turkey carcass, use 6 cups/1.5 L sodium-reduced chicken broth instead of the turkey stock. (See page 62 for the recipe for low-sodium chicken stock or use store-bought.)

For a main-course soup and to increase fibre, add 1 can (19 oz/540 mL) chickpeas or kidney beans, drained. Other possible additions include green peas, chopped fresh spinach, asparagus, chopped broccoli, diced potato, squash, turnip and chopped fresh herbs such as basil, dill or pesto.

Chicken Noodle Soup
Use a carcass from a roast chicken to make the stock. Reduce the water to 8 cups (2 L).

PER SERVING: 88 calories, 5 g protein, 2 g total fat, 1 g saturated fat, 5 mg cholesterol, 11 g carbohydrate, 1 g fibre, 164 mg sodium, 267 mg potassium

Basic Chicken Stock

Making your own chicken stock is a great solution for those of you on a sodium-restricted diet—you'll definitely want to avoid using stock cubes or canned stock, both of which are high in sodium. Any pieces of chicken can be used to make the stock, even a whole chicken (giblets removed), though backs and necks are the least expensive. Ask at your local butcher or poultry store if they sell just the bones.

4 lb	chicken, whole or pieces	2 kg
12 cups	cold water	3 L
2	carrots, chopped	2
2	onions, chopped	2
2	stalks celery, chopped	2
2	bay leaves	2
6	black peppercorns	6
2	sprigs fresh thyme (or pinch each dried thyme, basil and marjoram)	2

In stockpot, combine chicken and water; bring to boil. Skim off any scum. Add carrots, onions, celery, bay leaves, peppercorns and thyme; simmer, uncovered, for 4 hours.

Remove from heat and strain; cover and refrigerate stock until any fat congeals on surface. Remove fat layer and discard.

MAKES 8 CUPS (2 L)

Refrigerate for up to 2 days or freeze for up to 2 months. Freeze homemade chicken stock in ice-cube trays (then transfer to a plastic bag) or ½ cup (125 mL) container and use in cooking whenever you want extra flavour without added salt.

MAKE AHEAD: Refrigerate for up to 2 days or freeze for up to 2 months. Freeze homemade chicken stock in ice-cube trays (then transfer to a plastic bag) or ½-cup (125 mL) container and use in cooking whenever you want extra flavour without added salt.

NOTE: This recipe has 4 mg sodium per 1 cup (250 mL) compared with 750 to 1000 mg of sodium in the same amount of canned ready-to serve or canned condensed broth prepared with an equal amount of water. Broth prepared from cubes may contain up to 1100 mg of sodium per cup (250 mL).

To reduce the amount of sodium in stock made from cubes, which are typically high in sodium, double the amount of water called for. Or look for low-sodium stock cubes or prepared stock.

VARIATIONS:

Easiest Chicken Stock
Pour all the pan drippings from a roast chicken into a jar; cover and refrigerate. Discard fat from top once it has congealed. Use remaining gelatinous mixture to flavour soups or dilute with water for stock. Store in refrigerator for up to 1 week.

Beef, Veal or Lamb Stock
Use beef, veal or lamb bones instead of chicken. For added flavour, roast bones before simmering in water. Spread bones in roasting pan and bake in 400°F (200°C) oven for 1 hour or until browned; transfer to stockpot and continue as in Basic Chicken Stock recipe.

PER 1 CUP (250 mL): 3 calories, trace protein, trace total fat, trace saturated fat, 3 mg cholesterol, trace carbohydrate, 0 g fibre, 4 mg sodium, 11 mg potassium

Arugula Salad with Grilled Chèvre

Arugula and chèvre are two of my favourite foods. To have them together is heaven. This salad makes a fabulous first course for a dinner party. A vinaigrette dressing also works well in this salad (see salad dressings pp. 95 to 98).

8-oz	chèvre (soft goat cheese) log (15% BF), chilled	250 g
1	egg, beaten	250 mL
1 cup	homemade whole-grain bread crumbs	250 mL
3 cups	arugula, large stems removed, torn	750 mL
8 cups	red leaf or Boston lettuce, torn	2 L
1 tbsp	olive oil	15 mL

DRESSING

¼ cup	low-fat plain yogurt	50 mL
2 tsp	white wine vinegar	10 mL
2 tsp	olive oil	10 mL
1 tsp	minced fresh tarragon (or ¼ tsp/1 mL dried)	5 mL
½ tsp	each Dijon mustard and freshly ground pepper	2 mL
¼ tsp or less	salt	1 mL or less

DRESSING: In bowl, whisk together yogurt, vinegar, oil, tarragon, mustard, pepper and salt.

SALAD: Slice cheese into 8 rounds; dip in egg then in bread crumbs to coat all sides. Toss arugula and lettuce with dressing; divide among 8 salad plates.

In nonstick skillet, heat oil over medium heat. Cook chèvre, turning once, for 3 to 5 minutes or until crisp and golden outside and slightly melted inside. Place a round on each salad.

MAKES 8 SERVINGS

MAKE AHEAD: Refrigerate dressing and breaded chèvre rounds for up to 2 hours. Toss the salad and grill chèvre just before serving.

PER SERVING: 111 calories, 6 g protein, 8 g total fat, 4 g saturated fat, 27 mg cholesterol, 4 g carbohydrate, 1.5 g fibre, 223 mg sodium, 203 mg potassium

Arugula and Boston Lettuce Salad with Walnut Oil Vinaigrette

A simple salad is often the best, especially if the dressing uses a flavourful oil, such as walnut or hazelnut. Use any combination of fresh greens in season. Because it is simple, this salad complements a variety of dishes, making it a good buffet offering.

1	head Boston or leaf lettuce	1
Half	bunch arugula, escarole or watercress	Half
1	small head radicchio	1

WALNUT OIL VINAIGRETTE

2 tbsp	walnut oil	25 mL
2 tbsp	fresh lemon juice or rice vinegar	25 mL
1 tbsp	water	15 mL
¼ tsp or less	salt and freshly ground pepper	1 mL or less

Separate leaves of lettuce, arugula and radicchio; wash and dry well. Tear bite-size pieces into salad bowl.

WALNUT OIL VINAIGRETTE: In small dish, combine oil, lemon juice, water, and salt and pepper; mix well. Pour over salad and toss to mix.

MAKES 8 SERVINGS

NOTE: Nut oils add a subtle, delicious note to salads. Store in the refrigerator.

VARIATION:

Roasted Red Pepper and Chèvre Divide salad among 8 individual plates. Cut 2 roasted red peppers in thin strips. Dice 4 oz (125 g) chèvre (soft goat cheese). Top each individual salad with red pepper strips and chèvre.

PER SERVING: 41 calories, 1 g protein, 4 g total fat, 0 g saturated fat, 0 mg cholesterol, 2 g carbohydrate, 1 g fibre, 81 mg sodium, 149 mg potassium

Greek Salad

I serve this salad at least once a week in the summer—for lunch on the weekend or for dinner with grilled chicken or lamb. Sometimes I add sweet red pepper, artichokes, capers or chopped red onion, but never lettuce. When you use ripe, juicy tomatoes, you'll be surprised at how little dressing you need. If you can't find Kalamata olives, use any other Greek olive.

4	large tomatoes, cut in chunks	4
2	medium cucumbers or 1 English cucumber, cut in chunks	2
4 oz	light feta cheese, crumbled (1 cup/250 mL)	125 g
2 tbsp	crumbled dried oregano	25 mL
2 tbsp	fresh lemon juice	25 mL
1 tbsp	olive oil	15 mL
	Freshly ground pepper	
10	black Kalamata olives	10

In shallow salad bowl or on platter, combine tomatoes, cucumbers, cheese, oregano, lemon juice and olive oil. Season with pepper to taste. Toss gently to mix; sprinkle with olives. Serve at room temperature.

MAKES 8 SERVINGS

NOTE: To reduce the fat in this salad, omit the olives and olive oil, and omit or reduce the amount of cheese. Salad prepared without oil or olives and half the amount of cheese has about 2 g total fat per serving.

PER SERVING: 86 calories, 4 g protein, 6 g total fat, 2 g saturated fat, 5 mg cholesterol, 8 g carbohydrate, 1.5 g fibre, 290 mg sodium, 320 mg potassium

Lighthearted Caesar Salad

Here's a version of this very popular salad with less oil than usual and without the egg—but with no sacrifice in flavour. If you prefer a creamy dressing, substitute Creamy Garlic Dressing (p. 100) for this one.

2	slices bread (preferably whole wheat)	2
1	large clove garlic, halved	1
1	large head romaine lettuce	1
3 tbsp	freshly grated Parmesan cheese	50 mL

DRESSING

2 tbsp	fresh lemon juice	25 mL
2 tbsp	olive oil	25 mL
1 tbsp	water	15 mL
1 tbsp	freshly grated Parmesan cheese	15 mL
1 tsp	Dijon mustard	5 mL
1 tsp	Worcestershire sauce	1 tsp
1	anchovy fillet, minced, or 1 tsp (5 mL) anchovy paste	1
⅛ tsp or less	salt and freshly ground pepper	0.5 mL or less

Toast bread until browned and crisp. Rub cut side of garlic over both sides of bread; cut bread into cubes. Mince garlic to use in dressing.

DRESSING: In small bowl, combine garlic, lemon juice, oil, water, Parmesan, mustard, Worcestershire, anchovy, and salt and pepper; whisk to mix well.

Just before serving, tear romaine into salad bowl. Pour dressing over and toss to mix. Add croutons and cheese; toss again.

MAKES 5 SERVINGS

MAKE AHEAD: Wash lettuce; dry in salad spinner or between paper towels or tea towels. Wrap in paper towels or tea towels and place in a plastic bag; refrigerate for up to 1 day. Prepare dressing up to 1 day in advance. Store, covered, in the refrigerator; whisk again just before using. Prepare croutons up to 1 day in advance; store in airtight container.

For a crisp salad, tear lettuce and add dressing just before serving.

PER SERVING: 119 calories, 5 g protein, 8 g total fat, 2 g saturated fat, 5 mg cholesterol, 9 g carbohydrate, 3 g fibre, 272 mg sodium, 350 mg potassium

Quick Spinach Salad

It's easy to keep the ingredients for this salad on hand. I sometimes add croutons, chopped red or green onion, celery, mushrooms, grapefruit, apple, orange, tomatoes (cherry tomatoes work especially well), kidney beans or chickpeas. This salad pairs nicely with Everyday Vinaigrette. You might also try it with the Caesar variation of the Creamy Garlic Dressing (p. 100).

1 lb	spinach	500 g
¼ cup	crumbled light feta cheese or cubed skim-milk mozzarella cheese	50 mL
2 tbsp	sunflower seeds	25 mL
⅓ cup	Everyday Vinaigrette (p. 95)	75 mL

Trim, wash and dry spinach; tear into bite-size pieces to make about 10 cups (2.5 mL) lightly packed. Place in salad bowl. Add cheese and sunflower seeds. Pour dressing over and toss lightly.

MAKES 8 SERVINGS

PER SERVING: 64 calories, 3 g protein, 5 g total fat, 1 g saturated fat, 2 mg cholesterol, 3 g carbohydrate, 1 g fibre, 106 mg sodium, 253 mg potassium

Spinach Supper Salad

On a hot summer night, this salad makes a perfect light meal along with French bread, cold soup and, for dessert, fresh fruit. Present it attractively mounded in a large shallow bowl or arrange on individual salad plates. Sometimes I add sliced cooked beets, grated carrot, hearts of palm, artichoke hearts, chopped nuts, salmon, tuna, cooked chicken, fresh herbs or sunflower seeds. This salad is also delicious with Everyday Vinaigrette (p. 95).

4 cups	torn fresh spinach leaves (4 oz/125 g)	1 L
Half	head leaf lettuce, torn in bite-size pieces	Half
2 cups	alfalfa sprouts	500 mL
¼ cup	Buttermilk Herb Dressing (p. 99)	50 mL
4 oz	mushrooms, sliced	125 g
1	large tomato, cut in chunks	1
2	green onions, chopped	2
½ cup	crumbled light feta cheese (2 oz/60 g)	125 mL
1	hard-cooked egg, coarsely chopped	1

In large shallow salad bowl, toss spinach, lettuce and alfalfa sprouts with dressing.

Sprinkle with mushrooms, then tomato, onions, feta cheese and egg.

MAKES 2 MAIN-COURSE OR 6 SIDE-SALAD SERVINGS

NOTE: A main-course serving contributes 81% of the daily value for vitamin A and 95% for vitamin C. It is also a very high source of calcium, iron, folacin and fibre.

PER MAIN-COURSE SERVING: 225 calories, 18 g protein, 12 g total fat, 5 g saturated fat, 110 mg cholesterol, 17 g carbohydrate, 6 g fibre, 714 mg sodium, 1181 mg potassium

Tomato Slices with Chèvre and Basil

Thick slices of ripe, juicy tomatoes topped with fresh herbs is the perfect salad for summer meals. If fresh basil isn't available, use fresh parsley, oregano, coriander or dill.

3	large tomatoes (at room temperature)	3
3 tbsp	crumbled chèvre (soft goat cheese) or light feta cheese	50 mL
2 tsp	balsamic vinegar or fresh lemon juice	10 mL
	Freshly ground pepper	
3 tbsp	chopped fresh basil, plus more to taste	50 mL
	Watercress or arugula (optional)	

Cut tomatoes into thick slices; arrange on individual plates or large platter. Sprinkle with cheese, then vinegar; season with pepper to taste. Just before serving, chop basil, sprinkle over tomatoes. Garnish plate with watercress (if using).

MAKES 6 SERVINGS

NOTE: It's best to chop basil just before serving; chopped basil will darken upon standing for too long.

PER SERVING: 31 calories, 2 g protein, 1 g total fat, 1 g saturated fat, 2 mg cholesterol, 4 g carbohydrate, 1 g fibre, 22 mg sodium, 225 mg potassium

Tomato Raita

This Indian salad is the ideal match for curries or spicy foods, and it adds a colourful note to the meal. I also like to have it for lunch spooned into pita bread pockets along with Hummus (p. 4) and shredded lettuce.

1½ cups	chopped peeled and seeded cucumber	375 mL
1 tsp	salt	5 mL
2	medium tomatoes	2
1 tbsp	finely chopped onion	15 mL
1 cup	low-fat or extra-thick plain yogurt	250 mL
¼ cup	chopped fresh parsley	50 mL
2 tbsp	chopped fresh coriander (cilantro)	25 mL
1 tsp	ground cumin	5 mL
⅛ tsp or less	salt and freshly ground pepper	0.5 mL or less

Sprinkle cucumber with salt; let stand for about 40 minutes. Rinse under cold running water; pat dry. Core tomatoes; cut into ½-inch (1 cm) cubes. In bowl, toss together cucumber, tomatoes and onion; drain off any liquid. Combine yogurt, parsley, coriander and cumin; pour over vegetables and mix lightly. Season with salt and pepper.

MAKES 6 SERVINGS, ¾ CUP (175 mL) EACH

MAKE AHEAD: Cover and refrigerate (omitting tomatoes) for up to 4 hours; add tomatoes just before serving.

VARIATIONS:

Cucumber Raita
Use 3 cups (750 mL) chopped cucumbers; omit tomatoes.

Cucumber Mint Raita
Add ¼ cup (50 mL) chopped fresh mint. Serve with grilled meats such as Souvlaki of Lamb (p. 313).

PER SERVING: 40 calories, 3 g protein, 1 g total fat, 0 g saturated fat, 2 mg cholesterol, 6 g carbohydrate, 1 g fibre, 277 mg sodium, 263 mg potassium

Orange and Fennel Salad

This crunchy, juicy salad is a good choice for a buffet or a meal with strong flavours.

1	small bulb fennel (about 12 oz/375 g)	1
4	oranges	4
2	green onions, chopped	2
2 tbsp	chopped fresh parsley (preferably flat-leaf Italian)	25 mL
¼ tsp or less	salt and freshly ground pepper	1 mL or less
	Boston lettuce or spinach leaves or Belgian endive	

GARLIC VINAIGRETTE

1 tbsp	fresh lemon juice	15 mL
¼ tsp	minced fresh garlic	1 mL
¼ tsp	Dijon mustard	1 mL
2 tbsp	olive oil	25 mL

Trim base and top of fennel; discard outer leaves. Slice very thinly. Cut a slice from top and bottom of each orange and discard. Cut away peel from oranges so that no white pith remains. Slice oranges. In bowl, combine fennel, oranges, onions and parsley.

GARLIC VINAIGRETTE: In small bowl, whisk together lemon juice, garlic and mustard; whisk in oil. Pour over orange mixture; toss to coat. Season with salt and pepper.

Serve on a bed of lettuce or spinach or with Belgian endive spears.

MAKES 8 SERVINGS

MAKE AHEAD: Cover and refrigerate dressed salad for up to 6 hours.

PER SERVING: 75 calories, 1 g protein, 4 g total fat, 0 g saturated fat, 0 mg cholesterol, 11 g carbohydrate, 3 g fibre, 99 mg sodium, 301 mg potassium

Roasted Beet and Orange Salad

I had a wonderful beet salad in Ronda, in southern Spain, made with smoked salmon, cheese and oranges. This is my version of it. You could also add slices of apple, pear, fennel or radishes.

1 lb	beets (about 4 medium) (unpeeled)	500 g
1	large orange (or blood orange)	1
1 tbsp	fresh lemon juice	15 mL
1 tbsp	olive oil	15 mL
Pinch	each salt, freshly ground pepper and granulated sugar	Pinch
2 to 4 oz	thickly sliced smoked salmon (optional)	60 to 125 g
3 tbsp	crumbled light feta cheese (optional)	50 mL
1	bunch watercress or arugula	1
2 tbsp	chopped green onion	25 mL
2 to 4 oz	thickly sliced smoked salmon (optional)	60 to 125 g
3 tbsp	crumbled light feta cheese (optional)	50 mL

Trim beets; prick several times with a fork and place on baking sheet. Roast in 425°F (220°C) oven for 40 minutes or until fork-tender (new beets cook much faster than old beets). When cool, peel and cut into cubes.

Cut peel from orange and cut orange into sections; set aside, saving any juice.

In small bowl, mix together lemon juice, olive oil, salt, pepper and sugar. Just before serving, line four individual salad plates with watercress. Top with beets, orange segments and green onion. Pour any saved orange juice into lemon-oil mixture; drizzle over salads. Top with smoked salmon and feta (if using).

MAKES 4 SERVINGS

NOTE: One half cup (125 mL) of beets is very high in folate and is also a source of potassium and magnesium.

PER SERVING: 89 calories, 2 g protein, 4 g total fat, 0 g saturated fat, 0 mg cholesterol, 14 g carbohydrate, 3 g fibre, 69 mg sodium, 422 mg potassium

Coleslaw with Apple and Onion

Use new-crop, mild-flavoured, crisp cabbage in this tasty everyday summer salad. This slaw also makes a fine winter salad when lettuce and tomatoes are neither plentiful nor flavourful.

2 cups	finely shredded cabbage	500 mL
1	medium carrot, grated	1
Half	sweet green pepper, chopped	Half
1	apple, cored and chopped (unpeeled)	1
2	green onions, chopped	2
¼ tsp or less	salt and freshly ground pepper	1 mL or less

YOGURT DRESSING

¼ cup	low-fat plain yogurt	50 mL
2 tbsp	light mayonnaise	25 mL
1 tsp	fresh lemon juice	5 mL
¼ tsp	dried dillweed (or 2 tbsp/25 mL chopped fresh)	1 mL

In serving bowl, combine cabbage, carrot, green pepper, apple and onions.

YOGURT DRESSING: Combine yogurt, mayonnaise, lemon juice and dillweed, mixing well. Pour over salad and toss to mix. Season with salt and pepper.

MAKES 4 SERVINGS, ½ CUP (125 mL) EACH

MAKE AHEAD: Cover and refrigerate for up to 1 day.

NOTE: One serving is very high in vitamin A and is a good source of vitamin C and folacin.

PER SERVING: 74 calories, 2 g protein, 3 g total fat, 1 g saturated fat, 3 mg cholesterol, 12 g carbohydrate, 2 g fibre, 222 mg sodium, 266 mg potassium

Purple Vegetable Slaw

This salad is a fabulous accompaniment to grilled meats or Marinated Baked Tofu (p. 166), or serve with soup for a light meal.

2 cups	finely shredded red cabbage	500 mL
¼ tsp	salt	1 mL
½ cup	canned red kidney beans, drained and rinsed	125 mL
½ cup	corn kernels	125 mL
⅓ cup	chopped fresh coriander (cilantro)	75 mL
1	tomato, diced	1
1	green onion, chopped	1
2 tbsp	balsamic or red wine vinegar	25 mL
1 tbsp	sesame oil	15 mL
¼ tsp	crushed red pepper flakes	1 mL
1	clove garlic, minced	1
	Freshly ground pepper	

Sprinkle cabbage with the ¼ tsp (1 mL) salt; set aside. In bowl, combine kidney beans, corn, coriander, tomato, green onion, vinegar, oil, red pepper flakes and garlic; mix well. Add cabbage, and pepper to taste.

MAKES 4 SERVINGS

MAKE AHEAD: Cover and refrigerate for up to 1 day.

PER SERVING: 96 calories, 3 g protein, 4 g total fat, 1 g saturated fat, 0 mg cholesterol, 14 g carbohydrate, 3 g fibre, 229 mg sodium, 303 mg potassium

Snow Pea and Red Pepper Buffet Salad

This colourful dish is a good addition to a buffet any time of year. To make a larger amount, double salad ingredients, but use the same amount of dressing.

¾ lb	snow peas	375 g
2 tbsp	sesame seeds	25 mL
½ lb	mushrooms, sliced	250 g
1	small sweet red pepper, cut in thin strips	1

WALNUT-ORANGE DRESSING

1	clove garlic, minced	1
⅓ cup	orange juice	75 mL
3 tbsp	apple cider or white wine vinegar	50 mL
1 tsp	granulated sugar	5 mL
¼ tsp	salt	1 mL
2 tbsp	olive or walnut oil	25 mL
	Freshly ground pepper	

Top and string peas; blanch in boiling water for 2 minutes or until bright green and slightly pliable. Drain and rinse under cold water; dry thoroughly and set aside.

In ungreased skillet over medium heat, cook sesame seeds, shaking pan often, for 2 minutes or until lightly browned. Set aside.

WALNUT-ORANGE DRESSING: In food processor or bowl, combine garlic, orange juice, vinegar, sugar and salt. With machine running or while mixing, gradually add oil.

In salad bowl, combine snow peas, mushrooms and red pepper. Just before serving, add dressing and sesame seeds; toss to mix.

MAKES 8 SERVINGS

MAKE AHEAD: The salad can be prepared up to 1 day in advance; however, to keep the snow peas' bright green colour, add the dressing just before serving.

NOTE: Nut oils, such as walnut oil, add a delicious flavour to salads. Use with tossed green salads or as suggested here. Store walnut oil in refrigerator and use within a few months, as it can become rancid.

PER SERVING: 76 calories, 3 g protein, 5 g total fat, 1 g saturated fat, 0 mg cholesterol, 7 g carbohydrate, 2 g fibre, 76 mg sodium, 226 mg potassium

Broccoli Buffet Salad

My sister-in-law Ann Braden makes this salad for our summer-cottage family reunions. She sometimes adds cooked, crumbled bacon. If you are able to keep it chilled, this is a great salad for packed lunches.

3 cups	broccoli florets (about 1 bunch)	750 mL
½ cup	chopped red onion	125 mL
¼ cup	sunflower seeds	50 mL
½ cup	raisins	125 mL
½ cup	light feta cheese, crumbled	125 mL
⅛ tsp or less	salt and freshly ground pepper	0.5 mL or less

DRESSING

½ cup	low-fat plain yogurt	125 mL
3 tbsp	light mayonnaise	50 mL
2 tbsp	granulated sugar	25 mL
1 tbsp	fresh lemon juice	15 mL

In salad bowl, combine broccoli, onion, sunflower seeds, raisins and cheese.

DRESSING: In bowl, stir together yogurt, mayonnaise, sugar and lemon juice; pour over salad and toss to mix. Season with salt and pepper. Cover and refrigerate for 2 hours.

MAKES 6 SERVINGS

MAKE AHEAD: Cover and refrigerate for up to 2 days.

NOTE: The fat in this salad comes equally from the sunflower seeds, feta cheese and mayonnaise. To reduce the fat, use half the amount of each.

PER SERVING: 166 calories, 6 g protein, 8 g total fat, 2 g saturated fat, 8 mg cholesterol, 21 g carbohydrate, 2 g fibre, 277 mg sodium, 325 mg potassium

Melon and Bean Salad

Juicy melon balls, red kidney beans and strips of sweet red pepper make a colourful combination that will perk up anything from cold turkey to meatloaf to sandwiches. If you like, white kidney beans can be substituted for red.

1	small cantaloupe or honeydew melon	1
2	green onions (including tops)	2
1	small sweet red pepper	1
1	can (19 oz/540 mL) red or white kidney beans, drained and rinsed	1
1	clove garlic, minced	1
2 tbsp	chopped fresh parsley	25 mL
2 tbsp	fresh lemon juice	25 mL
2 tbsp	olive oil	25 mL
¼ tsp or less	salt and freshly ground pepper	1 mL or less

Cut melon in half; scoop out seeds. With melon baller, scoop out balls (or cut into cubes) to make about 2 cups (500 mL). Cut onions and red pepper into thin 1-inch (2.5 cm) strips.

In salad bowl, combine melon, onions, red pepper, beans, garlic and parsley; toss to mix. Whisk together lemon juice and oil; pour over salad and toss to mix. Season with salt and pepper; toss again. Cover and refrigerate until serving time.

MAKES 8 SERVINGS, ½ CUP (125 mL) EACH

MAKE AHEAD: Cover and refrigerate for up to 2 days.

NOTE: One serving is an excellent source of vitamin C and folacin; it's a good source of vitamin A and also provides fibre.

PER SERVING: 101 calories, 4 g protein, 4 g total fat, 1 g saturated fat, 0 mg cholesterol, 14 g carbohydrate, 4 g fibre, 228 mg sodium, 309 mg potassium

White Kidney Bean Salad

Cannellini, or white kidney beans, make a tasty salad when teamed with summer garden vegetables. Add cucumber and tomato and you have a gazpacho-like flavour. If white kidney beans are not available, use red. Serve as part of a salad plate, with hamburgers or cold chicken, or toss with spinach for a substantial salad.

1	can (19 oz/540 mL) white kidney beans, drained and rinsed (about 2 cups/500 mL)	1
⅔ cup	chopped English cucumber	150 mL
⅔ cup	chopped Spanish or sweet onion	150 mL
1	sweet green pepper, chopped	1
1	large tomato, chopped	1
¼ cup	chopped fresh coriander (cilantro) or parsley	50 mL
2 tbsp	fresh lemon juice, plus more to taste	25 mL
1 tbsp	olive oil	15 mL
¾ tsp	ground cumin, plus more to taste	4 mL
⅛ tsp or less	salt and freshly ground pepper	0.5 mL or less
	Lettuce (optional)	

In bowl, combine beans, cucumber, onion, green pepper, tomato, coriander, lemon juice, oil, cumin, salt and pepper. Taste and season with more lemon juice, cumin, and pepper. Serve on its own or on a bed of lettuce.

MAKES 6 SERVINGS, ¾ CUP (175 mL) EACH

MAKE AHEAD: Cover and refrigerate for up to 3 days.

NOTE: One serving is an excellent source of folacin and is high in vitamin C, potassium and fibre.

VARIATION:

Jiffy White Kidney Bean Salad
Keep a can of white kidney beans on hand for a salad that can be made at a moment's notice—without the bother of chopping vegetables. Toss 1 can (19 oz/540 mL) drained and rinsed white kidney beans with 2 tbsp (25 mL) olive oil; 2 cloves garlic, minced; 1 cup (250 mL) chopped fresh parsley; and salt, pepper and fresh lemon juice to taste. Makes 4 servings

PER SERVING: 113 calories, 5 g protein, 3 g total fat, 0 g saturated fat, 0 mg cholesterol, 18 g carbohydrate, 5 g fibre, 249 mg sodium, 392 mg potassium

Green Bean Salad with Buttermilk Dressing

Serve this colourful salad with grilled meats, fish or chicken. The Buttermilk Herb Dressing is the perfect match for the beans and bacon.

1 lb	green beans, trimmed	500 g
1 cup	coarsely chopped fresh parsley	250 mL
⅓ cup	thinly sliced red onion	75 mL
1	sweet yellow pepper, thinly sliced	1
3	slices bacon, cooked and crumbled	3
½ cup	Buttermilk Herb Dressing (p. 99)	125 mL

In large pot of boiling water, cook beans for 1 minute; drain and rinse under cold water. Pat dry. In salad bowl, toss together beans, parsley, onion, yellow pepper and bacon. Add dressing and toss.

MAKES 6 SERVINGS

MAKE AHEAD: Cover and refrigerate for up to 1 day; add dressing up to 1 hour before serving.

PER SERVING: 77 calories, 4 g protein, 4 g total fat, 1 g saturated fat, 7 mg cholesterol, 9 g carbohydrate, 2 g fibre, 202 mg sodium, 347 mg potassium

Red Bean Salad with Feta and Peppers

My aim for this recipe was to create an easy-to-make, nutrient-packed dish that would keep for a few days in the refrigerator and still taste terrific. Apart from their great taste, texture and colour, the beans add fibre, protein and iron; red pepper, vitamin C; cabbage, vitamin C and fibre; and light feta cheese, protein and calcium (it is also a lower-fat cheese than many). Serve this salad for lunch with whole-wheat bread—in a packed lunch or for a quick supper with a soup, sandwich or omelette.

1	can (19 oz/540 mL) kidney beans, drained and rinsed	1
1	sweet red pepper, chopped	1
2 cups	finely chopped cabbage	500 mL
2	green onions, chopped	2
4 oz	light feta cheese*, cubed (1 cup/250 mL)	125 g
¼ cup	chopped fresh parsley	50 mL
1	clove garlic, minced	1
2 tbsp	fresh lemon juice	25 mL
1 tbsp	canola or olive oil	15 mL

In salad bowl, combine beans, red pepper, cabbage, onions, cheese, parsley, garlic, lemon juice and oil; toss to mix.

MAKES 4 MAIN-COURSE SERVINGS, 1½ CUP (375 mL) EACH

*Or part-skim mozzarella

MAKE AHEAD: Cover and refrigerate for up to 3 days.

NOTE: Brassica vegetables include cabbage, broccoli, cauliflower, brussels sprouts and kale. Studies suggest that consumption of these vegetables may reduce the risk of certain cancers.

PER SERVING: 224 calories, 13 g protein, 8 g total fat, 3 g saturated fat, 10 mg cholesterol, 27 g carbohydrate, 8 g fibre, 657 mg sodium, 588 mg potassium

Chickpea Salad with Red Onion and Tomato

Chickpeas, or garbanzo beans as they are also known, are now as popular in North America as they are in Mediterranean countries. Serve this substantial salad as part of a salad plate with a green salad and dark bread for a light yet high-fibre lunch or supper. It's ideal as part of a meatless meal—chickpeas supply protein and are high in fibre and iron.

1	can (19 oz/540 mL) chickpeas, drained and rinsed	1
2 tbsp	finely chopped red onion or green onions	25 mL
2	cloves garlic, minced	2
1	tomato, diced	1
½ cup	chopped fresh parsley	125 mL
2 tbsp	fresh lemon juice	25 mL
1 tbsp	olive oil	15 mL
¼ tsp or less	each salt and freshly ground pepper	1 mL or less

In salad bowl, combine chickpeas, onion, garlic, tomato, parsley, lemon juice, oil, salt and pepper; toss to mix. Chill for 2 hours to allow flavours to develop before serving.

MAKES 6 SERVINGS, ½ CUP (125 mL) EACH

MAKE AHEAD: Cover and refrigerate for up to 1 day.

NOTE: One serving is a high source of folacin.

PER SERVING: 109 calories, 4 g protein, 3 g total fat, 0 g saturated fat, 0 mg cholesterol, 16 g carbohydrate, 3 g fibre, 254 mg sodium, 222 mg potassium

Southwest Rice and Bean Salad

This salad is well-suited for summer buffets, picnics, ski lunches or just to have on hand in the refrigerator for a fast meal. One serving of this salad is high in dietary fibre; the beans make it an excellent source of folate and a good source of magnesium.

1 tsp	canola or olive oil	5 mL
1 cup	long-grain rice	250 mL
1	can (19 oz/540 mL) red kidney beans	1
1	can (19 oz/540 mL) black beans or pinto or romano beans	1
1½ cups	frozen peas, thawed	375 mL
1 cup	sliced celery	250 mL
1	jalapeño pepper, chopped, or 1 can (4 oz/114 mL) green chili peppers, drained and chopped	1
½ cup	chopped red onion	125 mL
½ cup	chopped fresh coriander (cilantro) or parsley	125 mL

VINAIGRETTE

⅓ cup	red wine vinegar	75 mL
¼ cup	canola or olive oil	50 mL
¼ cup	water	50 mL
1 tsp	minced fresh garlic	5 mL
¼ tsp	freshly ground pepper	1 mL

In saucepan, heat oil over medium heat; add rice and stir to coat well. Add 2 cups (500 mL) boiling water; cover and simmer for 20 minutes or until water is absorbed and rice is tender. Transfer to salad bowl and let cool.

Drain and rinse kidney and black beans; add to salad bowl. Add peas, celery, jalapeño or chili peppers, onion and coriander. Set aside.

VINAIGRETTE: In food processor or bowl, combine vinegar, oil, water, garlic, and pepper; mix well. Pour over salad and toss to mix.

MAKES 12 SERVINGS, ¾ CUP (175 mL) EACH

MAKE AHEAD: Cover and refrigerate for up to 2 days.

VARIATION:

Pasta and Bean Salad
Substitute 3 cups (750 mL) cooked orzo (rice-shaped pasta) for the rice.

NOTE: Leftover cooked rice can be used in this recipe: about 3 cups (750 mL) cooked rice equals 1 cup (250 mL) uncooked.

PER SERVING: 188 calories, 7 g protein, 5 g total fat, 0 g saturated fat, 0 mg cholesterol, 28 g carbohydrate, 5 g fibre, 220 mg sodium, 303 mg potassium

Elizabeth Baird's Curried Lentil, Wild Rice and Orzo Salad

This recipe is from *Canadian Living* magazine's Elizabeth Baird, who served this at her niece's wedding. It's also a good choice for buffets and picnics, and as a vegetarian meal. I've adapted it slightly by replacing some of the oil with water.

½ cup	wild rice	125 mL
⅔ cup	green or brown lentils	150 mL
½ cup	orzo*	125 mL
½ cup	currants	125 mL
¼ cup	chopped red onion	50 mL
⅓ cup	slivered almonds, toasted (optional)	75 mL

DRESSING

¼ cup	white wine vinegar	50 mL
2 tbsp	water	25 mL
1 tsp	ground cumin	5 mL
1 tsp	Dijon mustard	5 mL
½ tsp	each granulated sugar, salt and ground coriander	2 mL
¼ tsp	each turmeric, paprika, nutmeg and ground cardamom	1 mL
Pinch	each cinnamon, ground cloves and cayenne pepper	Pinch
¼ cup	canola or olive oil	50 mL

In separate pots of boiling water, cook wild rice for 35 to 40 minutes, lentils for 25 to 30 minutes and orzo for 5 minutes or until each is tender but not mushy. Drain well and transfer to large bowl. Add currants and onion; set aside.

DRESSING: In small bowl whisk together vinegar, water, cumin, mustard, sugar, salt, coriander, turmeric, paprika, nutmeg, cardamom, cinnamon, cloves and cayenne; whisk in oil. Pour over rice mixture and toss gently.

Let cool completely; cover and refrigerate for at least 4 hours. Serve sprinkled with almonds.

MAKES 8 SERVINGS

*Orzo is tiny, rice-shaped pasta, available in Italian food stores and most supermarkets.

MAKE AHEAD: Cover and refrigerate for up to 2 days.

VARIATION:

Curried Lentil, Rice and Raisin Salad
Substitute raisins for currants, long-grain converted rice for orzo. Cook rice in boiling water for 20 minutes or until tender but not mushy; drain well.

PER SERVING: 224 calories, 8 g protein, 8 g total fat, 1 g saturated fat, 0 mg cholesterol, 33 g carbohydrate, 4 g fibre, 166 mg sodium, 319 mg potassium

Wild Rice, Bulgur and Tomato Salad

Ever since my friend and terrific cook Susan Pacaud brought this salad to our gourmet club dinner, I have made it often for summer barbecues and buffet dinners.

¾ cup	medium bulgur	175 mL
1½ cups	sodium-reduced chicken broth	375 mL
¾ cup	wild rice, rinsed and drained	175 mL
2	large tomatoes, diced	2
1 cup	chopped fresh parsley	250 mL
¼ cup	finely chopped green onion	50 mL

LEMON VINAIGRETTE

¼ cup	fresh lemon juice	50 mL
2	cloves garlic, minced	2
½ tsp	salt	2 mL
¼ cup	olive oil	50 mL
	Freshly ground pepper	

Soak bulgur in 6 cups (1. 5 L) hot water for 1 hour; drain well. Meanwhile, in saucepan, bring broth and rice to boil; cover, reduce heat and simmer for 40 to 45 minutes or until rice splays, is tender-crisp but not soft, and most of the liquid is absorbed. Drain if necessary; let cool. In salad bowl, combine bulgur, rice, tomatoes, parsley and onion.

LEMON VINAIGRETTE: In food processor or bowl, combine lemon juice, garlic and salt; blend well. Add oil and process or whisk until mixed. Season with pepper to taste. Pour over salad; stir to mix. Chill before serving.

MAKES 10 SERVINGS, ½ CUP (125 mL) EACH

MAKE AHEAD: Cover and refrigerate for up to 2 days.

NOTE: See page 114 for more on bulgur.

PER SERVING: 139 calories, 4 g protein, 6 g total fat, 1 g saturated fat, 0 mg cholesterol, 20 g carbohydrate, 3 g fibre, 209 mg sodium, 238 mg potassium

Warm Scallop Salad

My friend Donna Osler serves this salad as a first course at dinner parties. It's a good choice: it tastes fabulous, and it serves as both a fish course and a salad.

1	bunch arugula	1
8 cups	torn mixed greens	2 L
2 tsp	canola oil	10 mL
1 tbsp	grated gingerroot	15 mL
1	clove garlic, minced	1
¼ cup	diced sweet red pepper	50 mL
1 lb	large scallops	500 g
¼ cup	dry sherry	50 mL
¼ cup	chopped fresh coriander (cilantro)	50 mL

VINAIGRETTE

2 tbsp	sesame oil	25 mL
1	clove garlic, minced	1
1 tbsp	fresh lemon juice	15 mL
1 tsp	sodium-reduced soy sauce	5 mL
¼ tsp	granulated sugar	1 mL

VINAIGRETTE: In large bowl, mix sesame oil, garlic, lemon juice, soy sauce and sugar.

Add arugula and greens and toss well. Divide among plates.

In skillet, heat oil over medium heat; cook gingerroot, garlic and red pepper, stirring, for 2 minutes. Add scallops, sherry and coriander; cover and cook for 3 minutes or until scallops are opaque through to centre, turning once. Using slotted spoon, divide scallops among plates. Increase heat to high and cook until pan liquid is reduced slightly; drizzle over salads.

MAKES 6 APPETIZER OR 3 MAIN-COURSE SERVINGS

MAKE AHEAD: Prepare vinaigrette and measure out all other ingredients up to 1 day in advance.

NOTE: If arugula is unavailable, substitute watercress.

If using frozen scallops, be sure they are completely thawed before using.

PER APPETIZER SERVING:
155 calories, 15 g protein, 7 g total fat, 1 g saturated fat, 25 mg cholesterol, 7 g carbohydrate, 2 g fibre, 192 mg sodium, 617 mg potassium

Marinated Shrimp and Mango Salad

For years, I've been part of a women's gourmet dinner group. This is one of our favourite starter salads, but it would also make a spectacular luncheon dish. My friend Ellen Wright makes it with chicken and says it is equally good.

2 lb	large peeled raw shrimp (or thawed and completely dried)	1 kg
1 tsp	canola oil	5 mL
2	bunches watercress (8 cups/2 L lightly packed)	2
1 cup	packed fresh coriander (cilantro) sprigs	250 mL
2	sweet red peppers, cut in thin strips	2
2	large ripe mangoes, peeled and cut in thin strips	2

SHRIMP MARINADE

2 tsp	each ground cumin, ground coriander and paprika	10 mL
⅔ cup	low-fat plain yogurt	150 mL
2 tbsp	minced gingerroot	25 mL
1 tbsp	minced fresh garlic	15 mL
2	fresh jalapeño peppers, seeded and chopped, or 1 tbsp (15 mL) chopped bottled peppers	2
	Grated rind of 1 lime	
¼ tsp or less	salt and freshly ground pepper	1 mL or less

DRESSING

½ cup	mango chutney	125 mL
⅓ cup	fresh lime juice	75 mL
3 tbsp	canola oil	50 mL
Dash	hot pepper sauce	Dash

SHRIMP MARINADE: In small nonstick skillet, dry-roast cumin, coriander and paprika over medium heat, stirring occasionally, for about 2 minutes or until darkened slightly and fragrant. Let cool.

In large bowl, stir together yogurt, gingerroot, garlic, jalapeño peppers, lime rind, roasted spices, and salt and pepper to taste. Add shrimp; mix to coat. Cover and refrigerate for 1 hour or for up to 1 day.

DRESSING: In food processor, purée chutney. Add lime juice, oil and hot pepper sauce; process to mix. Set aside.

In large nonstick skillet, heat oil over medium-high heat; cook shrimp and marinade, turning once, for 3 to 4 minutes or until shrimp are pink and opaque.

In large bowl, toss together watercress, coriander, red peppers, mangoes, shrimp and any marinade left in the pan, and dressing. Arrange on individual salad plates.

MAKES 12 APPETIZER SERVINGS OR 6 MAIN-COURSE SERVINGS

MAKE AHEAD: Marinate shrimp, covered, in the refrigerator for up to 1 day. Prepare dressing up to 1 day in advance; keep refrigerated until ready to use.

NOTE: Use whole sprigs of watercress and coriander but remove bottom of large, tough stems. You could also replace half watercress with arugula.

Chutney replaces some of the oil in the dressing in this recipe. Not only does it reduce the overall amount of fat, it adds flavour and helps to emulsify and thicken the dressing.

PER MAIN-COURSE SERVING:
391 calories, 35 g protein, 10 g total fat, 1 g saturated fat, 287 mg cholesterol, 42 g carbohydrate, 5 g fibre, 776 mg sodium, 841 mg potassium

Seafood Pasta Salad

Choose any short tubular or corkscrew pasta for this salad. Use fresh crab if it is available, instead of frozen. Imitation crab also works well.

2 cups	penne or other short pasta	500 mL
½ lb	sea scallops (not bay scallops)	250 g
¼ lb	snow peas, trimmed and strings removed	125 g
½ lb	cooked medium or small shrimp	250 g
¼ lb	frozen cooked or imitation crabmeat, drained and broken into chunks	125 g
Half	sweet red pepper, diced	Half
⅓ cup	chopped purple or green onion	75 mL
1 cup	Yogurt Herb Dressing (p. 99)	250 mL
⅛ tsp or less	salt and freshly ground pepper	0.5 mL or less

In large pot of boiling water, cook pasta until tender but firm, 7 to 10 minutes. Drain and rinse under cold water; drain thoroughly.

In pot of boiling water, cook scallops for about 3 minutes or until opaque in centre; drain. If large, cut in half or quarters.

In pot of boiling water, cook snow peas for 1 minute; drain. Rinse under cold water; drain. Slice in half diagonally.

In salad bowl, combine pasta, scallops, snow peas, shrimp, crabmeat, red pepper, onion and dressing; toss gently. Season with salt and pepper.

MAKES 8 SERVINGS

MAKE AHEAD: Cover and refrigerate (omitting snow peas) for up to 1 day. Wrap cooked snow peas in paper towels and refrigerate; to prevent discolouration, add to salad no more than 1 hour before serving.

NOTE: Shrimp are more flavourful when cooked in their shell, rather than peeled and deveined first. Cook in large pot of boiling water for 1 to 2 minutes or until shrimp turn pink; drain and cool under cold water. Remove shell and small dark vein running down back of shrimp.

PER SERVING: 201 calories, 18 g protein, 4 g total fat, 1 g saturated fat, 76 mg cholesterol, 22 g carbohydrate, 2 g fibre, 422 mg sodium, 316 mg potassium

Pasta Salad with Sweet Peppers and Dill

This is a terrific salad to have on hand in the refrigerator for a ready-made summer meal or a picnic. Feel free to add any of the usual salad ingredients to this dish, except lettuce. I often add black olives or artichokes. Vegetables can be crisply cooked, but I like the crunch of them raw. To serve as a main course, add shrimp, julienne strips of ham, chicken, tofu and/or cheese.

3 cups	penne (or 8 oz/250 g any pasta)	750 mL
1¼ cups	snow peas or green beans (4 oz/125 g)	300 mL
3 cups	small cauliflower pieces	750 mL
1 cup	thinly sliced carrots	250 mL
2	sweet peppers (red, yellow, green or purple or combination), chopped	2
2	green onions, chopped	2
1½ lb	large, cooked shrimp (optional)	750 g
½ cup	chopped fresh dill*	125 mL

DRESSING

2	cloves garlic, minced	2
¼ cup	white or red wine vinegar	50 mL
¼ cup	fresh lemon juice	50 mL
1 tsp	granulated sugar	5 mL
1 tsp	each dried basil and oregano	5 mL
½ tsp or less	each salt and freshly ground pepper	2 mL or less
⅓ cup	water	75 mL
¼ cup	olive oil	50 mL

In large saucepan of boiling water, cook pasta until tender but firm (taste for doneness after 2 minutes for fresh pasta, 5 minutes for dry). Drain and rinse under cold running water; drain thoroughly.

Blanch snow peas (or green beans if using) in boiling water for 2 minutes. Drain and rinse under cold running water; drain again. Cut diagonally into 2-inch (5 cm) lengths.

In large bowl, combine cauliflower, carrots, sweet peppers, onions, shrimp (if using), dill, snow peas and pasta; toss to mix.

DRESSING: In food processor or bowl, combine garlic, vinegar, lemon juice, sugar, basil, oregano, salt and pepper, mixing well. While processing or whisking, add water and oil, mixing well. Pour over salad; toss to mix.

MAKES 10 SERVINGS, 1 CUP (250 mL) EACH

*If fresh dill isn't available, substitute fresh parsley and/or basil.

MAKE AHEAD: Prepare salad but add only half of the dressing; cover and refrigerate for up to 1 day. Add remaining dressing just before serving.

NOTE: Instead of penne, try rotini, fusilli, truciolotti or broken lasagne noodles.

One serving provides 149% of an adult's daily requirement of vitamin C. It is also a very high source of vitamin A and folate.

PER SERVING: 184 calories, 5 g protein, 6 g total fat, 1 g saturated fat, 0 mg cholesterol, 28 g carbohydrate, 3 g fibre, 138 mg sodium, 283 mg potassium

Pasta Salad with Sun-Dried Tomatoes

Sun-dried tomatoes add flavour, colour and texture to this pasta salad. Use dry-packed tomatoes, which are lower in fat than those packed in oil. For variety, add artichoke hearts, celery, carrots, cauliflower, light feta cheese, cooked chicken or ham.

3 cups	penne, fusilli or macaroni (8 oz/250 g)	750 mL
1 cup	dry-packed sun-dried tomatoes	250 mL
1 cup	chopped green onions	250 mL
½ cup	chopped fresh parsley	125 mL
2 tbsp	freshly grated Parmesan cheese (optional)	25 mL

VINAIGRETTE

¼ cup	balsamic or apple cider vinegar	50 mL
⅓ cup	orange juice	75 mL
3 tbsp	olive oil	50 mL
1	clove garlic, minced	1
2 tsp	Dijon mustard	10 mL
1 tsp	each dried basil and oregano	5 mL
¼ tsp or less	salt and freshly ground pepper	1 mL or less

In large pot of boiling water, cook pasta until tender but firm; drain and rinse under cold water. Drain thoroughly.

Pour hot water over sun-dried tomatoes and let stand for 1 minute; drain, then coarsely chop. In large bowl, combine pasta, tomatoes, onions, parsley and Parmesan (if using).

VINAIGRETTE: Combine vinegar, orange juice, oil, garlic, mustard, basil and oregano; mix well. Pour over salad and toss to mix. Season with salt and pepper.

MAKES 8 SERVINGS

MAKE AHEAD: Cover and refrigerate for up to 2 days.

PER SERVING: 165 calories, 4 g protein, 6 g total fat, 1 g saturated fat, 0 mg cholesterol, 25 g carbohydrate, 2 g fibre, 253 mg sodium, 344 mg potassium

Thai Noodle Salad

All my kids love this quick salad. Keep a package of cellophane noodles or vermicelli rice noodles on hand to make it. Instead of spinach and red pepper, you might use grated carrot, chopped celery and frozen peas.

8 oz	rice vermicelli or cellophane (mung bean) thread noodles	250 g
2 cups	packed spinach leaves, cut in strips	500 mL
1	sweet red pepper, cut in thin strips	1
¼ cup	chopped fresh coriander (cilantro)	50 mL

THAI DRESSING

¼ cup	unsalted peanuts	50 mL
3 tbsp	minced gingerroot	50 mL
¼ cup	fresh lemon or lime juice	50 mL
¼ cup	water	50 mL
2 tbsp	sodium-reduced soy sauce	25 mL
1 tbsp	granulated sugar	15 mL
1 tbsp	canola or olive oil	15 mL
1 tsp	sesame oil	5 mL
¼ tsp	crushed red pepper flakes	1 mL

Prepare noodles according to package directions or cook in boiling water for 1 minute or until tender. (Or, soak in boiling water, for 2 to 4 minutes, until tender but still firm.) Drain and rinse under cold running water; drain thoroughly.

In salad bowl, toss noodles with spinach and red pepper.

THAI DRESSING: In food processor or blender, process peanuts and gingerroot until finely chopped. Add lemon juice, water, soy sauce, sugar, vegetable and sesame oils and red pepper flakes; process to mix.

Pour dressing over noodle mixture; toss to mix. Sprinkle with chopped coriander.

MAKES 6 SERVINGS

NOTE: Rice noodles come in a variety of shapes, including rice vermicelli, which are very thin. Cellophane thread noodles are made from ground mung beans and are tougher than rice noodles. Be careful not to overcook or oversoak the noodles or they will lose their crunchiness.

PER SERVING: 238 calories, 4 g protein, 6 g total fat, 1 g saturated fat, 0 mg cholesterol, 42 g carbohydrate, 3 g fibre, 218 mg sodium, 214 mg potassium

Singapore Noodle and Chicken Salad

Here's a tasty way to use up leftover barbecued chicken, or roast chicken or turkey. Blanched asparagus and/or green beans are nice additions to the salad.

¼ lb	thin noodles (capellini, spaghettini or rice vermicelli)	125 g
¼ cup	unsalted peanuts	50 mL
2	cloves garlic	2
2 tsp	chopped gingerroot	10 mL
1 tsp	granulated sugar	5 mL
¼ cup	water	50 mL
1 tbsp	sesame oil	15 mL
1 tbsp	sodium-reduced soy sauce	15 mL
1 tbsp	fresh lime juice	15 mL
½ tsp	hot chili paste or crushed red pepper flakes	2 mL
2	green onions, chopped	2
1 cup	thin strips cooked chicken	250 mL
1 cup	blanched julienned carrots	250 mL
¼ cup	packed chopped fresh coriander (cilantro)	50 mL

In large pot of boiling water, cook noodles until tender but firm. Drain and rinse under cold water; drain thoroughly.

In food processor, coarsely chop peanuts; set 2 tbsp (25 mL) aside. To food processor, add garlic, gingerroot and sugar; process for 30 seconds. Add water, sesame oil, soy sauce, lime juice and chili paste; process to mix.

Toss sauce with noodles. Add onions, chicken and carrots; toss to mix. Arrange on serving platter; sprinkle with coriander and reserved peanuts.

MAKES 6 SERVINGS

MAKE AHEAD: Cover and refrigerate for up to 1 day, garnishing with coriander and reserved peanuts when ready to serve.

NOTE: One serving is an excellent source of Vitamin A.

PER SERVING: 185 calories, 11 g protein, 7 g total fat, 1 g saturated fat, 21 mg cholesterol, 21 g carbohydrate, 2 g fibre, 131 mg sodium, 225 mg potassium

Asian Chicken Pasta Salad

A good choice for a luncheon, buffet or summer supper, this salad is wonderful served while still warm, though it can also be made ahead and served chilled or at room temperature.

MAKE AHEAD: Cover and refrigerate for up to 2 days.

PER SERVING: 290 calories, 22 g protein, 5 g total fat, 1 g saturated fat, 40 mg cholesterol, 39 g carbohydrate, 3 g fibre, 265 mg sodium, 345 mg potassium

1½ lb	boneless, skinless chicken breasts or thighs	750 g
½ cup	unseasoned rice vinegar	125 mL
¼ cup	sodium-reduced soy sauce	50 mL
3 tbsp	minced gingerroot	50 mL
2	cloves garlic, minced	2
1 tsp	granulated sugar	5 mL
1 lb	pasta or rice noodles*	500 g
4	medium carrots	4
2	sweet red, yellow or green peppers	2
8 oz	snow peas (optional)	250 g
2 tbsp	sesame oil	25 mL

Cut chicken into 2-inch (5 cm) julienne strips. In bowl, combine vinegar, soy sauce, gingerroot, garlic and sugar; stir in chicken. Cover and let stand for 30 minutes.

Meanwhile, in large pot of boiling water, cook pasta until tender but firm; drain. Rinse thoroughly under cold running water; drain and place in large salad bowl. Cut carrots and red peppers into julienne strips; set aside.

Using slotted spoon, remove chicken from marinade, reserving marinade. In large nonstick skillet, cook chicken over medium-high heat, stirring often, for 3 minutes or until no longer pink; add to pasta.

Add carrots and red peppers to skillet; stir-fry for 3 minutes. Transfer to bowl with pasta.

Add reserved marinade plus ½ cup (125 mL) water to skillet; bring to boil and boil gently for 5 minutes. Add snow peas (if using) to skillet; cover and cook for 1 minute. Pour mixture over pasta; add sesame oil and toss to mix.

MAKES 10 SERVINGS, 1 CUP (250 mL) EACH

*Use corkscrew-shaped pasta or broad rice or egg noodles broken into 4-inch (10 cm) pieces.

Chicken and Melon Salad

This main-course salad makes an elegant but easy lunch. The chicken can be cooked and all ingredients chopped a day in advance; then simply assemble the salad an hour or so before serving. Feel free to omit the grapes or honeydew melon, or substitute diced apple, pineapple or red or yellow pepper.

6 cups	cubed, cooked skinless chicken*	1.5 L
2 cups	honeydew melon or cantaloupe balls	500 mL
2 cups	chopped celery	500 mL
1 cup	seedless green or red grapes, cut in half	250 mL
1 cup	sliced water chestnuts (optional)	250 mL
½ cup	light sour cream	125 mL
½ cup	low-fat plain yogurt	125 mL
1 tsp	grated gingerroot (optional)	5 mL
½ tsp	curry powder, plus more to taste	2 mL
¼ tsp or less	salt and freshly ground pepper	1 mL or less

In large bowl, combine chicken, melon balls, celery, grapes and water chestnuts (if using). Combine sour cream, yogurt, gingerroot (if using) and curry powder until smooth; add salt, pepper and more curry powder, stirring gently into salad.

MAKES 8 SERVINGS, 1 CUP (250 mL) EACH

*For 6 cups (1.5 L) cubed cooked chicken, use two 2½ lb (1.25 kg) roasting chickens or 8 chicken breasts. To cook conventionally, cover whole chicken with water and simmer for 1 hour or until tender, skimming off foam occasionally. Let cool; discard skin and bones. See page 272 for how to microwave a whole chicken.

MAKE AHEAD: Cover and refrigerate cooked chicken and dressing separately for up to 1 day. Assemble salad up to 1 hour before serving.

PER SERVING: 230 calories, 32 g protein, 6 g total fat, 2 g saturated fat, 99 mg cholesterol, 11 g carbohydrate, 1 g fibre, 213 mg sodium, 628 mg potassium

Asparagus and Mushroom Salad

This salad is great for summer barbecues, buffets and to take to potlucks, because it goes with anything, tastes great and is easy to make. Green beans are also terrific served this way.

| 1 lb | asparagus | 500 g |
| 3 | large mushrooms, diced | 3 |

SESAME VINAIGRETTE

1 tbsp	unseasoned rice vinegar or white wine vinegar	15 mL
1 tbsp	sodium-reduced soy sauce	15 mL
1 tbsp	sesame oil	15 mL
¼ tsp	granulated sugar	1 mL
¼ tsp or less	salt and freshly ground pepper	1 mL or less
1 tbsp	toasted sesame seeds	15 mL

Cut or break off tough stem ends of asparagus. Peel stalks if large. In large pot of boiling water, cook asparagus until tender-crisp, about 4 minutes; drain. Cool under cold water; drain. Dry on paper towels.

SESAME VINAIGRETTE: Whisk together vinegar, soy sauce, sesame oil, sugar, and salt and pepper. Arrange asparagus on platter; pour vinaigrette over, rolling asparagus to coat.

Sprinkle with sesame seeds and mushrooms.

MAKES 6 SERVINGS

MAKE AHEAD: Prepare asparagus and dressing up to 1 day in advance. Cover cooked asparagus with damp paper towel or plastic wrap and refrigerate. Dress and garnish asparagus up to 1 hour before serving.

PER SERVING: 42 calories, 2 g protein, 3 g total fat, 0 g saturated fat, 0 mg cholesterol, 3 g carbohydrate, 1 g fibre, 192 mg sodium, 129 mg potassium

Citrus Quinoa Salad

Pronounced "keen-wah," the small grain-like seeds of this South American plant supply the same nutrients as grains like wheat, barley and rice. One-half cup (125 mL) cooked quinoa is high in magnesium and is also a source of iron and zinc. Look for it in select grocery stores and health food stores. Its crunchy texture makes an interesting and pleasing base for a salad. If you like, use sections of fresh orange instead of canned mandarin orange.

1 cup	quinoa	250 mL
1 cup	diced (unpeeled) cucumber	250 mL
½ cup	diced figs or dried apricots or raisins	125 mL
½ cup	drained canned mandarin orange sections, halved	125 mL
¼ cup	sunflower seeds or toasted almonds	50 mL
2	green onions, diced	2
2 tbsp	chopped fresh coriander (cilantro) or parsley	25 mL

DRESSING

1 tsp	grated lemon or lime rind	5 mL
3 tbsp	fresh lemon or lime juice	50 mL
1 tbsp	sesame oil	15 mL
1 tsp	granulated sugar	5 mL
¼ tsp	each ground cumin and coriander	1 mL

Rinse quinoa under cold running water; drain. In saucepan, bring 2 cups (500 mL) water to boil; stir in quinoa. Reduce heat, cover and simmer for 15 minutes or until water is absorbed and quinoa is translucent; drain and let cool. In salad bowl, combine quinoa, cucumber, figs, orange sections, sunflower seeds, onions and coriander.

DRESSING: In small bowl, mix lemon rind and juice, oil, sugar, cumin and coriander; pour over salad and toss to mix.

MAKES 8 SERVINGS, ½ CUP (125 mL) EACH

MAKE AHEAD: Cover and refrigerate for up to 3 days.

NOTE: Use these high-fat ingredients sparingly in your salads: nuts, avocados, bacon bits, high-fat cheese, olives, croutons prepared with added fat and, of course, high-fat salad dressings.

PER SERVING: 161 calories, 4 g protein, 5 g total fat, 1 g saturated fat, 0 mg cholesterol, 26 g carbohydrate, 3 g fibre, 8 mg sodium, 311 mg potassium

French Potato Salad with Tarragon Vinaigrette

The red-skinned potatoes look especially attractive in this salad; however, any type of potato will work well. For variety, add chopped chives, sliced celery or radish, corn kernels, or blanched snow peas or green beans.

2½ lb	small red potatoes (unpeeled)	1.25 kg
1 cup	chopped fresh parsley	250 mL
½ cup	chopped red onion	125 mL
¼ tsp or less	salt and freshly ground pepper	1 mL or less

TARRAGON VINAIGRETTE

⅓ cup	white wine vinegar	75 mL
2 tbsp	olive oil	25 mL
1 tbsp	grainy or Dijon mustard	15 mL
½ tsp	dried tarragon	2 mL

Scrub potatoes. In large pot of boiling water, cook potatoes until fork-tender; drain. Shake in pan over medium heat for 1 minute to dry potatoes. Cut into ¼-inch (5 mm) thick slices. In salad bowl, combine potatoes, parsley and onion.

TARRAGON VINAIGRETTE: In small bowl, whisk together vinegar, oil, mustard and tarragon; mix well. Pour over warm potatoes and toss to mix. Season with salt and pepper. Cover and let stand at room temperature for at least 1 hour.

MAKES 8 SERVINGS, 1 CUP (250 mL) EACH

MAKE AHEAD: Cover and refrigerate for up to 3 days.

VARIATION: Instead of Tarragon Vinaigrette, use 1 cup (250 mL) low-fat yogurt, ¼ cup (50 mL) light mayonnaise and ½ tsp (2 mL) dried tarragon.

PER SERVING: 139 calories, 3 g protein, 4 g total fat, 1 g saturated fat, 0 mg cholesterol, 24 g carbohydrate, 2 g fibre, 113 mg sodium, 493 mg potassium

Warm Potato and Tuna Salad

Served on a bed of lettuce along with fresh whole-wheat bread and sliced tomatoes or perhaps a bowl of soup, this salad is a meal in itself. Garnish with strips of anchovies, capers or slices of hard-cooked eggs.

2 lb	new red potatoes, cut into chunks (unpeeled)	1 kg
½ lb	green beans, halved (2 cups/500 mL)	250 g
4	green onions, chopped	4
2	stalks celery, chopped	2
1	sweet red pepper, chopped (optional)	1
½ cup	chopped fresh parsley	125 mL
1	can (6½ oz/170 g) water-packed tuna, drained and broken into chunks	1
⅛ tsp or less	salt and freshly ground pepper	0.5 mL or less

DRESSING

⅓ cup	tarragon or apple cider vinegar, plus more to taste	75 mL
3 tbsp	water	50 mL
2 tbsp	olive oil	25 mL
1 tbsp	Dijon mustard	15 mL
1 tbsp	anchovy paste	15 mL
1	clove garlic, minced	1
	Freshly ground pepper	

In saucepan, cover potatoes with water; bring to boil. Reduce heat and simmer until nearly tender, about 5 minutes. Add green beans; cook for 3 to 5 minutes or until tender-crisp; drain.

DRESSING: Whisk together vinegar, water, oil, mustard, anchovy paste, garlic, and pepper to taste; toss ¼ cup (50 mL) with hot potato mixture.

Add onions, celery, red pepper (if using) and parsley. Add half of remaining dressing and toss. Gently stir in tuna, without breaking up chunks. Season with salt and pepper. Just before serving, drizzle with remaining dressing. If necessary add more vinegar to taste. Serve warm or cold.

MAKES 8 SERVINGS, 1 CUP (250 mL) EACH

MAKE AHEAD: Cook green beans separately. Cover and refrigerate beans and potato mixture for up to 1 day. Remove from refrigerator 30 minutes before serving, adding green beans to potatoes.

NOTE: To save time, cut the potatoes into ¾-inch (2 cm) pieces so they will cook faster.

To reduce the sodium in this salad, use sodium-reduced canned tuna or fresh cooked tuna and omit anchovy paste.

VARIATION:

Warm Potato Salad
For a side-dish potato salad, omit tuna; green beans and red pepper are optional.

PER SERVING: 146 calories, 7 g protein, 4 g total fat, 1 g saturated fat, 7 mg cholesterol, 21 g carbohydrate, 2 g fibre, 262 mg sodium, 533 mg potassium

Red Potato Salad with Sour Cream and Chives

Red-skinned potatoes add colour to this salad, but any kind of new potato can be used. Light sour cream and low-fat yogurt combine to make a light yet creamy dressing that is much lower in fat than the traditional mayonnaise dressing. You might also use light mayonnaise mixed with non-fat sour cream or yogurt.

6	medium red potatoes (unpeeled)	6
½ cup	light sour cream	125 mL
½ cup	low-fat plain yogurt	125 mL
⅓ to ½ cup	finely chopped fresh chives or green onions	75 to 125 mL
½ tsp or less	salt	2 mL or less
	Freshly ground pepper	

Scrub potatoes. If large, cut in half or quarters. In saucepan of boiling water, cook potatoes until fork-tender; drain and return to pot. Shake in pan over medium heat for 1 minute to dry potatoes. Cut into ½-inch (1 cm) cubes; let cool and place in bowl.

Combine sour cream, yogurt and chives; toss with potatoes. Season with salt, and pepper to taste. Refrigerate until serving.

MAKES 10 SERVINGS, ½ CUP (125 mL) EACH

MAKE AHEAD: Cover and refrigerate for up to 8 hours.

NOTE: Don't peel the potatoes; the red skins are both attractive and flavourful; they also contain fibre and nutrients.

PER SERVING: 99 calories, 3 g protein, 1 g total fat, 1 g saturated fat, 3 mg cholesterol, 20 g carbohydrate, 2 g fibre, 143 mg sodium, 400 mg potassium

Tabbouleh

This Middle Eastern dish is popular as part of a summer salad plate for picnics or lunches. Bulgur adds a nutty flavour and texture, and mint lends a special fresh touch. If fresh mint isn't available, simply omit it.

1 cup	fine or medium bulgur	250 mL
2 cups	lightly packed chopped fresh parsley	500 mL
1 cup	finely chopped green onions	250 mL
¼ cup	olive oil	60 mL
⅓ cup	fresh lemon juice	75 mL
¼ to ½ cup	chopped fresh mint	50 to 125 mL
3	tomatoes, diced	3
1	cucumber, peeled, seeded and chopped	1
1 tsp or less	salt	5 mL or less
	Freshly ground pepper	

Soak bulgur for 30 minutes in enough hot water to cover by 2 inches (5 cm); drain well, pressing out excess water. Toss with parsley, onions, oil, lemon juice, mint, tomatoes and cucumber. Cover and refrigerate for at least 1 hour. Add salt; season with pepper to taste.

MAKES 12 SERVINGS, ½ CUP (125 mL) EACH

MAKE AHEAD: Cover and refrigerate for up to 1 day.

NOTE: One serving is a high source of folacin and a source of vitamin C and fibre.

PER SERVING: 95 calories, 2 g protein, 5 g total fat, 1 g saturated fat, 0 mg cholesterol, 12 g carbohydrate, 3 g fibre, 209 mg sodium, 227 mg potassium

SALAD DRESSINGS

Everyday Vinaigrette

I often add one of the ingredients listed as variations—especially fresh herbs.

2 tbsp	olive or canola oil	25 mL
2 tbsp	fresh lemon juice, rice vinegar, apple cider vinegar or balsamic vinegar	25 mL
2 tbsp	water	25 mL
1	small clove garlic, minced	1
1 tsp	Dijon mustard	5 mL
Pinch	each salt and freshly ground pepper	Pinch

In small measuring cup or bowl, or jar with screw top, combine oil, lemon juice, water, garlic, mustard, salt and pepper; mix well.

MAKES 6 TBSP (90 mL)

VARIATIONS:
Add one of the following to the dressing:

- 1 tsp (5 mL) sesame oil
- ¼ tsp (1 mL) ground cumin
- 1 tbsp (15 mL) freshly grated Parmesan cheese

Herb Dressing
Add 2 tbsp (25 mL) chopped fresh herbs (basil, dill or parsley or a combination).

Poppy Seed Dressing
Omit mustard and garlic. Add 1 tbsp (15 mL) poppy seeds and 1 tsp (5 mL) granulated sugar.

Ginger-Garlic Dressing
Use 1 tbsp (15 mL) each of canola oil and sesame oil; add 1 tsp (5 mL) finely minced gingerroot. Omit mustard.

NOTE: This vinaigrette has half the fat of a traditional vinaigrette. However, if you are wanting a really low-fat dressing, add 2 to 3 tbsp (25 to 50 mL) water to this vinaigrette or opt for one of the other dressing recipes in the book.

PER 1 TBSP (15 mL): 43 calories, 0 g protein, 5 g total fat, 1 g saturated fat, 0 mg cholesterol, 1 g carbohydrate, 0 g fibre, 21 mg sodium, 9 mg potassium

Orange Vinaigrette

Use this citrusy dressing with a tossed green salad or drizzle over cooked, cooled vegetables such as asparagus or green beans.

1	small clove garlic, minced	1
1 tbsp	fresh lemon juice	15 mL
½ tsp	Dijon mustard	2 mL
¼ tsp	granulated sugar	1 mL
¼ tsp or less	salt	1 mL or less
	Freshly ground pepper	
2 tbsp	olive oil	25 mL
¼ cup	fresh orange juice	50 mL
2 tbsp	finely chopped fresh parsley	25 mL

In small bowl, whisk together garlic, lemon juice, mustard, sugar, salt and pepper to taste; gradually whisk in oil. Whisk in orange juice, then parsley.

MAKES ½ CUP (125 mL)

MAKE AHEAD: Cover and refrigerate for up to 5 days.

NOTE: Salads aren't light if they're drowning in high-fat dressings. Homemade salad dressings take only minutes to prepare, taste fresher and are much less expensive than store-bought. The secret is adding herbs, mustard, garlic or other seasonings for flavour and replacing some of the oil in a traditional dressing with water, buttermilk, low-fat yogurt or juicy tomatoes.

PER 1 TBSP (15 mL): 35 calories, 0 g protein, 3 g total fat, 0 g saturated fat, 0 mg cholesterol, 1 g carbohydrate, 0 g fibre, 82 mg sodium, 25 mg potassium

Asian Vinaigrette

I often add a spoonful of chopped fresh basil and/or fresh coriander (cilantro) to this dressing. This goes well with any combination of colourful seasonal greens.

¼ cup	unseasoned rice vinegar	50 mL
2 tbsp	water	25 mL
2 tbsp	sesame oil	25 mL
2 tbsp	sodium-reduced soy sauce	25 mL
½ tsp	granulated sugar	2 mL
1	clove garlic, minced	1
1	green onion, minced	1

Whisk together vinegar, water, oil, soy sauce, sugar, garlic and onion.

MAKES ⅔ CUP (150 mL)

MAKE AHEAD: Cover and refrigerate for up to 3 days.

PER 1 TBSP (15 mL): 27 calories, 0 g protein, 3 g total fat, 0 g saturated fat, 0 mg cholesterol, 1 g carbohydrate, 0 g fibre, 100 mg sodium, 10 mg potassium

Mustard Garlic Vinaigrette

This is a good all-purpose vinaigrette.

2 tbsp	apple cider or white wine vinegar	25 mL
1 tbsp	Dijon mustard	15 mL
½ tsp	granulated sugar	2 mL
1	clove garlic, minced	1
⅓ cup	water	75 mL
⅓ cup	olive oil	75 mL
2 tsp	freshly grated Parmesan cheese	10 mL
¼ tsp or less	salt and freshly ground pepper	1 mL or less

In small bowl, mix together vinegar, mustard, sugar, garlic and water; gradually whisk in oil. Stir in Parmesan. Season with salt and pepper to taste.

MAKES 1 CUP (250 mL)

MAKE AHEAD: Cover and refrigerate for up to 1 week.

PER 1 TBSP (15 mL): 44 calories, 0 g protein, 5 g total fat, 1 g saturated fat, 0 mg cholesterol, 1 g carbohydrate, 0 g fibre, 65 mg sodium, 5 mg potassium

Parsley Dressing

This thick, creamy dressing is perfect to lightly coat spinach and green salads, and it can also be served as a dip for vegetables. It is much smoother and creamier when made in a blender rather than a food processor.

½ cup	coarsely chopped fresh parsley	125 mL
1 cup	low-fat cottage cheese	250 mL
1 tsp	Dijon mustard	5 mL
1 tsp	fresh lemon juice	5 mL
1 tsp	olive oil	5 mL
¼ tsp	freshly ground pepper	1 mL

In blender, finely chop parsley. Add cottage cheese, mustard, lemon juice, oil, and pepper; blend until well mixed.

MAKES 1 CUP (250 mL)

MAKE AHEAD: Cover and refrigerate for up to 3 days.

VARIATION:

Watercress Dressing
Substitute watercress leaves (stems removed, as they have too strong a flavour and also won't chop finely in blender) for the parsley.

PER 1 TBSP (15 mL): 16 calories, 2 g protein, 1 g total fat, 0 g saturated fat, 1 mg cholesterol, 1 g carbohydrate, 0 g fibre, 66 mg sodium, 25 mg potassium

Tomato Basil Dressing

For a starter salad, spoon this dressing over greens arranged on individual plates, then top with crumbled light feta cheese and/or sunflower seeds. Or toss with a pasta salad.

1 cup	finely chopped tomatoes	250 mL
¼ cup	chopped fresh basil	50 mL
1	clove garlic, minced	1
2 tbsp	chopped green onion	25 mL
2 tbsp	olive oil	25 mL
2 tbsp	fresh lemon juice or balsamic vinegar	25 mL
½ tsp	granulated sugar	2 mL
¼ tsp or less	each salt and freshly ground pepper	1 mL or less

In small bowl, combine tomatoes, basil, garlic, onion, oil, lemon juice, sugar, salt and pepper. Let stand for at least 15 minutes to allow flavours to meld.

MAKES 1 CUP (250 mL)

MAKE AHEAD: Cover and refrigerate for up to 1 day.

PER 1 TBSP (15 mL): 19 calories, 0 g protein, 2 g total fat, 0 g saturated fat, 0 mg cholesterol, 1 g carbohydrate, 0 g fibre, 37 mg sodium, 36 mg potassium

Buttermilk Herb Dressing

Buttermilk, made from low-fat milk, has only a trace of fat, yet it gives body and flavour to this creamy salad dressing.

¾ cup	buttermilk	175 mL
¼ cup	light mayonnaise	50 mL
3 tbsp	chopped fresh parsley	50 mL
1	small clove garlic, minced	1
½ tsp	Dijon mustard	2 mL
½ tsp	dried dillweed (or 3 tbsp/50 mL chopped fresh)	2 mL
¼ tsp or less	each salt and freshly ground pepper	1 mL or less

In small bowl, whisk together buttermilk, mayonnaise, parsley, garlic, mustard, dill, salt and pepper.

MAKES 1 CUP (250 mL)

MAKE AHEAD: Cover and refrigerate for up to 4 days.

PER 1 TBSP (15 mL): 17 calories, 0 g protein, 1 g total fat, 0 g saturated fat, 2 mg cholesterol, 1 g carbohydrate, 0 g fibre, 76 mg sodium, 25 mg potassium

Yogurt Herb Dressing

This creamy dressing goes well with pasta salads, green salads and potato salads.

1 cup	low-fat plain yogurt	250 mL
½ cup	light mayonnaise	125 mL
⅓ cup	chopped fresh parsley	75 mL
⅓ cup	chopped fresh dill*	75 mL
1	clove garlic, minced	1
1 tbsp	fresh lemon juice	15 mL
1 tsp	Dijon mustard	5 mL
¼ tsp or less	salt	1 mL or less
	Freshly ground pepper	

In bowl or large measuring cup, combine yogurt, mayonnaise, parsley, dill, garlic, lemon juice, mustard, salt and pepper. Using whisk or fork, mix well.

MAKES 1⅔ CUPS (400 mL)

*If fresh dill isn't available, substitute ½ tsp (2 mL) dried dillweed.

MAKE AHEAD: Cover and refrigerate for up to 1 week.

VARIATION:

Buttermilk Dill Dressing
Substitute 1 cup (250 mL) buttermilk for the yogurt.

NOTE: To reduce the fat content and for a lighter flavour and texture, substitute low-fat yogurt for half the mayonnaise in traditional salad dressing recipes, or use half yogurt and half sour cream or light mayonnaise.

PER 1 TBSP (15 mL): 20 calories, 1 g protein, 2 g total fat, 0 g saturated fat, 2 mg cholesterol, 1 g carbohydrate, 0 g fibre, 62 mg sodium, 30 mg potassium

Blue Cheese Dressing

Using low-fat yogurt instead of the mayonnaise that is traditionally used makes a lighter but equally tasty dressing that is much lower in fat and calories. It's perfect tossed with greens or spinach salad.

¼ cup	blue cheese, crumbled (about 1¼ oz/35 g)	50 mL
½ cup	low-fat plain yogurt	125 mL
Half	clove garlic, minced	Half
¼ tsp	Dijon mustard (or pinch dry mustard)	1 mL
	Freshly ground pepper	

In small bowl and using fork, mash half of the cheese until smooth. Stir in yogurt, garlic, mustard and pepper to taste, mixing well. Stir in remaining cheese.

MAKES ⅔ CUP (150 mL)

MAKE AHEAD: Cover and refrigerate for up to 3 days.

PER 1 TBSP (15 mL): 19 calories, 1 g protein, 1 g total fat, 1 g saturated fat, 3 mg cholesterol, 1 g carbohydrate, 0 g fibre, 55 mg sodium, 36 mg potassium

Creamy Garlic Dressing

Use this tasty, versatile dressing in pasta or potato salads, with any cooked, cooled leftover vegetables, or with spinach or lettuce salads.

½ cup	low-fat plain yogurt	125 mL
¼ cup	coarsely chopped fresh parsley	50 mL
2 tbsp	light mayonnaise	25 mL
1 tsp	Dijon mustard	5 mL
1	clove garlic, minced	1
¼ tsp or less	salt and freshly ground pepper	1 mL or less

In small bowl, mix yogurt, parsley, mayonnaise, mustard, garlic, and salt and pepper.

MAKES ⅔ CUP (150 mL)

VARIATIONS:
Add any of the following to the dressing:

- 2 tbsp (25 mL) chopped fresh basil

- 3 tbsp (50 mL) chopped fresh dill

- 1 to 2 tsp (5 to 10 mL) curry powder

- 2 tsp (10 mL) ground cumin

- 1 tsp (5 mL) dried tarragon or 1 tbsp (15 mL) fresh

- 2 tbsp (25 mL) chopped fresh coriander (cilantro)

- 1 to 2 tbsp (15 to 25 mL) crumbled blue cheese

CUCUMBER-DILL: Add ½ cup (125 mL) diced cucumber and ½ tsp (2 mL) dried dillweed

CAESAR: Add 1 to 2 tbsp (15 to 25 mL) freshly grated Parmesan cheese

PER 1 TBSP (15 mL): 17 calories, 1 g protein, 1 g total fat, 0 g saturated fat, 2 mg cholesterol, 1 g carbohydrate, 0 g fibre, 93 mg sodium, 38 mg potassium

GRAIN AND LEGUME SIDE DISHES

Spanish Rice with Coriander

Fresh coriander gives this traditional recipe an updated flavour. If it's unavailable, add 2 tsp (10 mL) ground cumin or curry powder along with the tomatoes.

3 cups	water or sodium-reduced vegetable broth	750 mL
1½ cups	long-grain rice	375 mL
2 tsp	olive oil	10 mL
1	medium onion, chopped	1
2	cloves garlic, minced	2
3	medium tomatoes, chopped	3
1	sweet green pepper, chopped	1
¼ tsp	red pepper flakes	1 mL
1 cup	frozen green peas	250 mL
¼ cup	each chopped fresh coriander (cilantro) and parsley	50 mL
¼ tsp or less	salt and freshly ground pepper	1 mL or less

In large saucepan, bring water to boil; add rice. Reduce heat, cover and simmer for 20 minutes or until rice is tender and liquid absorbed.

In large nonstick skillet, heat oil over medium heat; cook onion for 3 minutes or until tender. Add garlic, tomatoes, green pepper and red pepper flakes; cook, stirring occasionally, for 5 minutes. Stir in cooked rice, peas, coriander, parsley, and salt and pepper; cook, stirring, for 1 minute.

MAKES 6 SERVINGS

MAKE AHEAD: Cover and refrigerate for up to 1 day or freeze for up to 1 month.

VARIATIONS: For colour and variety, use half a sweet green pepper and half a yellow pepper. Drained canned tomatoes, chopped (1 to 1½ cups/250 to 375 mL) can also be used in this recipe instead of the fresh.

PER SERVING: 226 calories, 6 g protein, 2 g total fat, 0 g saturated fat, 0 mg cholesterol, 46 g carbohydrate, 3 g fibre, 125 mg sodium, 286 mg potassium

Wild Rice Pilaf

Smoky bacon adds a subtle depth of flavour to the rice. The attractive combination of wild, brown and white rice makes it a good dish to serve when entertaining. If you don't have brown rice, use half wild and half white.

2	slices bacon, diced	2
1	onion, diced	1
½ cup	wild rice	125 mL
3 cups	water or sodium-reduced chicken broth	750 mL
½ cup	brown rice	125 mL
½ cup	long-grain white rice	125 mL
¼ cup	chopped fresh parsley	50 mL
2 tbsp	chopped fresh basil	25 mL
¼ tsp or less	salt and freshly ground pepper	1 mL or less

In saucepan, cook bacon over medium heat for 3 minutes; add onion and cook, stirring, until tender, about 5 minutes.

Rinse wild rice under cold running water; drain. Add water to bacon and onion in saucepan; stir in wild rice and bring to boil. Add brown rice; cover and simmer for 15 minutes. Add white rice; cover and simmer for 25 minutes or until tender.

Stir in parsley, basil, and salt and pepper.

MAKES 8 SERVINGS

MAKE AHEAD: Cook rice but reduce cooking time from 25 minutes to 10 minutes; remove from heat and let cool. Refrigerate for up to 1 day. Reheat in 325°F (160°C) oven, covered, for 25 to 30 minutes or until hot. Stir in parsley, basil, and salt and pepper.

VARIATION:

Wild Rice Pilaf with Lemon and Raisins
Omit fresh basil. Add ½ cup (125 mL) raisins and 1 tsp (5 mL) grated lemon rind; stir in with parsley.

PER SERVING: 153 calories, 4 g protein, 3 g total fat, 1 g saturated fat, 4 mg cholesterol, 27 g carbohydrate, 2 g fibre, 127 mg sodium, 108 mg potassium

Lemon Parsley Rice Pilaf

Grated lemon rind lends a refreshing note to this rice. Serve with fish, chicken or meat.

1 tsp	canola or olive oil	5 mL
1 cup	chopped onion	250 mL
1½ cups	long-grain white or brown rice	375 mL
3 cups	sodium-reduced chicken or vegetable stock	750 mL
	Grated rind of 1 lemon	
1 tbsp	fresh lemon juice	15 mL
½ cup	coarsely chopped fresh parsley	125 mL
¼ tsp or less	salt and freshly ground pepper	1 mL or less

In heavy saucepan, heat oil over medium heat; cook onion for 5 minutes or until softened.

Stir in rice, then stock; bring to boil. Reduce heat, cover and simmer for 20 minutes for white rice, 40 minutes for brown, or until rice is tender.

Stir in lemon rind and juice, parsley, and salt and pepper.

MAKES 8 SERVINGS

MAKE AHEAD: Cover and refrigerate for up to 3 days; reheat gently.

PER SERVING: 144 calories, 4 g protein, 1 g total fat, 0 g saturated fat, 0 mg cholesterol, 30 g carbohydrate, 1 g fibre, 146 mg sodium, 126 mg potassium

Curried Fruit with Rice

Light and juicy fruits plus the spices in the curry blend make a fresh, pleasing flavour-and-texture combination. Along with rice, they go well with roast or grilled lamb or baked ham. Perfect for entertaining, the curried fruit looks terrific on a platter surrounded with the rice.

2 cups	cantaloupe or honeydew melon balls	500 mL
1 cup	diced fresh pineapple	250 mL
1 cup	sliced peeled peaches, strawberries, grapes and/or mandarin oranges	250 mL
1	banana, sliced	1
1 cup	sodium-reduced vegetable or chicken broth	250 mL
2 tsp	curry powder or paste	10 mL
1½ tsp	cornstarch	7 mL
½ cup	finely chopped chutney	125 mL
¼ cup	raisins	50 mL
2 tbsp	canola or olive oil	25 mL
5 cups	hot cooked rice	1.25 L
¼ cup	slivered almonds, toasted*	50 mL

In bowl, combine melon, pineapple, peaches (or combination) and banana; set aside.

In saucepan, combine stock, curry powder and cornstarch, mixing well; bring to boil over medium heat, stirring constantly. Combine reserved fruits, chutney and raisins; add to hot curry sauce. Add oil and stir.

Spoon hot rice around edge of shallow serving dish; spoon curry mixture into centre and garnish with almonds. Or serve rice and fruit mixture in separate serving dishes.

MAKES 8 SERVINGS

*To toast almonds, spread on baking sheet and roast in 350°F (180°C) oven for 5 to 8 minutes or until lightly golden.

MAKE AHEAD: Fruits and sauce can be prepared and set aside for up to 6 hours.

NOTE: Curry paste keeps its fresh flavour better than curry powder, which loses intensity over time. Bottled pastes keep well for months in the refrigerator.

One serving of this rice dish is a high source of vitamin C and vitamin A.

PER SERVING: 280 calories, 4 g protein, 6 g total fat, 1 g saturated fat, 0 mg cholesterol, 53 g carbohydrate, 3 g fibre, 244 mg sodium, 340 mg potassium

Brown Rice with Sherried Currants and Fresh Basil

This intriguing rice dish goes well with Tomatoes Florentine (p. 143), Baked Leeks au Gratin (p. 138) or fish or meat.

½ cup	currants	125 mL
2 tbsp	sherry	25 mL
1 tsp	canola or olive oil	5 mL
1	onion, chopped	1
2 cups	brown rice	500 mL
4 cups	sodium-reduced vegetable or chicken broth	1 L
⅓ cup	chopped fresh basil (or 1 tsp/5 mL dried)	75 mL
¼ tsp or less	salt and freshly ground pepper	1 mL or less

In bowl, soak currants in sherry; set aside.

In heavy saucepan, heat oil over medium heat. Add onion; cook, stirring, until tender. Add rice and stir to mix well.

Bring stock to boil; pour over rice. Stir in basil (if using dried), and salt and pepper. Simmer, covered, until water has been absorbed, about 40 minutes. Stir in currants and sherry and basil (if using fresh).

MAKES 8 SERVINGS

MAKE AHEAD: Refrigerate for up to 2 hours; reheat gently and add fresh basil just before serving.

NOTE: To reduce sodium, use a salt-free broth or Basic Chicken Stock (see p. 62) or water.

PER SERVING: 219 calories, 5 g protein, 2 g total fat, 0 g saturated fat, 0 mg cholesterol, 45 g carbohydrate, 3 g fibre, 163 mg sodium, 174 mg potassium

Rice with Black Beans and Ginger

This recipe is a favourite of my husband's. Be sure to use Chinese fermented black beans, not black turtle beans; you'll find them at Chinese markets (often sold in a plastic bag). Serve with fish, chicken or meats.

1 tbsp	canola or olive oil	15 mL
1 tbsp	minced fresh garlic	15 mL
1 tbsp	chopped onion or shallots	15 mL
1 tbsp	minced gingerroot	15 mL
1 cup	long-grain rice (basmati, jasmine or white)	250 mL
2 cups	boiling water	500 mL
¼ cup	Chinese fermented black beans	50 mL
1	green onion, chopped	1

In heavy or nonstick saucepan, heat oil over medium heat; cook garlic, onion and gingerroot for 1 minute, stirring. Add rice and water; simmer, covered, for 20 minutes or until rice is tender. Rinse black beans under cold water; stir into rice along with green onion.

MAKES 4 SERVINGS

MAKE AHEAD: Cover and refrigerate for up to 2 days.

VARIATIONS:

Rice with Black Beans, Ginger and Shrimp
Add 1 lb (500 g) peeled cooked shrimp after rice has been cooking for 15 minutes; continue with recipe.

Coconut Rice
Omit black beans and use 1 cup (250 mL) each water and light coconut milk instead of 2 cups (500 mL) water. Garnish with chopped fresh coriander (cilantro).

PER SERVING: 264 calories, 5 g protein, 4 g total fat, 0 g saturated fat, 0 mg cholesterol, 49 g carbohydrate, 2 g fibre, 237 mg sodium, 132 mg potassium

Chinese Vegetable Fried Rice

This is such a great way to use up leftover rice that I try to have leftovers. Oyster sauce lends a flavour punch; sesame oil and soy sauce could be added instead. Instead of tofu you could use diced cooked cold meat or chicken.

1 tbsp	canola or olive oil	15 mL
2 cups	diced zucchini	500 mL
1 cup	sliced celery	250 mL
4 cups	cold cooked rice*	1 L
¼ lb	diced tofu	125 g
1	sweet red pepper, diced	1
2	eggs, lightly beaten	2
1½ cups	bean sprouts (4 oz/125 g)	375 mL
⅓ cup	oyster sauce or sodium-reduced soy sauce	75 mL
½ cup	chopped green onions	125 mL

In large nonstick skillet, heat oil over high heat; stir-fry zucchini and celery for 2 minutes. Add rice; stir-fry for 1 minute. Add tofu and red pepper; stir-fry for 1 minute.

Make a well in centre; stir in eggs for 30 seconds. Add bean sprouts; stir-fry for 1 minute or until eggs are set. Stir in oyster sauce. Sprinkle with green onions.

MAKES 4 SERVINGS

*1⅓ cups (325 mL) uncooked parboiled long-grain rice yields about 4 cups (1 L) cooked.

MAKE AHEAD: Cover and set aside for up to 1 hour.

NOTE: To reduce sodium, omit oyster sauce (which adds 650 mg sodium per serving).

Canada's Food Guide recommends that adults have 6 to 8 servings of grain products and 7 to 10 servings of fruits and vegetables per day. One serving of Chinese Vegetable Fried Rice supplies two food guide servings of grains, two of vegetables, and about one-quarter meat and alternatives serving.

PER SERVING: 343 calories, 12 g protein, 8 g total fat, 1 g saturated fat, 93 mg cholesterol, 58 g carbohydrate, 4 g fibre, 721 mg sodium, 567 mg potassium

Peruvian Quinoa Pilaf

Quinoa (pronounced "keen-wha") is available in health food stores and some supermarkets. It has a mild flavour, making it a pleasant substitute for rice or other grains with meats, stir-fries or in salads. I like to garnish this pilaf with chopped fresh coriander (cilantro).

1 tbsp	olive oil	15 mL
Half	onion, chopped	Half
1	stalk celery (including leaves), diced	1
2	carrots, finely chopped	2
½ cup	quinoa	125 mL
1 cup	hot water or sodium-reduced vegetable broth	250 mL
1	bay leaf	1
	Grated rind from 1 medium lemon	
1 tbsp	fresh lemon juice	15 mL
½ cup	frozen peas, thawed	125 mL
¼ tsp or less	salt and pepper	1 mL or less

In nonstick saucepan, heat oil over medium heat; cook onion, celery and carrots, stirring occasionally, for 10 minutes.

In strainer, rinse quinoa under cold water; drain well and add to pan. Cook, stirring, for 1 minute.

Add water, bay leaf and lemon rind and juice; bring to boil. Reduce heat to medium-low; cover and simmer for 15 to 20 minutes or until liquid is absorbed and quinoa is tender. Discard bay leaf. Stir in peas; season with salt and pepper.

MAKES 3 SERVINGS

VARIATION:

Quinoa Squash Pilaf
Add 1 cup (250 ml) diced peeled butternut squash along with the water.

NOTE: Quinoa supplies many of the same nutrients that are found in whole grains. One half cup (125 mL) is high in magnesium, is a source of iron and zinc, and contains twice as much potassium as many grains.

PER SERVING: 189 calories, 6 g protein, 6 g total fat, 1 g saturated fat, 0 mg cholesterol, 29 g carbohydrate, 5 g fibre, 254 mg sodium, 400 mg potassium

Quick-and-Easy Spiced Couscous

This couscous is scented with a hint of cinnamon and allspice. It's a natural accompaniment for curries, chicken, lamb or pork.

2 cups	sodium-reduced chicken or vegetable broth or water	500 mL
1½ cups	couscous	375 mL
¼ tsp	each freshly ground pepper, allspice and cinnamon	1 mL
Pinch or less	salt	Pinch or less
1 tbsp	olive oil	15 mL

In saucepan, bring stock to boil; stir in couscous, pepper, allspice, cinnamon and salt. Remove from heat; cover and let stand for 5 minutes. Using two forks, fluff couscous. Stir in oil.

MAKES 6 SERVINGS

MAKE AHEAD: Cover and refrigerate for up to 1 day. Reheat, covered, in oven or microwave.

VARIATIONS:

Couscous with Tomato and Basil
Stir in 1 small finely chopped tomato and ¼ cup (50 mL) chopped fresh basil along with oil.

Couscous with Lemon and Fresh Basil
Prepare couscous as in recipe, omitting spices. Add ½ cup (125 mL) chopped fresh basil, 1 tsp (5 mL) grated lemon rind and 2 tbsp (25 mL) fresh lemon juice when fluffing couscous.

NOTE: Couscous, a staple of Moroccan cuisine, is made from semolina wheat and looks like a grain. The quick-cooking variety, which only needs to be soaked in boiling water, is available in most health food stores and supermarkets.

To reduce sodium, use a low-sodium stock (see p. 62).

PER SERVING: 198 calories, 7 g protein, 3 g total fat, 0 g saturated fat, 0 mg cholesterol, 36 g carbohydrate, 1 g fibre, 193 mg sodium, 159 mg potassium

Bulgur Pilaf with Fresh Basil, Mushrooms and Tomatoes

Dotted with vegetables and sprinkled with nuts, this makes a tasty side dish for meat or poultry, or to serve as part of a vegetarian dinner.

¾ cup	medium or coarse bulgur	175 mL
1 tbsp	olive oil	15 mL
1	onion, finely chopped	1
2	cloves garlic, minced	2
1½ cups	sliced mushrooms	375 mL
1	large tomato, diced	1
½ cup	chopped fresh basil*	125 mL
½ tsp or less	salt	2 mL or less
	Freshly ground pepper	
¼ cup	slivered almonds, toasted**	50 mL

NOTE: Bulgur has a slightly nutty flavour and a soft texture. Use it as you would rice or other grains: add to soups, serve as a side dish or as a main dish combined with vegetables, herbs and spices. (The coarse grind is best suited for hot side dishes; medium and fine, which are more tender, for salads.) One serving is a high source of fibre.

PER SERVING: 124 calories, 4 g protein, 5 g total fat, 1 g saturated fat, 0 mg cholesterol, 18 g carbohydrate, 4 g fibre, 203 mg sodium, 249 mg potassium

Place bulgur in bowl and add enough boiling water to cover by 2 inches (5 cm). Soak for 20 minutes or until tender. Drain thoroughly.

In nonstick skillet, heat oil. Add onion; cook, stirring, over medium heat until softened. Stir in garlic and mushrooms; cook until mushrooms are tender, about 3 minutes. Stir in bulgur, tomato, basil, salt, and pepper to taste; cook, stirring, for 2 to 3 minutes or until heated through. Sprinkle with almonds.

MAKES 6 SIDE-DISH SERVINGS

*If fresh basil is unavailable, use ½ cup (125 mL) chopped fresh parsley and 1 tbsp (15 mL) crushed dried basil.

**To toast almonds, spread on baking sheet and roast in 350°F (180°C) oven for 5 to 8 minutes or until lightly golden.

Roasted Red Peppers and Red Onion with Bulgur

Sweet red peppers are a colourful and flavourful addition to this dish. Regular cooking onions can also be used instead of red onions.

1 tbsp	olive oil	15 mL
1 cup	thinly sliced red onion	250 mL
1 cup	medium or coarse bulgur	250 mL
2 cups	boiling water	500 mL
1 tbsp	fresh lemon juice	15 mL
½ cup	chopped roasted sweet red peppers (see p. 22)	125 mL
¼ to ½ cup	chopped fresh parsley, basil or dill	50 to 125 mL
½ tsp	dried basil	2 mL
¼ tsp or less	salt and freshly ground pepper	1 mL

In small skillet, heat oil over medium heat; cook onion, stirring often, for 10 minutes or until tender.

Meanwhile, in saucepan, combine bulgur and water over low heat; simmer, covered, for 15 to 20 minutes or until liquid is absorbed. Stir in onion, lemon juice, red peppers, parsley, dried basil and salt and pepper.

MAKES 4 SERVINGS

MAKE AHEAD: Cover and refrigerate for up to 2 days.

NOTE: Both bulgur and cracked wheat are made from wheat berries. Bulgur is cooked first, then dried, then cracked. Cracked wheat is made from wheat berries that are cracked, then milled. They are available at health food store and provide high amounts of fibre.

VARIATION:

Roasted Peppers and Red Onion with Couscous or Rice
Prepare pepper and onion mixture but combine with cooked rice or couscous instead of bulgur.

PER SERVING: 171 calories, 5 g protein, 4 g total fat, 1 g saturated fat, 0 mg cholesterol, 32 g carbohydrate, 5 g fibre, 187 mg sodium, 225 mg potassium

Herb-Baked Polenta with Parmesan

For a long time, I wasn't interested in making polenta. I thought it very bland and probably difficult to make. It isn't; however, it does require stirring for 15 to 20 minutes unless you use the quick-cooking cornmeal (follow package instructions), but you can prepare it in advance. Toronto chef Mark Dowling makes the best polenta I've tasted. He adds flavour by cooking it with onions and herbs, then sprinkling it with cheese. Serve as part of a brunch or instead of a starch at dinner.

1	medium onion, minced	1
4 cups	water	1 L
½ tsp	each dried rosemary, thyme and salt	2 mL
1 cup	cornmeal	250 mL
1 tsp	olive oil	5 mL
¼ cup	freshly grated Parmesan cheese	50 mL

In large saucepan, cover and simmer onion and ¼ cup (50 mL) of the water for 5 minutes or until tender. Add remaining water, rosemary, thyme and salt; bring to boil.

Very gradually add cornmeal, stirring constantly (it should take at least 3 minutes). Continuing to stir, cook cornmeal over medium-low heat for 15 to 20 minutes or until very thick. (If it cooks for less than 15 minutes, cornmeal won't be cooked.)

Spray baking sheet with nonstick coating or canola oil. Evenly spread polenta over baking sheet in 9-inch (23 cm) square or circle about ¾ inch (2 cm) thick. Let cool.

Drizzle oil over polenta and brush to distribute evenly. Sprinkle with cheese. Cut into wedges or squares and separate slightly to have crisp edges. Bake in 375°F (190°C) oven for 12 to 15 minutes or until hot and golden. Serve hot.

MAKES 8 SERVINGS

MAKE AHEAD: Spread polenta on baking sheet, cover and refrigerate for up to 1 day. Drizzle with oil, sprinkle with cheese, then bake when ready to serve.

NOTE: To store grains, seal in airtight container and keep in cool dark place.

PER SERVING: 97 calories, 3 g protein, 2 g total fat, 1 g saturated fat, 3 mg cholesterol, 17 g carbohydrate, 1 g fibre, 199 mg sodium, 57 mg potassium

Polenta with Sautéed Mushrooms

For a light supper, top baked polenta with flavourful mushrooms. You can use a few wild mushrooms, fresh or dried, instead of some of the regular mushrooms.

PER SERVING: 175 calories, 6 g protein, 5 g total fat, 1 g saturated fat, 4 mg cholesterol, 28 g carbohydrate, 3 g fibre, 268 mg sodium, 345 mg potassium

1 tbsp	olive oil	15 mL
1	medium onion, chopped	1
1	small clove garlic, minced	1
1 lb	mushrooms, halved	500 g
⅓ cup	coarsely chopped fresh parsley	75 mL
	Freshly ground pepper	
	Herb-Baked Polenta with Parmesan (p. 111)	

In large nonstick skillet, heat oil over medium heat; cook onion and garlic until tender, about 5 minutes. Add mushrooms; stir-fry over high heat for 5 minutes or until tender and browned. Add parsley. Season with pepper to taste. Spoon over hot baked polenta.

MAKES 6 SERVINGS

Quick Lentils with Coriander and Mint

This is by far one of the best-tasting and easiest-to-make lentil dishes. I try to keep a can of lentils on my shelf so when my vegetarian children visit I can have a quick vegetable dish ready in minutes. Fresh mint and coriander add a special flavour, though you could use fresh basil instead of coriander. Serve with chicken, fish or meat, or as part of a meatless meal.

PER SERVING: 102 calories, 6 g protein, 3 g total fat, 0 g saturated fat, 0 mg cholesterol, 14 g carbohydrate, 3 g fibre, 283 mg sodium, 291 mg potassium

2 tsp	canola oil	10 mL
1	small onion, chopped	1
2 tsp	mild Indian curry paste	10 mL
1	tomato, chopped	1
1	can (19 oz/540 mL) lentils, drained and rinsed, or 2 cups (500 mL) cooked brown lentils	1
2 tbsp	each chopped fresh coriander (cilantro) and mint	25 mL
¼ tsp or less	salt and freshly ground pepper	1 mL or less

In nonstick skillet, heat oil over medium heat; add onion and cook until tender, about 5 minutes. Stir in curry paste until well mixed. Stir in tomato and lentils; cook until hot. Stir in coriander, mint, and salt and pepper.

MAKES 5 SERVINGS, ½ CUP (125 mL) EACH

Barley and Corn Casserole

This recipe is the result of a conversation I had with editor Kirsten Hanson, who told me that corn and barley is a nice combination. This dish goes well with any meats, fish or poultry or as part of a meatless meal. I like to serve it as an interesting alternative to rice. Be sure to save any leftover cobs of corn—it's easy to cut off kernels to use in this recipe.

1 tbsp	canola or olive oil	15 mL
1	onion, chopped	1
1 tbsp	minced fresh garlic	15 mL
1 cup	finely chopped carrots	250 mL
1 cup	pearl or pot barley	250 mL
3 cups	sodium-reduced vegetable broth	750 mL
2 cups	cooked or frozen corn kernels*	500 mL
½ cup	chopped fresh parsley or coriander (cilantro)	125 mL
¼ tsp or less	salt and freshly ground pepper	1 mL or less

In heavy flameproof casserole, heat oil over medium-high heat; cook onion, garlic and carrots for 4 minutes or until onion is softened. Stir in barley; pour in stock. Cover and bake in 350°F (180°C) oven for 1 hour.

Stir in corn, parsley, and salt and pepper. Bake for another 5 minutes or until heated through and barley is tender.

MAKES 8 SERVINGS

*If using frozen kernels, thaw under hot water, then drain well before using.

MAKE AHEAD: Cover and refrigerate for up to 2 days. To reheat, add ½ cup (125 mL) sodium-reduced broth or water and warm in microwave or oven.

NOTE: Soluble fibre, found in barley, oat bran and many legumes, may help to reduce blood cholesterol. Pot barley is not as refined as pearl barley, and therefore more nutritious. For more on barley, see Preparing Grains and Legumes (p. 114).

COMPARE:
1 cup (250 mL) corn kernels
Frozen
29 mg sodium
Canned
55 mg sodium

PER SERVING: 158 calories, 3 g protein, 3 g total fat, 0 g saturated fat, 0 mg cholesterol, 32 g carbohydrate, 4 g fibre, 260 mg sodium, 242 mg potassium

Preparing Grains and Legumes

GRAINS

Canada's latest food guide recommends to make at least half of the grain products in your daily diet whole grain. The less refined the grains are, the better they are for us. In general, grains are a good source of complex carbohydrates, fibre and protein and supply us with iron, calcium, phosphorus and B vitamins.

Here is a general guide for cooking grains. When you have package directions, follow them. As with beans, the cooking time will vary depending on the length of storage. Grains stored for a longer time will take longer to cook. Some grains (such as bulgur) come in a variety of sizes. The smaller the size, the faster the cooking time.

Grain and Use	Method of Cooking
CORN	
Cornmeal	
Tortillas, dumplings, stuffings, polenta, cereal, bread, muffins	For polenta and cereal: Add 1 cup (250 mL) cornmeal to 4 cups (1 L) boiling water. Simmer, covered, 25 to 30 minutes. For other uses: Follow package instructions or individual recipes.
WHEAT	
Bulgur	
Served like rice; pilafs, tabbouleh, stuffings, soups, salads, cereal	For salads, cover bulgur with hot water and soak 1 hour. Drain well. For other uses: Add 1 cup (250 mL) bulgur to 2 cups (500 mL) boiling water. Simmer, covered, 20 to 25 minutes (the finer the grain, the faster it will cook). Remove from heat, cover and let stand 10 minutes.
Couscous	
Served like rice with meats, poultry, stews	Follow package instructions for amount of liquid or add 1 cup (250 mL) couscous to 1½ cups (375 mL) boiling water. Cover. Remove from heat and let stand 5 minutes.
Wheat germ	
Crumb coatings; replaces nuts in cakes and cookies.	Add to muffins, breads, pancakes, granola. Follow package instructions or individual recipes.
Cracked wheat	
Served like rice; salads, cereals, breads, puddings	For cereal: Add 1 cup (250 mL) cracked wheat to 2 cups (500 mL) boiling water. Simmer, covered, 30 to 40 minutes. For other uses: Follow package instructions or individual recipes.

Grain and Use	Method of Cooking
WHEAT cont'd	
Wheat berries	
Pilafs, salads, baking, Swiss muesli	Add 1 cup (250 mL) wheat berries to 2 cups (500 mL) boiling water. Simmer, covered, 60 to 90 minutes.
Kasha (toasted buckwheat)	
Pilafs, stuffings, breads	Add 1 cup (250 mL) kasha to 2 cups (500 mL) boiling water. Simmer, covered, 10 to 15 minutes.
OATS	
Oat bran	
Cereal, muffins, cookies	For cereal: Follow package directions or add 1 cup (250 mL) oat bran to 3 cups (750 mL) boiling water. Cook 2 minutes. Remove from heat. Cover and let stand 2 to 4 minutes.
Rolled oats	
Cereal, granola, muesli, muffins, cakes, cookies, breads	For cereal: Add 1⅓ cups (325 mL) rolled oats to 2 cups (500 mL) boiling water. Follow package instructions for cooking time. For other uses: follow package instructions or individual recipes.
RICE	
White rice	
Pilafs, risottos, curries, stuffings, salads, soups, casseroles or with meats, desserts	Follow package instructions regarding rinsing. Add 1 cup (250 mL) rice to 2 cups (500 mL) boiling water. Simmer, covered, 15 to 20 minutes.
Brown rice	
Pilafs, stuffing, salads, soups, casseroles or with meats	Rinse. Add 1 cup (250 mL) brown rice to 2 cups (500 mL) boiling water. Simmer, covered, 45 to 60 minutes.
Whole grain brown rice	
Pilafs, stuffing, salads, soups, casseroles or with meats	Do not rinse. Is a parboiled brown rice and takes 20 minutes to cook.
Basmati rice	
Casseroles or with meats	Rinse. Add 1 cup rice (250 mL) to 1½ cups (375 mL) boiling water. Simmer, covered, 15 to 20 minutes.

Grain and Use	Method of Cooking
RICE cont'd	
Arborio rice	
Risotto, paella	Do not rinse. Add 1 cup (250 mL) Arborio rice to 3½ cups (875 mL) boiling water or stock. Total cooking time, 20 minutes. Or cook as directed in recipe.
Wild rice (actually a grass but treated like rice):	
Pilafs, curries, stuffings, salads, often mixed with other rices	Rinse. Add 1 cup (250 mL) wild rice to 3 cups (750 mL) boiling water. Simmer, covered, 45 to 60 minutes until rice splays; drain.
Red rice	
Salads, curries, moulds, desserts	Rinse. Add 1 cup (250 mL) red rice to 1¾ cups (425 mL) boiling water. Simmer, covered, 18 to 20 minutes.
Black rice	
Asian dishes, puddings	Rinse. Add 1 cup (250 mL) black rice to 1¾ cups (425 mL) boiling water. Simmer, covered, 35 to 40 minutes.
Wehani rice	
Pilafs or with meat	Follow package instructions or rinse and add 1 cup (250 mL) wehani rice to 2 cups (500 mL) boiling water. Simmer, covered, 30 minutes.
OTHER	
Pearl barley	
Pilafs, stuffings, stews, soups, hot cereal	Add 1 cup (250 mL) pearl barley to 2 cups (500 mL) boiling water. Simmer, covered, 45 minutes.
Pot barley	
Pilafs, stuffings, stews, soups, hot cereal	Add 1 cup (250 mL) pot barley to 2 cups (500 mL) boiling water. Simmer, covered, 60 minutes.
Quinoa	
Pilafs, stuffing, soups, salads, cereals, desserts	Rinse. Add 1 cup (250 mL) quinoa to 2 cups (500 mL) water. Bring to boil. Simmer, covered, 12 to 15 minutes.
Millet	
Pilafs, soups, bread, stuffings, puddings	Add 1 cup (250 mL) millet to 2 cups (500 mL) boiling water. Simmer, covered, 30 to 40 minutes.

LEGUMES

Legumes (which are the seeds of such plants as the lentil, garden pea, lima bean or kidney bean) are a source of protein almost as good as meat. Serve them with a grain or bread for a complete source of protein. Legumes are also excellent sources of B vitamins, iron and other minerals and a very high source of fibre. They are high in complex carbohydrates and, except for soybeans, low in fat. To store, seal in airtight containers and keep in cool dark place.

Instead of using canned beans in any of the bean recipes in this book, you can cook dried beans. They have a much nicer, firmer texture and are less expensive. Cooked beans freeze for up to 6 months.

Before cooking, dried legumes (except lentils and split peas) should be soaked to return moisture to them, to reduce cooking time, to save vitamins and minerals and to help reduce flatulence-causing sugars. Rinse and pick through before soaking to remove any grit or pebbles.

To reduce flatulence, change the soaking liquid a few times and drain the cooking water after 30 minutes, add fresh water, then cook until beans are tender. Rinse beans after cooking. Canned beans should be drained and well rinsed before use. Apparently the more you eat beans, the less you'll be bothered by flatulence. However, let your body become used to beans gradually.

LONG-SOAK METHOD

Cover dried beans with 3 to 4 times their volume of water and let stand for 8 hours or overnight.

QUICK-SOAK METHOD

Method 1: Place rinsed beans in large saucepan; add water to cover beans by at least 2 inches (5 cm). Bring to boil. Boil 2 minutes. Remove from heat; cover and let stand 1 hour. Drain and rinse.

Method 2: Place rinsed beans in large saucepan; add water to cover beans by at least 2 inches (5 cm). Bring to boil. Boil 10 minutes; drain. Cover with cold water. Let soak 30 minutes; drain.

COOKING

In a large saucepan, cover drained, soaked beans or lentils with 2½ times their volume of fresh water. Don't add salt. Bring to a boil; reduce heat and simmer, covered, until tender. See chart for cooking times. Drain if necessary.

YIELD

One cup (250 mL) dried beans or lentils yields 2 to 2½ cups (500 to 625 mL) cooked.

One can (19 oz/540 mL) beans equals 2 cups (500 mL) drained beans.

COOKING TIMES FOR BEANS, PEAS AND LENTILS

Adapted in part from the Food Advisory Division of Agriculture Canada

Legume	Soaking Method	Suggested Cooking Time
Black (turtle) beans	quick or overnight soak	1¾ hours
Cranberry (roman) beans	quick or overnight soak	45 minutes
Great northern beans	quick soak	60 minutes
	overnight soak	75 minutes
Kidney beans		
red	quick or overnight soak	60 minutes
white	quick soak	40 minutes
	overnight soak	60 minutes
Lentils		
brown	no soaking	30 minutes
green	no soaking	30 minutes
red	no soaking	10 minutes
Lima beans		
large	quick soak	20 minutes
	overnight soak	40 minutes
small	quick or overnight soak	35 minutes
Navy (pea) beans	quick soak	1¾ hours
	overnight soak	50 minutes
Peas		
whole yellow	quick soak	60 minutes
	overnight soak	40 minutes
split yellow	no soaking	75 minutes
split green	no soaking	75 minutes
Chickpeas (garbanzo beans)	quick soak	2 to 2½ hours
	overnight soak	1½ to 2½ hours
Pinto beans	quick or overnight soak	45 minutes
Small red beans	quick soak	50 minutes
	overnight soak	40 minutes
Soy beans	quick soak	3½ hours
	overnight soak	4 hours
Yellow-eyed beans	quick soak	60 minutes
	overnight soak	50 minutes

VEGETABLES

Buttermilk Mashed Potatoes

These creamy potatoes are fabulous. I'm often asked for ways to use leftover buttermilk; this is one of the best ways I know of. Instead of mashing, a potato ricer or food mill also works well. I usually use Yukon Gold potatoes in this recipe.

10	medium potatoes (about 3 lb/1.5 kg), peeled and quartered	10
2 cups	buttermilk	500 mL
1 tbsp	olive oil or soft margarine	15 mL
¼ cup	chopped green onion or chives	50 mL
Pinch	nutmeg	Pinch
½ tsp or less	salt and freshly ground pepper	2 mL or less

In large saucepan, cover potatoes with cold water; bring to boil and cook for 20 minutes or until fork-tender. Drain; return to low heat for 2 minutes to dry. Mash potatoes to remove all lumps. Gradually beat in buttermilk and oil. Stir in green onion and nutmeg. Season with salt and pepper.

MAKES 10 SERVINGS

MAKE AHEAD: Spoon prepared potatoes into lightly greased 8-cup (2 L) baking dish. Let cool, cover and refrigerate for up to 3 days. Do not freeze. To serve, let stand at room temperature for 30 minutes before reheating, covered, in 350°F (180°C) oven for 30 minutes.

VARIATIONS:

Garlic Mashed Potatoes
Add 8 to 10 peeled cloves garlic to potatoes before cooking; mash with potatoes.

Herbed Mashed Potatoes
Stir in ¼ cup (50 mL) chopped fresh dill or basil or parsley or a combination of these herbs to the mashed potatoes.

Mashed Potatoes with Celeriac (Celery Root)
Use 6 medium Yukon Gold potatoes, peeled and cut in chunks, and 1½ lb (750 g) celeriac, peeled and cut in chunks; put in pot and cover with water. Bring to a boil and simmer until tender, about 20 minutes. Drain and mash with enough milk until creamy. Season with ¼ tsp or less salt and freshly ground pepper.

PER SERVING: 150 calories, 4 g protein, 2 g total fat, 0 g saturated fat, 2 mg cholesterol, 30 g carbohydrate, 2 g fibre, 176 mg sodium, 529 mg potassium

Rosemary Garlic Roasted Potatoes

These potatoes pair well with roasted meat or poultry. And cooking them is simple—just pop them into the oven along with your roast or bird.

6 cups	peeled potato wedges (2 lb/1 kg)	1.5 L
1 tbsp	olive oil	15 mL
2 tsp	chopped fresh garlic	10 mL
2 tsp	chopped fresh or dried rosemary	10 mL
¼ tsp or less	salt and freshly ground pepper	1 mL or less

In large, shallow baking dish, toss potatoes with oil, garlic, rosemary, and salt and pepper. Bake, uncovered, in 325°F (160°C) oven for 1 hour or until fork-tender.

MAKES 6 SERVINGS

NOTE: The oven temperature can vary depending on what else is in the oven. Adjust cooking time accordingly.

PER SERVING: 109 calories, 2 g protein, 2 g total fat, 0 g saturated fat, 0 mg cholesterol, 21 g carbohydrate, 1 g fibre, 103 mg sodium, 340 mg potassium

New Potatoes with Mint Pesto

I try to make enough of these potatoes to have leftovers. They are equally tasty the next day hot, cold or tossed with a little vinaigrette or balsamic vinegar. To serve two to four more people, just add extra potatoes. Almonds can be used instead of pine nuts.

1	small clove garlic	1
½ cup	fresh mint	125 mL
¼ cup	fresh parsley	50 mL
1 tbsp	pine nuts, toasted*	15 mL
1 tbsp	each olive oil and water	15 mL
½ tsp or less	salt	2 mL or less
1½ lb	tiny new potatoes (about 6 cups/1.5 L)	750 g

Prepare mint pesto: In food processor, chop garlic. Add mint, parsley, pine nuts, oil, water and salt; process until nearly smooth.

Scrub potatoes; cut any large ones in half. In saucepan of boiling water, cook potatoes until tender; drain well. Heat potatoes in pan over low heat for 1 or 2 minutes to dry. Transfer to serving bowl; toss with pesto.

MAKES 6 SERVINGS

*Toast pine nuts in a skillet over medium heat for 3 to 5 minutes or until golden.

MAKE AHEAD: Prepare and refrigerate mint pesto for up to 1 day in advance.

NOTE: To prevent the nut oil from going rancid, store pine nuts in the freezer.

VARIATION:

New Potatoes with Dill
Toss hot cooked potatoes with chopped fresh dill, chives and 1 to 2 tsp (5 to 10 mL) each fresh lemon juice and olive oil. Season with ¼ tsp or less salt and freshly ground pepper.

PER SERVING: 110 calories, 2 g protein, 3 g total fat, 0 g saturated fat, 0 mg cholesterol, 19 g carbohydrate, 2 g fibre, 203 mg sodium, 399 mg potassium

Roasted Sesame-Chili French Fries

Everyone I've served these oven-baked "fries" to loves them. They are easy to make and much lower in fat than deep-fried ones.

4	baking potatoes (about 2 lb/1 kg)	4
1 tbsp	canola or olive oil	15 mL
2 tbsp	sesame seeds	25 mL
½ tsp	each chili powder, salt and freshly ground pepper	2 mL

Peel potatoes only if skins are tough or blemished; cut into ½-inch (1 cm) thick strips. Place in bowl and toss with oil to coat; sprinkle with sesame seeds, chili powder, salt and pepper. Spread on baking sheet and bake in 425°F (220°C) for 30 to 45 minutes or until tender and browned, turning occasionally.

MAKES 6 SERVINGS

VARIATIONS:

Roasted Sweet Potato Fries
Use sweet potatoes instead of baking potatoes.

Parmesan Roasted French Fries
Omit sesame seeds; toss hot cooked fries with freshly grated Parmesan cheese.

Herb Roasted French Fries
Omit sesame seeds and chili powder; add ½ tsp (2 mL) dried Italian seasoning or dried rosemary (or 1 to 2 tbsp/15 to 25 mL chopped fresh rosemary and thyme) before roasting.

PER SERVING: 152 calories, 3 g protein, 4 g total fat, 0 g saturated fat, 0 mg cholesterol, 27 g carbohydrate, 3 g fibre, 204 mg sodium, 521 mg potassium

Microwave Garlic Potatoes

This is my favourite fast potato dish in the summer and fall, when tiny red locally grown potatoes are readily available. It can be served hot or at room temperature, so you don't need to worry about split-second timing when serving with barbecued meats.

2 lb	small red potatoes (unpeeled)	1 kg
2 tbsp	olive oil	25 mL
1 tsp	minced fresh garlic	5 mL
⅓ cup	chopped fresh dill, basil or parsley	75 mL
¼ tsp or less	salt and freshly ground pepper	1 mL or less

Wash potatoes, then prick with fork. Arrange in single layer in microwaveable dish. Microwave, uncovered, on High for 10 to 13 minutes or until tender when pierced with fork, rearranging once.

Meanwhile, combine oil and garlic; let stand for at least 15 minutes and up to 30 minutes. Pour over hot cooked potatoes. Sprinkle with fresh dill and toss to mix; season with salt and pepper.

MAKES 6 SERVINGS

NOTE: The potatoes can be baked in a conventional oven or boiled, rather than microwaved, if you prefer. You can also substitute medium potatoes, cut in half.

PER SERVING: 143 calories, 2 g protein, 5 g total fat, 1 g saturated fat, 0 mg cholesterol, 24 g carbohydrate, 2 g fibre, 104 mg sodium, 461 mg potassium

Barbecued Potato Packets

Just scrub tender new potatoes, leaving the skin on for texture and nutrients. Instead of dried herbs, you can use 1 tbsp (15 mL) of any fresh herbs you have on hand—rosemary, basil, thyme, dill and/or oregano.

4	new potatoes, thinly sliced	4
1	onion, thinly sliced	1
1	clove garlic, minced	1
1 tbsp	olive oil	15 mL
¼ tsp	each dried thyme and rosemary	1 mL
¼ tsp or less	salt and freshly ground pepper	1 mL or less

Toss potatoes with onion, garlic, oil, thyme, rosemary, salt and pepper. Divide among 4 pieces of greased heavy-duty foil; wrap well to seal. Grill over medium heat for 20 minutes or until tender.

MAKES 4 SERVINGS

MAKE AHEAD: Prepare potatoes and refrigerate for up to 4 hours before grilling.

PER SERVING: 210 calories, 4 g protein, 4 g total fat, 1 g saturated fat, 0 mg cholesterol, 42 g carbohydrate, 4 g fibre, 157 mg sodium, 788 mg potassium

Mushroom-Stuffed Potatoes

This recipe comes from the PEI division of the Heart and Stroke Foundation of Canada. These tasty cheese-topped stuffed potatoes are a special treat.

4	baking potatoes (about 8 oz/250 g each)	4

STUFFING

2 tsp	canola or olive oil	10 mL
2 cups	chopped mushrooms	500 mL
½ cup	finely chopped onion	125 mL
¼ cup	finely chopped celery	50 mL
2 tbsp	finely chopped sweet red or green pepper	25 mL
¼ cup	finely chopped fresh parsley	50 mL
¼ cup	low-fat milk, plus more to taste	50 mL
	Freshly ground pepper	
½ cup	shredded part-skim Cheddar-type cheese	125 mL

Scrub potatoes; prick with fork. Bake in 400°F (200°C) oven for 50 to 60 minutes or until tender.

STUFFING: In saucepan, heat oil over medium heat; cook mushrooms, onion, celery and red pepper, stirring, until vegetables are tender.

Cut slice from top of each potato; scoop out pulp into bowl, reserving shells. Mash pulp until free of lumps. Stir in vegetables, parsley, milk, and pepper to taste. Add more milk to taste if necessary. Spoon mixture into shells, smoothing top. Sprinkle with cheese.

Bake in 400°F (200°C) oven for 10 minutes or until filling is hot and cheese is melted.

MAKES 4 SERVINGS

MAKE AHEAD: Freeze stuffed potatoes for up to 1 month. When ready to use, bake frozen in 400°F (200°C) oven for 50 to 60 minutes or until heated through. Top with cheese and bake until cheese melts, about 2 minutes.

MICROWAVE METHOD
Scrub potatoes; prick with fork. Microwave on High for 12 to 16 minutes or until almost tender. Let stand, covered, until tender.

Stuffing: In microwaveable dish, microwave oil on High for 5 seconds; stir in mushrooms, onion, celery and red or green pepper; microwave on High for 2 minutes. Stir; microwave on High for 1 minute longer or until vegetables are tender. Assemble stuffed potatoes as above.

Arrange potatoes in circle in microwave; cover with waxed paper. Microwave on High 1 minute per potato. (If potatoes have been refrigerated before microwaving, add 1 minute of cooking time for each potato.) Sprinkle with cheese; microwave for 1 to 2 minutes longer or until cheese melts.

Microwave frozen stuffed potatoes on High:

1 potato: 3 to 5 minutes
2 potatoes: 5 to 7 minutes
3 potatoes: 7 to 9 minutes
4 potatoes: 9 to 11 minutes

Sprinkle with cheese and microwave for 1 to 2 minutes longer or until cheese melts.

PER SERVING: 240 calories, 9 g protein, 5 g total fat, 2 g saturated fat, 9 mg cholesterol, 41 g carbohydrate, 4 g fibre, 127 mg sodium, 908 mg potassium

My Mother's Scalloped Potatoes

When my friend Elizabeth Baird was helping me name some of these recipes we both commented that this was the way our mothers made scalloped potatoes—hence the name. To save time, I slice the potatoes and chop the onions in a food processor, and warm the milk in the microwave.

8	medium potatoes*, peeled and thinly sliced	8
1	large onion, chopped	1
2 tbsp	all-purpose flour	25 mL
¼ tsp or less	salt and freshly ground pepper	1 mL or less
2 cups	hot low-fat milk	500 mL
1 cup	shredded part-skim Cheddar-type cheese	250 mL

Lightly oil 13- × 9-inch (3.5 L) baking dish or spray with nonstick coating. Arrange one-third of the potatoes over bottom; sprinkle with half of the onion, then half of the flour. Season with salt and pepper. Repeat layers; arrange remaining potatoes over top. Pour hot milk over. Sprinkle with cheese. Bake, uncovered, in 350°F (180°C) oven for 1 hour or until potatoes are tender.

MAKES 8 SERVINGS

*Use Yukon Gold or baking potatoes (not new potatoes).

PER SERVING: 223 calories, 9 g protein, 3 g total fat, 2 g saturated fat, 11 mg cholesterol, 40 g carbohydrate, 3 g fibre, 211 mg sodium, 685 mg potassium

Orange Sherried Sweet Potatoes

Sweet potatoes go well with turkey, goose and ham. Instead of sherry, you can substitute ginger, maple syrup or crushed pineapple, adjusting amount to taste.

4	sweet potatoes, unpeeled (about 2½ lb/1.25 kg)	4
1 tbsp	olive oil or soft margarine	15 mL
	Grated rind of half an orange	
¼ cup	fresh orange juice	50 mL
2 tbsp	sherry	25 mL
2 tbsp	packed brown sugar	25 mL
Pinch	freshly grated nutmeg	Pinch
¼ tsp or less	salt and freshly ground pepper	1 mL or less

In pot of boiling water, cook potatoes until tender, 30 to 40 minutes. Drain and let cool slightly; peel. (Or, peel, quarter and steam over simmering water until tender.)

While still warm, mash potatoes with oil, orange rind and juice, sherry, sugar, nutmeg, and salt and pepper. Return to saucepan and heat over medium heat until hot.

MAKES 5 SERVINGS

MAKE AHEAD: Cover and refrigerate potatoes in casserole dish for up to 2 days; reheat in microwave or in 350°F (180°C) oven for about 25 minutes or until hot.

NOTE: A serving of this dish provides over three times the daily value for vitamin A. It is also an excellent source of potassium and high in magnesium and fibre.

PER SERVING: 210 calories, 3 g protein, 3 g total fat, 0 g saturated fat, 0 mg cholesterol, 43 g carbohydrate, 5 g fibre, 217 mg sodium, 647 mg potassium

Rose Murray's Roasted Asparagus

My friend and cookbook author Rose Murray showed me how to cook asparagus this way. It has a slightly different texture and flavour from boiled asparagus and tastes delicious. Very thin asparagus might take less baking time; fat stalks are best for this recipe and might take a little longer. For extra flavour, sprinkle asparagus with freshly grated Parmesan cheese and/or balsamic vinegar after roasting.

1 lb	asparagus	500 g
2 tsp	olive oil	10 mL
¼ tsp or less	each salt and freshly ground pepper	1 mL or less

Break off tough ends of asparagus. Arrange asparagus in single layer on baking sheet. Drizzle with oil; turn to coat. Sprinkle with salt and pepper. Bake in 500°F (260°C) oven for about 8 minutes or until tender.

MAKES 4 SERVINGS

PER SERVING: 32 calories, 1 g protein, 2 g total fat, 0 g saturated fat, 0 mg cholesterol, 2 g carbohydrate, 1 g fibre, 154 mg sodium, 123 mg potassium

Foil-Steamed Spring Vegetables

These vegetables are terrific with fish or chicken. In winter, use parsnips, snow peas or beans instead of asparagus and cut the parsnips and carrots into ½-inch (1 cm) pieces. White pearl onions, which are the size of small grapes, are sold in 2-cup (500 mL) boxes. They keep for a month or two in a cool, dry place. If not available, use the white and tender green part of 2 to 3 bunches of green onions. You can also cook the vegetables on the barbecue.

8 oz	pearl onions	250 g
12 oz	young carrots	375 g
8 oz	asparagus	250 g
2 tbsp	water	25 mL
1 tbsp	olive oil	15 mL
1	bay leaf	1
¼ tsp or less	salt	1 mL or less
Pinch	white pepper	Pinch

In large pot of boiling water, blanch pearl onions for 2 minutes; remove with slotted spoon. Cut off root end and gently squeeze to remove skin. In same pot of boiling water, blanch carrots for 2 minutes; drain and rinse under cold running water. Drain again. Snap tough ends from asparagus.

On large piece of heavy-duty foil, arrange vegetables in single layer. Sprinkle with water and oil; add bay leaf, salt and pepper. Fold foil over vegetables and seal. Bake in 375°F (190°C) oven for 20 to 30 minutes or until vegetables are tender.

MAKES 6 SERVINGS

MAKE AHEAD: Prepare vegetables up to point of baking and set aside for up to 4 hours.

NOTE: One serving is a very high source of vitamin A (providing 73% of the daily value) and a high source of folacin.

PER SERVING: 58 calories, 1 g protein, 3 g total fat, 0 g saturated fat, 0 mg cholesterol, 8 g carbohydrate, 2 g fibre, 121 mg sodium, 247 mg potassium

Roasted Winter Vegetables

My mother taught me to roast vegetables. She just added them to the pan when roasting beef, pork or a chicken. They soaked up all the fat and drippings and were scrumptious. This lightened-up method uses broth and a little olive oil and is just as delicious. What's more, you don't need to cook a roast or a whole chicken to enjoy them. Roast extra vegetables and use the leftovers on pizza, or in a pasta, salad, sandwich or soup. You can also roast regular potatoes, any colour of peppers, carrots, onions, rutabagas and turnips.

2 cups	cubed (1½ inch/4 cm) peeled butternut squash (8 oz/250 g)	500 mL
2 cups	cubed (1½ inch/4 cm) peeled sweet potato (12 oz/375 g)	500 mL
3	medium leeks, trimmed and halved lengthwise, washed, cut crosswise into 2-inch (5 cm) chunks	3
1	large fennel, trimmed and cut lengthwise into sixths	1
3	medium parsnips (about 4 oz/125 g), peeled and cut in 1½ inch (4 cm) lengths	3
1	sweet red pepper, seeded and cut lengthwise into sixths	1
3 tbsp	olive or canola oil	50 mL
2 tbsp	chopped fresh rosemary (or 2 tsp/10 mL dried)	25 mL
¼ tsp or less	salt and freshly ground pepper	1 mL or less
1½ cups	sodium-reduced vegetable or chicken broth	375 mL

In roasting pan, toss together squash, sweet potato, leeks, fennel, parsnips, red pepper, oil, rosemary, and salt and pepper. Spread out in single layer.

Add stock; cover tightly with foil. Roast in 400°F (200°C) oven for 20 to 30 minutes or until liquid has evaporated and vegetables are almost tender. Remove foil and turn vegetables. Reduce heat to 375°F (190°C); roast, uncovered, for 15 to 30 minutes or until vegetables are very tender and golden.

MAKES 8 SERVINGS

MAKE AHEAD: Assemble vegetables in roasting pan up to 4 hours in advance; add stock just before roasting.

NOTE: To reduce sodium, use a low-sodium stock (see p. 62).

This dish is particularly high in vitamins and fibre.

PER SERVING: 155 calories, 3 g protein, 6 g total fat, 1 g saturated fat, 0 mg cholesterol, 26 g carbohydrate, 5 g fibre, 207 mg sodium, 580 mg potassium

Stir-Fried Vegetables with Ginger and Garlic

The colours and flavour combination of this dish complement any meat, from chicken to lamb to beef. You need only add rice to complete the main course. For a one-dish meal, add chicken, turkey, shellfish, ham or tofu to the stir-fry and serve over hot pasta.

1⅓ cups	green beans (4 oz/125 g)	325 mL
1	large stalk broccoli	1
Half	small cauliflower	Half
2	medium carrots	2
1	sweet red or yellow pepper	1
1½ cups	snow peas (4 oz/125 g)	375 mL
1	small zucchini	1
2 tbsp	canola or olive oil	25 mL
1	medium red onion, thinly sliced	1
4	large cloves garlic, minced	4
3 tbsp	minced gingerroot	50 mL
2 tbsp	sodium-reduced soy sauce	25 mL
	Freshly ground pepper	

Trim beans, then cut on the diagonal into 1½-inch (4 cm) lengths. Cut broccoli into florets. Peel stem; slice on the diagonal. Cut cauliflower into florets. Slice carrots on the diagonal.

In large pot of boiling water, blanch beans, broccoli, cauliflower and carrots separately just until tender-crisp. Remove and immediately rinse under cold running water to prevent further cooking; drain thoroughly.

Cut sweet pepper in 1-inch (2.5 cm) pieces, trim snow peas and slice zucchini on the diagonal; set aside.

Twenty minutes before serving, heat about 2 tsp (10 mL) of the oil in large nonstick skillet over medium-high heat. Add onion and one-third of the garlic; stir-fry for 3 to 4 minutes. Add zucchini and some of the gingerroot and more garlic; stir-fry for 3 minutes, adding more oil if necessary. If pan is full, transfer vegetables to baking dish and keep warm in 250°F (120°C) oven. Add as many of the blanched vegetables as you can stir-fry at one time, plus some of the garlic and ginger; stir-fry for 2 to 3 minutes or until hot. Add to baking dish; keep warm. Stir-fry remaining vegetables, adding a small amount of oil as necessary.

Stir-fry red pepper and snow peas until tender-crisp. Combine all vegetables; toss with soy sauce, and pepper to taste.

MAKES 8 SERVINGS

MAKE AHEAD: Prepare vegetables and blanch beans, broccoli, cauliflower and carrots up to 6 hours in advance.

NOTE: One serving is a very high source of vitamin C and vitamin A and a high source of folacin.

PER SERVING: 82 calories, 3 g protein, 4 g total fat, 0 g saturated fat, 0 mg cholesterol, 11 g carbohydrate, 3 g fibre, 156 mg sodium, 351 mg potassium

Grilled Fall Vegetables

Steaming the eggplant first shortens the grilling time and keeps it moist, which means you don't need to brush it with oil. Serve this side dish hot or at room temperature. I like to use the long, slender Japanese eggplant.

1	eggplant (about 12 oz/375 g)	1
2	zucchini (about 7 inches/18 cm each)	2
2 tbsp	olive oil	25 mL
3	sweet peppers (red, green and yellow)	3
2 tbsp	balsamic vinegar	25 mL
2 tbsp	chopped fresh thyme (or ¼ tsp/1 mL dried)	25 mL
1 tbsp	water	15 mL
¼ tsp or less	salt and freshly ground pepper	1 mL or less

Cut eggplant into ½-inch (1 cm) thick slices. Place in steamer in single layer; steam for 4 minutes. Cut zucchini diagonally into ¼-inch (5 mm) thick slices; brush with 1 tsp (5 mL) of the oil. Seed and cut peppers lengthwise into 8 pieces.

Grill vegetables in grill basket, in batches if necessary, over medium heat for 4 to 6 minutes on each side or until tender but firm. Transfer to serving bowl.

Whisk together remaining oil, vinegar, thyme, water, and salt and pepper. Pour over hot vegetables and toss to coat.

MAKES 6 SERVINGS

MAKE AHEAD: Cover and refrigerate for up to 1 day. Serve at room temperature.

NOTE: Sweet red peppers are a colourful, refreshing addition to rice, pasta and grain dishes. In the fall, when sweet red peppers are plentiful, roast or grill them to substitute for the canned or bottled pimientos or sweet red peppers. My husband, who does the barbecuing, has perfected his method for grilling sweet red peppers: Grill quartered peppers for about 10 minutes over medium-low heat, turning once. Then move them to the other side of the barbecue, off the direct heat, to continue cooking. Total cooking time varies but is about 20 to 30 minutes. Or, roast sweet red peppers in 400°F (200°C) oven for 20 to 30 minutes, turning once or twice, or until blackened and blistered. Scrape skin from peppers; discard seeds and cut in quarters or coarsely chop.

PER SERVING: 93 calories, 2 g protein, 5 g total fat, 1 g saturated fat, 0 mg cholesterol, 13 g carbohydrate, 4 g fibre, 104 mg sodium, 454 mg potassium

Glazed Brussels Sprouts with Pecans

This recipe can be easily doubled or tripled so that there's plenty to go around with a turkey dinner. Walnuts can be used instead of pecans—just make sure they're fresh.

2 cups	small brussels sprouts	500 mL
1 tbsp	canola or olive oil	15 mL
2 tsp	granulated sugar	10 mL
2 tbsp	coarsely chopped pecans	25 mL
¼ tsp or less	salt and freshly ground pepper	1 mL or less

Trim base of sprouts and outside leaves. Steam sprouts over boiling water for 8 to 10 minutes or until tender.

In skillet, heat oil over medium heat; add sugar and stir until melted. Add brussels sprouts and pecans, stirring to coat well; cook for 1 to 2 minutes. Season with salt and pepper.

MAKES 4 SERVINGS

NOTE: One serving is a very high source of vitamin C.

PER SERVING: 81 calories, 2 g protein, 6 g total fat, 0 g saturated fat, 0 mg cholesterol, 6 g carbohydrate, 2 g fibre, 156 mg sodium, 168 mg potassium

Middle-Eastern Eggplant Baked with Yogurt and Fresh Mint

This is one of the tastiest—and easiest—ways to prepare eggplant. It's especially good with lamb but also goes well with pork, beef and chicken. Or serve it as part of a buffet or meatless dinner.

3 tbsp	canola oil	50 mL
2 tbsp	water	25 mL
1	large onion, sliced	1
1	medium eggplant, unpeeled (about 1¼ lb/625 g)	1
1 cup	low-fat plain yogurt	250 mL
3 tbsp	chopped fresh mint and/or parsley	50 mL
2	cloves garlic, minced	2
¼ tsp or less	salt	1 mL or less
	Freshly ground pepper	
	Paprika	

In large nonstick skillet, heat 1 tsp (5 mL) of the oil and the water over medium heat; cook onion, stirring, for 5 minutes or until softened. Remove onion and set aside.

Cut eggplant into ¼-inch (5 mm) thick slices. Brush remaining oil over eggplant slices. In skillet over medium heat, cook eggplant (in batches) turning once, until tender, about 10 minutes (or arrange in a single layer on baking sheet and bake in 400°F (200°C) oven for 15 minutes or until tender and soft).

In ungreased shallow baking dish, arrange overlapping slices of eggplant alternating with onion.

In small bowl, stir together yogurt, fresh mint, garlic, salt, and pepper to taste; drizzle over eggplant slices. Sprinkle liberally with paprika. Bake in 350°F (180°C) oven until hot and bubbly, 10 to 15 minutes.

MAKES 8 SERVINGS

VARIATION: When tomatoes are in season, add slices of tomato between eggplant slices and onion in baking dish. Sprinkle top with grated low-fat mozzarella cheese.

PER SERVING: 88 calories, 2 g protein, 6 g total fat, 1 g saturated fat, 1 mg cholesterol, 8 g carbohydrate, 2 g fibre, 97 mg sodium, 174 mg potassium

Grilled Eggplant with Garlic and Rosemary

Eggplant cooked on the barbecue has a rich smoky flavour. Slice it ½ inch (1 cm) thick—thicker slices tend to burn before they have a chance to become tender inside. Serve with other grilled vegetables or broiled tomatoes.

1	eggplant (about 1 lb/500 g)	1
2 tbsp	olive or canola oil	25 mL
1 tbsp	water	15 mL
1	small clove garlic, minced	1
2 tsp	crushed dried rosemary (or 1 tbsp/15 mL fresh)	10 mL

Cut eggplant into ½-inch (1 cm) thick slices. Combine oil, water and garlic; brush over both sides of eggplant.

Grill on greased rack about 6 inches (15 cm) from medium-hot coals or on medium setting for 8 to 10 minutes (with lid down); turn and sprinkle with rosemary. Grill for 8 to 10 minutes longer or until lightly browned outside and soft and creamy inside. (Or, broil on baking sheet for 4 to 6 minutes per side.) Serve hot or warm.

MAKES 6 SERVINGS

VARIATION:

Eggplant, Tomato and Mozzarella Salad
Arrange overlapping slices of Grilled Eggplant with Garlic and Rosemary, thick slices of tomato and thin slices of low fat mozzarella cheese. Drizzle with Everyday Vinaigrette (p. 95).

PER SERVING: 58 calories, 0 g protein, 5 g total fat, 1 g saturated fat, 0 mg cholesterol, 5 g carbohydrate, 1 g fibre, 1 mg sodium, 64 mg potassium

Broccoli and Sweet Pepper Stir-Fry

This bright red, yellow and green vegetable dish tastes as good as it looks.

1	bunch broccoli (about 1 lb/500 g)	1
1	each sweet red and yellow pepper	1
1 tbsp	canola or sesame oil	15 mL
1	onion, chopped	1
1 to 2 tbsp	grated gingerroot	15 to 25 mL
¼ cup	sodium-reduced chicken broth	50 mL
1 tbsp	sodium-reduced soy sauce	15 mL
1 tbsp	toasted sesame seeds (optional)	15 mL

Peel tough broccoli stems. Cut stems and florets into pieces about 1½ inches (4 cm) long. Blanch in large pot of boiling water for 2 to 3 minutes or until bright green and tender-crisp; drain and cool under cold running water. Drain again and dry on paper towels. Core and seed peppers; cut into thin strips.

In large nonstick skillet or wok, heat oil over medium heat. Add onion and gingerroot; stir-fry for 1 minute. Add peppers and stir-fry for 2 to 3 minutes until tender, adding chicken stock when necessary to prevent sticking or scorching. Add broccoli; stir-fry until heated through. Sprinkle with soy sauce and sesame seeds (if using).

MAKES 8 SERVINGS

MAKE AHEAD: Prepare (including blanching of broccoli), cover and refrigerate vegetables for up to 1 day. Stir-fry just before serving.

VARIATION:

Broccoli and Carrot Stir-Fry
Use 2 cups (500 ml) sliced carrots instead of sweet peppers. Blanch along with broccoli.

NOTE: One serving is a very high source of vitamin C (providing 125% of the daily value) and a high source of vitamin A and folacin.

PER SERVING: 44 calories, 2 g protein, 2 g total fat, 0 g saturated fat, 0 mg cholesterol, 6 g carbohydrate, 1 g fibre, 99 mg sodium, 195 mg potassium

Broccoli and Red Pepper Casserole

This dish works equally well with cauliflower in place of broccoli, or use half of each. I like to serve it with turkey for Thanksgiving dinner.

2	bunches broccoli	2
1	sweet red pepper, sliced	1
1½ cups	low-fat milk	375 mL
3 tbsp	all-purpose flour	50 mL
	Grated rind of 1 lemon	
1 tsp	dried basil	5 mL
⅛ tsp or less	each salt and freshly ground pepper	0.5 mL or less
4 oz	light cream cheese, cubed	125 g

TOPPING

2 tsp	canola or olive oil	10 mL
1 cup	coarse fresh whole-wheat bread crumbs*	250 mL
¼ cup	freshly grated Parmesan cheese	50 mL
¼ tsp	dried basil	1 mL

Cut broccoli tops into florets; peel and slice stalk to make about 8 cups (2 L). In large pot of boiling water, cook broccoli for about 3 minutes or until tender-crisp. Drain well and blot with paper towels to dry. Transfer to a 9- × 13-inch (2.5 L) baking dish; sprinkle with red pepper.

In microwave-safe bowl, whisk together milk, flour, lemon rind, basil, salt and pepper. Microwave on High for 3 minutes, stopping every minute to whisk, or until bubbling and thickened; whisk in cream cheese until smooth. (Or, cook milk mixture in saucepan over medium heat, whisking for 5 minutes or until boiling and thickened; whisk in cream cheese.) Spread sauce over broccoli.

TOPPING: Mix oil with breadcrumbs, Parmesan and basil; sprinkle over top.

Bake, uncovered, in 375°F (190°C) oven for about 20 minutes or until bubbling and topping is golden. Let stand for 5 minutes before serving.

MAKES 8 SERVINGS

*If using ready-made fine dry bread crumbs, reduce the amount to ½ cup (125 mL).

MAKE AHEAD: After cooking, chill broccoli under cold running water and drain well. Combine broccoli and red peppers in baking dish. Whisk together and cook milk mixture; cover separately and refrigerate for up to 1 day. Just before baking, warm milk mixture to soften, then spread over vegetables; sprinkle with topping. Increase baking time to about 40 minutes.

PER SERVING: 140 calories, 7 g protein, 6 g total fat, 3 g saturated fat, 15 mg cholesterol, 16 g carbohydrate, 3 g fibre, 282 mg sodium, 418 mg potassium

Sesame Broccoli

Asian seasonings add tang to the broccoli in this dish.

1 tbsp	sesame seeds	15 mL
1	bunch broccoli (about 1 lb/500 g)	1
2 tbsp	orange juice	25 mL
2 tsp	sesame oil	10 mL
2 tsp	sodium-reduced soy sauce	10 mL
1 tsp	grated gingerroot	5 mL

In small pan, toast sesame seeds over medium heat for 3 minutes, shaking pan occasionally; set aside.

Cut broccoli into florets; peel stalks and diagonally slice. Boil broccoli for 5 to 6 minutes or steam until tender-crisp; drain and place in serving dish.

Combine orange juice, sesame oil, soy sauce and gingerroot; toss with broccoli. Sprinkle with sesame seeds.

MAKES 5 SERVINGS

VARIATION:

Sesame Carrots
Use 1 lb (500 g) carrots (about 6) peeled and cut into strips, instead of broccoli. Garnish with chopped fresh coriander (cilantro).

MAKE AHEAD: To prepare in advance, cook broccoli, then quickly cool in ice water; toast sesame seeds and mix seasonings. Just before serving, blanch broccoli in boiling water; drain and combine as in recipe.

NOTE: Studies suggest that consumption of brassica vegetables may reduce the risk of cancer, particularly of the bowel and colon. Brassica vegetables include cabbage, broccoli, cauliflower, turnips, rutabaga, collard greens, kale, kohlrabi, bok choy and brussels sprouts.

PER SERVING: 51 calories, 2 g protein, 3 g total fat, 0 g saturated fat, 0 mg cholesterol, 5 g carbohydrate, 2 g fibre, 95 mg sodium, 194 mg potassium

Spinach with Lemon and Nutmeg

Spinach adds a pretty colour to a plate and goes well with almost any fish, meat or poultry. This quick-cooking method maximizes spinach's nutrients.

1	bunch or pkg (10 oz/284 g) fresh spinach	1
2 tsp	fresh lemon juice	10 mL
2 tsp	canola or olive oil	10 mL
Pinch	nutmeg	Pinch
¼ tsp or less	salt and freshly ground pepper	1 mL or less

Rinse spinach and shake off excess water. In large saucepan, cover and cook spinach with just the water clinging to leaves over medium heat for 2 minutes or just until wilted; drain well. Stir in lemon juice, oil, nutmeg, and salt and pepper.

MAKES 3 SERVINGS

PER SERVING: 53 calories, 3 g protein, 3 g total fat, 0 g saturated fat, 0 mg cholesterol, 4 g carbohydrate, 3 g fibre, 174 mg sodium, 513 mg potassium

Sherried Green Beans with Sweet Red Peppers

This colourful vegetable dish goes well with any meat, fish or poultry. If fresh red peppers aren't available, substitute ½ cup (125 mL) diced bottled red peppers.

½ cup	cold water	125 mL
¼ cup	dry sherry	50 mL
2 tbsp	sodium-reduced soy sauce	25 mL
1 tbsp	minced gingerroot	15 mL
2 tsp	cornstarch	10 mL
1 tbsp	sesame oil	15 mL
1½ lb	green beans, stem ends and strings removed	750 kg
1 cup	diced sweet red pepper	250 mL

In saucepan, combine water, sherry, soy sauce, gingerroot and cornstarch; cook over medium-high heat, stirring constantly, until boiling and thickened. Remove from heat. Stir in sesame oil.

In separate saucepan of boiling water, cook beans for 6 to 8 minutes or until tender-crisp; drain. Pour hot sauce over beans; mix gently. Transfer to serving dish; sprinkle with red pepper.

MAKES 10 SERVINGS

MAKE AHEAD: Prepare sauce up to 3 hours in advance; reheat over medium-high heat, stirring continuously, or microwave on High for 1 minute, until hot.

MICROWAVE METHOD FOR SAUCE
In microwaveable dish, combine water, sherry, soy sauce, gingerroot and cornstarch; microwave on High for 3 to 4 minutes, stirring after each minute, until boiling and thickened. Let cool slightly. Add sesame oil.

PER SERVING: 44 calories, 1 g protein, 2 g total fat, 0 g saturated fat, 0 mg cholesterol, 6 g carbohydrate, 2 g fibre, 109 mg sodium, 199 mg potassium

Green Beans with Herbs and Pine Nuts

Green beans are a tasty and colourful addition to virtually any dinner.

2 tbsp	pine nuts or sunflower seeds	25 mL
1½ lb	green beans, trimmed	750 g
¼ cup	chopped fresh dill or parsley	50 mL
1 tbsp	olive oil	15 mL
2 tsp	fresh lemon juice	10 mL
¼ tsp or less	salt and freshly ground pepper	1 mL or less

Toast pine nuts in 350°F (180°C) oven for 5 minutes or until golden.

In large saucepan of boiling water, cook beans for 5 minutes or until tender-crisp. Drain thoroughly.

Add dill and olive oil; toss gently. Add lemon juice, and salt and pepper; toss again. Sprinkle with pine nuts.

MAKES 10 SERVINGS

MAKE AHEAD: Toast pine nuts; set aside. Cook beans; immediately plunge into cold water, then drain. Wrap in clean tea towel and refrigerate for up to 6 hours. Reheat in boiling water for 1 minute or until heated through; drain and continue with recipe.

PER SERVING: 41 calories, 1 g protein, 2 g total fat, 0 g saturated fat, 0 mg cholesterol, 5 g carbohydrate, 1 g fibre, 60 mg sodium, 173 mg potassium

Green Beans with Garlic, Balsamic Vinegar and Sesame Oil

This is the way I most often serve green beans. The recipe is very simple, yet it has the kick of garlic and the smooth richness of sesame oil making it full of flavour. In the summer I serve this at room temperature as a main-course salad. Garnish the platter, if you wish, with something colourful such as halved cherry tomatoes, or crunchy such as chopped cashews.

1½ lb	green beans	750 g
1	clove garlic, chopped	1
¾ tsp or less	salt	4 mL or less
1 tbsp	balsamic vinegar	15 mL
2 tbsp	dark sesame oil	25 mL

Remove stem ends from green beans. In large pot of boiling water, cook beans for 4 to 5 minutes or until tender; drain well. Meanwhile, on serving platter and using the back of a fork, crush garlic with salt to form paste; stir in vinegar, then oil.

Add hot, warm or cold green beans; stir to coat in garlic mixture and serve.

MAKES 8 SERVINGS

MAKE AHEAD: Cook beans, wrap in paper towels then place in plastic bag; refrigerate for up to 1 day. Make garlic mixture up to 2 hours in advance.

PER SERVING: 56 calories, 1 g protein, 4 g total fat, 1 g saturated fat, 0 mg cholesterol, 6 g carbohydrate, 2 g fibre, 222 mg sodium, 203 mg potassium

Cauliflower with Fresh Dill

Fresh dill goes well with most vegetables and is very good with cauliflower. This dish is also good served cold and makes a wonderful addition to a summer salad plate.

1	medium cauliflower	1
2 tbsp	fresh lemon juice	25 mL
1 tbsp	olive oil	15 mL
⅓ cup	lightly packed chopped fresh dill	75 mL
¼ tsp or less	salt and freshly ground pepper	1 mL or less
	Chopped sweet red pepper or tomato (optional)	

Remove leaves and stem from cauliflower; cut cauliflower into florets. Cook in large pot of boiling water, covered, for 10 minutes or until tender; drain. Transfer to serving dish.

Mix lemon juice with oil; pour over cauliflower and stir to mix. Sprinkle with dill, and salt and pepper; toss gently to mix. Garnish with red pepper (if using).

MAKES 6 SERVINGS

PER SERVING: 43 calories, 2 g protein, 3 g total fat, 0 g saturated fat, 0 mg cholesterol, 4 g carbohydrate, 1 g fibre, 112 mg sodium, 145 mg potassium

Tarragon Carrots

Onion and tarragon complement the natural sweetness of carrots and add extra colour. Cook the vegetables in the oven or microwave to retain the vitamins, and save time by slicing them in the food processor.

2 cups	thinly sliced carrots	500 mL
2	small onions, thinly sliced	2
2 tbsp	water	25 mL
1 tsp	crushed dried tarragon (or 1 tbsp/15 mL chopped fresh tarragon)	5 mL
¼ tsp or less	salt and freshly ground pepper	1 mL or less
2 tsp	olive oil	10 mL

Lightly oil large sheet of foil or 6-cup (1.5 L) microwaveable dish. Arrange carrots and onion in centre; sprinkle with water, tarragon, and salt and pepper. Wrap tightly or cover. Bake in 350°F (180°C) oven for 30 minutes, or microwave on High for 10 to 12 minutes, or until tender. Drizzle with oil.

MAKES 4 SERVINGS

MAKE AHEAD: Vegetables can be prepared a few hours in advance; cook just before serving.

NOTE: One serving is a very high source of vitamin A (providing approximately 140% of the daily value).

VARIATION:

Carrots with Coriander
Omit tarragon and sprinkle 2 to 3 tbsp (25 to 50 mL) chopped fresh coriander (cilantro) over cooked carrots just before serving.

PER SERVING: 62 calories, 1 g protein, 2 g total fat, 0 g saturated fat, 0 mg cholesterol, 10 g carbohydrate, 3 g fibre, 193 mg sodium, 247 mg potassium

Braised Carrots with Fennel

Tender new carrots teamed with mild licorice-tasting fennel is a lovely vegetable combination.

1	medium bulb fennel (about 12 oz/375 g)	1
1 cup	sodium-reduced vegetable or chicken broth	250 mL
2 cups	thinly sliced small carrots	500 mL
2 tbsp	chopped shallots or onion	25 mL
¼ cup	chopped fresh parsley	50 mL
¼ tsp or less	salt and freshly ground pepper	1 mL or less
	Freshly grated Parmesan cheese (optional)	

Trim stalk and base from fennel bulb and discard. Chop and save a few wispy fronds.

Remove outer layer of fennel bulb if discoloured or bruised. Cut bulb into ¼-inch (5 mm) thick pieces about 2 inches (5 cm) long.

In saucepan, bring chicken broth to boil; add carrots, shallots and fennel. Cover and simmer for 10 to 15 minutes or until vegetables are tender; uncover and boil to reduce liquid until nearly gone. Stir in parsley and reserved fennel fronds. Season with salt and pepper. Sprinkle with Parmesan, if desired. Serve hot.

MAKES 4 SERVINGS

NOTE: Choose young, slender carrots for this recipe—often sold with the green tops still attached.

PER SERVING: 51 calories, 2 g protein, 0 g total fat, 0 g saturated fat, 0 mg cholesterol, 11 g carbohydrate, 4 g fibre, 283 mg sodium, 494 mg potassium

Scalloped Cabbage and Tomato Gratin

This delicious dish adds a little protein to a meatless meal. It also goes well with hot or cold beef, pork and lamb.

4 cups	coarsely shredded cabbage	1 L
1	can (28 oz/796 mL) tomatoes, drained and chopped	1
2 tsp	granulated sugar	10 mL
1 tsp	crumbled dried oregano	5 mL
¼ tsp	each paprika and freshly ground pepper	1 mL
½ cup	shredded light Cheddar-style cheese	125 mL
1 cup	fresh whole-wheat bread crumbs	250 mL

In saucepan of boiling water, cook cabbage for about 6 minutes or until fork-tender; drain well. Spoon into lightly greased 6-cup (1.5 L) baking dish.

In bowl, combine tomatoes, sugar, oregano, paprika, and pepper; spoon evenly over cabbage. Sprinkle with cheese, then bread crumbs.

Bake, uncovered, in 350°F (180°C) oven for 30 minutes or until heated through.

MAKES 6 SERVINGS

MAKE AHEAD: Assemble casserole (except for bread crumbs), cover and refrigerate for up to 1 day. When ready to use, sprinkle with bread crumbs and bake as directed.

NOTE: One serving is a very high source of vitamin C.

PER SERVING: 76 calories, 4 g protein, 2 g total fat, 1 g saturated fat, 5 mg cholesterol, 11 g carbohydrate, 2 g fibre, 225 mg sodium, 243 mg potassium

Two-Cabbage Stir-Fry with Ginger and Onion

Red and green cabbage, stir-fried with fragrant ginger and onion, makes for a colourful vegetable dish that's especially good with pork and turkey. It's quick to make and can easily be doubled.

1 tbsp	unseasoned rice vinegar	15 mL
1 tbsp	water	15 mL
1 tsp	sodium-reduced soy sauce	5 mL
1 tsp	cornstarch	5 mL
1 tbsp	canola oil	15 mL
1 tsp	chopped gingerroot	5 mL
1	small onion, chopped	1
1 cup	thinly sliced red cabbage	250 mL
1 cup	thinly sliced green cabbage	250 mL

In small dish, mix together vinegar, water, soy sauce and cornstarch; set aside.

In nonstick skillet or wok, heat oil over medium heat. Add gingerroot and onion; stir-fry for 1 minute. Add red and green cabbage; stir-fry until tender, 3 to 5 minutes.

Pour in vinegar mixture and stir-fry until liquid comes to a boil, about 1 minute.

MAKES 3 SERVINGS

MAKE AHEAD: Prepare vinegar mixture and vegetables for up to 4 hours before cooking.

NOTE: Rice vinegar is a mild, sweet vinegar, available in the Chinese food section of many supermarkets. If unavailable, substitute apple cider vinegar and a pinch of granulated sugar.

Avoid seasoned rice vinegar; it contains a lot of salt.

PER SERVING: 70 calories, 1 g protein, 5 g total fat, 0 g saturated fat, 0 mg cholesterol, 7 g carbohydrate, 2 g fibre, 71 mg sodium, 150 mg potassium

Braised Red Cabbage

Here's a colourful and flavourful vegetable dish that's especially good with pork or poultry. To retain a bright red colour when cooking red cabbage, include an acid such as vinegar or lemon juice in the cooking liquid.

Half	medium red cabbage	Half
1	cooking apple	1
⅓ cup	water	75 mL
¼ cup	white wine vinegar	50 mL
¼ tsp or less	salt and freshly ground pepper	1 mL or less
2 tbsp	liquid honey or granulated sugar, plus more to taste	25 mL

Remove outer leaves and centre core of cabbage. Slice thinly to make about 5 cups/1.25 L. Peel, core and slice apple.

In large skillet or heavy saucepan, combine cabbage, apple, water and vinegar; bring to boil. Reduce heat and simmer, covered and stirring occasionally, for 50 to 60 minutes or until cabbage is very tender.

Season with salt, pepper and honey to make dish sweet and sour.

MAKES 4 SERVINGS

MAKE AHEAD: Cover and refrigerate for up to 2 days. Reheat to serve.

PER SERVING: 90 calories, 2 g protein, 0 g total fat, 0 g saturated fat, 0 mg cholesterol, 22 g carbohydrate, 4 g fibre, 182 mg sodium, 375 mg potassium

Baked Leeks au Gratin

Although leeks are available nearly all year round, they're in season and most reasonably priced during the fall. They're delicious with any cut of meat or poultry, or as part of an all-vegetable dinner.

4	large leeks	4
2 tsp	olive oil	10 mL
¼ tsp or less	salt and freshly ground pepper	1 mL or less
2 tbsp	freshly grated Parmesan cheese	25 mL
1 tsp	water	5 mL

Trim base and tough green leaves from leeks, leaving tender light green and white parts. Cut leeks in half lengthwise; wash under cold running water and drain.

Place leeks, cut side up, in single layer in microwaveable dish or on lightly oiled foil. Sprinkle with oil; season with salt and pepper to taste. Sprinkle with cheese. Add the water to dish. Cover dish or wrap in foil. Microwave on High for 10 minutes, or bake in 350°F (180°C) oven for 25 minutes, or until very tender.

MAKES 4 SERVINGS

MAKE AHEAD: Assemble leeks and set aside for up to 6 hours.

NOTE: Be sure to cook leeks until they are fork-tender. Undercooked leeks are tough and not as flavourful as well-cooked ones. Cooked and cooled leeks drizzled with Orange Vinaigrette (p. 96) or Tarragon Vinaigrette (used in the French Potato Salad, p. 91) are a marvellous first course.

PER SERVING: 82 calories, 2 g protein, 3 g total fat, 1 g saturated fat, 3 mg cholesterol, 12 g carbohydrate, 2 g fibre, 210 mg sodium, 140 mg potassium

Braised Red Peppers and Leeks

This dish goes well with lamb, pork or beef, but don't use more red pepper than called for—it could overpower the subtle flavour of the leeks.

6	medium leeks	6
1	large sweet red pepper	1
½ cup	sodium-reduced chicken broth or water	125 mL
1 tbsp	olive oil	15 mL
¼ tsp or less	salt and freshly ground pepper	1 mL or less

Trim base and tough green leaves from leeks, leaving tender light green and white parts. Cut leeks in half lengthwise; wash under cold running water and drain. Cut into ½-inch (1 cm) thick slices to make about 4 cups (1 L). Core and seed red pepper; cut into thin 1-inch (2.5 cm) strips.

In saucepan, combine chicken broth and leeks; cover and simmer for 5 to 10 minutes or until almost tender. Add red pepper; cover and simmer for 5 to 10 minutes or until tender. If too much liquid, uncover and cook for 1 to 2 minutes. Stir in oil, salt and pepper.

MAKES 4 SERVINGS

MAKE AHEAD: Cover and refrigerate for up to 2 days. Reheat gently in oven or microwave or on stove top.

NOTE: One serving is a very high source of vitamin C (providing 125% of the daily value) and a high source of iron, vitamin A and folacin.

MICROWAVE METHOD
In 10-inch (25 cm) round microwaveable dish, place leeks, cut side up, in single layer.

Add 1 tbsp (15 mL) water to dish. Drizzle with oil and season with salt and pepper. Cover dish and slightly vent; microwave on High for 5 minutes or until leeks are nearly tender. Add red peppers and cover and slightly vent; microwave on High for 2 minutes or until vegetables are tender.

PER SERVING: 101 calories, 2 g protein, 4 g total fat, 1 g saturated fat, 0 mg cholesterol, 17 g carbohydrate, 2 g fibre, 235 mg sodium, 254 mg potassium

Portobello Mushrooms with Sweet Peppers

Huge Portobello mushrooms have much more flavour than regular mushrooms and are easy to cook. If unavailable, use large, old-fashioned brown mushrooms or any kind of fresh mushrooms.

1 lb	portobello mushrooms	500 g
2 tbsp	canola or olive oil	25 mL
2	cloves garlic, minced (optional)	2
1	each sweet red and yellow pepper, cut in strips	1
¼ tsp or less	salt and freshly ground pepper	1 mL or less

Wash mushrooms quickly in a little water; pat dry. Cut into ¼-inch (5 mm) thick slices.

In large nonstick skillet, heat oil over high heat; cook garlic (if using), red and yellow peppers and mushrooms, shaking pan or stirring often, for 7 to 10 minutes or until vegetables are tender and any liquid from mushrooms has nearly disappeared. Sprinkle with salt and pepper.

MAKES 6 SERVINGS

NOTE: Portobello mushrooms are dark brown with 5- to 10-inch (12 to 25 cm) wide caps with prominent gills underneath. Because mushrooms are open and dirt is often in the gills, they need to be washed by quickly swishing through a bowl of water. When cooked, they turn mostly black.

PER SERVING: 71 calories, 3 g protein, 5 g total fat, 0 g saturated fat, 0 mg cholesterol, 6 g carbohydrate, 2 g fibre, 104 mg sodium, 361 mg potassium

Mashed Rutabaga with Carrots and Orange

Adding mashed carrots, along with a pinch of brown sugar and a splash of extra-virgin olive oil, mellows the rutabaga.

1	small rutabaga	1
4	carrots	4
2 tbsp	packed brown sugar	25 mL
2 tbsp	frozen orange juice concentrate*, thawed	25 mL
1 tbsp	canola or olive oil	15 mL
½ tsp	grated orange rind	2 mL
Pinch	freshly grated nutmeg	Pinch
¼ tsp or less	salt and freshly ground pepper	1 mL or less
	Chopped fresh parsley	

Peel rutabaga and carrots; cut into ¾-inch (2 cm) chunks. In separate pots of boiling water, cook rutabaga and carrots until very tender. Drain well and mash with potato masher or in food processor.

In serving dish, combine rutabaga, carrots, sugar, orange juice concentrate, oil, orange rind, nutmeg, and salt and pepper. Sprinkle with parsley.

MAKES 8 SERVINGS

*Or 2 to 4 tbsp (25 to 50 mL) fresh orange juice

MAKE AHEAD: Cover and refrigerate for up to 2 days. Reheat in microwave or oven. Sprinkle with parsley just before serving.

NOTE: The rutabaga is a root vegetable in the cabbage family and is often used interchangeably with turnips. Larger than a turnip, it has a thin, purplish yellow skin and pale yellow flesh. Turnips have a white and purplish tender skin with white flesh.

One serving of this dish is an excellent source of vitamin A and also provides vitamin C.

PER SERVING: 54 calories, 1 g protein, 2 g total fat, 0 g saturated fat, 0 mg cholesterol, 10 g carbohydrate, 1 g fibre, 97 mg sodium, 184 mg potassium

Parsnip Purée

Parsnips were one of the few vegetables I really disliked as a child. Now I absolutely love them, especially this way or cooked around a roast chicken. You can use carrots, turnips or squash instead of parsnips in this recipe. When buying parsnips, remember that the small ones are more tender and sweet than the older fat ones.

5	medium parsnips (about 1 lb/500 g)	5
2 tbsp	low-fat milk, plus more to taste	25 mL
1½ tsp	canola or olive oil	7 mL
1½ tsp	sherry (optional)	7 mL
Pinch	freshly ground nutmeg	Pinch
¼ tsp or less	salt and freshly ground pepper	1 mL or less

Peel parsnips and cut into chunks to make about 2½ cups (625 mL). In saucepan of boiling water, cook parsnips for 12 to 15 minutes or until tender; drain well. Transfer to food processor, blender or food mill; purée until smooth. Add milk, oil, sherry (if using), nutmeg, and salt and pepper; process or stir until smooth. Add additional milk if necessary to make a soft, creamy consistency. Return to saucepan to reheat or spoon into serving dish; cover and keep warm.

MAKES 4 SERVINGS

MAKE AHEAD: Cover and refrigerate for up to 2 days; reheat gently in oven or microwave.

NOTE: One serving is a very high source of folacin and a source of fibre..

Puréed vegetables, because of their creamy texture, are a good alternative to vegetables with cream sauce. Puréed parsnips team well with green beans, broccoli or other green vegetables that have been steamed or boiled. Serve with meats or poultry. For a slightly milder flavour, combine puréed parsnips or turnips with mashed potatoes.

PER SERVING: 103 calories, 2 g protein, 2 g total fat, 0 g saturated fat, 0 mg cholesterol, 21 g carbohydrate, 3 g fibre, 160 mg sodium, 396 mg potassium

Turnips Paysanne

Either white turnips or a yellow rutabaga can be used in this recipe, but the rutabaga will take longer to cook. To save time, use the food processor to slice the vegetables.

4 to 6	white turnips or 1 small rutabaga (about 2 lb/1 kg)	4 to 6
1 cup	sliced celery	250 mL
1 cup	sliced carrots	250 mL
1	large clove garlic, minced	1
1	onion, chopped	1
1 cup	sodium-reduced chicken or vegetable broth	250 mL
1 tbsp	olive oil	15 mL
¼ tsp or less	salt and freshly ground pepper	1 mL or less
¼ cup	chopped fresh parsley	50 mL

Peel and dice turnips. In heavy saucepan, combine turnip, celery, carrots, garlic, onion and broth; bring to boil. Cover, reduce heat and simmer until tender, about 20 minutes.

Uncover and cook until liquid is reduced to a glaze. Stir in oil, salt and pepper. Sprinkle with parsley.

MAKES 6 SERVINGS

MAKE AHEAD: Vegetables can be cooked and set aside for up to 4 hours; reheat and add parsley just before serving.

NOTE: One serving is a very high source of vitamin A and a high source of vitamin C.

PER SERVING: 69 calories, 2 g protein, 2 g total fat, 0 g saturated fat, 0 mg cholesterol, 11 g carbohydrate, 4 g fibre, 240 mg sodium, 396 mg potassium

Baked Squash with Ginger

Ginger is a particularly nice accent for squash. Grated orange rind also heightens the flavour and can be used instead of ginger. Serve with roast pork, chicken, turkey or fish.

2¼ lb	hubbard or butternut squash (or 2 acorn squash)	1 kg
2 tbsp	packed brown sugar	25 mL
1 tbsp	canola oil or soft margarine	15 mL
2 tsp	grated gingerroot (or 1 tsp/5 mL ground ginger)	10 mL
¼ tsp	salt, freshly ground pepper and freshly grated nutmeg	1 mL

Cut squash in half; scoop out seeds. Cover squash with foil and place on baking sheet. Bake in 400°F (200°C) oven for 40 to 60 minutes or until tender. (Or, place in microwaveable dish, partially cover and microwave on High for 10 to 15 minutes.)

Scoop out pulp; mash or purée with 2 or 3 on-off turns in food processor. Stir in sugar, oil, gingerroot, and salt, pepper and nutmeg. Transfer to baking dish and reheat, covered, in microwave or 350°F (180°C) oven until hot.

MAKES 6 SERVINGS

MAKE AHEAD: Cover and refrigerate for up to 2 days.

NOTE:

- An average-size acorn squash weighs about 1½ lb (750 g) and yields about 1½ cups (375 mL) cooked, mashed squash.

- A 1½-lb (750 g) chunk of hubbard squash, covered and microwaved on High for 10 minutes, yields 2¾ cups (675 mL) purée.

- A 3-lb (1.5 kg) whole butternut squash, peeled and cubed (about 11 cups/3 L) and steamed for 10 to 12 minutes or microwaved on High for 10 minutes, yields 4 cups (1 L) purée.

PER SERVING: 88 calories, 2 g protein, 3 g total fat, 0 g saturated fat, 0 mg cholesterol, 15 g carbohydrate, 2 g fibre, 107 mg sodium, 374 mg potassium

Sautéed Zucchini with Yogurt and Herbs

Sautéed zucchini dressed with yogurt or sour cream is one of my favourite quick-vegetable recipes.

1 lb	zucchini (about 3 small)	500 g
2 tsp	canola or olive oil	10 mL
1	small onion, sliced and separated into rings	1
½ tsp	crushed dried oregano and/or basil leaves (or 2 tbsp/25 mL chopped fresh)	2 mL
1 tsp	all-purpose flour	5 mL
⅓ cup	low-fat plain yogurt or light sour cream	75 mL
2 tbsp	chopped fresh parsley	25 mL
¼ tsp or less	salt and freshly ground pepper	1 mL or less

Trim ends from zucchini. In food processor or by hand, slice zucchini thinly.

In nonstick skillet, heat oil over medium heat. Add onion; cook, stirring, until tender. Add zucchini and oregano and/or basil (if using dried) and cook, stirring often, just until barely tender, about 5 minutes.

Mix flour into yogurt; stir into zucchini. Add parsley, oregano and/or basil (if using fresh), and salt and pepper. Stir to coat well.

MAKES 6 SERVINGS

PER SERVING: 39 calories, 1 g protein, 2 g total fat, 0 g saturated fat, 1 mg cholesterol, 5 g carbohydrate, 1 g fibre, 110 mg sodium, 223 mg potassium

Snow Peas with Mushrooms

Use any kind or combination of mushrooms in this easy vegetable dish. If using dried mushrooms such as porcini, soak in warm water to soften before cooking. A few ounces of dried wild mushrooms, rehydrated, mixed with some fresh brown mushrooms is a nice combination; the wild mushrooms will impart a distinctive flavour.

1 lb	snow peas	500 g
1 tbsp	olive oil	15 mL
½ lb	mushrooms, thickly sliced	250 g
¼ tsp or less	salt and freshly ground pepper	1 mL or less

Remove stem ends and strings from snow peas.

In large nonstick skillet, heat oil over medium-high heat; cook mushrooms, stirring or shaking pan, for 8 to 10 minutes or until browned, tender and any liquid has evaporated.

Blanch snow peas in boiling water for 2 to 4 minutes or until tender; drain well. Toss peas with mushrooms. Season with salt and pepper.

MAKES 8 SERVINGS

MAKE AHEAD: Cook mushrooms and blanch snow peas up to 4 hours in advance. After blanching snow peas, cool in ice water and drain thoroughly; to reheat, immerse in boiling water for 30 seconds or heat with mushrooms in skillet over medium heat.

VARIATION:

Celery and Mushroom Stir-Fry
Use 4 cups (1 L) sliced celery instead of snow peas; stir-fry with mushrooms. When tender, sprinkle with dash of sesame oil and sodium-reduced soy sauce to taste

PER SERVING: 43 calories, 2 g protein, 2 g total fat, 0 g saturated fat, 0 mg cholesterol, 5 g carbohydrate, 2 g fibre, 76 mg sodium, 207 mg potassium

Sprout and Snow Pea Stir-Fry

My friend Stevie Cameron is a fabulous cook. I came up with this recipe after tasting a similar dish at one of her dinner parties.

4 cups	snow peas (8 oz/250 g)	1 L
2 tsp	canola or olive oil	10 mL
2 tsp	minced fresh garlic	10 mL
2 tbsp	minced gingerroot	25 mL
2 cups	bean sprouts (4 oz/125 g)	500 mL
3 tbsp	water (optional)	50 mL
2 tsp	sodium-reduced soy sauce	10 mL

Remove stem ends and strings from snow peas. In large nonstick skillet or wok, heat oil over high heat. Add garlic, gingerroot and snow peas; stir-fry for 1 minute.

Add bean sprouts; stir-fry for 1 minute or until vegetables are tender-crisp, adding water if necessary to prevent burning. Stir in soy sauce.

MAKES 4 SERVINGS

PER SERVING: 62 calories, 3 g protein, 2 g total fat, 0 g saturated fat, 0 mg cholesterol, 8 g carbohydrate, 2 g fibre, 94 mg sodium, 208 mg potassium

Tomatoes Florentine

These tomatoes are an attractive make-ahead addition to a buffet table or dinner. Garlic enthusiasts could add a minced clove to the bread crumb topping.

6	tomatoes	6
2 tsp	olive oil	10 mL
1	small onion, finely chopped	1
1	clove garlic, minced	1
1	pkg (10 oz/300 g) frozen chopped spinach, thawed and drained	1
¼ tsp or less	each salt and freshly ground pepper	1 mL or less

TOPPING

2 tbsp	fine fresh bread crumbs	25 mL
2 tbsp	chopped fresh parsley	25 mL
2 tbsp	freshly grated Parmesan cheese	25 mL

Slice off top of each tomato. Scoop out pulp to halfway down tomato (save for sauce or soup).

In skillet, heat oil. Add onion and garlic; cook over medium heat for 3 minutes or until tender. Stir in spinach, salt and pepper. Spoon mixture into tomatoes. Arrange tomatoes in ovenproof serving dish or on baking sheet.

TOPPING: Combine bread crumbs, parsley and cheese; sprinkle over tomatoes. Bake in 400°F (200°C) oven for 20 minutes or until heated through.

MAKES 6 SERVINGS

MAKE AHEAD: Assemble, cover and set tomatoes aside at room temperature for up to 4 hours before heating.

NOTE: One serving is a very high source of vitamin A and a high source of vitamin C and folacin.

PER SERVING: 52 calories, 3 g protein, 2 g total fat, 1 g saturated fat, 2 mg cholesterol, 6 g carbohydrate, 2 g fibre, 174 mg sodium, 264 mg potassium

For more vegetarian recipes, see these sections: Appetizers, Soups, Salads, Pasta Selections. And see Chinese Vegetable Fried Rice recipe on page 106.

Elizabeth Baird's Mushroom Risotto

My friend and cookbook author Elizabeth Baird makes a delicious risotto. Dried porcini mushrooms, or any specialty fresh or dried mushrooms, can be used instead of some of the regular mushrooms. If the mushrooms are dried, be sure to use the mushroom soaking liquid as part of the stock.

3 cups	sodium-reduced vegetable broth	750 mL
2 tbsp	olive oil	25 mL
1	medium onion, chopped	1
1	clove garlic, minced	1
6 cups	sliced mushrooms (1 lb/500 g)	1.5 L
½ cup	coarsely chopped sweet red pepper	125 mL
1½ cups	Arborio rice	375 mL
1 cup	dry white wine or sodium-reduced vegetable broth	250 mL
¼ tsp or less	salt and freshly ground pepper	1 mL or less
½ cup	chopped green onions	125 mL
	Chopped fresh parsley	
¼ cup	freshly grated Parmesan cheese	50 mL

In saucepan, bring broth to low simmer. Meanwhile, in wide shallow saucepan or large skillet, heat half of the oil over medium-high heat; cook onion, garlic, mushrooms and red pepper, stirring, for about 10 minutes or until tender and most of the liquid released by mushrooms has evaporated.

Add rice, stirring to coat. Stir in about half of the wine; cook, stirring often, until wine is absorbed, about 2 minutes. Add remaining wine and cook, stirring often, until wine is absorbed.

Add hot broth, ¼ cup (50 mL) at a time and stirring after each addition, until all of the stock is absorbed and rice has swelled to double its size and is tender but still a little firm, about 20 minutes.

Stir in remaining oil, and extra stock if necessary to make risotto creamy and moist. Season with salt and pepper. Spoon into warmed pasta bowls and sprinkle with onions, parsley and cheese.

MAKES 4 MAIN-COURSE SERVINGS

NOTE: When making a risotto, you stir a little stock at a time into the rice until it is absorbed; this takes about 20 to 25 minutes. The result is a lovely creamy dish—without any cream. If you have guests, have them visit with you in the kitchen while you stir, or, better yet, get them to stir.

PER SERVING: 441 calories, 11 g protein, 10 g total fat, 2 g saturated fat, 6 mg cholesterol, 74 g carbohydrate, 5 g fibre, 595 mg sodium, 558 mg potassium

Beet Risotto

Dana McCauley, Toronto food writer and chef, helped test some of the recipes in my book *Smart Cooking* and contributed this colourful risotto. This versatile dish is best served immediately, as a first course or as a main course.

2½ cups	sodium-reduced vegetable broth	625 mL
2½ cups	water	625 mL
2 tsp	canola or olive oil	10 mL
½ cup	finely chopped onion	125 mL
2	cloves garlic, minced	2
1	small bay leaf	1
1½ cups	Arborio rice	375 mL
1½ cups	chopped cooked beets (or one 14-oz/398 mL can, drained and chopped)	375 mL
	Finely grated lemon rind from 1 lemon	
1 tbsp	fresh lemon juice	15 mL
⅓ cup	grated Parmesan cheese	75 mL
¼ to ½ tsp	freshly ground pepper	1 to 2 mL
¼ cup	chopped fresh parsley	50 mL

In saucepan, bring broth and water to low simmer. Meanwhile, in shallow wide nonstick saucepan or large skillet, heat oil over medium heat. Add onion, garlic and bay leaf; cook, covered and stirring often, for 5 minutes or until onion is softened.

Add rice, stirring constantly for 2 minutes or until rice is evenly coated. Add 1 cup (250 mL) of the hot broth; cook, stirring constantly, until liquid is absorbed. Add remaining hot broth ½ cup (125 mL) at a time, cooking and stirring until each addition is absorbed before adding next. This should take 20 to 25 minutes total cooking time.

Stir in beets, lemon rind and lemon juice; cook for 1 minute longer or until rice is soft and creamy but still slightly crunchy and beets are heated through. Stir in cheese and pepper. Discard bay leaf. Place in large shallow bowl; sprinkle with parsley.

MAKES 4 MAIN-COURSE SERVINGS

NOTE: For best results, choose a short-grain rice, which is less likely to break during cooking and will remain firm to the bite. Italian Arborio, which is starchier than most types of rice—the starch helps give risotto its creamy texture—is a good choice. One serving of risotto is a very high source of folacin.

PER SERVING: 381 calories, 10 g protein, 6 g total fat, 2 g saturated fat, 7 mg cholesterol, 71 g carbohydrate, 4 g fibre, 468 mg sodium, 303 mg potassium

Green Vegetable Risotto

Shannon Graham, who has worked with me on all my books, came up with this delicious rice dish, which has less fat than a traditional risotto. This risotto also works well as a side dish with chicken, a green salad and whole-grain bread.

4 cups	sodium-reduced vegetable broth	1 L
1 tbsp	canola or olive oil	15 mL
½ cup	sliced green onions	125 mL
1 cup	Arborio or Italian short-grain white rice	250 mL
1 cup	sliced green beans	250 mL
12	snow peas	12
1 cup	coarsely chopped zucchini	250 mL
¼ cup	chopped fresh parsley	50 mL
½ cup	freshly grated Parmesan cheese	125 mL
	Freshly ground pepper	

In saucepan, bring broth to low simmer. Meanwhile, in large nonstick skillet, heat half of the oil over medium heat; cook green onions until softened, about 3 minutes. Add rice and stir to coat. Add about half of the broth, ¼ cup (50 mL) at a time, cooking and stirring until each addition is absorbed before adding next, about 8 minutes in total.

Stir in green beans; cook for 2 minutes. Stir in snow peas and zucchini. Stir in remaining stock, ¼ cup (50 mL) at a time, cooking and stirring until each addition is absorbed before adding next, 10 to 15 minutes in total or until rice is creamy and firm.

Stir in parsley, Parmesan, remaining oil, and pepper to taste. Serve immediately.

MAKES 4 MAIN-COURSE SERVINGS, 8 SIDE-DISH SERVINGS

MAKE AHEAD: Risotto tastes best as soon as it's cooked, but leftovers are still good when reheated the next day.

PER MAIN-COURSE SERVING:
318 calories, 10 g protein, 8 g total fat, 3 g saturated fat, 11 mg cholesterol, 51 g carbohydrate, 4 g fibre, 658 mg sodium, 314 mg potassium

El Paso Pilaf

Tom Ney developed this tasty recipe for Project LEAN, a low-fat educational program I was involved with in the United States. My friend and agent Denise Schon always makes this dish when she goes camping.

2 tsp	olive oil	10 mL
½ cup	chopped onion	125 mL
1	can (14 oz/398 mL) red kidney beans, drained and rinsed	1
2½ cups	sodium-reduced vegetable broth or water	625 mL
1 cup	long-grain rice	250 mL
1 cup	fresh or frozen corn kernels	250 mL
1 cup	chunky salsa	250 mL
¼ cup	dry green lentils	50 mL
¼ cup	chopped sweet red or green pepper	50 mL
½ tsp	chili powder	2 mL
1	clove garlic, minced	1
12	thick slices tomato (optional)	12

In large saucepan, heat oil over medium heat; cook onion for 5 minutes or until tender but not browned. Add beans, broth, rice, corn, salsa, lentils, sweet pepper, chili powder and garlic; bring to boil. Reduce heat, cover and simmer for 20 to 25 minutes or until rice and lentils are tender and most of the liquid is absorbed. Serve over tomato slices (if using).

MAKES 6 SERVINGS

NOTE: If you are on a sodium-restricted diet, use water instead of broth.

PER SERVING: 266 calories, 10 g protein, 3 g total fat, 0 g saturated fat, 0 mg cholesterol, 52 g carbohydrate, 7 g fibre, 533 mg sodium, 474 mg potassium

Indonesian Fried Rice

This curried rice dish is a great way to use up leftover rice. Add tofu if desired. Garnish with chopped coriander (cilantro).

4 cups	water	1 L
2 cups	whole-grain or long-grain rice	500 mL
1 tbsp	canola or olive oil	15 mL
1	medium onion, chopped	1
1	stalk celery, chopped	1
1	medium carrot, diced	1
2	cloves garlic, chopped	2
1 tbsp	grated gingerroot	15 mL
1 tbsp	sodium-reduced soy sauce	15 mL
1 tsp	each curry paste* and ground cumin	5 mL
¼ tsp	hot pepper sauce or hot chili paste	1 mL
1	sweet green pepper, diced	1
1 cup	shredded cabbage	250 mL
½ cup	frozen peas	125 mL
¼ tsp or less	salt	1 mL or less
½ cup	unsalted dry roasted peanuts, chopped	125 mL

In saucepan, bring water to boil; add rice. Reduce heat, cover and simmer for 20 minutes for long-grain white rice or whole-grain brown rice, 40–45 minutes for regular brown rice, or just until tender (don't overcook).

Meanwhile, in large heavy saucepan, heat oil over medium-high heat; cook onion until softened, stirring constantly. Add celery, carrot, garlic, gingerroot, soy sauce, curry paste, cumin and hot pepper sauce; cook, stirring, for 2 minutes. Add green pepper, cabbage and peas; cook for 2 minutes.

Add rice and cook, stirring gently, until heated through and rice is light brown. Season with salt and add chopped peanuts. Serve hot.

MAKES 6 MAIN-COURSE SERVINGS

*Use a mild, medium or hot paste depending on your preference. Curry paste can be substituted with equal amounts of curry powder.

NOTE: People sometimes avoid brown rice because it requires more cooking time than white rice. Look for whole-grain parboiled varieties that cook in less than 20 minutes.

MAKE AHEAD: Rinse cooked rice under cold running water; drain well and pat dry. Refrigerate for up to 1 day.

VARIATIONS: Non-vegetarians might add 8 oz (250 g) peeled, deveined and halved medium shrimp along with green pepper, cabbage and peas. Or, before adding cooked rice, add 2 cups (500 mL) diced cooked chicken, ham, pork or lamb and heat thoroughly.

PER SERVING: 357 calories, 10 g protein, 11 g total fat, 1 g saturated fat, 0 mg cholesterol, 57 g carbohydrate, 6 g fibre, 252 mg sodium, 311 mg potassium

Indian Rice with Lentils and Mushrooms

Easy to make, this caramelized-onion-topped rice dish is delicious.

1 tbsp	canola or olive oil	15 mL	
2½ cups	sliced onions	625 mL	
3 cups	sodium-reduced vegetable broth	750 mL	
2 cups	mushrooms, quartered	500 mL	
1 cup	whole-grain or basmati rice	250 mL	
½ cup	green lentils	125 mL	
1 tbsp	minced gingerroot	15 mL	
¼ tsp	hot pepper sauce or to taste	1 mL	
1 to 2 tsp	curry powder or Indian curry paste	5 to 10 mL	
½ tsp	cinnamon	2 mL	
2	cloves garlic, minced	2	
½ cup	chopped fresh parsley	125 mL	
¼ tsp or less	salt and freshly ground pepper	1 mL or less	

In heavy nonstick skillet, heat oil over low heat; cook onions, stirring occasionally, for 25 minutes or until very tender and lightly browned. Meanwhile, in saucepan, combine broth, mushrooms, rice, lentils, gingerroot, hot pepper sauce, curry powder, cinnamon and garlic; bring to boil. Reduce heat, cover and simmer for 25 minutes or until rice and lentils are tender and most of the liquid is absorbed. (If mixture is dry before lentils are cooked, add additional water or broth and cook until lentils are tender.) Stir in parsley, and salt and pepper. Top each serving with some fried onions.

MAKES 4 MAIN-COURSE SERVINGS, 8 SIDE-DISH SERVINGS

MAKE AHEAD: Cover and refrigerate for up to 1 day, though tastes best when just made.

NOTE: Make your own curry powder if you have the time. See page 246 for directions.

Bottled Indian curry pastes are milder than Thai curry pastes.

PER MAIN-COURSE SERVING:
352 calories, 13 g protein,
6 g total fat, 1 g saturated fat,
0 mg cholesterol,
63 g carbohydrate, 9 g fibre,
602 mg sodium, 649 mg potassium

Barley, Green Pepper and Tomato Casserole

Serve this casserole as a main course along with a tossed salad and whole-wheat toast or pita bread. Crumbled light feta cheese is a nice addition.

1 cup	pot barley	250 mL
3 cups	hot sodium-reduced vegetable broth or water	750 mL
2	onions, chopped	2
1	sweet green pepper, chopped	1
2	large tomatoes, cut in chunks	2
1 tsp	dried oregano	5 mL
¼ tsp or less	salt and freshly ground pepper	1 mL or less
2 cups	shredded reduced-fat old Cheddar cheese	500 mL
	Fresh basil, coriander (cilantro) or parsley to taste	

In baking dish, combine barley, stock, onions, green pepper, tomatoes, oregano and salt and pepper to taste; stir to mix. Cover and bake in 350°F (180°C) oven for 45 minutes. Stir in cheese and bake, uncovered, for 20 minutes or until barley is tender and most of the liquid has been absorbed. Sprinkle with fresh herbs.

MAKES 6 SERVINGS

PER SERVING: 266 calories, 14 g protein, 8 g total fat, 4 g saturated fat, 21 mg cholesterol, 37 g carbohydrate, 5 g fibre, 611 mg sodium, 336 mg potassium

Speedy Lentils and Beans with Tomatoes and Cheese

This is one of the fastest family dinner dishes I know how to make, but even better than that, everyone loves it. Packed with nutrients, high in fibre yet low in fat, canned beans and lentils make it quick to prepare. This dish can be seasoned in any number of ways: instead of rosemary you can add crushed red pepper flakes, chili, curry or oregano to taste.

1 tbsp	canola or olive oil	15 mL
1	large onion, chopped	1
2	stalks celery, sliced	2
1	can (19 oz/540 mL) kidney beans, drained and rinsed	1
1	can (19 oz/540 mL) lentils, drained and rinsed	1
1	can (19 oz/540 mL) low-sodium tomatoes, drained	1
½ tsp	dried rosemary and/or thyme	2 mL
	Freshly ground pepper	
1½ cups	shredded part-skim Cheddar or mozzarella cheese	375 mL

In flameproof casserole, heat oil over medium heat; cook onion and celery until onion is softened. Add beans, lentils, tomatoes, rosemary and/or thyme and pepper to taste; stir and break up tomatoes with back of spoon. Bring to simmer. Sprinkle with cheese; broil until cheese melts.

MAKES 6 SERVINGS (ABOUT 1 CUP/250-mL EACH)

MICROWAVE METHOD
In microwaveable casserole, combine oil, onion and celery; cover and cook on High for 3 to 4 minutes or until onion is softened. Add beans, lentils, tomatoes (break up with back of spoon), rosemary and pepper to taste; cover and microwave on High for 5 minutes or until heated through. Sprinkle with cheese and microwave until cheese melts and is bubbly.

PER SERVING: 245 calories, 17 g protein, 8 g total fat, 4 g saturated fat, 16 mg cholesterol, 28 g carbohydrate, 7 g fibre, 598 mg sodium, 602 mg potassium

Bulgur Wheat, Tofu and Sweet Peppers

This tasty main-course vegetarian dish is a good source of protein and fibre.

½ cup	coarse or medium bulgur	125 mL
2 tsp	olive oil	10 mL
2	cloves garlic, minced	2
1 tsp	each ground cumin and coriander	5 mL
1	sweet red pepper, cut in strips	1
6 oz	firm-style tofu, cut in cubes (1 cup/250 mL)	175 g
⅓ cup	water	75 mL
2 tbsp	wine vinegar or apple cider vinegar	25 mL
⅛ tsp	hot pepper sauce	0.5 mL
Half	pkg (10 oz/284 g) fresh spinach, washed, stemmed and cut in strips (4 cups/1 L)	Half
2 tbsp	unsalted sunflower seeds	25 mL
½ tsp or less	salt	2 mL or less
	Freshly ground pepper	

NOTE: One serving of this dish is very high in fibre. It is also an excellent source of vitamin C, iron, vitamin A and folacin, and a good source of calcium.

PER SERVING: 210 calories, 10 g protein, 9 g total fat, 1 g saturated fat, 0 mg cholesterol, 26 g carbohydrate, 6 g fibre, 440 mg sodium, 519 mg potassium

Place bulgur in bowl and add enough boiling water to cover by 2 inches (5 cm); soak for 20 minutes. Drain thoroughly in sieve.

In large nonstick skillet, heat oil over medium heat. Add garlic; cook for a few seconds. Stir in cumin and coriander; stir in red pepper. Cover and cook for 5 minutes.

Stir in tofu, then add bulgur, water, vinegar and hot pepper sauce; cook, uncovered, for 2 minutes or until bulgur is nearly tender, stirring often. Add spinach; cook, stirring, for 2 to 3 minutes or until slightly wilted. Add sunflower seeds, salt, and pepper to taste.

MAKES 3 SERVINGS

Rice Baked with Spinach, Parsley and Cheese

Avoid the pitfall of high-fat vegetarian dishes by using a flavourful lower-fat cheese. Serve with Tomato, Eggplant and Zucchini Gratin (p. 159) and toasted whole-wheat bread.

1 cup	long-grain brown or basmati rice	250 mL
1 tbsp	olive oil	15 mL
1	medium onion, chopped	1
1	clove garlic, minced	1
1 lb	spinach leaves	500 g
3	eggs, beaten	3
1½ cups	shredded Danbo Light or reduced-fat Swiss cheese	375 mL
½ cup	low-fat milk	125 mL
⅓ cup	chopped fresh parsley	75 mL
¾ tsp or less	salt	4 mL or less
½ tsp	each dried basil and thyme	2 mL
Pinch	each cayenne and freshly ground pepper	Pinch
¼ cup	slivered almonds, toasted*	50 mL
2 tbsp	freshly grated Parmesan cheese	25 mL

In pot of boiling water, cook rice 20 minutes for basmati, 40 minutes for brown; drain and rinse under cold water; drain. Transfer to large bowl.

Meanwhile, in skillet, heat oil over medium heat; cook onion and garlic until tender. In saucepan, cook spinach in small amount of water just until wilted; drain, squeeze dry and chop.

To rice, stir in onion mixture, spinach, eggs, Danbo, milk, parsley, salt, basil, thyme, cayenne and pepper. Transfer to greased 11- × 7-inch (2 L) glass baking dish. Sprinkle with almonds and Parmesan.

Bake, covered, in 350°F (180°C) oven for 25 minutes. Uncover and bake for another 10 minutes or until golden.

MAKES 8 SERVINGS

*To toast almonds, spread on baking sheet and roast in 350°F (180°C) oven for 5 to 8 minutes or until lightly golden.

MAKE AHEAD: Assemble dish, then cover and set aside for up to 2 hours before baking.

NOTE: Danbo Light is a Danish cheese with good flavour and texture that has an 13% butterfat content, making it one of the lower-fat cheeses. Use it in sandwiches and cooking.

Substituting 1 cup (250 mL) of 13% BF cheese for the same amount of regular (about 30% BF) cheese will reduce fat per serving by 6 grams, in a recipe that makes four servings.

VARIATION: Use ¼ cup (50 mL) chopped fresh basil and 1 tbsp (15 mL) chopped fresh thyme instead of dried basil and thyme.

PER SERVING: 232 calories, 14 g protein, 10 g total fat, 3 g saturated fat, 82 mg cholesterol, 23 g carbohydrate, 3 g fibre, 486 mg sodium, 419 mg potassium

Beans with Tomatoes and Spinach

It seems that something that tastes as good as this dish should be harder to make. Serve as a quick dinner or lunch along with a green salad. Sometimes I cook a pound (500 g) of extra-lean ground beef along with the onions, and add chili powder.

PER SERVING: 209 calories, 12 g protein, 3 g total fat, 0 g saturated fat, 0 mg cholesterol, 36 g carbohydrate, 12 g fibre, 356 mg sodium, 963 mg potassium

1 tbsp	olive oil	15 mL
2	cloves garlic, minced	2
2	onions, sliced	2
1	can (28 oz/796 mL) low-sodium diced tomatoes	1
1	can (19 oz/540 mL) red kidney beans, drained and rinsed	1
1	can (19 oz/540 mL) romano beans, drained and rinsed	1
1 tsp	dried oregano	5 mL
1	pkg (10 oz/284 g) fresh spinach (or 1 bunch) stems removed	1
	Freshly ground pepper	

In large nonstick or heavy saucepan or casserole, heat oil over medium heat; cook garlic and onions, stirring occasionally, for 5 minutes or until softened. Add tomatoes, kidney beans, romano beans and oregano; simmer 5 minutes. Stir in spinach. Season with pepper to taste.

MAKES 6 SERVINGS, ⅔ CUP (150 mL) EACH

Tuscan White Kidney Beans and Tomato

You'll want to have a little of this left over—it's delicious cold. Good as a main course with a green salad and whole-wheat pita bread, it's a high-fibre dinner that's easy to make.

1 tbsp	olive oil	15 mL
1	onion, thinly sliced	1
1	clove garlic, minced	1
1	large tomato, coarsely chopped	1
1	small sweet green or red pepper, diced	1
½ tsp	crushed dried basil (or 3 tbsp/50 mL chopped fresh)	2 mL
½ tsp	crushed dried oregano	2 mL
1	can (19 oz/540 mL) white kidney beans, drained and rinsed	1
	Freshly ground pepper	
½ cup	chopped fresh parsley	125 mL

In small heavy saucepan, heat oil over medium heat. Add onion; cook until tender. Stir in garlic, tomato and green pepper; cook for 1 minute. Stir in basil (if using dried), oregano, kidney beans, and pepper to taste; simmer over low heat for 5 minutes or until heated through and flavours are blended. Stir in parsley and basil (if using fresh).

MAKES 2 SERVINGS

MAKE AHEAD: Cover and refrigerate for up to 1 day. Add fresh herbs just before serving.

NOTE: One serving has a whopping 16 grams of fibre. Health professionals recommend we get about 25 to 35 grams of fibre daily.

One serving is also an excellent source of iron, folacin and vitamin C and is high in vitamin A.

PER SERVING: 324 calories, 16 g protein, 8 g total fat, 1 g saturated fat, 0 mg cholesterol, 50 g carbohydrate, 16 g fibre, 610 mg sodium, 1094 mg potassium

Old-Fashioned Baked Beans

I make these to have after skiing. Homemade beans are a treat and great for feeding a crowd—not to mention being good for us. The beans need to be soaked overnight or quick soaked, so plan ahead.

1 lb	dry white pea (navy) beans	500 g
2	medium onions, sliced	2
¼ cup	molasses	50 mL
2 tbsp	tomato paste or ½ cup (125 mL) ketchup	25 mL
1 tbsp	packed brown sugar	15 mL
1 tbsp	vinegar	15 mL
1 tsp or less	salt	5 mL or less
½ tsp	dry mustard	2 mL
¼ tsp	freshly ground pepper or red pepper flakes	1 mL
4 cups	hot water	1 L
2	slices bacon (2 oz/50 g), chopped (optional)	2

Rinse beans; discard any discoloured ones. In large saucepan, soak beans in water overnight or quick soak (see p. 118); drain. Add water to cover by at least 2 inches (5 cm), bring to boil and simmer for 30 minutes; drain.

In bean pot or 8-cup (2 L) casserole, spread onion slices. Mix molasses, tomato paste, sugar, vinegar, salt, mustard and pepper; pour into casserole. Add drained beans and hot water; sprinkle with bacon (if using).

Cover and bake in 250°F (120°C) oven for 6 hours; uncover and bake for 1 hour longer, adding enough water if necessary to keep beans covered.

MAKES 8 SERVINGS, ABOUT ¾ CUP (175 mL) EACH

NOTE: Soaking the beans before cooking will return moisture to them, reduce cooking time, save vitamins and minerals and help reduce flatulence-causing sugars.

PER SERVING: 236 calories, 12 g protein, 1 g total fat, 0 g saturated fat, 0 mg cholesterol, 47 g carbohydrate, 9 g fibre, 307 mg sodium, 725 mg potassium

Curried Lentils with Coriander

This is an adaptation of a recipe from Hajra Wilson, a volunteer for the Heart and Stroke Foundation of Ontario. She uses a combination of dhal (lentils): black, pink, split and green. I tested the recipe using all green lentils—the flavour is wonderful.

2 cups	green lentils	500 mL
2 tbsp	canola or olive oil	25 mL
2	medium onions, chopped	2
1 tsp	each ground ginger, coriander, cumin and turmeric	5 mL
1 tsp	minced fresh garlic	5 mL
½ tsp or less	salt	2 mL or less
3	whole cloves	3
3	whole cardamom	3
1	3-inch (8 cm) stick cinnamon (or ½ tsp/2 mL ground)	1
¼ tsp	crushed red pepper flakes	1 mL
1 cup	chopped tomatoes (fresh or canned)	250 mL
⅓ cup	chopped green onions (including tops)	75 mL
¼ cup	chopped fresh coriander (cilantro)	50 mL

Wash lentils in cold water; drain. In saucepan, bring 6 cups (1.5 L) water and lentils to boil; reduce heat, cover and simmer for 20 to 30 minutes or until tender. Drain.

Meanwhile, in large saucepan over medium heat, combine oil, onions, ginger, coriander, cumin, turmeric, garlic, salt, cloves, cardamom, cinnamon and red pepper flakes; cook for 10 minutes or until onions are softened, stirring frequently.

Add tomatoes and drained lentils; simmer over low heat for 3 minutes. Discard cloves, cardamom and cinnamon stick. Stir in green onions and coriander. Serve hot.

MAKES 8 SERVINGS, ABOUT ½ CUP (125 mL) EACH

NOTE: One-half cup (125 mL) cooked lentils is high in fibre and contains 8 grams of protein and no fat. It is also an excellent source of folacin and a good source of potassium and iron.

PER SERVING: 211 calories, 13 g protein, 4 g total fat, 0 g saturated fat, 0 mg cholesterol, 32 g carbohydrate, 7 g fibre, 154 mg sodium, 633 mg potassium

Potato, Bean and Tomato Stew with Basil

This fast and easy main dish is gentle on the budget, full of flavour and packed with nutrients. It is also delicious made with 1 tsp (5 mL) fresh rosemary instead of basil.

1 tbsp	olive oil	15 mL
1	medium onion, chopped	1
2	large cloves garlic, minced	2
½ tsp	paprika	2 mL
3	large tomatoes, coarsely chopped*	3
¼ cup	packed, chopped fresh basil (or 1 tsp/5 mL dried)	50 mL
1 tsp	dried oregano	5 mL
2	medium potatoes, peeled and diced	2
1 cup	water or sodium-reduced vegetable broth	250 mL
1	can (19 oz/540 mL) chickpeas, drained and rinsed	1
¼ tsp or less	salt and freshly ground pepper	1 mL or less
½ cup	chopped fresh parsley	125 mL

In large heavy saucepan, heat oil over medium heat; cook onion until tender, about 5 minutes. Add garlic, paprika, 2 of the tomatoes, basil (if using dried) and oregano; simmer, stirring often, for 5 minutes.

Add potatoes and water; cover and boil for 5 minutes, stirring occasionally. Add chickpeas; reduce heat and simmer for 5 minutes or until potatoes are tender.

Add remaining tomato, basil (if using fresh), and salt and pepper; heat for 1 minute. Serve garnished with parsley in large shallow bowls.

MAKES 3 MAIN-COURSE SERVINGS

*Instead of fresh tomatoes, you can use 1 can (28 oz/796 mL) low-sodium tomatoes, undrained.

MAKE AHEAD: Cover and refrigerate potato-chickpea mixture for up to 2 days. Reheat gently before adding remaining tomato, basil, salt and pepper.

PER SERVING: 351 calories, 12 g protein, 7 g total fat, 1 g saturated fat, 0 mg cholesterol, 63 g carbohydrate, 11 g fibre, 535 mg sodium, 1166 mg potassium

Tomato, Eggplant and Zucchini Gratin

Long, narrow Japanese eggplants or very small eggplants work best for this recipe. Traditionally in this type of Mediterranean dish, all the vegetables would be first sautéed in oil. This method is faster to prepare and much lower in fat.

1 tbsp	olive oil	15 mL
1	onion, sliced	1
3 cups	sliced mushrooms (½ lb/250 g)	750 mL
2	cloves garlic, minced	2
4	medium tomatoes, chopped	4
½ tsp	dried marjoram	2 mL
¼ tsp	dried thyme	1 mL
¼ tsp or less	salt and freshly ground pepper	1 mL or less
2	zucchini or small yellow summer squash (about 4 oz/125 g each)	2
2	small eggplant (about 4 oz/125 g each)	2
1 cup	fresh bread crumbs	250 mL
½ cup	freshly grated Parmesan cheese	125 mL

In nonstick skillet, heat 1 tsp (5 mL) of the oil over medium-high heat; cook onion, mushrooms, garlic and 2 tbsp (25 mL) water, stirring, for 3 minutes or until softened. Add tomatoes, marjoram, thyme, and salt and pepper; cook for 20 minutes or until thickened, stirring often.

Slice zucchini and eggplants diagonally into ¼-inch (5 mm) thick slices. Toss eggplant with remaining oil.

Spread ½ cup (125 mL) tomato sauce in 13- × 9-inch (3.5 L) glass baking dish. Layer with half of the zucchini, eggplant and sauce; repeat layers.

Mix bread crumbs with cheese; sprinkle over top. Bake, uncovered, in 400°F (200°C) oven for 35 minutes or until bubbling.

MAKES 4 MAIN-COURSE SERVINGS

MAKE AHEAD: Assemble gratin up to 1 hour in advance. Sprinkle with bread crumbs and cheese just before baking.

VARIATION: If fresh herbs are available, use 2 tbsp (25 mL) chopped fresh marjoram and 1 tbsp (15 mL) chopped fresh thyme instead of dried marjoram and thyme.

NOTE: Make fresh bread crumbs by chopping 2 slices of day-old bread in a food processor. Or rub bread over a grater. Packaged bread crumbs are dry and very fine and not as nice as fresh bread crumbs for a topping.

PER SERVING: 202 calories, 11 g protein, 9 g total fat, 4 g saturated fat, 15 mg cholesterol, 22 g carbohydrate, 6 g fibre, 478 mg sodium, 703 mg potassium

Winter Vegetable Stew

Serve this satisfying yet light stew in large shallow soup or pasta bowls. Other vegetables can be added to or substituted for the vegetables suggested. Broccoli, green beans, cooked kidney beans or chickpeas, asparagus in season, snow peas or other quick-cooking vegetables can be added to the stew when you add the zucchini.

1 tbsp	canola or olive oil	15 mL
2	onions, coarsely chopped	2
4	large cloves garlic, minced	4
2	leeks	2
2	potatoes	2
2	carrots	2
1	sweet potato	1
Quarter	small rutabaga	Quarter
3 cups	water (preferably vegetable cooking water) or sodium-reduced vegetable broth	750 mL
1½ tsp	each crushed dried oregano and thyme	7 mL
1	small zucchini, cut in chunks (unpeeled)	1
1 cup	canned chickpeas, drained and rinsed	250 mL
¼ tsp or less	salt and freshly ground pepper	1 mL or less
⅓ cup	chopped fresh parsley	75 mL
⅓ cup	freshly grated Parmesan cheese	75 mL

In large nonstick saucepan, heat oil over medium heat. Add onions and garlic; cook, stirring occasionally, until tender. Discard tough green parts of leeks; cut leeks in half lengthwise and wash under cold running water. Cut into ¾-inch (2 cm) pieces; add to saucepan.

Peel potatoes, carrots, sweet potato and rutabaga; cut into 1-inch (2.5 cm) cubes and add to pan. Stir in water, oregano and thyme; bring to boil. Cover and simmer until vegetables are tender, about 30 minutes. Stir in zucchini, chickpeas and salt and pepper; simmer for 5 minutes or until all vegetables are tender, adding more water if desired. Ladle into bowls; sprinkle with parsley and Parmesan.

MAKES 4 SERVINGS

MAKE AHEAD: Cover and refrigerate for up to 2 days.

NOTE: One serving of this stew is a very high source of vitamin A (about 150% of the daily value), folacin and fibre; it is also a high source of vitamin C and calcium.

When making any kind of stew, try to make it a day in advance and refrigerate. Any fat will solidify on the surface and then can easily be removed. As well, stews always taste better the next day, once flavours have had a chance to blend and develop.

PER SERVING: 301 calories, 10 g protein, 7 g total fat, 2 g saturated fat, 7 mg cholesterol, 52 g carbohydrate, 8 g fibre, 441 mg sodium, 929 mg potassium

Harvest Vegetable Curry

Serve this colourful and flavourful main-course vegetable dish over couscous, bulgur or brown rice. The chickpeas and grain complement each other to form complete protein.

2	carrots, sliced	2
2 cups	cubed peeled squash (about 1-inch/2.5 cm pieces)	500 mL
2 cups	broccoli florets	500 mL
1	sweet red pepper, cut in strips	1
1	small (6-inch/15 cm) yellow zucchini, cut in chunks	1
1	red onion, cut in thin wedges	1
1	can (19 oz/540 mL) chickpeas, drained and rinsed	1
1 tbsp	olive oil	15 mL
2 tbsp	minced gingerroot	25 mL
1 tbsp	curry powder or paste	15 mL
1 tsp	ground cumin	5 mL
3	cloves garlic, minced	3
¼ tsp	crushed red pepper flakes	1 mL
½ cup	sodium-reduced vegetable broth or water	125 mL
2 tbsp	fresh lemon juice	25 mL
3 cups	hot cooked brown rice, couscous or bulgur	750 mL
¼ cup	chopped fresh coriander (cilantro) or parsley	50 mL

Steam carrots and squash for 5 minutes. Add broccoli, red pepper, zucchini and red onion; steam for 5 minutes. Add chickpeas; steam for 3 to 5 minutes or until all vegetables are tender-crisp.

Meanwhile, in small saucepan, heat oil over medium heat; cook gingerroot, curry powder, cumin, garlic and red pepper flakes, stirring often, for 2 minutes. Add broth and lemon juice; simmer, covered, for 2 minutes. Toss vegetables with sauce.

Serve over hot rice. Sprinkle with coriander or parsley.

MAKES 4 MAIN-COURSE SERVINGS

NOTE: If you don't have a large steamer, cook vegetables in as little water as possible, or microwave the carrots, squash and zucchini together, covered, on High for 6 minutes, then add chickpeas and microwave for another minute. I simmer the broccoli, onion and sweet pepper together in a small amount of water for 5 minutes or until tender-crisp, then drain and toss all the vegetables with the curry mixture.

PER SERVING: 402 calories, 13 g protein, 7 g total fat, 1 g saturated fat, 0 mg cholesterol, 76 g carbohydrate, 11 g fibre, 335 mg sodium, 865 mg potassium

Chickpea Burgers

Hot pickled peppers add zing to these burgers. Tuck them into pita pockets or buns with yogurt, fresh coriander (cilantro), lettuce and tomatoes. Or serve the mixture wrapped in a soft tortilla.

2 tsp	canola or olive oil	10 mL
3	green onions (including tops), chopped	3
2	cloves garlic, minced	2
1 tsp	each dried oregano and chili powder	5 mL
1 cup	diced sweet red or green pepper and/or ¼ to ½ cup (50 to 125 mL) chopped pickled hot peppers	250 mL
Half	tomato, chopped	Half
1	can (19 oz/540 mL) chickpeas, drained and rinsed	1
⅓ cup	fine dry bread crumbs	75 mL
2 tbsp	chopped fresh coriander (cilantro) or parsley	25 mL
¼ tsp or less	salt and freshly ground pepper	1 mL or less
8 tbsp	shredded reduced-fat Cheddar cheese	100 mL

In nonstick skillet, heat 1 tsp (5 mL) of the oil over medium heat; cook onions, garlic, oregano and chili powder, stirring, for 2 minutes. Add red pepper and/or hot peppers, and tomato: cook, stirring, for about 3 minutes or until red pepper is tender and liquid is evaporated.

In food processor, mix pepper mixture with chickpeas; transfer to bowl. Stir in bread crumbs, parsley, and salt and pepper until well combined. Pressing firmly, shape into 4 burgers.

In nonstick skillet, heat remaining oil over medium heat. Cook burgers for 4 minutes on each side or until heated through. Sprinkle each burger lightly with Cheddar cheese.

MAKES 4 SERVINGS

MAKE AHEAD: Wrap uncooked burgers well and refrigerate for up to 3 days or freeze for up to 1 month. Thaw before cooking.

VARIATION:

Chickpea, Tomato and Coriander Tortilla Wraps Omit bread crumbs. Spoon unshaped chickpea burger mixture down centre of 4 large soft flour tortillas. Top with diced tomato, drizzle of yogurt, chopped fresh coriander (cilantro) and shredded lettuce or spinach. Fold one side, then ends, over filling and roll up. Makes 4 servings

PER SERVING: 237 calories, 12 g protein, 7 g total fat, 2 g saturated fat, 8 mg cholesterol, 33 g carbohydrate, 5 g fibre, 555 mg sodium, 374 mg potassium

Bean and Vegetable Burritos

My kids really like these. They're easy to prepare, especially if you have salsa or spicy tomato sauce on hand. Serve with yogurt.

1 tsp	canola or olive oil	5 mL
2	medium onions, chopped	2
3	cloves garlic, minced	3
1	sweet red or green pepper, chopped	1
1 cup	finely diced zucchini	250 mL
1	large carrot, grated	1
2 tsp	chili powder	10 mL
1 tsp	each dried oregano and ground cumin	5 mL
1 cup	Winter Salsa (p. 3)*	250 mL
1	can (14 oz/398 mL) red kidney beans, drained, rinsed and mashed	1
5	9-inch (23 cm) flour tortillas	5
⅔ cup	shredded reduced-fat Cheddar cheese	150 mL

In nonstick skillet, heat oil over medium heat; cook onions, stirring occasionally, for 3 minutes. Add garlic, red pepper, zucchini and carrot; cook, stirring often, for 5 minutes. Stir in chili powder, oregano and cumin.

Stir ⅔ cup (150 mL) of the Winter Salsa into mashed beans. Spread about ⅓ cup (75 mL) bean mixture in thin layer over each tortilla, leaving about a 1-inch (2.5 cm) border; cover with vegetable mixture. Roll up each tortilla and place seam side down in lightly oiled 13- × 9-inch (3.5 L) baking dish.

Bake in 400°F (200°C) oven for 15 minutes. Sprinkle with cheese and bake for 5 minutes longer. Serve with remaining salsa.

MAKES 5 SERVINGS

*Instead of Winter Salsa, you can use any prepared salsa or even spicy tomato sauce.

NOTE: Flour tortillas are available at most supermarkets. Check in the refrigerator section if you can't find them with the baked goods.

PER SERVING: 328 calories, 15 g protein, 8 g total fat, 3 g saturated fat, 8 mg cholesterol, 49 g carbohydrate, 9 g fibre, 707 mg sodium, 650 mg potassium

Jiffy Mexican Burritos

This is the way my kids make burritos. They spread the tortillas with mashed beans, top with grated cheese and chopped vegetables or salsa, then roll up to bake or microwave.

PER SERVING: 280 calories, 12 g protein, 7 g total fat, 3 g saturated fat, 12 mg cholesterol, 42 g carbohydrate, 6 g fibre, 687 mg sodium, 392 mg potassium

1	can (14 oz/398 mL) refried or kidney beans*	1
⅓ cup	salsa	75 mL
1½ tsp each	chilli powder, dried oregano and cumin	75 mL
6	9-inch (23 cm) flour tortillas	6
1	medium tomato, chopped	1
4	small green onions, chopped	4
Half	sweet green pepper, chopped (optional)	Half
½ cup	shredded part-skim mozzarella cheese	125 mL
	Shredded lettuce	
	Tomato and Cucumber Salsa (p. 2) or Winter Salsa (p. 3) or taco sauce	
	Light sour cream or low-fat plain yogurt	

Combine beans, salsa and spices; mix well. Thinly spread about ¼ cup (50 mL) bean mixture over each tortilla, leaving 1-inch (2.5 cm) border. Sprinkle tomato, green onions, green pepper (if using) and half the cheese over tortillas.

Roll up each tortilla and place, seam side down, in lightly greased baking dish. Bake in 400°F (200°C) oven for 10 minutes. Sprinkle with remaining cheese; bake for 5 minutes longer or until heated through and cheese melts. (Or, cover with waxed paper and microwave on Medium-High for 2 to 4 minutes or until heated through.)

Serve each burrito on a bed of shredded lettuce. Pass salsa or taco sauce and light sour cream or yogurt separately.

MAKES 6 SERVINGS

*If using kidney beans, drain and rinse under cold water, then mash.

Quinoa-Stuffed Peppers

This quinoa mixture is delicious as a stuffing for sweet peppers—red, green or purple—or on its own. I keep dried sliced Chinese mushrooms on hand and often use them when I don't have fresh ones.

½ cup	quinoa	125 mL
4	sweet green peppers	4
1 tsp	canola or olive oil	5 mL
1	medium onion, chopped	1
8	mushrooms, quartered (or ¼ cup/50 mL dried mushrooms)*	8
1 cup	cooked or frozen corn kernels	250 mL
2 tbsp	minced fresh coriander (cilantro) or parsley	25 mL
1 tbsp	sodium-reduced soy sauce	15 mL
2 tsp	sesame oil	10 mL
2 tsp	chopped fresh garlic	10 mL
Pinch	red pepper flakes	Pinch
¼ cup	fresh whole-wheat bread crumbs (see p. 159)	50 mL
8 tbsp	shredded part-skim mozzarella cheese	100 mL

Rinse quinoa under cold water; drain. In saucepan, bring 1 cup (250 mL) water to boil; stir in quinoa. Reduce heat, cover and simmer for 15 minutes or until water is absorbed and quinoa is translucent.

Cut off ½ inch (1 cm) from tops of green peppers; remove seeds. In large saucepan of boiling water, cook peppers for 5 minutes or until tender-crisp. Remove and drain upside down.

In skillet, heat oil over medium heat; cook onion until tender. Stir in mushrooms, quinoa, corn, half the coriander, soy sauce, sesame oil, garlic and red pepper flakes; stuff into peppers.

Mix bread crumbs and cheese. Sprinkle peppers with bread crumb mixture and remaining coriander. Bake in greased 8-inch (2 L) square baking dish in 350°F (180°C) oven for 30 minutes or until heated through.

MAKES 4 SERVINGS

*If using dried mushrooms, soak in hot water for 5 minutes; drain, discard tough stems and slice.

MAKE AHEAD: Assemble stuffed peppers, cover and refrigerate for up to 4 hours. Sprinkle with bread crumbs and coriander (cilantro) just before baking.

VARIATION:

Quinoa Pilaf
Prepare quinoa mixture but omit bread crumbs and green peppers.

PER SERVING: 242 calories, 10 g protein, 8 g total fat, 2 g saturated fat, 10 mg cholesterol, 35 g carbohydrate, 5 g fibre, 236 mg sodium, 606 mg potassium

Moroccan Vegetable Couscous

Here's a great example of how tasty and nutritious vegetarian cooking can be. Instead of couscous, you can use rice, orzo (rice-shaped pasta) or bulgur. Season to taste with more coriander (cilantro) and lemon juice if desired.

2 tbsp	olive oil	25 mL
3	onions, chopped	3
2 tbsp	minced gingerroot	25 mL
1 tsp	each turmeric, cinnamon and granulated sugar	5 mL
1 tsp	each ground coriander and ground cumin	5 mL
2½ cups	cubed peeled sweet potato	625 mL
2 cups	water or sodium-reduced vegetable broth	500 mL
1 cup	sliced carrots	250 mL
¼ tsp	crushed dried hot red pepper flakes	1 mL
1	sweet green or red pepper, chopped	1
1½ cups	cubed firm-style tofu or 2 cups (500 mL) cooked chickpeas*	375 mL
1	pkg (10 oz/284 g) fresh spinach, stems removed and coarsely chopped	1
¼ cup	chopped fresh coriander (cilantro)	50 mL
1 tbsp	fresh lemon juice	15 mL
½ tsp or less	each salt and freshly ground pepper	2 mL or less
1½ cups	couscous	375 mL

In large nonstick skillet, heat oil over medium heat. Stir in onions, gingerroot, turmeric, cinnamon, sugar, coriander and cumin; cook, stirring often, for 5 minutes or until onions are softened. Add sweet potato, water, carrots and hot pepper flakes; cook, covered and stirring occasionally, for 15 minutes or until sweet potatoes are almost tender.

Add green pepper, tofu and spinach; cook, stirring frequently, for 5 minutes or until potatoes are fork-tender and spinach is wilted. Stir in coriander and lemon juice. Season with salt and pepper.

Meanwhile, in saucepan, bring 2½ cups (625 mL) water to boil; add couscous, cover and remove from heat. Let stand for 5 minutes; fluff with fork, then spoon into individual bowls or plates. Top with vegetable mixture.

MAKES 6 SERVINGS

*If using canned chickpeas, use one can (19 oz/540 mL), drained and rinsed.

MAKE AHEAD: Cover and refrigerate up to 1 day. Add water if necessary when reheating.

NOTE: One serving is an excellent source of vitamin A (almost twice the daily value), iron and folacin, and a good source of vitamin C and calcium. It also contains a very high amount of fibre.

PER SERVING: 361 calories, 14 g protein, 8 g total fat, 1 g saturated fat, 0 mg cholesterol, 60 g carbohydrate, 6 g fibre, 288 mg sodium, 782 mg potassium

Chilled Cucumber Mint Soup p. 33

Marinated Shrimp and Mango Salad p. 81

Purple Vegetable Slaw p. 71

Fresh Tomato Pizza p. 172

Grilled Halibut Fillets with Fresh Tomato-Basil Salsa p. 216
Green Vegetable Risotto p. 147

Quick and Easy Salmon Fillets with Watercress Sauce p. 212
New Potatoes with Mint Pesto p. 122

Vegetable Tofu Stir-Fry

Serve this flavourful dish over rice, noodles, bulgur or couscous.

¾ lb	firm tofu	375 g
4 tsp	cornstarch	20 mL
1 tbsp	canola or vegetable oil	15 mL
1	medium onion, chopped	1
1	carrot, thinly sliced	1
2	stalks celery, sliced	2
1	sweet red or yellow pepper, cut into chunks	1
1 cup	frozen peas	250 mL
1 cup	diced zucchini	250 mL
4	green onions, chopped	4
3	cloves garlic, minced	3
¼ cup	chopped unsalted roasted peanuts (optional)	50 mL

TOFU MARINADE

⅓ cup	unseasoned rice vinegar or apple cider vinegar	75 mL
1 tbsp	sodium-reduced soy sauce	15 mL
2 tbsp	sesame oil	25 mL
1½ tsp	granulated sugar	7 mL
¼ tsp	red pepper flakes or hot chili paste	1 mL

TOFU MARINADE: In bowl, combine vinegar, soy sauce, sesame oil, sugar and red pepper flakes.

Cut tofu into ½-inch (1 cm) cubes; add to marinade. Cover and marinate in refrigerator for 1 hour, stirring occasionally. Drain tofu marinade into small dish; stir in cornstarch, mixing well.

In large nonstick skillet, heat oil over high heat; stir-fry onion, carrot and celery for 3 minutes. Add red pepper, peas, zucchini, green onions and garlic; stir-fry for 3 minutes or until tender-crisp. Add tofu; stir-fry for 1 minute.

Whisk marinade-cornstarch mixture; add to pan and cook for 1 minute or until thickened. Garnish with peanuts (if using).

MAKES 4 SERVINGS

MAKE AHEAD: Marinate tofu for up to 1 day in advance.

NOTE: If firm tofu is unavailable, place regular tofu in sieve over bowl, weigh down and drain for 1 hour or overnight.

PER SERVING: 245 calories, 10 g protein, 14 g total fat, 2 g saturated fat, 0 mg cholesterol, 21 g carbohydrate, 4 g fibre, 196 mg sodium, 486 mg potassium

Marinated Baked Tofu

This is one of the very best ways to cook tofu. It's delicious baked in this mixture of ginger and soy sauce.

10 oz	extra-firm tofu	300 g
2 tbsp	sodium-reduced soy sauce	25 mL
1 tbsp	dark sesame oil	15 mL
1 tbsp	minced gingerroot	15 mL

Cut tofu into slices slightly larger than ½ inch (1 cm) thick. In 8-inch (2 L) square glass baking dish just large enough to hold tofu in single layer, combine soy sauce, sesame oil and gingerroot. Arrange tofu in dish, turning to coat both sides with mixture. Let marinate for 15 to 30 minutes. Bake in 375°F (190°C) oven for 20 minutes, turning after 10 minutes.

MAKES 3 SERVINGS

MAKE AHEAD: Marinate tofu, covered and refrigerated, for up to 1 day. Baked tofu can be covered and refrigerated for up to 1 day; reheat or eat cold.

PER SERVING: 138 calories, 10 g protein, 10 g total fat, 2 g saturated fat, 0 mg cholesterol, 3 g carbohydrate, 0 g fibre, 364 mg sodium, 153 mg potassium

Tofu Alfredo

It's easy to slip some tofu into your diet with this tasty pasta recipe from Susan Van Hezewijk, a talented home economist who retested many of the recipes in the third edition of *The New Lighthearted Cookbook*. This is especially nice served with a few grilled shrimp on top.

½ lb	spaghetti	250 g
1	pkg (10 oz/300 g) soft silken tofu	1
2 tsp	olive oil	10 mL
4	cloves garlic, minced	4
¼ tsp or less	each salt and freshly ground pepper	1 mL or less
½ cup	chopped fresh basil	125 mL
¼ cup	freshly ground Parmesan cheese (optional)	50 mL

In large pot of boiling salted water, cook pasta for 8 to 10 minutes or until tender but firm; drain, reserving ⅓ cup (75 mL) of the cooking water.

Meanwhile, purée tofu in food processor or blender; set aside.

In saucepan, heat oil over low heat. Add garlic and cook, stirring, until softened but not coloured. Stir in tofu, reserved cooking liquid, salt and pepper just until warmed through.

Toss pasta in sauce; place on serving plate and top with basil and Parmesan (if using).

MAKES 4 SERVINGS, 1 CUP (250 mL) EACH

VARIATION: Use garlic-flavoured oil instead of minced garlic and olive oil, as a shortcut.

NOTE: Tofu, made from soybeans, is a good source of soy protein. Add firm tofu to salads, soups, pastas and stir-fries; add soft tofu to spreads, dips or salad dressings. When choosing soy beverages, read the label and choose ones fortified with calcium and vitamin D.

PER SERVING: 273 calories, 11 g protein, 5 g total fat, 1 g saturated fat, 0 mg cholesterol, 45 g carbohydrate, 3 g fibre, 153 mg sodium, 211 mg potassium

Thai Noodles with Broccoli

Here's a quick and easy stir-fry with Thai flavours.

4 oz	rice vermicelli noodles	125 g
5 cups	small broccoli florets	1.25 L
1 tbsp	canola or olive oil	15 mL
2	cloves garlic, minced	2
1½ cup	cubed firm tofu	375 mL
1	fresh red chili pepper, seeded and chopped (or ¼ tsp/1 mL dried hot red pepper flakes)	1
3 tbsp	oyster or hoisin sauce	50 mL
2 tbsp	fresh lime juice	25 mL
1 tbsp	fish sauce	15 mL
1 tbsp	minced gingerroot	15 mL
1 tsp	granulated sugar	5 mL
3	green onions, chopped	3
1 tbsp	toasted sesame seeds (optional)	15 mL

Soak rice noodles in warm water for 15 minutes; drain.

In large pot of boiling water, cook broccoli for 2 minutes; add noodles and cook for 1 minute or until tender; drain.

Meanwhile, in wok or large nonstick skillet, heat oil over medium heat. Add garlic and tofu; cook, stirring, for 1 minute. Stir in chili pepper, oyster sauce, lime juice, fish sauce, gingerroot and sugar; cook, stirring, for 1 minute. Add noodle mixture; cook, stirring, for 1 minute. Sprinkle with green onions and sesame seeds.

MAKES 4 SERVINGS

NOTE: One serving is an excellent source of vitamin C, vitamin A and folacin.

PER SERVING: 287 calories, 12 g protein, 8 g total fat, 1 g saturated fat, 0 mg cholesterol, 44 g carbohydrate, 4 g fibre, 788 mg sodium, 583 mg potassium

Tofu Vegetable Shish Kabobs

My daughter-in-law, Jesse Pierce, makes these kabobs at the cottage in the summer. The longer the tofu marinates, the more flavourful it will be. She soaks wooden skewers in water for at least 15 minutes before using to prevent them from charring.

2 tbsp	each apple cider vinegar and sodium-reduced soy sauce	25 mL
1 tbsp	sesame oil	15 mL
1 tbsp	minced gingerroot	15 mL
1½ tsp	granulated sugar	7 mL
½ tsp	hot chili paste or hot pepper sauce	2 mL
10 oz	extra-firm tofu, cut into 16 pieces (about ½ inch/1 cm)	300 g
1	red onion, quartered and separated into pieces	1
1	sweet red, yellow or green pepper, cut in 1-inch (2.5 cm) pieces	1
1	yellow or green zucchini, cut in ¾-inch (2 cm) thick slices	1
3	wooden skewers	3
	Coriander (cilantro) leaves (optional)	

In large bowl, combine vinegar, soy sauce, sesame oil, gingerroot, sugar and hot chili paste; add tofu and stir to coat. Let stand for at least 1 hour or cover and refrigerate for up to 1 day.

Add onion, red pepper and zucchini to tofu mixture; stir to coat with marinade. Reserving marinade, alternately thread pieces of tofu, then coriander leaves (if using), zucchini, pepper and onion onto skewers.

Place on greased grill over medium-high heat; close lid and cook, turning once and basting occasionally with reserved marinade, for 8 to 10 minutes or until browned.

MAKES 3 SERVINGS

MAKE AHEAD: Marinate tofu, covered and refrigerated, for up to 1 day. Cover and set aside threaded skewers for up to 2 hours, basting with marinade occasionally.

NOTE: There are many ways to use tofu. Marinate ½-inch (1 cm) thick slices or cubes of firm tofu in this marinade or in soy sauce, sesame oil and chopped gingerroot; bake in 375°F (190°C) oven for 15 minutes, or broil, barbecue or add to stir-fries.

Add small chunks of plain or marinated firm tofu to pasta sauces, chili, tacos, soups, stews and salads.

Mix chopped medium tofu with onion, celery, light mayonnaise and fresh herbs or a touch of curry or cumin. Use as a sandwich filling.

Add soft tofu to spreads, dips or salad dressings.

PER SERVING: 171 calories, 12 g protein, 9 g total fat, 1 g saturated fat, 0 mg cholesterol, 14 g carbohydrate, 3 g fibre, 258 mg sodium, 556 mg potassium

Quick Tomato, Broccoli and Red Onion Pizza

Pizza makes a great snack or a quick supper, and juicy vegetable toppings make a pleasing combination of flavours.

1	12-inch (30 cm) uncooked pizza crust	1
¼ cup	tomato sauce*	50 mL
1½ tsp	dried oregano	7 mL
Half	sweet green pepper, chopped	Half
1	medium tomato, sliced	1
1 cup	small broccoli florets	250 mL
½ cup	thinly sliced red onion rings	125 mL
2 tbsp	chopped fresh basil (or ¼ tsp/1 mL dried)	25 mL
1 cup	shredded part-skim mozzarella cheese	250 mL
Pinch	crushed red pepper flakes	Pinch

Place pizza crust on nonstick baking sheet or pizza pan. Spread tomato sauce over crust; sprinkle with oregano. Arrange green pepper, tomato, broccoli, onion and basil over sauce. Sprinkle with cheese, then red pepper flakes.

Bake in 450°F (230°C) oven for 10 minutes or until cheese is bubbly.

MAKES 4 SERVINGS

*To reduce sodium, instead of tomato sauce, use 2 tbsp (25 mL) tomato paste mixed with 2 tbsp (25 mL) water.

NOTE: You can make your own great-tasting pizza in less time than it takes to have one delivered. You'll save money as well. See page 174 for a whole-wheat pizza dough recipe. Or, pick up ready-made pizza crusts at any supermarket to keep on hand in the refrigerator or freezer (frozen crusts don't need to be thawed before using). You might also buy ready-made pizza dough, either fresh or frozen, if you have the time to roll it out. For other quick crusts, use pita bread rounds, English muffins, Armenian- or Italian-style flatbread, or large flour tortillas, or make pizza subs using French bread halved lengthwise.

PER SERVING: 315 calories, 16 g protein, 10 g total fat, 4 g saturated fat, 19 mg cholesterol, 44 g carbohydrate, 6 g fibre, 548 mg sodium, 426 mg potassium

Sweet Pepper and Mushroom Pizza

Vegetable toppings make the best-tasting pizza—juicy and flavourful. See above for more on pizza crusts.

2	12-inch (30 cm) uncooked pizza crusts	2
¾ cup	water	175 mL
¼ cup	tomato paste	50 mL
1½ tsp	dried oregano	7 mL
Half	sweet red pepper, cut in strips	Half
Half	sweet yellow or green pepper, cut in strips	Half
1 cup	sliced mushrooms	250 mL
1	small onion, thinly sliced	1
2 cups	shredded part-skim mozzarella cheese	500 mL

Place each pizza crust on nonstick baking sheet or pizza pan. Combine water, tomato paste and oregano; spread over each crust. Arrange red and yellow peppers, mushrooms and onion on each crust. Sprinkle with cheese. Bake in 450°F (230°C) oven for 12 minutes or until cheese is bubbly.

MAKES 8 SERVINGS

NOTE: Feel free to add your own favourite vegetable toppings, or try zucchini, broccoli, cauliflower, artichokes, sliced tomato or eggplant. Vegetable toppings add fibre, vitamins and minerals, and take only seconds to prepare. Avoid salty or higher fat toppings such as anchovies, olives and high-fat cheese.

PER SERVING: 302 calories, 15 g protein, 10 g total fat, 4 g saturated fat, 19 mg cholesterol, 41 g carbohydrate, 5 g fibre, 466 mg sodium, 354 mg potassium

Fresh Tomato Pizza

I don't like too much cheese on my pizzas because it makes for a salty, greasy pizza. Instead I love to add fresh basil. This version has far less fat than the regular cheese variety, and is especially nice when Armenian- or Italian-style flatbread is used as the crust. To serve as an appetizer, cut into bite-size squares.

1	12-inch (30 cm) pizza crust or flatbread round	1
1 cup	shredded part-skim mozzarella cheese	250 mL
½ cup	very thinly sliced onion (preferably Spanish or sweet)	125 mL
2 tbsp	chopped fresh basil (or 1 tsp/5 mL dried)	25 mL
1 to 2 tsp	dried oregano	5 to 10 mL
2	large tomatoes, thinly sliced	2
2 tbsp	freshly grated Parmesan cheese	25 mL

On baking sheet, sprinkle pizza crust with mozzarella, onion and half of the basil and oregano. Arrange tomato slices over top; sprinkle with Parmesan and remaining basil and oregano. Bake in 450°F (230°C) oven for 15 minutes or until cheese is bubbly.

MAKES 4 SERVINGS

MAKE AHEAD: Assemble pizza, cover and set aside at room temperature for up to 1 hour or refrigerate for up to 3 hours before baking.

VARIATIONS:
Choose low-fat, low-calorie pizza toppings. On top of the tomatoes, sprinkle one or two of the following:

- chopped jalapeño or sweet peppers
- chopped purple peppers
- sliced rehydrated sun-dried tomatoes
- caramelized onion
- artichoke hearts, halved
- lightly cooked asparagus or broccoli
- wild or button mushrooms
- arugula
- fresh or dried figs, sliced
- chèvre (soft goat cheese) or feta cheese
- fresh herbs such as basil, coriander, oregano
- non-vegetarians might add slivers of barbecued shrimp, chicken or meats; avoid bacon and pepperoni, both high in sodium and fat

Pesto Pizza
Spread ⅓ cup (75 mL) Pesto (p. 41) over pizza base. Top with any combination of pizza toppings, including roasted vegetables, goat cheese, mushrooms and sliced fresh tomatoes or cherry tomatoes.

PER SERVING: 317 calories, 17 g protein, 11 g total fat, 4 g saturated fat, 22 mg cholesterol, 41 g carbohydrate, 5 g fibre, 513 mg sodium, 399 mg potassium

Deep-Dish Vegetable Pizza

This scrumptious pizza is very filling. Two slices are plenty for dinner along with a salad.

	Whole-Wheat Pizza Dough (p. 174)	
1 cup	tomato sauce	250 mL
1 tbsp	minced fresh garlic	15 mL
1 tsp	each crushed dried oregano and basil	5 mL
1 tsp	canola or olive oil	5 mL
2 cups	thinly sliced onions	500 mL
2 cups	sliced mushrooms	500 mL
	Freshly ground pepper	
4 cups	broccoli pieces (about ¾ inch/2 cm)	1 L
2½ cups	shredded part-skim mozzarella cheese	625 mL

Divide dough into 2 portions.* Roll out pieces to fit two 10-inch (25 cm) round quiche or cake pans that are at least 1 inch (2.5 cm) deep.

In small bowl, combine tomato sauce, garlic, oregano and basil; set aside.

In nonstick skillet, heat oil over medium heat. Add onions; cook, stirring, over medium-low heat for 5 to 10 minutes or until tender. Add mushrooms; cook over medium heat, stirring occasionally, until lightly browned and liquid has evaporated. Season with pepper to taste; set aside.

In large pot of boiling water, cook broccoli for 2 minutes or until bright green; drain and cool under cold running water to prevent any further cooking. Drain well and set aside.

Spread tomato mixture over dough. Cover with broccoli, then with mushroom mixture. Sprinkle with cheese. Bake in 450°F (230°C) oven for 25 to 35 minutes or until crust is browned and top is bubbly.

MAKES 8 SERVINGS

*This method makes a thick crust. If you want a thin crust, divide dough into three portions and freeze the extra dough to make another pizza later.

NOTE: One serving is a very high source of vitamin C, folacin and fibre and a high source of iron, vitamin A and calcium.

PER SERVING: 330 calories, 17 g protein, 11 g total fat, 4 g saturated fat, 19 mg cholesterol, 46 g carbohydrate, 6 g fibre, 635 mg sodium, 518 mg potassium

Whole-Wheat Pizza Dough

Use this basic dough for any type of pizza. It's very quick and easy to make in a food processor, too. Whole-wheat flour adds colour, flavour, fibre and vitamins. See page 172 for topping suggestions.

1 tsp	granulated sugar	5 mL
1 cup	warm water	250 mL
1	pkg active dry yeast (1 tbsp/15 mL)	1
1½ cups	all-purpose flour (approx)	375 mL
1½ cups	whole-wheat flour (approx)	375 mL
1 tsp or less	salt	5 mL or less
2 tbsp	canola oil	25 mL

In large mixing bowl, dissolve sugar in warm water. Sprinkle yeast over water and let stand for 10 minutes or until foamy. Meanwhile, in separate bowl, combine all-purpose and whole-wheat flours and salt.

Stir oil into foamy yeast mixture. Stir in about half of the flour mixture. Add more flour, mixing until dough can be gathered into a slightly sticky ball (you may need a little more or less than 3 cups/750 mL of flour).

On lightly floured surface, knead dough for about 5 minutes or until smooth and elastic, adding flour as necessary to prevent dough from sticking to working surface. Cut dough in half; cover with waxed paper and let stand for 10 minutes.

On lightly floured surface, use a rolling pin to roll each piece of dough into 12-inch (30 cm) circle, about ¼-inch (5 mm) thick. Transfer rounds to 2 lightly oiled pizza pans or baking sheets. Carefully, using fingers, stretch dough into large circles.

Let dough rise for about 15 minutes before adding toppings. For a thicker crust, let dough rise for 30 minutes. Add toppings of your choice just before baking.

Bake in lower half of 475°F (240°C) oven for 13 to 16 minutes or until crust is golden brown and cheese is bubbly.

MAKES TWO 12-INCH (30 CM) PIZZA ROUNDS

MAKE AHEAD: Freeze dough for up to 3 weeks.

NOTE: One serving is a very high source of iron, folacin and fibre.

VARIATIONS:

Food Processor Dough
In measuring cup, combine sugar and warm water; add yeast and let stand until foamy. In food processor bowl, combine whole-wheat flour, 1 cup (250 mL) of the all-purpose flour and salt. Add oil to yeast mixture. While processing, pour yeast mixture into feed tube. Process 30 seconds. Turn onto floured board and knead in enough of the remaining flour to prevent dough from sticking to board. Roll out as directed.

Larger Regular Pizza
This recipe also makes two 16- × 12-inch (40 × 30 cm) rectangular pizzas. Bake in 475°F (240°C) oven for 13 to 15 minutes or until crust is crisp and top is bubbling.

PER ¼ PIZZA: 198 calories, 6 g protein, 4 g total fat, 0 g saturated fat, 0 mg cholesterol, 35 g carbohydrate, 4 g fibre, 296 mg sodium, 146 mg potassium

Pasta with Tomatoes, Cheese and Jalapeños

Keep a jar of pickled jalapeños in your refrigerator to add zing to this easy pasta dish. Vary the amount or kind of hot pepper, depending on your tastes. Serve with toasted whole-wheat buns and a green salad.

12 oz	linguine or other pasta	375 g
2 tbsp	minced fresh garlic	25 mL
1 cup	coarsely chopped parsley	250 mL
2 tbsp	chopped pickled jalapeño peppers	25 mL
2 tbsp	olive oil	25 mL
3	large tomatoes, chopped	3
1 cup	freshly grated Parmesan or Romano cheese	250 mL

In large pot of boiling water, cook linguine until tender yet firm; drain.

Meanwhile, in food processor, chop garlic, parsley and peppers until fine.

In nonstick skillet, heat oil over high heat; cook garlic mixture and tomatoes for 1 minute or until hot. Toss with linguine. Add cheese and toss to mix.

MAKES 6 SERVINGS

NOTE: Any leftovers can be covered and refrigerated; to reheat, add a spoonful or two of water, cover and microwave until hot.

VARIATION: Use 1 can (28 oz/ 796 mL) tomatoes, undrained (chopped), instead of fresh. Cook garlic mixture in oil for 1 minute; add tomatoes and simmer, uncovered, for 5 minutes. Toss with pasta and cheese.

PER SERVING: 344 calories, 15 g protein, 10 g total fat, 4 g saturated fat, 15 mg cholesterol, 48 g carbohydrate, 4 g fibre, 314 mg sodium, 335 mg potassium

Penne with Tomato, Black Olives and Feta

I make this pasta dish often in the fall, when tomatoes are at their best. Try locally grown tomatoes from farmers' markets.

1 lb	penne, fusilli or other short pasta	500 g
1 tbsp	olive oil	15 mL
1 tbsp	minced fresh garlic	15 mL
4	large tomatoes, cut in chunks	4
⅓ cup	black olives, pitted and halved	75 mL
½ cup	crumbled light feta cheese	125 mL
½ cup	chopped fresh parsley	125 mL
½ cup	chopped fresh basil (or 1 tbsp/15 mL dried)	125 mL
¼ cup	freshly grated Parmesan cheese	50 mL

In large pot of boiling water, cook pasta until tender but firm; drain and return to pot to keep warm.

Meanwhile, in large nonstick skillet, heat oil over medium heat; stir in garlic. Add tomatoes and cook, stirring, for 3 minutes or until heated through.

Transfer to pot with drained pasta; add olives, feta cheese, parsley and basil; toss gently to mix. Sprinkle each serving with Parmesan.

MAKES 6 MAIN-COURSE SERVINGS

PER SERVING: 379 calories, 15 g protein, 8 g total fat, 3 g saturated fat, 8 mg cholesterol, 63 g carbohydrate, 6 g fibre, 302 mg sodium, 382 mg potassium

Pasta e Fagioli

This hearty pasta-and-bean dish proves that healthy eating is not expensive. If you have the time, to save money, reduce sodium and improve texture and flavour, instead of using canned beans, cook dried beans and peas; use 2 cups (500 mL), cooked, of each.

2 cups	small pasta or broken noodles (6 oz/175 g)	500 mL
1 tbsp	olive oil	15 mL
1	large onion, chopped	1
2	medium carrots, chopped	2
2 tsp	minced fresh garlic	10 mL
¼ tsp	crushed red pepper flakes	1 mL
1 tsp	each dried basil, rosemary and oregano	5 mL
1	can (28 oz/796 mL) plum tomatoes, undrained, chopped	1
1	can (19 oz/540 mL) kidney beans, drained and rinsed	1
1	can (19 oz/540 mL) chickpeas, drained and rinsed	1
¼ tsp or less	salt and freshly ground pepper	1 mL or less
2 tbsp	freshly grated Parmesan cheese	25 mL
½ cup	chopped fresh parsley	125 mL

In large pot of boiling water, cook pasta until tender but firm; drain.

Meanwhile, in large saucepan, heat oil over medium heat; cook onion, carrots, garlic and red pepper flakes until tender. Add basil, rosemary, oregano and tomatoes; bring to boil. Add beans, chickpeas and cooked pasta; mix gently and simmer for 2 minutes.

Season with salt and pepper. Serve in soup bowls and sprinkle with Parmesan, then parsley.

MAKES 6 SERVINGS, 1¼ CUPS (300 mL) EACH

MAKE AHEAD: If you don't like last-minute dinner party cooking but want to serve pasta, take a tip from chefs. They usually cook (making sure they don't overcook) pasta a few hours before serving, then drain it and keep it in cold water. Just before serving, they reheat it in boiling water for 1 minute. When possible, prepare the sauce ahead of time and reheat. Otherwise, chop and measure all sauce ingredients, then it's easy to cook it at the last minute.

PER SERVING: 353 calories, 16 g protein, 5 g total fat, 1 g saturated fat, 2 mg cholesterol, 63 g carbohydrate, 11 g fibre, 668 mg sodium, 764 mg potassium

Pasta Provençal

Use medium-size penne or seashell pasta (conchiglie) in this recipe. Zucchini, grilled eggplant, capers or black olives can also be added. If you have a vegan in your family, they will appreciate this recipe (minus the Parmesan).

8 oz	penne or seashell pasta	250 g
1 tbsp	olive oil	15 mL
1	large onion, chopped	1
1	sweet green or red pepper, chopped	1
2 tbsp	minced fresh garlic	25 mL
8 oz	mushrooms, sliced	250 g
1	can (28 oz/796 mL) tomatoes, chopped	1
¼ tsp	red pepper flakes	1 mL
1¼ cups	diced extra-firm tofu	300 mL
⅓ cup	packed chopped fresh parsley	75 mL
⅓ cup	packed chopped fresh basil (or 1½ tsp/7 mL dried)	75 mL
¼ cup	freshly grated Parmesan cheese	50 mL

In pot of boiling water, cook pasta for 7 to 10 minutes or until tender but firm; drain.

Meanwhile, in large nonstick saucepan, heat oil over medium heat; cook onion, green pepper, garlic and mushrooms for 5 to 8 minutes or until tender. Add tomatoes and red pepper flakes; boil for 6 minutes or until thickened slightly.

Add tofu, parsley and basil. Toss with pasta; sprinkle with Parmesan.

MAKES 4 SERVINGS

MAKE AHEAD: Prepare, cover and refrigerate sauce for up to 1 day. Add tofu, parsley, basil and pasta before serving.

NOTE: I go easy on the amounts of spices, herbs and seasonings in these recipes, assuming that anyone who likes spicier tastes will add more. It's much easier to add spice than to take it away.

PER SERVING: 426 calories, 21 g protein, 11 g total fat, 2 g saturated fat, 6 mg cholesterol, 66 g carbohydrate, 7 g fibre, 370 mg sodium, 870 mg potassium

Penne with Creamy Tomato Sauce

Creamy pasta dishes can be low in fat. Using light ricotta cheese and low-fat milk keeps the fat down in this easy-to-make dish.

1 tbsp	olive oil	15 mL
1	onion, chopped	1
2	cloves garlic, minced	2
1	can (28 oz/796 mL) tomatoes	1
¼ tsp	hot red pepper flakes or chili paste	1 mL
½ cup	chopped fresh parsley	125 mL
2 tbsp	chopped fresh oregano (or 1 tbsp/15 mL crushed dried)	25 mL
1 cup	light ricotta cheese	250 mL
¼ cup	2% milk	50 mL
1 lb	penne (about 5 cups/1.25 L)	500 g
¼ tsp or less	salt and freshly ground pepper	1 mL or less
¼ cup	freshly grated Parmesan cheese	50 mL

In heavy saucepan, heat oil over medium heat. Add onion and garlic; cook for 3 minutes. In food processor or blender, purée tomatoes and add to saucepan along with hot red pepper flakes; bring to boil. Reduce heat and simmer, uncovered, for 20 minutes or until thickened. Add parsley and oregano; remove from heat. In food processor or blender, purée ricotta and milk until smooth; stir into tomato mixture.

Meanwhile, in large pot of boiling water, cook penne for 8 to 10 minutes or until tender but firm. Drain well and toss with sauce. Season with salt and pepper. Sprinkle with Parmesan.

MAKES 6 SERVINGS

NOTE: Don't substitute milk with 1% or less MF for 2% milk in this recipe—it will result in a less creamy, thinner pasta sauce.

One serving is a very high source of iron and folacin and a high source of calcium, vitamin C, vitamin A and fibre.

PER SERVING: 403 calories, 18 g protein, 8 g total fat, 3 g saturated fat, 10 mg cholesterol, 66 g carbohydrate, 5 g fibre, 396 mg sodium, 452 mg potassium

Pasta with Sweet Peppers, Cheese and Basil

This colourful pasta dish makes a great supper: it will make four servings (unless you have teenage boys!) if you serve it with a vegetable such as broccoli or green beans, a salad and French bread. Don't use canned olives for this dish.

PER SERVING: 373 calories, 16 g protein, 10 g total fat, 5 g saturated fat, 13 mg cholesterol, 57 g carbohydrate, 5 g fibre, 602 mg sodium, 340 mg potassium

8 oz	rigatoni or fusilli	250 g
1 tsp	olive oil	5 mL
1	small onion, minced	1
1	clove garlic, minced	1
1	each medium sweet red and yellow pepper, cut in strips	1
1	large tomato, chopped	1
½ cup	finely shredded fresh basil (or 2 tsp/10 mL dried)	125 mL
1 cup	crumbled light feta cheese (4 oz/125 g)	250 mL
6	black olives (preferably Kalamata), pitted and sliced	6

In large pot of boiling water, cook pasta until tender but firm; drain and return to pot.

Meanwhile, in large nonstick skillet, heat oil over medium heat; cook onion and garlic for 3 minutes. Add red and yellow peppers; cook for 3 minutes, stirring often. Add tomato; cook until peppers are tender, about 2 minutes. Add to hot pasta along with basil, cheese and olives; toss well.

MAKES 4 SERVINGS

Fettuccine with Pesto Sauce

Pesto, a vibrant Italian sauce made with fresh basil, garlic and Parmesan is perfect with pasta. This version of pesto has less oil than most and no pine nuts so it is lower in fat and calories without any loss in flavour

12 oz	fettuccine	375 g
¼ tsp or less	salt and freshly ground pepper	1 mL or less
	Freshly grated Parmesan cheese	

PESTO SAUCE

3	cloves garlic	3
1½ cups	packed fresh basil	375 mL
½ cup	freshly grated Parmesan cheese	125 mL
2 tbsp	olive oil	25 mL

In large pot of boiling water, cook fettuccine for 8 to 10 minutes or until tender but firm.

PESTO SAUCE: Meanwhile, with food processor on, drop garlic through tube; process until chopped. Add basil; process to chop. Add Parmesan and olive oil; process until smooth. Remove ½ cup (125 mL) of the pasta cooking liquid and add to sauce; process until smooth.

Drain pasta and toss with pesto sauce. Sprinkle with salt, pepper, and Parmesan to taste.

MAKES 6 SERVINGS

VARIATIONS: Add cooked large shrimps, halved slow-roasted regular cherry tomatoes, grilled vegetables, rehydrated sun-dried tomatoes cut into strips, black olives or strips of grilled chicken.

NOTE: Use any leftover Pesto Sauce by spreading it on pizza, instead of tomato sauce. Add a spoonful to soups or stews or salad dressings, spread it on chicken or salmon before grilling, stuff it under the skin of chicken, or add it to pasta salads.

PER SERVING: 290 calories, 11 g protein, 8 g total fat, 2 g saturated fat, 7 mg cholesterol, 43 g carbohydrate, 3 g fibre, 227 mg sodium, 137 mg potassium

Fettuccine with Fresh Tomatoes, Basil and Shrimp

Use any kind or shape of pasta you like in this easy dish—my husband likes long types, whereas I prefer short. For a vegetarian dish, omit the shrimp and add cubes of firm tofu or chickpeas. Try using tomatoes from your local farmers' market—they're often more flavourful than the ones found in supermarkets.

8 oz	fettuccine or other pasta	250 g
1 tbsp	olive oil	15 mL
2 tbsp	minced fresh garlic	25 mL
3	large tomatoes, coarsely chopped	3
1 lb	peeled and deveined large shrimp*	500 g
⅓ cup	each chopped fresh basil and parsley	75 mL
½ cup	freshly grated Parmesan cheese	125 mL
¼ tsp or less	salt and freshly ground pepper	1 mL or less

In large pot of boiling water, cook pasta until tender but firm; drain and return to pot.

Meanwhile, in nonstick skillet, heat oil over medium-high heat; cook garlic, stirring, for 1 minute. Add tomatoes; cook, stirring, for 2 minutes. Add shrimp; cook until heated through and pink in colour, about 2 minutes for cooked shrimp, 4 minutes if using raw shrimp. Add to hot pasta along with basil, parsley, Parmesan, and salt and pepper; toss to mix.

MAKES 4 SERVINGS, 2 CUPS (500 mL) EACH

*If using frozen shrimp, thaw completely and drain thoroughly before using.

NOTE: Heritage tomatoes, often available at local farmers' markets, are grown from seeds saved from old varieties, as opposed to the hybrid tomatoes you find in the supermarkets.

They come in a wide range of sizes and colours—from red to purple to striped—and taste wonderful.

PER SERVING: 433 calories, 37 g protein, 9 g total fat, 3 g saturated fat, 225 mg cholesterol, 49 g carbohydrate, 5 g fibre, 604 mg sodium, 612 mg potassium

Easy Linguine with Scallops and Spinach

Tasty and colourful, this quick pasta dish is also relatively low in fat, high in complex carbohydrates and a very high source of iron and folacin.

8 oz	linguine	250 g
½ cup	sodium-reduced chicken broth or white wine	125 mL
1	onion, minced	1
8 oz	scallops (halved if large)	250 g
⅓ cup	light cream cheese	75 mL
2 tbsp	chopped fresh dill or 1 tsp (5 mL) dried basil	25 mL
1 tsp	grated lemon rind	5 mL
2 cups	shredded spinach	500 mL
¼ tsp or less	salt and freshly ground pepper	1 mL or less
2 tbsp	freshly grated Parmesan cheese	25 mL

In large pot of boiling water, cook linguine until tender but firm; drain and return to pot.

Meanwhile, in small saucepan, bring stock to simmer; add onion and scallops. Cover and simmer for 4 minutes or until scallops are opaque throughout. (Time will vary depending on size of scallops: bay scallops will cook in about 2 minutes.) Using slotted spoon, remove scallops to bowl and keep warm.

Stir cream cheese, dill and lemon rind into hot cooking liquid; stir over medium heat until smooth. Pour over pasta and toss. Add spinach and scallops; toss. Season with salt and pepper. Sprinkle each serving with Parmesan.

MAKES 3 SERVINGS

VARIATION: To reduce the calories and cholesterol in this dish, substitute low-fat cottage cheese for the light cream cheese. Purée cottage cheese in a blender or food processor or pass through a sieve, then stir into cooking liquid with lemon rind and dill.

PER SERVING: 441 calories, 28 g protein, 8 g total fat, 4 g saturated fat, 45 mg cholesterol, 63 g carbohydrate, 4 g fibre, 669 mg sodium, 528 mg potassium

Pasta with Shrimp, Zucchini and Mushrooms

Pasta picks up the delicate shrimp flavour in this wonderful, light dish. Penne or rigatoni work well in this recipe, though feel free to use whatever kind of pasta you have on hand. I also like to add fresh herbs, such as basil or dill.

1 lb	penne or rigatoni	500 g
3 tbsp	olive oil	50 mL
4	small (about 7-inch/18 cm) zucchini, julienned	4
8 oz	mushrooms, sliced	250 g
2 lb	large raw shrimp, peeled and deveined	1 kg
3	cloves garlic, minced	3
1	large tomato, diced	1
½ cup	chopped fresh parsley	125 mL
¼ cup	freshly grated Parmesan cheese	50 mL
2 tbsp	fresh lemon juice	25 mL
¼ tsp or less	salt and freshly ground pepper	1 mL or less

In large pot of boiling water, cook pasta until tender but firm; drain and return to pot.

Meanwhile, in large nonstick skillet, heat 1 tbsp (15 mL) of the oil over high heat; stir-fry zucchini and mushrooms until tender-crisp, about 3 minutes. Transfer to bowl.

In skillet, heat remaining oil over high heat; cook shrimp and garlic, stirring, for 3 minutes or until shrimp are opaque. Add tomato and cook for 1 minute.

Add shrimp and zucchini mixtures (including all liquids) to pot with hot pasta. Add parsley, cheese and lemon juice; toss to mix. Season with salt and pepper.

MAKES 8 SERVINGS

PER SERVING: 382 calories, 29 g protein, 8 g total fat, 2 g saturated fat, 183 mg cholesterol, 47 g carbohydrate, 4 g fibre, 336 mg sodium, 508 mg potassium

Capellini with Clam Sauce and Sweet Red Peppers

Capellini are the thinnest of pasta noodles, though this recipe works well with any kind of pasta. Whole-wheat noodles add a boost of fibre. Serve this easy-to-make dish with steamed snow peas or a tossed spinach salad. It's a great choice for company when you don't have much preparation time.

2	sweet red peppers	2
1 tbsp	olive oil	15 mL
	Freshly ground pepper	
4	cloves garlic, minced	4
1 cup	dry white wine	250 mL
2	cans (5 oz/142 g each) clams, drained	2
1 tsp	chopped fresh thyme (or ½ tsp/2 mL crushed dried)	5 mL
Pinch	hot red pepper flakes	Pinch
½ cup	minced fresh parsley	125 mL
¼ tsp or less	salt	1 mL or less
8 oz	capellini or other pasta	250 g
½ cup	grated Parmesan cheese	125 mL

Core and seed red peppers; cut into thin strips.

In heavy nonstick skillet, heat half of the oil over medium heat. Add red peppers and half of the garlic; cook, stirring often, until peppers are tender, about 10 minutes. Season with freshly ground pepper.

Meanwhile, in saucepan, heat remaining oil over medium heat. Add remaining garlic; cook, stirring, for 1 minute. Add wine, clams, thyme and hot pepper flakes; simmer for 5 minutes. Add parsley, and salt and more pepper.

Meanwhile, in large pot of boiling water, cook capellini until tender but firm; drain and arrange on warm plates. Pour sauce over pasta; surround with sautéed red peppers. Sprinkle pasta with Parmesan.

MAKES 4 MAIN-COURSE OR 8 APPETIZER SERVINGS

MAKE AHEAD: Prepare red peppers and sauce; cover and refrigerate for up to 2 hours.

NOTE: One serving is high in fibre and is an excellent source of vitamin C (providing close to twice the daily value), vitamin A, folacin and iron.

PER MAIN-COURSE SERVING: 433 calories, 22 g protein, 12 g total fat, 3 g saturated fat, 35 mg cholesterol, 50 g carbohydrate, 4 g fibre, 388 mg sodium, 488 mg potassium

Linguine with Scallops and Leeks

Serve this linguine with baby carrots, a tossed salad and garlic bread.

1 tbsp	olive oil	15 mL
2 cups	chopped leeks (white and light green parts only)	500 mL
2 tbsp	all-purpose flour	25 mL
1½ cups	2% milk	375 mL
½ cup	dry white wine	125 mL
1 lb	scallops	500 g
¼ cup	chopped Italian (flat-leaf) parsley	50 mL
2 tbsp	chopped fresh chives or green onions	25 mL
8 oz	linguine	250 g
½ cup	freshly grated Parmesan cheese	125 mL
¼ tsp or less	salt and freshly ground pepper	1 mL or less

In large nonstick skillet, heat oil over medium-low heat; cook leeks, covered, for 10 minutes or until tender. (If mixture sticks to pan, add 1 tbsp/15 mL water, or more.)

Sprinkle flour over leeks; cook, stirring, for 1 minute. Gradually add milk, stirring constantly; bring to simmer. Cook, stirring, for 2 to 3 minutes or until thickened. Gradually whisk in wine until mixture is smooth.

Add scallops to leek mixture; cook over low heat for 2 to 3 minutes or until scallops are opaque. Stir in parsley and chives.

Meanwhile, in large pot of boiling water, cook linguine until tender but firm; drain and return to saucepan. Pour leek mixture into hot pasta; add Parmesan, and salt and pepper and toss gently.

MAKES 4 SERVINGS, 2 CUPS (500 mL) EACH

MAKE AHEAD: Prepare leek mixture up to 3 hours in advance. Add scallops and remaining ingredients as directed when ready to serve.

NOTE: Don't substitute milk with 1% or less MF for 2% milk in this recipe—it will result in a less creamy, thinner pasta sauce.

For the best taste, grate your own Parmesan cheese: it's easy to do in a food processor or with a hand grater and it will have much more flavour than pre-grated cheese. I sometimes put a piece of Parmesan cheese and a grater on the table so everyone can grate their own as they wish.

PER SERVING: 471 calories, 35 g protein, 11 g total fat, 4 g saturated fat, 56 mg cholesterol, 53 g carbohydrate, 3 g fibre, 563 mg sodium, 619 mg potassium

Lighthearted Fettuccine Alfredo

This light version of a classic has a surprisingly rich flavour.

8 oz	fettuccine or spaghetti	250 g
1 cup	2% cottage cheese	250 mL
¼ cup	freshly grated Parmesan cheese	50 mL
¼ cup	2% milk	50 mL
1	egg	1
¼ tsp	nutmeg	1 mL
¼ tsp	freshly ground pepper	1 mL
½ cup	chopped fresh parsley or basil	125 mL

In large pot of boiling water, cook fettuccine until tender but firm; drain and return to saucepan.

Meanwhile, in food processor, process cottage cheese until smooth. Add Parmesan, milk, egg, nutmeg and pepper; blend until smooth. Pour into saucepan with hot cooked pasta; cook over medium heat for 1 minute or until thickened, stirring constantly. Sprinkle with parsley. Serve immediately.

MAKES 4 SERVINGS

VARIATIONS:

Add one or more of the following:

- 1 cup (250 mL) chopped cooked ham
- 1 can (7½ oz/220 g) salmon, drained and flaked
- 1 can (6½ oz/184 g) tuna, drained and flaked
- 1 cup (250 mL) frozen peas, thawed
- ½ cup (125 mL) corn kernels or chopped green onion
- 1 cup (250 mL) cooked sliced mushrooms
- 1 cup (250 mL) cooked julienned carrots, zucchini, sweet peppers or leeks
- 4 cups (1 L) cooked broccoli florets

NOTE: Don't substitute milk with 1% or less MF for the 2% milk called for in this recipe—it will result in a less creamy, thinner pasta sauce.

PER SERVING: 315 calories, 19 g protein, 6 g total fat, 3 g saturated fat, 58 mg cholesterol, 45 g carbohydrate, 3 g fibre, 352 mg sodium, 190 mg potassium

Pasta with Broccoli, Mushrooms and Cauliflower in Basil-Cream Sauce

Your family will love this quick and easy pasta dish. The variety of vegetables you can use is limitless—try adding carrots, snow peas, celery or green beans. Evaporated milk gives a rich creamy sauce with a minimum of fat.

4 cups	broccoli florets	1 L
4 cups	cauliflower florets	1 L
4 oz	whole-wheat noodles or spaghettini	125 g
1 tbsp	olive or canola oil	15 mL
3	cloves garlic, minced	3
2½ cups	thickly sliced mushrooms	625 mL
½ cup	chopped fresh basil (or 4 tsp/20 mL crushed dried)	125 mL
4 tsp	all-purpose flour	20 mL
½ tsp or less	each salt and freshly ground pepper	2 mL or less
1	can (370 mL) 2% evaporated milk (or 1½ cups/375 mL 2% milk)	1
¼ cup	freshly grated Parmesan cheese	50 mL

In large pot of boiling water, cook broccoli and cauliflower until tender-crisp, about 5 minutes. With slotted spoon, remove vegetables and set aside. Add pasta to boiling cooking water; cook until al dente (tender but firm), about 10 minutes. Drain well.

Meanwhile, in nonstick skillet, heat oil over medium heat. Add garlic; cook, stirring, for 30 seconds. Increase heat to medium-high. Add mushrooms and basil (if using dried); cook for 3 to 5 minutes until mushrooms are browned and tender, stirring often. Sprinkle evenly with flour, salt and pepper; cook, stirring, for 1 minute.

Stir in milk; boil for 1 minute. Stir in broccoli, cauliflower and Parmesan; cook for 1 minute. Stir in basil (if using fresh). Add noodles and toss to combine well.

MAKES 4 SERVINGS

NOTE: One serving is a very high source of calcium, vitamin C, folacin and fibre and a high source of iron and vitamin A.

PER SERVING: 318 calories, 19 g protein, 9 g total fat, 3 g saturated fat, 13 mg cholesterol, 46 g carbohydrate, 7 g fibre, 545 mg sodium, 884 mg potassium

Family Favourite Spaghetti

A quick dinner that over the years has been my kids' favourite is this spaghetti with meat sauce. Sometimes I use only tomato paste, other times, crushed tomatoes with added purée, sometimes both tomato paste and tomatoes. I often add chopped red or green peppers and sliced mushrooms, a bag of fresh spinach (chopped), arugula or parsley. You can also add sun-dried tomatoes or rehydrated dried mushrooms.

1 lb	lean ground beef	500 g
2	onions, chopped	2
4	large cloves garlic, minced	4
1	can (5½ oz/156 mL) tomato paste	1
1	can (28 oz/796 mL) diced tomatoes	1
1 cup	water	250 mL
2 tbsp	dried oregano	25 mL
1 tsp	dried basil (or ¼ cup/50 mL fresh)	5 mL
½ tsp	dried thyme	2 mL
¼ tsp	freshly ground pepper or hot pepper flakes	1 mL
1 lb	spaghetti	500 g
2 tbsp	freshly grated Parmesan cheese	25 mL

In large heavy skillet, brown beef over medium heat; pour off all fat. Stir in onions and garlic; cook, stirring occasionally until softened.

Stir in tomato paste, tomatoes, water, oregano, basil, thyme and pepper; bring to boil. Reduce heat and simmer for 10 minutes. Add water if too thick. Taste and adjust seasoning if desired.

Meanwhile, in large pot of boiling water, cook spaghetti until tender but firm; drain and arrange on plates. Spoon sauce over each serving. Sprinkle with Parmesan and pass additional cheese at the table.

MAKES 6 SERVINGS

VARIATIONS:
For a vegetarian version, omit beef and add tofu or cooked chickpeas or beans.

Tomato Basil Sauce
Omit beef, spaghetti and cheese, adding instead 1 tsp (5 mL) olive oil and 1 cup (250 mL) coarsely chopped fresh basil or 1 cup (250 mL) chopped fresh parsley and increase dried basil to 2 tbsp (25 mL). Cook onions and garlic in olive oil; add fresh basil or parsley just before using sauce.

PER SERVING: 486 calories, 27 g protein, 10 g total fat, 4 g saturated fat, 41 mg cholesterol, 73 g carbohydrate, 7 g fibre, 281 mg sodium, 921 mg potassium

Italian Sausage, Red Pepper and Mushroom Rigatoni

This is a dish that often comes to mind when I stop at the store at 6 p.m. wondering what to cook for dinner. I like to use hot Italian sausage or, for a less spicy version, sweet Italian sausage or some of each. You can chop the onions and garlic in the food processor to save time. In tomato season, I use three or four fresh tomatoes instead of canned.

1 lb	hot Italian sausage	500 g
1 lb	rigatoni, penne or corkscrew pasta	500 g
1 tsp	canola or olive oil	5 mL
1	large onion, chopped	1
4	cloves garlic, minced	4
2	sweet red peppers, cut in chunks	2
2 cups	thickly sliced mushrooms	500 mL
1	can (28 oz/796 mL) diced tomatoes	1
2 tsp	dried basil	10 mL
2 tsp	dried oregano	10 mL
	Freshly ground pepper	
½ cup	chopped fresh parsley, dill or basil	125 mL
2 tbsp	freshly grated Parmesan cheese, plus more to taste	25 mL

In skillet, cook sausage over medium heat until no longer pink in centre, 15 to 20 minutes. Drain well; cut into thin slices.

Meanwhile, in large pot of boiling water, cook pasta until tender but firm; drain and return to pot.

In nonstick pan, heat oil over medium heat; cook onion until tender, about 5 minutes. Add garlic, red peppers and mushrooms; cook, stirring often for 5 minutes. Add tomatoes, basil and oregano; simmer, uncovered, for 5 minutes. Add cooked sausage, and pepper to taste. Pour over pasta; toss to mix. Sprinkle with parsley and Parmesan; toss again. Pass extra Parmesan at the table.

MAKES 8 SERVINGS

VARIATION:

Pasta with Shrimp and Tomatoes
Substitute 1 lb (500 g) large cooked shrimp for the sausage, or use ½ lb (250 g) each cooked shrimp and sausage. Add shrimp to tomato mixture when adding cooked sausage.

PER SERVING: 396 calories, 17 g protein, 13 g total fat, 4 g saturated fat, 23 mg cholesterol, 53 g carbohydrate, 5 g fibre, 624 mg sodium, 522 mg potassium

Sue Zach's Beef and Pasta Casserole for a Crowd

This crowd-pleasing recipe is from my friend Sue Zacharias. Serve with a green or Caesar salad.

1 lb	penne (5 cups/1.25 L uncooked)	500 g
1 tsp	canola oil	5 mL
2 lb	extra-lean ground beef	1 kg
3	onions, finely chopped	3
2	cloves garlic, minced	2
8 oz	mushrooms, sliced	250 g
2	stalks celery, sliced	2
1	sweet green pepper, chopped	1
1	large can (13 oz/369 mL) tomato paste	1
4 cups	water	1 L
2 tsp	each dried oregano and basil	10 mL
1	pkg (10 oz/284 g) fresh spinach, cooked, drained and chopped	1
¾ lb	part-skim mozzarella cheese, cut in small cubes	375 g
¼ tsp or less	salt and freshly ground pepper	1 mL or less
1 cup	fresh bread crumbs	250 mL
¼ cup	chopped fresh parsley	50 mL
½ cup	freshly grated Parmesan cheese	125 mL

In large pot of boiling water, cook pasta until tender but firm, about 10 minutes, or according to package directions. Drain and rinse under cold running water; drain and set aside.

In large nonstick skillet or Dutch oven, heat oil over medium heat. Add beef, onions and garlic; cook, stirring, for a few minutes or until beef is no longer pink. Drain off fat. Add mushrooms, celery and green pepper; cook for 5 minutes, stirring occasionally. Stir in tomato paste, water, oregano and basil; simmer, covered, for 30 minutes.

Combine meat sauce, spinach, pasta and mozzarella cheese; season with salt and pepper. Spoon into lightly greased 16-cup (4 L) casserole. Sprinkle with bread crumbs, parsley, then Parmesan. Bake, uncovered, in 350°F (180°C) oven for 45 minutes or until bubbly.

MAKES 14 SERVINGS

VARIATION: This recipe can be made with other short pasta, such as fusilli or rotini.

MAKE AHEAD: Cover and refrigerate for up to 2 days in advance. Remove from refrigerator 1 hour before baking. Unbaked dish can also be covered and frozen for up to 1 month. Defrost in refrigerator 2 days or in microwave, if in glass dish.

PER SERVING: 361 calories, 28 g protein, 11 g total fat, 5 g saturated fat, 52 mg cholesterol, 39 g carbohydrate, 5 g fibre, 327 mg sodium, 832 mg potassium

Family Favourite Lasagna

This is your classic lasagna made as healthy as possible by using lean beef, tomato paste (not tomato sauce, which is higher in sodium), 2% cottage cheese (not ricotta or cream cheese) and low-fat or part-skim mozzarella (not regular mozzarella or Cheddar) to keep sodium, fat and cholesterol at a minimum.

12 oz	extra-lean ground beef	375 g
2	onions, chopped	2
2	cloves garlic, minced	2
1	can (19 oz/540 mL) tomatoes, undrained	1
1 cup	water	250 mL
1	can (5½ oz/156 mL) tomato paste	1
2 tsp	dried oregano	10 mL
1 tsp	dried basil	5 mL
	Freshly ground pepper	
1 tsp	granulated sugar, plus more to taste (optional)	5 mL
9	lasagna noodles (8 oz/250 g)	9
2 cups	low-fat cottage cheese	500 mL
1½ cups	shredded part-skim mozzarella cheese	375 mL
1	egg, lightly beaten	1
½ cup	freshly grated Parmesan cheese	125 mL

In large nonstick skillet or Dutch oven, cook beef over medium heat for about 5 minutes or until browned, breaking up with fork; pour off fat. Add onions and garlic; cook for 3 to 5 minutes or until softened. Add tomatoes, breaking up with fork. Add water, tomato paste, oregano and basil; bring to boil. Reduce heat to medium-low and simmer uncovered, stirring occasionally, for 20 minutes or until mixture has spaghetti sauce consistency. Season with pepper to taste. If too acidic, add 1 tsp (5 mL) granulated sugar or to taste.

In large pot of boiling water, cook lasagna noodles for 10 to 12 minutes or until tender but firm. Drain and rinse under cold water; drain well.

Combine cottage cheese, mozzarella, egg and half of the Parmesan.

Cover bottom of 13- × 9-inch (3.5 L) baking dish sparingly with some of the tomato sauce; top with layer of lasagna noodles. Cover with half of the cheese mixture. Repeat with remaining sauce, noodles and cheese mixture to make 3 layers of each, then a final layer of tomato sauce. Sprinkle with remaining Parmesan cheese.

Bake, uncovered, in 350°F (180°C) oven for 45 minutes or until hot and bubbly. Remove from oven and let stand for 5 to 10 minutes before serving.

MAKES 9 SERVINGS

VARIATION:

Vegetarian Lasagna
Omit beef (and egg, if desired). Instead, in a nonstick pan, heat 1 tbsp (15 mL) canola or olive oil over medium heat; add 8 cups (2 L) shredded unpeeled zucchini, 1 sweet red pepper, chopped, and 12 oz (375 g) coarsely chopped mushrooms along with onions and garlic. Cook until tender. Continue with recipe.

PER SERVING: 319 calories, 28 g protein, 10 g total fat, 5 g saturated fat, 62 mg cholesterol, 30 g carbohydrate, 3 g fibre, 528 mg sodium, 618 mg potassium

Mushroom and Sweet Pepper Lasagna

Sweet peppers and mushrooms make this a delicious variation on an old favourite.

| 9 | lasagna noodles (8 oz/250 g) | 9 |
| 1 | pkg (8 oz/250 g) fresh spinach, trimmed | 1 |

TOMATO SAUCE

1 tsp	canola or olive oil	5 mL
1	large onion, chopped	1
12 oz	fresh mushrooms, sliced	375 g
3	cloves garlic, minced	3
¼ cup	chopped fresh parsley	50 mL
1½ tsp	each dried basil and oregano	7 mL
¼ cup	tomato paste	50 mL
1	can (28 oz/796 mL) diced (no salt added) tomatoes, undrained	1
2	sweet red, yellow or green peppers, coarsely chopped	2
¼ tsp or less	salt and freshly ground pepper	1 mL or less

FILLING

2 cups	skim-milk cottage cheese or light ricotta	500 mL
⅓ cup	freshly grated Parmesan cheese	75 mL
1 tsp	dried oregano	5 mL
2½ cups	shredded part-skim mozzarella cheese (15% B.F.)	625 mL

TOMATO SAUCE: In large nonstick skillet, heat oil over medium heat; cook onion and mushrooms for 5 minutes or until tender, stirring often. Stir in garlic, parsley, basil, oregano, tomato paste and tomatoes. Simmer, uncovered, for 10 minutes. Add sweet peppers; simmer for 10 minutes or until sauce is thickened. Season with salt and pepper.

Meanwhile, in large pot of boiling water, cook noodles for 8 to 10 minutes or until tender but firm. With tongs, transfer to cold water. Drain and set aside in single layer on dampened tea towel. Add spinach to boiling pasta water, cook for 1 minute. Drain in sieve, pressing out liquid with back of spoon, chop coarsely, set aside.

FILLING: Combine cottage cheese, half of the Parmesan and the oregano; mix well.

ASSEMBLY: In 13- × 9-inch (3.5 L) baking dish, spread 1 cup (250 mL) tomato sauce over bottom. Top with layer of noodles. Cover with half of the cottage cheese mixture, then one-third of the mozzarella cheese, one half of the spinach and one-third of the remaining sauce. Add another layer of noodles; spread with remaining cottage cheese mixture and spinach. Layer with half of the remaining mozzarella, then half of the remaining sauce and a final layer of noodles. Top with remaining sauce and mozzarella, then remaining Parmesan.

Bake, covered, in 350°F (180°C) oven for 30 minutes. Uncover and bake for 10 to 15 minutes longer or until hot and bubbly. Remove from oven and let cool for 5 minutes before serving.

MAKES 8 SERVINGS

MAKE AHEAD: Assemble lasagna, cover and refrigerate for up to 1 day. Add 15 minutes to baking time. Or, bake lasagna, let cool, wrap with heavy-duty foil and freeze for up to 1 month, thaw in refrigerator about 48 hours. Add 20 minutes to baking time while covered.

VARIATION:

Italian Sausage Lasagna
Add 1 lb (500 g) Italian sausage (I use half sweet and half hot sausage). Omit oil and cook sausage in nonstick skillet over medium-high heat until firm and nearly cooked through, about 15 minutes; remove and cut into thin slices. Discard fat from pan and continue cooking vegetables. Return sausage to pan and add tomato sauce.

PER SERVING: 332 calories, 28 g protein, 10 g total fat, 5 g saturated fat, 32 mg cholesterol, 35 g carbohydrate, 5 g fibre, 486 mg sodium, 718 mg potassium

Pad Thai

An everyday dish in Thailand, this wonderful noodle recipe is from Vancouver chef Karen Barnaby. Pad Thai has many versions, often with stir-fried meat or chicken. Rice noodles are available at many supermarkets; choose the wide flat rice noodles called jantaboon. If these aren't available, use Chinese rice noodles or vermicelli, or even Italian capellini.

8 oz	flat rice noodles	250 g
1 tbsp	canola or olive oil	15 mL
1 tbsp	minced fresh garlic	15 mL
2 cups	thinly sliced cabbage	500 mL
8 oz	large shrimp, peeled and deveined (optional)	250 g
4 oz	firm tofu, cubed	125 g
2	eggs, lightly beaten	2
3 cups	bean sprouts	750 mL
1 cup	julienned green onions	250 mL
½ cup	chopped fresh coriander (cilantro)	125 mL
¼ cup	chopped unsalted peanuts	50 mL
	Lime wedges	

SEASONING SAUCE

1½ tbsp	fish sauce	22 mL
2 tbsp	unseasoned rice vinegar	25 mL
2 tbsp	ketchup	25 mL
2 tbsp	water	25 mL
2 tbsp	packed brown sugar or molasses	25 mL
1½ tbsp	sodium-reduced soy sauce	22 mL
½ tsp	crushed red pepper flakes or fresh chili paste	2 mL

Cover rice noodles in hot water; soak for 10 minutes until soft or according to package directions. Drain well.

SEASONING SAUCE: In small bowl, combine fish sauce, vinegar, ketchup, water, sugar, soy sauce and red pepper flakes; set aside.

In large nonstick skillet, heat oil over medium-high heat; stir in garlic, cabbage and shrimp. Stir-fry for 5 minutes; stir in tofu. Push mixture to side of pan; pour in eggs and stir to scramble. Stir in sauce and bring to a boil.

Add drained noodles; toss to mix well. Add 2 cups (500 mL) of the bean sprouts and green onions; stir until mixed and heated through.

Transfer to serving platter or individual plates. Sprinkle with coriander, peanuts and remaining bean sprouts. Garnish with lime wedges.

MAKES 5 MAIN-COURSE SERVINGS, 8 SIDE-DISH SERVINGS

NOTE: Fish sauce, made from salted, fermented fish, is a flavouring used in much of Southeast Asian cooking. Thai fish sauce is known as nam pla; Vietnamese as nuoc nam. Both are available in Asian grocery stores and some supermarkets. Fish sauce keeps on the shelf for at least a year.

PER MAIN-COURSE SERVING:
344 calories, 11 g protein,
10 g total fat, 2 g saturated fat,
74 mg cholesterol,
55 g carbohydrate, 4 g fibre,
715 mg sodium, 368 mg potassium

Make-Ahead Party Thai Noodles

This noodle dish is particularly suitable for a buffet or when entertaining, as it can be made in advance and reheated. I use spaghetti rather than rice noodles in this dish because it keeps very well in the refrigerator should you prepare the dish a day in advance.

8 oz	spaghetti	250 g
Half	each sweet red and yellow pepper, cut in thin strips	Half
½ cup	chopped fresh coriander (cilantro)	125 mL
⅓ cup	chopped green onion	75 mL
4 cups	bean sprouts	1 L

SAUCE

¼ cup	unseasoned rice vinegar or apple cider vinegar	50 mL
¼ cup	hoisin sauce	50 mL
2 tbsp	hot water	25 mL
1 tbsp	sesame oil	15 mL
1 tbsp	sodium-reduced soy sauce	15 mL
1 tbsp	minced gingerroot	15 mL
1½ tsp	packed brown sugar	7 mL
1½ tsp	minced fresh garlic	7 mL
½ tsp	dry mustard	2 mL
½ tsp	chili paste or hot pepper sauce	2 mL

In large pot of boiling water, cook pasta until tender but firm; drain. Transfer to 12- × 8-inch (3 L) baking dish.

SAUCE: Combine vinegar, hoisin sauce, water, oil, soy sauce, gingerroot, sugar, garlic, mustard and chili paste. Set one-third of the sauce aside; stir remaining sauce into noodles.

Stir in red and yellow peppers, coriander, onion and bean sprouts. Add remaining sauce; bake, covered, in 350°F (180°C) oven for 20 to 30 minutes or until hot.

MAKES 8 SIDE-DISH SERVINGS

MAKE AHEAD: Prepare noodles, sauce and vegetables; combine as directed, (do not add reserved sauce or bake) then cover and refrigerate for up to 1 day. Before baking, let stand at room temperature for 1 hour; add reserved sauce and bake for 30 to 40 minutes.

PER SERVING: 165 calories, 5 g protein, 3 g total fat, 0 g saturated fat, 0 mg cholesterol, 30 g carbohydrate, 2 g fibre, 205 mg sodium, 153 mg potassium

Singapore Noodles with Pork

You can prepare these spicy noodles in a variety of ways: use chicken or beef instead of pork; for a side dish, omit pork; for vegetarians, substitute diced firm tofu for the pork; for special occasions, add large shrimp. Instead of red pepper, use two large carrots, cut in thin strips.

¼ cup	unseasoned rice vinegar or fresh lemon juice	50 mL
¼ cup	sodium-reduced soy sauce	50 mL
2 tbsp	packed brown sugar	25 mL
½ tsp	chili paste or hot pepper sauce	2 mL
8 oz	medium rice vermicelli noodles or very thin regular noodles	250 g
1 tbsp	canola or olive oil	15 mL
1 tbsp	curry powder or 1 tsp (5 mL) curry paste	15 mL
2 tbsp	minced fresh garlic	25 mL
2 tbsp	minced gingerroot	25 mL
1	sweet red pepper, thinly sliced	1
½ lb	lean pork, cut in thin strips	250 g
4 cups	bean sprouts	1 L
1½ cups	frozen peas, thawed	375 mL
½ cup	diagonally sliced green onions	125 mL
¼ cup	chopped fresh coriander (cilantro)	50 mL

Combine vinegar, soy sauce, sugar and chili paste; set aside.

Cook noodles according to package directions; drain.

Meanwhile, in large nonstick skillet, heat oil over medium-high heat; stir in curry powder, garlic and gingerroot; cook for 10 seconds. Add red pepper; stir-fry for 1 minute. Add pork; stir-fry for 3 minutes or until no longer pink inside. Add noodles, bean sprouts, peas and soy sauce mixture; cook, stirring, for 2 minutes or until heated through.

Transfer to platter; sprinkle with onions and coriander.

MAKES 4 SERVINGS

NOTE: These Singapore Noodles are quite mild. Add more chili paste or hot pepper sauce to taste to spice them up, if you like.

PER SERVING: 456 calories, 21 g protein, 8 g total fat, 2 g saturated fat, 37 mg cholesterol, 75 g carbohydrate, 7 g fibre, 652 mg sodium, 555 mg potassium

Szechuan Beef with Noodles

Vacuum-packed chow mein or Cantonese-style steamed noodles are fast and easy to prepare. They're often available in the fresh vegetable section of the supermarket. If unavailable, use vermicelli or other thin noodles. Don't use the canned chow mein noodles, which are fried and high in fat.

1 tbsp	canola or olive oil	15 mL
2	onions, sliced	2
4	cloves garlic, minced	4
2 tbsp	minced gingerroot	25 mL
¾ lb	lean beef, thinly sliced	375 g
3	tomatoes, cut in chunks	3
2	sweet green peppers, cut in strips	2
3 tbsp	oyster sauce	50 mL
2 tbsp	sodium-reduced soy sauce	25 mL
1½ tsp	hot chili paste	7 mL
4 cups	bean sprouts	1 L
8 oz	fresh chow mein noodles or vermicelli	250 g
2 tbsp	chopped unsalted peanuts	25 mL
6	green onions, diagonally sliced	6

In wok or large deep nonstick skillet, heat oil over high heat; stir-fry onions for 2 minutes. Add garlic, ginger and beef; stir-fry for 2 minutes or until beef is browned. Add tomatoes, green peppers, oyster sauce, soy sauce and chili paste; stir-fry for 2 minutes. Stir in bean sprouts.

Meanwhile, in large pot of boiling water, cook chow mein noodles for 2 minutes or until heated through; drain. (If using vermicelli, cook for 6 to 8 minutes or until tender but firm; drain.) Toss with beef mixture. Sprinkle with peanuts and green onions.

MAKES 4 SERVINGS

NOTE: Oyster sauce is a rich, dark brown sauce made from soy sauce and oysters (but with no fishy taste). It is available in Asian markets and most supermarkets and will keep indefinitely in the refrigerator.

PER SERVING: 425 calories, 33 g protein, 9 g total fat, 1 g saturated fat, 77 mg cholesterol, 56 g carbohydrate, 7 g fibre, 735 mg sodium, 1057 mg potassium

Spicy Beef Chow Mein

Here is my version of this popular Chinese dish. It is only mildly spicy, so if you like hot foods, at least double the amount of red pepper flakes called for. Use Cantonese-style steamed noodles or other cooked noodles—it's a great way to use up leftovers.

¼ cup	water	50 mL
1 tbsp	sodium-reduced soy sauce	15 mL
1 tbsp	ketchup	15 mL
1 tbsp	Worcestershire sauce	15 mL
2 tsp	sesame oil	10 mL
1 tsp	granulated sugar	5 mL
1 tsp	canola or peanut oil	5 mL
2 tsp	minced fresh garlic	10 mL
⅛ tsp	crushed red pepper flakes	0.5 mL
8 oz	lean beef, cut in thin ¼-inch (5 mm) wide strips	250 g
3	green onions, cut lengthwise, then diagonally in 2-inch (5 cm) pieces	3
4 cups	thinly sliced cabbage	1 L
1 cup	coarsely grated carrot	250 mL
4 cups	fresh chow mein or Cantonese noodles or cooked pasta (spaghetti, fettuccine)	1 L

In bowl, combine water, soy sauce, ketchup, Worcestershire sauce, sesame oil and sugar; set aside.

In large nonstick skillet, heat canola oil over medium-high heat, cook garlic and red pepper flakes for 10 seconds. Add beef; stir-fry for 1 minute. Add green onions, cabbage and carrots; stir-fry for 3 minutes. Add pasta and sauce; heat through, about 1 minute, stirring gently to coat.

MAKES 4 SERVINGS

VARIATION: Substitute pork or boneless chicken for beef.

PER SERVING: 338 calories, 21 g protein, 6 g total fat, 1 g saturated fat, 24 mg cholesterol, 50 g carbohydrate, 5 g fibre, 279 mg sodium, 536 mg potassium

Thai Noodles with Chicken and Broccoli

Serve this dish as a main course, or omit the chicken and serve as a side with fish, poultry or any grilled meats.

8 oz	spaghettini or thin noodles	250 g
4 cups	broccoli florets (1 bunch)	1 L
2	carrots, cut in julienne strips	2
2 tsp	canola or olive oil	10 mL
1 tbsp	minced gingerroot	15 mL
3	cloves garlic, minced	3
¾ lb	boneless, skinless chicken breasts or thighs, cut in thin strips	375 g
¼ cup	chopped fresh coriander (cilantro)	50 mL

SAUCE

½ cup	sodium-reduced chicken broth	125 mL
3 tbsp	apple cider vinegar or unseasoned rice vinegar	50 mL
3 tbsp	sodium-reduced soy sauce	50 mL
2 tbsp	peanut butter	25 mL
1 tbsp	granulated sugar	15 mL
1 tbsp	sesame oil	15 mL
1½ tsp	chili paste or hot pepper sauce	7 mL

SAUCE: Whisk together broth, vinegar, soy sauce, peanut butter, sugar, sesame oil and chili paste. Set aside.

In large pot of boiling water, cook noodles for 5 minutes. Add broccoli and carrots; cook for 2 to 3 minutes or until noodles are tender yet firm. Drain and set aside.

In large nonstick skillet, heat oil over high heat; stir-fry ginger and garlic for 30 seconds. Add chicken; stir-fry for 3 to 5 minutes or until no longer pink inside.

Stir sauce; add to skillet and bring to boil. Remove from heat; toss with noodles and vegetables. Sprinkle with coriander. Serve in large bowls.

MAKES 4 SERVINGS

MAKE AHEAD: Prepare sauce up to 4 hours in advance.

PER SERVING: 463 calories, 32 g protein, 12 g total fat, 2 g saturated fat, 50 mg cholesterol, 57 g carbohydrate, 6 g fibre, 623 mg sodium, 703 mg potassium

Kids' Easy Macaroni and Cheese with Vegetables

This is a quick and easy version of pasta that most children will enjoy.

1 cup	macaroni or other small pasta (4 oz/125 g)	250 mL
2	medium carrots, thinly sliced	2
1 cup	frozen peas	250 mL
⅓ cup	2% milk*	75 mL
2 tbsp	light cream cheese	25 mL
½ tsp	dried basil (or 2 tbsp/25 mL chopped fresh)	2 mL
½ cup	shredded part-skim mozzarella or reduced-fat Cheddar cheese	125 mL
1 tbsp	freshly grated Parmesan cheese	15 mL
1	green onion, chopped	1
¼ tsp or less	salt and freshly ground pepper	1 mL or less

In large pot of boiling water, cook pasta until tender but firm; drain.

Meanwhile, steam or boil carrots for 4 minutes. Add peas and cook until carrots are tender-crisp, about 3 minutes. Drain and return to pot.

In small saucepan over medium heat or in microwave, heat milk until steaming. Whisk in cream cheese until smooth; stir in basil. Add to pasta along with vegetables, mozzarella and Parmesan cheeses and onion; toss to mix. Season with salt and pepper to taste.

MAKES 3 SERVINGS, 1½ CUPS (375 mL) EACH

*Or use whatever milk you have in the refrigerator.

VARIATION: Instead of cream cheese, whisk 1 egg into ⅓ cup (75 mL) cold milk; pour over hot cooked macaroni and stir over low heat for 1 minute. Add mozzarella and vegetables; stir and cook for another minute or until cheese has melted and sauce thickened slightly.

PER SERVING: 283 calories, 15 g protein, 7 g total fat, 4 g saturated fat, 23 mg cholesterol, 39 g carbohydrate, 5 g fibre, 471 mg sodium, 275 mg potassium

Tomato Ham Pasta Dinner for One

Any shaped pasta can be used, but for a more interesting looking dish, try one with a unique shape, such as farfalle or radiatore. Use the leftover broccoli in a stir-fry, a soup or an omelette.

1 cup	farfalle or other shaped pasta (2 oz/60 g)	250 mL
1 cup	broccoli florets	250 mL
1 tsp	canola or olive oil	5 mL
1	small tomato, coarsely chopped	1
Half	clove garlic, minced	Half
1 tbsp	chopped fresh basil (or ¼ tsp/1 mL dried)	15 mL
1	thin slice ham, smoked turkey or firm tofu (1 oz/30 g), cut in strips	1
1 tbsp	freshly grated Parmesan cheese	15 mL
	Freshly ground pepper	

In pot of boiling water, cook pasta until tender but firm, about 10 minutes. About 2 minutes before pasta is cooked, add broccoli. Cook until tender-crisp; drain.

Meanwhile, in nonstick skillet, heat oil over medium-high heat; cook tomato, garlic, basil and ham, stirring often, until tomato is heated through, about 2 minutes. Pour over drained pasta and broccoli; toss to mix. Sprinkle with Parmesan. Season with pepper to taste.

MAKES 1 SERVING

PER SERVING: 354 calories, 17 g protein, 9 g total fat, 2 g saturated fat, 21 mg cholesterol, 52 g carbohydrate, 6 g fibre, 452 mg sodium, 568 mg potassium

Tomato Clam Sauce for Pasta

Serve this tasty, quick sauce over any kind of hot cooked pasta. Using crushed tomatoes saves time and results in a thicker sauce.

1 tbsp	olive oil	15 mL
1	medium onion, chopped	1
1	clove garlic, minced	1
1	can (28 oz/796 mL) crushed or diced tomatoes	1
1	bay leaf	1
1 tbsp	each dried basil and oregano	15 mL
Pinch	crushed red pepper flakes	Pinch
1	can (5 oz/142 g) clams, undrained	1
½ tsp	granulated sugar (optional)	2 mL
½ cup	chopped fresh parsley	125 mL

In saucepan, heat oil over medium heat; cook onion, stirring often, until tender. Add garlic, tomatoes, bay leaf, basil, oregano, red pepper flakes and clams; simmer, uncovered, for 5 minutes or until flavours are blended. Discard bay leaf. Taste and add sugar (if using). Stir in parsley.

MAKES 4 CUPS (1 L), ENOUGH FOR 1 LB (500 G) PASTA, 6 MAIN-COURSE SERVINGS

PER SERVING: 93 calories, 6 g protein, 3 g total fat, 0 g saturated fat, 8 mg cholesterol, 13 g carbohydrate, 3 g fibre, 223 mg sodium, 568 mg potassium

Cooking Pasta

Cook pasta in a large pot of boiling water, using about 16 cups (4 L) of water for every pound (500 g) of pasta. Add pasta all at once, stirring to make sure noodles don't stick together. Boil, uncovered, stirring occasionally. Be sure to have the sauce ready before the pasta is finished cooking (overcooked, soft, gluey pasta isn't appealing); then toss pasta with sauce and serve immediately.

Fresh pasta cooks quickly, sometimes in as little time as 2 minutes. Dried pasta takes longer, usually at least 7 minutes, sometimes 10 to 12 minutes. Begin tasting to see whether pasta is done before the suggested cooking time; pasta is cooked when it's al dente—tender but firm, not mushy—and has lost its raw starch taste. Drain in a colander, then toss immediately with sauce, butter or oil as specified in recipe to prevent pasta from sticking together. Because pasta cools quickly, it's important to warm the serving platter or individual plates. When using cooked pasta in salads, rinse under cold running water to prevent sticking; drain well.

When entertaining, you can cook pasta a few hours in advance, drain, then rinse under cold water to prevent the noodles from sticking together. Just before serving, reheat in boiling water for 1 or 2 minutes, then toss with sauce.

HOW MUCH PASTA TO COOK?

Appetites for pasta vary widely depending on what else you are eating with the meal, your age, your size, the type of meal and other factors. Catelli recommends 85 grams of dry pasta as a standard serving size and provides this guide to estimate the measure.

85 g dry (approximate) equals:

LONG PASTA

- spaghetti, vermicelli, fettuccine, linguine: bunch ¾ inch (2 cm) in diameter

SHAPED PASTA

- alphabet, soup noodles, stars, rings: ½ cup (125 mL)

- macaroni, small seashells: ¾ cup (175 mL)

- penne, radiatore, fusilli, wagon wheels, small bows (farfalle): 1 cup (250 mL)

- large shells, rigatoni: 1⅓ cups (325 mL)

- rotini, medium bows (farfalle); fine, medium and broad noodles: 1⅔ cups (400 mL)

Fish Fillets with Lemon and Parsley

The fillets in this simple recipe are tender and moist. If using frozen fillets, thaw and separate them before cooking for best results. Use fillets at least 1 inch (2.5 cm) thick. Fresh basil can be substituted for the parsley if you like.

1 lb	fillets (Pacific halibut or perch, tilapia, catfish, snapper or cod)	500 g
¼ tsp or less	salt and freshly ground pepper	1 mL or less
2 tbsp	chopped fresh parsley	25 mL
1 tbsp	fresh lemon juice	15 mL
2 tsp	canola or olive oil	10 mL

Place fillets in lightly greased baking or microwaveable dish just large enough to hold them in single layer. Sprinkle with salt and pepper. Combine parsley, lemon juice and oil; drizzle over fish.

Bake, uncovered, in 450°F (230°C) oven for 7 to 10 minutes or until fish flakes easily when tested with fork. Or cover with vented waxed paper or parchment and microwave on High for 3 to 4 minutes. Sprinkle with additional lemon juice.

MAKES 4 SERVINGS

NOTE: Fish is an excellent source of protein and is generally low in fat and calories.

PER SERVING: 145 calories, 24 g protein, 5 g total fat, 1 g saturated fat, 36 mg cholesterol, 0 g carbohydrate, 0 g fibre, 208 mg sodium, 522 mg potassium

Lemon-Tarragon Sole Fillets

Broiling is an easy way to cook any kind of fish fillets or steaks. This recipe is a lighter version of my mother's West Coast one.

2 tbsp	light mayonnaise	25 mL
2 tbsp	low-fat plain yogurt	25 mL
1 tsp	all-purpose flour	5 mL
½ tsp	dried tarragon	2 mL
1 tsp	finely chopped lemon rind	5 mL
1 lb	Pacific sole, salmon or sea bass fillets	500 g

In small bowl, mix together mayonnaise, yogurt, flour, tarragon and lemon rind. Arrange fillets in single layer on baking sheet; spread with mayonnaise mixture. Broil 6 to 8 inches (15 to 20 cm) from heat for 5 to 10 minutes or until fish is opaque. (Time will vary depending on thickness of fish; ¼-inch/1 cm thick fillets will take only 5 minutes.)

MAKES 4 SERVINGS

MAKE AHEAD: Prepare fillets, cover and refrigerate for up to 2 hours in advance.

PER SERVING: 134 calories, 22 g protein, 4 g total fat, 1 g saturated fat, 63 mg cholesterol, 2 g carbohydrate, 0 g fibre, 145 mg sodium, 333 mg potassium

Baked Breaded Fish Fillets with Almonds

You can use any kind of fresh or frozen and thawed fillets in this easy-to-make fish dish. Whole-wheat bread crumbs instead of white bread crumbs not only add fibre but are much more attractive in colour.

1	egg, lightly beaten	1
¼ cup	low-fat milk	50 mL
1⅓ cups	fresh whole-wheat bread crumbs	325 mL
1 tsp	dried oregano and/or basil	5 mL
¼ tsp or less	each salt and freshly ground pepper	1 mL or less
1 lb	Pacific sole, halibut, cod or haddock fillets	500 g
2 tbsp	fresh lemon juice	25 mL
2 tbsp	water	25 mL
1 tbsp	olive oil	15 mL
3 tbsp	sliced almonds	50 mL
3 tbsp	chopped green onions	50 mL

In shallow dish, combine egg and milk. On plate, mix bread crumbs, oregano, salt and pepper. Dip fillets in egg mixture, then in crumbs. Arrange in single layer on greased baking sheet. Combine lemon juice, water and oil; drizzle over fish. Sprinkle with almonds. Bake, uncovered, in 425°F (220°C) oven for 10 minutes or until fish is opaque. Sprinkle with onions.

MAKES 4 SERVINGS

MAKE AHEAD: Cover and refrigerate breaded fillets up to 30 minutes in advance. Drizzle sauce over fish just before baking.

PER SERVING: 193 calories, 24 g protein, 8 g total fat, 1 g saturated fat, 84 mg cholesterol, 5 g carbohydrate, 1 g fibre, 219 mg sodium, 393 mg potassium

Swordfish with Capers, Basil and Olives

Swordfish is moist and juicy as long as it is not overcooked and is well suited to this easy Provençal-type dish. If swordfish is unavailable, use fresh Pacific cod, sea bass or halibut fillets.

2	cloves garlic	2
¼ cup	lightly packed fresh Italian (flat-leaf) parsley	50 mL
¼ cup	lightly packed fresh basil	50 mL
1 tbsp	capers, drained	15 mL
6	black olives, pitted and chopped	6
3	anchovies, chopped	3
1½ tsp	olive oil	7 mL
1½ lb	swordfish (1 inch/2.5 cm thick)	750 g

In food processor, chop garlic then add parsley, basil, capers, olives, anchovies and oil; chop coarsely.

Place fish on lightly greased baking sheet; evenly spread herb mixture over fish.

Bake in 375°F (190°C) oven for 10 to 12 minutes or until opaque throughout. (Time will vary depending on thickness of fish.)

MAKES 4 SERVINGS

MAKE AHEAD: Assemble fillets; cover and refrigerate for up to 4 hours in advance.

NOTE: Olives can be high in fat and sodium, so use in moderation.

PER SERVING: 239 calories, 35 g protein, 9 g total fat, 2 g saturated fat, 69 mg cholesterol, 1 g carbohydrate, 1 g fibre, 382 mg sodium, 557 mg potassium

Fish Provençal

Any kind of fish fillet is delicious topped with this zesty tomato, olive and caper sauce. Cooking time will vary depending on the thickness of the fish. If you like, instead of poaching, you could grill, broil or microwave the fish (see p. 230), then top with this sauce.

1 lb	Pacific halibut, snapper, black sea bass, sole or other fillets	500 g

SAUCE

½ tsp	olive oil	2 mL
1 tbsp	chopped green onion or shallots	15 mL
½ tsp	minced fresh garlic	2 mL
¾ cup	drained canned or fresh tomatoes, chopped	175 mL
¼ tsp	dried basil (or 1 tbsp/15 mL chopped fresh)	1 mL
2 tbsp	chopped black olives	25 mL
1 tbsp	capers	15 mL
	Freshly ground pepper	

In skillet of gently simmering water, cover and poach fish over medium heat for 5 minutes or until fish is opaque. Drain well; transfer to serving platter and keep warm.

SAUCE: Meanwhile, in small saucepan, heat oil over medium heat; cook onion and garlic for 2 minutes. Add tomatoes and basil; simmer for 3 minutes, stirring occasionally. Stir in olives, capers, and pepper to taste. Spoon sauce over fish.

MAKES 4 SERVINGS

MAKE AHEAD: Prepare sauce up to 1 hour before serving; reheat gently.

PER SERVING: 143 calories, 24 g protein, 4 g total fat, 1 g saturated fat, 36 mg cholesterol, 2 g carbohydrate, 1 g fibre, 220 mg sodium, 603 mg potassium

Cod Fillets with Red Peppers and Onions

Sautéed sweet red pepper strips and onion rings spooned over lightly cooked cod fillets is a colourful, easy fish dish both family and friends will enjoy.

1 tbsp	olive oil	15 mL
1	sweet red pepper, cut in thin strips	1
4	thin slices red onion	4
1 tsp	minced fresh garlic	5 mL
½ tsp	dried oregano (or 1 tbsp/15 mL fresh)	2 mL
1 lb	Pacific cod fillets, cut in 4 pieces	500 g
2 tbsp	chopped fresh parsley	25 mL
	Freshly ground pepper	

PER SERVING: 136 calories, 21 g protein, 4 g total fat, 1 g saturated fat, 49 mg cholesterol, 3 g carbohydrate, 1 g fibre, 71 mg sodium, 291 mg potassium

In nonstick skillet, heat oil over medium heat; add red pepper and sauté for 1 minute.

Separate onion into rings and add to pan along with garlic and oregano; cook for 3 minutes. Push vegetables to edge of pan.

Add fish; cover and cook for 3 minutes. Turn fish; cover and cook for 2 to 3 minutes longer or until fish is opaque. Sprinkle fish with parsley; season with pepper to taste. Spoon red pepper mixture over fish and serve.

MAKES 4 SERVINGS

Swordfish with Lime Coriander Marinade

These flavourful fillets are easy to prepare and quick to cook. You can substitute rainbow trout, black cod (sablefish) or Pacific halibut fillets or steaks for the swordfish. Serve with wedges of lime and garnish the plate with sprigs of coriander.

1½ lb	swordfish fillets or steaks, 1 inch (2.5 cm) thick	750 g
¼ cup	chopped fresh coriander (cilantro)	50 mL
	Grated rind from 1 medium lime	
¼ cup	fresh lime juice	50 mL
2 tbsp	olive oil	25 mL
2	cloves garlic, minced	2
1 tsp	minced canned or fresh green chilies (optional)	5 mL
¼ tsp or less	each salt and pepper	1 mL or less

VARIATION:

Grilled Fillets with Lime Coriander Marinade
Marinate fillets. Grease and preheat barbecue to medium heat; grill fillets for 3 to 5 minutes on each side, or until fish is opaque and flakes easily when tested with fork.

PER SERVING: 239 calories, 34 g protein, 10 g total fat, 2 g saturated fat, 66 mg cholesterol, 1 g carbohydrate, 0 g fibre, 226 mg sodium, 505 mg potassium

Place fillets in 8-inch (2 L) square baking dish. Whisk together coriander, lime rind and juice, oil, garlic, chilies, salt and pepper; pour over fillets. Cover and marinate for 30 minutes.

Bake in 425°F (220°C) oven for 10 to 15 minutes or until fish flakes easily when tested with fork.

MAKES 4 SERVINGS

Halibut Poached with Tomatoes, Artichokes and Mushrooms

You can use any type of white fish fillets or steaks, such as Pacific cod, sole or haddock, in this moist and savoury fish dish. Serve over pasta or rice.

1 tbsp	olive oil	15 mL
1½ cups	thickly sliced mushrooms	375 mL
1	clove garlic, minced	1
3	tomatoes, seeded and cut in chunks	3
½ tsp	crushed dried basil (or ¼ cup/50 mL chopped fresh)	2 mL
Pinch	crushed dried thyme	Pinch
1 lb	Pacific halibut fillets	500 g
1	can (14 oz/398 mL) artichoke hearts, drained and halved	1
¼ tsp or less	salt and freshly ground pepper	1 mL or less
Pinch	granulated sugar (optional)	Pinch

In heavy saucepan or nonstick skillet, heat oil over medium-high heat. Add mushrooms and garlic; cook, stirring often, until mushrooms are tender. Add tomatoes, basil (if using dried) and thyme; bring to simmer. Add halibut and artichokes; cover and simmer for 3 minutes. Uncover and cook for 2 to 5 minutes longer or until fish is opaque. Sprinkle with fresh basil (if using). Season with salt and pepper.

MAKES 4 SERVINGS

NOTE: One serving is a high source of vitamin C and a very high source of folacin and fibre.

PER SERVING: 211 calories, 27 g protein, 6 g total fat, 1 g saturated fat, 36 mg cholesterol, 13 g carbohydrate, 6 g fibre, 393 mg sodium, 1029 mg potassium

Microwave Fillets with Mushrooms and Ginger

The tantalizing flavours of Asian seasonings, mushrooms and green onions combine to complement the tender fillets of sole or any white fish fillets you like. But best of all, this dish takes less than 10 minutes to make from start to finish.

6	medium mushrooms, sliced	6
1	green onion, chopped	1
2	Pacific sole or other fillets (about 4 oz/125 g each)	2
1 tsp	grated gingerroot	5 mL
1 tsp	sesame oil	5 mL
1 tsp	dry sherry	5 mL
1 tsp	sodium-reduced soy sauce	5 mL

Spread mushrooms and green onion in microwaveable dish large enough to hold fillets in a single layer. Cover and microwave on High for 2 minutes; pour off any liquid.

Push mushrooms and onions to edge of dish; arrange fillets in single layer in centre.

Combine gingerroot, oil, sherry and soy sauce; spread evenly over fillets. Spoon mushrooms and onions on top. Cover and microwave on High for 2 to 3 minutes. Let stand, covered, for 1 to 2 minutes or until fish flakes when tested with a fork.

MAKES 2 SERVINGS

PER SERVING: 144 calories, 23 g protein, 4 g total fat, 1 g saturated fat, 60 mg cholesterol, 4 g carbohydrate, 1 g fibre, 184 mg sodium, 510 mg potassium

Hoisin-Glazed Halibut

All my tasters loved this dish, whether it was made with swordfish, tuna, Pacific cod or salmon; in the oven, on the grill or in the microwave. Strips of green onion or chives add a fresh colourful garnish to the plate.

2 tbsp	hoisin sauce	25 mL
1 tsp	minced gingerroot	5 mL
1 tsp	sesame oil	5 mL
¼ tsp	chili paste (optional)	1 mL
4	halibut fillets, 1 inch (2.5 cm) thick (about 4 oz/125 g each	4

In small bowl, mix together hoisin sauce, gingerroot, oil and chili paste (if using).

Spread over each side of fish. Place on greased grill or on broiler pan or on baking sheet. Grill over medium heat with lid down, basting occasionally with any remaining hoisin mixture, for 5 minutes. Turn and grill for another 5 minutes or until fish flakes easily when tested with fork. (Or bake in 425°F/220°C oven for 10 minutes.)

MAKES 4 SERVINGS

VARIATION:

Hoisin-Glazed Cod or Salmon Steaks
Use Pacific cod or salmon instead of halibut. Simply spread with hoisin sauce; barbecue over medium-high heat with lid down, for 3 to 5 minutes per side or until fish flakes when tested with fork.

NOTE: You can also microwave the Hoisin-Glazed Halibut on High for 5 minutes instead of grilling or baking.

PER SERVING: 119 calories, 20 g protein, 3 g total fat, 0 g saturated fat, 31 mg cholesterol, 2 g carbohydrate, 0 g fibre, 116 mg sodium, 439 mg potassium

Baked Salmon Trout with Papaya-Cucumber Salsa

Whole baked fish is a wonderful dish for entertaining. It's a treat to have, looks spectacular and is easy to prepare. The stuffing is light and flavourful, and salsa instead of the usual rich butter sauce is refreshing. Salmon trout vary in size; a 3-pound (1.5 kg) trout will weigh about 1½ lb (750 g) after it has been cleaned and boned (have your fishmonger do this). Do serve the fish with heads on, as they look more attractive. If papaya isn't available for the salsa, use diced, unpeeled red apple or mango or melon.

2	salmon trout (about 3 lb/1.5 kg each) or salmon, cleaned and boned	2
2 cups	sliced mushrooms	500 mL
⅓ cup	minced shallots	75 mL
1 tsp	olive oil	5 mL
2 cups	packed chopped fresh spinach	500 mL
¼ cup	chopped fresh dill	50 mL
¼ tsp or less	salt and freshly ground pepper	1 mL or less
1	lemon, thinly sliced	1
8	sprigs fresh dill	8

PAPAYA-CUCUMBER SALSA

2 cups	finely diced English cucumber (unpeeled)	500 mL
2 cups	diced peeled papaya	500 mL
2 tbsp	white wine vinegar or fresh lime juice	25 mL
2 tbsp	chopped fresh dill	25 mL
	Freshly ground pepper	

Wash fish and pat dry; arrange in greased baking dish. In microwaveable dish, combine mushrooms and shallots; sprinkle with oil. Microwave, uncovered, on High for 2 minutes or until softened. (Or, cook in nonstick skillet over medium heat until softened.)

Combine mushroom mixture, spinach and dill; season with salt and pepper. Stuff fish cavities so that stuffing stays in place without sewing. Arrange lemon slices in row on top of fish. Top with dill sprigs.

Bake fish in 400°F (200°C) oven for 25 minutes or until fish is opaque. (Test by making small cut at thickest part of fish.)

PAPAYA-CUCUMBER SALSA: Meanwhile, in bowl, combine cucumber, papaya, vinegar and dill; season with pepper to taste.

Using spatulas, transfer cooked fish to large serving platter. Spoon Papaya-Cucumber Salsa around fish. To serve, discard skin.

MAKES 8 SERVINGS WITH 4 CUPS/1 L SALSA

MAKE AHEAD: Prepare salsa up to 1 day ahead; drain off liquid before serving.

PER SERVING: 228 calories, 31 g protein, 8 g total fat, 2 g saturated fat, 88 mg cholesterol, 7 g carbohydrate, 2 g fibre, 158 mg sodium, 864 mg potassium

Baked Whole Salmon Stuffed with Mushrooms and Artichokes

This easy-to-prepare fish looks and tastes terrific. Garnish the serving platter with fresh dill sprigs, parsley or watercress and lemon or cucumber slices. Use any combination of mushrooms—regular, oyster, Portobello, cremini or porcini. If you're lucky enough to have leftovers, this dish is also delicious cold.

5½ lb	whole wild salmon, cleaned, scaled, head and tail on	2.5 kg
STUFFING		
1 tsp	olive oil	5 mL
¼ lb	each white, brown, shiitake and oyster mushrooms, chopped	125 g
1	can (14 oz/398 g) artichokes, drained and coarsely chopped	1
½ cup	lightly packed chopped fresh dill	125 mL
	Creamy Dill Sauce (p. 325)	

STUFFING: In nonstick skillet, heat oil over medium-high heat; cook mushrooms, stirring often, for about 5 minutes or until softened. Stir in artichokes; cook for 1 minute. Remove from heat; stir in dill.

Lightly stuff cavity of salmon with mushroom mixture. Using heavy needle and thread, stitch opening of fish together. Place fish on ungreased baking sheet. Bake, uncovered, in 450°F (230°C) oven for 50 minutes or until small cut in centre of fish shows meat is opaque. Transfer fish to serving platter. Pass Creamy Dill Sauce separately.

MAKES 12 SERVINGS

MAKE AHEAD: Stuff fish up to 6 hours in advance; cover and refrigerate. Remove from refrigerator 30 minutes before baking, or increase baking time 5 to 10 minutes.

NOTE: For easier serving, ask your fishmonger to remove the bones while leaving the fish whole.

PER SERVING: 201 calories, 28 g protein, 7 g total fat, 1 g saturated fat, 69 mg cholesterol, 5 g carbohydrate, 2 g fibre, 122 mg sodium, 771 mg potassium

Quick and Easy Salmon Fillets with Watercress Sauce

Fresh wild salmon steaks or fillets are a wonderful treat and I like them best when simply cooked—either grilled, broiled or cooked wrapped in foil. In summer, dress them up with this watercress sauce; in winter, serve with Lime Ginger Mayonnaise (p. 323).

4	wild salmon fillets or steaks, 1 inch (2.5 cm) thick (about 5 oz/150 g each	4
1 tbsp	fresh lemon juice	15 mL
	Freshly ground pepper	
	Watercress sprigs	

WATERCRESS SAUCE

1 cup	light sour cream	250 mL
¼ cup	low-fat plain yogurt	50 mL
½ cup	finely chopped fresh watercress	125 mL
2 tbsp	chopped fresh parsley	25 mL
1 tbsp	chopped fresh chives or green onions	15 mL
2 tsp	freshly grated Parmesan cheese	10 mL
¼ tsp or less	salt and freshly ground pepper	1 mL or less

On large, lightly oiled piece of foil, or microwave-safe dish, arrange salmon in single layer. Sprinkle with lemon juice, and pepper to taste. Fold foil over salmon and seal; place on baking sheet. Bake in 400°F (200°C) oven for about 15 minutes. Or, in microwave-safe dish, cover loosely; microwave on High for 5 minutes or until fish is opaque and flakes easily with fork.

WATERCRESS SAUCE: Combine sour cream, yogurt, chopped watercress, parsley, chives, Parmesan, and salt and pepper; stir until well mixed.

Arrange salmon on plates and garnish with sprig of watercress. Pass sauce separately.

MAKES 4 SERVINGS

MAKE AHEAD: Cover and refrigerate sauce for up to 1 day.

NOTE: The only way to ruin good-quality fish is to overcook it. If fillets or steaks are ¾ to 1 inch (2 to 2.5 cm) thick, you'll be much less likely to overcook them than if they are thin. Cooking times in this recipe are based on 1-inch (2.5 cm) thick steaks.

The watercress sauce makes a wonderful dip for fresh vegetables.

PER SERVING: 262 calories, 32 g protein, 11 g total fat, 4 g saturated fat, 87 mg cholesterol, 8 g carbohydrate, 0 g fibre, 304 mg sodium, 775 mg potassium

Barbecued Salmon Fillets

What could be better for a quick summer meal than barbecued salmon? Sometimes I don't add anything to the salmon; its delicate flavour and smoky taste from the barbecue is all that is needed. Other times I spread hoisin sauce over top or sprinkle it with fresh lemon juice, or use this recipe.

1 tsp	grated lemon rind	5 mL
2 tbsp	fresh lemon juice	25 mL
1 tbsp	olive oil	15 mL
2 tbsp	chopped fresh dill*	25 mL
4	wild salmon fillets (about 1½ lb/750 g total)	4
¼ tsp or less	salt and freshly ground pepper	1 mL or less

Combine lemon rind, juice, oil and dill. Pour over salmon; marinate for 15 minutes at room temperature.

Spray grill or broiler pan with nonstick coating; cook salmon skin side down about 4 inches (10 cm) from medium-high heat, turning halfway through cooking time, for 8 to 10 minutes per inch (2.5 cm) of thickness or until fish is opaque. (If fillet is thin and the barbecue lid is closed, turning may not be necessary.) Season with salt and pepper.

MAKES 4 SERVINGS

*Or 2 tsp (10 mL) dried dillweed or 1 tsp (5 mL) crumbled dried rosemary.

MAKE AHEAD: Marinate salmon, covered and refrigerated, for up to 4 hours; remove from refrigerator 10 minutes before cooking.

VARIATION:

Hoisin-Glazed Salmon
Spread hoisin sauce over fillets or steaks. Grill over medium-high heat with lid closed, for 4 to 5 minutes per side or until fish flakes when tested with fork.

NOTE: I usually start cooking the salmon skin side down on the grill; however, others do the reverse. Do whichever works best for you.

PER SERVING: 213 calories, 30 g protein, 9 g total fat, 2 g saturated fat, 78 mg cholesterol, 0 g carbohydrate, 0 g fibre, 217 mg sodium, 656 mg potassium

Salmon Salad Fajitas

There is a fabulous combination of flavours and textures in this easy-to-make meal. If you have leftover cooked salmon, use it instead of canned.

1	can (7½ oz/213 g) salmon, drained	1
¼ cup	low-fat plain yogurt	50 mL
2 tbsp	light sour cream	25 mL
¼ tsp	chili powder	1 mL
1	medium carrot, grated	1
1	green onion, chopped	1
1	tomato, diced	1
1	small avocado, cut in chunks (optional)	1
¼ cup	chopped fresh coriander (cilantro)	50 mL
¼ tsp or less	salt and freshly ground pepper	1 mL or less
4	soft 8-inch (20 cm) flour tortillas	4
4	large leaves leaf lettuce	4

In bowl, combine salmon, yogurt, sour cream and chili powder. Add carrot, onion, tomato, avocado, if using, and coriander. Season with salt and pepper; stir gently.

Stack tortillas; wrap in foil and warm in 350°F (180°C) oven for 5 minutes. Lay each tortilla flat; top with lettuce leaf. Spoon salmon mixture down one side of tortilla; roll up.

MAKES 4 SERVINGS

MAKE AHEAD: Cover and refrigerate salmon mixture for up to 2 hours in advance.

PER SERVING: 278 calories, 14 g protein, 9 g total fat, 2 g saturated fat, 13 mg cholesterol, 34 g carbohydrate, 3 g fibre, 711 mg sodium, 491 mg potassium

Light Salmon Loaf with Dill

Fresh dill adds a wonderful flavour to this moist loaf. Make the bread crumbs by processing two slices of bread in a food processor. Serve with Yogurt Remoulade (p. 326).

1 tbsp	soft margarine or olive oil	15 mL
1	medium onion, chopped	1
1 cup	sliced mushrooms	250 mL
1 cup	diced celery	250 mL
2	eggs	2
1	can (7½ oz/213 g) salmon	1
1 cup	fresh homemade bread crumbs	250 mL
⅔ cup	low-fat milk	150 mL
¼ cup	chopped fresh dill*	50 mL
	Freshly ground pepper	

In skillet, melt margarine over medium heat; cook onion, mushrooms and celery, stirring, for about 5 minutes or until tender-crisp. In bowl, lightly beat eggs; add mushroom mixture. Drain salmon liquid into egg mixture. Flake salmon and mash bones; add to bowl along with bread crumbs, milk, dill, and pepper to taste. Stir lightly to mix.

Transfer to lightly greased 8½- × 4½-inch (1.5 L) loaf pan. Place in larger pan and pour in enough hot water to come 1 inch (2.5 cm) up sides of pan. Bake, uncovered, in 350°F (180°C) oven for 45 to 55 minutes or until firm to the touch. Pour off any liquid.

MAKES 4 SERVINGS

*If fresh dill is unavailable, substitute fresh parsley plus 1 tsp (5 mL) dried dillweed.

MICROWAVE METHOD
Cover and microwave loaf on High for 7 minutes; let stand for 5 minutes.

VARIATION: Substitute 1½ cups (375 mL) diced (unpeeled) zucchini for the mushrooms and celery.

PER SERVING: 215 calories, 15 g protein, 12 g total fat, 3 g saturated fat, 109 mg cholesterol, 12 g carbohydrate, 1 g fibre, 393 mg sodium, 472 mg potassium

Grilled Halibut Fillets with Fresh Tomato-Basil Salsa

The salsa adds great colour and flavour to the fish, though the halibut is tasty enough to serve on its own if you're in a hurry. Use fillets or steaks.

4	Pacific halibut fillets or steaks (about 6 oz/170 g each)	4
2 tbsp	fresh lemon juice	25 mL
1 tbsp	olive oil	15 mL
1 tsp	dried crushed rosemary	5 mL
¼ tsp or less	salt and freshly ground pepper	1 mL or less

TOMATO-BASIL SALSA

½ cup	diced ripe tomatoes	125 mL
¼ cup	coarsely chopped fresh basil or coriander (cilantro)	50 mL
2 tbsp	finely chopped green onions	25 mL
1 tbsp	red wine vinegar	15 mL
1 tbsp	olive oil	15 mL
½ tsp	grated lemon rind	2 mL
¼ tsp or less	salt and freshly ground pepper	1 mL or less

Place halibut steaks in large shallow dish. Combine lemon juice, oil and rosemary; season with salt and pepper. Pour marinade over halibut and turn to coat both sides. Cover and refrigerate for about 30 minutes.

Place fish on greased broiler pan or greased grill 4 inches (10 cm) from heat; cook for about 10 minutes per inch (2.5 cm) of thickness, turning once, or until fish flakes when tested with a fork.

TOMATO-BASIL SALSA: Meanwhile, in small bowl and using whisk, blend together tomatoes, basil, onions, vinegar, oil and lemon rind. Season with salt and pepper. To serve, spoon 3 tbsp (45 mL) over each steak.

MAKES 4 SERVINGS, WITH ¾ CUP (175 mL) SALSA

MICROWAVE METHOD
Place marinated steaks in single layer in microwaveable dish; cover and microwave on High for 4 to 5 minutes (for ¾-inch/2 cm thick steaks) or until fish flakes.

NOTE: Be sure to use microwave-safe covers when covering food for cooking in the microwave. I prefer using waxed paper or parchment paper. There is some controversy about the use of plastic in microwave ovens, even when deemed microwave-safe. When in doubt, don't use.

PER SERVING: 223 calories, 36 g protein, 7 g total fat, 1 g saturated fat, 54 mg cholesterol, 2 g carbohydrate, 1 g fibre, 313 mg sodium, 845 mg potassium

Grilled Trout with Light Tartar Sauce

This fish can also be cooked in foil. A few capers, a little Dijon mustard, chopped green onions or chives can be added to the tartar sauce. Garnish trout with lemon slices and fresh dill.

4	sprigs fresh dill	4
4	whole rainbow trout (about 9 oz/255 g each) or 1½ lb (750 g) trout fillets	4
¼ tsp or less	salt and freshly ground pepper	1 mL or less

LIGHT TARTAR SAUCE

¼ cup	low-fat plain yogurt	50 mL
¼ cup	light mayonnaise	50 mL
¼ cup	finely chopped dill pickle	50 mL
2 tbsp	chopped fresh dill	25 mL
	Freshly ground pepper	

LIGHT TARTAR SAUCE: Stir together yogurt, mayonnaise, pickle, dill, and pepper to taste.

Place dill sprig in each trout cavity; sprinkle cavity with salt and pepper. Place trout on greased grill over medium-high heat; cover and grill, turning once, for 10 to 15 minutes (about 7 to 10 minutes if cooking fillets) or until fish is opaque. Serve with tartar sauce.

MAKES 4 SERVINGS

MAKE AHEAD: Prepare tartar sauce, cover and refrigerate, for up to 3 days in advance.

VARIATION: Instead of barbecuing, bake trout on baking sheet in 450°F (230°C) oven for 10 minutes for every inch (2.5 cm) of thickness of fish. To foil-steam, wrap in foil and bake, adding 5 minutes to baking time.

NOTE: Light Tartar Sauce is delicious with any fish, or with chicken or turkey burgers.

PER SERVING (with 3 tbsp/45 mL tartar sauce): 199 calories, 23 g protein, 10 g total fat, 2 g saturated fat, 72 mg cholesterol, 3 g carbohydrate, 0 g fibre, 418 mg sodium, 483 mg potassium

Teriyaki Orange Fish Fillets

This flavourful easy-to-make dish is low in both calories and fat.

1 lb	fish fillets (perch, sole, haddock)	500 g
1 tsp	grated orange rind	5 mL
½ cup	orange juice	125 mL
1 tbsp	minced onion	15 mL
1 tbsp	sodium-reduced soy sauce	15 mL
1 tsp	grated gingerroot	5 mL
½ tsp	granulated sugar	2 mL
1 tbsp	water	15 mL
1 tsp	cornstarch	5 mL

In large skillet, arrange fish in single layer. In small bowl, mix together orange rind and juice, onion, soy sauce, gingerroot and sugar; pour over fish. Bring to boil; reduce heat to simmer and cook, covered, for 3 to 5 minutes or until fish is opaque and flakes easily when tested with fork.

Remove fish to serving platter, reserving orange mixture in skillet. Mix water with cornstarch until smooth; pour into skillet and bring to boil, stirring. Pour orange sauce over fish.

MAKES 4 SERVINGS

PER SERVING: 130 calories, 22 g protein, 2 g total fat, 0 g saturated fat, 48 mg cholesterol, 5 g carbohydrate, 0 g fibre, 218 mg sodium, 382 mg potassium

Lemon Sesame Tuna Fillets

Tuna is tender and moist as long as it isn't overcooked—it should be still red in the centre; when it's overcooked it becomes dry. Garnish tuna with toasted brown or black sesame seeds.

4	tuna fillets or steaks, 1 inch (2.5 cm) thick (about 1½ lb/750 g)	4
1	green onion, chopped	1
Pinch	freshly ground pepper	Pinch

LEMON-SOY MARINADE

2 tbsp	fresh lemon juice	25 mL
1 tbsp	sodium-reduced soy sauce	15 mL
1 tbsp	sesame or vegetable oil	15 mL

LEMON-SOY MARINADE: Combine lemon juice, soy sauce and oil; pour over tuna fillets in baking dish. Cover and refrigerate for at least 30 minutes.

Place fish on greased grill or sauté pan over high heat; cook for 1 to 2 minutes or until brown to a depth of ⅛ inch (3 mm). Turn and cook for another 1 to 2 minutes or until brown to a depth of ⅛ inch (3 mm) and still red in centre. Remove from heat, cover and let stand until desired degree of doneness is reached (it continues to cook upon standing). Sprinkle with green onion and pepper.

MAKES 4 SERVINGS

MAKE AHEAD: Prepare marinade up to 4 hours ahead; cover and refrigerate. Remove from refrigerator 10 minutes before cooking.

VARIATION:

Grilled Tuna Fillet Burgers
Use 4 oz (125 g) fillets ½ inch (1 cm) thick. Grill for 2 to 4 minutes and serve in a toasted whole-wheat bun with lettuce and sliced tomato.

PER SERVING: 247 calories, 40 g protein, 8 g total fat, 2 g saturated fat, 71 mg cholesterol, 0 g carbohydrate, 0 g fibre, 131 mg sodium, 606 mg potassium

Coconut Shrimp Curry

This dish is terrific for dinner parties—it's quick and easy to make, looks great and has fabulous flavour. Serve over basmati or jasmine rice along with green beans or snow peas.

1 tsp	canola oil	5 mL
1	onion, chopped	1
3	cloves garlic, minced	3
3 tbsp	minced gingerroot	50 mL
1 tsp	ground cumin	5 mL
1 tsp	garam masala	5 mL
1 to 2 tbsp	mild Indian curry paste	15 to 25 mL
1 tsp	grated lemon rind	5 mL
1	sweet red pepper, chopped	1
1	tomato, diced	1
1 cup	light coconut milk	250 mL
1 lb	jumbo shrimp, peeled, deveined	500 g
2 tbsp	fresh lemon juice	25 mL
¼ cup	chopped fresh coriander (cilantro), mint or basil	50 mL
¼ tsp or less	salt and freshly ground pepper	1 mL or less

In nonstick skillet, heat oil over medium heat; add onion and cook, stirring often, until tender, about 5 minutes. Stir in garlic, gingerroot, cumin, garam masala, curry paste and lemon rind; cook 1 minute. Add red pepper and tomato; cook, stirring, for 2 minutes. Add coconut milk and bring to a simmer.

Stir in shrimp and cook 3 to 4 minutes until shrimp is pink and cooked. Stir in lemon juice, coriander, and salt and pepper. Serve over hot rice.

MAKES 4 SERVINGS

MAKE AHEAD: Prepare coconut milk mixture; cover and refrigerate for up to 6 hours. Reheat gently, then add shrimp and remaining ingredients as directed.

NOTE: Garam masala, a blend of ground spices often including pepper, cardamom, cinnamon and cumin, is available at Indian markets and many supermarkets.

Canned coconut milk is available at many supermarkets and Asian markets. If this recipe is made with regular coconut milk instead of light, it has 238 calories and 13 grams of fat per serving.

PER SERVING (of curry only):
195 calories, 22 g protein,
7 g total fat, 3 g saturated fat,
180 mg cholesterol,
10 g carbohydrate, 2 g fibre,
492 mg sodium, 507 mg potassium

Shrimp and Scallops in Coconut Milk

This popular dish for entertaining contains a flavourful combination of ginger, garlic, lemon and coriander. It's easy to make and looks attractive, too. Coconut milk adds a creamy texture and delightful taste yet is rather high in fat, so I use a moderate amount of the light variety. Serve over rice with Garlic Balsamic Vinegar and Sesame Oil (p. 135).

MAKE AHEAD: Prepare coconut milk mixture up to 2 hours in advance. Cover and set aside until ready to use.

PER SERVING: 190 calories, 27 g protein, 5 g total fat, 2 g saturated fat, 193 mg cholesterol, 7 g carbohydrate, 1 g fibre, 375 mg sodium, 470 mg potassium

1	medium lemon	1
1 tbsp	vegetable oil	15 mL
½ cup	chopped onion	125 mL
6	cloves garlic, minced	6
¼ cup	finely chopped gingerroot	50 mL
1 tbsp	all-purpose flour	15 mL
¾ cup	light coconut milk	175 mL
¼ cup	white wine	50 mL
¼ tsp	crushed red pepper flakes	1 mL
1½ lb	extra-large shrimp (raw or cooked), peeled and deveined	750 g
8 oz	large scallops	250 g
¼ tsp or less	salt and freshly ground pepper	1 mL or less
⅓ cup	each chopped fresh parsley and coriander (cilantro)	75 mL
3	green onions, finely chopped	3

Grate rind and squeeze juice from lemon; set aside. In large nonstick saucepan, heat oil over medium heat; cook onion, garlic and gingerroot, stirring, until tender, about 5 minutes. Sprinkle with flour and stir to mix. Stir in coconut milk, wine, lemon rind and juice and red pepper flakes; bring to simmer, stirring constantly.

Stir in shrimp and scallops; cover and cook, stirring occasionally, for 5 to 10 minutes or until shrimp are pink and scallops are opaque. Season with salt and pepper. Stir in parsley and coriander; sprinkle with green onions.

MAKES 6 SERVINGS

Rice Pilaf with Shrimp and Snow Peas

This pilaf is golden yellow like paella. Saffron lovers should add more saffron to taste. Serve with a tossed salad and fresh bread.

1 tsp	canola or olive oil	5 mL
1	onion, chopped	1
¼ tsp	each turmeric and freshly ground pepper	1 mL
Pinch	cayenne	Pinch
1 cup	basmati, or long-grain white or brown rice	250 mL
2 cups	sodium-reduced hot vegetable or chicken broth	500 mL
½ tsp	saffron threads	2 mL
½ lb	snow peas, trimmed	250 g
½ to 1 lb	cooked peeled large shrimp	250 to 500 g
½ cup	chopped fresh parsley or dill	125 mL
2	medium tomatoes, chopped	2
¼ tsp or less	salt	1 mL or less
	Lemon wedges	

In large nonstick skillet, heat oil over medium-low heat; cook onion, turmeric, pepper and cayenne, stirring occasionally, for 5 minutes or until onion is softened. Stir in rice, broth and saffron; bring to boil. Reduce heat to low; simmer, covered, for 20 minutes (40 minutes if using brown rice) or until liquid is absorbed.

Meanwhile, in pot of boiling water, cook snow peas for 1 minute; drain. To rice mixture, add snow peas, shrimp, parsley and tomatoes; cook over medium heat, tossing gently, for about 3 minutes or until hot. Season with salt. Garnish each plate with lemon wedge.

MAKES 4 SERVINGS

MAKE AHEAD: Cover and refrigerate pilaf for up to 4 hours; reheat gently.

VARIATIONS:

Bulgur Pilaf with Shrimp and Snow Peas
Substitute 1½ cups (375 mL) bulgur for the rice and increase broth to 3½ cups (875 mL); cook for 15 minutes.

Chicken or Tofu Pilaf
Substitute cubes of cooked boneless chicken breast or Marinated Baked Tofu (p. 168) for the shrimp.

PER SERVING: 339 calories, 19 g protein, 3 g total fat, 0 g saturated fat, 111 mg cholesterol, 58 g carbohydrate, 4 g fibre, 517 mg sodium, 489 mg potassium

Teriyaki Salmon and Shrimp Skewers

Serve these skewers of salmon and shrimp over a bed of fragrant jasmine or basmati rice. Sometimes I add a few tablespoons of hoisin sauce, chopped fresh coriander and some hot pepper sauce to the marinade. I often use scallops as well as salmon and shrimp.

8 oz	extra-large raw shrimp	250 g
12 oz	skinless wild salmon, cut in ¾-inch (2 cm) cubes	375 g
4	stalks asparagus (or 8 cherry tomatoes)	4
8	large mushrooms	8
8	large seedless green grapes	8

TERIYAKI MARINADE

2 tbsp	sodium-reduced soy sauce	25 mL
2 tbsp	sherry	25 mL
1 tbsp	sesame or olive oil	15 mL
1 tbsp	grated gingerroot	15 mL
2 tsp	granulated sugar	10 mL
8	8-inch (20 cm) wooden skewers	8

TERIYAKI MARINADE: In large bowl, combine soy sauce, sherry, oil, gingerroot and sugar, mixing to dissolve sugar. Peel and remove black veins from shrimp; add to bowl along with salmon, stirring to coat well. Cover and refrigerate for 30 minutes.

Snap off tough ends of asparagus; peel stalks if desired. Blanch in boiling water for 3 minutes; drain and plunge into cold water. Drain and cut into 1½-inch (4 cm) lengths.

On wooden skewers alternately thread salmon, asparagus, shrimp, mushrooms and grapes. Brush with marinade.

Preheat broiler. Place skewers on broiler pan or grill; cook for 3 to 5 minutes, turning once, or until fish is opaque.

MAKES 4 MAIN-COURSE OR 8 APPETIZER SERVINGS

MAKE AHEAD: Marinate shrimp and salmon in refrigerator for up to 8 hours. Cover and refrigerate skewers for up to 2 hours; brush occasionally with marinade.

NOTE: One serving is a high source of iron and a very high source of folacin.

To prevent scorching, soak wooden skewers in water for at least 30 minutes before threading with food.

VARIATION:

Lemon-Garlic Salmon and Shrimp Brochettes
Instead of Teriyaki Marinade, combine 2 tbsp (25 mL) fresh lemon or lime juice, 1 tbsp (15 mL) sesame or olive oil, 2 cloves minced garlic, ¼ tsp (1 mL) each salt and pepper; marinate salmon and shrimp in lemon mixture for 15 minutes. Thread salmon and shrimp onto skewers with vegetables, brush with lemon mixture and broil as directed. Serve with Creamy Dill Sauce (p. 325).

PER MAIN-COURSE SERVING:
216 calories, 28 g protein,
8 g total fat, 1 g saturated fat,
137 mg cholesterol,
7 g carbohydrate, 1 g fibre,
277 mg sodium, 724 mg potassium

Spicy Scallops

Hot Chinese chili paste adds a little fiery flavour to scallops. Serve with rice and snow peas and sprouts or stir-fried bok choy or broccoli. I like to use the regular-size scallops, rather than the tiny bay scallops, for this recipe.

2 tsp	canola or olive oil	10 mL
1 tbsp	minced gingerroot	15 mL
3 tbsp	chopped green onion	50 mL
1 lb	scallops	500 g
SAUCE		
2 tbsp	sherry	25 mL
1 tbsp	sodium-reduced soy sauce	15 mL
1 tbsp	sesame oil	15 mL
1 tsp	granulated sugar	5 mL
½ tsp	chili paste or hot pepper sauce	2 mL

SAUCE: Stir together sherry, soy sauce, oil, sugar and chili paste. Set aside.

In nonstick skillet, heat oil over high heat; stir-fry gingerroot and onion for 10 seconds. Add scallops; cook for about 30 seconds on each side or until lightly browned. Stir in sauce; stir-fry for about 2 minutes or just until scallops are opaque throughout.

MAKES 4 SERVINGS

MAKE AHEAD: Prepare sauce up to one day in advance.

NOTE: Three ounces (90 g) of steamed scallops (about 7 scallops) has only 1 g fat, 96 calories and 36 mg cholesterol.

Be careful not to overcook scallops. They cook very quickly and soon become dry.

PER SERVING: 167 calories, 19 g protein, 7 g total fat, 1 g saturated fat, 37 mg cholesterol, 5 g carbohydrate, 0 g fibre, 325 mg sodium, 399 mg potassium

Steamed Mussels with Tomatoes and Fennel

Cultured mussels, which require almost no preparation time, are available in many supermarkets—making this a fast and easy dish that's perfect for a small casual dinner party or Sunday night supper. The tomato sauce can be prepared ahead, but cook the mussels at the last minute.

4 lb	mussels	2 kg
1 tbsp	olive oil	15 mL
1	onion, chopped	1
4	cloves garlic, finely chopped	4
1	can (28 oz/796 mL) low-sodium plum tomatoes, drained and chopped	1
1 tsp	fennel seeds	5 mL
3 tbsp	chopped fresh parsley	50 mL
	Freshly ground pepper	
½ cup	dry white wine or water	125 mL
1	shallot, minced (optional)	1
2 tbsp	chopped green onions	25 mL

Rinse mussels; cut off any hairy beards. Discard any that do not close when lightly tapped or any that are cracked. Place in large pot and set aside.

In large skillet, heat oil over medium heat; cook onion and half of the garlic, stirring occasionally, until tender. Add tomatoes and fennel seeds; cook for 5 minutes. Add parsley, and pepper to taste; mix well.

Meanwhile, in small bowl, combine wine, shallot (if using) and remaining garlic; pour over mussels. Cover and bring to boil; reduce heat and simmer for 5 minutes or until mussels open. Discard any that do not open.

Using a slotted spoon, transfer mussels to individual bowls (pasta or large soup bowls). Stir ½ cup of mussel cooking liquid into tomato mixture; spoon over mussels. Garnish with green onions.

MAKES 4 SERVINGS

NOTE: Most of the sodium in this dish is from the salty liquid released by the mussels when they open during cooking. To reduce the sodium, we have used a minimum of the mussel cooking liquid.

PER SERVING: 205 calories, 18 g protein, 7 g total fat, 1 g saturated fat, 38 mg cholesterol, 15 g carbohydrate, 2 g fibre, 274 mg sodium, 541 mg potassium

Mussels, Tomatoes and Rice

When the mussels open, their liquid adds a delicate seafood flavour to the rice in this paella-type dish.

1 tbsp	olive oil	15 mL
¾ cup	long-grain converted rice	175 mL
2	cloves garlic, minced	2
¼ tsp	turmeric	1 mL
Pinch	hot pepper flakes	Pinch
1	bay leaf	1
1 tsp	saffron threads (optional)	5 mL
1½ cups	chopped tomatoes*	375 mL
⅔ cup	bottled clam juice or sodium-reduced chicken broth	150 mL
½ cup	dry white wine	125 mL
2 lb	mussels	1 kg
¼ cup	chopped fresh parsley	50 mL

In large skillet, heat oil over medium heat; cook rice, garlic, turmeric, hot pepper flakes, bay leaf and saffron (if using), stirring often, for 2 minutes. Stir in tomatoes, clam juice and wine; bring to boil. Reduce heat to medium-low; cover and simmer for 15 minutes.

Meanwhile, wash mussels and remove any beards. Discard any mussels that have broken shells or open shells that do not close when tapped. Nestle mussels into rice mixture; cover and cook until mussels open and rice is tender, 5 to 8 minutes. Discard any mussels that do not open. Discard bay leaf. Sprinkle with parsley.

MAKES 3 SERVINGS

*You can substitute 1 can (19 oz/540 mL) tomatoes, drained and chopped, for the fresh, if you like.

NOTE: Don't refrigerate mussels wrapped in plastic; instead, remove from plastic bag and place in bowl, cover with ice and refrigerate. Ten large mussels are an excellent source of protein and iron, a good source of folacin and zinc, and are low in fat.

PER SERVING: 323 calories, 16 g protein, 7 g total fat, 1 g saturated fat, 27 mg cholesterol, 45 g carbohydrate, 2 g fibre, 382 mg sodium, 519 mg potassium

Cioppino

Here's an excellent dish for a dinner party. The shellfish make it look and taste special, yet it is easy to prepare and has a nice light broth. Serve in bowls with toasted cheese bread or with grilled slices of Italian bread, rubbed with a cut clove of garlic and drizzled with olive oil, and a green salad.

1 tbsp	olive oil	15 mL
1	onion, chopped	1
4	cloves garlic, minced	4
1	sweet red pepper, chopped	1
1	can (28 oz/796 mL) tomatoes, undrained	1
1 cup	dry red or white wine	250 mL
1	bottle (8 oz/240 mL) clam juice	1
⅓ cup	chopped fresh parsley	75 mL
½ tsp	each dried basil, oregano and fennel seeds	2 mL
¼ tsp	hot pepper sauce or red pepper flakes	1 mL
1 lb	white fish fillets*	500 g
1 lb	mussels (in shells)	500 g
1 lb	crab legs (in shells), cut in 3-inch (8 cm) pieces	500 g
1 lb	large shrimp, peeled and deveined	500 g
¼ cup	chopped fresh basil	50 mL
¼ tsp or less	freshly ground pepper	1 mL or less

In large saucepan, heat oil over medium heat; cook onion, garlic and red pepper, stirring often, until onion is tender, 5 to 8 minutes. Stir in tomatoes, breaking up with knife. Add wine, clam juice, parsley, dried basil, oregano, fennel seeds and hot pepper sauce; bring to boil. Reduce heat and simmer, uncovered, for 20 minutes, stirring occasionally.

Cut fish fillets into 2-inch (5 cm) pieces. Scrub mussels and remove beards; discard any that don't close when tapped.

Add fillets, mussels and crab (if uncooked); cover and simmer for 2 minutes. Stir in shrimp and fresh basil and crab (if cooked); simmer for 3 to 5 minutes or until shrimp turn pink and mussel shells open. Discard any mussels that don't open. Season with pepper.

MAKES 6 SERVINGS

*Use any fresh, firm white fish fillets—Pacific cod, Pacific halibut or swordfish (U.S. or Canadian).

MAKE AHEAD: Cover and refrigerate cooked vegetable mixture for up to 6 hours; reheat before adding fish and shellfish.

NOTE: Use Dungeness, Kona or stone crab. Crab can be left in the shell or removed. If shell is left on, crack the legs so it is easy to remove the meat. If crab isn't available, use lobster (shelled and cooked is easiest) or add small clams or ½ lb (250 g) scallops along with the fish, or increase mussels to 2 lb (1 kg).

PER SERVING: 172 calories, 21 g protein, 4 g total fat, 1 g saturated fat, 137 mg cholesterol, 11 g carbohydrate, 2 g fibre, 706 mg sodium, 647 mg potassium

Easy Fish and Tomato Stew

Serve in shallow bowls with bread or over pasta, couscous, rice or boiled potatoes. Fennel adds a wonderful complementary flavour to fish. Use the seeds or ¼ cup (50 mL) chopped fresh leaves, or a pinch of anise, or a tablespoon or two (15 to 25 mL) of Pernod liqueur. The wine is optional but the stew tastes much better when it's included. To dress up this stew for a special occasion, or when unexpected guests arrive, add scallops, shrimp, mussels, clams and/or crab.

2 tsp	olive oil	10 mL
1	medium onion or leek, chopped	1
1½ tsp	minced fresh garlic	7 mL
1	large stalk celery, chopped	1
¼ tsp	fennel seeds	1 mL
⅛ tsp	crushed red pepper flakes	0.5 mL
1	can (28 oz/796 mL) tomatoes, undrained, chopped	1
¼ cup	dry white wine (optional)	50 mL
1 lb	fresh or frozen fish fillets (Pacific sole, halibut, cod)	500 g
¼ cup	chopped fresh parsley or coriander (cilantro)	50 mL
¼ tsp or less	salt and freshly ground pepper	1 mL or less

In nonstick saucepan, heat oil over medium heat; cook onion and garlic until softened, about 5 minutes. Add celery, fennel seeds, red pepper flakes, tomatoes and wine (if using); bring to boil. Reduce heat and simmer for 5 minutes. Add fish and cook until fish is opaque, about 5 minutes for fresh, 10 minutes for frozen. Add parsley and season with salt and pepper. (Most fish will break up into pieces as you stir in the salt and pepper; if not, cut into pieces before serving.)

MAKES 4 SERVINGS

VARIATION:

Easy Fish Stew with Scallops, Shrimp and Mussels
Along with the fresh or thawed fish, add 1 lb (500 g) mussels (in shells, washed and debearded; see page 232); cover and simmer 3 minutes. Add 4 oz (125 g) each scallops and medium to small shrimp (peeled, fresh or cooked). Cover and simmer another 3 minutes or until mussels open. Add parsley and continue as directed in recipe. Discard any mussels that don't open.

NOTE: If you keep the ingredients for this recipe on hand in your freezer and pantry, you can make a meal in minutes—even when your refrigerator is bare. If using frozen fish, use individually frozen fillets rather than those frozen in a block and, if possible, thaw before using. (However, if using a frozen block, increase cooking time to 20 minutes or until fish is opaque.)

PER SERVING: 173 calories, 24 g protein, 4 g total fat, 1 g saturated fat, 60 mg cholesterol, 11 g carbohydrate, 2 g fibre, 509 mg sodium, 777 mg potassium

Shrimp and Chicken Jambalaya

This make-ahead version of a Creole classic is mild to medium-hot. Add more pepper or hot pepper sauce if you want it hotter. Instead of shrimp, you could add ½ lb (250 g) lean smoked cubed ham. This recipe is part of a Christmas buffet menu I developed for *Canadian Living* magazine.

1 tbsp	olive oil	15 mL
2 cups	chopped onion	500 mL
2 cups	chopped celery	500 mL
1	sweet green pepper, chopped	1
3 oz	diced smoked ham or sausage (andouille or kielbasa)	75 g
1½ lb	boneless skinless chicken breasts or thighs, cubed	750 g
2 tbsp	minced fresh garlic	25 mL
2	bay leaves	2
2 tsp	dried oregano	10 mL
1 tsp	dried thyme	5 mL
½ tsp	each cayenne and freshly ground pepper	2 mL
1	can (28 oz/796 mL) low-sodium tomatoes	1
1	can (7½ oz/213 mL) no-salt-added tomato sauce	1
4 cups	water	1 L
2½ cups	long-grain white rice	625 mL
1 lb	large raw shrimp, peeled	500 g
1	sweet red pepper, chopped	1
½ cup	chopped green onions	125 mL
½ cup	chopped fresh parsley	125 mL

In large Dutch oven, heat oil over medium-high heat; cook onion and celery for 3 minutes. Add green pepper, ham, chicken, garlic, bay leaves, oregano, thyme, cayenne and pepper; cook, stirring, for 3 minutes. Add tomatoes, tomato sauce and water; bring to boil. Stir in rice and shrimp; boil for 1 minute. Bake, covered, in 350°F (180°C) oven for 25 minutes or until rice is tender. Discard bay leaves. Stir in red pepper and green onions; sprinkle with parsley.

MAKES 8 SERVINGS

MAKE AHEAD: Cover and refrigerate for up to 1 day. To reheat, stir in 1 cup (250 mL) hot water; bake, covered, in 350°F (180°C) oven for 1 hour and 15 minutes or until hot.

PER SERVING: 441 calories, 38 g protein, 5 g total fat, 1 g saturated fat, 146 mg cholesterol, 60 g carbohydrate, 4 g fibre, 313 mg sodium, 934 mg potassium

Buying and Cooking Fish and Shellfish

Fish and shellfish are good nutritional buys, and are good for you because they contain heart-healthy omega-3 fat. (See page 444 for more details on the benefits of omega-3 fats.) Most varieties of fish are low in fat and calories, and even the varieties that are higher in fat, such as salmon, are on a par with extra-lean ground beef when it comes to fat content. This means you don't have to worry about fat when choosing the kind of fish to buy and can eat it two to three times a week. The important thing to remember is to serve a variety of fish in moderate-sized portions and use little or no extra fat when you prepare it.

Cod, haddock, halibut, perch, pickerel, pollock, red snapper, sole, crab, crayfish, lobster, shrimp and scallops also have less than 3 grams of fat per 90 g (3 oz) serving. However, this doesn't mean it is fine to fry fish in added fat or to serve it with a butter-laden sauce. Remember, 4 oz (125 g) sole, snapper, cod or haddock has 1 g fat or less, but 1 tbsp (15 mL) of butter has 11 g fat and 1 tbsp (15 mL) of oil has 14 g fat.

Fish is also an excellent source of protein and the B-vitamin niacin and provides iron, thiamin and riboflavin. It's a good source of potassium, a mineral that is believed to protect against high blood pressure.

BUYING, STORING AND COOKING FISH

BUYING FRESH FISH

When possible, buy fish the day you will cook it. The best test for freshness is to use your nose—the fish should have a mild fishy or seawater odour. Anything stronger means the fish has been out of the water too long. Look for:

- a mild smell

- glistening, firm flesh that springs back when touched

- very firmly attached scales

- clear, bright, convex (not sunken) eyes

STORING FRESH FISH

- If not cleaned, clean as soon as possible.

- Wipe with a damp cloth, wrap in waxed paper and place in covered container.

- Store in coldest part of the refrigerator.

- Cook as soon as possible (same day for store-bought, within 4 days if freshly caught).

BUYING FROZEN FISH

Look for:

- glazed fish coated with ice

- shiny, solidly frozen flesh with no signs of drying or freezer burn (white spots)

- tightly wrapped package with no sign of frost or ice crystals inside

STORING FROZEN FISH

- Keep fish at 0°F (-18°C) or lower for ideal storage.

- Store fatty fish (salmon, mackerel, lake trout) for a maximum of 2 months.

- Store lean fish (cod, haddock, ocean perch, pike, sole) for a maximum of 6 months.

COOKING TIMES

- Measure fish at the thickest part (stuffed or not).

- Allow 10 minutes' cooking time per inch (2.5 cm) of thickness for fresh fish; add 2 to 3 minutes extra for frozen fillets, double the time for fish frozen in a block. If wrapped in foil, add 5 minutes for fresh, 10 minutes for a frozen block. This applies to all fish and all cooking methods (if in oven, cook at 450°F/230°C).

- Fish is cooked when flesh is opaque and it flakes and separates into solid moist sections when firmly prodded with a fork.

COOKING METHODS

STEAMING (STOVE TOP)

Pour 2 inches (5 cm) of water in a steamer and bring to a boil. Season and wrap fish securely in cheesecloth. Place on a rack over boiling water. Cover and begin timing (see above).

BROILING

Place fish on broiler pan. Follow manufacturer's instructions regarding preheating and leaving oven door open while broiling. Adjust rack so top of food is about 3 inches (7.5 cm) from heat.

BAKING

Place whole fish, with skin, on baking pan (line with foil if desired); season to taste with salt, pepper, a sprinkle of lemon juice and/or herbs. Bake in preheated 450°F (230°C) oven for required time.

OVEN STEAMING

Place fresh or frozen fish on lightly greased foil on baking sheet. Season with salt, pepper and herbs (parsley, dill, chives or basil) to taste. Sprinkle with lemon juice or white wine. Wrap securely in foil. Bake in preheated 450°F (230°C) oven for required time, adding 5 minutes for fresh fish and 10 minutes for frozen because of being wrapped in foil.

POACHING

Place fish on greased heavy-duty foil. Season with salt and pepper to taste; add chopped onion and celery. Wrap, using double folds to make package watertight. Place in rapidly boiling water and simmer for required cooking time. (Fish may also be wrapped in cheesecloth and poached in court bouillon or fish stock.)

MICROWAVING

Place fish in microwaveable dish. Season with salt and pepper to taste. Cover with parchment paper or waxed paper, turning back corner to allow steam to escape. Estimate cooking time at 3 to 4 minutes per pound (500 g), plus 2 to 3 minutes' standing time. Microwave on High or according to appliance manual.

GRILLING

Place fish (for fillets, I prefer skin side down) on lightly greased grill. Close cover and grill over medium or low heat, turning once, until fish is opaque and flakes. Cooking time will vary depending on the thickness of fish and distance from coals; 1-inch (2.5 cm) thick salmon steaks will take 8 to 10 minutes over medium heat.

SKILLET COOKING

If fish is washed or marinated, pat dry. Lightly oil (½ tsp/2 mL olive oil) a nonstick skillet. Add fish and cook over medium-high heat, turning once. Fish fillets or steaks about ¾ inch (2 cm) thick will take 2 to 3 minutes per side.

BUYING, STORING AND COOKING SHELLFISH

SHRIMP

Buying frozen shrimp

The larger the shrimp, the fewer there are per pound (500 g). Most packages state how many shrimp there are per pound. For example, you'll usually get 11 to 15 per pound with jumbo shrimp; for extra-large 16 to 20; large 21 to 30; medium 31 to 35; small 36 to 45; and very small about 100. Canadian or U.S. shrimp, farmed or wild, are recommended over imported.

Thawing shrimp

Thaw shrimp in the refrigerator in a sealed container for 8 hours or overnight, or place sealed package in cold water for 30 to 60 minutes. Once thawed, use immediately; do not refreeze.

Cleaning shrimp

Using scissors, cut shell of shrimp along centre of back. Pull off shell, leaving tail intact if desired. Cut shallow slit down centre back and pull out intestinal vein if showing; rinse shrimp.

Cooking shrimp

Frozen shrimp is often sold cooked and needs only to be thawed and reheated. Overcooking toughens them. For the most flavour, cook raw shrimp in the shell. You can steam, boil, or sauté shrimp, or broil or roast in the oven, grill on the barbecue or in a grill pan. To grill, place in a single layer in grill basket or thread onto wooden skewers, starting at tail end, through centre of shrimp.

MUSSELS

Buying mussels

Buy medium size, about 18 to the pound (500 g) cultured (farmed) mussels; they are easy to clean and have more meat than wild ones. Buy and use only those mussels with closed shells. The fresher the mussel, the better it tastes.

Storing mussels

Don't refrigerate mussels stored in plastic or submerged in water; instead remove from plastic bag and place in bowl, cover with slightly wet paper towel or with newspaper that has some ice on top, and refrigerate. Mussels should be used preferably within 24 hours, at the latest by the second day.

Cleaning mussels

Debeard the mussels just before cooking. Under running water, lightly scrub shells with a brush to remove grit. With your fingers or a small pair of pliers, pull off the beard (the clump of dark threads).

Cooking mussels

Discard any mussels with cracked or open shells before cooking. Cook mussels in a large covered pot with a little water or white wine, parsley and garlic, or according to the recipe. Mussels are cooked when the shells open. Discard any cooked mussels with unopened shells.

Provençal Saffron Chicken

I've lightened up this recipe, which I learned at Lydie Marshall's cooking school in Nyons, France. It is a splendid entertaining dish, especially in the fall, when tomatoes are at their best. Sometimes I omit the saffron and serve this with saffron rice. It's also nice served with mashed potatoes and a green salad.

4 lb	skinless chicken parts or legs	2 kg
1 tsp	each paprika and turmeric	5 mL
½ tsp or less	each salt and freshly ground pepper	2 mL or less
2 tbsp	olive oil	25 mL
1 tsp	saffron threads	5 mL
6	medium onions, thinly sliced (6 cups/1.5 L)	6
1 tsp	granulated sugar	5 mL
8	large cloves garlic, chopped	8
6	large tomatoes (3½ lb/1.75 kg) peeled and coarsely chopped or 2 cans (19 oz/540 mL each) tomatoes, chopped	6
2 tbsp	chopped gingerroot	25 mL
1 tsp	coarsely grated lemon rind	5 mL
⅔ cup	pitted green olives	150 mL

Arrange chicken in large shallow glass baking dish. In small bowl, mix paprika, turmeric, salt and pepper; stir in 1 tbsp (15 mL) of the oil; spread over chicken. Cover and refrigerate for at least 4 hours or for up to 24 hours.

In small dish, pour 2 tbsp (25 mL) hot water over saffron; let stand for 20 minutes.

In large nonstick skillet, heat remaining oil over medium-high heat; brown chicken; transfer to plate. Add onions, sugar and any remaining marinade to skillet; cook over medium heat, stirring occasionally, until tender, about 10 minutes. Add garlic, tomatoes and gingerroot; cook for 10 minutes.

Return chicken to pan. Stir in lemon rind and saffron with liquid. Cover and simmer for 20 to 25 minutes or until juices run clear when chicken is pierced. Add olives; cook just until warmed.

MAKES 8 SERVINGS

MAKE AHEAD: Marinate chicken for up to 1 day. Cook chicken as directed, then cover and refrigerate, up to 1 day in advance. Add olives when reheating.

NOTE: Removing the skin from chicken parts before cooking significantly reduces fat.

PER SERVING: 331 calories, 41 g protein, 11 g total fat, 2 g saturated fat, 120 mg cholesterol, 16 g carbohydrate, 4 g fibre, 418 mg sodium, 924 mg potassium

Chicken with Lemons, Olives and Coriander

Serve this delightful chicken dish with basmati rice or couscous and a green vegetable or salad.

1 tbsp	extra-virgin olive oil	15 mL
1½ lb	each skinless chicken thighs and breasts	750 g
2 tsp	ground cumin	10 mL
2 tbsp	minced gingerroot	25 mL
2 tbsp	fresh lemon juice	25 mL
½ tsp or less	each salt and freshly ground pepper	2 mL or less
1	lemon, cut in halves	1
6 to 12	green or black olives	6 to 12
3 tbsp	chopped fresh coriander (cilantro)	50 mL

In large nonstick skillet, heat oil over high heat; add chicken and brown on all sides. Stir in cumin and gingerroot; cook 1 minute; add lemon juice, salt and pepper. Cover and cook over medium-low heat, turning often, until chicken is tender, about 35 to 45 minutes.

Add lemon pieces, olives and coriander. Cover and simmer 5 minutes.

MAKES 6 SERVINGS

MAKE AHEAD: Cover and refrigerate up to 1 day. Reheat, covered, in microwave or skillet.

PER SERVING: 252 calories, 38 g protein, 9 g total fat, 2 g saturated fat, 120 mg cholesterol, 3 g carbohydrate, 0 g fibre, 347 mg sodium, 475 mg potassium

Chicken Dijon

This is one of my all-time favourite recipes, mainly because it's so easy to make and tastes so good. Crisp and juicy, this chicken can be prepared ahead of time and served hot, warm or cold. I make the bread crumbs in the food processor from at least one-day-old whole-wheat bread.

¼ cup	low-fat plain yogurt	50 mL
2 to 3 tbsp	Dijon mustard	25 to 50 mL
1 cup	fresh whole-wheat bread crumbs	250 mL
1 tsp	crushed dried thyme	5 mL
¼ tsp or less	each salt and freshly ground pepper	1 mL or less
4	skinless chicken breasts or legs (boned if desired)	4

In small bowl, combine yogurt and mustard. In shallow bowl, mix bread crumbs, thyme, salt and pepper.

Spread each piece of chicken with mustard mixture, then roll in bread-crumb mixture. Place chicken in single layer on lightly greased baking sheet. Bake in 350°F (180°C) oven for 45 to 50 minutes for bone-in chicken, 30 minutes for boneless, or until golden brown and meat is no longer pink.

MAKES 4 SERVINGS

MAKE AHEAD: Unbaked chicken can be covered and refrigerated for up to 2 hours. Bake as directed. Baked chicken can be covered and refrigerated for up to 2 days.

NOTE: In Chicken Dijon the skin is removed to reduce the fat content; the mustard mixture and bread-crumb coating keep the chicken moist. Make the crumbs from whole-wheat bread; it is higher in fibre and has a more attractive colour for crumbs than white bread. They are quick to make using a food processor.

PER SERVING: 181 calories, 32 g protein, 3 g total fat, 1 g saturated fat, 80 mg cholesterol, 5 g carbohydrate, 1 g fibre, 372 mg sodium, 440 mg potassium

Sherry Chicken Breasts Stuffed with Zucchini and Carrots

Light yet full of flavour, these make-ahead chicken breasts are perfect for a dinner party.

6	boneless skinless chicken breasts (1½ lb/750 g)	6
12	large spinach leaves	12
1 tsp	canola or olive oil	5 mL
½ cup	sherry	125 mL
STUFFING		
1 tbsp	canola or olive oil	15 mL
1	onion, chopped	1
2	cloves garlic, minced	2
1 cup	coarsely grated zucchini	250 mL
½ cup	coarsely grated carrot	125 mL
½ tsp	dried thyme	2 mL
½ cup	fresh bread crumbs	125 mL
2 tbsp	chopped fresh parsley	25 mL
1	egg white	1
¼ tsp or less	each salt and freshly ground pepper	1 mL or less

Between sheets of waxed paper, pound chicken to ¼ inch (5 mm) thickness.

Remove tough stems from spinach; rinse spinach. With just the water clinging to leaves, cook spinach for 1 minute or just until wilted; drain and set aside.

STUFFING: In nonstick skillet, heat oil over medium heat; cook onion and garlic for 3 minutes. Stir in zucchini, carrot and thyme; cook, stirring often, for 5 minutes or until tender. Remove from heat. Add bread crumbs, parsley, egg white, salt and pepper; mix well.

Cover top of each chicken breast with 2 spinach leaves; spread stuffing evenly over spinach. Carefully roll up each breast and tie each end with cotton string.

In large nonstick skillet, heat oil over medium heat; cook stuffed breasts for 5 minutes, turning often. Pour in sherry; reduce heat to medium-low and cook, covered, for 10 to 12 minutes or until chicken is no longer pink inside, turning to coat in sauce for last 2 minutes.

Let stand for 5 minutes. Untie each roll and slice diagonally into 3 or 4 slices.

MAKES 6 SERVINGS

MAKE AHEAD: Assemble stuffed chicken breasts, cover and refrigerate, up to 8 hours in advance.

VARIATION:

Chicken Breasts Stuffed with Mushrooms and Leeks
Omit onion, zucchini and carrot from stuffing. Substitute 1½ cups (375 mL) finely chopped mushrooms and ¾ cup (175 mL) chopped white of leek.

PER SERVING: 198 calories, 28 g protein, 5 g total fat, 1 g saturated fat, 67 mg cholesterol, 7 g carbohydrate, 2 g fibre, 210 mg sodium, 569 mg potassium

Sautéed Chicken with Mushrooms and Onions

A rich-tasting dish for family or guests, this is a natural partner for broiled tomatoes, a green vegetable and rice. Any kind of mushrooms can be used—domestic, wild or dried. Try shiitake, porcini, Portobello, oyster or a combination.

¾ lb	each skinless chicken breasts and thighs	375g
¼ tsp	paprika	1 mL
2 tsp	canola or olive oil	10 mL
1	onion, thinly sliced	1
3 cups	thickly sliced mushrooms*	750 mL
¼ cup	low-fat plain yogurt	50 mL
1 tsp	all-purpose flour	5 mL
¼ tsp or less	salt and freshly ground pepper	1 mL or less

Sprinkle chicken with paprika. In large nonstick skillet, heat oil over medium-high heat; cook chicken until browned all over, about 5 minutes on each side. Reduce heat to medium-low; cover and cook for 10 minutes longer on each side or until juices run clear when chicken is pierced. If necessary to prevent burning, add a spoonful or two of water or mushroom soaking liquid if using dried mushrooms. Remove from pan and keep warm.

Add onion and mushrooms to pan; cook over medium heat, stirring often, for 5 to 10 minutes or until tender.

In small bowl, combine yogurt and flour; stir into onion mixture. Season with salt and pepper. Return chicken to pan and spoon sauce over top; cook over medium-low heat for 1 to 2 minutes or until hot.

MAKES 3 SERVINGS

*If using only dried mushrooms, soak 1 or 2 ounces (30 to 60 g) of dried mushrooms in small amount of hot water for 15 to 30 minutes or until soft; drain (saving liquid for a soup or sauce) and slice.

NOTE: One serving is a high source of iron.

PER SERVING: 292 calories, 41 g protein, 10 g total fat, 2 g saturated fat, 121 mg cholesterol, 9 g carbohydrate, 2 g fibre, 320 mg sodium, 755 mg potassium

Stir-Fry for One

Stir-fries are a quick and easy meal for one or two people and an excellent way to use up a piece of broccoli or half a red pepper lurking in the refrigerator—add a few more vegetables and they can easily be stretched to make an extra serving. Don't be put off by the long list of ingredients—they take only a minute or two to put together and taste delicious. Serve over hot rice or noodles.

¼ lb	boneless chicken	125 g
1 tsp	cornstarch	5 mL
1 tbsp	sherry or dry white wine	15 mL
1	stalk broccoli or celery	1
½	sweet red pepper	½
2 tsp	canola oil	10 mL
1	clove garlic, minced	1
1 tsp	minced gingerroot	5 mL

SEASONING SAUCE

1 tbsp	water	15 mL
1 tbsp	sherry or white wine	15 mL
½ tsp	cornstarch	2 mL
1 tsp	sodium-reduced soy sauce	5 mL

Cut chicken into thin strips about 2 inches (5 cm) long.

In bowl, mix cornstarch and sherry; stir in chicken and let stand for 10 minutes or up to 2 hours. Cut broccoli into florets and red pepper into thin strips.

SEASONING SAUCE: In small bowl, combine water, sherry, cornstarch and soy sauce; mix well.

In wok or nonstick skillet, heat oil over high heat. Add garlic, gingerroot and chicken; stir-fry for 1 minute. Add broccoli and red pepper; stir-fry for 2 minutes or until tender-crisp, adding water if necessary to prevent scorching. Stir in seasoning sauce and stir-fry for another minute.

MAKES 1 SERVING

VARIATION: Use well-trimmed beef or pork instead of chicken.

PER SERVING: 254 calories, 16 g protein, 11 g total fat, 1 g saturated fat, 29 mg cholesterol, 21 g carbohydrate, 5 g fibre, 270 mg sodium, 730 mg potassium

Breast of Chicken and Spinach with Tarragon Mushroom Sauce

This recipe may look lengthy but it isn't hard to make. Because most of the preparation can be done in advance, it's ideal for a dinner party. Serve with Two-Cabbage Stir-Fry with Ginger and Onion (p. 137) or Parsnip Purée (p. 140) and brown rice.

1 lb	fresh spinach	500 g
1 tsp	fresh lemon juice	5 mL
1 tsp	canola or olive oil	5 mL
¼ tsp or less	salt and freshly ground pepper	1 mL or less
1 cup	Tarragon and Mushroom Sauce (p. 327)	250 mL
4 oz	enoki mushrooms (optional)	125 g

CHICKEN

¼ cup	all-purpose flour	50 mL
1 tsp	crushed dried thyme	5 mL
¼ tsp or less	salt	1 mL or less
	Freshly ground pepper	
1	egg, lightly beaten	1
1 tbsp	water	15 mL
½ cup	fresh bread crumbs	125 mL
¼ cup	freshly grated Parmesan cheese	50 mL
4	boneless skinless chicken breasts (about 1 lb/500 g)	4

CHICKEN: On plate, combine flour, thyme, salt, and pepper to taste. In shallow bowl, combine egg and water. On another plate, combine bread crumbs and cheese. Coat chicken pieces with seasoned flour; shake off excess. Dip into egg mixture, then roll in crumb mixture. Set aside.

Trim stems from spinach. Wash and shake off water; place in saucepan with just the water clinging to leaves. Cover and cook over medium-high heat until wilted. Drain thoroughly; squeeze out excess liquid and chop coarsely. Toss with lemon juice, oil, and salt and pepper.

On lightly greased baking sheet or in microwaveable dish, bake chicken in 400°F (200°C) oven for 15 minutes, or microwave, loosely covered with waxed paper, on High for 5 to 6 minutes, or until chicken is no longer pink inside. If microwaving, let stand for 1 to 2 minutes (cooking time will vary, depending on thickness of chicken).

Place chicken on top of spinach. Garnish with a few spoonfuls of Tarragon and Mushroom Sauce. Sprinkle with raw enoki mushrooms (if using). Pass the remainder of the sauce separately.

MAKES 4 SERVINGS

MAKE AHEAD: Cook spinach a few hours in advance; reheat in microwave or on stove, then add lemon juice, butter, and salt and pepper. Refrigerate prepared unbaked chicken for 20 minutes or for up to 2 hours. Tarragon Mushroom Sauce can be covered and refrigerated for up to 2 days.

NOTE: Enoki mushrooms have long, thin stems and small, round heads. Raw, they add a woodsy flavour to dishes and are lovely as a garnish. They are available at some supermarkets, in specialty vegetable stores and in Asian markets.

One serving of this recipe provides 90% of the daily value for vitamin A; it is also an excellent source of iron and folacin and high in calcium.

PER SERVING: 264 calories, 34 g protein, 8 g total fat, 2 g saturated fat, 106 mg cholesterol, 14 g carbohydrate, 3 g fibre, 686 mg sodium, 906 mg potassium

Crispy Herbed Chicken

I keep a small jar of herb-seasoned flour on hand so I can make this chicken dish quickly—it's one of my children's favourites. The herb-seasoned flour need not be limited to the herbs I've suggested here; feel free to include whichever herbs you like—just be sure to use the crushed dried leaf form, not powdered or ground.

| 6 | skinless chicken legs, thighs or breasts (about 2 lb/1 kg, bone-in) | 6 |
| ⅓ cup | (approx) warm water | 75 mL |

HERB-SEASONED FLOUR

2 tbsp	flour	25 mL
2 tsp	dried herbs (crushed oregano, thyme, tarragon and/or Italian seasonings)	10 mL
¼ tsp or less	salt and freshly ground pepper	1 mL or less

Rinse chicken under cold running water and pat dry with paper towels. Place chicken in single layer in lightly greased shallow roasting pan or baking dish.

HERB-SEASONED FLOUR: Combine flour with dried herbs; season with salt and pepper to taste. Use small sieve or spoon to sprinkle Herb-Seasoned Flour over chicken.

Pour warm water down side of pan, not directly over chicken. Bake, uncovered, in 375°F (190°C) oven for 40 to 50 minutes or until chicken is no longer pink inside, basting occasionally with liquid in pan to brown top of chicken. Add more water if there's not enough liquid in pan for basting.

MAKES 6 SERVINGS

NOTE: If you wish to make a larger amount of Herb-Seasoned Flour to keep on hand, in small jar with lid, combine ½ cup (125 mL) all-purpose flour, 2 tsp (10 mL) each crushed dried basil, oregano and thyme, 1 tsp (5 mL) each salt, pepper, dried tarragon and paprika. Cover and shake to mix; store at room temperature. Makes about ⅔ cup (150 mL).

COMPARE:
% calories from fat

Roast chicken breast with skin on
42

Roast chicken breast without skin
12

PER SERVING: 168 calories, 24 g protein, 7 g total fat, 2 g saturated fat, 87 mg cholesterol, 2 g carbohydrate, 0 g fibre, 187 mg sodium, 236 mg potassium

Roast Chicken with Lemon Thyme Apple Stuffing

I don't usually follow a recipe when making stuffing for chicken. First I make bread crumbs in the food processor using whole-wheat bread, then I chop an onion and add herbs and whatever else I have on hand—apples, celery or mushrooms. Here's one I often make. This recipe makes 9 cups (1.75 L) stuffing, enough for two 5-lb (2.4 kg) roasting chickens. Wrap extra stuffing in foil and bake for 20 minutes. For 1 chicken, halve recipe.

2	chickens (5 lb/2.2 kg each) or 1 capon (9 lb/4.5 kg)	2

STUFFING

3 cups	soft bread crumbs	750 mL
3	apples, peeled, cored and chopped	3
2	onions, chopped	2
3	stalks celery (including leaves), chopped	3
3 tbsp	fresh thyme, chopped (or 2 tsp/10 mL dried)	50 mL
	Grated rind from 1 lemon	
¼ tsp or less	salt and freshly ground pepper	1 mL or less

Wipe cavity of chicken; pat dry inside and out with paper towel.

In large bowl, mix bread crumbs, apples, onions, celery, thyme and lemon rind until well blended. Season with salt and pepper.

Fill the cavity of the chicken; truss the chicken with string and place on rack, breast side up, in a roasting pan. Roast in 325°F (160°C) oven for about 35 minutes per pound (500 g), or until juices run clear when chicken is pierced with fork.

MAKES 12 SERVINGS OF 4 OZ (125 g) SKINLESS LIGHT AND DARK MEAT WITH ¹⁄₁₂ OF STUFFING

NOTE: To truss a chicken, use cotton string to tie the legs and wings close to the body. This prevents the legs and wings from becoming overcooked and dried out before the rest of the chicken is cooked.

If making a bread stuffing, use fairly fresh bread, or moisten stale bread with chicken stock; add chopped onions, celery and apple instead of oil or butter. Or, instead of stuffing, place apple slices, onion wedges, mushrooms and/or orange sections in cavity. Slip garlic slivers, fresh herbs, sliced fresh gingerroot between flesh and skin or place in cavity.

VARIATION:

Mushroom Onion Stuffing
Omit apples and lemon. Add 1½ cups (375 mL) coarsely chopped mushrooms and 1 tsp (5 mL) dried sage (or 1 tbsp/15 mL chopped fresh); celery is optional.

PER SERVING (skinless meat):
273 calories, 34 g protein,
9 g total fat, 2 g saturated fat,
101 mg cholesterol,
12 g carbohydrate, 1 g fibre,
214 mg sodium, 381 mg potassium

Jamaican Jerk Chicken

Spicy Jamaican jerk seasoning was traditionally used when cooking dried meats in a large pot over an open fire. The jerk marinade in this recipe is delicious with chicken or roast pork. I prefer to use a jalapeño pepper instead of the traditional Scotch bonnet pepper because the jalapeño is not as hot.

1	onion, quartered	1
1	Scotch bonnet* or hot pepper, halved	1
3	cloves garlic, halved	3
4	green onions, coarsely chopped	4
¼ cup	orange juice	50 mL
¼ cup	sodium-reduced soy sauce	50 mL
1 tbsp	canola or olive oil	15 mL
1 tbsp	red or white wine vinegar	15 mL
1 tsp	each dried thyme and ground allspice	5 mL
½ tsp	each cinnamon and curry powder	2 mL
¼ tsp or less	freshly ground pepper	1 mL or less
2 lb	skinless chicken pieces	1 kg

In food processor, purée onion, hot pepper, garlic and green onions. Add orange juice, soy sauce, oil, vinegar, thyme, allspice, cinnamon, curry powder, and pepper; process to mix.

Pour marinade over chicken pieces; cover and refrigerate for 2 hours or longer, turning occasionally.

Grill over high heat for about 20 minutes on each side, or bake in 325°F (160°C) oven for 40 minutes, or until no longer pink inside.

MAKES 4 SERVINGS

*A Scotch bonnet pepper is fiery hot. You can substitute jalapeño, serrano or banana pepper. Wear rubber gloves when handling. To lessen the heat, discard the seeds.

MAKE AHEAD: Marinate chicken for up to 2 days.

NOTE: The term "jerk" refers to a traditional method of preserving meats: cutting them into strips and drying them in the sun. I use regular chicken in this recipe.

Omitting the soy sauce will lower the sodium to 110 mg per serving.

PER SERVING: 252 calories, 39 g protein, 8 g total fat, 2 g saturated fat, 120 mg cholesterol, 4 g carbohydrate, 1 g fibre, 376 mg sodium, 504 mg potassium

Grilled Tandoori Chicken

The Indian yogurt-and-spice marinade makes the chicken moist and flavourful. Serve with rice and a green vegetable such as asparagus, green beans or broccoli. Instead of the spices listed here, you can also use a tablespoon (15 mL) of tandoori spice blend.

1 tbsp	Dijon mustard	15 mL
1 tbsp	canola oil	15 mL
½ cup	low-fat plain yogurt	125 mL
2 tbsp	minced gingerroot	25 mL
1 tsp	each ground cumin and ground coriander	5 mL
½ tsp	ground turmeric	2 mL
¼ tsp	cayenne	1 mL
2 tbsp	fresh lemon juice	25 mL
2 lb	skinless chicken pieces	1 kg

Place mustard in mixing bowl; whisk in oil, drop by drop, until well blended. Stir in yogurt and gingerroot; set aside.

In skillet over medium heat, cook cumin, coriander, turmeric and cayenne 1 to 2 minutes or until fragrant; stir into yogurt mixture; add lemon juice and mix well.

Arrange chicken in shallow dish or place in plastic bag; pour yogurt-spice mixture over chicken and be sure to coat all pieces. Cover and refrigerate for at least 8 hours and up to 24 hours.

On greased grill over medium heat or under broiler, grill chicken for 15 to 20 minutes on each side (15 minutes if top is down on barbecue) or until chicken is tender and juices run clear when chicken is pierced with fork. Watch carefully and turn to prevent burning.

MAKES 4 SERVINGS

VARIATION:

Roasted Tandoori Chicken
Bake in 400°F (200°C) oven for 30 minutes or until juices run clear when pierced with a fork.

PER SERVING: 278 calories, 40 g protein, 10 g total fat, 2 g saturated fat, 121 mg cholesterol, 4 g carbohydrate, 0 g fibre, 226 mg sodium, 537 mg potassium

Curried Chicken Crêpes

This delicious dish is terrific as a make-ahead brunch, lunch or dinner. It's even quicker and easier to make if you keep crêpes on hand in the freezer. Cooked turkey, shrimp or pork can be used instead of chicken. Serve with Arugula and Boston Lettuce Salad with Walnut Oil Vinaigrette (p. 65).

PER SERVING: 225 calories, 24 g protein, 5 g total fat, 1 g saturated fat, 50 mg cholesterol, 20 g carbohydrate, 1 g fibre, 337 mg sodium, 441 mg potassium

2 tsp	canola oil	10 mL
½	medium onion, chopped	½
½ cup	diced celery	125 mL
1 tbsp	all-purpose flour	15 mL
1½ tsp	curry powder or paste or to taste	7 mL
¼ tsp	salt	1 mL
½ cup	sodium-reduced chicken broth	125 mL
1½ cups	diced cooked chicken (about ¾ lb/375 g boneless chicken breasts)	375 mL
¼ cup	light sour cream	50 mL
¼ cup	low-fat plain yogurt	50 mL
8	Basic Crêpes (p. 402)	8
	Plain yogurt, chutney and green grapes for garnish	

In saucepan, heat oil; over medium heat, cook onion and celery, stirring, until onion is softened. Add flour, curry powder and salt; cook, stirring, for 1 minute.

Whisk in chicken broth and bring to simmer while whisking. Reduce heat to low and simmer, stirring, for 2 minutes. Remove from heat and stir in chicken, sour cream and yogurt. Add more curry powder to taste.

Place 2 or 3 large spoonfuls of chicken mixture across centre of each crêpe. Roll up and place seam side down in lightly greased shallow baking dish.

Bake in 375°F (190°C) oven for 20 minutes or microwave on High for 2 minutes or until heated through. Top each serving with a spoonful of yogurt and another of chutney; garnish plate with grapes.

MAKES 4 SERVINGS OF 2 CRÊPES EACH

Curried Chicken and Shrimp

This dish makes for no-stress entertaining. To save time, buy peeled shrimp and boneless chicken. Place small bowls of toasted slivered almonds, chopped green onions, chopped fresh coriander, raisins and chutney on the table for guests to sprinkle over their servings.

1 tbsp	canola or olive oil	15 mL
1 lb	boneless skinless chicken, cubed	500 g
3	cloves garlic, minced	3
2 cups	chopped Spanish onion	500 mL
2 tbsp	minced gingerroot	25 mL
2 tbsp	curry powder or Indian curry paste	25 mL
2	tomatoes, chopped (about 2 cups/500 mL)	2
1 lb	peeled large shrimp (raw or cooked)	500 g
7 cups	hot cooked rice	1.75 L

In large nonstick saucepan, heat oil over medium heat; cook chicken, stirring often, for 5 minutes or until chicken is no longer pink inside. Remove chicken and set aside.

Add garlic, onion and gingerroot to saucepan; cook, stirring occasionally, for 4 minutes or until softened. Stir in curry powder; cook for 30 seconds. Add tomatoes; increase heat to high and cook for about 3 minutes or until mixture has thickened.

Reduce heat to medium-low. Add shrimp and chicken; cover and simmer for 5 minutes or until shrimp are pink and chicken is heated through.

To serve, spread rice on platter; spoon curry mixture on top.

MAKES 8 SERVINGS

NOTE: Make your own curry powder if you have the time: combine 2 tsp (10 mL) each ground cardamom and coriander, 1 tsp (5 mL) each cinnamon and ground cumin and ½ tsp (2 mL) each cayenne and turmeric.

MAKE AHEAD: Cook chicken; add to tomato mixture, then cover and refrigerate for up to 1 day. Reheat before adding shrimp.

PER SERVING: 345 calories, 28 g protein, 5 g total fat, 1 g saturated fat, 145 mg cholesterol, 45 g carbohydrate, 2 g fibre, 164 mg sodium, 436 mg potassium

Indian-Style Chicken with Yogurt and Spices

I love the subtle spicing in this chicken dish. It is very mild; if you prefer more heat, add more hot pepper flakes. In India, in stew-type dishes such as this one, the chicken is most often cooked without the skin. Serve over basmati rice.

MAKE AHEAD: Cover and refrigerate up to 1 day (omitting garnish of fresh coriander). Reheat in oven or on stovetop.

PER SERVING: 247 calories, 31 g protein, 10 g total fat, 2 g saturated fat, 91 mg cholesterol, 7 g carbohydrate, 1 g fibre, 398 mg sodium, 478 mg potassium

1 cup	low-fat plain yogurt	250 mL
1 tsp or less	salt	5 mL or less
¼ tsp	hot pepper flakes	1 mL
⅓ cup	finely chopped fresh coriander (cilantro)	75 mL
2 tbsp	canola oil	25 mL
1 tbsp	each ground cumin and ground coriander	15 mL
10	cardamom pods	10
6	whole cloves	6
1	stick cinnamon (3 inches/8 cm)	1
3	bay leaves	3
5	large cloves garlic, minced	5
3 tbsp	minced gingerroot	50 mL
2 lb	each skinless chicken breast and thighs	1 kg
3 tbsp	blanched slivered almonds	50 mL
3 tbsp	raisins	50 mL

Mix yogurt with salt, hot pepper flakes and ¼ cup (50 mL) of the fresh coriander; set aside.

In large nonstick pan or Dutch oven, heat oil over medium-high heat. When hot, add cumin, ground coriander, cardamom, cloves, cinnamon, bay leaves, garlic and gingerroot; stir, then add chicken a few pieces at a time to brown. When browned on both sides, remove chicken to large plate.

Return browned chicken and any juices to pan. Stir in yogurt mixture and bring to a simmer. Reduce heat to low, cover and cook for 20 minutes. Uncover, increase heat and simmer gently until sauce is reduced and thickened slightly, about 20 minutes, stirring occasionally. Stir in almonds and raisins.

Sprinkle with remaining fresh coriander. Serve over hot rice. (Remove cardamom, cloves, cinnamon stick and bay leaves, if possible.)

MAKES 8 SERVINGS

Grilled Asian Chicken on Arugula with Tiny Tomatoes and Black Olives

I got the idea for this dish at an after-tennis dinner at my friend Marg Churchill's. The colourful platter of tossed greens topped with hoisin chicken combines two courses into one dish—perfect for elegant yet casual entertaining. Serve this tasty dish with crusty bread or Lemon Parsley Rice Pilaf (p. 103). I sometimes add other garnishes, such as sliced cooked beets, artichoke hearts and/or avocado wedges, and then sprinkle everything with chopped fresh coriander or basil.

½ cup	Asian Sauce (p. 329)	125 mL
6	skinless chicken breasts or 3 lb (1.5 kg) skinless chicken parts	6
1 tbsp	dark sesame oil	15 mL
1 tbsp	unseasoned rice vinegar	15 mL
Dash	hot pepper sauce	Dash
8 cups	arugula or torn mixed lettuces	2 L
¼ tsp or less	salt and freshly ground pepper	1 mL or less
2 cups	cherry or grape tomatoes	500 mL
6	black olives	6

Spread Asian Sauce over chicken; cover and refrigerate for 4 hours.

Grill chicken over high heat for 15 to 20 minutes on each side or until no longer pink inside.

Meanwhile, combine oil, vinegar and hot pepper sauce; toss with arugula, and salt and pepper. Arrange on large serving platter. Arrange grilled chicken on arugula. Garnish with tomatoes and olives.

MAKES 6 SERVINGS

MAKE AHEAD: Marinate chicken for up to 1 day.

VARIATION:

Oven-Baked Asian Chicken
Instead of grilling chicken, place on baking sheet and bake in 375°F (190°C) oven for 20 to 30 minutes for boneless or 45 minutes with bones or until no longer pink inside.

PER SERVING: 224 calories, 32 g protein, 5 g total fat, 1 g saturated fat, 79 mg cholesterol, 10 g carbohydrate, 2 g fibre, 561 mg sodium, 621 mg potassium

Szechuan Orange-Ginger Chicken

This popular recipe is much easier and faster to make than it may look. Asian dishes from the Szechuan region of China are usually spicy hot—add more chili paste to this dish if you like it hot; if you prefer a milder taste, use less chili paste. Serve with rice.

1 lb	boneless skinless chicken breasts	500 g
1	sweet green pepper	1
1	sweet red pepper	1
1	orange	1
1 tsp	bottled chili paste or ¼ tsp (1 mL) dried hot pepper flakes	5 mL
2 tbsp	sherry	25 mL
1 tbsp	sodium-reduced soy sauce	15 mL
1 tsp	granulated sugar	5 mL
1 tsp	cornstarch	5 mL
2 tbsp	canola oil	25 mL
3	cloves garlic, minced	3
1 tbsp	minced gingerroot	15 mL
	Chopped fresh coriander (cilantro) (optional)	

Cut chicken into 1-inch (2.5 cm) squares; set aside. Halve green and red peppers and remove ribs and seeds; cut into 1-inch (2.5 cm) squares.

Finely grate the orange rind. Squeeze orange and reserve ¼ cup (50 mL) of the juice.

In small bowl, combine reserved orange juice, chili paste, sherry, soy sauce, sugar and cornstarch; stir until smooth.

In wok or large nonstick skillet, heat half the oil over high heat; add chicken and stir-fry for 3 minutes or until browned and no longer pink. Remove chicken. Add remaining oil, orange rind, garlic and gingerroot; stir-fry for 10 seconds. Add peppers and stir-fry for 1 minute. Add chili paste mixture and bring to boil. Return chicken to wok and stir until heated through. Sprinkle with coriander (if using).

MAKES 4 SERVINGS

NOTE: Bottled chili paste is available in some supermarkets and most Asian grocery stores. Dried chili peppers can be substituted. The seeds in fresh or dried peppers are very hot; for a milder taste, omit the seeds.

PER SERVING: 235 calories, 27 g protein, 9 g total fat, 1 g saturated fat, 67 mg cholesterol, 10 g carbohydrate, 1 g fibre, 210 mg sodium, 490 mg potassium

Chicken and Snow Peas in Black Bean Sauce

You can find the fermented (or salted) black beans (often in a plastic bag) in Chinese food stores. They keep for years and are also delicious in Rice with Black Beans and Ginger (p. 105). Don't substitute black turtle beans. You could add a sliced sweet red pepper. Serve with rice or noodles.

1 lb	boneless skinless chicken breasts or thighs	500 g
1 tbsp	canola or olive oil	15 mL
3 tbsp	Chinese fermented black beans, rinsed	50 mL
4	cloves garlic, minced	4
2 tbsp	minced gingerroot	25 mL
¼ tsp	crushed red pepper flakes	1 mL
2 cups	snow peas, trimmed	500 mL
SAUCE		
½ cup	sodium-reduced chicken broth or water	125 mL
2 tbsp	sodium-reduced soy sauce	25 mL
1 tbsp	sherry	15 mL
2 tsp	granulated sugar	10 mL
1½ tsp	cornstarch	7 mL
1 tsp	sesame oil	5 mL

SAUCE: Combine broth, soy sauce, sherry, sugar, cornstarch and sesame oil; set aside.

Slice chicken thinly; set aside.

In large nonstick skillet, heat oil over high heat; stir-fry black beans, garlic, gingerroot and red pepper flakes for 15 seconds. Add chicken; stir-fry for 2 minutes. Add snow peas; stir-fry for 2 minutes.

Stir sauce; add to skillet and stir-fry over medium heat for 1 minute or until chicken is no longer pink inside.

MAKES 4 SERVINGS

MAKE AHEAD: Prepare sauce and slice chicken; cover and refrigerate for up to 4 hours.

PER SERVING: 233 calories, 30 g protein, 7 g total fat, 1 g saturated fat, 67 mg cholesterol, 11 g carbohydrate, 2 g fibre, 634 mg sodium, 586 mg potassium

Asian Chicken Lettuce Wraps

This is a great dish for casual entertaining or when you want something a little different. Set the table with a platter of the cooked chicken, one of lettuce and one with remaining ingredients. Give each person some sauce. Diners make up their own lettuce wraps filled with chicken, noodles and herbs.

¾ cup	Asian Sauce (p. 329)	175 mL
6	boneless skinless chicken breasts, cut in strips	6
½ lb	rice vermicelli noodles	250 g
2	heads Boston or soft leaf lettuce	2
1	cucumber, halved lengthwise and thinly sliced	1
3 cups	bean sprouts	750 mL
½ cup	fresh mint	125 mL
½ cup	fresh coriander (cilantro)	125 mL

Mix ⅓ cup (75 mL) of the Asian Sauce with chicken; cover and refrigerate for 4 hours.

In large saucepan of boiling water, cook noodles for 1 minute or according to package directions; drain and rinse under cold water. Drain again and toss with 2 tbsp (25 mL) of Asian Sauce.

On serving platter, arrange lettuce leaves. On another platter, arrange cucumber, bean sprouts, mint, coriander and noodles. Divide remaining sauce among 6 small dishes.

In nonstick skillet, stir-fry chicken over high heat for 3 to 5 minutes or until no longer pink inside; transfer to lettuce-lined serving platter.

Let each person spread Asian Sauce on a lettuce leaf, then top with chicken, noodles, cucumber, bean sprouts, mint and coriander. Using fingers, roll up and eat.

MAKES 6 SERVINGS

MAKE AHEAD: Marinate chicken in Asian Sauce and cook and toss noodles up to 1 day in advance. Platters can be assembled (omitting chicken), covered and refrigerated, for up to 4 hours. Cook chicken just before serving.

VARIATION:

Barbecue Asian Chicken
Marinate whole boneless skinless chicken breasts (rather than strips) in Asian sauce. Grill chicken over high heat for about 4 minutes on each side or until meat is no longer pink inside. Cut into strips; place on serving platter with other wrap ingredients.

PER SERVING: 387 calories, 36 g protein, 3 g total fat, 1 g saturated fat, 80 mg cholesterol, 52 g carbohydrate, 5 g fibre, 630 mg sodium, 746 mg potassium

Chicken Fondue in Ginger Broth

This is an easy yet elegant supper for family or guests. By using chicken broth instead of oil for cooking, and by including vegetables as well as low-fat sauces, fat and calories are kept to a minimum. Serve with rice.

PER SERVING (without sauce):
183 calories, 29 g protein,
2 g total fat, 1 g saturated fat,
67 mg cholesterol,
12 g carbohydrate, 4 g fibre,
248 mg sodium, 952 mg potassium

FONDUE COOKING BROTH

4 cups	sodium reduced chicken broth	1 L
⅔ cup	white wine or ¼ cup (50 mL) apple cider or unseasoned rice vinegar	150 mL
2	lemon slices	2
2	large cloves garlic, minced	2
2 tbsp	minced gingerroot	25 mL
2 tsp	granulated sugar	10 mL

CHICKEN AND VEGETABLE TRAY

1 lb	boneless skinless chicken breasts	500 g
Half	bunch broccoli	Half
1	small yellow summer squash or zucchini	1
2 cups	torn Swiss chard or romaine lettuce	500 mL
1	sweet red or green pepper	1
4 oz	mushrooms	125 g
	Hot Chili Sauce (p. 330)	
	Garlic Sauce (p. 330)	

FONDUE COOKING BROTH: In fondue pot, electric skillet or electric wok, combine chicken broth, white wine, lemon slices, garlic, gingerroot and sugar. Just before serving, heat to simmer.

CHICKEN AND VEGETABLE TRAY: Cut chicken into ¾-inch (2 cm) pieces; place on serving platter. Cut broccoli, summer squash, Swiss chard and sweet pepper into bite-sized pieces; arrange along with mushrooms on separate platter.

Using long fondue forks, spear chicken or vegetables; dip into simmering fondue broth to cook. Cook chicken pieces until no longer pink inside, and vegetables until tender-crisp. Serve with Hot Chili Sauce and Garlic Sauce for dipping.

MAKES 4 SERVINGS

Thai Chicken Curry in Coconut Milk

The combination of flavours in this easy-to-make yet exotic dish is mouth-watering. Use Thai red or green curry paste in this recipe; simply add a little more to make this saucy chicken dish hotter and spicier. Sometimes I add large shrimp and sliced Japanese eggplant. Serve this curry with basmati rice and a green vegetable.

1 tbsp	canola or olive oil	15 mL
1 to 2 tsp	red curry paste (medium)	5 to 10 mL
1¼ lb	boneless skinless chicken, cut in cubes	625 g
1	onion, coarsely chopped	1
1	sweet red pepper, cut in thin strips	1
	Grated rind of 1 medium lemon	
1 cup	light coconut milk	250 mL
2 tbsp	fish sauce or sodium reduced soy sauce	25 mL
1 tbsp	fresh lemon juice	15 mL
⅓ cup	chopped fresh coriander (cilantro)	75 mL

In large nonstick skillet, heat oil over high heat: stir-fry curry paste for 30 seconds. Add chicken; stir-fry for 2 minutes. Stir in onion; stir-fry for 2 minutes. Add red pepper and lemon rind; stir-fry for 1 minute or until onion is softened. Stir in coconut milk, fish sauce and lemon juice; bring to simmer. Cook for about 2 minutes or until liquid is reduced slightly. Stir in coriander.

MAKES 4 SERVINGS

VARIATION: Instead of the lemon rind and juice, use 6 chopped kaffir lime leaves, the "spine" removed. (I freeze fresh kaffir lime leaves, available at Asian markets, to have on hand.)

NOTE: Canned light coconut milk is available in some supermarkets. If you can't find it, use ½ cup (125 mL) regular coconut milk mixed with an equal amount of water.

PER SERVING: 252 calories, 34 g protein, 9 g total fat, 4 g saturated fat, 83 mg cholesterol, 7 g carbohydrate, 1 g fibre, 818 mg sodium, 647 mg potassium

Simmered Chicken Dinner

Here's one of the fastest and easiest ways to cook a chicken, potato and vegetable dinner—all in one pot. It's also a good way to introduce children to new vegetables. This dish has sweet potatoes, which are not overpowering or as dried out as baked ones can sometimes be. You can use carrots, turnips or squash cubes instead of sweet potatoes.

PER SERVING: 319 calories, 16 g protein, 7 g total fat, 2 g saturated fat, 37 mg cholesterol, 50 g carbohydrate, 6 g fibre, 242 mg sodium, 1016 mg potassium

3 lb	chicken pieces, skinned	1.5 kg
4 cups	water	1 L
2	slices bacon, cut in pieces	2
3	leeks or medium onions	3
2	bay leaves	2
1 tsp	dried thyme	5 mL
5	red potatoes, halved	5
1	large sweet potato (12 oz/375 g), peeled and cut into chunks	1
Half	small head cabbage	Half
1	clove garlic, minced	1
¼ cup	chopped fresh parsley	50 mL
¼ tsp or less	salt and freshly ground pepper	1 mL or less

If using a whole chicken, remove skin first, then cut into pieces. In large pot, combine chicken, water and bacon; bring to boil and skim off any foam.

Halve leeks lengthwise and clean under running water; cut into 2-inch (5 cm) lengths. If using onions, cut into quarters. Add leeks to pot along with bay leaves, thyme and red and sweet potatoes; cover and simmer for 10 minutes.

Cut cabbage into 1-inch (2.5 cm) wedges and add to pot; cover and simmer for 10 minutes or until vegetables are tender.

Using slotted spoon, transfer chicken and vegetables to six large soup bowls. Remove bay leaves. Increase heat to high; boil liquid for 3 to 5 minutes or until reduced to about 3 cups (750 mL). Stir in garlic, parsley, and salt and pepper; ladle over each portion.

MAKES 6 SERVINGS

Chicken and Vegetable Stew with Parsley Dumplings

This one-pot chicken dinner is a light version of an old-fashioned favourite. Add ½ cup (125 mL) white wine to the stew when adding peas, if desired.

4	skinless chicken breasts (2 lb/1 kg) or 2 lb (1 kg) skinless chicken parts	4
4	small potatoes, quartered	4
2	each carrots and onions, quartered	2
2	stalks celery, sliced	2
1½ cups	cubed peeled rutabaga	375 mL
1½ cups	cubed peeled sweet potato	375 mL
4 cups	water or sodium-reduced chicken broth	1 L
½ tsp	each dried thyme, sage and salt	2 mL
¼ tsp or less	freshly ground pepper	1 mL or less
1 cup	frozen peas	250 mL

DUMPLINGS

1 cup	all-purpose flour	250 mL
2 tbsp	chopped fresh parsley	25 mL
2 tbsp	soft margarine	25 mL
1½ tsp	baking powder	7 mL
¼ tsp or less	salt	1 mL or less
½ cup	low-fat milk	125 mL

In large saucepan, combine chicken, potatoes, carrots, onions, celery, rutabaga, sweet potato, water, thyme, sage, salt and pepper; bring to boil over high heat. Reduce heat to medium-low; simmer, covered, for 20 minutes. Stir in peas.

DUMPLINGS: In food processor or by hand, combine flour, parsley, margarine, baking powder and salt until mixture is in coarse crumbs. Stir in milk; drop by tablespoonfuls onto hot stew to make 4 to 6 mounds.

Cover and simmer (don't boil hard and don't lift lid) for 15 minutes or until dumplings have risen.

MAKES 4 SERVINGS

MAKE AHEAD: Cook chicken and vegetable stew up to 1 day in advance; cover and refrigerate. Make dumplings when ready to serve.

PER SERVING: 635 calories, 54 g protein, 10 g total fat, 2 g saturated fat, 111 mg cholesterol, 82 g carbohydrate, 9 g fibre, 852 mg sodium, 1733 mg potassium

Moroccan Chicken Stew with Couscous

I like to serve this when entertaining—for a buffet—because it tastes terrific, can be prepared in advance and is easily eaten with a fork, so no knives are needed. Brown or white rice can be served instead of couscous. Turnip can be used as well as or instead of sweet potato.

1¼ lb	boneless skinless chicken, cubed	625 g
3	onions, thinly sliced	3
2 cups	water	500 mL
1 tbsp	minced gingerroot	15 mL
1 tsp	each turmeric, cinnamon and granulated sugar	5 mL
½ tsp	saffron (optional)	2 mL
1	sweet potato, peeled and cubed	1
4	carrots, cut in chunks	4
1 cup	canned or cooked chickpeas, drained and rinsed	250 mL
¼ cup	dried currants	50 mL
2 tbsp	fresh lemon juice	25 mL
1	small zucchini (6 oz/170 g), cut in chunks	1
3 tbsp	each chopped fresh parsley and coriander (cilantro)	50 mL
¼ tsp or less	salt and freshly ground pepper	1 mL or less
1½ cups	couscous	375 mL

In nonstick skillet or saucepan, cook chicken over high heat until brown on all sides and no longer pink inside, about 5 minutes; remove chicken to plate and set aside. Reduce heat to medium and add onions; cook, stirring occasionally, for 5 minutes or until softened.

Add water, gingerroot, turmeric, cinnamon, sugar and saffron (if using); bring to simmer. Add sweet potato and carrots; cover and simmer for 20 minutes. Stir in chickpeas, currants and lemon juice. Add zucchini and chicken; cover and simmer for 10 minutes or until vegetables are tender. Add parsley and coriander; season with salt and pepper.

Cook couscous according to package directions or see page 114. Serve with stew.

MAKES 6 SERVINGS

MAKE AHEAD: Cover and refrigerate cooked chicken and chickpea mixture for up to 2 days. Bring to simmer before adding zucchini and chicken and continuing with recipe.

PER SERVING (including couscous): 422 calories, 30 g protein, 4 g total fat, 1 g saturated fat, 62 mg cholesterol, 66 g carbohydrate, 7 g fibre, 329 mg sodium, 815 mg potassium

Baked Chicken Breasts with Mango Chutney Sauce

This easy-to-make chicken dish is moist and tender. Dress up the plate with a slice of fresh mango and a sprig of watercress. Serve with chutney and basmati rice cooked in sodium-reduced chicken broth and a teaspoon or two (5 to 10 mL) of chopped gingerroot.

⅓ cup	mango chutney	75 mL
⅓ cup	low-fat plain yogurt	75 mL
1 tbsp	each Dijon mustard and minced gingerroot	15 mL
2 tsp	all-purpose flour	10 mL
2 lb	skinless chicken breasts (about 4, bone-in)	1 kg

In small bowl, stir together chutney, yogurt, mustard, gingerroot and flour. Arrange chicken, bone side down, in single layer in baking dish; spoon chutney mixture over top.

Bake, uncovered, in 350°F (180°C) oven for 45 minutes or until chicken is no longer pink in centre. Remove from oven; let stand for 5 minutes. Spoon any baking juices over top before serving.

MAKES 4 SERVINGS

MAKE AHEAD: Assemble chicken for baking; cover and refrigerate for up to 3 hours.

PER SERVING: 298 calories, 44 g protein, 3 g total fat, 1 g saturated fat, 111 mg cholesterol, 20 g carbohydrate, 1 g fibre, 560 mg sodium, 621 mg potassium

Grilled Chicken Breast Burgers with Caramelized Onions and Sun-Dried Tomatoes

The idea for these chicken burgers came from Browne's Bistro in Toronto, which serves the most wonderful grilled chicken sandwich with a sun-dried tomato pesto and sautéed onions. Serve with coleslaw or a tossed salad.

1 tbsp	olive oil	15 mL
4 cups	thinly sliced Spanish onions	1 L
¼ cup	chopped dry-packed sun-dried tomatoes	50 mL
1	large clove garlic, minced	1
1 to 2 tbsp	water	15 to 30 mL
4	boneless skinless chicken breasts (about 1 lb/500 g)	4
4	whole-wheat buns or Kaiser rolls	4

In large nonstick skillet, heat oil over medium-low heat; cook onions, stirring occasionally, for 20 to 30 minutes or until tender and golden. Add tomatoes, garlic and 1 tbsp (15 mL) water; cook for 5 minutes, adding another tablespoon (15 mL) water if needed to prevent sticking.

Meanwhile, place chicken on greased grill over medium heat; grill for about 4 minutes on each side or until no longer pink inside.

Toast buns. Spoon some of the onion mixture onto bottom halves. Top with chicken, then remaining onion mixture and bun tops.

MAKES 4 SERVINGS

MAKE AHEAD: Prepare onion-tomato mixture up to 1 day in advance; cover and refrigerate until ready to reheat.

PER SERVING: 357 calories, 33 g protein, 8 g total fat, 2 g saturated fat, 67 mg cholesterol, 40 g carbohydrate, 6 g fibre, 468 mg sodium, 779 mg potassium

Burgers with Coriander-Yogurt Sauce

Serve these burgers on whole-wheat buns, on thick slices of toasted French bread, or in a pita pocket with shredded lettuce and tomato. I love them made with fresh coriander, but you can also use fresh dill, basil or parsley.

1 lb	lean ground turkey or chicken	500 g
1	small onion, finely chopped	1
1	egg white	1
2 tbsp	fresh soft bread crumbs	25 mL
2 tbsp	chopped fresh coriander (cilantro) or ¼ cup (50 mL) chopped fresh parsley	25 mL
½ tsp	Worcestershire sauce	2 mL
Dash	hot pepper sauce	Dash

CORIANDER-YOGURT SAUCE

½ cup	low-fat plain yogurt	125 mL
2 tbsp	diced tomato	25 mL
1 tbsp	chopped green onion	15 mL
1 to 2 tbsp	chopped fresh coriander (cilantro)	15 to 25 mL
½ tsp	prepared horseradish	2 mL
½ tsp	Dijon mustard	2 mL

In bowl, combine ground poultry, onion, egg white, bread crumbs, coriander, Worcestershire and hot pepper sauce; mix well. Form into 5 patties.

CORIANDER-YOGURT SAUCE: In small bowl, combine yogurt, tomato, onion, coriander, horseradish and mustard; mix well.

Grill, broil or cook patties in nonstick skillet over medium heat for 4 minutes per side or until patties are no longer pink inside. Place on bun and top with spoonful of sauce.

MAKES 5 SERVINGS

VARIATION: Use lean ground beef, lamb or pork for the patties.

PER SERVING: 166 calories, 18 g protein, 8 g total fat, 2 g saturated fat, 61 mg cholesterol, 4 g carbohydrate, 0 g fibre, 117 mg sodium, 269 mg potassium

Ginger-Garlic Chicken Burgers

Serve these juicy, delicious burgers in a bun with sliced tomato and lettuce, or as patties along with stir-fried bok choy and rice or Roasted Sesame-Chili French Fries (p. 122).

1 lb	lean ground chicken	500 g
1	egg (or 2 egg whites)	1
2	green onions, chopped	2
1 tbsp	sodium-reduced soy sauce	15 mL
1 tbsp	cornstarch	15 mL
2 tsp	minced gingerroot	10 mL
2	cloves garlic, minced	2
1 tbsp	chopped fresh coriander (cilantro) or parsley	15 mL
	Freshly ground pepper	

In bowl, combine chicken, egg, onions, soy sauce, cornstarch, gingerroot, garlic, coriander, and pepper to taste; mix gently. Form into 4 patties (mixture will be moist) about ½ inch (1 cm) thick.

Broil on greased broiler pan or baking sheet for 6 minutes or until browned on top; turn and broil for 2 to 3 minutes or until no longer pink inside.

MAKES 4 SERVINGS

MAKE AHEAD: Cover and refrigerate uncooked patties for up to 4 hours..

PER SERVING (1 patty):
192 calories, 22 g protein, 10 g total fat, 3 g saturated fat, 136 mg cholesterol, 3 g carbohydrate, 0 g fibre, 213 mg sodium, 621 mg potassium

Herb and Buttermilk Barbecued Chicken

This delicious chicken recipe is from food writer Vicki Burns. Buttermilk is low in fat yet thick and creamy, perfect for marinating. If it's not available, substitute 2% evaporated milk.

3 lb	chicken parts, skinned	1.5 kg

BUTTERMILK MARINADE

¾ cup	buttermilk	175 mL
2 tbsp	Dijon mustard	25 mL
2	cloves garlic, minced	2
2 tsp	each dried oregano, basil, thyme and rosemary	10 mL
¼ tsp or less	each salt and freshly ground pepper	1 mL or less

BUTTERMILK MARINADE: In large bowl, combine buttermilk, mustard, garlic, oregano, basil, thyme, rosemary, salt and pepper.

Add chicken, turning pieces to coat. Cover and refrigerate for 3 hours, turning occasionally.

Place chicken on greased grill over medium heat; grill, turning occasionally, for 30 to 40 minutes or until juices run clear when chicken is pierced.

MAKES 6 SERVINGS

MAKE AHEAD: Marinate chicken for up to 1 day.

VARIATION:

Baked Buttermilk Herb Chicken
Marinate chicken. Spread ¾ cup (175 mL) cornmeal on plate. Remove chicken from marinade; coat each piece with cornmeal. Bake on baking sheet in 350°F (180°C) oven for 45 minutes or until juices run clear when chicken is pierced with fork.

NOTE: Despite its name, buttermilk is not high in fat and is well suited for lower-fat cooking and baking. Try other recipes in this book calling for buttermilk to use up the carton (see index).

PER SERVING: 177 calories, 30 g protein, 5 g total fat, 1 g saturated fat, 91 mg cholesterol, 2 g carbohydrate, 0 g fibre, 210 mg sodium, 370 mg potassium

Grilled Lemon Chicken with Rosemary

As my days get busier and busier, my cooking seems to get simpler and simpler. Now that I have a flourishing rosemary plant growing in the garden (I keep it in the sunroom in the winter), this is how I often cook chicken.

4	boneless skinless chicken breasts (about 1 lb/500 g)	4
¼ cup	fresh lemon juice	50 mL
2	large sprigs fresh rosemary (or 1 tbsp/15 mL dried)	2
¼ tsp or less	salt and freshly ground pepper	1 mL or less

In shallow dish, arrange chicken in single layer. Pour lemon juice over chicken and turn to coat both sides. Separate rosemary needles from stem; sprinkle over chicken. Season with salt and pepper.

Let stand at room temperature for 20 minutes or cover and refrigerate for up to 6 hours. Spray grill with nonstick vegetable coating. Grill chicken over hot coals or on medium-high setting for 4 to 5 minutes on each side or until meat is no longer pink inside.

MAKES 4 SERVINGS

VARIATION:

Grilled Lemon Chicken with Garlic and Oregano
Omit rosemary and instead sprinkle 2 minced cloves garlic and 1 to 2 tsp (5 to 10 mL) dried oregano over chicken.

PER SERVING: 126 calories, 26 g protein, 2 g total fat, 0 g saturated fat, 67 mg cholesterol, 0 g carbohydrate, 0 g fibre, 131 mg sodium, 320 mg potassium

Lemon Pepper Turkey Loaf

Serve this tasty turkey loaf either hot with mashed potatoes, baked squash and green beans, or cold in a sandwich.

1	pkg (10 oz/300 g) frozen spinach, thawed	1
1 lb	lean ground turkey	500 g
1	small onion, chopped	1
1	egg, lightly beaten	1
1	slice whole-wheat bread, crumbled	1
1	clove garlic, minced	1
2 tsp	grated lemon rind	10 mL
½ tsp or less	each salt and freshly ground pepper	2 mL or less
Pinch	nutmeg	Pinch
	Thin slices of peeled lemon	

Squeeze excess water from spinach; chop finely. In bowl, combine spinach, turkey, onion, egg, bread crumbs, garlic, lemon rind, salt, pepper and nutmeg; mix gently.

Transfer mixture to 6-cup (1.5 L) baking dish, smoothing top. Arrange lemon slices on top. Bake in 350°F (180°C) oven for 40 minutes or until no longer pink in centre and meat thermometer registers 185°F (85°C). Let stand for 10 minutes. Pour off any liquid.

MAKES 4 SERVINGS

MAKE AHEAD: Assemble loaf; cover and refrigerate for up to 3 hours.

PER SERVING: 236 calories, 25 g protein, 11 g total fat, 3 g saturated fat, 121 mg cholesterol, 9 g carbohydrate, 3 g fibre, 486 mg sodium, 451 mg potassium

Turkey and Potato Hash

This tasty recipe is handy when you want to use up the remains of a turkey, chicken, ham or roast. Since the hash isn't fried, it's important to use a large nonstick skillet.

2	large potatoes, thinly sliced (about 3 cups/750 mL)	2
1½ cups	water	375 mL
1	large onion, chopped	1
1½ cups	diced cooked turkey (6 oz/175 g)	375 mL
1½ tsp	Worcestershire sauce	7 mL
1 tsp	minced fresh garlic	5 mL
2	green onions, chopped	2
1 tsp	olive oil	5 mL
Dash	hot pepper sauce	Dash
¼ tsp or less	salt and freshly ground pepper	1 mL or less

In large nonstick skillet, bring potatoes, water and onion to boil; cover and cook over medium heat for 10 minutes or until vegetables are tender.

Add turkey, Worcestershire, garlic, green onions, oil and hot pepper sauce; mix well. Cook, uncovered, over medium heat for about 5 minutes or until mixture begins to sizzle and water has evaporated.

With spatula, scrape up crusty bits and stir them into mixture. Cook for 10 minutes longer or until mixture is lightly browned, stirring often and scraping up brown bits from bottom of pan. Season with salt and pepper.

MAKES 3 SERVINGS

PER SERVING: 265 calories, 24 g protein, 5 g total fat, 1 g saturated fat, 53 mg cholesterol, 31 g carbohydrate, 3 g fibre, 285 mg sodium, 809 mg potassium

Make-Ahead Turkey Divan

This recipe is from Shannon Graham, my friend and co-worker who has helped with recipe testing for all my cookbooks. It's a good way to use up leftover turkey or chicken. The sauce is very fast and easy to prepare in the microwave. I prefer to cook the broccoli in boiling water, rather than in the microwave—it's just as fast and the broccoli is more tender and brighter in colour.

1	bunch broccoli	1
1 tbsp	canola oil	15 mL
¼ cup	all-purpose flour	50 mL
2 cups	low-fat milk	500 mL
⅔ cup	shredded part-skim milk mozzarella cheese	150 mL
2 tbsp	freshly grated Parmesan cheese	25 mL
	Freshly ground pepper	
12 oz	sliced cooked turkey or chicken (about 3 cups/750 mL)	375 g
	Paprika	

Cut broccoli into large pieces; peel stems and quarter lengthwise. Cut into 3-inch (8 cm) pieces. In large pot of boiling water, cook broccoli for 2 to 3 minutes or until tender-crisp; drain well. Place in ungreased 12- × 8-inch (3 L) baking dish.

In saucepan, stir oil and flour; whisk in milk, whisking until smooth; cook over medium heat, stirring frequently, until thickened. Add mozzarella cheese and 1 tbsp (15 mL) of the Parmesan; stir until melted. Season with pepper to taste.

Arrange turkey on top of broccoli; pour cheese sauce over and spread evenly. Sprinkle with remaining Parmesan, and paprika to taste. Bake, covered, in 350°F (180°C) oven for 25 minutes. Uncover and bake for 5 minutes longer or until hot and bubbling.

MAKES 5 SERVINGS

MICROWAVE METHOD
In 12- × 8-inch (3 L) microwaveable dish, cover broccoli plus 2 tbsp (25 mL) water with vented waxed paper; microwave on High for 4 to 6 minutes or until tender-crisp. Drain and set aside.

In 4-cup (1 L) microwaveable bowl, stir oil and flour until smooth; whisk in milk until smooth. Microwave on High for 5 to 7 minutes or until thickened, whisking after 2 minutes and then every minute.

Stir in mozzarella cheese and 1 tbsp (15 mL) of the Parmesan until melted. Add pepper to taste. Arrange turkey on top of broccoli; pour cheese sauce over and spread evenly. Sprinkle with remaining Parmesan and paprika to taste. Cover with waxed paper; microwave on Medium-high for 5 to 8 minutes or until heated through. Let stand for 2 to 3 minutes.

VARIATION: If you don't have any leftover turkey, you can poach a turkey breast to use in this recipe. In large pot, bring 6 cups (1.5 L) water to boil. Add 1½ lb (750 g) bone-in turkey breast, skin side down. Reduce heat to medium; cover and simmer for 20 to 25 minutes or until no longer pink inside. Remove from water, let cool, then slice and measure amount needed.

PER SERVING: 229 calories, 21 g protein, 9 g total fat, 4 g saturated fat, 43 mg cholesterol, 16 g carbohydrate, 2 g fibre, 222 mg sodium, 509 mg potassium

Tarragon-Orange Grilled Turkey

Turkey scaloppine is lean, low in calories and fast and easy to cook. If you can't find it in the store, buy chicken cutlets or boneless, skinless chicken breasts and flatten them between waxed paper. Or buy a turkey breast, then cut the meat into thin slices and freeze the extra. Veal scallopini can be used instead of turkey.

1 lb	turkey or chicken scaloppine	500 g
¼ cup	orange juice	50 mL
1 tsp	grated orange rind	5 mL
3	medium cloves garlic, minced	3
1 tsp	dried tarragon	5 mL
¼ tsp or less	salt and freshly ground pepper	1 mL or less
	Thin slices of orange	

Place turkey in shallow dish. Combine orange juice and rind, garlic and tarragon; pour over turkey and turn to coat both sides. Sprinkle with salt and pepper. Let stand for 5 minutes at room temperature.

Spray grill with nonstick coating. Grill turkey over high heat or broil for about 2 minutes on each side or until no longer pink. Garnish with orange slices.

MAKES 4 SERVINGS

MAKE AHEAD: Marinate turkey, covered and refrigerated, for up to 4 hours.

VARIATION:

Garlic and Herb Grilled Turkey Scaloppine
Omit orange juice, orange rind and tarragon. Add ½ tsp (2 mL) each dried thyme, rosemary and oregano, and 2 tbsp (25 mL) each olive oil and fresh lemon juice.

PER SERVING: 140 calories, 25 g protein, 2 g total fat, 1 g saturated fat, 59 mg cholesterol, 3 g carbohydrate, 0 g fibre, 206 mg sodium, 322 mg potassium

Thai Barbecued Turkey Scaloppine

Serve these tasty turkey slices with rice or noodles and a refreshing salad such as Purple Vegetable Slaw (p. 71). For a spicier flavour, add more red pepper flakes or chili paste.

2 tbsp	chopped fresh coriander (cilantro) or parsley	25 mL
2 tbsp	fish sauce or sodium-reduced soy sauce	25 mL
2 tbsp	fresh lemon or lime juice	25 mL
1 tbsp	water	15 mL
1 tsp	granulated sugar	5 mL
1 tsp	vegetable oil	5 mL
¼ tsp	freshly ground pepper	1 mL
¼ tsp	crushed red pepper flakes or hot chili paste	1 mL
1 lb	turkey scaloppine	500 g

Combine coriander, fish sauce, lemon juice, water, sugar, oil, pepper and red pepper flakes; mix well.

Place turkey in shallow dish; pour marinade over top. Cover and refrigerate for 1 hour, turning occasionally.

Place turkey on greased grill over high heat; grill for about 2 minutes on each side or until no longer pink inside.

MAKES 4 SERVINGS

MAKE AHEAD: Marinate turkey for up to 1 day.

NOTE: Scaloppine are thin slices of meat, usually veal. Turkey is an excellent, less expensive alternative; if you can't find turkey scaloppine, buy turkey or chicken breast and cut it into thin slices.

PER SERVING: 141 calories, 25 g protein, 3 g total fat, 1 g saturated fat, 59 mg cholesterol, 1 g carbohydrate, 0 g fibre, 581 mg sodium, 293 mg potassium

Turkey and Fruit Curry

Juicy melons, mangoes or peaches add a festive touch and cooling flavour to this quick curry dish. The sauce is also good with shrimp or hard-cooked eggs. If using the sauce for shrimp, use half chicken stock and half clam juice.

3 cups	large chunks cooked turkey or chicken	750 mL
2 cups	melon balls, sliced mango or peaches	500 mL

CURRY SAUCE

3 tbsp	canola or olive oil	50 mL
1	onion, chopped	1
1	clove garlic, minced	1
4 tsp	curry powder or Indian curry paste	20 mL
½ tsp	each chili powder and ground cumin	2 mL
⅓ cup	all-purpose flour	75 mL
2 cups	sodium-reduced chicken broth	500 mL
½ tsp or less	salt	2 mL or less
	Freshly ground pepper	

CURRY SAUCE: In saucepan, heat oil over medium-low heat. Add onion, garlic, curry powder, chili powder and cumin; cook, stirring, until onion is tender. Stir in flour, mixing well. Stir in broth; bring to boil, stirring; simmer, uncovered, for 5 minutes. Add salt; season with pepper to taste.

Stir in turkey; cook for 3 minutes. Add melon and cook, stirring, until heated through, 2 to 3 minutes.

MAKES 6 SERVINGS

MAKE AHEAD: Cover and refrigerate sauce for up to 2 days. Reheat gently, then continue with recipe.

NOTE: This is a lovely buffet dish: it's easy to eat without a knife and can be prepared in advance. (Add melon just before serving.) It can be easily doubled or tripled for more guests. You can substitute chicken for the turkey and can also include shrimp. Plan on about 4 oz (125 g) snow peas per person or use less and serve another vegetable as well.

One serving is a high source of iron.

PER SERVING: 243 calories, 23 g protein, 11 g total fat, 2 g saturated fat, 53 mg cholesterol, 13 g carbohydrate, 1 g fibre, 442 mg sodium, 497 mg potassium

Cranberry-Glazed Turkey Breast

When I first cooked a whole turkey breast for my family, we were all amazed at how tender and juicy it was. This recipe is now a family favourite. It's extremely easy and splendid for Sunday dinners, Thanksgiving or other holiday dinners when you don't want to cook a whole turkey.

3 lb	bone-in thick piece of turkey breast	1.5 kg
1½ cups	fresh cranberry sauce or 1 can (14 oz/398 mL) whole cranberry sauce	375 mL
¼ cup	packed brown sugar	50 mL
¼ cup	sodium-reduced soy sauce	50 mL
2 tbsp	fresh lemon juice	25 mL
1 tbsp	chopped gingerroot (or 1 tsp/5 mL ground ginger)	15 mL
1 tbsp	Dijon mustard (or 1 tsp/5 mL dry mustard)	15 mL
1	large clove garlic, minced	1

Remove skin and fat from turkey; place, meat side up, in baking dish sprayed with nonstick cooking spray or lined with foil.

In bowl, combine cranberry sauce, sugar, soy sauce, lemon juice, gingerroot, mustard and garlic; spread about ⅓ cup (75 mL) over turkey.

Roast, uncovered, in 325°F (160°C) oven for 1½ hours or until thermometer inserted in thickest part registers 170°F (77°C), basting every 30 minutes. Cover loosely with foil and let stand for 15 minutes before slicing. Microwave remaining cranberry mixture until hot; pass separately.

MAKES 6 SERVINGS

NOTE: You can reduce sodium by 135 mg per serving by using only 2 tbsp (25 mL) of soy sauce in this recipe.

PER SERVING: 325 calories, 41 g protein, 4 g total fat, 1 g saturated fat, 94 mg cholesterol, 31 g carbohydrate, 1 g fibre, 428 mg sodium, 491 mg potassium

Turkey Vegetable Casserole

This is a scrumptious way to use up cooked turkey or chicken and makes a fine dish for a buffet.

1 cup	long-grain rice	250 mL
1½ tsp	olive or canola oil	7 mL
½ cup	coarsely chopped fresh parsley	125 mL
1	onion, chopped	1
3	cloves garlic, minced	3
1½ cups	finely chopped carrots	375 mL
1½ cups	chopped celery	375 mL
½ lb	mushrooms, thinly sliced (3 cups/750 mL)	250 g
4 cups	cooked turkey chunks (1 lb/500 g)	1 L

CREAMY HERB SAUCE

2 tbsp	soft margarine	25 mL
¼ cup	all-purpose flour	50 mL
2½ cups	low-fat milk	625 mL
½ tsp	each dried tarragon, salt and freshly ground pepper	2 mL
½ tsp	dried thyme	2 mL

TOPPING

½ cup	fresh whole-wheat bread crumbs	125 mL
¼ cup	chopped fresh parsley	50 mL

In saucepan, bring 2 cups (500 mL) water to boil; add rice and ½ tsp (2 mL) of the oil. Reduce heat, cover and simmer for 20 minutes. Toss with 2 tbsp (25 mL) of the parsley; spoon into greased 13- × 9-inch (3.5 L) baking dish.

Meanwhile, in large nonstick saucepan, heat remaining oil over low heat; cook onion, garlic and carrots for 5 minutes, stirring often. Add celery, mushrooms and remaining parsley; cook, stirring, for 5 to 10 minutes or until softened. Add a spoonful or two of water when necessary to prevent scorching. Stir in turkey.

CREAMY HERB SAUCE: In saucepan, melt margarine over medium-low heat; whisk in flour and cook, stirring, for 1 minute. Gradually add milk, whisking constantly; cook for 5 minutes or until bubbling and thickened. Add tarragon, salt, pepper and thyme. Stir sauce into turkey mixture; spread over rice.

TOPPING: Combine bread crumbs and parsley; sprinkle over casserole. Bake in 325°F (160°C) oven for 40 to 50 minutes or until heated through.

MAKES 8 SERVINGS

MAKE AHEAD: Combine turkey mixture and sauce, cover and refrigerate for up to 2 days, or cool in refrigerator, then freeze for up to 2 weeks. Thaw in refrigerator for 2 days; let stand at room temperature for 25 minutes before sprinkling with topping and baking.

PER SERVING: 314 calories, 27 g protein, 9 g total fat, 2 g saturated fat, 57 mg cholesterol, 32 g carbohydrate, 2 g fibre, 301 mg sodium, 565 mg potassium

Roast Turkey with Sausage, Apple and Herb Stuffing

Traditional roast turkey is still my dish of choice for Christmas and Thanksgiving dinners.

14 lb	turkey	6.5 kg
	Sausage, Apple and Herb Stuffing (p. 269)	
4	sprigs fresh rosemary and/or thyme	4

Remove neck and giblets from body cavity of turkey. Discard gizzard and heart. Cover and refrigerate neck and liver for gravy. Rinse turkey under cold running water; dry skin and cavities with paper towels.

Loosely stuff neck and body cavity with stuffing. Fold neck skin over cavity and skewer to back. Secure legs by tying together with string. Lift wings and fold behind back or tie to sides of turkey with string. Place rosemary and/or thyme sprigs between body of turkey and each leg and wing.

Place turkey, breast side up, on rack in roasting pan. Cover with loose tent of lightly greased foil, shiny side down, leaving sides open. Roast in 325°F (160°C) oven for 3¾ to 4 hours or until juices run clear when turkey is pierced and thermometer inserted into thigh reads 180°F (82°C). Remove foil for last 30 minutes of cooking, so turkey can brown.

Remove from oven and let stand, covered with foil, for 20 to 30 minutes before carving.

MAKES 14 SERVINGS OF 3.5 OZ (100 g) SKINLESS LIGHT MEAT WITH ½ CUP (125 mL) STUFFING

NOTE: Avoid pre-basted turkeys or ones injected with fat. You are paying a high price for added fat, which is usually hydrogenated or saturated.

PER SERVING: 223 calories, 33 g protein, 5 g total fat, 1 g saturated fat, 74 mg cholesterol, 11 g carbohydrate, 2 g fibre, 283 mg sodium, 407 mg potassium

Cornish Hens with Porcini Mushroom and Basil Stuffing

I love the taste of Cornish hens but for years I've avoided cooking them because I thought a whole hen was one serving, which is too much, or that they had to be deboned, which is fiddly. Since I've discovered that cooked Cornish hens are very easy to cut in half, I now serve them for dinner party fare. I use dried porcini mushrooms because of their woodsy flavour. You can also use other fresh or dried mushrooms, such as shiitake or Portobello.

1 oz	dried porcini mushrooms	30 g
1 tbsp	olive oil	15 mL
8 oz	fresh mushrooms, coarsely chopped (2½ cups/625 mL)	250 g
1	leek (white part only), thinly sliced (1½ cups/375 mL)	1
1	large clove garlic, minced	1
½ tsp or less	salt	2 mL or less
¼ tsp	freshly ground pepper	1 mL
2 cups	soft fresh bread crumbs	500 mL
⅓ cup	packed fresh basil, chopped	75 mL
2 tbsp	sherry	25 mL
3	Cornish hens (about 1⅓ lb/670 g each)	3

SHERRY GRAVY

1 cup	combination of mushroom soaking liquid and sodium-reduced chicken broth	250 mL
2	green onions, minced	2
1	clove garlic, minced	1
1 tbsp	all-purpose flour	15 mL
2 tbsp	sherry	25 mL

Rinse porcini mushrooms under cold water to remove grit. Place in small bowl and pour in 1 cup (250 mL) very hot water; let stand for 30 minutes or until softened. Drain, reserving liquid. Chop any large mushrooms.

In skillet, heat oil over medium heat; cook fresh mushrooms, leek and garlic for 5 minutes, stirring often. Season with salt and pepper.

In bowl, stir together leek mixture, bread crumbs, ¼ cup (50 mL) reserved mushroom liquid and porcini mushrooms, basil and sherry. Stuff into hen cavities. Use skewers to fasten closed. Tie legs together with cotton string; tuck wings under backs.

Place on rack in roasting pan. Roast in 375°F (190°C) oven, basting 2 or 3 times, for 50 to 60 minutes or until juices run clear when hens are pierced. Transfer to warmed platter: tent with foil.

cont'd . . .

NOTE: Fresh bread crumbs are very easy to make. Use one or two day-old bread slices and process in a food processor or pass over a hand grater to form crumbs. Don't substitute store-bought fine dry bread crumbs.

PER SERVING (skin removed):
274 calories, 32 g protein, 9 g total fat, 2 g saturated fat, 131 mg cholesterol, 16 g carbohydrate, 2 g fibre, 404 mg sodium, 543 mg potassium

SHERRY GRAVY: Pour pan juices into gravy separator or measuring cup; skim off fat. Add reserved mushroom soaking liquid, then chicken stock; set aside. In same roasting pan, cook green onions and garlic, stirring, for 2 minutes. Sprinkle with flour; cook, stirring, for 1 minute. Whisk in chicken broth mixture and sherry: simmer, whisking, for 3 to 5 minutes or until thickened slightly.

Using kitchen scissors, cut hens along each side of the backbone. Using scissors or large knife, cut rib cage to divide hens in half. Pile stuffing in centre of each half. Serve drizzled with gravy.

MAKES 6 SERVINGS

Sausage, Apple and Herb Stuffing

In the fall, I often use McIntosh apples; in the winter, Golden Delicious or Spy. Stuff the bird just before cooking.

¼ lb	bulk turkey sausage	125 g
6 cups	day-old whole-wheat bread cubes (about 9 slices)	1.5 L
½ cup	chopped celery	125 mL
½ cup	chopped onion	125 mL
2	small apples, peeled and chopped	2
2 tbsp	each chopped fresh sage and basil (or ½ tsp/2 mL each dried)	25 mL
1½ tsp	dried savory	7 mL
2 tsp	chopped fresh thyme or oregano	10 mL
½ tsp or less	each salt and freshly ground pepper	2 mL or less

In small nonstick skillet, cook sausage over medium heat for 5 to 7 minutes or until no longer pink, breaking up meat with fork.

In large bowl, combine sausage, bread, celery, onion, apples, sage, basil, savory, thyme, salt and pepper.

MAKES ABOUT 8 CUPS (2 L), ENOUGH FOR ONE 14 LB (6.5 KG) TURKEY OR 14 SERVINGS

MAKE AHEAD: Refrigerate stuffing in airtight container for up to 2 days or freeze for up to 4 weeks. Thaw slightly in refrigerator before using to stuff the turkey.

NOTE: Pan juices with the fat removed or cranberry sauce with chutney, port or brandy added for interest are flavourful alternatives to gravy.

PER SERVING (generous ½ cup):
67 calories, 3 g protein,
1 g total fat, 0 g saturated fat,
6 mg cholesterol, 11 g carbohydrate,
2 g fibre, 219 mg sodium,
104 mg potassium

Moroccan Rabbit Tagine

This dish, unlike most traditional rabbit dishes, is low in added fat and spiked with North African seasonings. Serve with plain couscous, rice or bulgur.

2 tsp	canola or olive oil	10 mL
1 tbsp	chopped fresh garlic	15 mL
2	onions, sliced	2
2 tbsp	chopped gingerroot	25 mL
1 tsp	each ground coriander, ground cumin and turmeric	5 mL
½ tsp	cinnamon	2 mL
¼ tsp or less	each salt and freshly ground pepper	1 mL or less
1	skinned rabbit (3 lb/1.5 kg), cut in pieces	1
3 cups	chopped peeled sweet potato	750 mL
2 cups	chopped peeled carrots	500 mL
2 cups	chopped peeled parsnips	500 mL
1	can (28 oz/796 mL) tomatoes	1
1 cup	pitted prunes	250 mL
¼ cup	chopped fresh parsley and/or coriander (cilantro)	50 mL

In large flameproof casserole, heat oil over medium-high heat; cook garlic, onions, gingerroot, ground coriander, cumin, turmeric, cinnamon, salt and pepper, stirring often, for 3 minutes. Add rabbit; cook for 5 minutes or until lightly browned. Add potato, carrots, parsnips and tomatoes; bring to boil.

Bake, covered, in 325°F (160°C) oven for 35 minutes. Add prunes; bake for 5 minutes or until rabbit is tender, meat easily falls away from bone and vegetables are fork-tender. Stir in parsley and/or coriander.

MAKES 6 SERVINGS

MAKE AHEAD: Bake tagine for 35 minutes, as directed; then cover and refrigerate for up to 1 day or freeze for up to 2 weeks. Thaw completely. Reheat in 350°F (180°C) oven, uncovered, for 30 to 40 minutes or until bubbly. Add prunes and parsley and/or coriander near end of baking time.

VARIATION:

Moroccan Chicken Tagine
Substitute 3 lb (1.5 kg) bone-in skinless chicken pieces for rabbit.

NOTE: A tagine is a North African stew, typically served over couscous. I don't know if rabbit tagines are popular in Morocco, but this one tastes wonderful.

PER SERVING: 462 calories, 39 g protein, 12 g total fat, 3 g saturated fat, 98 mg cholesterol, 52 g carbohydrate, 8 g fibre, 378 mg sodium, 1447 mg potassium

Cooking Poultry

Chicken and turkey (without skin) are low-fat sources of protein. Dark meat has a little more fat than white meat. (Duck and goose have a much higher fat content.) To keep the fat at a minimum, remove the skin and any visible fat from poultry pieces before cooking; for whole birds, cut the skin away before eating—but don't remove before cooking, as the poultry will take longer to cook and will dry out. Baking and broiling are the best cooking methods; frying adds to the fat intake.

THAWING POULTRY

Leave in original wrapper (make sure it's well wrapped). Cover with cold water and allow 1 hour per pound (500 g); change water every half hour. Or, in refrigerator, allow 1 day for every 5 lb (2.2 kg).

ROASTING A CHICKEN OR TURKEY

- Truss bird with kitchen twine or string, tying wings and legs close to body (this prevents them from becoming overcooked and dried out before the rest of the chicken is cooked). Do not use synthetic twine.

- Place bird on rack in roasting pan. This makes it easier to remove the bird and keeps it from cooking in its own juices and fat.

- Cover turkey lightly with foil (shiny side down); remove foil during last hour of roasting to brown top. (Chicken cooks in less time so usually doesn't over-brown if left uncovered.)

- Various factors affect the cooking time. For example, fresh turkeys take longer than thawed. Don't overcook, as it will be dry.

- Transfer cooked bird to platter; let stand for 15 minutes before carving to let juices settle.

ROASTING TIMES FOR WHOLE CHICKENS AND TURKEYS

Chicken

in 325°F (160°C) oven

20 minutes per lb (500 g)

Weight	Stuffed	Unstuffed
3½ lb (1.75 kg)	1¾ to 2 hours	1¾ to 2 hours
5 lb (2.2 kg)	2½ to 3 hours	2½ to 3 hours

Turkey

in 325°F (160°C) oven

Weight	Stuffed	Unstuffed
6 to 8 lb (3.0 to 3.5 kg)	3 to 3¼ hrs	2½ to 2¾ hrs
8 to 10 lb (3.5 to 4.5 kg)	3¼ to 3½ hrs	2¾ to 3 hrs
10 to 12 lb (4.5 to 5.5 kg)	3½ to 3¾ hrs	3 to 3¼ hrs
12 to 16 lb (5.5 to 7.0 kg)	3¾ to 4 hrs	3¼ to 3½ hrs
16 to 22 lb (7.0 to 10.0 kg)	4 to 4½ hrs	3½ to 4 hrs

POULTRY DONENESS TEMPERATURES

Meat thermometer should be inserted into the inner thigh or thickest part of the bird.

Chicken

Stuffed	185°F (85°C) or 165°F (73°C) in the dressing
Unstuffed	185°F (85°C)

Turkey

Stuffed	180°F (82°C)
Unstuffed	170°F (75°C)

Bird is cooked when drumstick moves easily in socket and juices from thigh run clear when pierced with knife tip and white meat has no trace of pink.

If cooking a turkey, remove it from the oven or barbecue once cooked; cover with foil and let stand for 15 to 20 minutes before carving.

MICROWAVING WHOLE CHICKEN

Microwaving keeps the meat moist and is an easy way to cook chicken or turkey when you want to remove the meat from the bone to use in salad.

Tie wings and legs tightly to body with cotton string. Place bird on microwaveable rack in shallow microwaveable dish; cover with waxed paper, but don't tuck in waxed paper or bird will stew.

For a 2½ lb (1.25 kg) chicken, microwave on High for 17 to 20 minutes (about 8 minutes per pound/500 g), turning dish occasionally, until juices run clear when thigh is pierced or meat thermometer registers 185°F (85°C) when inserted in thickest part.

Transfer bird to carving board; cover with tent of foil; let chicken stand for 10 to 15 minutes before using. Pour cooking juices into container and refrigerate or freeze. Fat will rise to the surface and solidify; lift fat off and discard. Use remaining liquid for stock or for making sauces or soups.

Garlic-Soy Marinated Beef Skewers

This is a good choice for buffets or barbecues when you don't want to use a fork. Soak wooden skewers in water for 15 minutes before threading with beef. Top round steak is a lean cut that works well here. You could also use lean boneless pork. Serve with Thai Peanut Sauce (p. 329) or use the sauce with Lettuce Wrap Pork (p. 299) or sprinkle with chopped fresh coriander.

	Wooden skewers	
¼ cup	sodium-reduced soy sauce	50 mL
2 tbsp	dry sherry	25 mL
2 tbsp	packed brown sugar	25 mL
1 tbsp	minced fresh garlic	15 mL
1 lb	lean beef, 1 inch (2.5 cm) thick	500 g

In 13- × 9-inch (3.5 L) baking dish, stir together soy sauce, sherry, sugar and garlic until sugar dissolves.

Slice beef into ¼-inch (5 mm) thick strips about 7 inches (18 cm) long and 1 inch (2.5 cm) wide. Thread strips onto skewers; place in soy sauce mixture, turning to coat. Cover and refrigerate for 4 hours, turning occasionally.

Broil or grill for about 2 minutes on each side or until desired doneness, brushing with remaining marinade.

MAKES 6 SERVINGS

MAKE AHEAD: Marinate beef skewers for up to 1 day.

PER SERVING: 105 calories, 17 g protein, 2 g total fat, 1 g saturated fat, 35 mg cholesterol, 3 g carbohydrate, 0 g fibre, 295 mg sodium, 244 mg potassium

Beef and Asparagus Stir-Fry

Make the most of asparagus season with this fast, easy dinner. To save time, buy beef ready-cut for stir-frying. Pork, chicken or turkey can also be used. Serve over rice or noodles.

1 lb	asparagus	500 g
¾ lb	lean boneless beef	375 g
1 tbsp	canola or olive oil	15 mL
1 tbsp	minced gingerroot	15 mL
2	cloves garlic, minced	2
¼ cup	water	50 mL
3	green onions, diagonally sliced	3
SAUCE		
⅓ cup	water	75 mL
2 tbsp	sherry	25 mL
2 tbsp	sodium-reduced soy sauce	25 mL
2 tbsp	apple cider or wine vinegar	25 mL
1 tbsp	cornstarch	15 mL
1 tsp	granulated sugar	5 mL
	Crushed red pepper flakes or hot chili paste	

SAUCE: Combine water, sherry, soy sauce, vinegar, cornstarch, sugar and red pepper flakes.

Cut asparagus diagonally into 1½-inch (4 cm) lengths; cut beef into thin slices.

In large nonstick skillet, heat oil over high heat; stir-fry gingerroot and garlic for 30 seconds. Add meat and stir-fry until no longer pink; transfer to plate.

Add asparagus; stir-fry for 30 seconds. Add water; cover and cook for 3 minutes or until tender-crisp. Return meat mixture to pan along with green onions and sauce; cook, stirring, for 1 minute or until thickened.

MAKES 4 SERVINGS

MAKE AHEAD: Prepare sauce and slice asparagus and beef, cover and refrigerate for up to 8 hours in advance.

NOTE: Stir-frying is a quick and easy cooking method. By frying foods in a small amount of oil over high heat and stirring continuously and vigorously, they are seared and quickly cooked—meats are tender and vegetables crisp. Once you have tried a few stir-fry recipes, you'll find it easy to improvise and make up your own. Stir-frying is a great way to use up leftover raw vegetables and to stretch a small amount of meat, chicken or seafood. By cutting meats and vegetables on the diagonal, meats will be tenderized, and the largest possible surface area of the food is exposed to the heat. For easier slicing, partially freeze meat before cutting.

PER SERVING: 171 calories, 21 g protein, 5 g total fat, 1 g saturated fat, 36 mg cholesterol, 8 g carbohydrate, 1 g fibre, 325 mg sodium, 564 mg potassium

Ginger Beef and Broccoli Stir-Fry

Marinating sliced beef in a mixture of cornstarch and sodium-reduced soy sauce even for ten minutes tenderizes and flavours the beef considerably in this family favourite dish. The sherry also adds taste and tenderizes but it can be omitted. Serve over rice or Chinese noodles.

1 tbsp	each cornstarch, unseasoned rice vinegar and sherry	15 mL
½ tsp	each hot pepper sauce and sesame oil	2 mL
2 tbsp	minced gingerroot	25 mL
1 lb	stir-fry beef strips	500 g
2 tsp	canola or olive oil	10 mL
1	onion, sliced	1
3	cloves garlic, minced	3
6 cups	broccoli pieces (1 inch/2.5 cm) (about 1 lb/500 g)	1.5 L
½ cup	water	125 mL

SAUCE

½ cup	water	125 mL
2 tbsp	sodium-reduced soy sauce	25 mL
1 tbsp	cornstarch	15 mL

In bowl, mix cornstarch, vinegar, sherry, hot pepper sauce, sesame oil and half of the gingerroot; stir in beef strips to coat. Let stand for at least 10 minutes.

SAUCE: In small bowl, mix together water, soy sauce and cornstarch; set aside.

In nonstick skillet or wok, heat 1 tsp (5 mL) of the oil over high heat; stir-fry beef, in two batches, until browned. Transfer to side plate.

Reduce heat to medium-high. Add remaining oil; stir-fry onion, garlic and remaining gingerroot for 1 minute. Stir in broccoli and water; cover and steam for 3 minutes.

Return beef to pan. Stir sauce and add to pan; bring to boil, stirring to coat beef well.

MAKES 4 SERVINGS

MAKE AHEAD: Marinate beef, covered and refrigerated, for up to 2 hours.

NOTE: To save time, buy stir-fry strips of beef or thinly slice 1 lb (500 g) of sirloin tip or inside round or other lean cut of beef. To keep meat as lean as possible, trim all fat.

PER SERVING: 244 calories, 30 g protein, 6 g total fat, 1 g saturated fat, 48 mg cholesterol, 18 g carbohydrate, 4 g fibre, 405 mg sodium, 996 mg potassium

Beef and Pepper Stir-Fry

Choose red, yellow and green sweet peppers when they are in season. At other times, use broccoli, cauliflower, onions or carrots. Serve with hot cooked pasta or rice tossed with a few drops of hot pepper sauce.

1 lb	boneless lean beef, cut in thin 2-inch-long strips	500 g (5 cm)
1 tbsp	canola or olive oil	15 mL
2	cloves garlic, minced	2
2 tbsp	minced gingerroot	25 mL
2	sweet peppers (1 yellow, 1 green or red), cut in strips	2
2 cups	bean sprouts or snow peas	500 mL
2 tbsp	water (optional)	25 mL
2 tbsp	sodium-reduced soy or oyster sauce	25 mL

MARINADE

1 tbsp	cornstarch	15 mL
1 tbsp	sherry	15 mL
2 tsp	sodium-reduced soy sauce	10 mL

MARINADE: In bowl, stir together cornstarch, sherry and soy sauce until smooth.

Add beef and stir to coat. Marinate at room temperature for 10 minutes.

In nonstick skillet or wok, heat oil over high heat; stir-fry beef, garlic and gingerroot for 3 minutes or until beef is browned. Transfer to plate and set aside.

Add sweet peppers to skillet; stir-fry for 3 minutes. Add bean sprouts; cook for 1 minute or until vegetables are tender-crisp, adding water if necessary to prevent scorching. Stir in soy sauce. Return beef to pan and toss to mix and reheat.

MAKES 4 SERVINGS

NOTE: Use lean cuts of beef such as grilling or marinating steaks or stir-fry strips from the flank, round, rump or sirloin with all visible fat removed.

PER SERVING: 214 calories, 28 g protein, 6 g total fat, 1 g saturated fat, 48 mg cholesterol, 11 g carbohydrate, 1 g fibre, 421 mg sodium, 728 mg potassium

Stir-Fry Beef Curry

The wonderful flavours of curry and the quick cooking of a beef and vegetable stir-fry make for an easy, delicious dinner. Serve over mashed potatoes or rice.

12 oz	top round beef steak	350 g
1 tbsp	minced gingerroot	15 mL
2 tsp	canola or olive oil	10 mL
1 tsp	medium curry powder or paste	5 mL
½ tsp	each ground cinnamon and ground coriander	2 mL
2	carrots, thinly sliced on diagonal	2
3 cups	sliced cabbage	750 mL
1	apple, cored and cut in chunks	1
¾ cup	water	175 mL
1 tbsp	fresh lemon juice	15 mL
½ tsp	cornstarch	2 mL
¼ cup	chopped green onions	50 mL
½ tsp	each salt and granulated sugar	2 mL
¼ tsp	freshly ground pepper	1 mL

Slice meat diagonally across the grain into thin strips; set aside.

In small bowl, combine gingerroot, oil, curry powder, cinnamon and coriander. In large nonstick skillet, cook half of the spice mixture over medium heat, stirring, for 1 minute. Increase heat to high. Add beef; stir-fry for 2 minutes or until browned yet still pink inside. Transfer to plate.

Reduce heat to medium. Add remaining spice mixture, carrots, cabbage and apple; cook, stirring, for 1 minute. Add water, mixing well; cover and simmer for 3 minutes.

Mix lemon juice with cornstarch; stir into pan along with green onions, salt, sugar and pepper. Simmer, stirring constantly, for 2 to 3 minutes or until vegetables are tender. Stir in beef and any accumulated juices until heated through.

MAKES 4 SERVINGS

NOTE: One serving is very high in vitamin A and is a good source of iron.

PER SERVING: 170 calories, 20 g protein, 5 g total fat, 1 g saturated fat, 36 mg cholesterol, 12 g carbohydrate, 3 g fibre, 365 mg sodium, 581 mg potassium

Easy Oven Beef and Vegetable Stew

This is the easiest stew to make and tastes wonderful. Sometimes I add parsnips along with the carrots, and then frozen green peas just before serving. Make the stew on the weekend and you'll probably have enough left over for a meal during the week. Or make it during the week, to bring with you to the cabin or cottage.

1½ lb	stewing beef	750 g
¼ cup	all-purpose flour	50 mL
6	small onions, halved	6
2	large potatoes, cut in chunks (about 1 lb/500 g)	2
4	large carrots, peeled and cut in chunks	4
3	cloves garlic, minced	3
2 cups	peeled, diced rutabaga	500 mL
3 cups	water	750 mL
1¼ cups	sodium-reduced beef broth	300 mL
1	can (7½ oz/213 mL) tomato sauce	1
1 tsp	dried thyme	5 mL
1 tbsp	dried oregano	15 mL
¼ tsp or less	each salt and freshly ground pepper	1 mL or less
2	bay leaves	2
½ tsp	grated orange rind (optional)	2 mL

Remove all visible fat from beef; cut beef into 1-inch (2.5 cm) cubes.

In large casserole or Dutch oven, toss beef with flour. Add onions, potatoes, carrots, garlic, rutabaga, water, beef broth, tomato sauce, thyme, oregano, salt, pepper, bay leaves and orange rind (if using); stir to mix.

Bake, covered, in 325°F (160°C) oven for 2½ to 3 hours, stirring occasionally (if you remember). Remove bay leaves.

MAKES 8 SERVINGS

NOTE: The flavour of a stew is usually better the second day. Make it a day in advance and refrigerate. Any fat will solidify on top and can easily be removed.

Compare mg sodium for about ⅔ cup (150 mL) stew:

This recipe	388
Canned beef and vegetable stew	685

PER SERVING: 226 calories, 19 g protein, 6 g total fat, 2 g saturated fat, 35 mg cholesterol, 25 g carbohydrate, 4 g fibre, 388 mg sodium, 895 mg potassium

No-Fuss Pot Roast with Onions

The onions impart a wonderful, familiar flavour to both the beef and the gravy. An easy dish for Sunday dinner.

3 cups	thinly sliced onions	750 mL
3	cloves garlic, minced	3
3 lb	lean bottom round roast	1. 5 kg
	Freshly ground pepper	
¼ cup	water	50 mL
1 tbsp	cornstarch	15 mL
1 tbsp	cold water	15 mL

In casserole or Dutch oven, spread half of the onions and garlic. Place roast on top. Cover with remaining onions and garlic. Sprinkle with pepper to taste.

Pour in ¼ cup (50 mL) water. Cover and cook in 325°F (160°C) oven for 2½ to 3 hours or until meat is tender. Transfer meat and onions to serving platter; cover loosely with foil. Let stand for 15 minutes to make carving easier.

Meanwhile, add enough water to pan liquids, if necessary, to make 1 cup (250 mL); spoon off fat from top of liquid. Dissolve cornstarch in 1 tbsp (15 mL) cold water; stir into pan juices. Cook over medium-high heat, stirring, for 2 to 3 minutes or until gravy boils and thickens. Strain if desired. Cut roast into thin slices and serve with gravy.

MAKES 8 SERVINGS

PER SERVING: 250 calories, 40 g protein, 7 g total fat, 3 g saturated fat, 89 mg cholesterol, 5 g carbohydrate, 1 g fibre, 66 mg sodium, 434 mg potassium

Pot-Au-Feu

This French savoury classic consists of a pot roast of beef and vegetables slowly simmered together. Serve along with mashed or boiled potatoes in individual large shallow bowls and pour cooking broth over top. It's best to make this recipe a day in advance and refrigerate it overnight so the fat will solidify on top for easy removal. Serve with horseradish.

2 lb	boneless sirloin tip, rib or blade roast of beef, all visible fat removed	1 kg
6 cups	water	1.5 L
1 tsp	crushed dried thyme	5 mL
1	bay leaf	1
6	peppercorns	6
2	large carrots, cut in chunks	2
2	medium onions, quartered	2
1	small white turnip (or ¼ yellow rutabaga), peeled and cut in ½-inch (1 cm) cubes	1
2	stalks celery, sliced	2
Quarter	small cabbage, cut in wedges	Quarter
¼ tsp or less	each salt and freshly ground pepper	1 mL or less

Be sure roast is securely tied. Place in large deep saucepan or flameproof casserole and add water. Bring to boil over medium heat; remove any scum. Add thyme, bay leaf and peppercorns; simmer for 3 hours or until tender. Skim off fat, or refrigerate overnight then remove fat.

Add carrots, onions and turnip to hot stock; cover and simmer for 30 to 40 minutes or until vegetables are nearly tender. Add celery and cabbage; cook for 15 minutes or until vegetables are fork-tender. Season with salt and pepper.

Remove meat to platter; let stand for 10 minutes before carving. Discard bay leaf. Keep vegetables warm; serve with meat and pour broth over top.

MAKES 8 SERVINGS

MAKE AHEAD: Cover and refrigerate stew for up to 2 days.

NOTE: One serving is an excellent source of vitamin A and zinc, and a good source of iron.

VARIATION:

Crock Pot Method for Pot-Au-Feu
For a medium-size Crock Pot, cut recipe in half. Reduce liquid to 2 cups (500 mL) and use low-sodium beef stock. Add all vegetables except cabbage. Cover and cook on low for 8 to 9 hours. Add cabbage, cook for 1 hour. Add salt and pepper.

PER SERVING: 175 calories, 25 g protein, 5 g total fat, 2 g saturated fat, 56 mg cholesterol, 6 g carbohydrate, 2 g fibre, 144 mg sodium, 383 mg potassium

Beef Filet Roasted with Mustard Peppercorn Crust

This most tender cut of beef is the perfect choice for a special dinner. Serve with Tarragon and Mushroom Sauce (p. 327) or Yogurt Béarnaise Sauce (p. 326) and with asparagus or green beans, and the Buttermilk Mashed Potatoes celeriac variation (p. 121).

2½ lb	beef tenderloin	1.2 kg
¼ cup	Dijon mustard	50 mL
2 tsp	minced fresh garlic	10 mL
2 tbsp	black peppercorns	25 mL

Trim any fat or muscle covering from meat; place meat in roasting pan. Combine mustard and garlic; spread over beef. In clean coffee grinder or with mallet, crush peppercorns; pat onto mustard coating. Let stand at room temperature for 1 hour.

Roast in 425°F (220°C) oven for 10 minutes. Reduce heat to 350°F (180°C); roast for 25 minutes or until medium-rare. Remove and let stand for 10 minutes before carving.

MAKES 8 SERVINGS

NOTE: Beef will continue to cook as it stands; temperature will rise 5°F (3°C).

MAKE AHEAD: Add toppings to beef, cover and refrigerate for up to 1 day. Remove from refrigerator 1 hour before roasting, or if roasting directly from refrigerator, add at least 5 minutes to roasting time.

VARIATION: To serve cold, roast as directed; let cool completely before slicing and serving cold— ideal for a summer party or large gathering.

PER SERVING: 212 calories, 30 g protein, 9 g total fat, 4 g saturated fat, 69 mg cholesterol, 2 g carbohydrate, 0 g fibre, 251 mg sodium, 329 mg potassium

Family Favourite Marinated Flank Steak

This recipe came from my friend Diane Gilday years ago. It is still a favourite with both our families. My daughter, Susie, now serves it at parties. Whether served hot or cold, it's tender, flavourful and one of the leanest cuts of beef. Best when marinated at least one day in advance.

1 lb	flank steak	500 g
¼ cup	sodium-reduced soy sauce	50 mL
2 tbsp	wine or apple cider vinegar	25 mL
2 tbsp	granulated sugar or liquid honey	25 mL
1 tbsp	canola or olive oil	15 mL
1 tbsp	grated gingerroot (or 1 tsp/5 mL ground ginger)	15 mL
2 cloves	garlic, minced	2

Trim any fat from steak. Place meat in shallow dish or plastic bag. Combine soy sauce, vinegar, sugar, oil, gingerroot and garlic; pour over meat. Cover and refrigerate for at least 24 hours, or let stand at room temperature for up to 1 hour, turning occasionally.

Discarding marinade, broil steak for 3 to 4 minutes on each side or until desired doneness. Slice thinly on angle across the grain.

MAKES 4 SERVINGS

MAKE AHEAD: Marinate steak in refrigerator for up to 3 days. If serving cold, cook, cover and refrigerate for up to 1 day; slice just before serving.

PER SERVING: 222 calories, 26 g protein, 10 g total fat, 4 g saturated fat, 46 mg cholesterol, 4 g carbohydrate, 0 g fibre, 320 mg sodium, 372 mg potassium

Hoisin-Garlic Flank Steak

This Asian-style marinade tenderizes a lean cut of beef while adding extra flavour. The longer it marinates, the more tender the steak.

1 lb	flank steak	500 g

ASIAN MARINADE

2 tbsp	hoisin sauce	25 mL
1 tbsp	each unseasoned rice vinegar*, sherry and liquid honey	15 mL
1 tsp	sesame oil	5 mL
1 tsp	grated orange rind	5 mL
3	cloves garlic, minced	3
Pinch	crushed red pepper flakes or chili paste	Pinch

Place meat in shallow dish or plastic bag.

ASIAN MARINADE: Combine hoisin sauce, vinegar, sherry, honey, oil, orange rind, garlic and red pepper flakes; pour over meat. Cover and refrigerate for at least 1 hour or up to 24 hours.

Discarding marinade, grill or broil steak for 5 to 8 minutes on each side or until medium-rare. Let stand for 3 minutes before slicing thinly on an angle across the grain.

MAKES 4 SERVINGS

*If unseasoned rice vinegar is unavailable, use apple cider or red or white wine vinegar.

MAKE AHEAD: Marinate steak for up to 1 day. To serve cold, grill marinated steak, cover and refrigerate for up to 1 day; slice just before serving.

PER SERVING: 214 calories, 26 g protein, 9 g total fat, 4 g saturated fat, 46 mg cholesterol, 4 g carbohydrate, 0 g fibre, 119 mg sodium, 363 mg potassium

Hamburgers au Poivre

These peppery hamburgers are drizzled with a shallot-yogurt sauce that turns an ordinary meal into a dressed-up plate.

1 lb	extra-lean ground beef	500 g
1 to 2 tsp	peppercorns	5 to 10 mL
1 tsp	canola or olive oil	5 mL
1 tbsp	finely chopped shallots*	15 mL
1 tbsp	red wine vinegar	15 mL
1 tsp	all-purpose flour	5 mL
¼ cup	low-fat plain yogurt or light sour cream	50 mL
1 tbsp	chopped fresh parsley and/or coriander	15 mL (cilantro)

Divide meat into 4 portions and shape into hamburger patties.

Put peppercorns on large piece of waxed paper, foil or plastic bag. Using bottom of heavy skillet or pan or with side of cleaver or in mini-chopper, crack peppercorns coarsely. Spread peppercorns out. Press patties onto peppercorns; turn patties over and sprinkle any remaining peppercorns over top, pressing to adhere.

In nonstick skillet, heat oil over high heat. Add patties and cook for 2 to 3 minutes or until browned; turn and cook for 1 to 2 minutes or until no longer pink inside, reducing heat if necessary to prevent burning. Transfer to plate and keep warm.

Pour off any fat in pan; reduce heat to medium. Add shallots; cook for 1 minute. Add vinegar; cook for 1 minute, scraping up brown bits from bottom of pan. Remove from heat.

Mix flour with yogurt; stir into skillet, mixing well. Stir in parsley and/or coriander. Place patties on individual plates; spoon sauce over patties.

MAKES 5 SERVINGS

*If shallots are unavailable, use cooking onions.

MAKE AHEAD: Cover and refrigerate uncooked patties with peppercorns for up to 6 hours in advance.

PER SERVING: 157 calories, 20 g protein, 7 g total fat, 3 g saturated fat, 49 mg cholesterol, 2 g carbohydrate, 0 g fibre, 63 mg sodium, 301 mg potassium

Hamburger and Noodle Skillet Supper

When fresh tomatoes aren't in season, use cherry tomatoes or a whole 14-oz (398 mL) can of tomato sauce or tomatoes. Instead of zucchini or sweet peppers, you can use chopped celery, frozen peas or corn.

PER SERVING: 294 calories, 22 g protein, 10 g total fat, 4 g saturated fat, 72 mg cholesterol, 29 g carbohydrate, 5 g fibre, 308 mg sodium, 677 mg potassium

3 cups	egg noodles or 1 cup (250 mL) small pasta (4 oz/125 g)	750 mL
1 lb	lean ground beef	500 g
1	onion, chopped	1
1	small zucchini, cut in thin 2-inch (5 cm) long strips	1
1	sweet green or red pepper, cubed	1
1¼ cups	sliced mushrooms (4 oz/125 g) (optional)	300 mL
4	tomatoes, cubed	4
½ cup	tomato sauce	125 mL
¼ cup	chopped fresh parsley	50 mL
1 tsp	each dried basil and oregano	5 mL
¼ tsp or less	salt and freshly ground pepper	1 mL or less

In large pot of boiling water, cook pasta until tender but firm; drain.

Meanwhile, in large skillet or Dutch oven, cook beef over medium heat, stirring to break up, for about 5 minutes or until browned; pour off fat. Add onion; cook for about 4 minutes or until tender. Add zucchini, sweet pepper and mushrooms (if using); cook, stirring, over medium-high heat for about 5 minutes or until tender-crisp.

Add tomatoes, tomato sauce, parsley, basil and oregano; simmer for 5 minutes. Stir in noodles. Season with salt and pepper.

MAKES 5 SERVINGS

Family Favourite Shepherd's Pie

My mother always made shepherd's pie from leftover Sunday roast beef, gravy and mashed potatoes. However, I usually make shepherd's pie using ground meat—beef, pork or lamb. If you don't have leftover mashed potatoes, boil 5 medium potatoes; drain and mash with milk.

1 lb	lean ground beef, pork or lamb, or a combination of these	500 g
2	medium onions, chopped	2
2	large cloves garlic, minced	2
1	carrot, minced	1
⅓ cup	tomato paste	75 mL
⅔ cup	water	150 mL
1 tsp	dried thyme	5 mL
1 tbsp	Worcestershire sauce	15 mL
¼ tsp or less	salt and freshly ground pepper	1 mL or less
2 cups	mashed potatoes	500 mL
	Paprika	

In skillet over medium heat, cook beef, stirring to break up meat, until brown; pour off fat. Add onions, garlic and carrot; cook until tender. Add tomato paste, water, thyme, Worcestershire, and salt and pepper. Simmer for 5 minutes, stirring up any brown bits from bottom of pan.

Spoon meat mixture into 8-cup (2 L) baking or microwave-safe dish; spread mashed potatoes evenly on top. Sprinkle with paprika to taste. Bake in 375°F (190°C) oven for 35 minutes or until heated through, or microwave on High for 9 minutes.

MAKES 5 SERVINGS

VARIATION: This dish is equally good made with 1 can (7½ oz/213 mL) tomato sauce instead of tomato paste and water, but it is higher in sodium.

COMPARE: Sodium (mg per serving) when made with:

Tomato paste plus water	480
Tomato sauce	688

PER SERVING: 258 calories, 20 g protein, 9 g total fat, 4 g saturated fat, 48 mg cholesterol, 26 g carbohydrate, 4 g fibre, 480 mg sodium, 785 mg potassium

Meat Loaf with Herbs

Here's an updated version of an old classic. Serve with Tomato Salsa (p. 3) or Mango Salsa (p. 322) and Roasted Sesame-Chili French Fries (p. 122) or Barley and Corn Casserole (p. 113). Leftovers are always delicious hot or cold or in sandwiches.

1	slice bread, crumbled	1
¼ cup	low-fat milk	50 mL
1	onion, minced	1
1	stalk celery (with leaves), minced	1
¼ cup	chopped fresh parsley	50 mL
¼ cup	minced sweet green or red pepper	50 mL
1 tsp	dried thyme (or 1 tbsp/15 mL fresh)	5 mL
1 tbsp	chopped fresh rosemary or oregano	15 mL
1	clove garlic, minced	1
1	egg, lightly beaten	1
¼ cup	ketchup	50 mL
1½ tsp	Worcestershire sauce	7 mL
¼ tsp or less	each salt and freshly ground pepper	1 mL or less
1 lb	extra-lean ground beef	500 g

In large bowl, combine bread crumbs and milk. Stir in onion, celery, parsley, green pepper, thyme, rosemary, garlic, egg, ketchup, Worcestershire, salt and pepper; mix well. Add beef; mix lightly. Transfer to 9- × 5-inch (2 L) loaf pan.

Bake in 350°F (180°C) oven for 1 hour or until meat thermometer registers 170°F (75°C); drain off fat. Let stand for 10 minutes; cut into thick slices.

MAKES 4 SERVINGS

MAKE AHEAD: Cover and refrigerate uncooked meat loaf for up to 3 hours in advance.

NOTE: To reduce the amount of sodium, substitute 2 tbsp (25 mL) tomato paste for the ketchup in this recipe; sodium will then be 337 mg per serving.

PER SERVING: 255 calories, 27 g protein, 10 g total fat, 4 g saturated fat, 108 mg cholesterol, 14 g carbohydrate, 1 g fibre, 505 mg sodium, 567 mg potassium

Beef, Tomato and Rice Stuffed Peppers with Tomato Basil Sauce

This flavourful main course can be tucked away in the freezer to have on hand. For a truly attractive dish, use a colourful variety of peppers. Tiny baby peppers are a nice choice when serving this dish in a buffet.

12	medium sweet red, green, yellow or purple peppers (or 24 baby peppers)	12
12 oz	lean ground beef	350 g
1	onion, finely chopped	1
2 cups	cooked rice (1 cup/250 mL uncooked)	500 mL
1½ cups	drained canned or chopped fresh tomatoes	375 mL
½ cup	tomato sauce*	125 mL
1 tbsp	Worcestershire sauce	15 mL
¾ tsp or less	salt	3 mL or less
1½ cups	Tomato Basil Sauce (p. 189)	375 mL

Slice top off each pepper; chop tops and reserve for filling. Remove core, seeds and membranes from peppers. Blanch peppers in boiling water for 3 minutes; drain and set aside.

In large nonstick skillet or saucepan, cook beef, onion and chopped pepper until beef is no longer pink and onions are tender. Drain off fat. Stir in rice, tomatoes, tomato sauce, Worcestershire and salt; simmer for 2 minutes. Spoon meat mixture into peppers. Bake in 350°F (180°C) oven for 20 minutes or until hot. Serve with Tomato Basil Sauce to spoon over top.

MAKES 6 SERVINGS

*Instead of tomato sauce, you can mix ¼ cup (50 mL) tomato paste with ¼ cup (50 mL) water, or use ½ cup (125 mL) ketchup.

MAKE AHEAD: Stuffed unbaked peppers can be covered and refrigerated for up to 1 day or frozen for up to 1 month. Cook frozen or thawed peppers in microwave or conventional oven.

NOTE: One serving is an excellent source of vitamin A, vitamin C (678%) and folacin and a good source of iron. It also contains a very high amount of fibre.

VARIATION: Instead of Tomato Basil Sauce, sprinkle stuffed peppers with freshly grated Parmesan cheese or low-fat mozzarella cheese before baking.

PER SERVING: 275 calories, 16 g protein, 7 g total fat, 2 g saturated fat, 30 mg cholesterol, 41 g carbohydrate, 6 g fibre, 598 mg sodium, 951 mg potassium

Beef and Vegetable Chili

If you are cooking for a family, this is an easy and quick meal. It's easily reheated—handy if people are eating at different times—and is nice for a packed lunch. I often add a can of pork and beans or another type of cooked beans, such as pinto, black, romano or chickpeas. Sometimes I top it with light sour cream, grated reduced-fat Cheddar cheese and chopped green onions.

1 lb	lean ground beef	500 g
2	medium onions, chopped	2
2	large cloves garlic, minced	2
1 cup	each chopped celery and carrots	250 mL
1 cup	chopped sweet green or red pepper	250 mL
3 tbsp	chili powder	50 mL
1 tsp	each oregano and ground cumin	5 mL
½ tsp	(approx) crushed red pepper flakes	2 mL
1	can (28 oz/796 mL) tomatoes, whole or diced	1
2	cans (19 oz/540 mL each) red kidney beans, drained and rinsed	2
1½ cups	frozen or fresh cooked corn kernels	375 mL
1 tbsp	fresh lemon juice	15 mL

In large nonstick skillet or saucepan, cook beef over medium-high heat, breaking up with fork, until browned, about 5 minutes. Pour off fat. Add onions, garlic, celery, carrots, green pepper, chili powder, oregano, cumin and red pepper flakes; cook for 5 to 10 minutes or until onions are tender, stirring often.

Add tomatoes, kidney beans, corn and lemon juice; cover and simmer for 10 minutes or until vegetables are tender. Add water if too thick. Taste and adjust seasoning, adding more chili powder and red pepper flakes if desired.

MAKES 6 SERVINGS

MICROWAVE METHOD

In 12-cup (3 L) microwaveable bowl, combine beef, onions, garlic, celery, carrots, green pepper, chili powder, oregano, cumin and red pepper flakes; mix well, breaking up beef.

Microwave on High for 7 to 9 minutes or until meat is no longer pink, stirring once. Stir in tomatoes, kidney beans, corn and lemon juice; cover with waxed paper. Microwave on High for 5 minutes; stir well. Microwave on Medium-high for about 20 minutes or until desired thickness. Taste and adjust seasoning with more chili powder and red pepper flakes if desired.

VARIATION:

Vegetarian Chili
Omit beef, adding instead an extra can of kidney or other beans and additional sweet peppers and other vegetables such as chopped broccoli or cauliflower. Heat 2 tbsp (25 mL) canola oil in large saucepan; add onions, garlic, celery, carrots and green pepper. Prepare as directed.

PER SERVING: 366 calories, 27 g protein, 9 g total fat, 3 g saturated fat, 40 mg cholesterol, 48 g carbohydrate, 14 g fibre, 674 mg sodium, 1218 mg potassium

Beef Fajitas

This family pleaser is a cinch to make. If you have pickled jalapeño peppers on hand, add them to taste instead of red pepper flakes.

6	soft 8-inch (20 cm) flour tortillas	6
1 tsp	canola or olive oil	5 mL
½ lb	extra-lean ground beef	250 g
1	onion, chopped	1
1	sweet red or green pepper, cut in thin strips	1
2	cloves garlic, minced	2
1 tsp	ground coriander or chili powder	5 mL
1 tsp	ground cumin	5 mL
	Crushed red pepper flakes, hot chili paste or hot red pepper sauce to taste	
½ cup	each shredded lettuce, tomato salsa, low-fat plain yogurt	125 mL
¼ cup	chopped fresh coriander (cilantro)	50 mL

Stack tortillas and wrap in foil; heat in 325°F (160°C) oven for 5 to 10 minutes or until warmed through.

Meanwhile, in large nonstick skillet, heat oil over high heat; cook beef and onion, breaking up meat with spoon, for 1 minute. Add red pepper, garlic, ground coriander, cumin and red pepper flakes; cook for 5 minutes or until beef is no longer pink.

Spoon mixture evenly onto centre of each tortilla; top with lettuce, salsa, yogurt and coriander. Roll up.

MAKES 6 SERVINGS

MAKE AHEAD: Prepare beef filling; cover and refrigerate for up to 3 hours; reheat in microwave or over low heat.

VARIATION: Substitute lean ground chicken or turkey for the beef.

PER SERVING: 271 calories, 14 g protein, 8 g total fat, 2 g saturated fat, 21 mg cholesterol, 35 g carbohydrate, 3 g fibre, 483 mg sodium, 373 mg potassium

Easy Veal Cutlets with Tarragon Sauce

Don't let the ease of this recipe fool you into thinking it's not suitable for guests. Because such a tiny amount of fat is used, it's important to have a nonstick skillet. Use either veal scaloppine or thin cutlets.

1 tsp	canola or olive oil	5 mL
1 lb	veal cutlets	500 g
½ cup	dry white wine or sodium-reduced chicken or veal broth	125 mL
½ tsp	dried tarragon (or 1 tbsp/15 mL chopped fresh)	2 mL
1 tsp	all-purpose flour	5 mL
¼ cup	low-fat plain yogurt	50 mL
¼ tsp or less	salt and freshly ground pepper	1 mL or less

In large nonstick skillet, heat oil over high heat; add veal and brown on both sides, about 2 minutes per side. Watch carefully: if veal is overcooked, it toughens. Remove and set aside.

Add wine and tarragon, stirring to scrape up brown bits from bottom of pan. Cook until liquid is reduced by half, about 2 minutes. Remove from heat.

Mix flour with yogurt; stir into pan liquid and mix well. Return veal to pan and turn to coat with sauce. Season with salt and pepper.

MAKES 4 SERVINGS

VARIATION:

Chicken Breasts with Tarragon Sauce

Pound 1 lb (500 g) chicken breasts between waxed paper until about ¼ inch (5 mm) thick so they will cook faster and appear larger (or use chicken or turkey cutlets).

In large nonstick skillet, heat oil over high heat; cook chicken for about 5 minutes or until browned on both sides. Add wine and tarragon; reduce heat to medium and cook, uncovered, for about 5 minutes or until chicken is no longer pink inside and liquid is reduced by half.

Transfer chicken to a plate; mix flour into yogurt; stir into pan liquid until mixed well. Return chicken to pan and coat with sauce; season with salt and pepper to taste.

PER SERVING: 153 calories, 26 g protein, 2 g total fat, 0 g saturated fat, 70 mg cholesterol, 2 g carbohydrate, 0 g fibre, 197 mg sodium, 332 mg potassium

Buying and Cooking Beef

Many people have stopped eating red meat or reduced their consumption drastically out of concern, in part, about its fat content. Although red meat isn't essential for good health, it is the best source of heme iron, which is more easily absorbed by our bodies than the iron we get from vegetables. It is also a concentrated source of many nutrients, including vitamin B12, which we can't get from conventional vegetables. I'm not recommending plate-size steaks fried in butter, but 4 oz (125 g) of grilled sirloin once in a while is a different matter.

BUYING BEEF

In general, when buying beef, choose leaner cuts, such as round steak (inside is leanest), sirloin and sirloin tip, rump, eye of round, strip loin, tenderloin and flank. Choose the type of ground beef depending on what you are cooking.

FAT CONTENT OF GROUND BEEF

Type	Maximum % fat (by raw weight)
Extra lean	10 %
Lean	17 %
Medium	23 %
Regular	30 %

COOKING BEEF

- Use *extra lean* ground beef when you can't pour off the fat (e.g., shepherd's pie or stuffing for pasta), or where other fats are in same dish.

- Anyone on a low-fat diet should use extra-lean ground meat whenever possible.

REDUCING THE FAT WHEN COOKING BEEF

- Trim off all visible fat.

- Use a nonstick pan to brown meat, or cook in a heavy pan to prevent burning.

- Grill, broil or roast on a rack, or microwave instead of frying.

- Pour or spoon off any visible fat from stews or baked dishes. Or prepare a day ahead, refrigerate and remove hardened fat.

- Cut off any fat from cooked meat before eating.

- Serve small portions.

BEEF DONENESS TEMPERATURES

Doneness	Internal Temp. When Cooked
Rare	140°F (60°C)
Medium rare	145°F (63°C)
Medium	160°F (70°C)
Well done	170°F (75°C)

Beef will continue to cook when it is taken out of the oven, so it should be removed from the oven 3–5°F prior to reaching the desired doneness.

It is important to cook ground beef until it is well done in order to kill any bacteria. Roasts and steaks can be eaten a little rare, as long as they are well cooked on the outside. Be sure to have a clean plate to put the cooked meat on and clean utensils, not the ones already used for the raw meat.

PORK

Brochette of Pork with Lemon and Herb Marinade

Herbs and lemon add tang to this easy-to-prepare dish. Use pork tenderloin or any other lean cut of pork. Zucchini or blanched slices of carrot can be used instead of the vegetables. Serve with Lemon Parsley Rice Pilaf (p. 103) and a green salad. Soak the wooden skewers for about 10 minutes before using to prevent charring.

PER SERVING: 248 calories, 26 g protein, 11 g total fat, 3 g saturated fat, 69 mg cholesterol, 12 g carbohydrate, 3 g fibre, 61 mg sodium, 692 mg potassium

	Wooden skewers	
1 lb	boneless lean pork	500 g
	Grated rind and juice of 1 lemon	
2	large cloves garlic, minced	2
2 tsp	dried basil (or 2 tbsp/25 mL fresh)	10 mL
1 tsp	dried thyme (or 1 tbsp/15 mL fresh)	5 mL
2 tbsp	chopped fresh parsley	25 mL
2 tsp	olive or canola oil	10 mL
1	sweet green or red pepper, cut in squares	1
2	onions, quartered and separated into pieces	2
16	cherry tomatoes or fresh pineapple chunks*	16

Cut pork into 1-inch (2.5 cm) cubes. In bowl, combine lemon rind and juice, garlic, basil, thyme, parsley and oil. Add pork and toss to coat well. Cover and marinate in refrigerator for 4 hours or overnight.

Alternately thread pork, green pepper, onions and cherry tomatoes onto soaked wooden skewers. On greased grill over medium heat or under broiler, grill brochettes, turning often, for 15 minutes or until just a hint of pink remains inside pork.

MAKES 4 SERVINGS

*Pineapple chunks packed in their own juice can be used instead of fresh pineapple.

Pork Tenderloin with Rosemary and Thyme

Pork tenderloin is ideal for a dinner party any time of year. In fall, serve with squash or sweet peppers, in summer with Tomatoes Florentine (p. 143), in spring with Rose Murray's Roasted Asparagus (p. 126) and in winter with Braised Red Cabbage (p. 138). In good weather, barbecue for 18 to 25 minutes instead of roasting.

2 tbsp	Dijon mustard	25 mL
1 tsp	dried rosemary (or 1 tbsp/15 mL fresh)	5 mL
½ tsp	crushed dried thyme (or 1 tbsp/15 mL fresh)	2 mL
¼ tsp	coarsely ground black pepper	1 mL
1 lb	pork tenderloin	500 g
	Fresh rosemary sprigs	

In small bowl, combine mustard, rosemary, thyme and pepper; spread over pork. Place in roasting pan. Roast in 350°F (180°C) oven for 30 to 40 minutes or until just slightly pink inside. To serve, cut into thin slices. Garnish with fresh rosemary.

MAKES 3 SERVINGS

NOTE: The tenderloin is one of the leanest and most tender cuts of pork.

One serving is a high source of iron.

PER SERVING: 227 calories, 37 g protein, 7 g total fat, 2 g saturated fat, 85 mg cholesterol, 2 g carbohydrate, 0 g fibre, 320 mg sodium, 551 mg potassium

Pork Tenderloin Teriyaki

Pork tenderloin is delicious marinated, then grilled just until moist and juicy. Serve with Mango Salsa (p. 322) and Grilled Fall Vegetables (p. 129).

2 tbsp	sodium-reduced soy sauce	25 mL
2 tbsp	sherry	25 mL
1 tbsp	canola or olive oil	15 mL
1 tbsp	finely chopped gingerroot	15 mL
1 tsp	granulated sugar	5 mL
1	clove garlic, minced	1
2	pork tenderloins (about 9 oz/255 g each)	2

Combine soy sauce, sherry, oil, gingerroot, sugar and garlic.

Place pork in plastic bag; pour in marinade. Refrigerate for 2 hours.

Reserving marinade, place pork on greased grill over medium-high heat. Grill for 18 to 25 minutes or until meat thermometer registers 160°F (70°C) for medium or 170°F (75°C) for well done, turning occasionally and brushing with marinade.

Remove from grill; tent with foil and let stand for 5 minutes. Cut diagonally into thin slices.

MAKES 6 SERVINGS

MAKE AHEAD: Cover and refrigerate sauce for up to 2 days. Marinate pork for up to 1 day in advance.

VARIATION:

Oven-Roasted Pork Tenderloin Teriyaki
In roasting pan or on baking sheet, roast marinated pork in 350°F (180°C) oven for 40 to 50 minutes or until meat thermometer registers 160°F to 170°F (70°C to 75°C). (Cooking time is based on meat coming straight from refrigerator. If meat is at room temperature, cooking time will be less.)

PER SERVING: 140 calories, 20 g protein, 5 g total fat, 1 g saturated fat, 48 mg cholesterol, 1 g carbohydrate, 0 g fibre, 156 mg sodium, 309 mg potassium

Pork Tenderloin with Orange Ginger Sauce

Pork tenderloin is very easy to cook; just be careful not to overcook it or it will be too dry. Serve with Buttermilk Mashed Potatoes (p. 121) and Green Beans with Garlic, Balsamic Vinegar and Sesame Oil (p. 135).

1 lb	pork tenderloin	500 g
1	medium carrot, peeled	1
4	green onions or 1 leek	4
¼ cup	water	50 mL
1 tsp	grated gingerroot	5 mL
½ tsp	minced fresh garlic	2 mL
1 cup	orange juice	250 mL
½ tsp	grated orange rind	2 mL
1 tbsp	cornstarch	15 mL
Pinch	red pepper flakes	Pinch
¼ tsp or less	salt and freshly ground pepper	1 mL or less

In roasting pan, roast pork in 350°F (180°C) oven for 30 to 40 minutes or until meat thermometer registers 160°F to 170°F (70°C to 75°C), juices run clear when pork is pierced and just a hint of pink remains inside.

Meanwhile cut carrot and green onions into thin 2-inch (5 cm) long strips.

About 15 minutes before serving, prepare sauce: In heavy saucepan, bring carrot and water to simmer; cover and cook for 5 minutes longer. Add green onions, gingerroot and garlic; cover and simmer for 1 minute.

Combine orange juice and rind, cornstarch and red pepper flakes; mix well. Pour over carrot mixture and bring to boil, stirring constantly. Cook, stirring, for 2 minutes longer. Season with salt and pepper.

Cut pork into thin, round slices and arrange on dinner plates; spoon sauce over.

MAKES 4 SERVINGS

PER SERVING: 207 calories, 28 g protein, 5 g total fat, 2 g saturated fat, 64 mg cholesterol, 11 g carbohydrate, 1 g fibre, 209 mg sodium, 594 mg potassium

Lemon Ginger Pork Loin with Mango Salsa

This strong-flavoured marinade gives pork a rich and satisfying taste. Fresh and light, Mango Salsa (p. 322) is a perfect accompaniment.

4 lb	boneless pork loin roast (centre cut), trimmed of fat	2 kg

MARINADE

¼ cup	lemon marmalade	50 mL
2 tbsp	sherry	25 mL
2 tbsp	chopped gingerroot	25 mL
2 tsp	minced fresh garlic	10 mL
2 tsp	Dijon mustard	10 mL
2 tsp	sodium-reduced soy sauce	10 mL
2 tsp	sesame oil	10 mL
1 tsp	grated lemon rind	5 mL

MARINADE: In small bowl, combine marmalade, sherry, gingerroot, garlic, mustard, soy sauce, sesame oil and lemon rind.

Place roast in large plastic bag and pour marinade over; tie shut and refrigerate for at least 4 hours or up to 24 hours, rotating bag occasionally.

Remove roast from bag, leaving as much marinade as possible clinging to roast. Set roast on rack in roasting pan.

Roast, uncovered, in 350°F (180°C) oven for 2 to 2½ hours or until meat thermometer registers 160°F (70°C) and juices run clear when roast is pierced. Let stand for 15 minutes before carving into thin slices.

MAKES 12 (3.5 OZ/100 g TRIMMED LEAN) SERVINGS

PER SERVING: 191 calories, 32 g protein, 4 g total fat, 2 g saturated fat, 68 mg cholesterol, 4 g carbohydrate, 0 g fibre, 99 mg sodium, 428 mg potassium

Lettuce Wrap Pork

Whenever we go out for Chinese food in Vancouver, my niece and nephew, Ashley and Jayson Elliott, always pick a dish similar to this. Serve as an appetizer or as part of a main course and let diners wrap their own.

6	dried Chinese mushrooms	6
2 tsp	sesame oil	10 mL
¾ lb	extra-lean pork or pork tenderloin, ground	375 g
10	water chestnuts, chopped	10
1	stalk celery, chopped	1
3	green onions, chopped	3
2 tsp	minced gingerroot	10 mL
2 tbsp	unseasoned rice vinegar or sherry	25 mL
2 tbsp	hoisin sauce	25 mL
1 tbsp	sodium-reduced soy sauce	15 mL
12	leaves iceberg lettuce	12
SAUCE		
2 tbsp	each hoisin sauce, unseasoned rice vinegar or sherry, and sodium-reduced soy sauce	25 mL
1 tsp	minced gingerroot	5 mL

SAUCE: In small serving dish, combine hoisin sauce, vinegar, soy sauce and gingerroot.

Remove tough stems from mushrooms. Cover mushrooms with hot water and let soak for 15 minutes; drain and chop.

In nonstick skillet, heat oil over high heat; stir-fry pork for 3 minutes; pour off any liquid. Add water chestnuts, celery, onions, gingerroot and mushrooms; stir-fry until pork is no longer pink. Stir in vinegar and hoisin and soy sauces.

Spoon onto platter; surround with lettuce. Let each person spoon a little pork mixture onto a lettuce leaf, drizzle with sauce and roll up to enclose filling.

MAKES 4 MAIN-COURSE SERVINGS

MAKE AHEAD: Cook pork mixture, cover and refrigerate for up to 1 day; reheat in microwave or over medium heat.

NOTE: Omitting the sauce in this recipe will reduce the sodium to less than 350 mg.

PER SERVING: 224 calories, 23 g protein, 7 g total fat, 2 g saturated fat, 48 mg cholesterol, 18 g carbohydrate, 2 g fibre, 710 mg sodium, 502 mg potassium

Pork with Broccoli Stir-Fry

Pork tenderloin is quick and easy to slice, but any lean cut of pork is fine for this recipe. I keep a bottle of hoisin sauce on hand in the refrigerator and like to add a splash to stir-fries for extra flavour. Omit it if you want to reduce the sodium in this dish. Serve over hot rice or pasta.

12 oz	lean boneless pork	375 g
1 tbsp	cornstarch	15 mL
1 tbsp	sodium-reduced soy sauce	15 mL
1 tbsp	sherry	15 mL
1	bunch broccoli	1
1 tbsp	canola oil	15 mL
2	cloves garlic, minced	2
2 tbsp	minced gingerroot	25 mL
¼ cup	water	50 mL
2 tbsp	hoisin sauce	25 mL

Slice pork thinly across the grain. In bowl, stir together cornstarch, soy sauce and sherry; add pork and stir to coat well.

Separate broccoli into florets; peel stalks, then cut into 1½-inch (4 cm) pieces.

In wok or large nonstick skillet, heat oil over high heat. Add pork mixture; stir-fry for 2 minutes or until meat is lightly browned. Stir in garlic, gingerroot and broccoli; stir-fry for 2 minutes. Add water; cover and steam for 2 minutes or until broccoli is tender-crisp. Stir in hoisin sauce.

MAKES 4 SERVINGS

NOTE: Lean cuts of pork come from the leg (roast, chop and cutlets), picnic shoulder and loin (tenderloin and centre).

VARIATION: Substitute 12 oz (375 g) sliced boneless chicken or turkey for pork.

PER SERVING: 233 calories, 21 g protein, 10 g total fat, 3 g saturated fat, 52 mg cholesterol, 14 g carbohydrate, 3 g fibre, 341 mg sodium, 599 mg potassium

Chinese Pork and Vegetables

When my children were young they liked this dish without the hot red pepper flakes. Now that they are adults, they probably wish I would double the heat. You may want to add sherry, hot pepper sauce or chili paste, or perhaps more gingerroot or hot red pepper flakes to taste. Serve on a bed of hot fluffy rice.

2 tsp	canola or olive oil	10 mL
1 lb	lean boneless pork, cut in thin strips	500 g
4	cloves garlic, minced	4
1	onion, sliced	1
5	stalks celery, diagonally sliced	5
4	carrots, diagonally sliced	4
2 tbsp	chopped fresh gingerroot	25 mL
4 cups	thinly sliced cabbage	1 L
½ cup	hot sodium-reduced chicken broth	125 mL
2 tbsp	sodium-reduced soy sauce	25 mL
¼ tsp	crushed hot red pepper flakes	1 mL
1 tbsp	cornstarch	15 mL
2 tbsp	cold water	25 mL

In large nonstick skillet, heat oil over high heat. Add pork and stir-fry until pork is no longer pink. Add garlic, onion, celery, carrots and gingerroot; stir-fry until onion is tender.

Stir in cabbage, broth, soy sauce and hot red pepper flakes; cook, covered, for 3 to 4 minutes or until vegetables are tender-crisp. Blend cornstarch with cold water; add to skillet; cook, stirring constantly, until sauce thickens.

MAKES 4 SERVINGS

MAKE AHEAD: Cover and refrigerate prepared ingredients for up to 8 hours before cooking.

NOTE: One serving is an excellent source of vitamin A and a good source of iron, vitamin C, dietary fibre and folacin.

PER SERVING: 274 calories, 27 g protein, 11 g total fat, 3 g saturated fat, 69 mg cholesterol, 17 g carbohydrate, 4 g fibre, 470 mg sodium, 808 mg potassium

Chickpea and Pork Curry

This is a mild-flavoured curry; add more curry powder or paste to taste. Serve over rice or with a green salad.

½ lb	lean ground pork	250 g
1 tbsp	minced fresh garlic	15 mL
1	white of leek (or 1 onion), chopped	1
1 tbsp	minced gingerroot	15 mL
1 tbsp	all-purpose flour	15 mL
1 to 2 tsp	curry powder or paste	5 to 10 mL
½ tsp	each ground coriander and ground cumin	2 mL
¼ tsp or less	each freshly ground pepper and salt	1 mL or less
1½ cups	cubed peeled butternut squash	375 mL
1 cup	coarsely shredded carrot	250 mL
1 cup	cubed peeled potato	250 mL
1 cup	water	250 mL
1	can (19 oz/540 mL) chickpeas, drained and rinsed	1
1	apple, cored and chopped	1
¼ cup	chopped fresh coriander (cilantro) or basil (optional)	50 mL

In nonstick saucepan, brown pork over medium heat; pour off fat. Add garlic, leek and gingerroot; cook for 2 minutes. Add flour, curry powder, coriander, cumin, pepper and salt; cook, stirring, for 1 minute.

Add squash, carrot, potato and water; bring to boil. Reduce heat, cover and simmer for 10 minutes. Add an extra ½ cup (125 mL) water if too dry.

Add chickpeas and apple; cover and cook until vegetables are tender. Sprinkle with coriander.

MAKES 4 SERVINGS

MAKE AHEAD: Cover and refrigerate curry for up to 1 day.

VARIATION: Ground pork adds to the flavour and is inexpensive, but ground beef, chicken or turkey can also be used. For a vegetarian meal, omit meat and instead sauté garlic, leek and gingerroot in 1 tbsp (15 mL) canola or olive oil.

PER SERVING: 322 calories, 18 g protein, 8 g total fat, 2 g saturated fat, 34 mg cholesterol, 47 g carbohydrate, 7 g fibre, 432 mg sodium, 786 mg potassium

Mexican Pork Stew

My son John really likes this stew. Cubed pork cooks much faster than chops or a roast, making this ideal for a quick family dinner. Add crushed hot pepper flakes to taste and any other vegetables in season, such as eggplant or zucchini. Serve with boiled new potatoes or over hot noodles.

1 lb	boneless pork (butt, shoulder)	500 g
1 tsp	canola or olive oil	5 mL
1	large onion, coarsely chopped	1
1	clove garlic, minced	1
2 tsp	chili powder	10 mL
1 tsp	each ground cumin and dried oregano	5 mL
½ tsp	dried thyme	2 mL
1	can (19 oz/540 mL) tomatoes	1
1	small sweet green pepper, coarsely chopped	1
¼ tsp	each salt, freshly ground pepper and granulated sugar	1 mL
2 tbsp	chopped fresh parsley and/or coriander	25 mL

Trim any visible fat from pork; cut into 1-inch (2.5 cm) cubes. In nonstick skillet, heat oil over medium-high heat. Add pork a few pieces at a time and cook until lightly browned on all sides.

Add onion and garlic; cook, stirring, for 5 minutes or until onion is tender. Stir in chili powder, cumin, oregano and thyme; cook for 1 minute. Stir in tomatoes, breaking up with back of spoon; add green pepper, salt, pepper and sugar; bring to boil. Reduce heat and simmer, covered, for 15 minutes. Stir in parsley.

MAKES 4 SERVINGS

MAKE AHEAD: Cover and refrigerate stew for up to 2 days.

NOTE: One serving is a very high source of vitamin C and a high source of iron.

PER SERVING: 203 calories, 23 g protein, 7 g total fat, 2 g saturated fat, 65 mg cholesterol, 12 g carbohydrate, 3 g fibre, 382 mg sodium, 660 mg potassium

Skillet Sausage and Rice Paella

Hot and spicy Italian sausage is perfect in this easy rice dish. You can also use sweet (mild) Italian sausages, but then add more hot pepper sauce or a pinch of red pepper flakes.

¾ lb	extra-lean Italian turkey sausage (hot or sweet), thickly sliced	375 g
1	onion, chopped	1
2	cloves garlic, minced	2
1	sweet green or yellow pepper, cut in chunks	1
2	tomatoes, coarsely chopped	2
1	bay leaf	1
¼ tsp	turmeric	1 mL
Dash	hot pepper sauce or hot chili paste	Dash
1 cup	short-grain rice (Spanish or Italian)	250 mL
2 cups	boiling water or sodium-reduced chicken broth	500 mL
1 cup	frozen peas, thawed	250 mL
	Freshly ground pepper	

In large nonstick skillet, cook sausages over medium heat for 10 minutes or until browned. Pour off fat. Add onion and garlic; cook until softened. Add green pepper, tomatoes, bay leaf, turmeric and hot pepper sauce; stir in rice, then water and simmer, uncovered, stirring occasionally for 20 minutes or until rice is tender and most liquid is absorbed. Stir in peas, and add pepper to taste. Discard bay leaf.

MAKES 4 SERVINGS

MAKE AHEAD: Cover and refrigerate paella for up to 24 hours. Reheat in microwave or over medium heat.

VARIATION:

Chicken and Rice Paella
Substitute pieces of skinless chicken (1 lb/500 g) for sausage. Increase hot pepper sauce to ¼ to ½ tsp (1 to 2 mL). Add 1 tsp (5 mL) saffron threads when adding broth. Fat per serving is then cut to 4 grams.

NOTE: Short-grain risotto-style rice will give a creaminess to the dish, but brown rice is more nutritious. For faster cooking use parboiled brown rice, which only takes about 20 minutes.

To reduce sodium, use a low-sodium stock (see p. 62).

PER SERVING: 351 calories, 21 g protein, 6 g total fat, 2 g saturated fat, 91 mg cholesterol, 53 g carbohydrate, 4 g fibre, 634 mg sodium, 303 mg potassium

Honey Garlic Roast Pork

For easy entertaining, this is one of my favourites. While the pork is roasting, rich aromas will fill your kitchen. Serve with Mango Salsa (p. 322) or chutney, Sesame Broccoli (p. 133) and My Mother's Scalloped Potatoes (p. 125).

4 lb	boneless pork loin roast	2 kg
MARINADE		
2 tbsp	sodium-reduced soy sauce	25 mL
2 tbsp	sherry	25 mL
2 tbsp	liquid honey	25 mL
2 tbsp	minced gingerroot	25 mL
2	cloves garlic, minced	2

MARINADE: Combine soy sauce, sherry, honey, gingerroot and garlic.

Trim any visible fat from meat. Place roast in large plastic bag and pour marinade over. Tie bag shut and refrigerate for at least 4 hours, rotating bag occasionally.

Remove roast from bag, reserving marinade and leaving as much ginger and garlic bits as possible clinging to roast. Set roast on rack in roasting pan. Roast, uncovered and basting occasionally with marinade, in 325°F (160°C) oven for 2 hours or until meat thermometer registers 160°F (70°C). Let stand for 15 minutes before carving.

MAKES 12 (3.5 OZ/100 g TRIMMED LEAN) SERVINGS

MAKE AHEAD: Marinate pork in refrigerator for up to 2 days.

PER SERVING: 182 calories, 32 g protein, 4 g total fat, 2 g saturated fat, 68 mg cholesterol, 3 g carbohydrate, 0 g fibre, 125 mg sodium, 429 mg potassium

Chutney-Glazed Ham

I often will cook a ham when I want a no-fuss meal to feed a crowd and have leftovers. Ham is a good choice because it is easy to serve and to eat, and you don't have to worry about over- or under-cooking it. Serve with Curried Fruit with Rice (p. 104), or chutney and Foil-Steamed Spring Vegetables (p. 126) or Grilled Fall Vegetables (p. 129). Since ham is high in sodium it is a good idea to try to balance the meal by choosing vegetable dishes, such as the ones above that are low in sodium. Wild Rice Pilaf (p. 103) is a lower sodium rice dish.

7 lb	part-skinned, semi-boneless ham (shank or butt; fully cooked or cook-before-eating)	3.5 kg
GLAZE		
½ cup	packed brown sugar	125 mL
¼ cup	chutney	50 mL
¼ cup	plum or peach jam	50 mL
1 tbsp	Dijon mustard	15 mL
1 tbsp	wine vinegar	15 mL
1	clove garlic, minced	1
Dash	hot pepper sauce	Dash

GLAZE: Combine sugar, chutney, jam, mustard, vinegar, garlic and hot pepper sauce; set aside.

Remove skin and all but ¼-inch (5 mm) thick layer of fat on ham. Place, fat side up, in roasting pan. Bake in 325°F (160°C) oven for 1¾ hours for fully cooked ham, or 2¼ hours for cook-before-eating ham.

Brush with half of the glaze; bake for another 30 minutes. Brush with remaining glaze; bake for 15 minutes or until meat thermometer reaches 140°F (60°C) for ready-to-eat ham or 160°F (70°C) for cook-before-eating ham. Remove from oven and let stand for 10 minutes before slicing. Serve hot or cold.

MAKES 12 (3.5 OZ/100 g TRIMMED LEAN) SERVINGS

MAKE AHEAD: To serve ham cold, cover and refrigerate cooked ham for up to 2 days.

NOTE: Hams may be fresh, cured, or cured-and-smoked. The usual colour for cured ham is deep rose or pink; fresh ham (which is not cured) has the pale pink or beige colour of a fresh pork roast; country hams and prosciutto (which are dry cured) range from pink to mahogany colour. Hams are either ready-to-eat or not. Ready-to-eat hams include prosciutto and fully cooked hams. Fresh hams must be cooked by the consumer before eating (follow the directions on the package).

PER SERVING: 194 calories, 27 g protein, 4 g total fat, 1 g saturated fat, 70 mg cholesterol, 14 g carbohydrate, 0 g fibre, 923 mg sodium, 416 mg potassium

Baked Ham with Marmalade Mustard Glaze

I like to cook ham in a liquid (wine, port, Madeira, meat stock, orange or apple juice or a combination of these liquids) because it makes a flavourful and moist ham. For a whole ham, use the same amount of liquid but double the glaze recipe. Serve with mango salsa and Baked Squash with Ginger (p. 141) or Snow Peas with Mushrooms (p. 142) and Rosemary Garlic Roasted Potatoes (p. 121) or Wild Rice Pilaf (p. 103). All these dishes are low in sodium, which balances the higher sodium content of the ham.

PER SERVING: 155 calories, 27 g protein, 4 g total fat, 1 g saturated fat, 70 mg cholesterol, 4 g carbohydrate, 0 g fibre, 846 mg sodium, 403 mg potassium

8 lb	semi-boneless ham (shank or butt)	4 kg
2 cups	orange juice	500 mL
1 cup	Madeira or port wine	250 mL
GLAZE		
¼ cup	packed brown sugar	50 mL
¼ cup	orange marmalade	50 mL
2 tbsp	Dijon or grainy mustard	25 mL

GLAZE: In small bowl, combine sugar, marmalade and mustard; set aside.

Remove skin and all but ¼-inch (5 mm) thick layer of fat on ham. Diagonally score fat side of ham to form diamond shapes; place fat side up in roasting pan. In saucepan, bring orange juice and Madeira to simmer; pour over ham.

Bake in 325°F (160°C) oven, basting occasionally, for 1¾ hours for fully cooked ham, or 2¼ hours for cook-before-eating ham.

Brush one-third of the glaze over ham. Cook for 45 minutes longer, brushing with remaining thirds of glaze every 15 minutes, or until meat thermometer reaches 140°F (60°C) for ready-to-eat ham or 160°F (70°C) for cook-before-eating ham.

Remove from oven and let stand for 10 minutes before slicing. Serve hot or cold.

MAKES 16 (3.5 OZ/100 g TRIMMED LEAN) SERVINGS

Cauliflower and Ham Gratin

Ham and cauliflower seem like a natural combination. Dill adds extra flavour, while red pepper adds colour and crunch.

½	head cauliflower	½
1½ tbsp	soft margarine	20 mL
2 tbsp	all-purpose flour	25 mL
1 cup	low-fat milk	250 mL
¼ cup	freshly grated Parmesan cheese	50 mL
¼ cup	grated Danbo Light or part-skim (16% MF) mozzarella cheese	50 mL
¼ cup	packed chopped fresh dill*	50 mL
	Freshly ground pepper	
½ to 1 cup	diced cooked ham (2 oz/60 g)	125 to 250 mL
½	sweet red pepper, coarsely chopped	125
⅓ cup	fresh bread crumbs	75 mL

Cut cauliflower into florets, about 2-inch (5 cm) pieces. In large pot of boiling water, blanch cauliflower for 5 minutes or until tender-crisp; drain and set aside.

In saucepan, melt margarine; add flour and cook over low heat, stirring, for 1 minute. Pour in milk and bring to simmer, stirring constantly. Simmer, stirring, for 2 minutes. Add Parmesan and Danbo, dill, and pepper to taste; cook, stirring, until cheese melts.

In lightly greased 8 cup (2 L) shallow baking dish, arrange cauliflower, ham and red pepper; pour sauce evenly over. Sprinkle with bread crumbs. Bake in 375°F (190°C) oven for 30 minutes or until bubbly.

MAKES 4 SERVINGS

*If fresh dill is unavailable, use ¼ cup (50 mL) fresh parsley plus 1 tsp (5 mL) dried dillweed.

NOTE: Use the remaining cauliflower in stir-fries, salads or soups.

PER SERVING: 175 calories, 12 g protein, 9 g total fat, 3 g saturated fat, 21 mg cholesterol, 13 g carbohydrate, 1 g fibre, 442 mg sodium, 299 mg potassium

Buying and Cooking Pork

BUYING PORK

Pork tenderloins, the leanest cut of pork, range in size from 8 oz to 1 lb (250 to 500 g). Plan on buying 5 to 6 oz (150 to 175 g) per person when entertaining.

Other lean cuts of pork are ham, back bacon, leg (roast, chop and cutlets) and centre loin.

Various boneless pork cuts including pork shoulders are often featured in supermarket specials. Cut the meat into cubes or strips, discarding fat, and use in stews and stir-fries or on skewers. Package them in 1-lb (500 g) portions (or a size to suit your household) and freeze until needed.

COMPARE:

Per 3½ Oz (100 G) Serving:	g fat
pork, loincut, lean and fat, fried	28
spareribs, braised, lean and fat	25
pork loin, centre cut, lean and fat, broiled	20
pork loincut, lean only, roasted	12
pork loin, center cut, lean only, broiled	9
pork tenderloin, lean only, roasted	5

COOKING PORK

Pork used to be cooked until well done to ensure that it was safe to eat. Today, trichinosis from pork is virtually nonexistent in Canada. According to Agriculture Canada, this organism, if present, is destroyed when pork is cooked to an internal temperature of 137°F (58°C), well below the recommended 160°F (70°C). Also, because pork is leaner, it should be cooked at a lower oven temperature to medium doneness with just a hint of pink remaining. Cooking to a higher temperature will dry it out and make it tough. Of course, ground pork and sausage should be cooked thoroughly.

PORK DONENESS TEMPERATURE (ROASTING)

Doneness	Internal Temp. When Removed from Oven
Medium	160°F (70°C)

Onions Stuffed with Lamb and Spinach

Tender, juicy onions are filled with a tasty, fragrant Middle Eastern stuffing. Use any kind of large onion—Spanish, red or regular cooking onions—3½ to 4 inches (9 to 10 cm) in diameter (or use 8 medium onions). Serve with couscous, cooked rice or bulgur.

5	large onions	5
½ lb	lean ground lamb	250 g
¼ tsp	each cinnamon, allspice and ground cumin	1 mL
2 cups	packed chopped fresh spinach	500 mL
1	egg	1
1 cup	coarse fresh bread crumbs	250 mL
¼ tsp or less	salt and freshly ground pepper	1 mL or less
1 cup	hot sodium-reduced broth (lamb or beef)	250 mL

Peel onions; cut slice off tops, then off root ends so they will stand. Cut cone shape into top of each onion; remove cone. Using melon baller or teaspoon, hollow out onions to make ½-inch (1 cm) thick shells; chop removed onion to make 1½ cups (375 mL).

Blanch shells in boiling water for 5 minutes. Remove and drain upside down on rack.

In nonstick pan, cook lamb over medium heat, stirring to break up, for 3 minutes or until browned; pour off fat. Add chopped onion, cinnamon, allspice and cumin; cook until onion is tender.

Add spinach and cook until wilted. Remove from heat. Stir in egg, bread crumbs, and salt and pepper. Spoon into onion shells.

Place stuffed shells in baking pan. Pour hot broth into pan. Bake in 375°F (190°C) oven for 30 minutes. Cover with foil and bake for 10 minutes longer or until onion is tender.

MAKES 5 SERVINGS

MAKE AHEAD: Assemble stuffed onions, cover and refrigerate for up to 4 hours.

NOTE: Use store-bought sodium-reduced beef or lamb broth or make your own low-sodium lamb broth:

Bring 1 lamb shank, 8 cups (2 L) water, bay leaf and 1 chopped onion to boil; simmer for 1 hour. Remove lamb and cut meat from bone; reserve for other use. Refrigerate broth for 4 hours or overnight; skim all fat.

PER SERVING: 171 calories, 12 g protein, 6 g total fat, 2 g saturated fat, 63 mg cholesterol, 18 g carbohydrate, 3 g fibre, 313 mg sodium, 435 mg potassium

Ground Lamb with Spinach and Feta

Pork or beef can be used instead of lamb in this satisfying dish. Serve over basmati rice.

¾ lb	lean ground lamb	375 g
1	onion, minced	1
2 tsp	minced fresh garlic	10 mL
1	stalk celery, chopped	1
1	pkg (10 oz/300 g) chopped frozen spinach, thawed and squeezed dry	1
2 tsp	dried oregano	10 mL
¼ tsp or less	salt and freshly ground pepper	1 mL or less
⅓ cup	crumbled light feta cheese	75 mL
1	tomato, diced	1
½ cup	low-fat plain yogurt	125 mL

In large nonstick skillet, cook lamb, onion, garlic and celery over medium-high heat for 5 minutes or until vegetables are tender. Pour off any liquid. Add spinach, oregano, and salt and pepper; cook for 2 minutes or until heated through.

Remove from heat. Crumble in cheese. Top with tomato, then drizzle with yogurt.

MAKES 4 SERVINGS

MAKE AHEAD: Crumble cheese over cooked lamb mixture, cover and refrigerate for up to 4 hours. Reheat in microwave or over medium heat.

VARIATION:

Lamb and Feta Pita Pockets
Cut pitas in half, then slide knife into each half to form pocket. Warm in 325°F (160°C) oven for 5 minutes. Line pitas with lettuce; spoon in lamb mixture.

PER SERVING: 210 calories, 21 g protein, 10 g total fat, 4 g saturated fat, 55 mg cholesterol, 10 g carbohydrate, 3 g fibre, 425 mg sodium, 552 mg potassium

Lamb Chops Dijon

Here's a fast, tasty way to cook lamb chops. Buy chops at least 1 inch (2.5 cm) thick. The zippy mustard mixture is also great spread over lamb racks or leg.

12	loin lamb chops (about 2½ lb/1.25 kg)	12
3 tbsp	Dijon mustard	50 mL
2 tsp	dried rosemary	10 mL
¼ to ½ tsp	coarsely ground black pepper	1 to 2 mL

Remove excess fat from chops; arrange in single layer on broiler pan. In small bowl, combine mustard, rosemary and pepper. Spread over chops.

Broil or grill 4 inches (10 cm) from heat for 5 minutes; turn and cook for 4 to 6 minutes longer for medium rare or until desired degree of doneness.

MAKES 6 SERVINGS

VARIATION:

Lamb Racks Dijon
Use 3 racks of lamb (about 1 lb/500 g each) trimmed of fat. Combine ½ cup (125 mL) Dijon mustard, 2 tbsp (25 mL) dried rosemary and 2 tsp (10 mL) coarsely ground pepper; spread over racks. Roast in 425°F (220°C) oven or barbecue with lid closed for 15 to 20 minutes for medium rare. Remove from heat, let stand for 5 minutes then cut in half between bones. Makes 6 servings.

PER SERVING (Trimmed Lean): 166 calories, 22 g protein, 8 g total fat, 3 g saturated fat, 68 mg cholesterol, 1 g carbohydrate, 0 g fibre, 250 mg sodium, 289 mg potassium

Souvlaki of Lamb

Greece is famous for its souvlaki or skewered lamb, which is seasoned with lemon juice and oregano. The Greeks don't usually put vegetables on the skewers, but it's more colourful when you include them—and they add extra flavour. Boneless lamb loins are available in the frozen-food sections of supermarkets if you can't find fresh lamb. Serve the skewers on hot rice with Tomato Raita (p. 68).

4	wood or metal skewers	4
1 lb	boneless lamb loin or leg	500 g
2 tbsp	fresh lemon juice plus more to taste	25 mL
1 to 2 tsp	crumbled dried oregano	5 to 10 mL
¼ tsp or less	salt and freshly ground pepper	1 mL or less
8	small onions	8
1	small sweet red pepper	1
1	small sweet yellow or green pepper	1

Cut lamb into 1-inch (2.5 cm) cubes. Place in glass dish or plate; sprinkle with lemon juice, oregano, and salt and pepper to taste. Blanch onions in boiling water for 10 to 15 minutes or until almost tender; drain and let cool enough to handle. Cut off root ends; squeeze off skins. Seed red and yellow peppers; cut into 1½-inch (4 cm) pieces.

Alternately thread lamb and vegetables onto metal skewers or wooden skewers that have been soaked in water.

Place skewers on broiler rack or grill about 5 inches (12 cm) from heat; cook, turning once or twice, for 8 to 12 minutes or until meat is brown outside but still pink inside. Sprinkle with additional lemon juice and pepper.

MAKES 4 SERVINGS

MAKE AHEAD: Cover and refrigerate lamb in lemon juice mixture for up to 1 day.

Assemble skewers, cover and refrigerate for up to 2 hours in advance.

NOTE: Soak wooden skewers in water for 15 minutes before threading to prevent charring.

One serving provides a very high source of vitamin C.

PER SERVING: 184 calories, 19 g protein, 5 g total fat, 2 g saturated fat, 68 mg cholesterol, 15 g carbohydrate, 3 g fibre, 183 mg sodium, 391 mg potassium

Navarin of Lamb

Adapted from Lucy Waverman's beautifully flavoured navarin of lamb and wild rice, this dish has sweet mild garlic and the special note of rosemary. Serve with rice, noodles or potatoes.

2 lb	lean boneless lamb (e.g., leg)	1 kg
1 tsp	granulated sugar	5 mL
¼ tsp or less	salt and freshly ground pepper	1 mL or less
1 tbsp	canola or olive oil	15 mL
2 tbsp	all-purpose flour	25 mL
2 cups	sodium-reduced beef or homemade lamb broth	500 mL
1	clove garlic, minced	1
1 tbsp	tomato paste	15 mL
	Bouquet garni*	
1	long strip orange rind (orange part only)	1
1 tbsp	fresh rosemary (or 1 tsp/5 mL dried)	15 mL

VEGETABLES

5	carrots	5
3	small white turnips or 1 yellow rutabaga (about 1 lb/500 g)	3
10	small onions (or 1 cup/250 mL pearl onions)	10

GARLIC GARNISH

4	heads garlic	4
½ cup	low-fat milk	125 mL

*Bouquet garni: Tie 2 sprigs fresh parsley, 1 sprig fresh thyme and 1 bay leaf in hollow of 1 stalk of celery or place in cheesecloth bag (if you don't have fresh thyme, use ½ tsp/2 mL dried).

Trim any visible fat from lamb; cut into bite-size cubes. Sprinkle with sugar, and salt and pepper. In large heavy Dutch oven or nonstick pan, heat oil over medium heat. Add meat a few pieces at a time and brown well.

Remove meat from pan and pour off fat; return meat to pan. Sprinkle with flour; cook over medium heat, stirring constantly, for 1 minute or until flour has browned. Add broth, garlic, tomato paste, bouquet garni and orange rind; bring to boil, stirring to scrape up brown bits from bottom of pan.

Cover and bake in 325°F (160°C) oven for 1 hour. Let cool, then refrigerate until cold. Remove fat from surface of stew; discard orange rind and bouquet garni.

VEGETABLES: Peel carrots and turnips; cut into ¾-inch (2 cm) pieces. Peel onions. (If using pearl onions, blanch in boiling water for 1 minute; drain, cut off root end and gently squeeze to remove skin.)

cont'd . . .

NOTE: By using homemade broth without salt (see p. 62), you will reduce the sodium to 160 mg per serving.

MAKE AHEAD: Bake lamb, cover and refrigerate for up to 1 day. Gently reheat before adding vegetables.

NOTE: One serving is a very high source of vitamin A.

PER SERVING: 226 calories, 23 g protein, 7 g total fat, 3 g saturated fat, 72 mg cholesterol, 17 g carbohydrate, 3 g fibre, 296 mg sodium, 496 mg potassium

GARLIC GARNISH: Separate garlic heads into cloves. Place in small saucepan along with milk; bring to boil and boil for 2 minutes. Reduce heat to low; cover and simmer until soft. Drain and let cool; gently squeeze to remove skins. Set aside.

About 45 minutes before serving, gently reheat lamb mixture, stirring to prevent scorching. Add vegetables and simmer, covered, for 30 to 40 minutes or until vegetables are tender, adding water if necessary. (For a thicker gravy, add 2 tbsp/25 mL flour mixed with ½ cup/125 mL water or broth; bring to boil and cook, stirring, until thickened slightly.) Add rosemary and garnish with garlic cloves.

MAKES 8 SERVINGS

Lamb Shank and Vegetable Stew

Lamb shanks are inexpensive and add rich flavour to this stew. If possible, make it a day in advance, then cover and refrigerate it to allow the flavour to develop and the stew to thicken. The next day, remove any fat that has solidified on top.

1¼ lb	lamb shanks	625 g
6	small onions	6
6	small potatoes, cut in chunks (1 lb/500 g)	6
Half	small turnip, peeled and cubed	Half
3	large carrots, cut in chunks	3
3	cloves garlic, minced	3
4 cups	water	1 L
1	can (7½ oz/213 mL) tomato sauce	1
1 tsp	each dried thyme and rosemary	5 mL
¼ tsp	freshly ground pepper	1 mL
1	bay leaf	1
1 tsp	grated orange rind	5 mL
2 tbsp	all-purpose flour (optional)	25 mL

Trim any visible fat from lamb. In large casserole or Dutch oven, combine lamb shanks, onions, potatoes, turnip, carrots, garlic, water, tomato sauce, thyme, rosemary, pepper, bay leaf and orange rind; stir to mix.

Bake, covered, in 325°F (160°C) oven for 3 hours, stirring occasionally. Discard bay leaf. Remove lamb from stew; cut meat from bones and return meat to stew.

To thicken stew if desired, mix flour with ⅓ cup (75 mL) cold water until smooth; whisk into stew and stir until thickened, about 1 minute.

MAKES 6 SERVINGS

NOTE: Although the amount of lamb may appear small, one serving of this stew is filling. Lamb shanks are high in fat, so it is best to use a small amount.

PER SERVING: 239 calories, 13 g protein, 2 g total fat, 1 g saturated fat, 29 mg cholesterol, 43 g carbohydrate, 5 g fibre, 245 mg sodium, 958 mg potassium

Marinated Leg of Lamb with Coriander

Boneless butterflied legs of lamb are available in the frozen-food sections of many supermarkets or fresh at butcher stores. This marinade is also delicious with lamb chops and rack of lamb. An easy dish to prepare in advance, marinated leg of lamb is easy to transport (in a plastic bag) to the cottage or camp. Serve with Tomatoes Florentine (p. **143**), Buttermilk Mashed Potatoes (p. **121**) and Cucumber Mint Raita (p. 68).

1	boneless butterflied leg of lamb (about 3 lb/1.5 kg boned)	1
¼ tsp or less	salt and freshly ground pepper	1 mL or less
	Dijon mustard or horseradish (optional)	

MARINADE

1 tbsp	coriander seeds	15 mL
½ cup	fresh lemon juice	125 mL
2 tbsp	olive or canola oil	25 mL
1	small onion, chopped	1
1 tbsp	grated gingerroot	15 mL
2	cloves garlic, chopped	2
1 tsp	black peppercorns, crushed	5 mL

MARINADE: In skillet, toast coriander seeds over medium heat for 5 minutes, shaking pan occasionally. Let cool, then crush seeds. Combine crushed seeds, lemon juice, oil, onion, gingerroot, garlic and peppercorns.

Trim any visible fat from lamb. If meat is not of even thickness, slash thickest section and open up, book fashion. Place lamb in plastic bag and coat both sides with marinade. Tie bag closed; refrigerate for 24 to 48 hours, turning occasionally. Remove lamb from refrigerator about 1 hour before cooking.

Remove lamb from bag, leaving as many seeds or ginger bits as possible clinging to meat. Place on grill or broiler rack; broil about 6 inches (15 cm) from heat for about 12 minutes on each side for rare, and 15 to 20 minutes on each side for medium or until meat thermometer reaches desired temperature (see Note on following page). Transfer to cutting board; tent with foil and let stand for 5 minutes. Season with salt and pepper. Slice thinly across the grain. Serve with mustard or horseradish.

MAKES 8 SERVINGS

MAKE AHEAD: Marinate lamb in refrigerator for at least 1 day and up to 2 days.

VARIATION:

Grilled Butterflied Leg of Lamb with Lemon and Garlic
Omit coriander seeds and gingerroot from marinade; add 1 tsp (5 mL) each lemon rind and dried rosemary (or 2 tbsp/25 mL chopped fresh rosemary) and increase garlic to 3 large cloves.

PER SERVING: 215 calories, 30 g protein, 9 g total fat, 4 g saturated fat, 107 mg cholesterol, 2 g carbohydrate, 0 g fibre, 122 mg sodium, 221 mg potassium

Lemon Grass–Marinated Leg of Lamb

This lamb dish a good choice for entertaining. As well as having an intriguing flavour, it's marinated in advance, it cooks fairly quickly and it's boneless for easy serving. In the summer, I barbecue it; in the winter, broil.

1	boneless butterflied leg of lamb (about 3 lb/1.5 kg boned)	1

MARINADE

3	stalks lemon grass*	3
1 tbsp	finely chopped onion	15 mL
3 tbsp	fresh lemon juice	50 mL
2 tbsp	fish sauce or sodium-reduced soy sauce	25 mL
1½ tsp	minced fresh garlic	7 mL
1 tsp	packed brown sugar	5 mL
½ tsp	hot pepper sauce	2 mL

MARINADE: Cut off top one-third of each lemon grass stalk; trim off outside leaves and roots. Finely chop remaining stalk; combine with onion, lemon juice, fish sauce, garlic, sugar and hot pepper sauce.

Trim any visible fat from lamb; place lamb in bowl or plastic bag; pour marinade over. Cover and refrigerate for at least 12 hours, turning occasionally.

Remove lamb from refrigerator about 1 hour before cooking. Broil about 6 inches (15 cm) from heat for 12 to 15 minutes on each side for rare, 15 to 20 minutes on each side for medium. Remove from heat; let stand for 10 minutes. Slice thinly across the grain.

MAKES 8 SERVINGS

*If fresh lemon grass is unavailable, use 2 tbsp (25 mL) dried, or grated rind of 1 lemon.

MAKE AHEAD: Marinate lamb for at least 12 hours and up to 2 days.

NOTE: It is best to let a frozen leg of lamb thaw in the refrigerator for 2 days, rather than defrosting in the microwave or on the kitchen counter, to retain the most meat juices and for the best texture. Lamb is juicy and tender when cooked just until it is pink or medium rare.

Fresh lemon grass is available at many supermarkets (check the vegetable section) and at Asian markets.

VARIATIONS:

Barbecued Leg of Lamb
Grill over high heat for 15 to 20 minutes on each side for medium rare, 25 to 30 minutes on each side for well done.

Lamb Tenderloins or Loins
Marinate up to 2 lb (1 kg) of tenderloins in this marinade for 1 hour or up to 2 days. Grill or broil over high heat for 3 to 4 minutes for tenderloins, 6 minutes for loins, or until still pink inside, turning once or twice.

NOTE: Meat thermometer should register:

140°F (60°C) for rare

145°F (63°C) for medium rare

160°F (70°C) for medium

170°F (75°C) for well done

PER SERVING: 200 calories, 30 g protein, 8 g total fat, 3 g saturated fat, 107 mg cholesterol, 1 g carbohydrate, 0 g fibre, 315 mg sodium, 222 mg potassium

Ginger Apricot Stuffed Lamb

This is an enticing dish any time of year. If you make it in the spring when bright orange grape-sized fresh kumquats are available, add them as an attractive and interesting edible garnish.

3 lb	boneless leg or shoulder of lamb, ready for stuffing (about 5 lb/2.2 kg, bone-in)	1.5 kg

STUFFING

1 tsp	canola or olive oil	5 mL
1	small onion, chopped	1
⅔ cup	coarsely chopped dried apricots	150 mL
1 tbsp	minced gingerroot	15 mL
1 tsp	grated lemon rind	5 mL
¼ tsp or less	salt and freshly ground pepper	1 mL or less

GLAZE

2 tbsp	apricot jam	25 mL
2 tbsp	Dijon mustard	25 mL
1 tsp	ground ginger	5 mL

GARNISH

8	apricots (fresh or canned), halved and pitted	8
8	sprigs fresh rosemary or watercress	8
8	small ripe kumquats (optional)	8

STUFFING: In nonstick skillet, heat oil over medium heat. Add onion; cook until softened. Stir in apricots, gingerroot, lemon rind, and salt and pepper. Place stuffing in lamb cavity and sew or tie together. Place on rack in roasting pan. Roast in 325°F (160°C) oven for 1½ hours.

GLAZE: Combine jam, mustard and ginger; brush over lamb. Roast for 15 minutes longer or until lamb is brown outside and pink inside. Transfer to serving platter; tent with foil and let stand for 15 minutes before carving. Arrange apricots, rosemary and kumquats (if using) around lamb.

MAKES 8 (100 g TRIMMED WITH STUFFING) SERVINGS

MAKE AHEAD: Stuff lamb, cover and refrigerate for up to 6 hours. Remove from refrigerator 1 hour before roasting.

NOTE: One serving is a very high source of iron and a high source of vitamin A.

Tiny orange kumquats are the smallest of the citrus fruits. They are usually eaten unpeeled and are often blanched and added to salads. For a garnish, leave the stems and small leaves attached.

PER SERVING: 275 calories, 31 g protein, 9 g total fat, 3 g saturated fat, 107 mg cholesterol, 18 g carbohydrate, 2 g fibre, 220 mg sodium, 536 mg potassium

Lamb Pilaf Supper for One

I like to use lamb in this recipe because of the flavour it gives to the rice, but you can also use pork, beef or chicken—cooked or raw. Buy any small piece of lamb and freeze the extra. Double the recipe to serve two. Add chopped parsley, basil, dill or coriander just before serving if you have some on hand.

PER SERVING: 367 calories,
21 g protein, 4 g total fat,
1 g saturated fat, 43 mg cholesterol,
63 g carbohydrate, 7 g fibre,
403 mg sodium, 633 mg potassium

Half	medium onion, finely chopped	Half
2 oz	tender boneless lamb, pork or beef, trimmed of any fat and cut in ½-inch (1 cm) cubes or ¼ cup (50 mL) cooked cubed meat	50 g
¼ cup	long-grain rice	50 mL
¼ cup	finely diced celery or carrot	50 mL
1 tbsp	currants or raisins	15 mL
⅛ tsp	allspice	0.5 mL
Quarter	bay leaf	Quarter
½ cup	boiling water	125 mL
½ cup	frozen peas, thawed	125 mL
1	small tomato, coarsely chopped	1
⅛ tsp or less	salt and freshly ground pepper	0.5 mL or less

Spray nonstick saucepan or small skillet with nonstick coating or ½ tsp (2 mL) canola oil. Add onion and lamb; cook over medium heat, stirring often, until meat is browned and onion is tender, about 5 minutes. Add rice, celery, currants, allspice and bay leaf; stir. Pour in boiling water; cover and simmer for 15 minutes. Stir in peas, tomato, and salt and pepper; cook for 1 minute or until peas are hot and rice is tender. Discard bay leaf.

MAKES 1 SERVING

Buying and Cooking Lamb

Lamb is very versatile and, if not overcooked, tender and juicy. Lamb is available in a variety of cuts, and also ground. Racks, which are especially flavourful, are a real treat.

BUYING LAMB

Choose leaner cuts, such as the leg or loin. Lamb shanks are higher in fat.

COOKING LAMB

Should lamb be rare or well done? As with beef, this is a matter of personal taste. However, if it is too rare, it can be tough. If overcooked, it will be dry. Medium rare is best, so the meat is tender, juicy and pink on the inside.

LAMB DONENESS TEMPERATURES (ROASTING)

Doneness	Internal Temp. When Removed from Oven
Rare	140°F (60°C)
Medium rare	145°F (63°C)
Medium	160°F (70°C)
Well done	170°F (75°C)

SAUCES, MARINADES AND CONDIMENTS

Mango Salsa

I love the taste of this fresh mango relish. I like to serve it with roast chicken, turkey or pork because it's much easier than making a gravy at the last minute—not to mention that it's healthier for you. Papaya can be used instead of mango. Peel cucumber if skin is tough or waxed.

1	mango, peeled and finely diced	1
½ cup	finely diced red onion	125 mL
½ cup	finely diced cucumber	125 mL
2 tbsp	fresh lime juice	25 mL
½ tsp	grated lime rind	2 mL
¼ tsp	ground cumin	1 mL

In small bowl, combine mango, onion, cucumber, lime juice, lime rind and cumin. Cover and let stand for at least 1 hour.

MAKES 1½ CUPS (375 mL)

MAKE AHEAD: Cover and store in refrigerator for up to 4 hours.

PER 2 TBSP (25 mL): 16 calories, 0 g protein, 0 g total fat, 0 g saturated fat, 0 mg cholesterol, 4 g carbohydrate, 1 g fibre, 1 mg sodium, 49 mg potassium

Homemade Ketchup

This version tastes delicious, is a snap to make and is much lower in sodium than store-bought ketchup. Consider using it instead of barbecue sauce.

1 can	(5 ½ oz/156 mL) tomato paste	1
¼ cup	packed brown sugar	50 mL
¼ cup	water	50 mL
2 tbsp	apple cider vinegar	25 mL
¼ tsp	dry mustard	1 mL
¼ tsp	cinnamon	1 mL
Pinch	each ground cloves and allspice	Pinch

In jar or bowl, combine tomato paste, sugar, water, vinegar, mustard, cinnamon, cloves and allspice; mix well. Cover and refrigerate for at least 1 day, to allow flavours to develop.

MAKES 1 CUP (250 mL)

MAKE AHEAD: Cover and store in refrigerator for at least 1 day or up to 1 month.

PER 1 TBSP (15 mL): 22 calories, 0 g protein, 0 g total fat, 0 g saturated fat, 0 mg cholesterol, 5 g carbohydrate, 1 g fibre, 12 mg sodium, 123 mg potassium

Evelyn Barrigar's Fresh-Tasting Cucumber Relish

This recipe from my friend Evelyn Barrigar in Victoria, BC, makes the best relish I've ever tasted. Serve it cold with meats, chops or hamburgers.

4 cups	coarsely shredded peeled cucumbers* (about 3 large)	1 L
2 cups	chopped onions	500 mL
1	sweet red pepper, chopped	1
½	bunch celery, chopped	½
2½ cups	packed brown sugar	625 mL
1½ tsp	salt	7 mL
2⅓ cups	white vinegar	575 mL
6 tbsp	all-purpose flour	90 mL
½ tsp	ground turmeric	2 mL
½ tsp	dry mustard	2 mL

PER 1 TBSP (15 mL): 20 calories, 0 g protein, 0 g total fat, 0 g saturated fat, 0 mg cholesterol, 5 g carbohydrate, 0 g fibre, 31 mg sodium, 32 mg potassium

In large heavy saucepan, combine cucumbers, onions, red pepper, celery, sugar, salt and 1½ cups (375 mL) of the vinegar. Bring to boil over medium-high heat and boil for 15 minutes.

Meanwhile, in small bowl, blend together flour, turmeric, mustard and remaining vinegar until smooth; whisk into cucumber mixture. Boil for 15 minutes (reduce heat but maintain a boil), stirring and skimming off any foam. Be careful mixture doesn't burn.

Using sterilized utensils, ladle into sterilized jars, leaving ½-inch (10 mm) headspace. Seal with sterilized lids and bands. Process in boiling water canner for 15 minutes.

MAKES ABOUT 8 CUPS (2 L)

*If cucumbers have large seeds, remove and discard before shredding.

Monda Rosenberg's Lime Ginger Mayonnaise

Serve this mayonnaise with any fish or seafood. It's wonderful with salmon, including smoked salmon.

½ cup	light mayonnaise	125 mL
½ cup	low-fat plain yogurt	125 mL
	Grated rind of 1 lime	
2 tsp	fresh lime juice	10 mL
2 tsp	finely minced gingerroot	10 mL
1	clove garlic, minced	1

MAKE AHEAD: Cover and refrigerate for up to 24 hours.

PER 1 TBSP (15 mL): 28 calories, 0 g protein, 2 g total fat, 0 g saturated fat, 3 mg cholesterol, 1 g carbohydrate, 0 g fibre, 52 mg sodium, 23 mg potassium

In small bowl, stir together mayonnaise, yogurt, lime rind and juice, gingerroot and garlic. Cover and refrigerate for at least 1 hour to allow flavours to meld.

MAKES 1 CUP (250 mL)

Shannon Graham's Fresh Mint Sauce

Shannon Graham helped with the recipe testing for all my cookbooks. She likes to serve this sauce with roast leg of lamb.

3 tbsp	granulated sugar	50 mL
⅓ cup	apple cider vinegar	75 mL
¼ cup	water	50 mL
1½ tsp	cornstarch	7 mL
½ cup	firmly packed fresh mint, finely chopped	125 mL

In small saucepan, combine sugar, vinegar, water and cornstarch; bring to boil over medium heat, stirring constantly. Stir in mint; simmer for 3 minutes.

Transfer to sauce boat and let stand for 30 minutes to allow flavours to develop.

Serve with lamb chops or roast.

MAKES ½ CUP (125 mL)

MAKE AHEAD: Store, covered in refrigerator, for up to 2 months.

PER 1 TBSP (15 mL): 25 calories, 0 g protein, 0 g total fat, 0 g saturated fat, 0 mg cholesterol, 6 g carbohydrate, 1 g fibre, 3 mg sodium, 49 mg potassium

Pesto

Pesto is a fresh-tasting Italian sauce often paired with pasta, though it's also great with fish and poultry. Freeze pesto (in ice-cube trays, then transfer to plastic bag) to have on hand to flavour soups, salad dressings and sauces. This is higher in fat than most sauces in this book, but it is much lower in fat than most other pesto sauce recipes. A little of this extremely flavourful sauce goes a long way. A tablespoon or two added to a vegetable soup or minestrone will really liven it up.

2	cloves garlic	2
1 cup	lightly packed fresh basil	250 mL
½ cup	freshly grated Parmesan cheese	125 mL
2 tbsp	olive oil	25 mL

In food processor, chop garlic and basil. Add Parmesan and olive oil; process until smooth. Add a little hot water (2 to 4 tbsp/25 to 50 mL) or pasta cooking water to reach desired consistency.

MAKES ⅔ CUP (150 mL)

NOTE: Because pine nuts, commonly added to pesto, have been omitted, and the oil has been reduced from a traditional recipe, this pesto has about half the amount of fat of most pesto recipes.

VARIATION:

Pasta with Pesto Sauce
If making pesto to serve with pasta, add enough of the pasta cooking liquid to make sauce pourable without losing its thickness. Plan on at least 2 tbsp (25 mL) pesto sauce per person. Toss with hot cooked pasta and serve.

PER 2 TBSP (25 mL): 90 calories, 4 g protein, 8 g total fat, 2 g saturated fat, 8 mg cholesterol, 1 g carbohydrate, 0 g fibre, 144 mg sodium, 65 mg potassium

Creamy Dill Sauce

Serve with Baked Whole Salmon Stuffed with Mushrooms and Artichokes (p. 211) or any grilled or poached fish.

½ cup	low-fat plain yogurt	125 mL
½ cup	light sour cream*	125 mL
½ cup	chopped fresh dill	125 mL
2 tbsp	capers	25 mL
¼ tsp or less	salt and freshly ground pepper	1 mL or less

In small bowl, combine yogurt, quark, dill and capers. Season with salt and pepper.

MAKES 1¼ CUPS (300 mL)

*Or use puréed low-fat cottage cheese.

MAKE AHEAD: Cover and refrigerate sauce for up to 3 days.

PER 1 TBSP (15 mL): 10 calories, 1 g protein, 0 g total fat, 0 g saturated fat, 2 mg cholesterol, 1 g carbohydrate, 0 g fibre, 65 mg sodium, 27 mg potassium

Dill Mustard Sauce

This versatile sauce can be served with hot or cold fish dishes and seafood, with chicken or turkey, as a dressing for salads, or tossed with cold cooked pasta.

⅓ cup	low-fat plain yogurt	75 mL
⅓ cup	low-fat cottage cheese* or light sour cream	75 mL
¼ cup	chopped fresh dill**	50 mL
1½ tsp	Dijon mustard	7 mL
⅛ tsp or less	salt and freshly ground pepper	0.5 mL or less

In blender or bowl, combine yogurt, cottage cheese, dill and mustard; blend or whisk until smooth. Season with salt and pepper.

MAKES ⅔ CUP (150 mL)

*If using cottage cheese, combine in a blender (not a food processor) to achieve a smooth sauce.

**Fresh dill gives this sauce excellent flavour, but if unavailable, substitute 2 tbsp (25 mL) chopped fresh parsley and 1 tsp (5 mL) dried dillweed.

MAKE AHEAD: Cover and store in refrigerator for up to 2 days.

PER 1 TBSP (15 mL): 12 calories, 1 g protein, 0 g total fat, 0 g saturated fat, 1 mg cholesterol, 1 g carbohydrate, 0 g fibre, 79 mg sodium, 28 mg potassium

Yogurt Béarnaise Sauce

In this version of Béarnaise sauce, the classic accompaniment to steak, I use yogurt instead of butter and half the usual number of egg yolks—so I call it a halfway healthy sauce. Margie Glue, a cooking-school teacher, gave me the idea of using yogurt in a Béarnaise sauce. It's also delicious with grilled chicken, turkey, lamb or fish.

4 tsp	minced shallots or onions	20 mL
¼ cup	white wine	50 mL
1	small clove garlic, minced	1
1 tbsp	chopped fresh tarragon (or 1¼ tsp/6 mL dried)	15 mL
1 cup	2% plain yogurt	250 mL
2	egg yolks	2
1 tsp	cornstarch	5 mL
¼ tsp	granulated sugar	1 mL
⅛ tsp or less	salt, cayenne and freshly ground pepper	0.5 mL or less

In small saucepan, combine shallots, wine, garlic and tarragon (if using dried); bring to boil over medium heat. Boil until liquid is reduced to 1 tbsp (15 mL).

In top of non-aluminum double boiler or saucepan, beat together yogurt, egg yolks, cornstarch and sugar; add wine mixture. Cook over simmering water, stirring often, until sauce has thickened, about 20 minutes.

Remove from heat, add tarragon (if using fresh) and season with salt, cayenne and pepper to taste. Serve warm.

MAKES 1 CUP (250 mL), ENOUGH FOR 8 PEOPLE

NOTE: For best results, use 2% or richer yogurt; sauce made with 1% or fat-free yogurt will have a thin consistency.

MAKE AHEAD: Cover and store in refrigerator for up to 1 week. Reheat over hot water or in microwave on Low.

PER 2 TBSP (25 mL): 37 calories, 2 g protein, 2 g total fat, 1 g saturated fat, 49 mg cholesterol, 3 g carbohydrate, 0 g fibre, 61 mg sodium, 91 mg potassium

Yogurt Remoulade

This low-calorie, quick-to-prepare sauce is delicious with the Light Salmon Loaf with Dill (p. 215) or with grilled, poached or baked fish.

½ cup	low-fat plain yogurt	125 mL
2 tbsp	light sour cream	25 mL
2 tbsp	minced dill pickle	25 mL
1 tbsp	minced fresh parsley	15 mL
1 tsp	Dijon mustard	5 mL
¼ tsp	dried tarragon	1 mL

In small bowl, combine yogurt, sour cream, dill pickle, parsley, mustard and tarragon; mix thoroughly.

MAKES ⅔ CUP (150 mL)

PER 1 TBSP (15 mL): 11 calories, 1 g protein, 0 g total fat, 0 g saturated fat, 1 mg cholesterol, 1 g carbohydrate, 0 g fibre, 45 mg sodium, 37 mg potassium

Italian Sausage, Red Pepper and Mushroom Rigatoni p. 190

Lamb Chops Dijon p. 312
Tomatoes Florentine p. 143
Barley and Corn Casserole p. 113

Spicy Scallops p. 223
Sprout and Snow Pea Stir-Fry p. 143

Green Bean Salad with Buttermilk Dressing p. 75
Grilled Lemon Chicken with Rosemary p. 260

Harvest Vegetable Curry p. 161

Double Chocolate Brownies p. 380
Nectarine and Orange Compote p. 423

Yogurt Hollandaise

Use this sauce with vegetables, eggs or fish. It tastes like Hollandaise but is made with yogurt instead of butter.

1 cup	low-fat plain yogurt	250 mL
2 tsp	fresh lemon juice	10 mL
3	egg yolks	3
½ tsp or less	salt	2 mL or less
½ tsp	Dijon mustard	2 mL
Pinch	freshly ground pepper	Pinch
1 tbsp	chopped fresh dill or parsley (optional)	15 mL

In top of non-aluminum double boiler or saucepan, whisk together yogurt, lemon juice, egg yolks, salt, mustard and pepper. Heat over simmering water, stirring constantly, for 10 to 15 minutes or until thickened and sauce coats back of wooden spoon. (Sauce could become thinner after about 10 minutes of cooking, then will thicken again.) Stir in dill (if using). Serve warm.

MAKES 1¼ CUPS (300 mL)

NOTE: Use non-aluminum cookware when making egg-yolk mixtures—they will discolour in aluminum.

MAKE AHEAD: Sauce can be covered and refrigerated for up to 3 days. Reheat over hot, not boiling, water.

PER 1 TBSP (15 mL): 16 calories, 1 g protein, 1 g total fat, 0 g saturated fat, 29 mg cholesterol, 1 g carbohydrate, 0 g fibre, 71 mg sodium, 32 mg potassium

Tarragon and Mushroom Sauce

This sauce is similar in taste to a Béarnaise sauce but with much less fat. It is delicious served warm with lentil burgers, steak, meatballs and other meats or poultry.

1 tbsp	canola or olive oil	15 mL
1 cup	chopped fresh mushrooms (4 oz/125 g)	250 mL
2 tbsp	chopped green onion	25 mL
2 tbsp	all-purpose flour	25 mL
½ tsp	crushed dried tarragon	2 mL
2 cups	hot sodium-reduced beef, chicken or vegetable broth	500 mL

In saucepan, heat oil over medium heat. Add mushrooms and onion; cook, stirring occasionally, until tender and most of the liquid is evaporated. Sprinkle with flour and tarragon; cook, stirring, for 2 minutes.

Bring broth to boil; gradually pour into mushroom mixture, whisking constantly. Cook, whisking constantly, until boiling and thickened slightly. Simmer, uncovered, for 10 minutes or until reduced to about 1½ cups (375 mL). Serve warm.

MAKES 1½ CUPS (375 mL)

MAKE AHEAD: Cover and store in refrigerator for up to 2 days; reheat gently.

NOTE: To reduce sodium, use a low-sodium stock (see p. 62).

PER 1 TBSP (15 mL): 10 calories, 0 g protein, 1 g total fat, 0 g saturated fat, 0 mg cholesterol, 1 g carbohydrate, 0 g fibre, 49 mg sodium, 23 mg potassium

Everyday Marinade

Pour this marinade over beef, pork or lamb kabobs, steak, roast or chops, then cover and refrigerate for 1 hour or up to 24 hours, turning meat occasionally.

2	cloves garlic, minced	2
1	medium onion, chopped	1
¼ cup	wine vinegar	50 mL
1 tbsp	canola or olive oil	15 mL
1 tbsp	sodium-reduced soy sauce	15 mL
½ tsp	dry mustard or curry powder	2 mL

In small bowl, combine garlic, onion, vinegar, oil, soy sauce and mustard; mix well.

MAKES ½ CUP (125 mL), ENOUGH FOR UP TO 2 LB (1 KG) MEAT

VARIATION:

Ginger Marinade
Add 2 tbsp (25 mL) minced fresh gingerroot.

NOTE: Instead of using salt to add zip or counting on fat-marbled cuts for tenderness, let marinades tenderize and add flavour to lean meats. The Heart and Stroke Foundation of Canada recommends that we limit our salt intake to 1 tsp (5 mL) or less a day.

PER 1 TBSP (15 mL): 25 calories, 0 g protein, 2 g total fat, 0 g saturated fat, 0 mg cholesterol, 2 g carbohydrate, 0 g fibre, 67 mg sodium, 29 mg potassium

Teriyaki Marinade

Use this marinade on any kind of fish steaks or fillets, chicken wings, flank steak, lamb leg or pork tenderloin.

2 tbsp	sodium-reduced soy sauce	25 mL
2 tbsp	sherry	25 mL
2 tbsp	water	25 mL
1 tbsp	canola or olive oil	15 mL
1 tbsp	grated gingerroot	15 mL
1 tsp	granulated sugar (optional)	5 mL

In small bowl, combine soy sauce, sherry, water, oil, gingerroot and sugar (if using); mix well.

MAKES ½ CUP (125 mL), ENOUGH FOR 1 LB (500 G) OF BONELESS MEAT, FISH OR POULTRY

PER 1 TBSP (15 mL): 20 calories, 0 g protein, 2 g total fat, 0 g saturated fat, 0 mg cholesterol, 1 g carbohydrate, 0 g fibre, 133 mg sodium, 14 mg potassium

Thai Peanut Sauce

Use this hot Thai sauce for dipping Thai Pork Skewers (p. 20) or with your favourite satay recipe. This is lower in fat than most peanut sauces. Because it's hot and spicy, you'll probably want just a little.

1 cup	dry-roasted unsalted peanuts*	250 mL
1⅓ cups	water	325 mL
3	cloves garlic	3
2 tbsp	packed brown sugar	25 mL
2 tbsp	fresh lime juice	25 mL
1 tbsp	sodium-reduced soy sauce	15 mL
¼ tsp	crushed red pepper flakes	1 mL
1	piece (1 inch/2.5 cm) gingerroot, peeled and thinly sliced	1

In blender or food processor, combine peanuts, water, garlic, sugar, lime juice, soy sauce, red pepper flakes and gingerroot; process for 2 minutes. Pour into top of double boiler over boiling water; cook for 30 minutes, stirring occasionally. Serve warm.

MAKES 2 CUPS (500 mL)

*To roast peanuts, place on baking sheet and roast in 350°F (180°C) oven for 12 minutes.

MAKE AHEAD: Cover and store in refrigerator for up to 2 weeks.

PER 1 TBSP (15 mL): 31 calories, 1 g protein, 2 g total fat, 0 g saturated fat, 0 mg cholesterol, 2 g carbohydrate, 0 g fibre, 18 mg sodium, 37 mg potassium

Asian Sauce or Marinade

This is delicious as a marinade or as a sauce with chicken, pork, Chinese noodle dishes, shrimp or scallops. I love to use it as a marinade for skewered shrimp, scallops and cubes of salmon. Add more hot chili paste or red pepper flakes if you like. I sometimes add a dash of sesame oil and a teaspoon (5 mL) of five-spice powder. This sauce is higher in sodium than most of the other sauces in this book, but is very flavourful when mixed in a dish such as Chinese noodles—a little goes a long way.

½ cup	hoisin sauce	125 mL
2 tbsp	sodium-reduced soy sauce	25 mL
2 tbsp	unseasoned rice vinegar, scotch or sherry	25 mL
1 tbsp	minced gingerroot	15 mL
1 tbsp	minced fresh garlic	15 mL
¼ tsp	hot chili paste or crushed red pepper flakes	1 mL

Combine hoisin sauce, soy sauce, vinegar, gingerroot, garlic and hot chili paste.

MAKES ¾ CUP (175 mL)

MAKE AHEAD: Cover and store in refrigerator for up to 2 weeks.

NOTE: This sauce is thick and quite sweet. With pasta you might want to add more vinegar to taste. This is enough marinade for 3 lb (1.5 kg) skinless chicken thighs or legs.

PER 1 TBSP (15 mL): 27 calories, 1 g protein, 0 g total fat, 0 g saturated fat, 0 mg cholesterol, 5 g carbohydrate, 0 g fibre, 262 mg sodium, 23 mg potassium

Garlic Sauce

Serve with grilled chicken, lamb or beef, or as a dip with Herb Roasted French Fries (p. 122) or fresh vegetables.

½ cup	light sour cream and/or low-fat plain yogurt	125 mL
2	cloves garlic, minced	2
¼ cup	chopped fresh parsley	50 mL

In small bowl, combine sour cream and/or yogurt, garlic and parsley.

MAKES ½ CUP (125 mL)

VARIATION: Substitute chopped fresh basil or coriander to taste for the garlic and reduce the parsley to 1 tbsp (15 mL).

PER 1 TBSP (15 mL): 17 calories, 1 g protein, 1 g total fat, 0 g saturated fat, 3 mg cholesterol, 2 g carbohydrate, 0 g fibre, 17 mg sodium, 39 mg potassium

Hot Chili Sauce

Young children might prefer a milder version of this medium-hot sauce; others might double the fresh chili paste. Use for dipping. It's especially good with cooked large shrimp, Teriyaki Shrimp Wrapped with Snow Peas (p. 14) and Smoked Turkey–Wrapped Melon Balls (p. 23).

¼ cup	unseasoned rice vinegar*	50 mL
2 tbsp	granulated sugar	25 mL
2 tbsp	fresh lemon or lime juice	25 mL
1 tbsp	sodium-reduced soy sauce	15 mL
½ tsp	fresh chili paste or hot pepper sauce	2 mL

In small bowl, combine vinegar, sugar, lemon or lime juice, soy sauce and chili paste.

MAKES ½ CUP (125 mL)

*Or use 3 tbsp (50 mL) apple cider vinegar and 1 tbsp (15 mL) water.

PER 1 TBSP (15 mL): 16 calories, 0 g protein, 0 g total fat, 0 g saturated fat, 0 mg cholesterol, 4 g carbohydrate, 0 g fibre, 71 mg sodium, 10 mg potassium

Spicy Apricot or Plum Sauce

Use this dipping sauce with Thai Pork Skewers (p. 20), Teriyaki Shrimp Wrapped with Snow Peas (p. 14) or Spiced Meatballs (p. 29).

½ cup	apricot or plum jam	125 mL
2 tbsp	fresh lemon juice	25 mL
¼ tsp	crushed red pepper flakes or hot chili paste to taste	1 mL

Combine jam, lemon juice and red pepper flakes; mix well.

MAKES ⅔ CUP (150 mL)

PER 1 TSP (5 mL): 12 calories, 0 g protein, 0 g total fat, 0 g saturated fat, 0 mg cholesterol, 3 g carbohydrate, 0 g fibre, 2 mg sodium, 5 mg potassium

Blackberry Sauce

This sauce is delicious with turkey, chicken and ham. Conventional gravy is much higher in fat than this sweet yet tart sauce. Currant jelly can be used instead of blackberry.

1 cup	blackberry jelly	250 mL
⅓ cup	frozen orange juice concentrate	75 mL
⅓ cup	brandy	75 mL
¼ cup	red wine or balsamic vinegar	50 mL

In small saucepan, combine jelly, orange juice concentrate, brandy and vinegar. Heat over low heat until jelly is melted; stir well.

MAKES 2 CUPS (500 mL)

MAKE AHEAD: Cover and store in refrigerator for up to 1 week.

PER 1 TBSP (15 mL): 37 calories, 0 g protein, 0 g total fat, 0 g saturated fat, 0 mg cholesterol, 8 g carbohydrate, 0 g fibre, 3 mg sodium, 27 mg potassium

Shannon Graham's Pickled Beets

My husband likes the tartness of these pickled beets; however, you can add more sugar to taste if you prefer a sweeter pickled beet. These are extremely easy to make, especially if you have leftover cooked beets. They are a colourful addition to appetizer trays, salad plates, buffets and potluck dinners and are good with hot or cold meats.

9	medium beets (or 1½ lb/750 g trimmed baby beets)	9
1 cup	water	250 mL
1 cup	apple cider vinegar	250 mL
3 tbsp	granulated sugar	50 mL

Trim beets, leaving at least 1 inch (2.5 cm) of the stems attached. Place in saucepan and cover with warm water; bring to boil and simmer for 40 minutes or until tender. Drain and rinse under cold running water. Using fingers, slip off skins. Quarter or cut into thick slices and place in clean 4-cup (1 L) jar.

In saucepan, combine water, vinegar and sugar; heat until sugar dissolves. Pour over beets; cover and let cool.

MAKES 4 CUPS (1 L)

MAKE AHEAD: Cover and store in refrigerator for up to 1 month.

NOTE: Beets can be steamed, baked or microwaved as well as boiled. Don't peel beets before cooking, for they will "bleed" too much. Boiling and steaming take about the same time; baking takes longer. Large old beets take twice as long to cook as young beets.

To microwave 1½ lb (750 g) medium-to-small beets, place beets in microwave-safe dish; add ¼ cup (50 mL) water. Cover with lid or vented plastic wrap and microwave on High for 12 to 15 minutes or until tender.

The Heart and Stroke Foundation of Canada recommends that we limit our sodium intake to 2,300 mg or less per day—that's the equivalent of 1 tsp (5 mL) of salt. Pickles, especially dill pickles, can be very high in sodium; choose homemade pickled beets instead.

PER ¼ CUP (50 mL): 24 calories, 0 g protein, 0 g total fat, 0 g saturated fat, 0 mg cholesterol, 5 g carbohydrate, 1 g fibre, 22 mg sodium, 101 mg potassium

BREAKFAST AND BRUNCH

Crustless Vegetable Quiche

Not only is this lighter in fat and calories than a traditional quiche, it is much faster and easier to make.

1 tbsp	canola or olive oil	15 mL
½ cup	fine fresh bread crumbs	125 mL
1 cup	sliced mushrooms	250 mL
1 cup	chopped sweet red pepper	250 mL
3 cups	chopped fresh spinach leaves	750 mL
2	eggs	2
2	egg whites	2
1 cup	low-fat milk	250 mL
2	green onions, chopped	2
¼ cup	crumbled light feta cheese	50 mL
¼ cup	chopped fresh parsley	50 mL
2 tbsp	chopped fresh basil (or 1 tsp/5 mL dried)	25 mL
Dash	hot pepper sauce	Dash
2	medium tomatoes, sliced	2

Spread 1 tsp (5 mL) of the oil in 10-inch (25 cm) quiche dish or glass pie plate; sprinkle bottom and sides evenly with bread crumbs.

In large nonstick skillet, heat remaining oil over medium heat; cook mushrooms and red pepper, stirring, for 5 to 7 minutes or until tender and liquid has evaporated. Add spinach; cook, stirring, for 2 minutes or until wilted.

In large bowl, beat together eggs and egg whites; add milk. Stir in onions, cheese, parsley, basil, hot pepper sauce and spinach mixture. Spoon into prepared dish; top evenly with tomato slices.

Bake in 350°F (180°C) oven for 40 to 50 minutes or until firm to the touch and knife inserted in centre comes out clean.

MAKES 4 SERVINGS

MAKE AHEAD: Line pie plate with bread crumbs up to 2 hours in advance. Cover and refrigerate prepared egg-spinach mixture for up to 2 hours.

NOTE: Eggs are a nutritious food and, like many foods, should be eaten in moderation. Since the cholesterol is only in the egg yolk, mix extra egg whites with one whole egg when making omelettes and for baking.

An egg yolk contains 3 grams of protein and is an excellent source of vitamin B12, and a source of zinc and vitamins A, D and E. A whole egg contains 6 grams of protein.

PER SERVING: 171 calories, 11 g protein, 9 g total fat, 2 g saturated fat, 99 mg cholesterol, 14 g carbohydrate, 3 g fibre, 261 mg sodium, 592 mg potassium

Spinach and Zucchini Frittata

This frittata is ideal cut into wedges and served as a first course with toast and salad or sliced tomatoes for brunch, lunch or dinner. Or cut into small squares and serve warm or cold as hors d'oeuvres.

1 tsp	olive oil	5 mL
1	medium onion, chopped	1
1	clove garlic, minced	1
2 cups	thinly sliced unpeeled zucchini	500 mL
½ cup	grated part-skim mozzarella cheese	125 mL
¼ cup	chopped fresh parsley	50 mL
4	eggs, lightly beaten	4
1	pkg (10 oz/300 g) frozen chopped spinach, thawed and drained	1
½ tsp or less	salt	2 mL or less
¼ tsp	freshly ground pepper	1 mL
Pinch	ground nutmeg	Pinch

In nonstick skillet, heat oil over medium heat. Add onion and garlic; cook until onion is tender. Add zucchini; cook, stirring, for 5 minutes.

In bowl, combine cheese, parsley, eggs, spinach, salt, pepper and nutmeg; stir in zucchini mixture. Spoon into lightly greased 9-inch (23 cm) pie plate. Bake in 325°F (160°C) oven for 35 to 45 minutes or until set but still moist in centre. Serve hot or cold.

MAKES 4 MAIN-COURSE SERVINGS

NOTE: One serving is a very high source of vitamin A and folacin and a high source of calcium and iron.

PER SERVING: 161 calories, 13 g protein, 9 g total fat, 3 g saturated fat, 196 mg cholesterol, 8 g carbohydrate, 3 g fibre, 485 mg sodium, 411 mg potassium

Broccoli Frittata

This delicious Italian open-faced omelette is equally good for supper as it is brunch. Unlike a French omelette, which is cooked quickly over high heat and is creamy in the centre, a frittata is cooked slowly and is set or firm in the middle.

1	bunch broccoli (1 lb/500 g)	1
1 tbsp	olive or canola oil	15 mL
1 cup	sliced onions	250 mL
2 or 3	cloves garlic, minced	2 or 3
6	eggs, lightly beaten	6
¼ cup	low-fat milk (optional)	50 mL
2 tbsp	finely chopped fresh parsley	25 mL
1 tsp	salt	5 mL
¼ tsp	each ground nutmeg and freshly ground pepper	1 mL
½ cup	grated part-skim mozzarella cheese	125 mL

Trim tough ends from broccoli; peel stems. Cut stems and florets into ¾-inch (2 cm) pieces to make about 4 cups (1 L). Steam or cook in boiling water for 5 minutes or until crisp-tender; drain thoroughly.

In 10- to 12-inch (25 to 30 cm) nonstick skillet, heat oil over medium heat. Add onions and garlic; cook until onion is tender. Stir in broccoli.

Beat together eggs, milk, parsley, salt, nutmeg and pepper; pour over broccoli mixture and sprinkle with cheese.* Cover and cook over medium-low heat for 5 to 10 minutes or until set but still slightly moist on top. Place pan under broiler for 2 to 3 minutes to lightly brown top, leaving oven door slightly open. (If skillet handle isn't ovenproof, wrap it in foil. Since the oven door is open slightly most of the handle will not be directly under the heat.) Loosen edges of frittata; cut into pie-shaped wedges.

MAKES 6 SERVINGS

*Or, transfer egg mixture to greased 9-inch (23 cm) deep pie pan or 9-inch square (2 L) greased baking dish; sprinkle top with cheese and bake in 350°F (180°C) oven about 20 minutes or until top is golden and slightly puffed.

NOTE: One serving is a very high source of vitamin C and folacin and a high source of vitamin A.

PER SERVING: 153 calories, 11 g protein, 9 g total fat, 3 g saturated fat, 192 mg cholesterol, 8 g carbohydrate, 2 g fibre, 532 mg sodium, 304 mg potassium

Microwave Leek and Mushroom Flan

This brunch flan also makes a quick meatless dinner along with a green vegetable, salad and whole-wheat bun. Chopped onion can be used instead of leeks.

1 cup	thinly sliced leek (white part only)	250 mL
1 tsp	canola or vegetable oil	5 mL
8 oz	mushrooms, coarsely chopped (about 3 cups/750 mL)	250 g
2	eggs, lightly beaten	2
2	egg whites, lightly beaten*	2
2 tbsp	low-fat milk	25 mL
Pinch	paprika	Pinch
¼ tsp or less	salt and freshly ground pepper	1 mL or less

In 8- × 4-inch (1.5 L) microwaveable dish, toss leeks with oil. Cover with waxed or parchment paper and microwave on High for 1 minute. Add mushrooms; cover and microwave on High for 4 minutes or until mushrooms are nearly tender. Stir in eggs, egg whites, milk, paprika, and salt and pepper to taste. Microwave, uncovered, on Medium for 6 to 8 minutes or until mixture is set. Serve hot.

MAKES 2 SERVINGS

*Using egg whites makes this dish light in texture and keeps the cholesterol count down, as the cholesterol in eggs is found in the yolks.

VARIATION: This flan is also delicious made with 1 whole egg plus 3 egg whites. The cholesterol is then 94 mg per serving.

PER SERVING: 141 calories, 12 g protein, 8 g total fat, 2 g saturated fat, 187 mg cholesterol, 6 g carbohydrate, 2 g fibre, 416 mg sodium, 470 mg potassium

Omelette à la Jardinière

Don't relegate eggs to breakfast only. Accompanied by toasted whole-wheat bread and a spinach salad, this omelette makes a terrific instant lunch or dinner. For variety, add sliced mushrooms or chopped tomatoes and cook them along with the carrots.

½ tsp	canola or olive oil	2 mL
1	small onion, finely chopped	1
1	clove garlic, minced	1
⅓ cup	grated carrot	75 mL
¼ cup	chopped sweet green pepper	50 mL
¼ tsp or less	salt and freshly ground pepper	1 mL or less
2	whole eggs	2
3	egg whites	3
1 tbsp	water	15 mL
1 tsp	canola or olive oil	5 mL

In nonstick skillet, heat oil over medium heat; sauté onion and garlic, stirring, until tender. Stir in carrot and green pepper; cook, stirring, for 2 to 3 minutes or until carrot is wilted. Season with salt and pepper.

In bowl, beat eggs with water until blended. Heat 8- to 9-inch (20 to 23 cm) nonstick omelette pan or skillet over very high heat; heat oil until sizzling but not browned. Pour in eggs; cook, continuously shaking pan back and forth while stirring eggs quickly with fork to spread evenly over pan until eggs are thickened and almost set.

Spoon carrot mixture over eggs. Tilt pan and roll up omelette, or simply fold in half. Slide onto plate.

MAKES 2 SERVINGS

NOTE: One serving is a very high source of vitamin A and vitamin B12 and a high source of folacin.

A 2-egg omelette is easier to make than a 4-egg or larger omelette. It's important to use the correct size of pan: for a 2- to 3-egg omelette, use an omelette pan that's 7 inches (18 cm) in diameter at the bottom; for a 4-egg omelette, use an 8- to 9-inch (20 to 23 cm) pan.

PER SERVING: 155 calories, 12 g protein, 8 g total fat, 2 g saturated fat, 186 mg cholesterol, 7 g carbohydrate, 1 g fibre, 447 mg sodium, 265 mg potassium

Spanish Omelette

Although this light, colourful omelette is designed for someone who wants to avoid egg yolks, it's tasty enough to be a part of anyone's brunch repertoire. It's important to use a nonstick pan for this recipe.

2	egg whites	2
1 tbsp	low-fat milk	15 mL
Pinch	turmeric or paprika	Pinch
⅛ tsp or less	salt and freshly ground pepper	.05 mL or less
1 tsp	canola or olive oil	5 mL
2 tbsp	diced green or red pepper	25 mL
2 tbsp	finely chopped tomato	25 mL
1 tbsp	finely chopped green onion	15 mL

In bowl, whisk egg whites until frothy; add milk, turmeric, and salt and pepper. Heat large nonstick skillet over medium-high heat; add oil and swirl to coat bottom of pan.

Pour in egg mixture and shake pan over high heat until egg sets. Sprinkle pepper, tomato and onion over egg. Remove from heat and, using fork, lift one-third of omelette and fold it over centre, tilt pan and roll omelette over onto plate.

MAKES 1 SERVING

VARIATIONS: Add chopped cooked or raw vegetables, fresh herbs or a small amount of low-fat cheese or flaked fish such as salmon.

PER SERVING: 85 calories, 8 g protein, 5 g total fat, 0 g saturated fat, 1 mg cholesterol, 3 g carbohydrate, 1 g fibre, 410 mg sodium, 171 mg potassium

Eggs Florentine

This egg dish is perfect for entertaining at brunch or lunch, or even as a light supper, because the eggs, spinach and sauce can all be prepared in advance and gently reheated.

2	pkg (10 oz/284 g each) fresh spinach	2
1 tsp	canola or olive oil	5 mL
¼ tsp or less	salt, freshly ground pepper and freshly grated nutmeg	1 mL
2 tbsp	white vinegar	25 mL
6	eggs	6
¾ cup	Yogurt Hollandaise (p. 327), warmed	175 mL

Trim stems from spinach. Wash and shake off excess water; place in saucepan with just the water clinging to leaves. Cover and cook over medium-high heat until wilted. Drain thoroughly; squeeze out excess liquid and chop coarsely. Toss with oil, and salt, pepper and nutmeg. Return to saucepan; cover and keep warm.

Nearly fill large shallow pan or skillet with water and bring to boil; add vinegar. Reduce to simmer and break egg shells over pan, gently dropping eggs into water. Reduce heat until water is barely simmering; cook eggs for 3 to 5 minutes or until whites are firm and yolks are still soft, spooning water over yolks occasionally to cook slightly.

Spoon spinach onto warmed plates or serving dish. With slotted spoon, place 1 egg over each serving. Spoon about 2 tbsp (25 mL) Yogurt Hollandaise over each.

MAKES 6 SERVINGS

MAKE AHEAD: Poach eggs, then cool in ice water to prevent further cooking and refrigerate in bowl of water for up to 1 day; reheat in simmering water for about 30 seconds. Cook spinach, then cool under cold running water, drain and set aside for up to 2 hours, or cover and refrigerate for up to 24 hours. Chop and reheat before continuing. Yogurt Hollandaise can be made up to 3 days in advance; see page 327.

NOTE: One serving is a very high source of vitamin A (providing 79% of the daily value), a very high source of folacin, and a high source of calcium and iron.

VARIATION:

Asparagus with Poached Eggs
In spring, substitute cooked drained asparagus for the spinach. Arrange hot asparagus spears on warmed individual plates or serving dish; sprinkle with fresh lemon juice, salt and pepper. Top with poached egg and grated Parmesan or Yogurt Hollandaise. If desired, broil for a minute to brown.

PER SERVING: 132 calories, 11 g protein, 8 g total fat, 2 g saturated fat, 244 mg cholesterol, 5 g carbohydrate, 2 g fibre, 359 mg sodium, 518 mg potassium

Scrambled Eggs and Smoked Salmon on Focaccia

My friend Suzanne Kopas served this great dish to us one weekend at her cottage on Georgian Bay, Ontario. Buy a focaccia or flatbread about ¾ inch (2 cm) thick and 10 to 12 inches (25 to 30 cm) in diameter.

1 cup	light sour cream	250 mL
⅓ cup	finely chopped green onions	75 mL
2 tsp	Dijon mustard	10 mL
	Focaccia, about 12-inch (30 cm) round	
7	eggs	7
6	egg whites	6
⅓ cup	low-fat milk	75 mL
¼ tsp or less	salt	1 mL or less
½ tsp	freshly ground pepper	2 mL
2 tsp	canola or olive oil	10 mL
4 oz	thinly sliced smoked salmon, coarsely chopped (or tidbits)	125 g
2 tbsp	chopped fresh parsley and/or dill	25 mL

In small bowl, mix together sour cream, onions and mustard; set aside.

Heat focaccia in 350°F (180°C) oven for 10 minutes.

In bowl, whisk together eggs, egg whites, milk, salt and pepper.

In large nonstick skillet, heat oil over medium-high heat: add eggs and cook, stirring, until scrambled.

Spread sour cream mixture over hot focaccia: spoon scrambled eggs over top. Top with smoked salmon; sprinkle with parsley and/or dill. Cut into wedges, and serve warm or at room temperature.

MAKES 8 SERVINGS

MAKE AHEAD: Prepare uncooked egg mixture up to 1 hour in advance.

PER SERVING: 245 calories, 15 g protein, 11 g total fat, 3 g saturated fat, 173 mg cholesterol, 21 g carbohydrate, 1 g fibre, 465 mg sodium, 228 mg potassium

Apple Cinnamon Whole-Wheat Pancakes

Top these tasty pancakes with yogurt mixed with brown sugar or maple syrup or sliced fresh strawberries, peaches or blueberries.

½ cup	all-purpose flour	125 mL
½ cup	whole-wheat flour	125 mL
1 tbsp	granulated sugar	15 mL
1½ tsp	baking powder	7 mL
1 tsp	cinnamon	5 mL
¼ tsp	baking soda	1 mL
1	egg, lightly beaten	1
1 cup	low-fat milk	250 mL
½ cup	grated peeled apple	125 mL
1 tbsp	canola or olive oil	15 mL
½ tsp	soft margarine	2 mL

In bowl, combine all-purpose and whole-wheat flours, sugar, baking powder, cinnamon and baking soda.

Combine egg, milk, apple and oil; pour into flour mixture, stirring just until combined.

Heat nonstick skillet over medium heat until hot; add margarine to lightly grease. Pour in batter, ¼ cup (50 mL) for each pancake; cook until bubbles form on surface and underside is golden brown. Turn and cook just until bottom is lightly browned.

MAKES 3 SERVINGS OF 3 PANCAKES EACH

MAKE AHEAD: Combine dry ingredients up to 1 day in advance.

NOTE: All-purpose flour can be substituted for the whole wheat, but the pancakes won't be as high in fibre.

PER SERVING: 281 calories, 10 g protein, 8 g total fat, 2 g saturated fat, 66 mg cholesterol, 43 g carbohydrate, 4 g fibre, 321 mg sodium, 283 mg potassium

Upside-Down Apple Pancake

Make this fabulous-tasting pancake for a weekend breakfast or brunch. If you make it in two pie plates, it's easy to turn upside down onto regular plates and looks great. Top with yogurt mixed with a little honey or maple syrup.

2 tbsp	soft margarine	25 mL
¼ cup	granulated sugar	50 mL
2 tsp	cinnamon	10 mL
3	medium apples, peeled and sliced	3

BATTER

⅓ cup	all-purpose flour	75 mL
½ tsp	baking powder	2 mL
2	egg yolks	2
⅓ cup	low-fat milk	75 mL
4	egg whites	4
⅓ cup	granulated sugar	75 mL

In two 9-inch (23 cm) pie plates or one 13- × 9-inch (3.5 L) baking dish, melt margarine in 400°F (200°C) oven, about 2 minutes.

Combine sugar and cinnamon; sprinkle evenly over margarine. Bake for 2 minutes or until melted. Arrange apple slices in overlapping circles over top; bake for 10 minutes.

BATTER: Meanwhile, in bowl, combine flour and baking powder; blend in egg yolks and milk. In large bowl, beat egg whites until white and frothy; gradually beat in sugar until soft peaks form. Fold into milk mixture. Spread evenly over apples.

Bake for 15 to 20 minutes or until lightly browned. Loosen edges with knife; invert onto serving plate.

MAKES 6 SERVINGS

MAKE AHEAD: Best served immediately, but also good prepared a few hours in advance and served at room temperature.

NOTE: This pancake can just as easily be called a cake and served for dessert.

PER SERVING: 209 calories, 5 g protein, 6 g total fat, 1 g saturated fat, 64 mg cholesterol, 36 g carbohydrate, 2 g fibre, 103 mg sodium, 144 mg potassium

Banana Blender Pancakes

These scrumptious pancakes take just two minutes to prepare.

½ cup	all-purpose flour	125 mL
¼ cup	whole-wheat flour	50 mL
¼ cup	cornmeal*	50 mL
1 tbsp	granulated sugar	15 mL
1½ tsp	baking powder	7 mL
1	egg	1
1 cup	low-fat milk	250 mL
1 tbsp	canola or olive oil	15 mL
1	banana, diced	1
1 tsp	soft margarine	5 mL

In blender or food processor, blend together all-purpose and whole-wheat flours, cornmeal, sugar and baking powder. Add egg, milk and oil; process until mixed. Stir in banana.

Heat nonstick skillet over medium heat until hot; add margarine to lightly grease. Pour in batter, ¼ cup (50 mL) for each pancake; cook for about 1 minute or until bubbles form on surface and underside is golden. Turn and cook just until bottom is browned.

MAKES EIGHT 5-INCH (12 CM) PANCAKES

*Instead of cornmeal, substitute whole-wheat flour if desired. The pancakes are also tasty made with 1 cup (250 mL) all-purpose flour but won't be as nutritious.

MAKE AHEAD: Combine dry ingredients up to 1 day in advance.

NOTE: Top pancakes with maple syrup or fresh fruit or a mixture of either with low-fat yogurt—you'll never miss the butter or margarine.

PER SERVING (1 pancake):
121 calories, 4 g protein,
3 g total fat, 1 g saturated fat,
25 mg cholesterol,
19 g carbohydrate, 1 g fibre,
83 mg sodium, 146 mg potassium

Cornmeal Peach Pancakes

The peaches add juicy flavour to these thin pancakes; the cornmeal adds colour and crunch. If you like thick pancakes, add ¼ cup (50 mL) all-purpose flour.

¾ cup	cornmeal	175 mL
¾ cup	all-purpose flour	175 mL
½ cup	whole-wheat flour	125 mL
2 tbsp	granulated sugar	25 mL
1 tbsp	baking powder	15 mL
½ tsp	baking soda	2 mL
2	eggs	2
2 cups	low-fat milk	500 mL
2 tbsp	canola or olive oil	25 mL
1½ cups	chopped peaches (fresh or canned)	375 mL
1 tsp	soft margarine	5 mL

In large bowl, mix cornmeal, all-purpose flour, whole-wheat flour, sugar, baking powder and baking soda.

In medium bowl, beat eggs until light; stir in milk and oil. Pour into flour mixture. Add peaches; stir until dry ingredients are wet. (Don't worry about a few lumps.)

Heat nonstick skillet over medium heat until hot. Add margarine to lightly grease. Drop large spoonfuls of batter into skillet to form rounds; cook until bubbles form on surface and underside is golden brown. Turn pancakes and cook just until bottom is lightly browned.

MAKES 6 SERVINGS OF THREE 5-INCH (12 CM) PANCAKES EACH

VARIATIONS: Add blueberries or finely diced apple instead of peaches.

PER SERVING: 315 calories, 10 g protein, 8 g total fat, 2 g saturated fat, 66 mg cholesterol, 51 g carbohydrate, 4 g fibre, 323 mg sodium, 321 mg potassium

Swiss Fruit Muesli

Different from most of the packaged muesli in supermarkets, especially in its creamy texture, this delicious Swiss-style breakfast is a make-ahead meal in one dish. Rather than skipping breakfast on rushed mornings, pack this in individual serving-size containers and eat on the way to school or at work. Add fresh berries, peaches or other fruits in season.

½ cup	rolled oats (not instant)	125 mL
½ cup	hot water	125 mL
1 cup	low-fat plain yogurt	250 mL
¼ cup	granulated sugar	50 mL
¼ cup	raisins or chopped dried apricots	50 mL
2 tbsp	each oat bran and wheat bran	25 mL
1	apple, cored and diced	1

In bowl, combine oats and water; let stand for 10 minutes or until water is absorbed. Stir in yogurt, sugar, raisins, oat and wheat brans and apple.

MAKES 3 SERVINGS, ¾ CUP (175 mL) EACH

MAKE AHEAD: Cover and refrigerate for up to 3 days.

NOTE: One serving is a high source of calcium and fibre.

PER SERVING: 254 calories, 8 g protein, 3 g total fat, 1 g saturated fat, 5 mg cholesterol, 54 g carbohydrate, 4 g fibre, 61 mg sodium, 445 mg potassium

Leslie King's Muesli

My long-time friend Leslie King taught me how to make this muesli. In this simplified version, you measure only the first time you make it; after that you just add what you have on hand. Sometimes I add chopped dried figs or apricots and various kinds of nuts. Serve with milk or yogurt and top with any kind of fresh fruit—banana, strawberries or blueberries.

3 cups	rolled oats (not instant)	750 mL
½ cup	each oat bran and wheat bran	125 mL
1 cup	raisins or mixture of chopped dried fruits	250 mL
½ cup	toasted wheat germ	125 mL
½ cup	pumpkin seeds or sunflower seeds	125 mL

Spread rolled oats, oat bran and wheat bran on baking sheet; bake in 350°F (180°C) oven for 5 minutes. Shake pan or stir; bake for 2 to 5 minutes longer or until golden. Combine oat mixture, raisins, wheat germ and seeds; store in airtight container for up to 6 months.

MAKES 15 SERVINGS, ⅓ CUP (75 mL) EACH

PER SERVING: 136 calories, 5 g protein, 2 g total fat, 0 g saturated fat, 0 mg cholesterol, 27 g carbohydrate, 4 g fibre, 3 mg sodium, 239 mg potassium

Breakfast Bran-and-Fruit Mix

With this mixture on your kitchen shelf, breakfast can be ready in a jiffy—just add sliced apples, peaches, blueberries, strawberries or banana, and top with yogurt or milk.

2 cups	bran flakes	500 mL
1 cup	ready-to-eat bran cereal	250 mL
½ cup	sliced or chopped almonds, walnuts or pecans	125 mL
½ cup	chopped dried apricots	125 mL
½ cup	chopped prunes	125 mL
½ cup	raisins	125 mL

Combine bran flakes, All-Bran, almonds, apricots, prunes and raisins. Store in airtight container.

MAKES 10 SERVINGS, ½ CUP (125 mL) EACH

MAKE AHEAD: Store in airtight container for up to 2 months.

NOTE: One serving is a high source of iron and fibre.

PER SERVING: 134 calories, 3 g protein, 3 g total fat, 0 g saturated fat, 0 mg cholesterol, 28 g carbohydrate, 5 g fibre, 113 mg sodium, 401 mg potassium

Honey Raisin Granola

This easy-to-make granola recipe is one of the few that doesn't use oil. It is my staple breakfast topped with yogurt and fresh berries or banana. I often add dried cranberries or apricot along with the raisins.

5 cups	quick-cooking rolled oats (not instant)	1.25 L
1 cup	wheat bran	250 mL
½ cup	toasted wheat germ	125 mL
¼ cup	chopped walnuts or almonds	50 mL
¼ cup	each sesame seeds and sunflower seeds	50 mL
¾ cup	liquid honey	175 mL
1½ cups	raisins	375 mL

In large bowl, combine oats, bran, wheat germ, walnuts, sesame seeds and sunflower seeds; pour in honey, stirring to mix. Spread on 2 lightly greased baking sheets; squeeze together to form small clumps. Bake in 300°F (150°C) oven for 20 minutes or until golden brown, stirring often so granola will brown evenly. Stir in raisins. Let cool completely. Store in airtight containers.

MAKES 18 SERVINGS, ½ CUP (125 mL) EACH

MAKE AHEAD: Store in airtight container for up to 6 weeks.

NOTE: One serving is a high source of iron and fibre.

VARIATION:

Fresh Fruit, Granola and Yogurt Trifle
In individual serving dishes or large glass bowl, top Honey Raisin Granola with a layer of Lemon Yogurt Cream (p. 429) and a layer of fresh berries.

PER SERVING: 231 calories, 6 g protein, 5 g total fat, 1 g saturated fat, 0 mg cholesterol, 44 g carbohydrate, 5 g fibre, 4 mg sodium, 295 mg potassium

Blender Breakfast Smoothie

My daughter-in-law Jessica Pierce makes the best smoothies, often adding frozen or fresh mango, strawberries or other berries. My grandson Pierce likes them best when made with soy milk and enjoys them any time of day. Great for when you want breakfast or a snack on the run; it takes only a minute to make and is packed with nutrients.

1	banana, peach or nectarine, peeled and cut in chunks	1
½ cup	low-fat milk or plain low-fat yogurt	125 mL
1 tbsp	wheat bran	15 mL
1 tsp	liquid honey, granulated sugar or maple syrup (or more to taste)	5 mL

In blender or food processor, blend banana, milk, bran and honey until smooth. Pour into tall glass. Serve immediately.

MAKES 1 SERVING

NOTE: One serving is a high source of vitamin D and fibre.

PER SERVING: 186 calories, 6 g protein, 2 g total fat, 1 g saturated fat, 6 mg cholesterol, 41 g carbohydrate, 4 g fibre, 55 mg sodium, 683 mg potassium

Tofu Blender Drink

The recipe for this creamy-tasting orange drink is from Vancouver vegetarian dietitian and author Vesanto Melina. I think it's one of the best-tasting and easiest ways to use tofu. It's great for breakfast or a snack.

10 oz	tofu (about 1 pkg), drained	300 g
1 cup	frozen orange juice concentrate	250 mL
1½ cups	water	375 mL
1	ripe banana	1

In blender or food processor, combine tofu, orange juice, water and banana; blend until smooth.

MAKES 4 SERVINGS

MAKE AHEAD: Cover and refrigerate for up to 1 day; stir before serving.

NOTE: Three ounces (85 g) of tofu contain 6 grams of protein; it is an excellent source of folacin and a good source of calcium, iron and zinc.

PER SERVING: 181 calories, 6 g protein, 3 g total fat, 1 g saturated fat, 0 mg cholesterol, 34 g carbohydrate, 1 g fibre, 6 mg sodium, 737 mg potassium

BREADS AND MUFFINS

Shannon Graham's Crisp Cracker Bread

Crisp, thin cracker bread is very easy to make and much less expensive than store-bought versions. Arrange the flatbread in a wicker basket and serve with salads or soups, or break into small pieces and use instead of chips for dipping.

½ cup	sesame seeds	125 mL
½ cup	cracked wheat or bulgur	125 mL
1 cup	all-purpose flour	250 mL
1 cup	whole-wheat flour	250 mL
1 tbsp	granulated sugar	15 mL
½ tsp or less	salt	2 mL or less
½ tsp	baking soda	2 mL
⅓ cup	soft margarine	75 mL
¾ cup	buttermilk	175 mL

TOPPING

1	egg white	1
1 tbsp	water	15 mL
2 tbsp	poppy, sesame or caraway seeds	25 mL

In bowl, combine sesame seeds, cracked wheat, all-purpose and whole-wheat flours, sugar, salt and baking soda; cut in margarine. Add buttermilk; mix well.

Shape into 6 balls, each about the size of a lemon; roll out on lightly floured surface into circles less than ⅛ inch (3 mm) thick (as thin as you can). Using spatula, transfer to ungreased baking sheet.

TOPPING: Combine egg white and water; brush over top of circles. Sprinkle with poppy seeds, and salt to taste (if using). Bake in 400°F (200°C) oven for 8 to 10 minutes or until golden brown.

Let cool on wire rack until crisp. Break into smaller pieces and store in airtight container for up to 2 weeks.

MAKES 24 SERVINGS, 5 PIECES EACH

PER SERVING: 96 calories, 3 g protein, 5 g total fat, 1 g saturated fat, 0 mg cholesterol, 12 g carbohydrate, 2 g fibre, 109 mg sodium, 63 mg potassium

Whole-Wheat Zucchini Bread

This zucchini bread is lower in fat and cholesterol than most, yet it is moist and full of flavour.

1½ cups	all-purpose flour	375 mL
1½ cups	whole-wheat flour	375 mL
1 tbsp	cinnamon	15 mL
1 tsp	nutmeg	5 mL
1 tsp	each baking soda and baking powder	5 mL
½ tsp or less	salt	2 mL or less
¾ cup	raisins	175 mL
2	eggs	2
⅓ cup	canola oil	75 mL
¾ cup	low-fat plain yogurt	175 mL
¼ cup	low-fat milk	50 mL
1 cup	packed brown sugar	250 mL
2 tsp	pure vanilla extract	10 mL
2 cups	finely shredded unpeeled zucchini	500 mL

In bowl, combine all-purpose and whole-wheat flours, cinnamon, nutmeg, baking soda, baking powder, salt and raisins.

In large bowl, beat eggs until foamy; beat in oil, yogurt, milk, sugar and vanilla. Stir in zucchini. Add flour mixture and stir until combined.

Pour batter into 2 well-greased 8- × 4-inch (1.5 L) loaf pans. Bake in 350°F (180°C) oven for 55 minutes or until toothpick inserted in centre comes out clean. Remove from pan and let cool thoroughly before slicing.

MAKES 2 LOAVES, 13 SLICES EACH

VARIATION: To reduce the cholesterol to zero, substitute 4 egg whites for the 2 eggs.

PER SLICE: 133 calories, 3 g protein, 4 g total fat, 0 g saturated fat, 15 mg cholesterol, 23 g carbohydrate, 1 g fibre, 121 mg sodium, 144 mg potassium

Buttermilk Herb Quick Bread

Serve this textured flavourful bread any time—for breakfast or snacks, with salads, soups or bean dishes. Be sure to use the crumbled leaf form of herbs, not the ground.

1 cup	whole-wheat flour	250 mL
½ cup	all-purpose flour	125 mL
½ cup	cornmeal	125 mL
2 tsp	baking powder	10 mL
½ tsp	baking soda	2 mL
1 tsp	salt	5 mL
1 tsp	dried dillweed	5 mL
½ tsp	each crumbled dried oregano, basil and thyme	2 mL
½ tsp	fennel seeds (optional)	2 mL
1¼ cups	buttermilk or soured milk*	300 mL
1	egg, beaten	1
2 tbsp	liquid honey	25 mL
2 tbsp	canola or olive oil	25 mL
1 tbsp	sesame and/or flax seeds	15 mL

In bowl, combine whole-wheat and all-purpose flours, cornmeal, baking powder, baking soda, salt, dillweed, oregano, basil, thyme and fennel seeds (if using).

Combine buttermilk, egg, honey and oil; stir into flour mixture just until blended. Spoon into foil or waxed paper–lined 8- × 4-inch (1.5 L) loaf pan; sprinkle with sesame and/or flax seeds.

Bake in 350°F (180°C) oven for 45 to 55 minutes or until tester inserted in centre comes out clean. Turn out and cool on rack.

MAKES 15 SLICES

*To sour milk, spoon 1 tbsp (15 mL) fresh lemon juice or white vinegar into measuring cup; add milk to measure 1¼ cups (300 mL) and let stand for 10 minutes.

NOTE: Buttermilk has the same fat content as the milk it is made from—skim, 1% or 2%, so it isn't high in fat.

PER SLICE: 104 calories, 3 g protein, 3 g total fat, 0 g saturated fat, 13 mg cholesterol, 17 g carbohydrate, 2 g fibre, 265 mg sodium, 90 mg potassium

Whole-Wheat Raisin Soda Bread

This whole-wheat raisin quick bread warm from the oven or toasted is a nice treat. Substitute an equal amount of dried fruit mixture for the raisins, if you like.

2 cups	whole-wheat flour*	500 mL
1 cup	all-purpose flour	250 mL
½ cup	rolled oats	125 mL
3 tbsp	granulated sugar	50 mL
1 tbsp	baking powder	15 mL
1 tsp	baking soda	5 mL
1 tsp or less	salt	5 mL or less
¾ cup	raisins	175 mL
2 tbsp	canola or olive oil	25 mL
1¾ cups	buttermilk**	425 mL

MUESLI TOPPING

1	egg white	1
1 tbsp	each rolled oats, wheat germ, oat bran, sunflower seeds and sesame seeds	15 mL

In bowl, combine whole-wheat and all-purpose flours, rolled oats, sugar, baking powder, baking soda and salt; stir in raisins.

Add oil to buttermilk; pour into flour mixture. Stir to make soft dough.

Turn out onto lightly floured surface and knead about 10 times or until smooth. Place on greased baking sheet; shape into circle about 2½ inches (6 cm) thick. Cut large shallow X on top.

MUESLI TOPPING: Brush egg white over top of loaf. Combine rolled oats, wheat germ, oat bran and sunflower and sesame seeds; sprinkle over loaf.

Bake in 350°F (180°C) oven for 65 to 70 minutes or until toothpick inserted in centre comes out clean.

MAKES 1 LOAF, 20 SLICES

*If you don't have whole-wheat flour, use a total of 3¼ cups (800 mL) all-purpose flour.

**If buttermilk is not available, you can use soured milk. To sour milk, spoon 2 tbsp (25 mL) fresh lemon juice or white vinegar into measuring cup; add milk to measure 1¾ cups (425 mL) and let stand for 10 minutes.

MAKE AHEAD: Best eaten warm from oven, but keeps well for 2 to 3 days wrapped in a plastic bag or foil.

PER SLICE: 127 calories, 4 g protein, 3 g total fat, 0 g saturated fat, 1 mg cholesterol, 23 g carbohydrate, 2 g fibre, 252 mg sodium, 153 mg potassium

Olive and Rosemary Soda Bread

Quick and easy to prepare, this bread dough can be mixed in a few minutes, then popped into the oven. From breakfast to dinner, this bread suits any meal.

3 cups	whole-wheat flour	750 mL
1 cup	all-purpose flour	250 mL
2 tbsp	granulated sugar	25 mL
1 tbsp	baking powder	15 mL
1 tsp	baking soda	5 mL
1 tsp or less	salt	5 mL or less
¼ cup	finely chopped pitted black olives	50 mL
1½ tsp	dried whole-leaf rosemary (or 4 tsp/20 mL fresh)	7 mL
1¾ cups	buttermilk*	425 mL
3 tbsp	canola or olive oil	50 mL

In large bowl, combine whole-wheat and all-purpose flours, sugar, baking powder, baking soda and salt. Stir in olives and half of the rosemary. Add buttermilk and oil; stir to make soft dough. Turn out onto lightly floured surface; knead about 10 times until smooth.

Place dough on lightly greased baking sheet; flatten into circle about 2½ inches (6 cm) thick. Cut large X about ¼ inch (5 mm) deep on top. Brush top with water. Sprinkle with remaining rosemary. Bake in 350°F (180°C) oven for 40 to 50 minutes or until toothpick inserted in centre comes out clean.

MAKES 1 LARGE LOAF, 20 SLICES

*If buttermilk is not available, you can use soured milk. To sour milk, spoon 2 tbsp (25 mL) fresh lemon juice or white vinegar into measuring cup; add milk to measure 1¾ cups (425 mL) and let stand for 10 minutes.

MAKE AHEAD: Wrap in a plastic bag or foil and store for up to 2 days at room temperature or freeze for up to 5 weeks.

VARIATION:

Cranberry Lemon Soda Bread
Omit the olives, rosemary and whole-wheat flour. Use 4 cups (1 L) all-purpose flour and add 1 cup (250 mL) dried cranberries along with the flour. Add a beaten egg and grated rind from 1 lemon to the buttermilk mixture.

PER SLICE: 118 calories, 4 g protein, 3 g total fat, 0 g saturated fat, 1 mg cholesterol, 21 g carbohydrate, 2 g fibre, 235 mg sodium, 115 mg potassium

Blueberry Buttermilk Biscuits

My daughter, Susie, makes these biscuits every summer at the cottage for breakfast or brunch. If using frozen blueberries, don't thaw them before using.

1 cup	all-purpose flour	250 mL
1 cup	whole-wheat flour	250 mL
2 tbsp	granulated sugar	25 mL
1 tbsp	baking powder	15 mL
½ tsp	baking soda	2 mL
½ tsp or less	salt	2 mL or less
⅓ cup	salt-free soft margarine	75 mL
1 cup	blueberries	250 mL
1 cup	buttermilk or soured low-fat milk*	250 mL

In bowl, combine all-purpose and whole-wheat flours, sugar, baking powder, baking soda and salt. Using fingers or fork, rub in margarine until mixture resembles coarse crumbs.

Stir in blueberries; add buttermilk and mix lightly. Drop by spoonfuls into 10 mounds onto lightly oiled baking sheet. Bake in 425°F (220°C) oven for 12 to 15 minutes or until golden.

MAKES 10 BISCUITS

*To sour milk, spoon 1 tbsp (15 mL) fresh lemon juice or white vinegar into measuring cup; add milk to measure 1 cup (250 mL) and let stand for 10 minutes.

PER BISCUIT: 170 calories, 4 g protein, 7 g total fat, 1 g saturated fat, 1 mg cholesterol, 24 g carbohydrate, 2 g fibre, 301 mg sodium, 118 mg potassium

Raspberry Pecan Tea Bread

Frozen raspberries make this bread easy to prepare all year round. If using frozen raspberries, don't thaw before using.

1 cup	granulated sugar	250 mL
¼ cup	soft margarine	50 mL
1	egg	1
⅔ cup	low-fat milk	150 mL
1½ cups	all-purpose flour	375 mL
1 tsp	baking powder	5 mL
½ tsp	cinnamon	2 mL
½ cup	chopped pecans	125 mL
1 cup	raspberries (fresh or frozen)	250 mL

Line 8- × 4-inch (1.5 L) loaf pan with foil; grease lightly.

In large bowl, cream sugar with margarine. Beat in egg, then milk.

Mix flour, baking powder and cinnamon; stir into egg mixture until blended. Stir in pecans and raspberries.

Spoon into pan; bake in 350°F (180°C) oven for 60 to 70 minutes or until toothpick inserted in centre comes out clean. Let stand in pan for 3 minutes. Transfer foil and tea bread to rack; loosen foil and let cool completely before cutting.

MAKES 16 SLICES

MAKE AHEAD: Wrap in foil and store for up to 4 days or freeze for up to 1 month.

NOTE: Soft diet-style tub margarines contain more water than regular soft margarines and are not recommended for baking.

Choosing a healthy margarine: Choose a soft, spreadable margarine sold in a tub, not in stick or brick form. Look for margarines that are non-hydrogenated; they will be low in saturated fat and have no trans-fatty acids.

PER SLICE: 154 calories, 2 g protein, 6 g total fat, 1 g saturated fat, 12 mg cholesterol, 24 g carbohydrate, 1 g fibre, 53 mg sodium, 61 mg potassium

Apricot, Orange and Pecan Loaf

A favourite with my recipe tasters, this bread keeps very well. Serve for dessert, tea, snacks, or brunch or lunch with salad and soup.

1 cup	all-purpose flour	250 mL
1 cup	whole-wheat flour	250 mL
1 cup	raisins	250 mL
⅔ cup	skim-milk powder	150 mL
½ cup	packed brown sugar	125 mL
½ cup	finely chopped dried apricots	125 mL
⅓ cup	wheat germ	75 mL
¼ cup	chopped pecans or almonds	50 mL
2 tsp	baking powder	10 mL
½ tsp	baking soda	2 mL
½ tsp or less	salt	2 mL or less
3	eggs	3
	Grated rind from 1 orange	
¾ cup	fresh orange juice	175 mL
½ cup	canola oil	125 mL
½ cup	fancy molasses	125 mL
2	bananas	2

In large bowl, combine all-purpose and whole-wheat flours, raisins, skim-milk powder, sugar, apricots, wheat germ, pecans, baking powder, baking soda and salt.

In separate bowl or food processor, beat eggs until foamy; beat in orange rind and juice, oil, molasses and bananas until well mixed. Pour over dry ingredients and stir just until moistened.

Pour into 2 lightly greased 8- × 4-inch (1.5 L) loaf pans. Bake in 325°F (160°C) oven for 55 to 65 minutes or until toothpick inserted in centre comes out clean. Let cool in pan on wire rack for 15 minutes. Turn out onto rack and let cool completely.

MAKES 2 LOAVES, 18 SLICES EACH

MAKE AHEAD: Wrap well and store for up to 5 days or freeze for up to 5 weeks.

NOTE: Fancy molasses, also called light molasses, is the lightest in flavour and colour of the various types of molasses. Cooking (dark) molasses is darker, thicker, and not as sweet as fancy molasses. Blackstrap molasses is quite thick and bitter and is not often used in baking.

PER SLICE: 123 calories, 2 g protein, 4 g total fat, 0 g saturated fat, 16 mg cholesterol, 20 g carbohydrate, 1 g fibre, 83 mg sodium, 239 mg potassium

Cinnamon Carrot Bread

This carrot bread is packed with flavour as well as nutrients. It's great as an afternoon snack or with a packed lunch.

1 cup	raisins	250 mL
¾ cup	all-purpose flour	175 mL
¾ cup	whole-wheat flour	175 mL
2 tsp	cinnamon	10 mL
1 tsp	ground ginger	5 mL
1 tsp	each baking soda and baking powder	5 mL
½ tsp	nutmeg	2 mL
¼ tsp or less	salt	1 mL or less
1	egg	1
3 tbsp	canola oil	50 mL
¾ cup	low-fat plain yogurt	175 mL
½ cup	packed brown sugar	125 mL
1 tsp	pure vanilla extract	5 mL
1 cup	finely shredded carrot	250 mL

TOPPING

1 tbsp	rolled oats	15 mL
1 tbsp	oat bran	15 mL

Pour boiling water over raisins and let stand for 5 minutes; drain thoroughly.

Combine all-purpose and whole-wheat flours, cinnamon, ginger, baking soda, baking powder, nutmeg, salt and raisins; set aside.

In large bowl, beat egg until fluffy; beat in oil. Mix in yogurt, sugar and vanilla; stir in carrot. Add flour mixture; stir until combined. Pour into greased and foil or waxed paper–lined 8- × 4-inch (1.5 L) loaf pan.

TOPPING: Combine rolled oats and oat bran; sprinkle over batter.

Bake in 350°F (180°C) oven for 50 to 55 minutes or until toothpick inserted in centre comes out clean. Let stand in pan for 5 minutes. Remove from pan and let cool before slicing.

MAKES 13 SLICES

PER SLICE: 166 calories,
3 g protein, 4 g total fat,
1 g saturated fat, 15 mg cholesterol,
31 g carbohydrate, 2 g fibre,
191 mg sodium, 217 mg potassium

Flax Banana Muffins

Hot from the oven, these are wonderful for a weekend breakfast.

1 cup	ground flax seeds	250 mL
¾ cup	whole-wheat flour	175 mL
¾ cup	all-purpose flour	175 mL
½ cup	granulated sugar	125 mL
1 tbsp	baking powder	15 mL
1 tsp	cinnamon	5 mL
½ tsp	each salt, baking soda and ground ginger	2 mL
1 cup	raisins or dried cranberries	250 mL
1 cup	buttermilk or soured low-fat milk*	250 mL
3 tbsp	canola oil	50 mL
1	whole egg, lightly beaten	1
2	egg whites	2
1 cup	mashed ripe bananas	250 mL
2 tsp	flax seeds (optional)	10 mL

In bowl, combine ground flax seeds, whole-wheat and all-purpose flours, sugar, baking powder, cinnamon, salt, baking soda and ginger; stir in raisins to mix. Add buttermilk, oil, egg, egg whites and bananas; stir just until combined.

Spoon into nonstick or paper-lined muffin tins. Sprinkle with flax seeds (if using). Bake in 375°F (190°C) oven for about 20 minutes or until firm to the touch.

MAKES 12 MUFFINS

*To sour milk, spoon 1 tbsp (15 mL) fresh lemon juice or white vinegar into measuring cup; add milk to measure 1 cup (250 mL) and let stand for 10 minutes.

NOTE: Muffins are best eaten the day they're baked; freeze any leftovers. To serve, wrap 1 frozen muffin in a paper towel and microwave on high for 30 seconds. It will taste like it has just been baked.

PER MUFFIN: 242 calories, 6 g protein, 8 g total fat, 1 g saturated fat, 16 mg cholesterol, 39 g carbohydrate, 5 g fibre, 268 mg sodium, 326 mg potassium

Refrigerator Applesauce-Spice Bran Muffins

I like to make these moist and flavourful muffins when I have overnight guests because the batter can be prepared in advance and refrigerated, ready for baking.

3 cups	wheat bran	750 mL
2 cups	whole-wheat flour	500 mL
1 cup	all-purpose flour	250 mL
1½ cups	raisins or chopped dates	375 mL
1 tbsp	cinnamon	15 mL
1½ tsp	each baking powder and baking soda	7 mL
1 tsp	each salt, ground ginger and nutmeg	5 mL
	Grated rind of 1 lemon or orange	
1 cup	applesauce	250 mL
¾ cup	granulated sugar	175 mL
½ cup	canola oil	125 mL
3	eggs	3
2¼ cups	low-fat milk	550 mL
½ cup	fancy molasses	125 mL

In large bowl, combine wheat bran, whole-wheat and all-purpose flours, raisins, cinnamon, baking powder, baking soda, salt, ginger, nutmeg and rind.

In separate bowl, beat together applesauce, sugar, oil and eggs until well mixed. Stir in milk and molasses. Add to dry ingredients. Stir just enough to moisten, being careful not to overmix.

Spoon into lightly greased nonstick muffin tins. Bake in 400°F (200°C) oven for 20 minutes or until tops are firm to the touch.

MAKES 24 MUFFINS

MAKE AHEAD: Cover and refrigerate batter for up to 2 weeks. Freeze baked muffins for up to 1 month.

NOTE: One muffin is a high source of fibre.

PER MUFFIN: 205 calories, 5 g protein, 6 g total fat, 1 g saturated fat, 24 mg cholesterol, 37 g carbohydrate, 5 g fibre, 218 mg sodium, 354 mg potassium

Banana Apricot Bran Muffins

Start your day with one of these fruity muffins, a glass of milk and fresh fruit.

1½ cups	whole-wheat flour	375 mL
1 tbsp	baking powder	15 mL
½ tsp	baking soda	2 mL
½ tsp	salt	2 mL
¾ cup	chopped dried apricots	175 mL
1½ cups	well-mashed ripe bananas (about 4)	375 mL
⅔ cup	low-fat plain yogurt	150 mL
⅓ cup	liquid honey	75 mL
¼ cup	canola oil	50 mL
1	egg, lightly beaten	1
1 cup	ready-to-eat bran cereal (All-Bran, 100% Bran)	250 mL

In large bowl, combine flour, baking powder, baking soda and salt. Stir in apricots.

In separate bowl, whisk together bananas, yogurt, honey, oil and egg. Stir in bran cereal. Pour over flour mixture and stir just enough to moisten, being careful not to overmix.

Spoon into lightly greased nonstick muffin tins. Bake in 400°F (200°C) oven for 18 to 20 minutes or until tops are firm to the touch.

MAKES 12 MUFFINS

MAKE AHEAD: Store in airtight container for up to 2 days or freeze for up to 1 month.

NOTE: If your dried fruit has hardened, you can plump raisins, apricots and other fruits by steeping in hot water before using them in recipes. Plumping adds moisture while preventing the fruit from drawing moisture from the batter during baking.

One muffin is a high source of fibre.

PER MUFFIN: 204 calories, 5 g protein, 6 g total fat, 1 g saturated fat, 16 mg cholesterol, 38 g carbohydrate, 5 g fibre, 292 mg sodium, 445 mg potassium

Citrus Double-Bran Muffins

Chopped prunes add flavour and keep these delicious muffins moist.

1 cup	all-purpose flour	250 mL
½ cup	wheat bran	125 mL
½ cup	oat bran	125 mL
½ cup	granulated sugar	125 mL
1 tsp	each baking powder and baking soda	5 mL
¼ tsp or less	salt	1 mL or less
1 cup	chopped prunes or raisins	250 mL
1	egg, lightly beaten	1
1 cup	buttermilk or soured low-fat milk*	250 mL
¼ cup	canola oil	50 mL
	Grated rind of 1 lemon and 1 orange	
1 tbsp	sesame seeds	15 mL

In large bowl, combine flour, wheat bran, oat bran, sugar, baking powder, baking soda and salt. Stir in prunes.

In separate bowl, mix egg, buttermilk, oil, and lemon and orange rinds. Pour into flour mixture and stir just enough to moisten, being careful not to overmix.

Spoon into greased nonstick muffin tins. Sprinkle with sesame seeds. Bake in 375°F (190°C) oven for 20 minutes or until tops are firm to the touch.

MAKES 12 MUFFINS

*To sour milk, spoon 1 tbsp (15 mL) fresh lemon juice or white vinegar into measuring cup; add milk to measure 1 cup (250 mL) and let stand for 10 minutes.

MAKE AHEAD: Store in airtight container for up to 3 days or freeze for up to 2 weeks.

NOTE: All muffins are not created equal, and it's not only the size that varies. A muffin can be as nutritious as a slice of bread or as frivolous as a piece of cake, with as little as 2 grams of fat or as much as 20 grams. When buying muffins, the best bet nutritionally is a small low-fat muffin made with whole grains or bran. By regulation, a 50 to 100 gram muffin claiming to be low-fat may contain no more than 3 grams of fat. When making your own muffins, use whole grains and as little fat as possible.

PER MUFFIN: 182 calories, 4 g protein, 6 g total fat, 1 g saturated fat, 16 mg cholesterol, 32 g carbohydrate, 3 g fibre, 207 mg sodium, 220 mg potassium

Rhubarb Bran Muffins

In this recipe, use Stewed Rhubarb (p. 421) or rhubarb stewed with a minimum amount of liquid: just a spoonful or two.

¾ cup	wheat bran	175 mL
1 cup	whole-wheat flour	250 mL
½ cup	granulated sugar	125 mL
2 tsp	cinnamon	10 mL
1 tsp	each baking powder and baking soda	5 mL
½ cup	raisins	125 mL
1 cup	stewed rhubarb	250 mL
1	egg, lightly beaten	1
½ cup	buttermilk or low-fat plain yogurt	125 mL
¼ cup	canola oil	50 mL

In bowl, combine wheat bran, flour, sugar, cinnamon, baking powder and baking soda; stir in raisins.

Combine stewed rhubarb, egg, buttermilk and oil; pour into flour mixture and stir just until combined.

Spoon into greased nonstick muffin tins. Bake in 400°F (200°C) oven for 25 minutes or until tops are firm to the touch.

MAKES 12 MUFFINS

MAKE AHEAD: Store in airtight container for up to 2 days or freeze for up to 2 weeks.

NOTE: For tender muffins, mix batter as little as possible.

VARIATION:

Applesauce Bran Muffins
Substitute 1 cup (250 mL) applesauce for the rhubarb.

PER MUFFIN: 167 calories, 3 g protein, 5 g total fat, 1 g saturated fat, 16 mg cholesterol, 30 g carbohydrate, 3 g fibre, 148 mg sodium, 170 mg potassium

Carrot Bran Muffins

These easy-to-make muffins are great for breakfast, snacks or lunch. Grated apple could be substituted for carrot.

1½ cups	whole-wheat flour	375 mL
1½ cups	ready-to-eat bran cereal (All-Bran, 100% Bran)	375 mL
½ cup	packed brown sugar	125 mL
1 tbsp	cinnamon	15 mL
1 tsp	each baking powder and baking soda	5 mL
½ tsp or less	salt	2 mL or less
1 cup	raisins or chopped dates	250 mL
1 cup	grated carrots	250 mL
1¾ cup	buttermilk or soured low-fat milk*	425 mL
¼ cup	canola oil	50 mL
1	egg, lightly beaten	1
	Grated rind of 1 lemon or orange	

In large bowl, stir together flour, bran cereal, sugar, cinnamon, baking powder, baking soda, salt, raisins and carrots.

Add buttermilk, oil, egg and rind, stirring just until combined.

Spoon into greased nonstick muffin tins. Bake in 400°F (200°C) oven for 20 minutes or until tops are firm to the touch.

MAKES 12 MUFFINS

*To sour milk, spoon 2 tbsp (25 mL) fresh lemon juice or white vinegar into measuring cup; add milk to measure 1¾ cups (425 mL) and let stand for 10 minutes.

MAKE AHEAD: Wrap in plastic wrap and refrigerate for up to 2 days, or freeze for up to 1 month.

NOTE: Depending on the size of your tins, you could get 14 muffins from this recipe.

PER MUFFIN: 209 calories, 5 g protein, 6 g total fat, 1 g saturated fat, 17 mg cholesterol, 39 g carbohydrate, 6 g fibre, 354 mg sodium, 366 mg potassium

Oatmeal Carrot Muffins

Grated carrot adds flavour and helps keep the muffins moist. They are delicious in a packed lunch or for breakfast.

1¼ cups	buttermilk*	300 mL
1½ cups	quick-cooking rolled oats (not instant)	375 mL
1 cup	grated carrots	250 mL
½ cup	packed brown sugar	125 mL
¼ cup	canola oil	50 mL
2	eggs, lightly beaten	2
1½ tsp	grated orange rind	7 mL
1¼ cups	all-purpose flour	300 mL
¾ cup	raisins or other dried fruit	175 mL
1 tbsp	baking powder	15 mL
1 tsp	cinnamon or ground ginger	5 mL
½ tsp or less	salt	2 mL or less

In bowl, pour buttermilk over oats; stir to mix. Let stand for 5 minutes. Stir in carrots, sugar, oil, eggs and orange rind.

In large bowl, combine flour, raisins, baking powder, cinnamon and salt. Pour buttermilk mixture over top and stir just enough to moisten, being careful not to overmix.

Spoon into lightly greased nonstick muffin tins. Bake in 400°F (200°C) oven for 20 minutes or until tops are firm to the touch.

MAKES 12 MUFFINS

*If buttermilk is not available, you can use soured low-fat milk. To sour milk, spoon 4 tsp (20 mL) fresh lemon juice or white vinegar into measuring cup; fill to 1¼ cups (300 mL) with milk and let stand for 10 minutes.

MAKE AHEAD: Store in airtight container for up to 2 days or freeze for up to 1 month.

NOTE: The carrots in these muffins make each one a good source of vitamin A.

PER MUFFIN: 222 calories, 5 g protein, 7 g total fat, 1 g saturated fat, 32 mg cholesterol, 37 g carbohydrate, 2 g fibre, 221 mg sodium, 234 mg potassium

Pumpkin Raisin Muffins

These are my daughter Susie's favourite muffins to bake. They are so moist you don't need to spread anything on them.

1 cup	whole-wheat flour	250 mL
¾ cup	wheat bran	175 mL
⅔ cup	packed brown sugar	150 mL
2 tsp	cinnamon and baking powder	10 mL
½ tsp	each baking soda, salt and nutmeg	2 mL
1 cup	raisins	250 mL
1 cup	mashed or canned cooked pumpkin	250 mL
½ cup	low-fat plain yogurt or buttermilk	125 mL
⅓ cup	canola oil	75 mL
1	egg, lightly beaten	1

In large bowl, combine flour, wheat bran, sugar, cinnamon, baking powder, baking soda, salt and nutmeg. Stir in raisins.

In separate bowl, whisk together pumpkin, yogurt, oil and egg. Pour over flour mixture and stir just enough to moisten, being careful not to overmix.

Spoon into lightly greased nonstick muffin tins. Bake in 400°F (200°C) oven for 20 to 25 minutes or until tops are firm to the touch.

MAKES 12 MUFFINS

MAKE AHEAD: Store in airtight container for up to 2 days or freeze for up to 1 month.

NOTE: The pumpkin in these muffins makes each one an excellent source of vitamin A.

VARIATIONS:

Banana-Date Muffins
Instead of pumpkin and raisins, use 1 cup (250 mL) mashed banana and ½ cup (125 mL) chopped dates.

Cranberry Orange Muffins
Instead of pumpkin and raisins, use 1 cup (250 mL) each whole-berry cranberry sauce and dried cranberries and add 1 tsp (5 mL) grated orange rind.

PER MUFFIN: 199 calories, 4 g protein, 7 g total fat, 1 g saturated fat, 16 mg cholesterol, 34 g carbohydrate, 4 g fibre, 221 mg sodium, 290 mg potassium

Blueberry Lemon Muffins

Warm from the oven and bursting with fresh flavour, these muffins do not need a spread.

1 tbsp	fresh lemon juice	15 mL
1 cup	low-fat milk	250 mL
1	egg, beaten	1
¼ cup	canola oil	50 mL
¼ cup	fancy molasses	50 mL
1 cup	wheat bran	250 mL
¾ cup	whole-wheat flour	175 mL
¾ cup	all-purpose flour	175 mL
⅓ cup	packed brown sugar	75 mL
1½ tsp	grated lemon rind	7 mL
1½ tsp	baking powder	7 mL
½ tsp	baking soda	2 mL
1 cup	blueberries (fresh or frozen)	250 mL

In bowl, stir lemon juice into milk; let stand for 10 minutes to sour. Stir in egg, oil and molasses.

In large bowl, combine wheat bran, whole-wheat and all-purpose flours, sugar, lemon rind, baking powder and baking soda. Add milk mixture and blueberries; mix just until combined.

Spoon into nonstick or paper-lined muffin tins. Bake in 375°F (190°C) oven for 20 to 25 minutes or until firm to the touch.

MAKES 12 MUFFINS

NOTE: To make pouring the molasses from the measuring cup easier, first measure the oil in the measuring cup, transfer the oil to the bowl, then measure the molasses.

PER MUFFIN: 170 calories, 4 g protein, 6 g total fat, 1 g saturated fat, 17 mg cholesterol, 29 g carbohydrate, 3 g fibre, 111 mg sodium, 268 mg potassium

Apple Streusel Muffins

These moist cinnamon-flavoured muffins are perfect for breakfast or snack time.

1⅓ cups	whole-wheat flour	325 mL
½ cup	oat bran	125 mL
⅓ cup	granulated sugar	75 mL
1 tbsp	baking powder	15 mL
1 tbsp	cinnamon	15 mL
¼ tsp or less	salt	1 mL or less
1¼ cups	chopped peeled apple	300 mL
1	egg, lightly beaten	1
1 cup	low-fat milk	250 mL
¼ cup	canola oil	50 mL

TOPPING

2 tbsp	packed brown sugar	25 mL
¼ tsp	cinnamon	1 mL
¼ tsp	nutmeg	1 mL

In large bowl, mix together flour, oat bran, sugar, baking powder, cinnamon and salt. Stir in chopped apple.

In separate bowl, combine egg, milk and oil; stir into flour mixture just until moistened, being careful to not overmix. Spoon into nonstick or paper-lined muffin cups, filling three-quarters full.

TOPPING: Combine sugar, cinnamon and nutmeg; sprinkle over muffins.

Bake in 400°F (200°C) oven 15 to 20 minutes or until golden and firm to the touch.

MAKES 12 MUFFINS

PER MUFFIN: 150 calories, 4 g protein, 6 g total fat, 1 g saturated fat, 17 mg cholesterol, 24 g carbohydrate, 3 g fibre, 141 mg sodium, 140 mg potassium

Jalapeño Cornmeal Muffins

Creamed corn makes these muffins very moist, while jalapeño peppers add zing. Serve with a main course of chicken or ham or as part of a brunch menu.

1 cup	cornmeal	250 mL
1 cup	all-purpose flour	250 mL
1 tsp	baking powder	5 mL
1 tsp	baking soda	5 mL
¼ tsp or less	salt	1 mL or less
2 tbsp	chopped pickled jalapeño peppers	25 mL
1	egg, lightly beaten	1
1	can (10 oz/284 mL) creamed corn	1
1 cup	buttermilk or soured low-fat milk*	250 mL
¼ cup	canola oil	50 mL

In large bowl, combine cornmeal, flour, baking powder, baking soda and salt. Stir in jalapeño peppers.

In separate bowl, mix egg, corn, buttermilk and oil. Pour into flour mixture and stir just enough to moisten, being careful not to overmix.

Spoon into greased nonstick muffin tins. Bake in 375°F (190°C) oven for 25 to 30 minutes or until tops are firm to the touch.

MAKES 12 MUFFINS

*To sour milk, spoon 1 tbsp (15 mL) fresh lemon juice or white vinegar into measuring cup; add milk to measure 1¼ cups (300 mL) and let stand for 10 minutes.

MAKE AHEAD: Store in airtight container for up to 3 days or freeze for up to 2 weeks.

VARIATION:

Cornmeal and Cheddar Muffins
Before baking, sprinkle tops of muffins with grated old Cheddar cheese.

PER MUFFIN: 161 calories, 4 g protein, 6 g total fat, 1 g saturated fat, 16 mg cholesterol, 24 g carbohydrate, 1 g fibre, 301 mg sodium, 109 mg potassium

COOKIES, SQUARES AND BARS

Almond Meringues

It can be difficult to find tasty cookies that are low in fat. These are both.

¼ cup	slivered almonds	50 mL
3	egg whites	3
½ cup	granulated sugar	125 mL
1 tbsp	cornstarch	15 mL
¼ tsp	almond extract	1 mL

Toast almonds on baking sheet in 325°F (160°C) oven for 6 minutes or until golden. Let cool. Reduce oven temperature to 225°F (110°C).

In large bowl and using electric mixer, beat egg whites until soft peaks form; gradually beat in sugar, then cornstarch and almond extract until stiff peaks form. Fold in almonds.

Line baking sheets with foil, shiny side down. Drop batter by small spoonfuls onto prepared pan. Bake in 225°F (110°C) oven for 2 hours or until cookies can be easily removed from foil. Let cool.

MAKES 30 COOKIES

MAKE AHEAD: Store in airtight container for up to 1 month.

NOTE: For a crisper cookie, leave baked cookies in turned-off oven overnight.

PER COOKIE: 21 calories, 1 g protein, 0 g total fat, 0 g saturated fat, 0 mg cholesterol, 4 g carbohydrate, 0 g fibre, 6 mg sodium, 12 mg potassium

Daphna Rabinovitch's Meringue Kisses

Daphna Rabinovitch, a friend, chef and cookbook author, is a terrific cook. When Daphna made these light cookies, they disappeared before they hardly had time to cool. If miniature chocolate chips are unavailable, use any small chocolate chips.

3	egg whites	3
Pinch	salt	Pinch
¾ cup	granulated sugar	175 mL
¾ cups	miniature semisweet chocolate chips	175 mL
1 tsp	cornstarch or potato starch	5 mL
½ tsp	pure vanilla extract	2 mL

In bowl and using electric mixer, beat egg whites with salt until soft peaks form. Beat in sugar, 2 tbsp (25 mL) at a time, until stiff shiny peaks form. Sprinkle with chocolate chips, cornstarch and vanilla; gently fold into whites.

Using pastry bag fitted with 1-inch (2.5 cm) tip, or two spoons, pipe or shape into 1-inch (2.5 cm) kisses on foil-lined baking sheets. Bake in 300°F (150°C) oven, rotating pans halfway through, for 25 to 30 minutes or until just starting to turn golden and tops are firm to the touch. Let cool on foil for 10 minutes, then on racks.

MAKES 40 COOKIES

MAKE AHEAD: Cookies can be stored in airtight container for up to 10 days.

NOTE: These meringues are softer and chewier than the Almond Meringues (above) because they bake for a shorter time at a higher temperature.

I always use pure vanilla extract when baking, rather than imitation, which is wholly artificial and can leave a bitter aftertaste. Although pure vanilla is more expensive than imitation, less is needed and the taste is incomparable.

PER COOKIE: 32 calories, 0 g protein, 1 g total fat, 1 g saturated fat, 0 mg cholesterol, 6 g carbohydrate, 0 g fibre, 4 mg sodium, 15 mg potassium

Lacy Oatmeal Crisps

These crisp, buttery, classic cookies are perfect with fresh fruit for dessert.

½ cup	butter, softened	125 mL
¾ cup	packed brown sugar	175 mL
1	egg white	1
1 tsp	pure vanilla extract	5 mL
1 cup	quick-cooking rolled oats (not instant)	250 mL
2 tbsp	all-purpose flour	25 mL
¼ tsp	baking soda	1 mL

In bowl, using electric beater, cream butter with sugar until fluffy. Beat in egg white and vanilla. Stir in rolled oats, flour and baking soda until mixed.

Drop by teaspoonfuls (5 mL) 3 inches (8 cm) apart onto parchment or foil-lined baking sheets. Bake in 325°F (160°C) oven for about 5 to 6 minutes or until spread out into lacy shape and golden. Let cool on baking sheets.

MAKES 60 COOKIES

MAKE AHEAD: Store in airtight container (separate layers with waxed paper or foil) for up to 1 week.

PER COOKIE: 31 calories, 0 g protein, 2 g total fat, 1 g saturated fat, 4 mg cholesterol, 4 g carbohydrate, 0 g fibre, 18 mg sodium, 17 mg potassium

Orange Hazelnut Biscotti

These crunchy double-baked Italian cookies are meant to be dunked in tea, coffee, hot chocolate or dessert wine.

¾ cup	coarsely chopped (unskinned) hazelnuts	175 mL
1½ cups	all-purpose flour	375 mL
2 tsp	baking powder	10 mL
2	eggs	2
½ cup	packed brown sugar	125 mL
2 tsp	pure vanilla extract	10 mL
	Grated rind of 1 orange	
1	egg white	1

In large bowl, combine nuts, flour and baking powder.

In separate bowl, beat eggs, sugar, vanilla and orange rind; stir into flour mixture, mixing well to form stiff dough.

Shape dough into 2 logs each about 1 inch (2.5 cm) in diameter. Transfer to ungreased baking sheet. Brush tops with egg white. Bake in 350°F (180°C) oven for 25 minutes. Let cool for 5 minutes.

Slice diagonally into ½-inch (1 cm) thick slices. Arrange on baking sheet. Reduce temperature to 300°F (150°C) and bake for 25 minutes or until crisp and golden.

MAKES 36 COOKIES

MAKE AHEAD: Store in airtight container for up to 2 weeks.

VARIATION:

Almond Ginger Biscotti
Omit hazelnuts, vanilla extract and orange rind, substituting ½ cup (125 mL) coarsely chopped unblanched almonds, 1½ tsp (7 mL) ground ginger and 3 tbsp (50 mL) finely chopped crystallized ginger.

PER COOKIE: 52 calories, 1 g protein, 2 g total fat, 0 g saturated fat, 10 mg cholesterol, 8 g carbohydrate, 0 g fibre, 23 mg sodium, 40 mg potassium

Apple Cinnamon Cookies

The glaze adds a special touch to these old-fashioned, soft cookies.

½ cup	soft margarine	125 mL
1⅓ cups	packed brown sugar	325 mL
1	egg	1
1½ cups	grated peeled apple	375 mL
1 cup	raisins	250 mL
¼ cup	chopped almonds	50 mL
¼ cup	apple juice	50 mL
2 cups	whole-wheat flour	500 mL
2 tsp	cinnamon	10 mL
1 tsp	baking soda	5 mL
½ tsp or less	salt	2 mL or less
¼ tsp	ground cloves	1 mL

GLAZE (OPTIONAL)

1 cup	icing sugar	250 mL
2 tbsp	lemon juice	25 mL

In large bowl, cream margarine with sugar until fluffy; beat in egg. Add apple, raisins, almonds and apple juice; mix well.

In separate bowl, combine flour, cinnamon, baking soda, salt and cloves. Stir into apple mixture; mix well.

Drop by tablespoonfuls (15 mL) about 2 inches (5 cm) apart onto lightly greased baking sheets. Bake in 375°F (190°C) oven for 10 to 12 minutes or until evenly browned. Let stand on baking sheets for 1 to 2 minutes before removing to racks to let cool.

GLAZE: In small bowl, combine icing sugar and lemon juice until smooth. Spread over each cookie.

MAKES 60 COOKIES

MAKE AHEAD: Store in airtight container for up to 1 week or freeze for up to 1 month.

NOTE: Grated apple adds moistness and flavour to this low-fat cookie.

PER COOKIE (without glaze):
59 calories, 1 g protein,
2 g total fat, 0 g saturated fat,
3 mg cholesterol, 10 g carbohydrate,
1 g fibre, 57 mg sodium,
62 mg potassium

Lemon Sugar Cookies

Shannon Graham, who helps me with recipe testing, came up with these cookies, which everyone loves.

¼ cup	soft margarine	50 mL
⅔ cup	granulated sugar	150 mL
1	egg	1
2 tbsp	lemon juice	25 mL
1¼ cups	all-purpose flour	300 mL
⅓ cup	whole-wheat flour	75 mL
	Grated rind of 2 lemons	
½ tsp	baking soda	2 mL
1 tbsp	granulated sugar	15 mL

In large bowl and using electric mixer, cream margarine and sugar. Add egg and lemon juice; beat until light and fluffy.

In separate bowl, combine all-purpose flour, whole-wheat flour, lemon rind and baking soda. Stir into egg mixture; mix well. Shape tablespoonfuls (15 mL) of dough into balls; place about 2 inches (5 cm) apart on lightly greased baking sheets. Using back of fork, press to ¼ inch (5 mm) thickness. Sprinkle with sugar.

Bake in 350°F (180°C) oven for 10 minutes or until firm.

MAKES 40 COOKIES

NOTE: Diet or calorie-reduced margarines are not recommended for baking, as they contain more water than regular soft margarines.

PER COOKIE: 44 calories, 1 g protein, 1 g total fat, 0 g saturated fat, 5 mg cholesterol, 7 g carbohydrate, 0 g fibre, 27 mg sodium, 12 mg potassium

Oatmeal Raisin Cookies

These cookies are a family favourite, especially of my grandson Pierce.

½ cup	soft margarine	125 mL
¾ cup	granulated sugar	175 mL
½ cup	lightly packed brown sugar	125 mL
1	egg	1
1 cup	whole-wheat flour	250 mL
1 cup	quick-cooking oats (not instant)	250 mL
¼ cup	wheat germ	50 mL
1 tsp	baking powder	5 mL
1 tsp	baking soda	5 mL
1½ cups	raisins	375 mL

In mixing bowl, cream margarine; beat in granulated and brown sugars and egg, creaming together thoroughly. Add flour, oats, wheat germ, baking powder and baking soda; mix well. Stir in raisins.

Drop by spoonfuls onto lightly greased baking sheets. Flatten slightly with floured fork. Bake in 350°F (180°C) oven for 12 to 15 minutes or until light golden.

MAKES 40 COOKIES

MAKE AHEAD: Store in airtight container for up to 2 weeks or wrapped well and freeze for up to 1 month.

PER COOKIE: 83 calories, 1 g protein, 3 g total fat, 0 g saturated fat, 5 mg cholesterol, 14 g carbohydrate, 1 g fibre, 62 mg sodium, 79 mg potassium

Hermits

These old-fashioned favourites are made healthier by using whole-wheat flour and reducing the sugar and fat. Use chopped dates or any combination of dried fruits, such as apricots, raisins, cranberries or figs.

⅓ cup	soft margarine	75 mL
⅔ cup	packed brown sugar	150 mL
1	egg, lightly beaten	1
	Grated rind of 1 lemon	
¾ cup	all-purpose flour	175 mL
⅔ cup	whole-wheat flour*	150 mL
1½ tsp	baking powder	7 mL
½ tsp	each ground allspice and cinnamon	2 mL
¼ tsp	each ground cloves and nutmeg	1 mL
1 cup	chopped dried fruit	250 mL
¼ cup	low-fat milk	50 mL

In large bowl and with electric mixer, cream margarine; gradually add sugar, beating at medium speed until light and fluffy. Beat in egg and lemon rind.

In separate bowl, combine all-purpose flour, whole-wheat flour, baking powder, allspice, cinnamon, cloves and nutmeg; stir in dried fruit. Stir into creamed mixture along with milk, mixing well.

Drop by spoonfuls onto lightly greased baking sheets. Bake in 325°F (160°C) oven for 15 minutes or until golden. Let cool slightly before removing from baking sheet.

MAKES 30 COOKIES

*Instead of whole-wheat flour you can use a total of 1½ cups (375 mL) all-purpose flour.

NOTE: If the dried fruits are hard, plump them by steeping them in hot water (drain and dry thoroughly) before using them in recipes. Plumping adds moisture while preventing the fruit from drawing moisture from the batter during baking.

PER COOKIE: 72 calories, 1 g protein, 2 g total fat, 0 g saturated fat, 6 mg cholesterol, 12 g carbohydrate, 1 g fibre, 39 mg sodium, 75 mg potassium

Gingersnaps

These crisp cookies are great for packed lunches or with fresh fruit for dessert. They also freeze well.

¼ cup	soft margarine	50 mL
½ cup	fancy or cooking molasses	125 mL
½ tsp	baking soda	2 mL
1½ tsp	boiling water	7 mL
1¼ cups	all-purpose flour	300 mL
1½ tsp	ground ginger	7 mL
½ tsp	ground cinnamon	2 mL
⅛ tsp	ground cloves	0.5 mL
1 tsp	granulated sugar	5 mL

In small saucepan, melt margarine; add molasses and bring to boil, stirring constantly. Remove from heat; let cool for 15 minutes.

In small dish, combine baking soda and water; stir into molasses mixture.

In mixing bowl, sift 1 cup (250 mL) of the flour, ginger, cinnamon and cloves. Stir in molasses mixture until well combined. Add enough of the remaining flour to make dough that is easy to roll. Chill dough in refrigerator for 20 minutes.

On unfloured surface and using unfloured rolling pin, roll dough out to about ⅛ inch (3 mm) thickness. Cut into 2-inch (5 cm) rounds. Sprinkle with sugar. Bake on ungreased baking sheet in 375°F (190°C) oven for 5 to 8 minutes or until set.

MAKES 4 DOZEN COOKIES

PER COOKIE: 31 calories, 0 g protein, 1 g total fat, 0 g saturated fat, 0 mg cholesterol, 5 g carbohydrate, 0 g fibre, 23 mg sodium, 56 mg potassium

Easy Cranberry-Chocolate Cookies

These easy-to-make, crisp cookies are a favourite in my house.

⅔ cup	soft margarine	150 mL
1 cup	packed brown sugar	250 mL
1	egg, slightly beaten	1
1 tbsp	water	15 mL
1 cup	whole-wheat flour	250 mL
1 cup	oat bran	250 mL
¼ cup	wheat germ	50 mL
1 tsp	baking soda	5 mL
1 tsp	baking powder	5 mL
1 cup	chopped dried cranberries, raisins, or chopped dates	250 mL
½ cup	chocolate chips or chopped nuts	125 mL

In large bowl, cream margarine; beat in brown sugar, egg and water to mix thoroughly. Add flour, oat bran, wheat germ, baking soda and baking powder; mix well. Stir in dried cranberries and chocolate chips.

Drop batter by spoonfuls onto lightly greased baking sheets; flatten slightly with floured fork. Bake in 350°F (180°C) oven for 10 to 12 minutes or until light golden.

MAKES 3 DOZEN COOKIES

NOTE: Oat bran, an excellent source of soluble fibre, may help to reduce blood cholesterol.

VARIATION: For a very crisp cookie, use butter; for slightly less crisp, use soft margarine. Using a reduced-fat spread will produce a soft, chewy cookie.

PER COOKIE: 97 calories, 1 g protein, 5 g total fat, 1 g saturated fat, 5 mg cholesterol, 15 g carbohydrate, 1 g fibre, 78 mg sodium, 69 mg potassium

Easy Date and Walnut Squares

My sister-in-law Nancy Williams gave me the recipe for these yummy squares.

1	egg	1
2	egg whites	2
1 cup	granulated sugar	250 mL
3 tbsp	melted soft margarine	45 mL
1¼ cups	finely chopped dates, packed	300 mL
¼ cup	chopped walnuts	50 mL
⅓ cup	all-purpose flour	75 ml
1 tsp	baking powder	5 mL

In bowl and using electric mixer, beat egg, egg whites and sugar for about 5 minutes or until light in colour. Beat in margarine, dates and walnuts. Stir in flour and baking powder until well combined.

Pour into lightly greased 8-inch (2 L) square baking dish. Bake in 350°F (180°C) oven for 35 minutes or until set. Let cool completely before cutting into squares.

MAKES 20 SQUARES

VARIATION: A less sweet, more cake-like version of these squares makes a tasty choice for a packed lunch. Prepare above recipe but reduce sugar to ½ cup (125 mL) and increase flour to ½ cup (125 mL). When cool, sift 1 tsp (5 mL) icing sugar over squares.

PER SQUARE: 107 calories, 1 g protein, 3 g total fat, 0 g saturated fat, 9 mg cholesterol, 20 g carbohydrate, 1 g fibre, 39 mg sodium, 92 mg potassium

Best-Ever Date Squares

Sometimes called matrimonial cake, these are my husband's favourite squares.

2 cups	packed chopped pitted dates (12 oz/375 g)	500 mL
1 cup	cold coffee	250 mL
2 tbsp	packed brown sugar	25 mL
	Grated rind and juice of half an orange	
1 tbsp	fresh lemon juice	15 mL

CRUMB MIXTURE

1¼ cups	all-purpose flour	300 mL
1 tsp	baking powder	5 mL
½ tsp	baking soda	2 mL
½ tsp or less	salt	2 mL or less
⅔ cup	soft margarine	150 mL
1¼ cups	quick-cooking oats (not instant)	300 mL
¾ cup	lightly packed brown sugar	175 mL

In small saucepan, combine dates, coffee, brown sugar and orange rind; bring to boil. Reduce heat and simmer, uncovered, until soft enough to mash and consistency of jam (runny but easy to spread), about 10 minutes. Remove from heat; stir in orange and lemon juices. Let cool.

CRUMB MIXTURE: In bowl, stir together flour, baking powder, baking soda and salt. With pastry blender or 2 knives, cut in butter until size of small peas. Stir in oats and sugar.

Press half of crumb mixture firmly into lightly greased 9-inch (2.5 L) square cake pan. Spread date mixture evenly over crumb mixture. Top with remaining crumbs, pressing lightly. Bake in 325°F (160°C) oven for 25 minutes or until lightly browned. Let cool in pan. Cut into squares.

MAKES 25 SQUARES

MAKE AHEAD: Cover and refrigerate for up to 5 days.

PER SQUARE: 154 calories, 2 g protein, 5 g total fat, 1 g saturated fat, 0 mg cholesterol, 26 g carbohydrate, 2 g fibre, 130 mg sodium, 157 mg potassium

Light Lemon Squares

This is a lighter version of a favourite square.

1 cup	all-purpose flour	250 mL
¼ cup	granulated sugar	50 mL
¼ cup	butter, softened	50 mL
2 tbsp	low-fat plain yogurt	25 mL

TOPPING

¾ cup	granulated sugar	175 mL
2 tbsp	all-purpose flour	25 mL
½ tsp	baking powder	2 mL
¼ tsp or less	salt	1 mL or less
2	eggs	2
	Grated rind of 1 large lemon	
¼ cup	lemon juice	50 mL
2 tsp	icing sugar	10 mL

In food processor or bowl, mix together flour, sugar, butter and yogurt until just combined.

Press into 8-inch (2 L) square cake pan lightly coated with cooking spray. Bake in 325°F (160°C) oven for 25 minutes or until golden.

TOPPING: In food processor or bowl, combine sugar, flour, baking powder, salt, eggs and lemon rind and juice; mix well.

Pour topping over base. Bake for 30 minutes or until top is set. Let cool in pan. Sift icing sugar over top. Cut into squares.

MAKES 16 SQUARES

MAKE AHEAD: Store in airtight container for up to 1 week or freeze for up to 2 weeks.

VARIATION: The traditional lemon square recipe uses ½ cup (125 mL) butter in the base. In this recipe, the fat is cut in half by replacing some of the butter with yogurt.

PER SQUARE: 119 calories, 2 g protein, 4 g total fat, 1 g saturated fat, 23 mg cholesterol, 20 g carbohydrate, 0 g fibre, 80 mg sodium, 29 mg potassium

Almond Apricot Squares

Apricots add extra flavour to these tasty, attractive squares.

¾ cup	packed dried apricots	175 mL

BASE

¼ cup	soft margarine	50 mL
1 cup	all-purpose flour	250 mL
¼ cup	granulated sugar	50 mL
2 tbsp	low-fat plain yogurt	25 mL

TOP

2	eggs	2
½ cup	granulated sugar	125 mL
Pinch	salt	Pinch
½ cup	slivered almonds	125 mL

In small saucepan, combine apricots with enough water to cover. Cover and bring to boil; remove from heat. (Alternatively, place apricots in microwaveable dish, add just enough water to cover. Cover and microwave on High for 1 minute.) Let stand for 1 minute. Drain, let cool and chop apricots finely; set aside.

BASE: In bowl and using pastry blender or 2 knives, cut butter into flour until it resembles fine crumbs. Stir in sugar and yogurt, combining well. Press evenly into lightly greased 8-inch (2 L) square cake pan. Bake in 350°F (180°C) oven for 20 minutes.

TOP: Meanwhile, in bowl, beat eggs with sugar and salt until light; stir in apricots. Pour over base. Sprinkle almonds evenly over top.

Bake in 350°F (180°C) oven for 30 minutes or until set and golden brown. Let cool slightly in pan. Cut into squares.

MAKES 18 SQUARES

MAKE AHEAD: Refrigerate in airtight container for up to 5 days or freeze for up to 3 weeks.

PER SQUARE: 120 calories, 2 g protein, 5 g total fat, 1 g saturated fat, 21 mg cholesterol, 18 g carbohydrate, 1 g fibre, 31 mg sodium, 117 mg potassium

Granola Energy Squares

These easy-to-make squares are great at lunch or for a snack and are a tasty alternative to store-bought granola bars.

½ cup	butter, melted	125 mL
¾ cup	corn syrup	175 mL
2 cups	quick-cooking oats (not instant)	500 mL
1 cup	wheat bran	250 mL
1 cup	sunflower seeds	250 mL
1 cup	chopped dried apricots, dates or raisins, or a combination (6 oz/170 g)	250 mL
½ cup	chopped nuts (walnuts, almonds, pecans)	125 mL
¼ cup	sesame seeds	50 mL

In large bowl, combine butter and corn syrup; stir in oats, bran, sunflower seeds, dried fruit, nuts and sesame seeds.

Firmly press into lightly greased 9- × 13-inch (2.5 L) cake pan; bake in 350°F (180°C) oven for 15 minutes or until golden. Let cool and cut into squares.

MAKES 40 SQUARES

MAKE AHEAD: Store in airtight container for up to 1 week or freeze for up to 2 months.

PER SQUARE: 105 calories, 2 g protein, 6 g total fat, 2 g saturated fat, 6 mg cholesterol, 13 g carbohydrate, 2 g fibre, 25 mg sodium, 138 mg potassium

Double Chocolate Brownies

These rich-tasting brownies are amazingly low in calories. They are even moister when made with Splenda.

⅔ cup	all-purpose flour	150 mL
½ cup	granulated sugar or Splenda	125 mL
⅓ cup	unsweetened cocoa powder	75 mL
1 tsp	baking powder	5 mL
¼ tsp or less	salt	1 mL or less
1 tsp	pure vanilla extract	5 mL
1 tsp	instant coffee granules	5 mL
¼ cup	soft margarine	50 mL
2	eggs	2
½ cup	unsweetened applesauce	125 mL
½ cup	chocolate chips	125 mL

In bowl, stir together flour, sugar, cocoa, baking powder and salt.

Mix vanilla and coffee to dissolve coffee. In mixing bowl, beat butter, eggs and vanilla mixture for 1 minute. Add applesauce and beat just until blended.

Fold in flour mixture and chocolate chips just until blended.

Spread evenly in greased 8-inch (2 L) square pan. Bake in 350°F (180°C) oven for about 12 minutes until outside edges are firm. Cool on rack.

MAKES 16 BROWNIES

MAKE AHEAD: Store in covered container in refrigerator for up to 1 week.

PER BROWNIE: 111 calories, 2 g protein, 5 g total fat, 2 g saturated fat, 23 mg cholesterol, 16 g carbohydrate, 1 g fibre, 89 mg sodium, 68 mg potassium

Date and Almond Meringue Bars

One of my mother's recipes, these bars go well with frozen desserts such as Louise Saunder's Grapefruit Ice (p. 424) or other fruit sorbets.

1¾ cups	chopped dates	425 mL
¾ cup	water	175 mL
⅓ cup	soft margarine	75 mL
⅓ cup	granulated sugar	75 mL
2	eggs, separated	2
1 tsp	pure vanilla extract	5 mL
¾ cup	all-purpose flour	175 mL
¾ cup	whole-wheat flour	175 mL
1 tsp	baking powder	5 mL
½ cup	packed brown sugar	125 mL
¼ cup	slivered almonds (optional)	50 mL

In saucepan, simmer dates and water until mixture is thick and soft, about 4 minutes.

In mixing bowl, cream margarine; beat in granulated sugar, mixing well. Beat in egg yolks and vanilla until well mixed. Beat in all-purpose and whole-wheat flours and baking powder until mixed. Pat into lightly greased 9-inch (2.5 L) square cake pan. Spread date paste on top.

In bowl, beat egg whites until soft peaks form; gradually beat in brown sugar until stiff peaks form. Spread over date mixture. Sprinkle with almonds (if using). Bake in 350°F (180°C) oven for 30 to 35 minutes or until golden.

MAKES 25 SQUARES

MAKE AHEAD: Squares are best the same day but can be stored in airtight container for up to 5 days or frozen for up to 3 weeks.

PER SQUARE: 115 calories, 2 g protein, 3 g total fat, 0 g saturated fat, 15 mg cholesterol, 22 g carbohydrate, 2 g fibre, 41 mg sodium, 122 mg potassium

Pineapple Carrot Bars

These delicious squares will be especially appreciated by those who don't like overly sweet desserts. They lasted about 10 minutes in my house!

½ cup	packed brown sugar	125 mL
2 tbsp	canola oil	25 mL
1 tsp	pure vanilla extract	5 mL
1	egg	1
1 cup	whole-wheat flour	250 mL
1 tbsp	cinnamon	15 mL
1 tsp	baking powder	5 mL
1 tsp	baking soda	5 mL
1 cup	finely grated carrots	250 mL
⅔ cup	drained crushed unsweetened pineapple	150 mL
½ cup	raisins	125 mL
¼ cup	low-fat milk	50 mL

In large bowl, combine sugar, oil, vanilla and egg. Stir well and set aside.

In separate bowl, combine flour, cinnamon, baking powder and baking soda; add to sugar mixture, stirring well. Stir in carrots, pineapple, raisins and milk.

Pat mixture into 13- × 9-inch (3.5 L) baking pan lightly coated with cooking spray. Bake in 350°F (180°C) oven for 25 minutes or until top is golden. Let cool before cutting into bars.

MAKES 24 BARS

MAKE AHEAD: Store in refrigerator, loosely covered, for up to 2 days.

PER BAR: 65 calories, 1 g protein, 2 g total fat, 0 g saturated fat, 8 mg cholesterol, 12 g carbohydrate, 1 g fibre, 74 mg sodium, 87 mg potassium

Cranberry Apricot Bars

Packed with fruit and fibre, these muffin-like bars are perfect for a breakfast on the run, a lunch-box treat or a quick snack.

2 cups	bran flakes	500 mL
1 cup	whole-wheat flour	250 mL
⅔ cup	packed brown sugar or half sugar and half Splenda*	150 mL
2 tsp	baking soda	10 mL
½ tsp or less	salt	2 mL or less
1 cup	buttermilk or soured low-fat milk**	250 mL
¼ cup	canola oil	50 mL
2	eggs	2
	Grated rind of 1 orange	
1 cup	chopped dried apricots	250 mL
1 cup	dried cranberries or chopped dates	250 mL
⅓ cup	chopped almonds	75 mL

In food processor, combine bran flakes, flour, sugar, baking soda and salt; process for 1 second.

Add buttermilk, oil, eggs and orange rind; process until blended. Stir in apricots, dates and almonds.

Spread in greased 13- × 9-inch (3.5 L) baking dish. Bake in 375°F (190°C) oven for 25 minutes or until toothpick inserted in centre comes out clean. Let cool before cutting into squares.

MAKES 20 SQUARES

*Splenda is a no-calorie sweetener that works in baked goods, the same as sugar.

**To sour milk, spoon 1 tbsp (15 mL) fresh lemon juice or white vinegar into measuring cup; add milk to measure 1 cup (250 mL) and let stand for 10 minutes.

MAKE AHEAD: Wrap individual squares in plastic wrap and store in cookie tin for up to 2 days or freeze for up to 1 month.

NOTE: For a softer, moister bar, soak apricots in hot water for 10 minutes, then drain, before using.

PER SQUARE: 146 calories, 3 g protein, 5 g total fat, 1 g saturated fat, 19 mg cholesterol, 26 g carbohydrate, 3 g fibre, 234 mg sodium, 238 mg potassium

DESSERTS

DESSERT SAUCES

Raisin Cupcakes with Lemon Icing

This recipe is from my mother-in-law, Olive Lindsay. The cupcakes are a hit with all the grandchildren.

1½ cups	raisins	375 mL
1½ cups	all-purpose flour	375 mL
1 tsp	baking soda	5 mL
1 tsp	cinnamon	5 mL
¼ tsp	ground cloves	1 mL
¾ cup	granulated sugar	175 mL
¼ cup	low-fat plain yogurt or buttermilk	50 mL
2 tbsp	soft margarine	25 mL
1	egg, beaten	1

LEMON ICING

¾ cup	sifted icing sugar	175 mL
1 tbsp	low-fat plain yogurt	15 mL
½ tsp	grated lemon rind	2 mL
½ tsp	fresh lemon juice	2 mL

PER CUPCAKE: 216 calories, 3 g protein, 3 g total fat, 0 g saturated fat, 16 mg cholesterol, 47 g carbohydrate, 1 g fibre, 143 mg sodium, 176 mg potassium

Spray muffin tins with nonstick coating or line with paper liners. In saucepan, cover raisins with water; bring to boil. Reduce heat and simmer for 20 minutes; drain, reserving ½ cup (125 mL) liquid. Let cool.

In bowl, sift together flour, baking soda, cinnamon and cloves.

In separate large bowl, beat sugar, yogurt and margarine until well mixed. Add egg and beat well. Stir in reserved cooled liquid alternately with dry ingredients, making two additions of each. Add cooled raisins and mix well.

Spoon into prepared muffin tins. Bake in 375°F (190°C) oven for 20 to 25 minutes or until toothpick inserted in centre comes out clean. Let cool.

LEMON ICING: In small bowl, combine sugar, yogurt, lemon rind and juice; mix until smooth. Spread on cooled cupcakes.

MAKES 12 CUPCAKES

Chocolate Banana Cupcakes

Perfect for a family celebration, these attractive cupcakes make good use of chocolate chips because a few go a long way when studding the tops.

¾ cup	mashed ripe bananas (2 small)	175 mL
¾ cup	buttermilk	175 mL
¾ cup	packed brown sugar	175 mL
¼ cup	corn syrup	50 mL
3 tbsp	canola oil	50 mL
2 tsp	pure vanilla extract	10 mL
1¾ cups	all-purpose flour	425 mL
¼ cup	unsweetened cocoa powder, sifted	50 mL
1 tsp	baking soda	5 mL
½ tsp	salt	2 mL
½ cup	chocolate chips	125 mL
1 tbsp	icing sugar	15 mL

In bowl, mix bananas, buttermilk, brown sugar, corn syrup, oil and vanilla.

In another bowl, mix together flour, cocoa, baking soda and salt; sprinkle over banana mixture and stir just until moistened.

Spray muffin pans with nonstick cooking spray; spoon in batter, filling two-thirds full. Sprinkle chocolate chips over top. Bake in 400°F (200°C) oven for 15 to 20 minutes or until toothpick inserted in centre comes out clean. Let cool in pans on rack. Sift icing sugar over top.

MAKES 12 CUPCAKES

MAKE AHEAD: Store in airtight container for up to 2 days.

NOTE: Buttermilk has the same fat content as the milk it is made from—skim, 1% or 2%, so it isn't high in fat.

PER CUPCAKE: 228 calories, 3 g protein, 6 g total fat, 2 g saturated fat, 1 mg cholesterol, 43 g carbohydrate, 2 g fibre, 234 mg sodium, 198 mg potassium

Orange Sponge Cake

This cake is delicious on its own, iced with Orange Icing (p. 395) or served with sorbet, fresh fruit or dessert sauces—especially Raspberry Coulis (p. 425). Make sure you use large eggs at room temperature for this recipe.

4	eggs, separated	4
¾ cup	granulated sugar	175 mL
1 tbsp	grated orange rind	15 mL
½ cup	fresh orange juice	125 mL
1 cup	all-purpose flour	250 mL
1 tsp	baking powder	5 mL
Pinch	salt	Pinch
2 tsp	icing sugar	10 mL

In mixing bowl, beat together egg yolks, sugar, and orange rind and juice until very light in colour. Add flour and baking powder; beat until combined.

In separate bowl, beat egg whites and salt until stiff peaks form. Mix a small amount of whites into yolk mixture, then fold yolk mixture into whites.

Pour batter into ungreased 10-inch (4 L) tube pan with removable bottom. Bake in 325°F (160°C) oven for 45 to 55 minutes or until golden brown and cake springs back when lightly touched. Invert and let hang to cool completely before removing from pan. Sift icing sugar over top.

MAKES 12 SLICES

NOTE: To make a larger cake, double recipe. Baking time will then be 55 minutes.

PER SLICE: 118 calories, 3 g protein, 2 g total fat, 1 g saturated fat, 62 mg cholesterol, 22 g carbohydrate, 0 g fibre, 46 mg sodium, 54 mg potassium

Elizabeth Baird's Chocolate Angel Food Cake

My friend Elizabeth Baird, former food director of *Canadian Living* magazine, made this fabulous cake for my birthday. More flavourful than regular angel food cake, it is still nearly fat-free. Serve with Vanilla Cream (p. 429) and fresh berries.

¾ cup	sifted cake-and-pastry flour	175 mL
1½ cups	granulated sugar	375 mL
¼ cup	unsweetened cocoa powder	50 mL
1½ cups	egg whites (about 11 large eggs), at room temperature	375 mL
1 tbsp	fresh lemon juice	15 mL
1 tsp	cream of tartar	5 mL
½ tsp or less	salt	2 mL or less
1 tsp	pure vanilla extract	5 mL
½ tsp	almond extract	2 mL
	Icing sugar	

Onto piece of waxed paper, sift together flour, ¾ cup (175 mL) of the sugar, and cocoa. Sift again; set aside.

In large nonplastic bowl, beat egg whites until foamy. Add lemon juice, cream of tartar and salt; beat until soft peaks form. Gradually add remaining sugar, 2 tbsp (25 mL) at a time, beating until glossy and stiff peaks form. Sprinkle with vanilla and almond extract. Sift one-quarter of the cocoa mixture at a time over egg whites, folding in each addition with rubber spatula.

Scrape into ungreased 10-inch (4 L) angel food tube pan. Run spatula through batter to eliminate large air pockets; smooth top. Bake in 350°F (180°C) oven for 40 to 45 minutes or until cake springs back when lightly touched.

Invert pan onto neck of large bottle unless pan has legs attached; let cake hang until cool. Loosen edges with knife; remove cake from pan. Place on plate; place doily over top and dust with icing sugar. Remove doily.

MAKES 12 SLICES

MAKE AHEAD: Store at room temperature for up to 2 days or freeze for up to 1 month.

VARIATION:

Traditional Angel Food Cake
Prepare above recipe using 1¼ cups (300 mL) sifted cake-and-pastry flour; omit cocoa powder.

PER SLICE: 141 calories, 4 g protein, 0 g total fat, 0 g saturated fat, 0 mg cholesterol, 31 g carbohydrate, 1 g fibre, 149 mg sodium, 139 mg potassium

Gingerbread Cake

Grated fresh gingerroot adds an extra flavour dimension to this moist cake, but ground ginger also works well. This cake is delicious topped with stewed sliced apples (see Apple Filling in Apple-Pecan Phyllo Crisps, p. 406), or serve with fresh fruit, Microwave Rhubarb Sauce (p. 421), Caramel Sauce (p. 430) or ice cream.

½ cup	packed brown sugar	125 mL
¼ cup	soft margarine	50 mL
	Grated rind of 1 orange	
1	egg	1
1	egg white	1
1 cup	applesauce	250 mL
½ cup	fancy molasses	125 mL
¼ cup	grated gingerroot	50 mL
1½ cups	sifted cake-and-pastry flour	375 mL
1 tsp	baking soda	5 mL
1 tsp	baking powder	5 mL
½ tsp	salt	2 mL

In bowl and using electric mixer, beat brown sugar, margarine and orange rind until smooth. Beat in egg and egg white, beating well after each addition. Mix in applesauce, molasses and gingerroot until smooth.

In a separate bowl combine flour, baking soda, baking powder and salt; gradually beat into sugar mixture, beating for 2 to 3 minutes.

Transfer to 8-inch (2 L) square cake pan. Bake in 350°F (180°C) oven for 40 minutes or until cake pulls away from sides of pan and toothpick inserted in centre comes out clean. Serve warm or cold.

MAKES 12 SLICES

MAKE AHEAD: Cover with foil and refrigerate for up to 4 days or freeze for up to 2 weeks.

VARIATION: Add 2 tsp (10 mL) ground ginger and 1 tsp (5 mL) cinnamon to the dry ingredients instead of using fresh gingerroot.

PER SLICE: 173 calories, 3 g protein, 5 g total fat, 1 g saturated fat, 16 mg cholesterol, 32 g carbohydrate, 2 g fibre, 298 mg sodium, 319 mg potassium

Pumpkin Spice Cake

Serve this flavourful, moist cake with coffee or for dessert with fruit or with Lemon Yogurt Cream (p. 429) or Caramel Sauce (p. 430). Buttermilk and pumpkin purée take the place of fat in this dark, spicy, raisin-studded cake.

1¾ cups	granulated sugar or 1 cup sugar plus ¾ cup (175 mL) Splenda	425 mL
¼ cup	soft margarine	50 mL
1	egg	1
¾ cup	buttermilk	175 mL
1	can (14 oz/398 mL) pumpkin purée	1
1 tbsp	grated orange rind	15 mL
1 tsp	pure vanilla extract	5 mL
1½ cups	all-purpose flour	375 mL
1½ cups	whole-wheat flour	375 mL
2 tsp	cinnamon	10 mL
2 tsp	baking powder	10 mL
1 tsp	baking soda	5 mL
½ tsp	each ground ginger, nutmeg and salt	2 mL
1 cup	raisins	250 mL

GLAZE

| ¼ cup | icing sugar or Splenda | 50 mL |
| 1½ tsp | orange juice | 7 mL |

Grease and flour 10-inch (25 cm) Bundt pan.

In bowl, beat sugar and Splenda (if using) with margarine; beat in egg until light. Beat in buttermilk, pumpkin, orange rind and vanilla.

Combine all-purpose and whole-wheat flours, cinnamon, baking powder, baking soda, ginger, nutmeg, salt and raisins; stir into pumpkin mixture just until combined.

Pour into pan; bake in 325°F (160°C) oven for 60 to 65 minutes or until toothpick inserted in centre comes out clean. Let cool on rack for 20 minutes; remove from pan.

GLAZE: Blend icing sugar with orange juice; drizzle over cooled cake.

MAKES 24 SMALL SLICES

MAKE AHEAD: Store in airtight container for up to 2 days or freeze for up to 1 month.

PER SLICE: 164 calories, 3 g protein, 3 g total fat, 0 g saturated fat, 8 mg cholesterol, 34 g carbohydrate, 2 g fibre, 165 mg sodium, 139 mg potassium

Applesauce Cranberry Cake

Full of flavour, this delicious moist cake looks attractive when made in a Bundt or tube pan. It's easy to make and keeps well. Serve with fresh fruit desserts, poached pears or sorbets.

1¾ cups	granulated sugar	425 mL
¼ cup	soft margarine, at room temperature	50 mL
1	egg	1
½ cup	low-fat plain yogurt	125 mL
2 cups	applesauce	500 mL
1 tsp	pure vanilla extract	5 mL
	Grated rind of 1 medium orange	
1½ cups	all-purpose flour	375 mL
1¼ cups	whole-wheat flour	300 mL
1 cup	dried cranberries or raisins	250 mL
¼ cup	wheat bran	50 mL
4 tsp	cinnamon	20 mL
2 tsp	baking soda	10 mL
½ tsp	ground nutmeg	2 mL

Lightly grease and flour a 10-inch (25 cm) Bundt pan.

In mixing bowl, beat sugar with margarine until well mixed. Beat in egg until light in colour. Beat in yogurt until mixed. Beat in applesauce, vanilla and orange rind.

In separate bowl, combine all-purpose and whole-wheat flours, cranberries, bran, cinnamon, baking soda and nutmeg; stir to mix. Pour over applesauce mixture and stir just until combined.

Pour into prepared pan and bake in 325°F (160°C) oven for 60 to 70 minutes or until toothpick inserted in centre comes out clean. Let cool in pan on rack for 20 minutes, then turn out onto rack and let cool completely.

MAKES 24 SMALL SLICES

MAKE AHEAD: Wrap well and refrigerate for up to 4 days or freeze for up to 1 month.

VARIATIONS: Top with low-fat Lemon Icing (p. 395) or Orange Icing (p. 395). Applesauce Cranberry Cake with either icing adds 27 calories per serving.

PER SLICE: 159 calories, 2 g protein, 3 g total fat, 0 g saturated fat, 8 mg cholesterol, 33 g carbohydrate, 2 g fibre, 138 mg sodium, 81 mg potassium

Apricot Almond Cake

This amazingly delicious moist cake is a lovely dessert accompanied by any fresh fruit, or serve as a coffee cake.

1½ cups	all-purpose flour	375 mL
¾ cup	granulated sugar or Splenda	175 mL
1 tsp	baking soda	5 mL
½ tsp or less	salt	2 mL or less
1	egg, lightly beaten	1
¾ cup	soured low-fat milk* or buttermilk	175 mL
¼ cup	canola oil	50 mL
½ tsp	almond extract	2 mL
8	fresh apricots (1 lb/500 g), chopped, or 1 can (14 oz/398 mL) apricots, thoroughly drained and chopped	8
3 tbsp	sliced almonds	50 mL

In large bowl, combine flour, sugar, baking soda and salt. Add egg, milk, oil and almond extract. Beat at medium speed until smooth, about 1 minute. Stir in apricots.

Spread in 8-inch (2 L) square cake pan lightly coated with cooking spray. Sprinkle almonds over top. Bake in 350°F (180°C) oven for 50 to 55 minutes or until toothpick inserted in centre comes out clean.

MAKES 12 SLICES

*To sour milk, spoon 2 tsp (10 mL) fresh lemon juice or white vinegar into measuring cup; add milk to measure ¾ cup (175 mL) and let stand for 10 minutes.

MAKE AHEAD: Cover with foil and store for 3 days or freeze for up to 2 weeks.

NOTE: If using canned apricots, be sure to first drain them very well on paper towels.

VARIATION: Instead of using high-fat whipped cream for a dessert topping, add sugar to taste to extra-thick yogurt and flavour with vanilla, liqueur or grated lemon rind. A deliciously low-fat alternative!

PER SLICE: 178 calories, 3 g protein, 6 g total fat, 1 g saturated fat, 16 mg cholesterol, 28 g carbohydrate, 1 g fibre, 215 mg sodium, 117 mg potassium

Prune Cake with Lemon Icing

Orange rind and juicy cooked prunes are a winning combination in this easy-to-make cake. It's ideal for dessert, along with fresh fruit, for packed lunches or for feeding a crowd of kids. Sprinkle it with icing sugar or ice with Lemon Icing (p. 395).

1½ cups	prunes	375 mL
¼ cup	soft margarine	50 mL
1 cup	low-fat plain yogurt	250 mL
¾ cup	packed brown sugar	175 mL
⅓ cup	granulated sugar	75 mL
2	eggs	2
1½ cups	all-purpose flour	375 mL
1 cup	whole-wheat flour	250 mL
2 tsp	baking powder	10 mL
1 tsp	cinnamon	5 mL
½ tsp	baking soda	2 mL
½ tsp or less	salt	2 mL or less
	Grated rind of 1 orange	
	Lemon Icing (p. 395) (optional)	

In saucepan or microwaveable dish, cover prunes with water and bring to boil. Let stand for 15 minutes or until cool; drain. Remove pits and chop prunes to make about 1½ cups (375 mL); set aside.

In mixing bowl, cream margarine; beat in yogurt and brown and granulated sugars until smooth. Beat in eggs until well mixed. Add all-purpose and whole-wheat flours, baking powder, cinnamon, baking soda, salt and orange rind; beat well. Stir in prunes.

Pour into lightly greased and floured 10-inch (25 cm) springform pan. Bake in 350°F (180°C) oven for 40 minutes or until toothpick inserted in centre comes out clean.

When cool, ice with Lemon Icing if desired.

MAKES 16 SMALL SLICES

MAKE AHEAD: Wrap well and store at room temperature for up to 3 days or freeze for up to 1 month. Defrost, wrapped, at room temperature.

NOTE: Prune Cake with Lemon Icing has 252 calories and 4 grams fat per serving.

PER SLICE (without icing):
207 calories, 4 g protein,
4 g total fat, 1 g saturated fat,
24 mg cholesterol,
40 g carbohydrate, 3 g fibre,
212 mg sodium, 246 mg potassium

Banana Cake with Orange Icing

I make this cake when I have overripe bananas to use up. It's delicious with or without icing. My mother often made this cake in a loaf pan.

¼ cup	soft margarine	50 mL
¾ cup	granulated sugar	175 mL
2	eggs	2
1 cup	mashed ripe bananas (about 3)	250 mL
1 tsp	grated orange rind (optional)	5 mL
1 tsp	pure vanilla extract	5 mL
2 cups	all-purpose flour	500 mL
2 tsp	baking powder	10 mL
1 tsp	baking soda	5 mL
½ cup	buttermilk or soured low-fat milk*	125 mL

ORANGE ICING

1½ cups	icing sugar	375 mL
2 tbsp	low-fat plain yogurt	25 mL
1 tsp	grated orange rind	5 mL
1 tsp	fresh orange juice	5 mL

In bowl, cream margarine; add sugar and beat well. Add eggs one at a time, beating well after each addition. Beat in bananas, orange rind (if using) and vanilla.

In a separate bowl mix together flour, baking powder and baking soda; beat into egg mixture alternately with buttermilk. Spray 9-inch (23 cm) springform or square pan with nonstick coating; spoon in batter.

Bake in 350°F (180°C) oven for 40 minutes or until cake springs back when pressed in centre or until toothpick inserted in centre comes out clean. Let cool in pan for 10 minutes; remove from pan and let cool on rack.

ORANGE ICING: In small bowl, combine sugar, yogurt, orange rind and juice; mix until smooth. Spread over cake. Cut into wedges.

MAKES 12 SLICES

*To sour milk, spoon 2 tsp (10 mL) fresh lemon juice or white vinegar into measuring cup; add milk to measure ½ cup (125 mL) and let stand for 10 minutes.

VARIATION:

Lemon Icing
Substitute lemon rind and juice for the orange rind and juice.

PER SLICE: 254 calories, 4 g protein, 5 g total fat, 1 g saturated fat, 31 mg cholesterol, 49 g carbohydrate, 1 g fibre, 230 mg sodium, 134 mg potassium

Lemon Tea Loaf

This tangy cake is an excellent choice to serve for dessert with fresh fruit or sorbet.

1 cup	granulated sugar	250 mL
¼ cup	soft margarine	50 mL
1	egg	1
2 tbsp	low-fat plain yogurt	25 mL
½ cup	low-fat milk	125 mL
1½ cups	all-purpose flour	375 mL
1 tsp	baking powder	5 mL
	Grated rind of 1 lemon	

GLAZE

	Juice of 1 lemon	
¼ cup	granulated sugar	50 mL

PER SLICE: 139 calories,
2 g protein, 3 g total fat,
1 g saturated fat, 12 mg cholesterol,
26 g carbohydrate, 0 g fibre,
53 mg sodium, 39 mg potassium

Line 8- × 4-inch (1.5 L) loaf pan with foil; grease lightly.

In large bowl, cream sugar and margarine. Beat in egg and yogurt; beat in milk. Mix flour and baking powder; beat into egg mixture until blended. Stir in lemon rind.

Spoon into prepared pan; bake in 350°F (180°C) oven for 1 hour or until toothpick inserted in centre comes out clean. Let cake stand in pan for 3 minutes.

GLAZE: Meanwhile, in small bowl, combine lemon juice and sugar, mixing well; pour over top of warm cake.

Remove foil and cake from pan and place on rack. Loosen foil and let cake cool completely before cutting.

MAKES 16 SMALL SLICES

Cinnamon Coffee Cake

Serve this easy-to-make extra-moist cake with fresh fruit or sorbet for any meal at any time of day.

1 cup	low-fat plain yogurt	250 mL
1 tsp	baking soda	5 mL
¼ cup	soft margarine	50 mL
1 cup	lightly packed brown sugar	250 mL
1	egg	1
1 tsp	pure vanilla extract	5 mL
1½ cups	all-purpose flour	375 mL
2 tsp	baking powder	10 mL

TOPPING

½ cup	lightly packed brown sugar	125 mL
1 tbsp	cinnamon	15 mL

In small bowl, combine yogurt and baking soda, mixing well; set aside. (Mixture will increase in volume.)

In large mixing bowl, beat margarine with sugar until well mixed. Add egg and vanilla; beat well, about 2 minutes. Mix flour and baking powder; add to margarine mixture alternately with yogurt mixture, making 3 additions of dry and 2 of wet. Spread half the batter in greased and floured 9-inch (2.5 L) square cake pan.

TOPPING: Combine sugar and cinnamon, mixing well. Sprinkle half over batter in pan.

Cover with remaining batter. Sprinkle with remaining topping. Bake in 350°F (180°C) oven for 35 minutes or until toothpick inserted in centre comes out clean. Let cool for 10 to 15 minutes in pan. Cut into squares.

MAKES 12 SLICES

MAKE AHEAD: Wrap in foil or plastic wrap and store at room temperature for up to 4 days or freeze for up to 1 month.

PER SLICE: 198 calories, 3 g protein, 5 g total fat, 1 g saturated fat, 16 mg cholesterol, 36 g carbohydrate, 1 g fibre, 236 mg sodium, 156 mg potassium

Streusel Plum Cake

Plums cooked in desserts are a favourite of mine. I like this cake because it isn't too sweet yet full of flavour. The glaze takes only minutes to prepare and makes the cake look fancy. Don't use a smaller pan than suggested here.

¼ cup	soft margarine	50 mL
¾ cup	granulated sugar	175 mL
2	eggs, separated	2
1¼ cups	all-purpose flour	300 mL
1 tsp	baking powder	5 mL
⅓ cup	low-fat milk	75 mL
3 cups	quartered fresh ripe plums or 2 cans (each 14 oz/398 mL) drained and halved plums	750 mL

TOPPING

½ cup	packed brown sugar	125 mL
1 tbsp	soft margarine	15 mL
1 tsp	cinnamon	5 mL

GLAZE (optional)

¼ cup	icing sugar	50 mL
1 tsp	milk	5 mL
¼ tsp	pure vanilla extract	1 mL

Lightly grease a 9-inch (2.5 L) or 10-inch (3 L) square cake pan or use a lightly greased springform pan.

In large bowl, cream together margarine, sugar and egg yolks until fluffy. Combine flour and baking powder; beat into egg mixture alternately with milk. Beat egg whites until stiff but not dry; fold into batter. Turn into prepared pan. Arrange plums on top.

TOPPING: In small bowl, combine brown sugar, margarine and cinnamon; mix well and sprinkle over fruit.

Bake in 350°F (180°C) oven for 35 to 45 minutes or until top is golden and toothpick inserted into cake comes out clean.

GLAZE: Combine icing sugar, milk and vanilla; mix well. Drizzle over cool cake.

MAKES 10 SLICES

NOTE: Any variety of plum works well in this recipe.

VARIATIONS:

Peach Streusel Cake
Instead of plums, use 2 to 3 fresh peaches sliced into wedges or 1 can (14 oz/398 mL) sliced peaches, thoroughly drained.

Apple Streusel Cake
Instead of plums, use 2 to 3 apples sliced into thin wedges. (If apples are unpeeled, the fibre content is higher.)

Pear Streusel Cake
Instead of plums, use 2 pears sliced into wedges or 1 can (14 oz/398 mL) sliced pears, thoroughly drained.

PER SLICE (without glaze):
249 calories, 4 g protein, 7 g total fat, 1 g saturated fat, 38 mg cholesterol, 44 g carbohydrate, 1 g fibre, 128 mg sodium, 163 mg potassium

Easy Chocolate Cake with Chocolate Buttermilk Icing

This dense, rich chocolate cake has all the taste but about half the fat of a regular chocolate cake. For the most intense chocolate flavour, use Dutch process unsweetened cocoa powder. Domestic brands are available in supermarkets.

2 tbsp	espresso powder or instant coffee granules	25 mL
½ cup	boiling water	125 mL
2¼ cups	all-purpose flour	550 mL
2 cups	granulated sugar	500 mL
¾ cup	unsweetened cocoa powder, sifted	175 mL
1½ tsp	each baking powder and baking soda	7 mL
½ tsp or less	salt	2 mL or less
1¾ cups	buttermilk	425 mL
2	eggs, beaten	2
¼ cup	canola oil	50 mL
2 tsp	pure vanilla extract	10 mL

CHOCOLATE BUTTERMILK ICING

½ cup	granulated sugar	125 mL
½ cup	unsweetened cocoa powder, sifted	125 mL
½ cup	buttermilk	125 mL
½ tsp	pure vanilla extract	3 mL

Dissolve espresso powder in boiling water; let cool. Grease or spray 13- × 9 inch (3.5 L) baking dish with nonstick cooking spray; line bottom with waxed paper.

In large bowl, mix flour, sugar, cocoa, baking powder, baking soda and salt. Beat in buttermilk, eggs, oil, vanilla and espresso mixture; beat at medium speed for 2 minutes.

Pour into prepared pan. Bake in 350°F (180°C) oven for 40 to 45 minutes or until top springs back when lightly touched. Let cool in pan on rack for 20 minutes. Remove from pan; let cool completely on rack. Spread with chocolate icing.

CHOCOLATE BUTTERMILK ICING: In small heavy saucepan, mix sugar with cocoa; whisk in buttermilk until smooth. Stirring constantly, cook over medium heat until simmering; cook, stirring constantly, for 2 minutes. Remove from heat; stir in vanilla. Let cool for 2 hours. (Icing will thicken upon cooling.)

MAKES 16 SMALL SLICES (WITH 1 CUP/250 mL ICING)

MAKE AHEAD: Cover and store cake for up to 2 days. Icing can be prepared up to 5 days in advance, covered by placing plastic wrap directly on surface.

NOTE: Adding coffee to chocolate dishes enhances the chocolate flavour.

PER SLICE: 274 calories, 5 g protein, 5 g total fat, 1 g saturated fat, 24 mg cholesterol, 51 g carbohydrate, 3 g fibre, 266 mg sodium, 198 mg potassium

Peach Crêpes with Grand Marnier Sauce

Crêpes are a hit any time of the year, but this version is particularly good in peach season. At other times, use 1½ cups (375 mL) fresh sliced strawberries. For a fancy dessert, it is surprisingly low in calories.

½ cup	low-fat plain yogurt	125 mL
1 tbsp	maple syrup or honey	15 mL
3	fresh peaches, peeled and sliced	3

GRAND MARNIER SAUCE

¾ cup	orange juice	175 mL
1 tbsp	cornstarch	15 mL
3 tbsp	Grand Marnier, Drambuie, or other orange liqueur	50 mL

8	Dessert Crêpes (p. 402)	8
	Sliced peaches, blueberries or other fresh berries for garnish	

In bowl, combine yogurt with syrup; stir until smooth. Add peaches and mix lightly.

GRAND MARNIER SAUCE: In saucepan, combine orange juice with cornstarch; whisk until smooth. Cook over medium heat, stirring constantly, until mixture thickens and comes to a boil; simmer for 2 minutes. Remove from heat and stir in liqueur.

Wrap crêpes in paper towels and heat in microwave on High for 30 seconds. Or heat in 350°F (180°C) oven for 5 to 10 minutes or until warm.

Spoon some peach mixture onto each crêpe; roll up and place on individual plates. Drizzle with warm sauce and garnish with fresh fruit.

MAKES 8 CRÊPES

PER CRÊPE: 113 calories, 3 g protein, 1 g total fat, 0 g saturated fat, 1 mg cholesterol, 20 g carbohydrate, 1 g fibre, 33 mg sodium, 194 mg potassium

Chocolate Crêpes with Banana Cream Filling

This is a fabulous light but fancy dessert. Even though there is a little bit of whipped cream in it, it is relatively low in fat—it has two egg whites instead of a whole egg and cocoa powder instead of higher-fat chocolate.

½ cup	Easy Chocolate Sauce (p. 431)	125 mL

CHOCOLATE CRÊPES

⅓ cup	all-purpose flour	75 mL
2 tbsp	unsweetened cocoa powder	25 mL
1 tbsp	granulated sugar or Splenda	15 mL
Pinch	salt	Pinch
2	egg whites, lightly beaten	2
⅓ cup	low-fat milk	75 mL
¼ cup	water	50 mL
1 tsp	soft margarine	5 mL

BANANA CREAM FILLING

¼ cup	whipping cream	60 mL
½ cup	low-fat plain yogurt or extra-thick yogurt	125 mL
2 tbsp	granulated sugar or Splenda	25 mL
½ tsp	pure vanilla extract	2 mL
3	bananas, sliced	3

In bowl, combine flour, cocoa, sugar and salt; make a well in centre. Add egg whites and whisk lightly to combine. Gradually whisk in milk and water until smooth.

Heat small nonstick crêpe pan or skillet over medium heat; brush with some of the margarine. For each crêpe, pour in 2 tbsp (25 mL) batter, swirling to cover bottom of pan; pour off any excess. Cook until edges begin to curl and crêpe no longer sticks; turn and cook for 30 seconds. Remove and set aside. Repeat with remaining batter, brushing pan with margarine as necessary.

BANANA CREAM FILLING: Whip cream; stir in yogurt, sugar and vanilla.

Spread about 2 tbsp (25 mL) filling over one half of each crêpe. Arrange overlapping banana slices over half of filling. Fold uncovered crêpe in half over filling; fold in half again. Arrange on dessert plates; drizzle with chocolate sauce.

MAKES 8 CRÊPES

MAKE AHEAD: Stack unfilled crêpes between waxed paper, wrap and refrigerate for up to 1 day or freeze for up to 1 month.

VARIATION: To reduce the amount of fat in the filling, use 1 cup (250 mL) extra-thick yogurt instead of whipping cream and increase sugar to ¼ cup (50 mL).

PER CRÊPE (with sauce):
146 calories, 4 g protein,
4 g total fat, 2 g saturated fat,
11 mg cholesterol,
26 g carbohydrate, 2 g fibre,
40 mg sodium, 284 mg potassium

Basic Crêpes

This all-purpose crêpe batter is low in cholesterol and fat. If you're on a low-cholesterol diet, use 2 whites instead of a whole egg. Prepare a batch of crêpes when you have time; freeze them, and you'll be able to make a main course such as Curried Chicken Crêpes (p. 245) or a luscious dessert of Peach Crêpes with Grand Marnier Sauce (p. 400) at a moment's notice.

½ cup	all-purpose flour	125 mL
Pinch	salt	Pinch
2	egg whites or 1 egg, lightly beaten	2
⅓ cup	low-fat milk	75 mL
⅓ cup	water	75 mL
½ tsp	soft margarine	2 mL

In bowl, combine flour and salt. Make a well in centre and add egg whites. While whisking, gradually add milk and water, whisking until mixture is smooth.

Heat small nonstick skillet or crêpe pan (6 to 8 inches/15 to 20 cm) over medium-high heat. Add margarine and brush over bottom of pan. Add 2 tbsp (25 mL) batter, swirling to lightly coat bottom of pan; pour off any excess. Cook until edges begin to curl and crêpe no longer sticks to pan. Turn crêpe and cook for a few seconds or until golden. Remove from pan and set aside. Repeat with remaining batter. You shouldn't need to add any more margarine.

MAKES EIGHT 8-INCH (20 CM) CRÊPES

VARIATION:

Dessert Crêpes
Add 2 tsp (10 mL) granulated sugar and ½ tsp (2 mL) each grated orange and lemon rind to batter.

MAKE AHEAD: Crêpes can be made in advance; stack between waxed paper and refrigerate for 1 day or freeze up to 1 month.

PER CRÊPE: 39 calories, 2 g protein, 0 g total fat, 0 g saturated fat, 1 mg cholesterol, 7 g carbohydrate, 0 g fibre, 22 mg sodium, 36 mg potassium

Berries with Orange Cream

Spoon this low-fat creamy sauce over juicy fresh strawberries. You'll enjoy it so much you'll want to try it over other fresh berries or sliced fruit or combinations of both. I love this sauce made with Grand Marnier; it's also good with rum or concentrated frozen orange juice.

| 3 cups | small strawberries | 750 mL |

ORANGE CREAM

½ cup	light sour cream	125 mL
3 tbsp	granulated sugar	50 mL
1 tbsp	orange liqueur or rum or concentrated frozen orange juice	15 mL
1 tbsp	low-fat plain yogurt	15 mL
½ tsp	grated orange rind	2 mL

ORANGE CREAM: Combine sour cream, sugar, orange liqueur, yogurt and orange rind; mix well.

Spoon sauce over individual bowls of berries.

MAKES 4 SERVINGS

MAKE AHEAD: Cover and refrigerate sauce for up to 4 days.

NOTE: Berries with ice cream makes a lovely dessert, but read the nutrition labels on ice cream products before buying—the fat and calorie content varies widely.

PER SERVING: 118 calories, 2 g protein, 2 g total fat, 1 g saturated fat, 7 mg cholesterol, 22 g carbohydrate, 2 g fibre, 35 mg sodium, 239 mg potassium

Honey-Lime Fruit Dip

Delicious at the beginning or end of a meal, this refreshing dip can be made with lime or lemon. Choose a colourful variety of fruit—melon and pineapple chunks, strawberries, grapes, wedges of apples, mango, papaya, pears and peaches, sections of orange or other seasonal fresh fruit. Arrange the fruit on a large platter with the dip in the centre and let guests help themselves.

1 cup	plain yogurt (preferably extra-thick or drained)	250 mL
3 tbsp	liquid honey	50 mL
	Grated rind of 1 lime	
1 tbsp	fresh lime juice	15 mL

In bowl, combine yogurt, honey and lime rind and juice; mix well. Cover and refrigerate for 30 minutes. (Mixture will thicken upon standing.) Before serving, taste and add more honey if necessary.

MAKES 4 SERVINGS, ¼ CUP (50 mL) EACH

MAKE AHEAD: Cover and refrigerate for up to 2 days.

VARIATION:

Honey Lime Sauce
This dip is equally delicious as a sauce for fruit desserts such as Plum Tart (p. 420), Rhubarb Apple Crisp (p. 414) or Peach Blueberry Crisp (p. 413).

NOTE: To drain yogurt, place 2 cups (500 mL) plain Balkan-style yogurt or a yogurt made without gelatin into sieve lined with cheesecloth or paper towel or yogurt drainer. Set sieve over bowl and refrigerate for 2 to 4 hours or until yogurt is reduced to 1 cup (250 mL). Discard liquid or use in soups or muffin batters or add to juice.

PER SERVING: 88 calories, 3 g protein, 1 g total fat, 1 g saturated fat, 4 mg cholesterol, 18 g carbohydrate, 0 g fibre, 44 mg sodium, 157 mg potassium

Mango Fool

Serve this creamy dessert garnished with sliced mango and any other fruit you like—try strawberries or mandarin oranges. Because there is no other fat in it, this dessert has room for a little whipping cream while still fitting into a healthy diet.

1½ cups	low-fat plain yogurt (no gelatin)	375 mL
1	ripe large mango	1
¼ cup	granulated sugar or Splenda	50 mL
¼ cup	whipping cream	60 mL

GARNISH (optional)

| 1 | mango, sliced | 1 |
| 1 cup | mandarin orange segments or small strawberries | 250 mL |

In cheesecloth-lined sieve set over bowl, drain yogurt in refrigerator for 1 to 2 hours or until yogurt is reduced to ¾ cup (175 mL). Discard liquid.

Peel mango; slice fruit from pit and purée in food processor. (You should have about 1¼ cups/300 mL.) Stir in sugar and yogurt. Whip cream; fold into mango mixture.

GARNISH: Serve in stemmed glasses or on dessert plates and top or surround with sliced mango, berries and/or orange segments.

MAKES 4 SERVINGS

MAKE AHEAD: Cover and refrigerate mango mixture for up to 4 hours. Transfer to serving dishes and garnish just before serving.

VARIATIONS:

Cherry Fool
Instead of mango, use 1 package (10 oz/300 g) frozen sweet dark pitted cherries, thawed and drained; purée. Reduce sugar to 2 tbsp (25 mL) and add 1 tbsp (15 mL) fresh lemon juice. Garnish with cherries.

Rhubarb Fool
Instead of mango, substitute 1 cup (250 mL) Microwave Rhubarb Sauce (made without strawberries) or Stewed Rhubarb (see p. 421). Garnish with raspberries, strawberries and/or blueberries.

PER SERVING: 193 calories, 5 g protein, 6 g total fat, 4 g saturated fat, 23 mg cholesterol, 30 g carbohydrate, 1 g fibre, 72 mg sodium, 330 mg potassium

Chris Klugman's Orange Yogurt Bavarian

Ontario chef Chris Klugman gave me the recipe for this lovely light dessert.

1	envelope unflavoured gelatin	1
1 cup	orange juice	250 mL
½ cup	low-fat plain yogurt	125 mL
	Grated rind of 1 orange	
2	egg whites	2
½ cup	granulated sugar	125 mL
¼ cup	skim milk	50 mL

In bowl, sprinkle gelatin over orange juice; let stand for 5 minutes to soften. Heat over simmering water until gelatin dissolves. Refrigerate until syrupy; stir in yogurt and orange rind until smooth.

In separate bowl, beat egg whites until soft peaks form; gradually beat in sugar until stiff peaks form. In another bowl, beat milk until frothy and tripled in volume.

Fold beaten whites, then whipped milk into orange mixture. Spoon into individual ramekins or serving dishes. Refrigerate until set, about 2 hours.

MAKES 8 SERVINGS, ½ CUP (125 mL) EACH

MAKE AHEAD: Prepare up to 1 day in advance. Store, covered, in the refrigerator.

NOTE: Cold skim milk whipped with an electric mixer quickly increases in volume and becomes light and frothy; ½ cup (125 mL) increases to 3 cups (750 mL). Whip just before using, as it will separate if left to stand. Once whipped, beat in about 2 tsp (10 mL) sugar to sweeten.

PER SERVING: 82 calories, 3 g protein, 0 g total fat, 0 g saturated fat, 1 mg cholesterol, 18 g carbohydrate, 0 g fibre, 29 mg sodium, 120 mg potassium

Apple-Pecan Phyllo Crisps

Once you are familiar with using phyllo pastry, this is a very easy—and delicious—dessert to make.

2	sheets phyllo pastry	2
2 tsp	soft margarine, melted	10 mL
2 tbsp	chopped pecans, toasted*	25 mL
1½ tsp	icing sugar	7 mL

APPLE FILLING

⅓ cup	packed brown sugar	75 mL
	Grated rind of half a lemon	
1 tbsp	fresh lemon juice	15 mL
½ tsp	cinnamon	2 mL
3 cups	sliced peeled apples	750 mL

Lay single sheet of phyllo on counter; brush with half of the margarine. Using scissors, cut crosswise into three 5-inch (12 cm) wide strips; fold each strip into thirds to form square shape. Using scissors, round off corners and gently mould into muffin cups. Repeat with remaining phyllo to make 6 shells. Bake in 400°F (200°C) oven for 5 minutes or until golden.

APPLE FILLING: In heavy skillet, combine sugar, lemon rind, lemon juice and cinnamon; cook over medium heat until bubbly. Add apples and cook, stirring often, for 5 minutes or until tender; let cool slightly.

Spoon apple mixture into prepared shells. Sprinkle with pecans; sift icing sugar over top. Serve warm or at room temperature.

MAKES 6 SERVINGS

*To toast pecans, cook in small skillet over medium-low heat for 1 to 2 minutes, stirring.

MAKE AHEAD: Store baked phyllo shells in airtight container for up to 3 days. Prepare apple filling up to 6 hours in advance. Spoon into prepared shells just before serving.

VARIATIONS: Fill baked phyllo crisps with fresh berries and drizzle with Lemon Yogurt Cream (p. 429) or fill with sliced bananas and drizzle with Easy Chocolate Sauce (p. 431) or Caramel Sauce (p. 430).

NOTE: Packages of phyllo dough containing about 20 paper-thin sheets are available at most supermarkets. Keep these tips in mind when using:

- Thaw before using.

- Unwrap package just before using. Cover phyllo with damp tea towel. Use sheets as you need them and re-cover. Stack right away to keep from drying out.

- Thoroughly wrap and freeze extra sheets as quickly as possible.

PER SERVING: 133 calories, 1 g protein, 4 g total fat, 0 g saturated fat, 0 mg cholesterol, 26 g carbohydrate, 1 g fibre, 62 mg sodium, 123 mg potassium

Strawberry Pavlova with Lemon Yogurt Sauce

Pavlova is one of my all-time favourite desserts to make. I use strawberries, raspberries, peaches, blueberries or a combination. I used to make it with whipping cream but now use a yogurt-based lemon sauce, which is fabulous.

3	egg whites (at room temperature)	3
Pinch	cream of tartar	Pinch
¾ cup	granulated sugar	175 mL
1 tsp	pure vanilla extract	5 mL
4 cups	strawberries, raspberries, peaches or blueberries	1 L

LEMON YOGURT SAUCE

4 cups	low-fat natural yogurt*	1 L
⅓ cup	granulated sugar	75 mL
2 tbsp	lemon juice	25 mL
	Grated rind of 1 lemon	

In large bowl, beat egg whites with cream of tartar until soft peaks form. Beat in sugar 1 tbsp (15 mL) at a time until stiff glossy peaks form. Beat in vanilla.

On foil-lined baking sheet, spread meringue into 10-inch (25 cm) circle, pushing up edge to form ring. Bake in 275°F (140°C) oven for 1½ hours or until firm to the touch. Turn off oven and leave meringue in oven to dry. Remove foil, then let cool and place meringue on serving platter.

Prepare fruit, slicing strawberries or peaches. Just before serving, spread lemon sauce over meringue; cover with fruit. Cut into wedges to serve.

LEMON YOGURT SAUCE: Place yogurt in cheesecloth-lined sieve set over bowl, or in yogurt drainer; refrigerate for at least 4 hours or overnight or until yogurt is about 2 cups (500 mL). Discard liquid.

In bowl, stir together drained yogurt, sugar, lemon juice and rind. Refrigerate for up to 3 days.

MAKES 8 SERVINGS

*Be sure to use Balkan-style yogurt or one made without gelatin.

VARIATION:

Individual Meringues with Berries and Lemon Sauce
Prepare meringue as in recipe. Spoon onto foil-lined baking sheet in bite-sized or 4- to 5-inch (10 to 12 cm) rounds. Using back of spoon, press down to indent and form shells. Bake and fill as directed in recipe.

PER SERVING: 218 calories, 8 g protein, 2 g total fat, 1 g saturated fat, 6 mg cholesterol, 44 g carbohydrate, 2 g fibre, 108 mg sodium, 421 mg potassium

Lemon Mousse with Raspberry Sauce

This dessert is lightened up by using only half the usual amount of whipping cream and no eggs.

1	envelope (7 g) unflavoured gelatin	1
¼ cup	cold water	50 mL
1 cup	granulated sugar or Splenda	250 mL
½ cup	fresh lemon juice (about 2 ½ large lemons)	125 mL
1 tbsp	grated lemon rind	15 mL
1¾ cups	low-fat plain yogurt	425 mL
¼ cup	whipping cream, whipped	50 mL

RASPBERRY SAUCE

1	pkg (10 oz/300 g) frozen unsweetened raspberries (partially thawed)	1
3 tbsp	icing sugar or Splenda	50 mL
1 tbsp	fresh lemon juice and/or Grand Marnier	15 mL

Sprinkle gelatin over water; let stand for 5 minutes or until softened. Stir over low heat until dissolved.

In bowl, whisk together sugar, lemon juice, lemon rind and yogurt; whisk in gelatin. Refrigerate until slightly thickened.

Fold in whipped cream. Spoon into 6-cup (1.5 L) serving bowl or individual sorbet or stemmed glasses. Chill for 2 hours.

RASPBERRY SAUCE: In blender, purée raspberries, sugar, lemon juice and/or Grand Marnier. Strain through sieve to remove seeds.

Spoon Raspberry Sauce onto plates; top with scoop of mousse. (Or, spoon sauce over mousse in sorbet glasses.)

MAKES 6 SERVINGS

MAKE AHEAD: Chill lemon mousse for up to 1 day. Refrigerate sauce for up to 3 days.

VARIATION:

Strawberry Sauce
Substitute strawberries for raspberries. Do not strain.

PER SERVING (without sauce):
256 calories, 6 g protein,
5 g total fat, 3 g saturated fat,
17 mg cholesterol,
50 g carbohydrate, 0 g fibre,
57 mg sodium, 282 mg potassium

Lemon Cream Meringues with Berries

I like to serve these at dinner parties or buffets—they taste scrumptious and are easy to serve and eat. For a buffet, arrange meringues on large platters and let guests help themselves.

MERINGUES

5	egg whites	5
¼ tsp	cream of tartar	1 mL
1 cup	granulated sugar	250 mL
1 tbsp	cornstarch	15 mL
	Grated rind of 1 lemon	
1 tsp	pure vanilla extract	5 mL

LEMON CREAM

2 cups	low-fat plain yogurt (gelatin free)	500 mL
⅔ cups	granulated sugar or Splenda	150 mL
¼ cup	cornstarch	50 mL
½ cup	fresh lemon juice	125 mL
½ cup	water*	125 mL
2	egg yolks, lightly beaten	2
	Grated rind of 2 lemons	
¾ cup	18% cream	175 mL

GARNISH

2 cups	sliced strawberries and/or raspberries	500 mL

MAKE AHEAD: Store baked, unfilled meringues in airtight container for up to 1 week. Cover Lemon Cream with plastic wrap and refrigerate for up to 1 day. Assemble meringues up to 2 hours before serving.

PER SERVING: 201 calories, 5 g protein, 4 g total fat, 2 g saturated fat, 43 mg cholesterol, 38 g carbohydrate, 1 g fibre, 60 mg sodium, 209 mg potassium

MERINGUES: In large bowl, beat egg whites with cream of tartar until soft peaks form. Beat in half the sugar, 1 tbsp (15 mL) at a time, until stiff glossy peaks form. Combine remaining sugar, cornstarch and lemon rind; gradually beat into egg whites. Beat in vanilla.

On parchment or foil-lined baking sheets, spoon meringue into twelve 4- to 5-inch (10 to 12 cm) rounds. Using back of spoon, press down on rounds to indent and form shells. Bake in 225°F (110°C) oven for 2½ to 3 hours or until firm to the touch and foil peels away easily from meringue. Remove foil; let cool on rack.

LEMON CREAM: In cheesecloth– or paper towel–lined sieve set over bowl, drain yogurt in refrigerator for 2 hours or until yogurt is reduced to 1 cup (250 mL). Discard liquid.

In non-aluminum saucepan, mix sugar and cornstarch. Add lemon juice and water; bring to boil, stirring constantly. Reduce heat and simmer gently for 3 minutes or until thickened. Whisk a little hot mixture into yolks; gradually stir back into saucepan. Cook over low heat, stirring, for 2 minutes; stir in lemon rind. Remove from heat and whisk in cream until mixed.

Let cool to room temperature (if in a hurry, stir over a bowl of ice). Whisk in drained yogurt. Spoon into meringues. Garnish with fruit.

MAKES 12 SERVINGS

*If using Splenda, add an additional½ cup (125 mL) water.

Fresh Plum Flan

This is a lovely fall dessert when plums are in season. In the winter, use 2 cans (each 14 oz/398 mL) plums, thoroughly drained. Use any kind or combination of fresh plums. Serve with Lemon Yogurt Cream (p. 429).

¾ cup	granulated sugar or ½ cup (125 mL) sugar plus ¼ cup (50 mL) Splenda	175 mL
⅓ cup	soft margarine, at room temperature	75 mL
2	eggs	2
1 cup	all-purpose flour	250 mL
1 tsp	baking powder	5 mL
1 tsp	grated orange or lemon rind	5 mL
¼ cup	low-fat milk	50 mL
3 cups	quartered pitted plums	750 mL
¼ to ½ cup	packed brown sugar	50 to 125 mL
1 tsp	cinnamon	5 mL

In large bowl and using electric mixer, cream together granulated sugar and margarine; beat in eggs one at a time, beating well after each addition.

Combine flour, Splenda (if using), baking powder and orange rind; beat into egg mixture alternately with milk, making three additions of flour mixture and two of milk.

Turn into greased 10-inch (25 cm) springform pan; combine brown sugar and cinnamon; sprinkle over batter. Arrange plums, cut side down, in circles on top.

Bake in 350°F (180°C) oven for 45 to 55 minutes or until top is golden and toothpick inserted into flan comes out clean. Serve warm or cold.

MAKES 10 SLICES

VARIATIONS:

Fresh Pear Flan
Instead of plums, substitute 2 fresh ripe pears, peeled, cored and cut into ¼-inch (5 mm) thick slices. Arrange slightly overlapping slices in circles on top, lightly pushing into batter.

Fresh Apple Flan
Instead of plums, use 2 large apples, peeled, cored and cut into ¼-inch (5 mm) thick slices. Arrange slightly overlapping slices in circles on top, lightly pushing into batter.

PER SLICE: 220 calories, 3 g protein, 7 g total fat, 1 g saturated fat, 38 mg cholesterol, 36 g carbohydrate, 1 g fibre, 129 mg sodium, 138 mg potassium

Raspberry Yogurt Flan

I love this easy-to-make cheesecake-type dessert. For such a rich-tasting finale, it is low in fat and calories. I also like to make this flan with blueberries or pears.

1½ cups	all-purpose flour	375 mL
½ cup	granulated sugar	125 mL
1½ tsp	baking powder	7 mL
⅓ cup	soft margarine	75 mL
2	egg whites	2
1 tsp	pure vanilla extract	5 mL
3 cups	fresh raspberries or 1 pkg (10 oz/300 g) individually frozen (not thawed)	750 mL

TOPPING

2 tbsp	all-purpose flour	25 mL
2 cups	low-fat plain yogurt	500 mL
1	egg, lightly beaten	1
⅔ cup	granulated sugar	150 mL
2 tsp	grated lemon rind	10 mL
1 tsp	pure vanilla extract	5 mL

In food processor or mixing bowl, combine flour, sugar, baking powder, margarine, egg whites and vanilla; mix well. Press onto bottom of 10-inch (3 L) square cake pan or springform or flan pan; sprinkle with raspberries.

Topping: In bowl, sprinkle flour over yogurt. Add egg, sugar, lemon rind and vanilla; mix until smooth. Pour over berries.

Bake in 350°F (180°C) oven for 70 minutes or until golden. Serve warm or cold.

MAKES 12 SLICES

VARIATIONS:

Pear Yogurt Flan
Use 5 peeled, thinly sliced small pears instead of raspberries. Substitute 1 tsp (5 mL) almond extract for the vanilla extract.

Blueberry Yogurt Flan
Use 3 cups (750 mL) blueberries, fresh or frozen (not thawed), instead of raspberries.

PER SLICE: 233 calories, 5 g protein, 6 g total fat, 1 g saturated fat, 17 mg cholesterol, 39 g carbohydrate, 2 g fibre, 150 mg sodium, 180 mg potassium

Peach Shortcake

Make this delicious dessert in peach season when peaches are ripe and juicy. At other times, use any fruit you like in this old-fashioned classic. When I'm in a hurry, I mix the biscuit dough in the food processor, then just pat the dough on the counter and cut it into rounds.

10	peaches, peeled and sliced	10
2 tbsp	granulated sugar	25 mL
1½ cups	Lemon Yogurt Cream (p. 429) or Quick Lemon Yogurt Sauce (p. 429)	375 mL

SWEET BISCUITS

2 cups	all-purpose flour	500 mL
2 tbsp	granulated sugar	25 mL
1 tbsp	baking powder	15 mL
¼ tsp or less	salt	1 mL or less
5 tbsp	salt-free soft margarine	75 mL
¾ cup	low-fat milk	175 mL

SWEET BISCUITS: In bowl, combine flour, sugar, baking powder and salt. Using 2 knives, cut in margarine until mixture resembles coarse crumbs. Stir in milk, mixing just until moistened. Gather mixture into ball; knead for 30 seconds and pat onto lightly floured surface to about ¾ inch (2 cm) thick.

Using 3-inch (8 cm) round cookie cutter or glass, cut out 10 rounds and place on baking sheet. Bake in 450°F (230°C) oven for 12 to 15 minutes or until golden.

In bowl, toss peaches with sugar. Split each biscuit in half and place bottoms on individual plates. Spoon some peaches on biscuit; cover with top biscuit. Spoon a few peach slices on top and pour Lemon Yogurt Cream over.

MAKES 10 SERVINGS

PER SERVING: 285 calories, 8 g protein, 7 g total fat, 1 g saturated fat, 4 mg cholesterol, 49 g carbohydrate, 3 g fibre, 212 mg sodium, 428 mg potassium

Lighthearted Strawberry Shortcake

The lemon, yogurt and light cream cheese in this wonderful dessert combine to make a refreshing, low-fat alternative to whipped cream.

¾ cup	light cream cheese	175 mL
1 cup	low-fat plain yogurt	250 mL
½ cup	granulated sugar	125 mL
	Grated rind of 2 lemons	
1	angel food cake (see traditional recipe, p. 389)	1
6 cups	sliced fresh strawberries	1.5 L

In food processor or bowl, combine cream cheese, yogurt, sugar and lemon rind; process or beat with electric mixer until smooth.

Cut cake horizontally into 3 layers. Spread one-third of the cheese mixture over first layer; arrange one-third of the berries on top. Repeat with remaining cake, cheese and berries to make 3 layers.

MAKES 12 SLICES

MAKE AHEAD: Refrigerate for up to 8 hours.

VARIATION:

Blueberry-Strawberry Shortcake
Add 2 cups (500 mL) blueberries. Arrange with strawberries.

PER SLICE: 251 calories, 7 g protein, 4 g total fat, 2 g saturated fat, 10 mg cholesterol, 49 g carbohydrate, 2 g fibre, 264 mg sodium, 286 mg potassium

Peach Blueberry Crisp

It's hard to find a better-tasting fall dessert than this one. If you cook it in a microwave, it takes only 10 minutes. I make crisps year round, using whatever fruit is in season. I love to add berries fresh or frozen to other fruits, such as apples, peaches, pears or plums. You can also add dried cranberries, cherries or raisins.

6 cups	peeled, sliced fresh peaches	1.5 L
2 cups	blueberries	500 mL
⅓ cup	packed brown sugar	75 mL
2 tbsp	all-purpose flour	25 mL
2 tsp	cinnamon	10 mL

TOPPING

1 cup	quick-cooking rolled oats (not instant)	250 mL
⅓ cup	packed brown sugar	75 mL
¼ cup	all-purpose or whole-wheat flour	50 mL
1 tsp	cinnamon	5 mL
3 tbsp	soft margarine, melted	50 mL

In 8-cup (2 L) baking dish, combine peaches and blueberries. Combine sugar, flour and cinnamon; add to fruit and toss to mix.

TOPPING: In small bowl, combine oats, sugar, flour and cinnamon; drizzle with margarine and toss to mix. Sprinkle over fruit mixture. Bake in 350°F (180°C) oven for 35 to 45 minutes, or microwave on High for 10 minutes or until bubbling and fruit is tender. Serve warm or cold.

MAKES 8 SERVINGS

MAKE AHEAD: Cover and refrigerate for up to 1 day.

PER SERVING: 251 calories, 3 g protein, 5 g total fat, 1 g saturated fat, 0 mg cholesterol, 50 g carbohydrate, 5 g fibre, 67 mg sodium, 404 mg potassium

Rhubarb Apple Crisp

The flavourful combination of apple and rhubarb is accented with a touch of lemon and cinnamon.

FILLING

⅔ cup	granulated sugar	150 mL
¼ cup	all-purpose flour	50 mL
1 tsp	grated lemon rind	5 mL
4 cups	fresh or frozen (thawed) rhubarb, cut in ½-inch (1 cm) pieces	1 L
4 cups	sliced apples	1 L

TOPPING

¾ cup	quick-cooking rolled oats (not instant)	175 mL
⅓ cup	packed brown sugar	75 mL
3 tbsp	whole-wheat flour	50 mL
1 tsp	cinnamon	5 mL
2 tbsp	soft margarine, melted	25 mL

FILLING: In bowl, combine sugar, flour and lemon rind; mix well. Add rhubarb and apples; stir to mix. Spoon into 8-cup (2 L) baking dish.

TOPPING: In bowl, combine rolled oats, sugar, flour and cinnamon. Add melted margarine and stir to mix; sprinkle over filling.

Bake in 375°F (190°C) oven for 40 to 50 minutes or until filling is bubbly and topping is brown. Serve warm or at room temperature.

MAKES 6 SERVINGS

NOTE: This crisp has far less fat than most recipes. Traditional recipes call for the butter or margarine to be cut in. Here, it is melted and tossed with the topping ingredients, which seems to make it go further.

Whether you should peel apples (or other fruits) when making desserts mainly depends on the condition of the skin and the type of dessert. In a crisp apple, as long as the skins are unwaxed, free of blemishes and look tender, I don't peel them. The thinner the apples are sliced, the less the peel is noticeable; as a bonus you will have more nutrients and fibre.

MICROWAVE METHOD
Prepare as above. Microwave, uncovered, on High for 9 minutes or until fruit is tender.

PER SERVING: 304 calories, 4 g protein, 5 g total fat, 1 g saturated fat, 0 mg cholesterol, 64 g carbohydrate, 5 g fibre, 60 mg sodium, 431 mg potassium

Berry Bread Pudding

I like this dessert because it isn't too sweet or rich but has fabulous flavour from the raspberries and strawberries. Top each serving with a spoonful of Quick Lemon Yogurt Sauce (p. 429).

Half	large loaf French bread	Half
1½ cups	low-fat milk	375 mL
½ cup	granulated sugar	125 mL
2 tsp	pure vanilla extract	10 mL
½ tsp	each nutmeg and cinnamon	2 mL
1 cup	chopped strawberries	250 mL
1 cup	raspberries	250 mL
2	eggs, beaten	2
1 tbsp	soft margarine	15 mL

Tear bread into 1-inch (2.5 cm) pieces to make 6 cups (1.5 L). In bowl, combine milk, sugar, vanilla, nutmeg and cinnamon; stir in bread and let stand for 10 minutes. Stir in strawberries, raspberries and eggs.

Meanwhile, in 8-inch (2 L) square baking dish, melt margarine in 350°F (180°C) oven; swirl to cover bottom of pan. Pour in batter; smooth top. Bake for 40 minutes or until puffed and browned. Serve warm.

MAKES 8 SERVINGS

PER SERVING (without sauce):
219 calories, 7 g protein,
4 g total fat, 1 g saturated fat,
49 mg cholesterol,
38 g carbohydrate, 2 g fibre,
277 mg sodium, 190 mg potassium

Lime Pudding Cake with Berries

This old-fashioned dessert is wonderful. Serve topped with fruit of your choice or on its own sprinkled with icing sugar.

¾ cup	granulated sugar	175 mL
2 tbsp	soft margarine	25 mL
	Grated rind of 3 limes or 2 lemons	
2	eggs, separated	2
⅓ cup	fresh lime or lemon juice	75 mL
¼ cup	all-purpose flour	50 mL
1 cup	low-fat milk	250 mL
2 cups	sliced strawberries or blueberries	500 mL

In mixing bowl, beat together sugar, margarine and lime or lemon rind. Beat in egg yolks, one at a time, beating well after each addition. Beat in lime or lemon juice, then flour and milk.

In separate bowl, beat egg whites until soft peaks form; fold into batter; pour into 6-cup (1.5 L) baking dish. Place in larger pan and pour in boiling water to come about 1 inch (2.5 cm) up sides of pan. Bake in 350°F (180°C) oven for 40 minutes. Spoon berries over top. Serve warm or cold.

MAKES 6 SERVINGS

PER SERVING: 210 calories,
4 g protein, 6 g total fat,
1 g saturated fat, 64 mg cholesterol,
36 g carbohydrate, 1 g fibre,
90 mg sodium, 189 mg potassium

Plum and Nectarine Cobbler

I used to make this dessert for Sunday dinners but thought it wasn't fancy enough for entertaining. Since I now think any homemade dessert is a treat, especially the comforting old-fashioned ones (with the sugar reduced), I decided to serve this at a dinner party—everyone asked for the recipe. Serve with Lemon Yogurt Cream (p. 429).

1 cup	granulated sugar	250 mL
3 tbsp	all-purpose flour	50 mL
2 tsp	finely grated orange rind	10 mL
2 tsp	cinnamon	10 mL
5 cups	coarsely chopped plums	1.25 L
5 cups	coarsely chopped nectarines	1.25 L

TOPPING

2 cups	all-purpose flour	500 mL
¼ cup	granulated sugar	50 mL
2 tsp	baking powder	10 mL
½ tsp	baking soda	2 mL
½ tsp or less	salt	2 mL or less
⅓ cup	salt-free soft margarine, in bits	75 mL
1⅓ cups	buttermilk	325 mL

In large bowl, combine sugar, flour, orange rind and cinnamon. Add plums and nectarines; toss to combine. Spread mixture in shallow glass 13- × 9-inch (3.5 L) baking dish; bake in 400°F (200°C) oven for 10 minutes.

TOPPING: Meanwhile, in large bowl, stir together flour, sugar, baking powder, baking soda and salt. Using fingers, rub in margarine until mixture is size of small peas. Make well in centre; pour in buttermilk. With fork, stir just until soft dough forms.

Drop dough by large spoonfuls in 12 evenly spaced mounds on hot fruit. Bake in 400°F (200°C) oven for 25 minutes or until top is golden and biscuit dough is cooked.

MAKES 12 SERVINGS

PER SERVING: 279 calories, 4 g protein, 6 g total fat, 1 g saturated fat, 1 mg cholesterol, 54 g carbohydrate, 3 g fibre, 232 mg sodium, 296 mg potassium

Rhubarb Strawberry Cobbler

I like to make this for Sunday family suppers or dinner parties. Tangy rhubarb mixed with sweet strawberries is a great combination. Serve with Quick Lemon Yogurt Sauce (p. 429).

¾ cup	granulated sugar	175 mL
2 tbsp	all-purpose flour	25 mL
1 tsp	cinnamon	5 mL
1 tsp	finely grated orange rind	5 mL
4 cups	coarsely chopped (¾-inch/2 cm pieces) rhubarb	1 L
2 cups	sliced strawberries	500 mL

TOPPING

1 cup	all-purpose flour	250 mL
2 tbsp	granulated sugar	25 mL
1 tsp	baking powder	5 mL
¼ tsp	baking soda	1 mL
¼ tsp or less	salt	1 mL or less
2 tbsp	salt-free soft margarine, chilled and cut in bits	25 mL
⅔ cup	buttermilk	150 mL

In bowl, combine sugar, flour, cinnamon and orange rind. Add rhubarb and strawberries; toss to mix. Spread mixture in 8-cup (2 L) shallow glass baking dish; bake in 400°F (200°C) oven for 10 minutes.

TOPPING: In large bowl, mix flour, sugar, baking powder, baking soda and salt. Using fingers or 2 knives, cut in margarine until mixture is size of small peas. With fork, stir in buttermilk until mixture is moistened and soft dough forms. Drop by spoonfuls in 6 evenly spaced mounds on hot fruit. Bake in 400°F (200°C) oven for 25 minutes or until top is golden and biscuit dough is cooked.

MAKES 6 SERVINGS

NOTE: Overly sweet desserts often need ice cream or whipped cream to balance the sweetness. When you cut down on the sugar in pies, cobblers and other desserts, as in these recipes, you will find that they don't need ice cream and are quite delicious on their own.

PER SERVING (without sauce):
277 calories, 4 g protein,
5 g total fat, 1 g saturated fat,
1 mg cholesterol,
56 g carbohydrate, 3 g fibre,
235 mg sodium, 387 mg potassium

Lemon and Fresh Blueberry Meringue Pie

Meringue on the bottom, lemon filling in the centre and blueberries on the top make a luscious, amazingly low-fat dessert that's also lower in calories than a pie made with traditional pastry.

MERINGUE CRUST

2	egg whites	2
½ cup	granulated sugar	125 mL
¼ tsp	cornstarch	1 mL
½ tsp	pure vanilla extract	2 mL

LEMON FILLING

½ cup	granulated sugar	125 mL
5 tbsp	cornstarch	75 mL
1½ cups	hot water	375 mL
2	egg yolks	2
	Grated rind of 1 lemon and half a medium orange	
⅓ cup	fresh lemon juice	75 mL

BLUEBERRY TOPPING

¼ cup	granulated sugar	50 mL
2 tsp	cornstarch	10 mL
⅓ cup	water	75 mL
1 tsp	fresh lemon juice	5 mL
2 cups	fresh blueberries	500 mL

MAKE AHEAD: Cover and store meringue crust in dry place at room temperature for up to 6 weeks. Assembled tart can be set aside for up to 6 hours.

PER SLICE: 198 calories, 2 g protein, 1 g total fat, 0 g saturated fat, 47 mg cholesterol, 46 g carbohydrate, 1 g fibre, 20 mg sodium, 51 mg potassium

MERINGUE CRUST: Line 8- or 9-inch (20 or 23 cm) pie plate with foil, dull side out. In medium bowl, beat egg whites until soft peaks form. Beat in sugar, 1 tbsp (15 mL) at a time, until stiff glossy peaks form. Beat in cornstarch, then vanilla. Spread into foil-lined pie plate, spreading meringue sides about ½ inch (1 cm) higher than pan. Bake in 275°F (140°C) oven for 1 hour. Reduce heat to 200°F (100°C); bake another 1½ hours or until firm and dry. Let cool slightly on rack. While still warm, remove meringue from pie plate and peel off foil. Return meringue shell to pie plate.

LEMON FILLING: In small non-aluminum heavy saucepan, mix sugar with cornstarch. Stir in water and bring to boil over medium heat, stirring constantly. Reduce heat and boil gently for 3 minutes, stirring constantly.

In small bowl, beat egg yolks lightly; whisk in a little hot mixture, then slowly pour yolk mixture into saucepan, stirring constantly. Cook over medium-low heat, stirring constantly, for 2 minutes. Remove from heat. Stir in grated lemon and orange rinds and lemon juice. Let cool slightly; pour into prepared pie shell.

cont'd . . .

BLUEBERRY TOPPING: In heavy saucepan, combine sugar and cornstarch; stir in water and lemon juice. Cook, stirring, over medium heat until mixture thickens, comes to boil and becomes clear. Remove from heat. Add blueberries, stirring to coat well; let cool to room temperature. Spoon over lemon filling. Refrigerate for 30 minutes before serving.

MAKES 8 SLICES

French Lemon Tart

It's hard to believe that something that tastes this good is so easy to make. This is a lightened-up version of the traditional French tart au citron with its thin, intense-flavoured filling. I make the crust in a flan pan. If using a store-bought pie shell or regular pie plate, reduce the volume of the filling by omitting the orange juice.

3	eggs	3
2	egg whites	2
¾ cup	granulated sugar	175 mL
	Grated rind of 2 medium lemons	
½ cup	fresh lemon juice	125 mL
¼ cup	fresh orange juice	50 mL
1	baked 9-inch (23 cm) pie shell (see Food Processor Easy-to-Make Pastry, p. 422)	1
2 tsp	icing sugar	10 mL

In bowl, using electric mixer, beat eggs, egg whites and sugar for 2 minutes or until creamy. Beat in lemon rind; continue beating and drizzle in lemon juice and orange juice. Place baked pie shell on baking sheet and fill with lemon mixture.

Bake in 350°F (180°C) oven for 25 to 30 minutes or until filling is slightly puffed, browned on top and barely set (may still wobble slightly in centre). If necessary, cover with foil to prevent over-browning. Let cool completely.

Just before serving, sift icing sugar over top.

MAKES 8 SLICES

MAKE AHEAD: Cover and refrigerate baked tart for up to 8 hours.

PER SLICE: 255 calories, 5 g protein, 8 g total fat, 1 g saturated fat, 70 mg cholesterol, 42 g carbohydrate, 1 g fibre, 39 mg sodium, 97 mg potassium

Plum Tart

I love cooked plums in desserts—they are sweet, juicy and flavourful. Use any kind of plums; however, if they are quite ripe and sweet, reduce sugar to ¾ cup (175 mL). This is the easiest and most foolproof method for making pastry. Serve with Honey-Lime Fruit Dip (p. 403) as a sauce or with Vanilla Frozen Yogurt (p. 427).

PASTRY

1¼ cups	all-purpose flour	300 mL
¼ cup	salt-free soft margarine	50 mL
2 tbsp	granulated sugar	25 mL
2 tsp	white vinegar	10 mL

FILLING

1 cup	granulated sugar	250 mL
⅓ cup	all-purpose flour	75 mL
1 tsp	cinnamon	5 mL
	Grated rind and juice of 1 lemon	
5 cups	quartered pitted fresh plums* (about 2 lb/1 kg)	1.25 L

PASTRY: In food processor, combine flour, margarine, sugar and vinegar; process with on-off motion until mixture resembles cornmeal. Firmly and evenly pat mixture into bottom and slightly up sides of 9-inch (23 cm) flan pan or pie plate.

FILLING: In bowl, combine sugar, flour, cinnamon and lemon rind. Add lemon juice and plums; toss to mix. Spoon evenly over pastry.

Place flan pan on baking sheet; bake in 400°F (200°C) oven for 50 to 60 minutes or until filling is bubbling and plums are fork-tender. (If top browns too quickly, cover loosely with foil.) Let stand for at least 1 hour before serving.

MAKES 6 SERVINGS

*If using large plums, cut into 8ths.

MAKE AHEAD: Set aside at room temperature for up to 6 hours.

PER SLICE: 393 calories, 4 g protein, 8 g total fat, 1 g saturated fat, 0 mg cholesterol, 78 g carbohydrate, 3 g fibre, 67 mg sodium, 267 mg potassium

Pear Pie with Apricots and Ginger

Ginger goes well with pears, but you could substitute 1 to 2 teaspoons (5 to 10 mL) of cinnamon instead if you like. Choose ripe yet firm pears, as they will keep their shape.

6 cups	sliced peeled pears (about 7)	1.5 L
½ cup	dried apricots, cut in strips	125 mL
	Grated rind of 1 lemon	
2 tbsp	fresh lemon juice	25 mL
1 tbsp	grated gingerroot (or 1 tsp/5 mL ground or 2 tbsp/25 mL chopped candied ginger)	15 mL
½ cup	granulated sugar or Splenda	125 mL
¼ cup	all-purpose flour	50 mL
3	sheets phyllo pastry	3
4 tsp	melted butter	20 mL

In bowl, combine pears, apricots, lemon rind, lemon juice and gingerroot. Mix sugar with flour; stir into fruit. Pour into deep 9- or 10-inch (23 or 25 cm) pie plate; cover lightly with foil.

Bake in 425°F (220°C) oven for 35 minutes or until pears are tender and filling is bubbling. Remove from oven; reduce heat to 375°F (190°C). Place one sheet of phyllo on work surface; brush lightly with butter. Scrunch gently with fingertips to cover ⅓ of top of pie; place on pie filling. Repeat with remaining phyllo to cover filling. Bake 7 to 10 minutes or until pastry is golden. Cover loosely with foil and cook another 5 minutes. Let cool at least 10 minutes before serving.

MAKES 8 SLICES

MAKE AHEAD: Set aside for up to 6 hours; serve hot or cold. To reheat, warm in 350°F (180°C) oven for 10 to 15 minutes.

NOTE: Use scissors to cut apricots into thin strips.

PER SLICE: 195 calories, 2 g protein, 3 g total fat, 1 g saturated fat, 5 mg cholesterol, 43 g carbohydrate, 4 g fibre, 60 mg sodium, 305 mg potassium

Berries with Microwave Rhubarb Sauce

Fresh berries add a delightful flavour to rhubarb sauce. Serve warm or cold with Gingerbread Cake (p. 390) or over Vanilla Frozen Yogurt (p. 427) or strawberries.

4 cups	chopped rhubarb (1¼ lb/625 g)	1 L
1	strip (3 inches/8 cm) orange rind	1
1 tbsp	water	15 mL
¾ cup	granulated sugar or Splenda to taste	175 mL
1 cup	raspberries or sliced strawberries	250 mL

In microwaveable dish, combine rhubarb, orange rind and water; cover with lid or vented waxed paper or parchment paper.

Microwave on High for 4 minutes; stir. Microwave for another 3 minutes or until rhubarb is tender. Stir in sugar until dissolved. Stir in berries.

MAKES 5 SERVINGS, ½ CUP (125 mL) EACH

NOTE: Don't peel the rhubarb, just wash. The skin provides colour and likely fibre and vitamins. (Discard the leaves.)

VARIATION:

Stewed Rhubarb
In saucepan, combine rhubarb, orange rind, sugar and water; cook over medium heat, stirring, until sugar dissolves. Simmer, uncovered and stirring occasionally, for 10 to 15 minutes or until rhubarb is tender.

PER SERVING: 149 calories, 1 g protein, 0 g total fat, 0 g saturated fat, 0 mg cholesterol, 37 g carbohydrate, 3 g fibre, 4 mg sodium, 319 mg potassium

Food Processor Easy-to-Make Pastry

This is a tender pastry using a minimum amount of fat. I tried to make pastry using vegetable oil, which is lower in saturated fat than butter or margarine, but the pastry was too tough.

1¼ cup	cake-and-pastry flour	300 mL
2 tbsp	granulated sugar	25 mL
¼ cup	salt-free soft margarine	50 mL
3 tbsp	(approx) cold water	50 mL
2 tsp	vinegar	10 mL

In food processor, combine flour and sugar. Add margarine, water and vinegar; process with on-off motion until mixture resembles coarse crumbs. Remove from processor and sprinkle evenly over pie plate. Firmly but evenly pat mixture into bottom and up sides of a 9-inch (23 cm) pie plate or flan pan.

MAKES 1 PIE SHELL, ENOUGH FOR 8 SERVINGS

MAKE AHEAD: Cover and refrigerate unbaked or baked crust for up to 1 day.

PER SERVING: 141 calories, 2 g protein, 6 g total fat, 1 g saturated fat, 0 mg cholesterol, 20 g carbohydrate, 0 g fibre, 3 mg sodium, 26 mg potassium

---

Baked Apples with Maple Yogurt Sauce

When choosing apples for baking, look for a large, firm, tall apple such as the Ida Red or the Northern Spy. For a juicier apple, the Mutsu also makes an excellent baked apple. If choosing a medium-sized apple, the tender, sweet McIntosh requires a shorter cooking time and only ¼ cup (50 mL) sugar.

4	apples	4
⅓ cup	packed brown sugar	75 mL
¼ cup	raisins	50 mL
2 tsp	cinnamon	10 mL
½ tsp	nutmeg	2 mL

MAPLE YOGURT SAUCE

¾ cup	low-fat plain yogurt	175 mL
¼ cup	maple syrup	50 mL

Core apples; remove top inch (2.5 cm) of peel. Make a shallow cut through skin around centre of each apple to prevent skin from bursting. Place apples upright in baking dish or pie plate.

In small bowl, combine brown sugar, raisins, cinnamon and nutmeg; spoon into centres of each apple. Add water to cover bottom of dish. Bake, uncovered, in 375°F (190°C) oven for 25 to 30 minutes for less firm apples, and up to 50 minutes for firm varieties, or until apples are tender when pierced with toothpick.

MAPLE YOGURT SAUCE: In bowl, combine yogurt and maple syrup. Pour over baked apples.

MAKES 4 SERVINGS

MICROWAVE METHOD
Apples baked in the microwave have tougher skins than oven-baked. Prepare as directed in recipe. Pierce skin in several places with toothpick to prevent skin from bursting. Cover with waxed paper; microwave on High for 6 to 9 minutes or until apples are almost tender. Let stand for 5 minutes. Serve with Maple Yogurt Sauce.

PER SERVING: 263 calories, 3 g protein, 1 g total fat, 1 g saturated fat, 3 mg cholesterol, 64 g carbohydrate, 3 g fibre, 42 mg sodium, 445 mg potassium

Nectarine and Orange Compote

Poached nectarines spiked with rum and a garnish of orange slices make a beautiful summer dessert. Add fresh berries or sliced yellow plums to taste.

4 cups	water	1 L
¾ cup	granulated sugar or Splenda	175 mL
6	nectarines	6
2	oranges	2
2 tbsp	fresh lemon or lime juice	25 mL
¼ cup	white rum (optional)	50 mL

In saucepan, bring water and sugar to boil, stirring until sugar dissolves.

Halve and pit the nectarines.

Using zester or vegetable peeler, cut thin strips of rind from one of the oranges; squeeze juice into hot syrup. Add orange rind and lemon juice. Add nectarines (syrup should cover fruit; if necessary cook in batches); simmer for 5 to 8 minutes or until fruit is tender when pierced. Place nectarines in bowl and pour hot syrup over top; let cool.

Slice remaining orange; halve each slice and add to bowl. Add rum (if using).

MAKES 8 SERVINGS

MAKE AHEAD: Cover and refrigerate for up to 1 day; serve at room temperature.

VARIATION:

Peach and Orange Compote
Substitute peaches for the nectarines.

PER SERVING: 131 calories, 1 g protein, 0 g total fat, 0 g saturated fat, 0 mg cholesterol, 33 g carbohydrate, 2 g fibre, 4 mg sodium, 258 mg potassium

Apricot, Orange and Fig Compote

I love to have a jar of this compote in the refrigerator, on hand for breakfast or dessert. I often add fresh fruit such as grapes, kiwi, banana or berries. It's also nice with a fresh mint garnish.

¾ cup	dried figs (about 4 oz/125 g)	200 mL
3 cups	water	750 mL
1 cup	dried apricot halves	250 mL
6	whole allspice	6
	Grated rind and juice of 1 lemon	
1 tbsp	liquid honey (optional)	15 mL
2	oranges, peeled and sliced	2

Trim off tough ends of figs.

In saucepan, combine water, figs, apricots, allspice and grated rind and juice of lemon; bring to boil. Cover and reduce heat; simmer for 20 minutes or until fruit is tender. Let cool. Stir in honey, if using, and oranges. Serve at room temperature or cold.

MAKES 8 SERVINGS

MAKE AHEAD: Cover and refrigerate for up to 5 days.

NOTE: One-half cup (125 mL) of orange juice is high in vitamin C and is a source of folacin. Folacin is required for growth and is especially important during pregnancy, particularly in the first month.

PER SERVING: 89 calories, 1 g protein, 0 g total fat, 0 g saturated fat, 0 mg cholesterol, 23 g carbohydrate, 3 g fibre, 6 mg sodium, 379 mg potassium

Louise Saunder's Grapefruit Ice

Fresh-squeezed grapefruit juice made into an ice is a delicious, refreshing dessert at any time of year. Arrange scoops of ice on individual plates with fresh grapefruit sections or other fresh fruit, or serve with cookies or squares.

2 cups	granulated sugar	500 mL
2 cups	water	500 mL
6	grapefruit	6
¼ cup	fresh lemon juice	50 mL

In saucepan, combine sugar and water, stirring to dissolve sugar. Bring to boil; boil for 5 minutes. Remove from heat. Grate rind from 1 of the grapefruits (grate only yellow part; the white part is too bitter); stir into syrup. Let cool.

Squeeze juice from all grapefruit to measure 4 cups (1 L). Stir grapefruit juice and lemon juice into cool syrup.

Freeze and serve according to instructions in Raspberry Sorbet (p. 425).

MAKES 12 SERVINGS

MAKE AHEAD: Freeze for up to 1 month.

NOTE: One serving is a very high source of vitamin C.

PER SERVING: 164 calories, 0 g protein, 0 g total fat, 0 g saturated fat, 0 mg cholesterol, 42 g carbohydrate, 0 g fibre, 2 mg sodium, 143 mg potassium

Fresh Strawberry Sorbet

Fresh ripe strawberries make a delicious easy-to-make sorbet. Serve with other fruit ices or sorbets and fresh fruit, or with Orange Yogurt Cream (p. 429).

1 cup	granulated sugar	250 mL
1 cup	water	250 mL
4 cups	strawberries, washed and hulled	1 L
	Juice of 2 oranges	
	Juice of 1 lemon	
	Unhulled strawberries	

In saucepan, bring sugar and water to boil, stirring to dissolve sugar; boil for 2 minutes. Let cool. In food processor or blender, purée strawberries. Add syrup, orange juice and lemon juice; mix to combine.

Freeze and serve according to instructions in Raspberry Sorbet (p. 425). Garnish each serving with strawberries.

MAKES 8 SERVINGS

MAKE AHEAD: Freeze for up to 1 month.

NOTE: One serving is a very high source of vitamin C.

PER SERVING: 129 calories, 1 g protein, 0 g total fat, 0 g saturated fat, 0 mg cholesterol, 33 g carbohydrate, 2 g fibre, 2 mg sodium, 170 mg potassium

Raspberry Sorbet with Strawberry Coulis

Coulis is a purée of fruits (or vegetables) used as a sauce and makes the base for a pretty dessert for summer. Don't strain the raspberry mixture; the seeds are an excellent source of fibre. This looks very attractive when different kinds of sorbets are served on each plate and garnished with fresh raspberries or other fresh fruits.

1	pkg (10 oz/300 g) frozen unsweetened raspberries	1
¾ cup	hot water	175 mL
½ cup	granulated sugar	125 mL

STRAWBERRY COULIS

| 1 | pkg (10 oz/300g) frozen strawberries | 1 |
| | Icing sugar | |

In food processor, purée raspberries. Combine hot water and sugar, stirring until sugar dissolves; add to raspberries and process to mix. Freeze according to instructions below.

STRAWBERRY COULIS: In blender or food processor, purée strawberries. If using unsweetened berries, add icing sugar to taste.

Sorbet should not be rock-hard. Transfer to refrigerator 15 to 30 minutes before serving or process in food processor. Spoon into individual dishes or stemmed glasses. Pour coulis over top. (Or, spoon sauce onto dessert plates; top with a scoop of sorbet.)

FREEZING INSTRUCTIONS

Method 1: Ice-cream machine: Follow manufacturer's instructions.

Method 2: Food processor: Freeze in shallow metal pan or bowl until almost firm. Break up mixture and process in food processor until smooth slush. Pour into airtight container and freeze until firm, about 1 hour.

Method 3: Hand method: Freeze in shallow metal pan or covered bowl until almost firm, about 3 hours. Beat by hand or electric mixer just until smooth and slushy. Pour into airtight container and freeze until firm, about 1 hour.

MAKES 6 SERVINGS

MAKE AHEAD: Freeze for up to 1 month.

NOTE: One serving is a very high source of vitamin C.

VARIATION:

Raspberry Coulis
Use 1 pkg (10 oz/300 g) raspberries instead of strawberries. Makes 1 cup (250 mL).

PER SERVING: 107 calories, 1 g protein, 0 g total fat, 0 g saturated fat, 0 mg cholesterol, 27 g carbohydrate, 3 g fibre, 2 mg sodium, 150 mg potassium

Monda Rosenberg's Citrus Frozen Yogurt with Mango

I had this dynamic dessert at a dinner party hosted by Monda Rosenberg, former *Chatelaine* magazine food editor. It was so wonderful that I immediately asked her for the recipe. The grated lemon and lime rind give the yogurt a fabulous fresh citrus flavour. You can use either store-bought frozen yogurt or homemade (see p. 427). It would also be lovely with fresh berries or peaches—in fact, any fresh fruit in season.

8 cups	vanilla low-fat frozen yogurt	2 L
2	lemons	2
2	limes	2
3	large ripe mangoes, peeled and sliced	3
	Fresh mint leaves	

Let frozen yogurt stand at room temperature just until it can be stirred, 15 to 30 minutes.

Finely grate rind from lemons and limes. Squeeze 1 tbsp (15 mL) each of the lime and lemon juice; set aside.

Turn softened yogurt into large bowl. Stir in rinds and juices until mixed. Spoon back into yogurt container; cover and freeze until hard, about 1 hour.

Arrange scoops of frozen yogurt on dessert plates. Attractively surround with mangoes; garnish with fresh mint.

MAKES 12 SERVINGS

MAKE AHEAD: Freeze citrus frozen yogurt for up to 1 month.

PER SERVING: 184 calories, 6 g protein, 2 g total fat, 1 g saturated fat, 7 mg cholesterol, 37 g carbohydrate, 1 g fibre, 83 mg sodium, 378 mg potassium

Vanilla Frozen Yogurt

Serve this frozen yogurt in place of ice cream. For a creamier frozen yogurt, drain the yogurt first before using.

2 cups	2% plain yogurt or drained yogurt*	500 mL
½ cup	granulated sugar	125 mL
2 tsp	pure vanilla extract	10 mL

In bowl, combine yogurt, sugar and vanilla, stirring to dissolve sugar. Pour into pan or ice-cream machine and freeze according to directions on page 425.

MAKES 4 SERVINGS, ½ CUP (125 mL) EACH

*To drain yogurt, place 4 cups (1 L) yogurt (made without gelatin) in cheesecloth-lined sieve set over bowl. Refrigerate for 3 to 4 hours or until yogurt is reduced to 2 cups (500 mL). Discard liquid or use in soups or muffin batters or add to juice.

PER SERVING: 184 calories, 6 g protein, 2 g total fat, 2 g saturated fat, 9 mg cholesterol, 34 g carbohydrate, 0 g fibre, 82 mg sodium, 287 mg potassium

Apricot Frozen Yogurt

Frozen yogurt made with a low-fat—2% butterfat or less—yogurt has much less fat than ice cream. But even better news is that yogurt tastes just as good as, if not better than, the old-fashioned favourite. Serve with fresh fruit or berries or garnish with fresh mint leaves.

1½ cups	dried apricots	375 mL
1½ cups	orange juice	375 mL
3 cups	low-fat plain yogurt	750 mL
1 tsp	grated orange rind	5 mL

In small saucepan or microwaveable dish, combine apricots with orange juice; bring to boil. Cover and simmer over medium heat for 10 to 12 minutes, or cover and microwave on High for 7 minutes, or until apricots are softened. Purée in food processor or blender or pass through food mill; let cool.

Combine apricot mixture, yogurt and orange rind; mix well. Freeze according to directions on page 425.

MAKES 8 SERVINGS

PER SERVING: 137 calories, 6 g protein, 2 g total fat, 1 g saturated fat, 6 mg cholesterol, 27 g carbohydrate, 2 g fibre, 67 mg sodium, 640 mg potassium

Raspberry Rhubarb Sauce

For a truly low-fat dessert, dress up strawberries, cherries, plums, blackberries or other fresh seasonal fruit with this delicious fruit sauce. You'll need about 1½ cups (375 mL) for 4 cups (1 L) of berries or cut fruit.

2½ cups	sliced (½ inch/1 cm thick) fresh or frozen rhubarb	625 mL
¾ cup	water	175 mL
½ cup	granulated sugar	125 mL
	Grated rind and juice of 1 lemon	
2 cups	fresh raspberries (or 1 cup/250 mL thawed unsweetened raspberries)*	500 mL
¼ tsp	cinnamon	1 mL

In saucepan, combine rhubarb, water, sugar and lemon rind; bring to boil over medium heat. Reduce heat and simmer for 10 to 15 minutes or until tender. Remove from heat; stir in lemon juice, raspberries and cinnamon. Serve warm or cool.

MAKES 3 CUPS (750 mL)

*If measuring raspberries while frozen, use 2 cups (500 mL); if thawed, about 1 cup (250 mL).

MAKE AHEAD: Refrigerate sauce in airtight container for up to 3 days.

NOTE: One serving is a very high source of vitamin C.

PER ½ CUP (125 mL): 98 calories, 1 g protein, 0 g total fat, 0 g saturated fat, 0 mg cholesterol, 25 g carbohydrate, 3 g fibre, 3 mg sodium, 221 mg potassium

Three-Berry Sauce

Spoon this delightful sauce over angel cake, Vanilla Frozen Yogurt (p. 427) or into meringue shells (see Strawberry Pavlova, p. 407).

3 cups	sliced strawberries	750 mL
1 cup	blueberries	250 mL
1 cup	raspberries	250 mL
¼ cup	granulated sugar	50 mL
2 tsp	cornstarch	10 mL
½ cup	cold water	125 mL

Wash and drain berries; place in bowl.

In small saucepan, combine sugar and cornstarch; add water. Cook, stirring, over medium heat until mixture comes to boil; boil for 1 minute. Pour over berries; stir well. Refrigerate for at least 1 hour or up to 24 hours.

MAKES 6 SERVINGS

PER SERVING: 81 calories, 1 g protein, 0 g total fat, 0 g saturated fat, 0 mg cholesterol, 20 g carbohydrate, 3 g fibre, 3 mg sodium, 172 mg potassium

Orange or Lemon Yogurt Cream

This sauce is delicious over fresh fruit, or as a dessert topping instead of whipped cream. Use extra-thick or Greek-style in this recipe, or, if it isn't available, drain the yogurt first.

1 cup	extra-thick plain yogurt*	250 mL
¼ cup	granulated sugar or Splenda plus more to taste	50 mL
1 tsp	grated orange or lemon rind	5 mL
1 tbsp	frozen orange juice concentrate or fresh lemon juice (optional)	15 mL

Stir together yogurt, sugar, rind and juice (if using). Taste and add more sugar if desired.

MAKES 1 CUP (250 mL)

*To make your own extra-thick yogurt, in cheesecloth-lined sieve set over bowl, drain 2 cups (500 mL) low-fat plain (no gelatin) yogurt in refrigerator for 4 hours or until yogurt is reduced to 1 cup (250 mL). Discard liquid or use in soups or muffin batters, or add to juice.

MAKE AHEAD: Cover and refrigerate for up to 1 week.

VARIATION:

Quick Lemon Yogurt Sauce
In small bowl, combine ¾ cup (175 mL) yogurt, 2 tbsp (25 mL) sugar and grated rind of 1 lemon. Cover and refrigerate for up to 3 days.

PER 2 TBSP (25 mL): 60 calories, 3 g protein, 1 g total fat, 0 g saturated fat, 3 mg cholesterol, 11 g carbohydrate, 0 g fibre, 43 mg sodium, 145 mg potassium

Vanilla Cream

Thanks go to my friend and fabulous cook Mary Holmes for this low-cal, lower-fat, crème fraîche–like sauce. If possible, make it a day in advance, as the sauce thickens considerably upon standing.

½ cup	light sour cream	125 mL
½ cup	2% milk	125 mL
½ cup	low-fat or extra-thick plain yogurt	125 mL
¼ cup	granulated sugar or Splenda	50 mL
1 tsp	pure vanilla extract	5 mL

Combine sour cream, milk, yogurt, sugar and vanilla; stir to dissolve sugar. Cover and refrigerate for at least 1 hour.

MAKES 1 ½ CUPS (375 mL)

MAKE AHEAD: Cover and refrigerate for up to 3 days.

NOTE: Vanilla Cream is delicious over fresh berries or any fresh fruit along with Gingerbread Cake (p. 390) or with any dessert instead of whipped cream.

PER 2 TBSP (25 mL): 39 calories, 1 g protein, 1 g total fat, 1 g saturated fat, 4 mg cholesterol, 7 g carbohydrate, 0 g fibre, 22 mg sodium, 57 mg potassium

Amaretto Custard Sauce

Serve this light sauce over berries or fresh fruit and top with toasted slivered almonds. Or, for a super-fast sauce, stir amaretto (almond liqueur) into slightly softened vanilla ice cream.

1 tbsp	granulated sugar	15 mL
2 tsp	cornstarch	10 mL
1 cup	low-fat milk	250 mL
1	egg yolk, whisked	1
2 tbsp	amaretto or coffee liqueur	25 mL

In small non-aluminum saucepan, combine sugar and cornstarch; stir in milk. Bring to simmer over medium heat, stirring constantly; reduce heat to low and cook, stirring, for 5 minutes or until thickened slightly.

Whisk about half of the hot mixture into yolk; whisk back into hot milk mixture. Cook, stirring, over low heat for 2 minutes or until thickened. Remove from heat and stir in amaretto. Let cool.

MAKES 1¼ CUPS (300 mL)

MAKE AHEAD: Cover and refrigerate for up to 2 days.

VARIATION:

Almond Custard Sauce
Substitute 1 tsp (5 mL) almond extract for the amaretto.

PER 2 TBSP (25 mL): 35 calories, 1 g protein, 1 g total fat, 0 g saturated fat, 20 mg cholesterol, 4 g carbohydrate, 0 g fibre, 12 mg sodium, 39 mg potassium

Caramel Sauce

Serve this wonderful caramel sauce hot or warm over frozen yogurt, or vanilla, chocolate or coffee ice cream, or with gingerbread, baked apples, poached pears or peaches.

1 cup	packed light brown sugar or ½ cup (125 mL) each brown sugar and Splenda	250 mL
½ cup	2% evaporated milk	125 mL
1 tbsp	soft margarine	15 mL
2 tbsp	light corn syrup	25 mL

In heavy saucepan, combine sugar, milk, margarine and corn syrup; over medium heat, stirring often, bring to simmer. Cook, stirring for 1 to 2 minutes until thickened slightly.

MAKES 8 SERVINGS, 1 CUP (250 mL) OR ¾ CUP (175 mL) IF MADE WITH SPLENDA

MAKE AHEAD: Sauce can be covered and refrigerated for up to 1 week.

PER 2 TBSP (25 mL): 145 calories, 1 g protein, 2 g total fat, 0 g saturated fat, 1 mg cholesterol, 32 g carbohydrate, 0 g fibre, 54 mg sodium, 147 mg potassium

Easy Chocolate Sauce

Spoon this sauce on ice cream, drizzle over bananas, pears or chocolate cake, or use as a dipping sauce for fresh fruit.

1 cup	unsweetened cocoa powder	250 mL
¾ cup	granulated sugar	175 mL
¾ cup	water	175 mL
½ cup	corn syrup	125 mL
1 tsp	pure vanilla extract	5 mL

In saucepan, combine cocoa and sugar; whisk in water and corn syrup. Bring to full boil over medium heat; boil for 2 minutes, stirring constantly. Remove from heat and stir in vanilla. Let cool (sauce will thicken upon cooling).

MAKES 2 CUPS (500 mL)

MAKE AHEAD: Refrigerate in airtight container for up to 2 weeks.

NOTE: Cocoa powder is made from solid chocolate with the cocoa butter removed, therefore it is much lower in fat than chocolate. Choose chocolate recipes using cocoa powder instead of chocolate if other fat ingredients such as butter or oil are in comparatively similar amounts.

VARIATION:

Chocolate Milk
Combine 2 tbsp (25 mL) Easy Chocolate Sauce with ¾ cup (175 mL) milk. Serve hot or cold.

PER 1 TBSP (15 mL): 39 calories, 0 g protein, 0 g total fat, 0 g saturated fat, 0 mg cholesterol, 10 g carbohydrate, 1 g fibre, 7 mg sodium, 39 mg potassium

Menus

SPRING

Quick-and-Easy Salmon Fillets with Watercress Sauce (p. 212) OR
 Grilled Halibut Fillets with Fresh Tomato-Basil Salsa (p. 216)

Green Vegetable Risotto (p. 147)

Rhubarb Strawberry Cobbler (p. 417)

Asparagus and Mushroom Salad (p. 89) OR Rose Murray's Roasted
 Asparagus (p. 126)

Chicken with Lemons, Olives and Coriander (p. 236) OR
 Grilled Lemon Chicken with Rosemary (p. 260)

Quick-and-Easy Spiced Couscous (p. 108)

French Lemon Tart (p. 419)

SUMMER

Chilled Cucumber Mint Soup (p. 33)

Spicy Scallops (p. 223) on Sprout and Snow Pea Stir-Fry (p. 143)

Tarragon Carrots (p. 136)

Strawberry Pavlova with Lemon Yogurt Sauce (p. 407)

Gazpacho (p. 31)

Grilled Asian Chicken on Arugula with Tiny Tomatoes and Black
 Olives (p. 248)

Green Beans with Garlic, Balsamic Vinegar and Sesame Oil (p. 135)

New Potatoes with Mint Pesto (p. 122)

Raspberry or Blueberry Yogurt Flan (p. 411)

Balkan Beet Cream Soup (p. 33)

Greek Salad (p. 65) OR Tomato Slices with Chèvre and Basil (p. 68)

Teriyaki Salmon and Shrimp Skewers (p. 222)

Lemon Parsley Rice Pilaf (p. 103) OR basmati rice

Peach Shortcake (p. 412)

FALL

Family Favourite Marinated Flank Steak (p. 282)
Grilled Fall Vegetables (p. 129) OR Braised Carrots with Fennel (p. 136)
Barbecued Potato Packets (p. 123)
Fresh Plum Flan (p. 410)

Pork Tenderloin with Rosemary and Thyme (p. 296) AND Mango
   Salsa (p. 322)
Tomatoes Florentine (p. 143)
Broccoli and Sweet Pepper Stir-Fry (p. 131)
Peach Blueberry Crisp (p. 413)

Arugula and Boston Lettuce Salad with Walnut Oil Vinaigrette (p. 65)
Grilled Tandoori Chicken (p. 244)
Roasted Red Peppers and Red Onion with Bulgur (pg. 110) OR
   Couscous with Tomato and Basil (Variation p. 108)
Poached pears with Caramel Sauce (p. 430)

WINTER

Sweet Potato and Ginger Soup (p. 37)
Lamb Racks Dijon (Variation p. 312)
Tomatoes Florentine (p. 143)
Barley and Corn Casserole (p. 113)
Lemon Cream Meringues with Berries (p. 409) OR Apple-Pecan Phyllo
   Crisps (p. 406)

Arugula Salad with Grilled Chèvre (p. 64)
Shrimp and Scallops in Coconut Milk (p. 220)
Green beans
Basmati rice
Chocolate Crêpes with Banana Cream Filling (p. 401)

SUNDAY FAMILY DINNER

Roast Chicken with Lemon Thyme Apple Stuffing (p. 242)
Baked Squash with Ginger (p. 141) OR Roasted Winter Vegetables (p. 127)
Buttermilk Mashed Potatoes (p. 121)
Blueberry Yogurt Flan (Variation p. 411) OR Rhubarb Apple Crisp (p. 414)

Arugula and Boston Lettuce Salad with Walnut Oil Vinaigrette (p. 65)
Easy Oven Beef and Vegetable Stew (p. 279)
Applesauce Cranberry Cake (p. 392) OR Fresh Plum Flan (p. 410)

Greek Salad (p. 65)
Brochette of Pork with Lemon and Herb Marinade (p. 295)
   OR Grilled Lemon Chicken with Rosemary (p. 260)
Barbecued Potato Packets (p. 123)
Lime Pudding Cake with Berries (p. 415)

BRUNCH

Fruit juice and soda water spritzers
Scrambled Eggs and Smoked Salmon on Focaccia (or flatbread) (p. 340)
Apricot, Orange and Fig Compote (p. 423) OR fresh fruit platter

Broccoli Frittata (p. 335)
Carrot Bran Muffins (p. 363) OR Blueberry Lemon Muffins (p. 366)
Fresh fruit platter
Tofu Blender Drink (p. 347)

SPECIAL SUNDAY BREAKFAST

Upside-Down Apple Pancake (p. 342)

Nectarine and Orange Compote (p. 423) OR fresh berries

EASY BREAKFAST

Honey Raisin Granola (p. 346)

Yogurt

Fresh berries

Apple Streusel Muffins (p. 367)

LUNCHEON

Curried Apple and Zucchini Soup (p. 48) OR Chilled Cucumber Mint
  Soup (p. 33)

Marinated Shrimp and Mango Salad (p. 81)

Berries with Orange Cream (p. 402) AND Almond Apricot Squares
  (p. 379) OR Peach Crêpes with Grand Marnier Sauce (p. 400)

Crudités with Creamy Fresh Dill Dip (p. 11) OR Black Bean and Corn
  Salsa (p. 2) with pita bread

Fresh Tomato Pizza (p. 172)

Double Chocolate Brownies (p. 380)

Creamy Corn Chowder with Dill (p. 55) OR Hearty Salmon Chowder
  (p. 58)

Olive and Rosemary Soda Bread (p. 353)

Lemon Mousse with Raspberry Sauce (p. 408) OR Streusel Plum Cake
  (p. 398)

ANYTIME EASY AND QUICK-TO-PREPARE SPECIAL DINNER

Sweet Potato and Ginger Soup (p. 37)

Beef Filet Roasted with Mustard Peppercorn Crust (p. 282)

Rose Murray's Roasted Asparagus (p. 126) OR Sesame Broccoli (p. 133)

Parsnip Puree (p. 140) OR Buttermilk Mashed Potatoes (p. 121) OR
　Mashed Potatoes with Celeriac (p. 121)

Monda Rosenberg's Citrus Frozen Yogurt with Mango (p. 426)

WINTER BUFFET SUPPERS

Snow Pea and Red Pepper Buffet Salad (p. 72)

Provençal Saffron Chicken (p. 235) AND Lemon Parsley Rice Pilaf (p. 103)
　OR Sue Zach's Beef and Pasta Casserole for a Crowd (p. 191)

Fresh Plum Flan (p. 410) OR Raspberry Yogurt Flan (p. 411)

SUMMER BUFFET SUPPERS

Tomato Slices with Chèvre and Basil (p. 68)

Elizabeth Baird's Curried Lentil, Wild Rice and Orzo Salad (p. 78)
　OR Southwest Rice and Bean Salad (p. 77)

Broccoli Buffet Salad (p. 73)

Chutney-Glazed Ham (p. 306)

Berries with Orange Cream (p. 402) AND Oatmeal Raisin Cookies (p. 373)

VEGETARIAN DINNERS

Hummus (p. 4) with vegetable crudités

Orange and Fennel Salad (p. 69)

Mushroom and Sweet Pepper Lasagna (p. 193)

Peach Crêpes with Grand Marnier Sauce (p. 400)
  OR Chocolate Crêpes with Banana Cream Filling (p. 401)

Elizabeth Baird's Mushroom Risotto (p. 145)

Sherried Green Beans with Sweet Red Peppers (p. 134)

Grilled Eggplant with Garlic and Rosemary (p. 131)

French Lemon Tart (p. 419)

Snow Pea and Red Pepper Buffet Salad (p. 72)

Harvest Vegetable Curry (p. 161) on rice OR Moroccan Vegetable
  Couscous (p. 166)

Grand Marnier Sauce (p. 400) over orange sections OR Apricot,
  Orange and Fig Compote (p. 423)

Purple Vegetable Slaw (p. 71)

Bean and Vegetable Burritos (p. 163)

Raspberry Sorbet with Strawberry Coulis (p. 425)

Arugula and Boston Lettuce Salad with Walnut Oil Vinaigrette (p. 65)

Peruvian Quinoa Pilaf (p. 107)

Tofu Vegetable Shish Kebobs (p. 170)

Raspberry Rhubarb Sauce (p. 428) over fresh berries
  OR Apple-Pecan Phyllo Crisps (p. 406)

Gazpacho (p. 31) OR Sweet Potato and Ginger Soup (p. 37)

Curried Lentils with Coriander (p. 157) OR Vegetarian Chili (p. 289)

Green Beans with Herbs and Pine Nuts (p. 134)

Three-Berry Sauce (p. 428) over fresh peaches OR pineapple or
  poached pears with Caramel Sauce (p. 430)

Glossary of Nutritional Terms

AMINO ACIDS

Amino acids are the building blocks of protein. There are twenty amino acids needed for proper human growth and function. Nine amino acids are considered "essential" because they must be provided by the diet; the body produces the remaining eleven as needed.

See also **Protein**.

ANTIOXIDANTS

Antioxidants are chemical compounds or substances that inhibit oxidation. Oxidation results in the formation of free radicals, which can have damaging effects on the body. Antioxidants are molecules that interact and stabilize free radicals, preventing the damage they may cause. Consuming foods with antioxidants, such as vegetables and fruit, is thought to protect body cells from the damaging effects of oxidation.

CAFFEINE

Caffeine is a mild stimulant found in coffee, tea, chocolate and some soft drinks and over-the-counter pain medication. Caffeine is a central nervous system stimulant, having the effect of temporarily warding off drowsiness and restoring alertness. Caffeine-containing products should be consumed in moderation.

CALCIUM

See **Minerals**.

CALORIES

Calories are the basic unit of measurement for the energy value of food and the energy needs of the body. To lose 1 pound (0.5 kg), you need to reduce your caloric intake by 3,500 calories. It is best not to aim to lose more than 1 to 2 pounds (0.5 to 1 kg) per week. Your caloric intake is affected both by the food you eat and the physical activity you do. Increasing your level of physical activity and reducing your food intake is the best way to obtain and maintain a healthy weight.

CARBOHYDRATES

Carbohydrates are classified according to their chemical structure and digestibility. The two main forms of carbohydrates are sugars (simple carbohydrates), such as fructose, glucose, and lactose; and starches (complex carbohydrates), found in foods such as starchy vegetables, grains, rice, breads and cereals. Fibre is another form of complex carbohydrate. The body breaks down or converts most carbohydrates (but not fibre), into glucose, which is absorbed into the bloodstream and is the body's primary source of fuel. As the glucose level rises in the body, the pancreas releases a hormone called insulin. Insulin is needed to move glucose from the blood into the cells, where it can be used as a source of energy.

Adults need to get 45 to 65 percent of their caloric intake from carbohydrates. This is about 225 to 325 grams of carbohydrate per day based on a 2,000-calorie diet. This amount is based on the minimum amount needed to produce enough glucose for the brain to function. The best carbohydrate choices include whole grains, legumes, beans, vegetables and fruit.

CHOLESTEROL

Cholesterol is a wax-like fatty substance produced in the liver and found in the blood and in all cells of the body. Cholesterol is important for good health and is needed for making cell walls, tissues, hormones, vitamin D and bile acid. When there is too much cholesterol in the blood, the buildup is stored on artery walls, causing the arteries to narrow and increasing your risk of developing a condition known as atherosclerosis. Low-density lipoprotein (LDL) cholesterol is referred to as "bad" cholesterol because it builds up on artery walls. High-density lipoprotein (HDL) cholesterol is called "good" cholesterol because it carries excess blood cholesterol back to the liver to be excreted from the body. Ideally, you should have high levels of HDL cholesterol and low levels of LDL cholesterol.

Cholesterol is also found in foods taken from animals, including egg yolks, meat, shellfish and full-fat dairy products. Dietary cholesterol is not found in plant-based foods. Dietary cholesterol can raise blood cholesterol, but not nearly as much as high-fat foods, especially those high in saturated and trans fat.

See also **Trans Fat.**

ESSENTIAL FATTY ACIDS

Essential fatty acids are the building blocks of fats. They are called "essential" fatty acids because, although they are needed for human health, the body can't produce them itself and so we must get them from our diet. Our need for essential fatty acids is met by linoleic acid (found in vegetable oils, especially corn, safflower and soybean oils), which is converted in the body into the essential fatty acid arachidonic acid. They help form cell membranes, aid in immune function and produce important hormones. Alpha linolenic acid is another essential fatty acid, which assists in the formation of EPA (eicosapentaenoic acid) and DHA (docosahexaenoic acid). Food sources include canola oil, fatty fish, flaxseed oil, sunflower seeds, walnuts and wheat germ.

See also **Omega-3 Fats** and **Omega-6 Fats.**

FAT

Fats add flavour and a pleasing texture to foods. Because they take longer to digest, fats continue to let us feel full even after the protein and carbohydrates are emptied from the stomach. Fats also help suppress our appetite and signal us to stop eating.

Along with proteins and carbohydrates, fat is one of the three nutrients used as energy sources by the body. The energy produced by fats is 9 calories per gram. Proteins and carbohydrates each provide 4 calories per gram. Total fat is the sum of saturated, monounsaturated and polyunsaturated fats.

A healthy eating pattern includes between 20 and 35 percent of your day's calories from fat. For a woman this means about 45 to 75 grams of fat a day. For a man this means about 60 to 105 grams of fat a day. For healthy eating, choose lower fat foods more often and choose fats wisely. Aim for more polyunsaturated and monounsaturated fat, and less trans and saturated fat.

See also **Monounsaturated Fat, Omega-3 Fats, Omega-6 Fats, Polyunsaturated Fat, Saturated Fat** and **Trans Fat.**

FIBRE

Dietary fibre is the indigestible component of plant foods. Fibre comes in two forms: soluble and insoluble.

Soluble fibre, which dissolves in water, helps lower blood cholesterol (when eaten as part of a lower fat diet) and may help control blood sugar in people with diabetes. Soluble fibre is found in lentils, legumes, oat bran, oatmeal, flaxseed, psyllium, barley and pectin-rich fruit such as apples, strawberries and citrus fruit.

Insoluble fibre, which retains water well, is called roughage. It may help lower the risk of some cancers, help in weight control and prevent constipation. Insoluble fibre is found in wheat bran; whole-wheat products; brown rice; some vegetables, including carrots, broccoli and peas; and some fruits, including pears.

A healthy adult needs 21 to 38 grams a day, but surveys show that the average daily Canadian intake is only about 14 grams. Fibre is found only in foods from plant origin, such as beans, fruits, vegetables and grains; there is no fibre in meat, fish or dairy products. High-fibre foods include:

12 or more grams of fibre:

1 cup (250 mL) lentils or beans

½ cup (125 mL) high-fibre bran cereal

6 to 8 grams:

1 cup (250 mL) blackberries or raspberries

½ cup (125 mL) bran flake cereal

½ cup (125 mL) figs or prunes

1 medium pear

1 cup (125 mL) cooked whole-grain pasta

4 to 5 grams:

1 cup (250 mL) broccoli, green beans, leafy greens or cabbage

1 cup (250 mL) blueberries or strawberries

1 medium apple or orange

1 cup (250 mL) cooked brown rice or oatmeal

2 slices whole-grain bread

FOLATE

See Vitamins.

GLYCEMIC INDEX

The glycemic index (GI) is a ranking of carbohydrate-containing foods according to their effect on blood sugar after they are digested. This makes it a useful tool for choosing carbohydrates that can help control blood sugar levels. Regulating blood sugars is a key strategy in preventing and controlling certain diseases, particularly both types 1 and 2 diabetes.

Foods have a low GI (<55), an intermediate GI (55-70), or a high GI (>70). Low GI foods, including oatmeal; oat bran; brown rice; barley; lentils; whole-grain, high-fibre breads; bulgur; sweet potatoes; apples; berries and peas, take longer to digest. They're absorbed more slowly by the body, resulting in more consistent blood sugar levels. These foods are generally relatively high in soluble fibre. High GI foods such as white bread, potatoes, cookies and watermelon are more quickly absorbed, causing blood sugar levels to rise quickly. Higher GI foods should generally be eaten less often. For a comprehensive table of the GI value of common foods, go to gilabs.com/main/tutorial_tables.php

IODINE
See **Minerals**.

IRON
See **Minerals**.

LACTOSE
Lactose is the natural sugar found in milk and milk products. It has to be broken down by an enzyme in the body called lactase into glucose and galactose before it can be absorbed by the body.

LYCOPENE
Lycopene is an antioxidant that lends red colour to red fruits and vegetables. Tomatoes especially have a high lycopene content. Studies have shown that lycopene may be protective for prostrate cancer, lung cancer and heart disease. Cooking foods containing lycopene increases the availability of the antioxidant.

MAGNESIUM
See **Minerals**.

MINERALS
Minerals are essential to maintain good health and promote proper metabolism and various other bodily functions. A varied and balanced diet should provide most of the essential nutrients you need each day. There are some exceptions, such as vitamin D, which is very difficult to obtain in the amount you need from your diet, and therefore a supplement is recommended. The function and foods sources of some of the key minerals are listed below.

Mineral	Function	Food Sources
Calcium	aids in the formation and maintenance of bones and teeth	milk and milk products, fortified soy beverages, canned sardines and salmon (including the bones), dark green leafy vegetables
Iodine	needed to make thyroid hormones	iodized salt, seafood, foods grown in iodine-rich soil
Iron	factor in red blood cell formation	meat, seafood, eggs, legumes, fortified cereals, dried fruits, whole grains, leafy greens, nuts and seeds

Magnesium	factor in energy metabolism, tissue formation and bone development	leafy green vegetables, legumes, whole-grain cereals and breads, meats, fish, poultry, eggs, nuts and milk
Potassium	required for normal cell function; needed for proper nerve, muscle and blood cell function	avocados, bananas, citrus and dried fruits, legumes and many vegetables, whole-grain products
Sodium	required for normal cell function and regulation of blood volume	table salt, seasonings, processed foods
Zinc	factor in energy metabolism and tissue formation	oysters, meat, yogurt, milk, eggs, wheat germ, nuts

MONOUNSATURATED FAT

Monounsaturated fat helps lower "bad" LDL cholesterol levels. These fats are found in olive oil, canola oil, peanut oils, non-hydrogenated margarines, avocado, nuts and seeds. Canada's Food Guide recommends that we include a small amount—2 to 3 tablespoons (30 to 45 mL)—of unsaturated fat in our daily diets.

NUTRITION INFORMATION ON FOOD PACKAGING

The nutrition label on pre-packaged foods is mandatory in Canada. The label includes the ingredients list, in descending order by weight, with the ingredient present in the largest amount listed first. The Nutrition Facts table includes information on serving size, calories, total fat, saturated fat, trans fat, cholesterol, sodium, carbohydrate, fibre, sugars, protein, vitamin A, Vitamin C, calcium and iron. Most of the nutrients include the % Daily Value, which tells you if there is a lot or a little of that particular nutrient in the food.

The product label may also include *nutrient content claims,* such as "low fat" or "high in fibre." Health Canada has set specific criteria for nutrient content claims. As well, food products may bear *health claims.* There are five approved health claims in Canada:

1. A healthy diet low in sodium and high in potassium may reduce the risk of high blood pressure.

2. A healthy diet adequate in calcium and vitamin D may reduce the risk of osteoporosis.

3. A healthy diet low in saturated fats and trans fats may reduce the risk of heart disease.

4. A healthy diet rich in vegetables and fruit may reduce the risk of certain cancers.

5. Non-fermentable carbohydrates in gums and hard candies may reduce dental caries.

OMEGA-3 FATS

Omega-3 fatty acids are considered essential fatty acids because they are needed for human health yet the body can't produce them itself. There are three types of omega-3 fatty acids: alpha-linolenic acid (ALA), eicosapentaenoic acid (EPA) and docosahexaenoic acid (DHA). Of the three, EPA and DHA are most readily used by the body. You get the EPA and DHA directly and efficiently from eating oily fish such as salmon, tuna, mackerel, herring and sardines. ALA is found primarily in flaxseed and flaxseed oils, walnuts and, in smaller amounts, dark green leafy vegetables. Omega-3 fatty acids help reduce stickiness and clotting of the blood, reducing the risk of stroke. They also help lower triglycerides (see **Triglycerides**), the form in which your body stores fat, and can reduce abnormal heart rhythms, or arrhythmias.

OMEGA-6 FATS

Omega-6 fatty acids are essential fatty acids that provide the body with linoleic acid. They help lower "bad" LDL cholesterol, but when eaten in large amounts are thought to also lower "good" HDL cholesterol levels. Omega-6 fat is liquid at room temperature and is found especially in safflower, sunflower, corn and soybean oils.

ORGANIC

Organic refers to crops that are grown, handled and processed without synthetic fertilizers, pesticides or herbicides, artificial ingredients or preservatives. Organic foods are not irradiated and shouldn't contain genetically engineered ingredients. Organic meat, poultry, eggs and dairy products come from animals that are given no antibiotics or growth hormones.

PHYTOCHEMICALS

Phytochemicals are naturally occurring compounds found in plants. Phytochemicals are thought to help prevent a number of diseases, including cancer and heart disease. They are found in vegetables and fruit, such as broccoli, cabbage, citrus fruits, apples, grapes, berries and onions, leeks and garlic. Some of the best-known phytochemicals are listed in the table below.

Phytochemical	Function	Food Sources
Allicin	thought to help reduce blood cholesterol and blood pressure levels	garlic, leeks, onions
Carotenoids	May have antioxidant properties to fight heart disease, certain types of cancer and degenerative eye disease.	Orange, yellow and red vegetables and fruit
Indoles Isothiocyanates	may help protect against colon cancer	bok choy, broccoli, brussels sprouts, cabbage, cauliflower, kale, rutabaga

Isoflavones	may help offset the effects of estrogen in breast and ovarian cancer	soybean products
Limonene	helps produce enzymes that help the body rid itself of cancer-causing substances	citrus fruits
Phytosterols	may help prevent colon cancer; may prevent cholesterol absorption from foods	soybeans

POLYUNSATURATED FAT
Polyunsaturated fat helps lower "bad" LDL cholesterol levels. These fats are found in safflower, sunflower and corn oils, non-hydrogenated margarines, nuts and seeds. Canada's Food Guide recommends that we include a small amount—2 to 3 tablespoons (30 to 45 mL)—of unsaturated fat in our daily diet.

POTASSIUM
Along with sodium, potassium helps maintain fluid balance and promotes proper metabolism and muscle function. It is thought that introducing some food sources of potassium, in addition to eating a healthy balanced diet, can help lower blood pressure. Food sources of potassium are avocados, bananas, citrus and dried fruits, legumes and many vegetables and whole-grain products.

See also **Minerals**.

PROTEIN
Protein is the nutrient that every cell in the human body needs for growth or repair. Protein is made up of amino acids. The human body requires twenty different amino acids to build all the protein it needs. Of these, eleven are made in the body, while the other nine, referred to as *essential amino acids,* must come from the diet. Animal protein provides all nine essential amino acids. Plant protein, with the exception of soy, lacks one or more essential amino acids. However, by combining plant proteins—for example, a grain with a legume—you can obtain all the essential amino acids.

SATURATED FAT
Saturated fat is what your body uses to make cholesterol, which can build up and be stored in your arteries, narrowing them and increasing the risk of developing a condition known as atherosclerosis. Saturated fats are found in fatty meats; full-fat milk products; butter; lard; coconut, palm and palm kernel oils; fast foods; snack foods; many ready-prepared foods and those containing hydrogenated vegetable oil.

SODIUM
Sodium in combination with chlorine make up table salt. Sodium helps maintain fluid balance and promotes proper metabolism and muscle

function. However, about one-third of people are sensitive to the sodium component of salt. This means that excess dietary salt can increase the amount of blood in the arteries, raising blood pressure and increasing the risk of heart disease and stroke.

The Heart and Stroke Foundation suggests that Canadians consume no more than 1 teaspoon (5 mL) of salt a day (2,300 mg), whether it comes from the salt shaker or the salt in processed and packaged foods.

See also **Minerals**.

SUGAR

Sugar contains simple carbohydrates but no other nutrients. Sugar may be listed in the ingredients list on food products as glucose, fructose, honey, cane juice, sucrose or syrup (corn, malt, golden, maple, refiners). Use the Nutrition Facts table to determine the total sugar content of the product. One teaspoon (4 grams) of sugar equals 15 calories.

See also **Lactose**, **Carbohydrate** and **Glycemic Index**.

TRANS FAT

A healthy diet limits the amount of trans fat. Trans fat is created when an unsaturated fat is processed or hydrogenated. Like saturated fat, trans fat raises LDL-cholesterol ("bad" cholesterol) levels. Trans fat is found in partially hydrogenated margarines, as well as in many crackers, cookies and commercially baked products, usually listed as "partially hydrogenated" or "vegetable oil shortening" in the ingredients list. Partially hydrogenated products are the biggest source of trans fat in the Canadian diet. Trans fats can also be found in deep-fried foods from fast food outlets.

To help you identify trans fat and other ingredients in foods, the amount of trans fat is listed on the Nutrition Facts table on food labels. These tables will help you identify and limit your intake of products high in trans fat.

TRIGLYCERIDES

Triglycerides are the most common form of dietary and body fat. High blood triglyceride levels are linked to an increased risk of heart disease. High blood triglyceride levels increase the tendency of the blood to clot; the greater the tendency of the blood to clot, the greater risk of a heart attack or stroke.

High triglycerides are associated with excess intake of simple sugars, refined carbohydrates, saturated fats, trans fats and alcohol. They are also linked to excess body weight, a sedentary lifestyle and poorly controlled diabetes.

VITAMINS

Much attention is now being paid to the role of vitamins in protecting against heart disease and certain cancers and keeping the immune system functioning well. It is important to get our vitamins from food and to not rely on supplements, as food contains fibre, energy and other important nutrients not found in supplements. Dark green and orange vegetables and orange fruits in particular are rich sources of vitamins and of natural plant chemicals called phytochemicals (see Phytochemicals). The table below lists key vitamins and their functions and major food sources.

Vitamin	Function	Food Sources
Vitamin A	aids in normal bone and tooth development; aids in the development and maintenance of night vision; aids in maintaining the health of the skin and membranes	salmon and other cold-water fish, egg yolks, fortified milk and dairy products; orange and yellow vegetables and fruit, leafy green vegetables
Beta Carotene	beta carotene is a form of Vitamin A	carrots, tomatoes, squash, pink grapefruit, sweet potatoes and Swiss chard
Vitamin B1 (Thiamine)	releases energy from carbohydrate; aids normal growth	pork, legumes, nuts and seeds, fortified cereals and grains
Vitamin B2 (Riboflavin)	factor in energy metabolism and tissue formation	fortified cereals and grains, lean meat and poultry, milk and other dairy products
Vitamin B3 (Niacin)	aids in normal growth and development; factor in energy metabolism and tissue formation	lean meats, poultry, seafood, milk, eggs, legumes, fortified breads and cereals
Vitamin B6	factor in energy metabolism and tissue formation	meat, fish, poultry, grains and cereals, green leafy vegetables, potatoes, soybeans
Vitamin B12	aids in red blood cell formation	all animal products
Folate	aids in red blood cell formation; may help prevent neural tube disorders; dietary folate is thought to protect against heart disease by keeping homocysteine level down	broccoli and other cruciferous vegetables, avocados, legumes, many raw vegetables

Vitamin	Function	Food Sources
Vitamin C	a factor in the development and maintenance of bones, cartilage, teeth and gums	citrus fruits and juices, melons, berries, peppers, broccoli, potatoes and other vegetables and fruit
Vitamin D	a factor in the formation and maintenance of bones and teeth; enhances calcium and phosphorus absorption and utilization; a growing body of evidence suggests a link between vitamin D and reduced risk for colorectal, breast and prostate cancers	fortified milk and yogurt, egg yolks, fatty fish
Vitamin E	protects the fat in body tissues from oxidation	eggs, vegetable oils, margarine, mayonnaise, nuts and seeds, fortified cereals
Vitamin K	essential for blood clotting; important to note that foods high in Vitamin K may interfere with some anticoagulant medication such as Warfarin	fish, liver, spinach, cabbage, cauliflower, broccoli and brussels sprouts

ZINC
See **Minerals**.

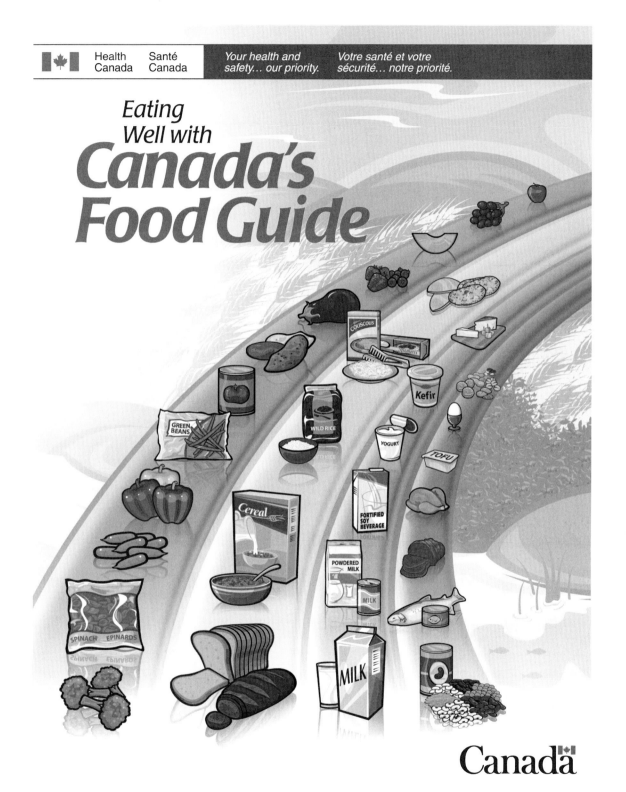

Health Canada　Santé Canada

Your health and safety... our priority.　Votre santé et votre sécurité... notre priorité.

Eating Well with
Canada's Food Guide

Canada

Recommended Number of *Food Guide Servings* per Day

	Children			Teens		Adults			
Age in Years	2-3	4-8	9-13	14-18		19-50		51+	
Sex	Girls and Boys			Females	Males	Females	Males	Females	Males
Vegetables and Fruit	4	5	6	7	8	7-8	8-10	7	7
Grain Products	3	4	6	6	7	6-7	8	6	7
Milk and Alternatives	2	2	3-4	3-4	3-4	2	2	3	3
Meat and Alternatives	1	1	1-2	2	3	2	3	2	3

The chart above shows how many Food Guide Servings you need from each of the four food groups every day.

Having the amount and type of food recommended and following the tips in *Canada's Food Guide* will help:

• Meet your needs for vitamins, minerals and other nutrients.

• Reduce your risk of obesity, type 2 diabetes, heart disease, certain types of cancer and osteoporosis.

• Contribute to your overall health and vitality.

What is One Food Guide Serving?
Look at the examples below.

Fresh, frozen or canned vegetables
125 mL (½ cup)

Leafy vegetables
Cooked: 125 mL (½ cup)
Raw: 250 mL (1 cup)

Fresh, frozen or canned fruits
1 fruit or 125 mL (½ cup)

100% Juice
125 mL (½ cup)

Bread
1 slice (35 g)

Bagel
½ bagel (45 g)

Flat breads
½ pita or ½ tortilla (35 g)

Cooked rice, bulgur or quinoa
125 mL (½ cup)

Cereal
Cold: 30 g
Hot: 175 mL (¾ cup)

Cooked pasta or couscous
125 mL (½ cup)

Milk or powdered milk (reconstituted)
250 mL (1 cup)

Canned milk (evaporated)
125 mL (½ cup)

Fortified soy beverage
250 mL (1 cup)

Yogurt
175 g
(¾ cup)

Kefir
175 g
(¾ cup)

Cheese
50 g (1 ½ oz.)

Cooked fish, shellfish, poultry, lean meat
75 g (2 ½ oz.)/125 mL (½ cup)

Cooked legumes
175 mL (¾ cup)

Tofu
150 g or
175 mL (¾ cup)

Eggs
2 eggs

Peanut or nut butters
30 mL (2 Tbsp)

Shelled nuts and seeds
60 mL (¼ cup)

Oils and Fats
· Include a small amount – 30 to 45 mL (2 to 3 Tbsp) – of unsaturated fat each day. This includes oil used for cooking, salad dressings, margarine and mayonnaise.
· Use vegetable oils such as canola, olive and soybean.
· Choose soft margarines that are low in saturated and trans fats.
· Limit butter, hard margarine, lard and shortening.

Make each Food Guide Serving count...
wherever you are – at home, at school, at work or when eating out!

▸ **Eat at least one dark green and one orange vegetable each day.**
- Go for dark green vegetables such as broccoli, romaine lettuce and spinach.
- Go for orange vegetables such as carrots, sweet potatoes and winter squash.

▸ **Choose vegetables and fruit prepared with little or no added fat, sugar or salt.**
- Enjoy vegetables steamed, baked or stir-fried instead of deep-fried.

▸ **Have vegetables and fruit more often than juice.**

▸ **Make at least half of your grain products whole grain each day.**
- Eat a variety of whole grains such as barley, brown rice, oats, quinoa and wild rice.
- Enjoy whole grain breads, oatmeal or whole wheat pasta.

▸ **Choose grain products that are lower in fat, sugar or salt.**
- Compare the Nutrition Facts table on labels to make wise choices.
- Enjoy the true taste of grain products. When adding sauces or spreads, use small amounts.

▸ **Drink skim, 1%, or 2% milk each day.**
- Have 500 mL (2 cups) of milk every day for adequate vitamin D.
- Drink fortified soy beverages if you do not drink milk.

▸ **Select lower fat milk alternatives.**
- Compare the Nutrition Facts table on yogurts or cheeses to make wise choices.

▸ **Have meat alternatives such as beans, lentils and tofu often.**

▸ **Eat at least two Food Guide Servings of fish each week.***
- Choose fish such as char, herring, mackerel, salmon, sardines and trout.

▸ **Select lean meat and alternatives prepared with little or no added fat or salt.**
- Trim the visible fat from meats. Remove the skin on poultry.
- Use cooking methods such as roasting, baking or poaching that require little or no added fat.
- If you eat luncheon meats, sausages or prepackaged meats, choose those lower in salt (sodium) and fat.

Enjoy a variety of foods from the four food groups.

Satisfy your thirst with water!

Drink water regularly. It's a calorie-free way to quench your thirst. Drink more water in hot weather or when you are very active.

Health Canada provides advice for limiting exposure to mercury from certain types of fish. Refer to www.healthcanada.gc.ca for the latest information.

Advice for different ages and stages...

Children

Following *Canada's Food Guide* helps children grow and thrive.

Young children have small appetites and need calories for growth and development.

- Serve small nutritious meals and snacks each day.
- Do not restrict nutritious foods because of their fat content. Offer a variety of foods from the four food groups.
- Most of all... be a good role model.

Women of childbearing age

All women who could become pregnant and those who are pregnant or breastfeeding need a multivitamin containing **folic acid** every day. Pregnant women need to ensure that their multivitamin also contains **iron**. A health care professional can help you find the multivitamin that's right for you.

Pregnant and breastfeeding women need more calories. Include an extra 2 to 3 Food Guide Servings each day.

Here are two examples:
- Have fruit and yogurt for a snack, or
- Have an extra slice of toast at breakfast and an extra glass of milk at supper.

Men and women over 50

The need for **vitamin D** increases after the age of 50.

In addition to following *Canada's Food Guide*, everyone over the age of 50 should take a daily vitamin D supplement of 10 µg (400 IU).

How do I count Food Guide Servings in a meal?

Here is an example:

Vegetable and beef stir-fry with rice, a glass of milk and an apple for dessert		
250 mL (1 cup) mixed broccoli, carrot and sweet red pepper	=	2 **Vegetables and Fruit** Food Guide Servings
75 g (2 ½ oz.) lean beef	=	1 **Meat and Alternatives** Food Guide Serving
250 mL (1 cup) brown rice	=	2 **Grain Products** Food Guide Servings
5 mL (1 tsp) canola oil	=	part of your **Oils and Fats** intake for the day
250 mL (1 cup) 1% milk	=	1 **Milk and Alternatives** Food Guide Serving
1 apple	=	1 **Vegetables and Fruit** Food Guide Serving

Eat well and be active today and every day!

The benefits of eating well and being active include:
- Better overall health.
- Lower risk of disease.
- A healthy body weight.
- Feeling and looking better.
- More energy.
- Stronger muscles and bones.

Be active

To be active every day is a step towards better health and a healthy body weight.

Canada's Physical Activity Guide recommends building 30 to 60 minutes of moderate physical activity into daily life for adults and at least 90 minutes a day for children and youth. You don't have to do it all at once. Add it up in periods of at least 10 minutes at a time for adults and five minutes at a time for children and youth.

Start slowly and build up.

Eat well

Another important step towards better health and a healthy body weight is to follow *Canada's Food Guide* by:

- Eating the recommended amount and type of food each day.
- Limiting foods and beverages high in calories, fat, sugar or salt (sodium) such as cakes and pastries, chocolate and candies, cookies and granola bars, doughnuts and muffins, ice cream and frozen desserts, french fries, potato chips, nachos and other salty snacks, alcohol, fruit flavoured drinks, soft drinks, sports and energy drinks, and sweetened hot or cold drinks.

Read the label

- Compare the Nutrition Facts table on food labels to choose products that contain less fat, saturated fat, trans fat, sugar and sodium.
- Keep in mind that the calories and nutrients listed are for the amount of food found at the top of the Nutrition Facts table.

Limit trans fat

When a Nutrition Facts table is not available, ask for nutrition information to choose foods lower in trans and saturated fats.

Nutrition Facts
Per 0 mL (0 g)

Amount	% Daily Value
Calories 0	
Fat 0 g	0 %
Saturates 0 g	0 %
+ Trans 0 g	
Cholesterol 0 mg	
Sodium 0 mg	0 %
Carbohydrate 0 g	0 %
Fibre 0 g	0 %
Sugars 0 g	
Protein 0 g	

Vitamin A	0 %	Vitamin C	0 %
Calcium	0 %	Iron	0 %

Take a step today...

✓ Have breakfast every day. It may help control your hunger later in the day.

✓ Walk wherever you can – get off the bus early, use the stairs.

✓ Benefit from eating vegetables and fruit at all meals and as snacks.

✓ Spend less time being inactive such as watching TV or playing computer games.

✓ Request nutrition information about menu items when eating out to help you make healthier choices.

✓ Enjoy eating with family and friends!

✓ Take time to eat and savour every bite!

For more information, interactive tools, or additional copies visit Canada's Food Guide on-line at:
www.healthcanada.gc.ca/foodguide

or contact:

Publications
Health Canada
Ottawa, Ontario K1A 0K9
E-Mail: publications@hc-sc.gc.ca
Tel.: 1-866-225-0709
Fax: (613) 941-5366
TTY: 1-800-267-1245

Également disponible en français sous le titre : Bien manger avec le Guide alimentaire canadien

This publication can be made available on request on diskette, large print, audio-cassette and braille.

Source: *Eating Well With Canada's Food Guide* (2007), Health Canada. Reproduced with the permission of the Minister of Public Works and Government Services Canada, 2009.

About the Nutrient Values

Nutrient values for the recipes were calculated by Food Intelligence (Toronto, Ontario). The primary database was the Canadian Nutrient File (version 2007 b) supplemented with information from USDA National Nutrient Database for Standard Reference (Release 21) and other sources. The computer-assisted calculations, using Genesis® R&D SQL (ESHA Research), were based on:

- imperial measurements, unless the recipe quantity would be typically purchased in metric measure, and the whole quantity or specified proportion of it used;

- smaller number of servings (i.e., larger serving) if there was a range;

- smaller ingredient quantity if there was a range, and first ingredient listed when there was a choice;

- unless otherwise specified, low-fat dairy products (1% milk and buttermilk, 1.5% yogurt, 2% cottage cheese, 5% sour cream and 19% light cream cheese); and

- medium-size vegetables and fruit (unless otherwise specified), and large eggs; and

- soft non-hydrogenated margarine.

Optional ingredients were not included.

In some recipes you will see, for example, "¼ tsp (1 mL) of salt *or less*." For these recipes the full amount of salt was calculated. You may find that you can use less than the recipe quantity of salt in other recipes as well.

Nutrient values for the recipes are rounded to whole numbers. Where a recipe serving is identified as an excellent or good source of a vitamin or mineral, this assessment is based on nutritional labelling criteria (2003 *Guide to Food Labelling and Advertising,* Canadian Food Inspection Agency). An excellent source provides 25 percent of the Daily Value for a nutrient (50% for vitamin C), and a good source provides 15 percent (30% for vitamin C). A source provides 5 percent of the Daily Value for a nutrient. A very high source of fibre provides 6 grams, a high source of fibre provides 4 grams and a source of fibre provides 2 grams.

Index